THE SOUND PATTERN
OF ENGLISH

THE SOUND PATTERN OF ENGLISH

NOAM CHOMSKY

MORRIS HALLE

The MIT Press
Cambridge, Massachusetts
London, England

To Roman Jakobson

Fourth printing, 1997
First MIT Press paperback edition 1991

© 1968, 1991 Noam Chomsky and Morris Halle

This book was printed in the United States of America.

Library of Congress Cataloging-in-Publication Data

Chomsky, Noam.
    The sound pattern of English / Noam Chomsky, Morris Halle.
      p.   cm.
    Originally published: New York : Harper & Row, 1968. Originally published in series: Studies in language.
    Includes bibliographical references (p.   ) and indexes.
    ISBN 0-262-03179-5. — ISBN 0-262-53097-X (pbk.)
    1. English language—Phonology. 2. English language—Grammar, Generative.
I. Halle, Morris. II. Title.
PE1133.C5 1991
421' .5—dc20
                                            90-19232
                                              CIP

PREFACE
TO THE PAPERBACK EDITION

In the preface to the original edition of this book we remarked that no treatment "that we have proposed has survived a course of lectures unchanged and we do not doubt that the same fate awaits the grammatical sketch that we develop here." While our record as prophets is in general rather unimpressive, in the present instance we were right on the money: few of the matters treated in this 1968 book have remained unaffected by the developments in phonology that have taken place in the past twenty years. In the light of this the question inevitably arises as to what reasons, other than vanity, cupidity, and/or lack of critical judgment on the part of the authors or our publisher, might justify reprinting this book at this time. Our answer is that while the solutions to many particular problems proposed in SPE are out of date, many of the theoretical issues raised there remain critical to phonology to this day, and in quite a number of instances the solutions proposed in SPE have yet to be improved upon. Moreover, there are few works in phonology that have quite the scope of SPE: it deals both with matters of broad theoretical importance as well as with numerous questions of detail; it attempts to contribute to the theoretical foundations of phonetics as well as of phonology and it embeds its central empirical topic—the phonology of modern English (General American)—on the one hand, in a discussion of parallel phenomena in other languages, and on the other hand, in an account of the historical evolution of the English vowel system.

It is for these reasons, we believe, that SPE remains—and will for some time in the future remain—a book that students of phonology should find worth reading and pondering and arguing with. And the existence of a potential audience of this kind justifies the reprinting of the book at this time.

NOAM CHOMSKY
MORRIS HALLE
AUGUST 1990

PREFACE

This study of English sound structure is an interim report on work in progress rather than an attempt to present a definitive and exhaustive study of phonological processes in English. We feel that our work in this area has reached a point where the general outlines and major theoretical principles are fairly clear and where we can identify the areas requiring additional intensive study with a reasonable expectation that further investigation within the same general framework will not significantly alter the overall picture we have presented, although it may well be that new and different insights—perhaps along the lines discussed in Chapter Nine—will lead to significant modifications. We have decided to publish this study in its present intermediate stage in the hope that it will stimulate criticism and discussion of basic issues and perhaps involve other investigators in the immense task of extending this sketch to the whole of English, providing the same sort of description for other languages, and enriching and sharpening (and, no doubt, revising in many ways) the phonological theory on which it is based.

This book is organized in the following way. Part I opens with an introductory chapter, Chapter One, in which background assumptions are briefly sketched. In Chapter Two of Part I our major conclusions with respect to phonological theory and the phonology of English are outlined. Also discussed are the possible implications of this work with regard to perceptual processes and the conditions under which knowledge of a language (and, presumably, knowledge of other sorts) can be acquired. We have tried in Part I to present an informal account of the main conclusions that we reach and to illustrate the kinds of data that support them. Thus, readers interested only in general conclusions may wish to read no further.

Part II of the book is an elaboration of the topics treated in Chapter Two of Part I. Chapters Three and Four examine in considerable detail two aspects of English sound structure which were only sketched in Chapter Two. In the course of this detailed investigation of English sound patterns and their underlying structure, certain rules of English phonology are developed. These rules are restated in Chapter Five, which concludes Part Two. The primary emphasis in Part II is on the phonology of English; theory is developed informally as needed for the exposition and analysis.

Part III deals with certain aspects of the historical evolution of the sound patterns revealed in the synchronic study in Part II.

Part IV is devoted to phonological theory. The informal discussion in Part I is expanded upon, and the theory presented in an ad hoc manner in Part II is systematically developed. The first chapter of Part IV—Chapter Seven—is concerned with universal phonetics, that is, with the general theory of linguistic representation of speech signals. Chapter Eight deals with the principles of organization of the phonological component of the grammar, that is, with the rules that relate syntactic structures to phonetically represented speech signals. In the ninth and concluding chapter, a proposal is presented for an extension of phonological theory that takes into account the intrinsic content of features. Part IV is not concerned with the structure of English but is intended rather as a contribution to universal grammar.

We have made no attempt to avoid redundancy or repetitiousness where we felt that this would assist the reader in following the analysis or argument. Thus, much of the discussion in Part I is repeated in Part II, with additional detail and analysis, and Part IV recapitulates, more systematically, much of the contents of Parts I and II. Each of the four parts of the book is very nearly self-contained. In particular, readers familiar with the general background of this work and its major conclusions as outlined in lectures and publications during the last few years might prefer to skip Part I altogether.

In writing the book we have had two classes of potential readers in mind: first, readers who are concerned only with the general properties of English sound structure, with the consequences of these properties for general linguistic theory, and with the implications of general linguistic theory for other fields; second, readers who are concerned with the detailed development of phonological theory and the theory of English, that is, English grammar. Part I of the book is directed to the first class of readers; Parts II, III, and IV, to the second.

One other point of clarification is needed. We have investigated certain topics in considerable detail and have neglected certain others in what might appear to be a rather idiosyncratic and unmotivated pattern. For example, we have studied the stress contours of English in some detail, but we say nothing about the gradations of aspiration that can easily be observed for English stop consonants. For one concerned solely with the facts of English, the gradations of stress may not seem more important than the gradations of aspiration. Our reason for concentrating on the former and neglecting the latter is that we are not, in this work, concerned exclusively or even primarily with the facts of English as such. We are interested in these facts for the light they shed on linguistic theory (on what, in an earlier period, would have been called "universal grammar") and for what they suggest about the nature of mental processes in general. It seems to us that the gradations of stress in English can be explained on the basis of very deep-seated and nontrivial assumptions about universal grammar and that this conclusion is highly suggestive for psychology, in many ways that we will sketch. On the other hand, gradations of aspiration seem to shed no light on these questions, and we therefore devote no attention to them. We intend no value judgment here; we are not asserting that one *should* be primarily concerned with universal grammar and take an interest in the particular grammar of English only insofar as it provides insight into universal grammar and psychological theory. We merely want to make it clear that this is our point of departure in the present work; these are the considerations that have determined our choice of topics and the relative importance given to various phenomena.

This general aim of our book also explains why we have not included a full discussion of exceptions and irregularities. Had our primary concern been the grammar of English, we would have said very little about the principle of the "transformational cycle" (see Chapters Two and Three) and its consequences (in particular, the properties of English stress contours), but we would have provided a complete account of irregular verbs, irregular plurals, exceptions to rules of stress placement and vowel alternation, etc. Since our main interest is, rather, in universal grammar, we have followed exactly the opposite course. We discuss the transformational cycle and its consequences in detail and we do not include an account of irregularities and exceptions, except insofar as these phenomena seem relevant to the formulation of general principles of English phonology. Given the goals of the research reported on here, exceptions to rules are of interest only if they suggest a different general framework or the formulation of deeper rules. In themselves they are of no interest.

We do not doubt that the segment of English phonology that we develop in detail is inaccurate in certain respects, perhaps in fundamental respects; and it is a near certainty that the phonological theory we propose will be shown to require substantial revision as research progresses. We mention many difficulties, inadequacies, and exceptions as we proceed. It would be a time-consuming but straightforward task to compile a complete list of exceptions, at least for the rules of word-level phonology. Given the purpose of this study such an effort would be beside the point unless it were to lead to the formulation of new and deeper rules that explained the exceptions or to a different theory that accounted both for the regularities that our rules express and for some of their defects and limitations. We see no reason to give up rules of great generality because they are not of even greater generality, to sacrifice generality where it can be attained. It seems hardly necessary to stress that if we are faced with the choice between a grammar G_1 that contains a general rule along with certain special rules governing exceptions and a grammar G_2 that gives up the general rule and lists everything as an exception, then we will prefer G_1. For this reason, citation of exceptions is in itself of very little interest. Counterexamples to a grammatical rule are of interest only if they lead to the construction of a new grammar of even greater generality or if they show some underlying principle is fallacious or misformulated. Otherwise, citation of counterexamples is beside the point.

We stress this point because of what seems to us a persistent misinterpretation, in linguistic discussion, of the significance of exceptions to rules—a misinterpretation which in part reflects a deeper misunderstanding as to the status of grammars or of linguistic theory. A grammar is a theory of a language. It is obvious that any theory of a particular language or any general theory of language that can be proposed today will be far from adequate, in scope and in depth. One of the best reasons for presenting a theory of a particular language in the precise form of a generative grammar, or for presenting a hypothesis concerning general linguistic theory in very explicit terms, is that only such precise and explicit formulation can lead to the discovery of serious inadequacies and to an understanding of how they can be remedied. In contrast, a system of transcription or terminology, a list of examples, or a rearrangement of the data in a corpus is not "refutable" by evidence (apart from inadvertence—errors that are on the level of proofreading mistakes). It is for just this reason that such exercises are of very limited interest for linguistics as a field of rational inquiry.

In addition to features of English phonology which seem of no general systematic importance, we have omitted from our discussion many topics about which we have not been able to learn enough, though they may very well be of considerable importance. For example, we have omitted pitch from consideration because we have nothing to add to the study of the phonetics of intonation and have not yet attempted to deal with the still quite open question of the systematic role of pitch contours or levels within the general framework of syntactic and phonological theory as we so far understand it. (See Stockwell (1960), Bierwisch (1966), Lieberman (1966) for discussion of these topics.) Thus pitch and terminal juncture will never be marked in the examples we present. As far as we have been able to determine, the various omissions and gaps have no serious bearing on the questions that we have dealt with, although, clearly, one must keep an open mind on this matter.

The dialect of English that we study is essentially that described by Kenyon and Knott (1944). We depart from their transcriptions occasionally, in ways that will be noted, and we also discuss some matters (e.g., stress contours beyond the word level) not included in their transcriptions. For the most part, however, we have used very familiar data of the sort presented in Kenyon and Knott. In fact, their transcriptions are very close to our own speech, apart from certain dialectal idiosyncrasies of no general interest, which we omit. It seems to us that the rules we propose carry over, without major modification, to many other dialects of English, though it goes without saying that we have not undertaken the vast and intricate study of dialectal variation. For reasons that we will discuss in detail, it seems to us very likely that the underlying lexical (or phonological) representations must be common to all English dialects, with rare exceptions, and that much of the basic framework of rules must be common as well. Of course, this is an empirical question, which must be left to future research. We will make only a few remarks about dialectal variation, where this seems to have some bearing on the problems we discuss.

The general point of view that underlies this descriptive study is one that several of us have been developing for more than fifteen years, at M.I.T. and elsewhere, at first independently, but increasingly as a joint effort. It is represented in such publications as Chomsky, *Syntactic Structures* (1957a); Halle, *The Sound Pattern of Russian* (1959); Chomsky, *Current Issues in Linguistic Theory* (1964); Katz and Postal, *An Integrated Theory of Linguistic Descriptions* (1964); Chomsky, *Aspects of the Theory of Syntax* (1965); Matthews, *Hidatsa Syntax* (1965); Katz, *The Philosophy of Language* (1966); Postal, *Aspects of Phonological Theory* (1968); and in many articles, reports, and dissertations. Much of the apparent novelty of this point of view is the result of historical accident. Although it naturally owes very much to the important studies, both of general linguistics and of English, that have been carried on during the past thirty or forty years, the approach that is developed in the works cited and that we follow here has much deeper roots in an older, largely forgotten, and widely disparaged tradition. (See Chomsky (1964, 1966a) and Postal (1964b) for discussion.) It seems to us accurate to describe the study of generative grammar, as it has developed during recent years, as fundamentally a continuation of this very rich tradition, rather than as an entirely novel departure.

We have been working on this book, with varying degrees of intensity, for about ten years, and have discussed and presented various aspects of this work at several stages of development. One or the other of us has lectured on this material at M.I.T. for the past seven years. No system of rules that we have proposed has survived a course of lectures unchanged, and we do not doubt that the same fate awaits the grammatical sketch that we develop here.

The research for this book was conducted largely at the Research Laboratory of Electronics, M.I.T., and has been partly assisted by grants from the National Science Foundation and, more recently, from the National Institute of Health (Grant 1 PO1 MH 13390–01).

It would be impossible for us, at this point, to acknowledge in detail the contribution that our students and colleagues have made to the clarification and modification of our ideas. We would like to thank Robert Lees and Paul Postal for their many invaluable comments and suggestions; Paul Kiparsky, Theodore Lightner, and John Ross for the questions they have raised and the answers they have supplied or forced us to find; Richard Carter, S. Jay Keyser, S. Y. Kuroda, James Sledd, Richard Stanley, and Robert Stockwell for reading and criticizing various parts of the book in different stages of its evolution. We owe thanks to Patricia Wanner, who has been in charge of typing the numerous versions of the manuscript, to Karen Ostapenko, Deborah MacPhail, and Michael Brame, who have prepared the Bibliography and Indexes, and to Florence Warshawsky Harris, our editor and former student, who has devoted a major part of her life during these last two years to seeing our difficult and forever unfinished manuscript through the press.

We dedicate the book to Roman Jakobson to mark, albeit belatedly, his seventieth birthday and to express our admiration and gratitude for his inspired teaching and his warm friendship which for so many years have enriched our lives.

Noam Chomsky
Morris Halle

CONTENTS

PART IV   PHONOLOGICAL THEORY

SEVEN · THE PHONETIC FRAMEWORK   293

PART I
GENERAL SURVEY

Chapter one

SETTING

1. Grammar

The goal of the descriptive study of a language is the construction of a grammar. We may think of a language as a set of sentences, each with an ideal phonetic form and an associated intrinsic semantic interpretation. The grammar of the language is the system of rules that specifies this sound-meaning correspondence.

The speaker produces a signal with a certain intended meaning; the hearer receives a signal and attempts to determine what was said and what was intended. The performance of the speaker or hearer is a complex matter that involves many factors. One fundamental factor involved in the speaker-hearer's performance is his knowledge of the grammar that determines an intrinsic connection of sound and meaning for each sentence. We refer to this knowledge—for the most part, obviously, unconscious knowledge—as the speaker-hearer's "competence." Competence, in this sense, is not to be confused with performance. Performance, that is, what the speaker-hearer actually does, is based not only on his knowledge of the language, but on many other factors as well—factors such as memory restrictions, inattention, distraction, nonlinguistic knowledge and beliefs, and so on. We may, if we like, think of the study of competence as the study of the potential performance of an idealized speaker-hearer who is unaffected by such grammatically irrelevant factors.

We use the term "grammar" with a systematic ambiguity. On the one hand, the term refers to the explicit theory constructed by the linguist and proposed as a description of the speaker's competence. On the other hand, we use the term to refer to this competence itself. The former usage is familiar; the latter, though perhaps less familiar, is equally appropriate. The person who has acquired knowledge of a language has internalized a system of rules that determines sound-meaning connections for indefinitely many sentences. Of course, the person who knows a language perfectly has little or no conscious knowledge of the rules that he uses constantly in speaking or hearing, writing or reading, or internal monologue. It is this system of rules that enables him to produce and interpret sentences that he has never before encountered. It is an important fact, too often overlooked, that in normal, everyday discourse one understands and produces new utterances with no awareness of novelty or innovation, although these normal utterances are similar to those previously produced or encountered only in that they are formed and interpreted by the same grammar, the same internalized system of rules. It is important to emphasize that there is no significant sense of "generalization" in which these new utterances can be described as generalizations from earlier experience, and no sense of the term "habit" in which the normal use of language can be described as some kind of "habit system" or as "habitual behavior." We cannot, in other words, characterize the internalized, mentally represented system of rules that we call the "grammar" in terms of any other significant concept of psychology.

To summarize, then, we use the term "grammar" to refer both to the system of rules represented in the mind of the speaker-hearer, a system which is normally acquired in early childhood and used in the production and interpretation of utterances, and to the theory that the linguist constructs as a hypothesis concerning the actual internalized grammar of the speaker-hearer. No confusion should result from this standard usage if the distinction is kept in mind.

2. Linguistic universals

General linguistics attempts to develop a theory of natural language as such, a system of hypotheses concerning the essential properties of any human language. These properties determine the class of possible natural languages and the class of potential grammars for some human language. The essential properties of natural language are often referred to as "linguistic universals." Certain apparent linguistic universals may be the result merely of historical accident. For example, if only inhabitants of Tasmania survive a future war, it might be a property of all then existing languages that pitch is not used to differentiate lexical items. Accidental universals of this sort are of no importance for general linguistics, which attempts rather to characterize the range of possible human languages. The significant linguistic universals are those that must be assumed to be available to the child learning a language as an a priori, innate endowment. That there must be a rich system of a priori properties—of essential linguistic universals—is fairly obvious from the following empirical observations. Every normal child acquires an extremely intricate and abstract grammar, the properties of which are much underdetermined by the available data. This takes place with great speed, under conditions that are far from ideal, and there is little significant variation among children who may differ greatly in intelligence and experience. The search for essential linguistic universals is, in effect, the study of the a priori *faculté de langage* that makes language acquisition possible under the given conditions of time and access to data.

It is useful to divide linguistic universals roughly into two categories. There are, first of all, certain "formal universals" that determine the structure of grammars and the form and organization of rules. In addition, there are "substantive universals" that define the sets of elements that may figure in particular grammars. For example, the theory of transformational generative grammar proposes certain formal universals regarding the kinds of rules that can appear in a grammar, the kinds of structures on which they may operate, and the ordering conditions under which these rules may apply. We shall study these questions in detail, in connection with the phonological component of a generative grammar. Similarly, general linguistic theory might propose, as substantive universals, that the lexical items of any language are assigned to fixed categories such as noun, verb, and adjective, and that phonetic transcriptions must make use of a particular, fixed set of phonetic features. The latter topic, once again, will occupy us in this book. We will be concerned with the theory of "universal phonetics," that part of general linguistics that specifies the class of "possible phonetic representations" of sentences by determining the universal set of phonetic features and the conditions on their possible combinations. The phonetic form of each sentence in each language is drawn from this class of possible phonetic representations.

3. *Phonetic representations*

What exactly is a phonetic representation? Suppose that universal phonetics establishes that utterances are sequences of discrete segments, that segments are complexes of a particular set of phonetic features, and that the simultaneous and sequential combinations of these features are subject to a set of specific constraints. For example, universal phonetics may provide us with the feature "consonantal," which distinguishes [+consonantal] phonetic segments such as [p], [t], [θ], [s], [š] from [−consonantal] phonetic segments such as [u], [i], [a]; and the feature "strident," which distinguishes [+strident] segments such as [s] and [š] from [−strident] segments such as [p], [t], and [θ]. Among the "simultaneous constraints" of universal phonetics would be the condition that no phonetic segment can be both [−consonantal] and [+strident]; the feature "strident" does not provide a further classification of the category of [−consonantal] segments. Among the "sequential constraints" might be certain conditions that assign a maximal length to a sequence of [+consonantal] phonetic segments, that is, to a consonant cluster. There will be many other constraints of both sorts, and they must be met by each phonetic representation in each language.

More specifically, a phonetic representation has the form of a two-dimensional matrix in which the rows stand for particular phonetic features; the columns stand for the consecutive segments of the utterance generated; and the entries in the matrix determine the status of each segment with respect to the features. In a full phonetic representation, an entry might represent the degree of intensity with which a given feature is present in a particular segment; thus, instead of simply subdividing segments into [+strident] and [−strident], as in the example just given, the entries in the row corresponding to the feature "strident" might indicate degrees along a differentiated scale of "stridency." The phonetic symbols [p], [t], [θ], [i], [u], etc., are simply informal abbreviations for certain feature complexes; each such symbol, then, stands for a column of a matrix of the sort just described.

To recapitulate, the phonetic representation of an utterance in a given language is a matrix with rows labeled by features of universal phonetics. The grammar of the language assigns to this phonetic representation a "structural description" that indicates how it is to be interpreted, ideally, in this language. More generally, we may say that the grammar of each language assigns a structural description to each member of the universal class of possible phonetic representations. For example, the grammar of every language will assign structural descriptions to phonetic representations such as (1) and (2):[1]

$$\begin{pmatrix}1\end{pmatrix} \qquad \text{ilvyɛ̃dradəmɛ̃} \qquad (\text{"il viendra demain"})$$

$$\begin{pmatrix}2\end{pmatrix} \qquad \text{hiylkʌm+təmarə} \qquad (\text{"he'll come tomorrow"})$$

---

[1] We omit much phonetic detail that should be specified in universal representations but that is irrelevant to the exposition here. This is the course we will generally follow in discussing particular examples. In the representation (2), and in other representations in this chapter, we include the "boundary symbol" +, which can be taken as specifying a certain type of transition between phonetic elements. Actually, however, we will suggest later that boundary symbols do not appear in phonetic representations.

The grammar of English will assign to (1) a structural description indicating that it is not a sentence of English at all, and to (2) a structural description that specifies the elements of which it is composed on the various linguistic levels, the manner of their organization, the interrelations of these abstract representations, and so on. The grammar of French will supply this information for (1), and will designate (2) as a nonsentence. Many elements of the class of possible phonetic representations will be designated as "semi-grammatical sentences," not well-formed but nevertheless interpretable by analogy to well-formed sentences in ways that are, for the moment, not well understood.[2]

4. Components of a grammar

The class of possible phonetic representations is of course infinite. Similarly, the class of phonetic representations designated as well-formed sentences in each human language is infinite. No human language has a limit on the number of sentences that are properly formed and that receive a semantic interpretation in accordance with the rules of this language. However, the grammar of each language must obviously be a finite object, realized physically in a finite human brain. Therefore, one component of the grammar must have a recursive property; it must contain certain rules that can be applied indefinitely often, in new arrangements and combinations, in the generation (specification) of structural descriptions of sentences. Every language, in particular, contains processes that permit a sentence to be embedded within another sentence, as the English sentence *John left* is embedded in the sentence *I was surprised that John left*. These processes can apply indefinitely often to form sentences of arbitrary complexity. For example, the sentence *I was surprised that John left* can itself be embedded in the context *Bill expected ———*, giving, finally, *Bill expected me to be surprised that John left*, after various obligatory modifications have taken place. There is no limit to the number of applications of such processes; with each further application, we derive a well-formed sentence with a definite phonetic and semantic interpretation.

The part of a grammar which has this recursive property is the "syntactic component," the exact form of which will not concern us here.[3] We will, however, make certain assumptions about the abstract objects generated by the syntactic component, that is, about the "syntactic descriptions" that can be formed by the application of its rules.

The syntactic component of a grammar assigns to each sentence a "surface structure" that fully determines the phonetic form of the sentence. It also assigns a far more abstract "deep structure" which underlies and partially determines the surface structure but is otherwise irrelevant to phonetic interpretation, though it is of fundamental significance for semantic interpretation. It is important to bear in mind that deep structures are very different from the surface structures to which we will restrict our attention and that they provide a great deal of information not represented in surface structures.

To recapitulate, a grammar contains a syntactic component which is a finite system of rules generating an infinite number of syntactic descriptions of sentences. Each such syntactic description contains a deep structure and a surface structure that is partially determined by the deep structure that underlies it. The semantic component of the grammar

---

[2] For discussion of this matter, which we will exclude from consideration henceforth, see Section IV of Fodor and Katz (1964), and pages 148 ff. of Chomsky (1965), as well as many other references.

[3] For recent discussion, see Katz and Postal (1964) and Chomsky (1965).

is a system of rules that assigns a semantic interpretation to each syntactic description, making essential reference to the deep structure and possibly taking into account certain aspects of surface structure as well. The phonological component of the grammar assigns a phonetic interpretation to the syntactic description, making reference only to properties of the surface structure, so far as we know. The structural description assigned to a sentence by the grammar consists of its full syntactic description, as well as the associated semantic and phonetic representations. Thus the grammar generates an infinite number of sentences, each of which has a phonetic and semantic representation; it defines an infinite sound-meaning correspondence, this correspondence being mediated by the abstract syntactic component and the structures it generates.

We are not concerned here with deep structures and the rules that generate them, the rules that relate them to surface structures, or the rules that assign semantic interpretations to syntactic descriptions. We are limiting our attention to surface structures, phonetic representations, and the rules that assign a phonetic representation (possibly several phonetic representations, in the case of free variation) to each surface structure.

5. Surface structures

The surface structures generated by the syntactic component have the following characteristics. Each consists of a string of minimal elements that we will call "formatives." Each formative is assigned to various categories that determine its abstract underlying form, the syntactic functions it can fulfill, and its semantic properties. For example, the formative *boy* will belong to the category of elements with initial voiced stops,[4] to the category "noun," to the category "animate," to the category "male," etc. This information about formatives will be presented in a "lexicon," which forms part of the syntactic component of the grammar. The organization of the lexicon will not concern us here; we simply assume that the full categorization of each formative is represented in the surface structure. In fact, we may think of the lexical entry of a formative as nothing other than a list of the categories to which it belongs. The categories are sometimes called "features." We will refer, as we proceed, to phonological, syntactic, and semantic features.

The surface structure must indicate how the string of formatives it contains is subdivided into "phrases," each phrase being a certain continuous substring of the string of formatives. The analysis of strings into phrases is a "proper bracketing" in the sense that phrases can overlap only if one is contained in the other. Thus, if A, B, C are formatives, the surface structure of the string ABC cannot specify AB as a phrase and BC as a phrase, for the string may be bracketed either as $((AB)C)$ or as $(A(BC))$ but not in both ways simultaneously.

The phrases furthermore are assigned to certain categories, and this information may be represented by putting labels on the brackets. Take, for example, the sentence (3):

$$\left(3\right) \qquad \textit{we established telegraphic communication}$$

In (3), the string underlying *we* is assigned to the same category as the string underlying

---

[4] This underlying representation will be abstract in a sense that we will later describe in detail. For example, although the formative *boy* is always represented phonetically with a back vowel, we will present evidence showing that it should be represented in surface structure—that is, before the phonological rules apply—with a front vowel.

telegraphic communication, namely, to the category "noun phrase." Similarly, the other phrases are assigned to certain universal categories.

We will make the empirical assumption that the surface structure of a sentence is precisely a proper bracketing of a string of formatives, with the bracketed substrings (the phrases) assigned to categories selected from a certain fixed universal set of categories. The complete string is assigned to the category "sentence"(S); the other phrases are also assigned to categories that are provided by general linguistic theory, such as the categories "noun phrase" (NP) and "verb phrase" (VP). These universal categories are on a par with the phonetic categories (bilabial closure, frontness, etc.) provided by universal phonetic theory. As we noted earlier, the categories of universal phonetic theory determine a certain infinite class of possible phonetic representations from which the phonetic forms of sentences of any human language are drawn. Similarly, the universal set of phrase categories (NP, VP, etc.), together with the universal lexical categories (noun, verb, adjective) and the universal lexical features that define the class of "possible formatives," provides us with an infinite class of possible surface structures, from which· the surface structures of sentences of any particular language are drawn. In other words, general linguistics should provide definitions, in terms independent of any particular language, for the notions "possible phonetic representation" and "possible surface structure." The grammar of each language relates phonetic representations to surface structures in a specific way; and, furthermore, it relates surface structures to deep structures, and, indirectly, to semantic interpretations, in ways that are beyond the scope of our present study.

To give a concrete example, the grammar of English might assign to the sentence (3) a surface structure which can be represented in the equivalent forms (4) and (5):[5]

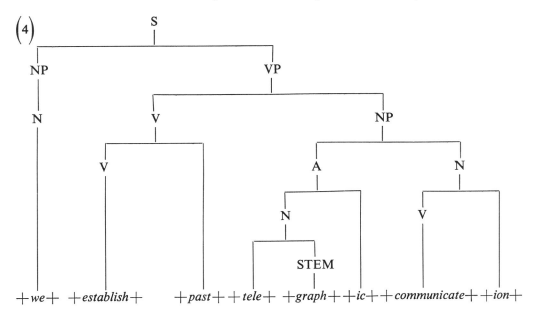

$\left(\begin{smallmatrix}5\end{smallmatrix}\right)$ [s [NP [N +we+]N]NP [VP [V [V +establish+]V +past+]V [NP [A [N +tele+ [STEM +graph+]STEM]N +ic+]A [N [V +communicate+]V +ion+]N]NP]VP]s

[5] Once again (see note 1), we omit details which are irrelevant here. We assume, for the purposes of this example, that the formatives are *we, establish, past, tele, graph, ic, communicate, ion*. The node labeled A represents the lexical category "adjective"; the other labels have been mentioned previously.

The interpretation of the notational devices used in (4) and (5) should be obvious. We intend these representations to indicate that the formative *we* is both an N and an NP, the formative *establish* a V, the formative string *tele graph* an N, the formative string *tele graph ic communicate ion* an NP, the full string an S, etc.[6] Furthermore, each formative has an analysis as a set of intersecting categories, in a way that we shall specify in more detail below. The + symbols represent formative boundaries which, by convention, automatically mark the beginning and end of each formative.

5.1. *LEXICAL AND PHONOLOGICAL REPRESENTATIONS*

To recapitulate, we presuppose, for our description of English sound patterns, a grammar with a syntactic component that assigns to each sentence a surface structure such as (4)-(5), that is, a proper labeled bracketing of a string of formatives. Our main concern here will be the "phonological component," that is, the system of rules that applies to a surface structure and assigns to it a certain phonetic representation drawn from the universal class provided by general linguistic theory. In particular, the phonological rules of English must assign to the surface structure (4)-(5) a phonetic representation much like (6):

$$(6) \qquad \text{wīyəstǽblišt+tèləgrǽfik+kəmyûwnəkéyšən}$$

The phonetic representation (6), corresponding to the underlying surface structure (4)-(5), is a feature matrix of the sort described earlier. In the surface structure, the individual formatives (for example, the lexical formatives *we, establish, tele, graph, communicate,* and the grammatical formatives *past, ic, ion*) will themselves be represented as feature matrices of an abstract sort, and we must now say a few words about this kind of representation. We shall distinguish between "lexical representations" and "phonological representations." We shall use the term "lexical representation" in reference to formatives which are provided directly by the lexicon, i.e., the lexical formatives as well as certain grammatical formatives which happen to appear in lexical entries. There may be other grammatical formatives introduced directly by the syntactic rules themselves. Thus the syntactic rules and the lexicon, applied in a manner that does not concern us here, provide for each utterance a representation as a string of formatives with surface structure.

Notice, however, that the surface structure must meet two independent conditions: first, it must be appropriate for the rules of phonological interpretation; second, it must be "syntactically motivated," that is, it must result from the application of independently motivated syntactic rules. Thus we have two concepts of surface structure: input to the phonological component and output of the syntactic component. It is an empirical question whether these two concepts coincide. In fact, they do coincide to a very significant degree, but there are also certain discrepancies. These discrepancies, some of which we discuss as we proceed, indicate that the grammar must contain certain rules converting the surface structures generated by the syntactic component into a form appropriate for use by the phonological component. In particular, if a linguistic expression reaches a certain level of complexity, it will be divided into successive parts that we will call "phonological phrases," each of which is a maximal domain for phonological processes. In simple cases the whole sentence is a single phonological phrase; in more complex cases the sentence may be re-analyzed as a sequence of phonological phrases. The analysis into phonological phrases

---

[6] Since in representations such as (4) the category labels are placed above the elements in the string that belong to these categories, one frequently speaks of the category as "dominating" a string or a part of a string. Thus, with respect to (4), we will say both that *we* "is an" N and that *we* "is dominated by" N.

depends in part on syntactic structure, but it is not always syntactically motivated in the sense just mentioned. If the syntactic component were to be connected to an orthographic rather than a phonetic output system, the reanalysis into phonological phrases would be unnecessary. Writers, unlike speakers, do not run out of breath, and are not subject to other physiological constraints on output that require an analysis into phonological phrases.

In addition to a reanalysis into phonological phrases in complex cases, the "readjust-ment rules" relating syntax to phonology make various other modifications in surface structures. It seems that in general these modifications involve elimination of structure, that is, deletion of nodes in representations such as (4) or of paired brackets in representa-tions such as (5). One can easily imagine why this should be so. Reasoning along lines suggested in Miller and Chomsky (1963, Part 2), let us suppose that perception involves a two-stage memory. The first stage is a short-term system quite limited in capacity and operating in real time in the sense that it must remain available for receiving the incoming signal, and the second stage is a very large system that operates on information supplied to it by the short-term real-time system. The short-term first stage must provide an initial analysis of the signal that is just sufficient in detail to permit the second-stage system to derive the deep structure and semantic interpretation. We might expect a language to be so designed that a very superficial analysis into phrases can be performed by a system with limited memory and heavy restrictions on access. To relate this speculation to the discussion of surface structure, it appears that the syntactic component of the grammar generates a surface structure Σ which is converted, by readjustment rules that mark phonological phrases and delete structure, to a still more superficial structure Σ'. The latter then enters the phonological component of the grammar. We might speculate, then, that a first stage of perceptual processing involves the recovery of Σ' from the signal using only the restricted short-term memory, and that a second stage provides the analysis into Σ and the deep structure that underlies it. From this point of view, it would be natural to suppose that the readjustment rules that form Σ' from Σ will have the effect of reducing structure. It is, incidentally, worthy of note that the transformations that form surface structures from deep structures also characteristically have the effect of reducing structure, in a sense which can be made precise.[7]

Let us return now to our discussion of lexical and phonological representations. We have used the term "lexical representation" to refer to the representation of formatives provided by the lexicon. As we have stated, however, the structures generated through the interaction of syntactic and lexical rules are not quite appropriate, in certain cases, for the application of the rules of the phonological component. They must be modified by certain readjustment rules (of a sort to which we will return in Chapter Eight, Section 6.5, noting, however, that our investigation of the effects of surface structure on phonetic representation has not yet reached a level of depth and complexity that requires a detailed, formal analysis of these processes).[8] These readjustment rules may somewhat modify the labeled bracketing of surface structure. They may also construct new feature matrices for certain strings of lexical and grammatical formatives. To take an obvious example, the verb *sing* will appear in the lexicon as a certain feature matrix, as will the verb *mend*. Using letters of the alphabet as informal abbreviations for certain complexes of features, i.e., certain columns of a feature matrix, we can represent the syntactically generated surface structure underlying the

---

[7] See Miller and Chomsky (1963). See also Ross (1967) for further relevant observations of a different sort on reduction of structure under transformations.

[8] See Bierwisch (1966) for a very interesting study of readjustment rules of the sort mentioned here.

forms *sang* and *mended* as [$_V$ [$_V$*sing*]$_V$ *past*]$_V$ and [$_V$ [$_V$*mend*]$_V$ *past*]$_V$, respectively, where *past* is a formative with an abstract feature structure introduced by syntactic rules. The readjustment rules would replace *past* by *d*, as a general rule; but, in the case of *sang*, would delete the item *past* with the associated labeled brackets, and would add to the *i* of *sing* a feature specification indicating that it is subject to a later phonological rule which, among other things, happens to convert *i* to *æ*. Designating this new column as *, the readjustment rules would therefore give the forms [$_V$*s*ng*]$_V$ and [$_V$ [$_V$*mend*]$_V$ *d*]$_V$, respectively. We shall refer to this representation—and in general to the representation given by the application of all readjustment rules—as the "phonological representation."

Other terms that might have been used in place of the terms just proposed are "morphophonemic representation" or "systematic phonemic representation." We have avoided these terms, however, because of the technical meaning they have been given in various theories of sound structure developed in modern linguistics. The term "morphophonemic representation" seems to us appropriate only if there is another linguistically significant level of representation, intermediate in "abstractness" between lexical (phonological) and phonetic and meeting the conditions placed on "phonemic representation" in modern structural linguistics. We feel, however, that the existence of such a level has not been demonstrated and that there are strong reasons to doubt its existence.[9] We will make no further mention of "phonemic analysis" or "phonemes" in this study and will also avoid terms such as "morphophonemic" which imply the existence of a phonemic level. Notice that the issue in this case is not terminological but rather substantive; the issue is whether the rules of a grammar must be so constrained as to provide, at a certain stage of generation, a system of representation meeting various proposed conditions. The references in note 9 explain our position, and we will say no more about the matter here.

5.2. *ON THE ABSTRACTNESS OF LEXICAL REPRESENTATIONS*

We have said that the underlying representations, lexical as well as phonological, are abstract as compared with phonetic representations, although both are given in terms of phonetic features. The meaning of this remark will become clearer as we proceed. There is, however, one very obvious sense in which the underlying representations are more abstract than the phonetic representations. Consider, for example, the word *telegraph*. This has several different variants in actual phonetic representations:[10]

$$(7) \qquad \overset{1}{\text{tel}}\text{ə}\overset{3}{\text{gr}}\text{æf}^{11} \qquad \text{(in isolation)}$$

$$(8) \qquad \overset{3}{\text{tel}}\text{ə}\overset{1}{\text{gr}}\text{æf} \qquad \text{(in the context ——— } ic; \text{ i.e., } telegraphic)$$

$$(9) \qquad \text{təl}\overset{1}{\text{e}}\text{grəf} \qquad \text{(in the context ——— } y; \text{ i.e., } telegraphy)$$

It is quite obvious, however, that this phonetic variation is not fortuitous—it is not of the

---

[9] We have presented our reasons for doubting the existence of a phonemic level, in the sense of modern linguistics, in various places. See Halle (1959), Chomsky (1964, 1966b), and Chomsky and Halle (1965), as well as Postal (1962, 1968), for arguments that seem to us fully convincing.

[10] Notice that in the sentence (6) it has still another representation because of the stress modifications that take place in that context.

[11] Stress levels are indicated here and throughout by numerals, with "1" representing primary stress, "2" representing secondary stress, etc. (See also note 3 in Chapter Two on this subject.)

same type as the variation between *I* and *we*, which depends on specific assignment of the latter to the category of plurality. Given the grammar of English, if we delete specific reference to the item *we*, there is no way to predict the phonetic form of the plural variant of *I*. On the other hand, the rules for English grammar certainly do suffice to determine the phonetic variation of *telegraph* without specific mention of this lexical item, just as they suffice to predict the regular variation between *cat* and *cats* without specifically mentioning the plural form. It is quite obvious that English grammar is complicated by the fortuitous variation between *I* and *we* but not by the totally predictable variation between *cat* and *cats*. Similarly, the grammar would be more complicated if *telegraph* did *not* undergo precisely the variation in (7)–(9): if, for example, it had one phonetic form in all contexts, or if it had the form (7) in the context —— *ic*, (8) in the context —— *y*, and (9) in isolation.

In short, the phonetic variation of *telegraph* in certain contexts is not an idiosyncratic property of this particular lexical item but is rather a matter of general rule, applying to many other lexical items as well. Regular variations such as this are not matters for the lexicon, which should contain only idiosyncratic properties of items, properties not predictable by general rule. The lexical entry for *telegraph* must contain just enough information for the rules of English phonology to determine its phonetic form in each context; since the variation is fully determined, the lexical entry must contain no indication of the effect of context on the phonetic form. In fact, as we shall see, the lexical representation for the word *telegraph* should be (10), where each of the symbols *t, e, . . .* is to be understood as an informal abbreviation for a certain set of phonological categories (distinctive features):[12]

$$\left(10\right) \qquad\qquad +\text{tele}+\text{græf}+$$

Thus the lexical representation is abstract in a very clear sense; it relates to the signal only indirectly, through the medium of the rules of phonological interpretation that apply to it as determined by its intrinsic abstract representation and the surface structures in which it appears.

An analogous argument can readily be constructed for the abstract nature of the phonological representations, i.e., those representations that are determined from lexical representations by application of certain readjustment rules (and which, for the most part, are in fact identical with lexical representations).

5.3. *ANALYSIS INTO WORDS*

One additional aspect of surface structure is crucial for our discussion. We will see that the phonological rules fall into two very different classes. Certain of these rules apply freely to phrases of any size, up to the level of the phonological phrase; others apply only to words. We must therefore assume that the surface structure of an utterance provides an analysis into a sequence of words. For example, the sentence (3), *we established telegraphic communication*, will be analyzed by its surface structure into the four successive words *we, establish+past, tele+graph+ic, communicate+ion*. The rules that form surface structure (or, perhaps, the readjustment rules discussed above) must provide this information, since it is required for the correct application of the rules of the phonological component of the grammar.

As a first approximation to the problem of analysis into words, let us assume that each lexical category (e.g., noun, verb, adjective) and each category that dominates a lexical

---

[12] In addition, the lexical entry will provide the other idiosyncratic syntactic information represented in (4)-(5), namely, the information that *graph* is a stem and *telegraph* is a noun.

category (e.g., sentence, noun phrase, verb phrase) automatically carries a boundary symbol # to the left and to the right of the string that belongs to it (i.e., that it dominates, in tree representations such as (4), or that it brackets, in bracket representations such as (5)). Under this assumption, we replace the representation (4) by (11) and modify (5) in a corresponding way:

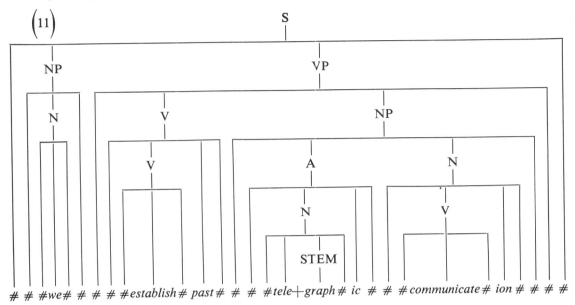

$$\text{\# \# \#} we \text{\#} \text{ \# \# \#} establish \text{\#} past \text{\#} \text{ \# \# \#} tele\!+\!graph \text{\#} ic \text{ \# \# \#} communicate \text{\#} ion \text{ \# \# \# \#}$$

Let us tentatively define a word as a string of formatives (one or more) contained in the context # # —— # # and containing no occurrences of # #.[13] Thus the words in (11) are *we*, *establish#past*, *tele+graph#ic*, and *communicate#ion*, as required. The principle just stated can be regarded, tentatively, as a universal principle for the interpretation of surface structures, and, as a first approximation, it works quite well. Among the readjustment rules discussed above, there will be some that modify the representation provided by this interpretive principle in ad hoc ways. For example, we shall see that although the boundary # is appropriate in *establish#ed*, as distinct from ordinary formative boundary (which we have been representing as +), it must be replaced by ordinary formative boundary in *tele+graph#ic* and *communicate#ion*, for reasons having to do with the applicability of certain phonetic rules.

To recapitulate, the rules of syntax will generate surface structures and a universal principle of interpretation will assign the boundary symbol # in certain places. The readjustment rules will modify the surface structure in various ad hoc ways, demarcating it into phonological phrases, eliminating some structure, and replacing some occurrences of # by +. The abstract object thus constructed (which we will also refer to as a "surface structure," or, if more explicitness is necessary, a "phonological surface structure," to contrast it with the syntactic surface structure generated by the syntactic component) enters the phonological component of the grammar and is converted by the phonological rules into a phonetic representation, in ways that we will specify in detail as we proceed. Certain of the phonological rules will apply only to words; others will apply freely to strings of formatives which may be words or subparts of words, or phrases that include words.

[13] See Chapter Eight, Section 6.2, for a more careful analysis of the notion "word."

We will find it convenient to use labeled bracketing such as (5) rather than tree diagrams such as (4) and (11) for the representation of surface structure in the presentation of phonological rules. Since, by convention, every lexical category or category dominating a lexical category has # boundaries associated with it on the left and right, we will sometimes omit reference to these boundaries in the statement of rules. For example, a rule of the form (12) is to be understood as applying to the string (13):

$$\left(12\right) \qquad\qquad A \;\rightarrow\; B \;\;/\; X \underline{\qquad} Y]_\mathbf{V}$$

$$\left(13\right) \qquad\qquad X A Y \#]_\mathbf{V}$$

Rule (12) states that an element of the type A is rewritten as a corresponding element of the type B when A appears in the context $X \underline{\qquad} Y$ (that is, with X to its left and Y to its right) and when the item in question is a verb, i.e., is dominated by V or, equivalently, is bracketed by $[_\mathbf{V} \;]_\mathbf{V}$. We will make these informal specifications more precise as we proceed.

6. Summary

The phonological component is a system of rules such as (12) that relates surface structures such as (11) to phonetic representations such as (6). As we proceed in our discussion, we will propose various specific hypotheses regarding the detailed form of representations such as (11) and (6), and we will also make specific proposals concerning the system of phonological rules that assign a phonetic interpretation to each surface structure.

We have already suggested that a phonetic representation such as (6) is actually a feature matrix in which the rows correspond to a restricted set of universal phonetic categories or features (voicing, nasality, etc.) and the columns to successive segments. We will propose further that such representations are mentally constructed by the speaker and the hearer and underlie their actual performance in speaking and "understanding." We will consider the question of the relation between such phonetic representations and actual speech signals, and the steps by which such representations might be constructed by the hearer on the occasion of reception of a speech signal. We have suggested, moreover, that each formative of the surface structure can also be represented as a feature matrix interpreted in a rather similar way, with rows corresponding to the universal phonetic and grammatical categories. The formative structure is much more abstract, however; its relation to the speech signal is not as direct as that of the phonetic representation.

We will propose that the rules of the phonological component have a fixed form and a specific organization, that they apply in a fixed manner determined by the labeled bracketing of the surface structure, and that they meet various additional conditions depending on their formal relations. These we propose as universal conditions, as aspects of general linguistic theory. We will try to show how, on the basis of these assumptions, many particular phenomena of English sound structure can be explained.

With these remarks on background assumptions, we can proceed to the analysis of English sound structure and of general phonological theory.

Chapter two

A SKETCH OF
ENGLISH PHONOLOGY AND
PHONOLOGICAL THEORY

1. The principle of the transformational cycle and its application to English stress contours

We turn here to the problem of how a surface structure of the sort described in the preceding chapter determines a phonetic representation.

It is well known that English has complex prosodic contours involving many levels of stress and pitch[1] and intricate processes of vowel reduction. It is clear even from a superficial examination that these contours are determined in some manner by the surface structure of the utterance. Furthermore, it is natural to suppose that in general the phonetic shape of a complex unit (a phrase) will be determined by the inherent properties of its parts and the manner in which these parts are combined, and that similar rules will apply to units of different levels of complexity. These observations suggest a general principle for the application of rules of the phonological component, namely, what we shall call the principle of the "transformational cycle."[2] Regarding a surface structure as a labeled bracketing (see representation (5) in Chapter One), we assume as a general principle that the phonological rules first apply to the maximal strings that contain no brackets, and that after all relevant rules have applied, the innermost brackets are erased; the rules then reapply to maximal strings containing no brackets, and again innermost brackets are erased after this application; and so on, until the maximal domain of phonological processes is reached. In terms of the tree representation of a surface structure (see representation (4) in Chapter One), the rules apply to a string dominated by a particular node A only after they have already applied to the strings dominated by each of the nodes dominated by A.

The actual operation of the transformational cycle can now be illustrated with some simple examples. It is clear, first of all, that there are at least two processes of stress

---

[1] As we explained in the Preface, we will have nothing to say about pitch in this study.

[2] This principle was first formulated in Chomsky, Halle, Lukoff (1956) in a slightly different but equivalent terminology. It has since been applied to phonetic study of a variety of different languages: French (Schane, 1965), Russian (Halle, 1963, Lightner, 1965a), Japanese (McCawley, 1965).

assignment in English. Thus *bláckboàrd*,[3] with a falling stress contour, must be distinguished from *blàck bóard*, with a rising contour. The elementary constituents, *black*, an adjective, and *board*, a noun, are the same in both cases; the difference lies in the way these constituents are combined, as reflected in their different surface structures, shown here in the two notations of the preceding chapter:

$\begin{pmatrix}1\end{pmatrix}$

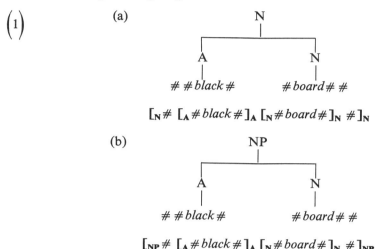

(a)

$[_N \# \ [_A \# black \#]_A \ [_N \# board \#]_N \ \#]_N$

(b)

$[_{NP} \# \ [_A \# black \#]_A \ [_N \# board \#]_N \ \#]_{NP}$

In case (1a), where the entire phrase belongs to the category "noun," the phonological rules must give the contour 13; in case (1b), where it belongs to the category "noun phrase," the rules must give the contour 21. According to the principle of the transformational cycle, the phonological rules apply first to the strings dominated by A and by N, the lowest-level categorial nodes of (1); in other words, the rules apply first to *black* and to *board*. In isolation, each of these would receive primary stress. We therefore might propose the rule:

$\begin{pmatrix}2\end{pmatrix}$ In monosyllables, the vowel receives primary stress.

Applying this rule to the structures of (1) and then erasing innermost brackets in accordance with the principle of the transformational cycle, we have, in the bracket notation, the representations (3a) and (3b):

$\begin{pmatrix}3\end{pmatrix}$ (a) $[_N \# \# bláck \# \ \# bóard \# \#]_N$ (b) $[_{NP} \# \# bláck \# \ \# bóard \# \#]_{NP}$

We must now apply rules that weaken the rightmost primary stress in case (3a) and that weaken the leftmost primary stress in case (3b). For many reasons, it is necessary to state the rules that determine stress contours as rules of placement of primary stress, rather than as rules of stress weakening. We will therefore formulate the rules that apply to (3) as processes that place primary stress on the leftmost and the rightmost syllables, respectively, and we will adopt the following convention: *when primary stress is placed in a certain*

---

[3] There are various conventions in use for marking stress, which, at least in part, appear to differ in factual content. We return to this matter later. Here, as mentioned in Chapter One, note 11, in place of the conventional symbols ´, ˆ, `, ˇ for primary, secondary, tertiary, and quaternary (zero) stress, respectively, we will simply use numerals, starting with 1 for primary stress. It should be kept in mind that the numbers go down as the stress goes up, admittedly a disadvantage of this notation. To minimize confusion, we will speak of strengthening and weakening stress, rather than of increasing and decreasing it.

position, then all other stresses in the string under consideration at that point are automatically weakened by one. We can now state the following two rules:

$\left(4\right)$ Assign primary stress to a primary-stressed vowel in the context

$$\text{---} \dots \overset{1}{\text{V}} \dots]_N$$

$\left(5\right)$ Assign primary stress to a primary-stressed vowel in the context

$$\overset{1}{\text{V}} \dots \text{---} \dots]_{NP}$$

In rules (4) and (5), the symbol V stands for "vowel," and $\overset{1}{\text{V}}$ stands for a vowel with primary stress. The dash indicates the position of the segment to which the rule applies. Thus rule (4) assigns primary stress to a primary-stressed vowel which is *followed* by another primary-stressed vowel in a noun, and rule (5) assigns primary stress to a primary-stressed vowel which is *preceded* by another primary-stressed vowel in a noun phrase. By the convention stated above, the actual effect of these rules is to weaken the other stresses in the string to which the rule applies. Thus, applying rule (4) to (3a), we derive the representation (6a); applying rule (5) to (3b), we derive the representation (6b).

$\left(6\right)$ (a) $\#\#bl\overset{1}{a}ck\#\#b\overset{2}{o}ard\#\#$ (b) $\#\#bl\overset{2}{a}ck\#\#b\overset{1}{o}ard\#\#$

We will refer to (4) as the Compound Rule and to (5) as the Nuclear Stress Rule.

It is important to observe that rules (4) and (5) make use of the bracketing given in the surface structure for their proper cyclic operation, and that the labels on the brackets, that is, the syntactic categories indicated in the surface structure, are necessary for determining the correct application of the rules.

To derive the stress contour for *blackboard*, we must apply still another rule, weakening the secondary stress on the second syllable to tertiary. This process can be formulated in the following way (with C_0 standing for a string of zero or more consonants):

$\left(7\right)$ Assign primary stress to a primary-stressed vowel in the context

$$\text{---} \dots \#\#C_0\overset{2}{V}C_0\#]_N$$

Application of rule (7) to (6a) gives the desired stress pattern 13 by the conventions established above; primary stress is placed on the first syllable, and the stress on the second syllable is automatically weakened to tertiary.

Clearly, both the Compound Rule and the Nuclear Stress Rule are of much greater generality than is indicated by the formulation we have given. Thus, rule (4) actually applies not only to compound nouns such as *blackboard*, but also to compound adjectives (*heart-$\overset{3}{broken}$*) and compound verbs ($\overset{1}{air}$-$\overset{3}{condition}$). It must therefore be extended to lexical categories in general. Similarly, the Nuclear Stress Rule applies not only to noun phrases, but to any phrase which is not a lexical category—for example, to verb phrases ($\overset{1}{read}$ the $\overset{2}{book}$), to adjective phrases ($\overset{2}{eager}$ to $\overset{1}{please}$), and to whole sentences ($\overset{2}{John}$ $\overset{1}{left}$). We therefore replace rules (4) and (5) by the formulations (8) and (9):

$\left(8\right)$ Assign primary stress to a primary-stressed vowel in the context

$$\text{---} \dots \overset{1}{\text{V}} \dots]_{NAV}$$

$\left(9\right)$ Assign primary stress to a primary-stressed vowel in the context

$$\overset{1}{\text{V}} \dots \text{---} \dots]_\alpha$$

where $]_\alpha$ stands for a bracket with any label except N, A, or V. We can make the notion "except" precise in a very simple way, namely, by requiring that the rules (8) and (9) apply in the order given. We can then take α in (9) to be simply a variable ranging over all categories. If rule (8) has applied, the resulting string will contain just one primary stress and thus will not fit the required context for (9). Therefore (9) will never apply when $\alpha = $ N, A, or V.

Using familiar notations, we can now formulate the Compound and Nuclear Stress Rules in the following way:

$$(10) \quad \begin{bmatrix} 1\ \text{stress} \\ V \end{bmatrix} \rightarrow [1\ \text{stress}] \quad / \quad \begin{cases} \underline{\quad} \dots \overset{1}{V} \dots]_{NAV} \\ \overset{1}{V} \dots \underline{\quad} \dots] \end{cases} \quad \begin{array}{l} \text{(a) \ COMPOUND RULE} \\ \text{(b) \ NUCLEAR STRESS RULE} \end{array}$$

In rule (10), we suppress the variable α. We interpret the rule as a sequence of two rules in accordance with the following quite general convention: a rule of the form (11) is an abbreviation for a sequence of rules of the form (12).

$$(11) \qquad\qquad X \rightarrow Y \quad / \quad \begin{cases} Z_1 \\ Z_2 \\ \vdots \\ Z_n \end{cases}$$

$$(12) \qquad\qquad \begin{array}{l} X \rightarrow Y \ / \ Z_1 \\ X \rightarrow Y \ / \ Z_2 \\ \qquad \vdots \\ X \rightarrow Y \ / \ Z_n \end{array}$$

The ith rule of (12) is interpreted as stating that any symbol meeting the condition X acquires the features listed as Y when it is in a context meeting the condition Z_i. In accordance with these conventions, which will be generalized as we proceed, the rules (10a)-(10b) have precisely the same content as the sequence (8)-(9).

The rules so far discussed illustrate two general observations that have proven valid in every careful study of phonological processes that has so far been undertaken within the framework of generative grammar, namely, the following:

(13) It is always possible to order the rules in a sequence and to adhere strictly to this ordering in constructing derivations without any loss of generality as compared to an unordered set of rules or a set ordered on a different principle.

(14) Such linear ordering makes it possible to formulate grammatical processes that would otherwise not be expressible with comparable generality.[4]

---

[4] We shall see later that certain qualifications are necessary in the formulation of (13) and (14).

   The observations (13), (14) are implicit in Bloomfield's "Menomini Morphophonemics" (1939). In Bever (1967), it is shown that the depth of ordering of Bloomfield's grammatical description is at least eleven; that is, from the linear sequence of rules constituting this grammar, a subsequence of eleven rules can be extracted with the property that the grammar becomes more complex if any two successive rules of this subsequence are interchanged in the ordering. In this same sense of depth of ordering, a depth of at least twenty-five is demonstrated in Chomsky (1951).

Neither of these statements is a necessary truth;[5] each represents an interesting and, for the present, reasonably well-confirmed empirical hypothesis. With the modification already stated as the principle of the transformational cycle, we will accept the empirical hypothesis

---

[5] This fact is sometimes overlooked in the case of (13). To illustrate the empirical character of (13), consider three hypothetical languages L_1, L_2, L_3, each containing the phonological segments A, B, X, Y and the lexical entries ABY, BAX. Suppose, furthermore, that in each of these languages it is a fact that B is realized as X before Y and that A is realized as Y before X. Thus the grammars contain the rules (α) and (β) as the most general statement of the facts:

$$(\alpha)\ B\ \rightarrow\ X\ /\ \text{---}\ Y$$

$$(\beta)\ A\ \rightarrow\ Y\ /\ \text{---}\ X$$

Suppose now that the lexical entries ABY and BAX are realized phonetically in the following ways in L_1, L_2, L_3:

In L_1	ABY is realized as YXY	BAX is realized as BYX
In L_2	ABY is realized as AXY	BAX is realized as XYX
In L_3	ABY is realized as AXY	BAX is realized as BYX

The facts of L_1 and L_2 can be accounted for by letting the rules (α) and (β) apply in different orders: in L_1 (α) precedes (β); in L_2 (β) precedes (α). Then in L_1 we will have the derivations of (I) for the lexical entries ABY and BAX, and in L_2 we will have the derivations of (II) for the same lexical entries:

(I)

ABY	BAX	
AXY		BY RULE (α)
YXY	BYX	BY RULE (β)

(II)

ABY	BAX	
	BYX	BY RULE (β)
AXY	XYX	BY RULE (α)

Hence the hypothetical languages L_1 and L_2 support the empirical generalizations (13) and (14). However, the facts of L_3 cannot be accounted for in this fashion. As we have just seen, neither the ordering (α), (β) nor the ordering (β), (α) will give the result required, namely, that ABY is realized as AXY and that BAX is realized as BYX. Nevertheless, rules (α) and (β) state the facts in the simplest and most general way. Therefore the hypothetical language L_3 refutes the empirical hypothesis (13). In fact, L_3 supports a different empirical hypothesis concerning rule ordering, namely, that rules be unordered and that they apply simultaneously, so that each derivation has only two steps. With this convention (call it the "simultaneous application" convention), we have the derivations (III), as required for L_3:

(III)

ABY		BAX	
AXY	BY RULE (α)	BYX	BY RULE (β)

The simultaneous application hypothesis was first made explicit by Z. S. Harris (1951, Appendix to §14.32), in a discussion of an example from Bloomfield (1939) in which statement (13) was explicitly assumed. It has since been restated several times by Lamb (1964 and elsewhere), who, however, introduced a new element into the discussion by his assumption that the simultaneous application hypothesis is simpler, in some absolute sense, than the hypothesis that rules apply in sequence, in a fixed order. We see no justification for such assumptions about an absolute sense of "simplicity," in this case, nor any relevance to such assumptions if they can be given sense. The issue seems to us an empirical one; that is, the issue is whether the case posited in the hypothetical language L_3 actually is representative of natural language. So far as we know, it is not. On the contrary, the empirical evidence in natural language rules against the hypothetical situation of L_3, and therefore against the simultaneous application hypothesis and in favor of the hypotheses (13), (14). We shall have more to say about this matter as we proceed. In fact, we shall note that there are situations, formally well defined, in which something like the simultaneous application hypothesis is correct, e.g., in the case of rules that switch values of a feature. (See Chapter Eight, Sections 3, 4.) Thus the situation is complex, but, we think, quite clear.
For further discussion, see Chomsky (1964, §4.2; 1967) and Chomsky and Halle (1965).

that the rules are linearly ordered as the basis for the work to be presented here, and will give many examples that support this hypothesis. We assume, then, the following principles:

$\begin{pmatrix}15\end{pmatrix}$ (a) The rules of the phonological component are linearly ordered in a sequence $R_1, \ldots, R_n$.

         (b) Each rule applies to a maximal string containing no internal brackets.

         (c) After applying the rule R_n, we proceed to the rule R_1.

         (d) Unless an application of R_n intervenes, the rule R_j cannot be applied after the rule R_i ($j < i$) has applied.

         (e) R_n is the rule: erase innermost brackets.

The joint effect of these principles is that the rules apply in a linear sequence to a minimal phrase of the surface structure, then reapply in the same sequence to the next larger phrase of the surface structure, and so on. When we speak of the principle of the "transformational cycle," we are referring to the empirical hypothesis (15). The statement of principle (15) is not yet sufficiently precise to resolve all questions as to how rules apply, and we will sharpen and refine it as we proceed.

In the technical terminology of the theory of generative grammar, the term "grammatical transformation" refers to a rule that applies to a string of symbols by virtue of some categorial representation of this string. We use the term "transformational" in referring to the principle just established since the rules in the cycle are transformational in the usual sense; that is, the domain of their applicability and the manner in which they apply is determined by the phrase structure of a string, not just by the sequence of elementary symbols of which the string is constituted.[6] More specifically, the application of the cyclical rules depends not only upon the formatives in the surface structure but also upon the way they are categorized. For example, the specification of N, A, or V is necessary for determining the applicability of the Compound Rule.

Notice, once again, that the principle of the transformational cycle is a very natural one. What it asserts, intuitively, is that the form of a complex expression is determined by a fixed set of processes that take account of the form of its parts. This is precisely what one would expect of an interpretive principle that applies to phrase markers, in this case, surface structures.[7]

Returning now to actual examples, let us consider the more complex phrases *black board-eraser* ("board eraser that is black"), *blackboard eraser* ("eraser for a blackboard"), and *black board eraser* ("eraser of a black board"), with the stress contours 213, 132, and 312, respectively.[8] Application of the rules discussed to the surface structure of these forms

---

[6] The rules involved here are, however, transformations of a very narrow and restricted class, the class referred to as "local transformations" in Chomsky (1965).

[7] Observe that the interpretive semantic rules must apply in accordance with essentially the same principle as the one stated here for the phonological rules, as has been pointed out by Fodor and Katz (1963) and by Katz and Postal (1964). The basic semantic rules apply to deep structures rather than to surface structures, however. In a sense the transformational syntactic rules also meet a similar cyclic condition. See Chomsky (1965, Chapter 3) for discussion

[8] Phoneticians might vary slightly in their description of the contours for these phrases. Whether these discrepancies are a matter of fact or of convention is a question to which we will return below. In any event, the matter is of little importance for the present. Our rules could be slightly modified to accommodate different decisions. For example, a slight revision of rule (7) would provide the contour 313 instead of 312 for the last example.

gives us the following derivations (with all occurrences of # suppressed):

$$\left(16\right)$$

(a) $[_{NP} [_{A}black]_{A} [_{N} [_{N}board]_{N} [_{N}eraser]_{N}]_{N}]_{NP}$
        1   1   RULE (2)
                                            1
    _____   _____   _____
                        1   2   RULE (10a)
                  _____
          2   1   3   RULE (10b)
    _____

(b) $[_{N} [_{N} [_{A}black]_{A} [_{N}board]_{N}]_{N} [_{N}eraser]_{N}]_{N}$
          1   1   RULE (2)
                                        1
    _____   _____   _____
          1   2   RULE (10a)
    _____
          1   3   2   RULE (10a)
    _____

(c) $[_{N} [_{NP} [_{A}black]_{A} [_{N}board]_{N}]_{NP} [_{N}eraser]_{N}]_{N}$
          1   1   RULE (2)
                                        1
                  _____   _____
          2   1   RULE (10b)
    _____
          3   1   2   RULE (10a)
    _____

These derivations illustrate the expository conventions that we will use henceforth. Let us now consider them in detail.

In the case of (16a), in the first cycle primary stress is placed on the minimal phrases *black* and *board*, which are monosyllables and therefore subject to rule (2). Also in the first cycle, primary stress is placed on *eraser* by a rule which we have not yet presented. Innermost brackets are then erased, and we return to the first of the linear sequence of transformational rules. The string now under consideration is (17), this being the only maximal string of (16a) which, at this point in the derivation, contains no internal brackets.

$$\left(17\right)$$

$$[_{N}bo\overset{1}{a}rd\ er\overset{1}{a}ser]_{N}$$

Rule (10a), the Compound Rule, is applicable to (17), and assigns primary stress on the first word, giving the stress contour 12 for this string by the conventions established previously. Since (10b) is inapplicable, we conclude this cycle, erasing innermost brackets. The string now under consideration is

$$\left(18\right)$$

$$[_{NP}bl\overset{1}{a}ck\ bo\overset{1}{a}rd\ er\overset{2}{a}ser]_{NP}$$

Rule (10a) is not applicable to this string, so we turn to rule (10b), the Nuclear Stress Rule, which assigns primary stress to *board*, weakening all other stresses in (18) by one. This gives the contour 213 as the final line of derivation (16a).

The derivation (16b) has the same first cycle as (16a), but for the second cycle, the string under consideration is the noun *blackboard* rather than the noun *board-eraser*. The

Compound Rule assigns to this noun the contour 12. Erasing innermost brackets, we proceed to the next cycle, considering now the noun *blackboard eraser* (whereas at the analogous stage of the derivation (16a), we considered the noun phrase *black board-eraser*). Being a noun, this string is subject to the Compound Rule, so that primary stress is placed on the first word, giving the contour 132.

Now consider the derivation (16c). The first cycle is exactly the same as in the other two derivations of (16). But in the second cycle we consider not the noun *board-eraser*, as in (16a), nor the noun *blackboard*, as in (16b), but the noun phrase *black board*, meaning "board that is black." To this, only the Nuclear Stress Rule applies, placing primary stress on the second word. This concludes the second cycle. In the third cycle we consider the noun *black board eraser*, which at this stage has the contour 211. The Compound Rule (10a) applies to this string, assigning primary stress to the leftmost primary-stressed vowel and weakening all the others. This gives the desired contour 312.[9]

To illustrate the transformational cycle with one more example, consider the noun phrase *John's blackboard eraser*, which undergoes the following derivation (where D stands for the category "determiner"):

$$\left(19\right) \quad [_{NP} \ [_D John's]_D \ [_N \ [_N \ [_A black]_A \ [_N board]_N \ ]_N \ [_N eraser]_N \ ]_N \ ]_{NP}$$

1		1	1	RULE (2)
				1
		1	2	RULE (10a)
		1	3	2	RULE (10a)
2		1	4	3	RULE (10b)

The phrase *blackboard eraser* undergoes the three-cycle derivation (16b); the determiner *John's* receives its primary stress on the first cycle. In the fourth cycle, the string under consideration is the noun phrase *John's blackboard eraser*, with the stress contour 1132. The Nuclear Stress Rule assigns primary stress to the rightmost primary-stressed vowel, weakening all others, and giving the stress contour 2143.[10]

Suppose that the phrase *John's blackboard eraser* appears in the context ——*was stolen*. The whole phrase in this case is a sentence, i.e., is bounded by $[_S \dots]_S$. The word *stolen* will receive primary stress on the first cycle, and *John's blackboard eraser* will have the derivation (19). In the final cycle, at the level of $[_S \dots]_S$, primary stress will be placed on *stolen* by the Nuclear Stress Rule, giving *John's blackboard eraser was stolen*.[11]

---

[9] Though examples (16a) and (16c) may appear somewhat artificial, the reality of the syntactic patterns they illustrate can hardly be doubted. They appear, for example, in such phrases as *American history-teacher*, meaning "American teacher of history," which is analogous to (16a) and has the same stress contour 213; and in *American-history teacher* meaning "teacher of American history," which is analogous to (16c) and also has the stress contour 312 (or 313—see note 8). We assume here that the word *American* receives primary stress on the second syllable, although we have not yet given the rules that determine this. Similarly, the phrases *civil rights bill* and *excess profits tax* are of the form illustrated in (16c), whereas *uncivil game warden* or *excessive profits tax* are of the form illustrated in (16a). There are many other exact or near minimal pairs, e.g., *civil engineering student* ("student of civil engineering" or "polite student of engineering"), *small boys school* ("school for small boys" or "boys' school that is small").

[10] See note 8.

[11] See note 8. To prevent *was* from receiving primary stress by rule (2), we restrict this rule, as a first approximation, to the lexical categories, namely, noun, adjective, verb. We assume, on syntactic grounds, that the auxiliary *be* is not introduced as a member of a lexical category.

Suppose that the phrase *John's blackboard eraser* appears in the context *take——*, the whole constituting a sentence (in this case, an imperative). The word *take* receives primary stress and *John's blackboard eraser* receives the contour 2143 by the derivation (19). In the final stage of the cycle, the Nuclear Stress Rule (10b) places primary stress on *black*, giving the final contour 23154.

These examples show how complex and varied phonetic representations are determined by very simple rules when the principle of the transformational cycle is presupposed; in other words, they illustrate the kind of evidence that can be offered in support of the hypothesis that it is the principle of the transformational cycle that underlies the phonetic interpretation of utterances. Observe that no rules at all are needed beyond those required for the most elementary phrases. The interplay of these rules in more complex phrases is determined by the principle of the transformational cycle, which is, it should be noted, not a rule of English grammar but rather a general principle governing the applicability of phonological rules in any grammar.

Notice that the rules, as presented, assign a different internal stress contour to the phrase *John's blackboard eraser* depending upon whether it appears in subject or object position in the surface structure. In subject position, as in the context *—— was stolen*, the contour of the phrase is 3254, with the same internal relations of stress as in the phrase in isolation, though weakened in each case by one degree. In object position, on the other hand, as in the context *take——*, the contour of the phrase is 3154, with internal relations that are different from those of the phrase in isolation. Similarly, a simple adjective-noun construction such as *sad plight* will have the contour 21 in isolation, the contour 32 in the context *his—— shocked us*, and the contour 31, with different internal relations, in *consider his——*. As the structure of the sentence becomes more complex, the internal relations of stress within a phrase of this sort will continually be modified. Thus in the sentence *my friend can't help being shocked at anyone who would fail to consider his sad plight*, the surface structure might indicate that the word *plight* terminates no less than seven phrases to which the Nuclear Stress Rule applies, so that successive applications of this rule would give the contour *sad plight* with superscript 8 on *sad* and superscript 1 on *plight*. Presumably, the actual internal relations of stress in *sad plight* are the same, in this case, as in *consider his sad plight*, or even in *sad plight* in isolation.

In connection with this problem, several comments are called for. First, it is very likely that certain readjustment rules of the sort mentioned in Chapter One, page 10, must be applied to surface structures before the application of phonological rules, deleting structure and restricting the number of applications of the transformational cycle (and, consequently, the fineness of stress differentiation). Second, it is necessary to formulate a principle for interpretation of phonetic representations that nullifies distinctions that go beyond a certain degree of refinement. Third, there may very well be additional principles that modify the convention weakening stress when primary stress is placed in a complex construction. Finally, it is necessary to take note of the qualifications with respect to phonetic representation in general that we discuss in the next section.

Before leaving the topic of stress contours within phrases, we should make it quite clear that the rules discussed above give accurate results only for very simple constructions. We have not investigated the problem of determining the stress contours of complex phrases of varying syntactic types; our investigation has been limited to the very restricted types of constructions that have been discussed in the literature on English phonetics and phonology of the past several decades. There is, for the moment, little useful data on more complex constructions. Such observations as have been made suggest that the problem of extending this description to a wider class of cases may be nontrivial. For example, Stanley Newman, in his important article on English intonation (1946), points out that in the sentence *he has plans to leave*, the contour on *plans to leave* is rising if the meaning is, roughly, " he intends to leave," but is falling if the meaning is " he has documents to leave." It is not at all clear what features of syntactic structure determine this difference. Another class of phenomena not accounted for are those involving obligatory contrastive stress (sometimes stress shift) as determined by syntactic parallelism, as in such sentences as *he wanted to study electrical rather than civil engineering*, or *instead of encouraging the teacher to make the work interesting, the school administrators actually* dis*courage her*. Many other problems can be cited, all indicating that many questions of fact and, perhaps, of principle still remain unresolved in this area.

2. *On the reality of phonetic representation*

Utilizing the principle of the transformational cycle, the speaker of English can determine the phonetic shape of an utterance on the basis of such rules as the Compound and Nuclear Stress Rules, even though the particular utterance may be quite new to him. He need not deal with the stress contour as a property of the utterance independent, in whole or in part, of its syntactic organization. There is no doubt that stress contours and many other phonetic properties are determined for new utterances with quite a bit of consistency among speakers. This is a fact that must be accounted for by an empirically adequate grammar. In the case of English we can approach an explanation by incorporating in the grammar such rules as the Compound and Nuclear Stress Rules and by postulating the principle of the transformational cycle. Before going on to investigate the rules of English in greater detail, let us briefly consider the question of how these rules and the general principles that govern their applicability relate to psychological processes and to physical fact.

We might suppose, on the basis of what has been suggested so far, that a correct description of perceptual processes would be something like this. The hearer makes use of certain cues and certain expectations to determine the syntactic structure and semantic content of an utterance. Given a hypothesis as to its syntactic structure—in particular its surface structure—he uses the phonological principles that he controls to determine a phonetic shape. The hypothesis will then be accepted if it is not too radically at variance with the acoustic material, where the range of permitted discrepancy may vary widely with conditions and many individual factors. Given acceptance of such a hypothesis, what the hearer "hears" is what is internally generated by the rules. That is, he will "hear" the phonetic shape determined by the postulated syntactic structure and the internalized rules.

Among the internalized rules are some that are particular to the language in question and thus must have been learned; there are others that simply play a role in setting the conditions on the content of linguistic experience. In the present case, it would be reasonable to suggest that the Compound and Nuclear Stress Rules are learned, while the principle of the transformational cycle, being well beyond the bounds of any conceivable method of "learning," is one of the conditions, intrinsic to the language-acquisition system, that determines the form of the language acquired. If this assumption is correct, we would expect the principle of the transformational cycle to be a linguistic universal, that is, to be consistent with the empirical facts for all human languages;[12] the Compound and Nuclear Stress Rules, on the other hand, might be in part language-specific.

We do not doubt that the stress contours and other phonetic facts that are recorded by careful phoneticians and that we will study here constitute some sort of perceptual reality for those who know the language in question. In fact we are suggesting a principled explanation for this conclusion. A person who knows the language should "hear" the predicted phonetic shapes. In particular, the careful and sophisticated impressionistic phonetician who knows the language should be able to bring this perceptual reality to the level of awareness, and there is ample evidence that phoneticians are capable of doing this. We take for granted, then, that phonetic representations describe a perceptual reality. Our problem is to provide an explanation for this fact. Notice, however, that there is nothing to suggest that these phonetic representations also describe a physical or acoustic reality in any detail. For example, there is little reason to suppose that the perceived stress contour must represent some physical property of the utterance in a point-by-point fashion; a speaker who utilizes the principle of the transformational cycle and the Compound and Nuclear Stress Rules should "hear" the stress contour of the utterance that he perceives and understands, whether or not it is physically present in any detail. In fact, there is no evidence from experimental phonetics to suggest that these contours are actually present as physical properties of utterances in anything like the detail with which they are perceived. Accordingly, there seems to be no reason to suppose that a well-trained phonetician could detect such contours with any reliability or precision in a language that he does not know, a language for which he cannot determine the surface structure of utterances.

Considerations of this sort lead us to suspect that the question of how highly differentiated the stress contours in a representation should be is of little significance. In a complex utterance with a rich surface structure, the rules outlined in the preceding section will lead to a stress contour of many levels. There may be no empirical sense to the question of whether the resulting representation is correct in full detail. Because of the completely impressionistic character of judgments of relative stress, decisions over a broad range are of little value. It is not at all surprising that there should be great difficulty, within impressionistic phonetics, in determining how many stress levels should be marked and how they are distributed in utterances that exceed a certain degree of complexity. The shape and the degree of differentiation of a stress contour are largely determined by obligatory rules and are therefore below the level of systematically significant representation. Once the speaker has selected a sentence with a particular syntactic structure and certain lexical items (largely or completely unmarked for stress, as we shall see), the choice of stress contour is not a matter subject to further independent decision.[13] That is, he need not make a

[12] In one sense, a general principle counts as a linguistic universal if it is compatible with the facts for all human languages. As linguists, of course, we are concerned not with principles that happen by accident to be universal in this sense, but rather with those that are universal in the domain of all possible human languages, that is, those that are in effect preconditions for the acquisition of language. (See the discussion in Chapter One, p. 4.) Such principles, and such alone, can serve to explain and account for the phenomena of particular languages. The distinction in question is not easy to draw, but is no less crucial for this reason.

   Notice, incidentally, that the transformational cycle might apply vacuously in a certain language, in particular if the language has very shallow surface structure. Thus a highly agglutinative language might be expected to offer little or no support for the principle of the transformational cycle, at least within the bounds of a word. This, if true, would be entirely irrelevant to the status of this principle as a linguistic universal.

[13] We assume that the position of emphatic stress is marked in the surface structure, and we neglect matters that we have assigned to the theory of performance (see Chapter One, p. 3).

choice among various "stress phonemes" or select one or another "superfix." With marginal exceptions, the choice of these is as completely determined as, for example, the degree of aspiration. Similarly, a hearer who has grasped the structure and morphemic constitution of an utterance from a rough sampling of the physical input need not attend to stress variation, to whatever extent this may actually be a physical property of utterances.

It is to be expected that determined phonetic features should be quite difficult for the user of the language to learn to identify, whether they involve stress or degree of aspiration (where undoubtedly there are many levels, predictable, at least roughly, by general rules).[14] The apparent ease with which phoneticians trained in the same conventions can, to a large extent, agree on the assignment of four or five stresses in utterances may very well be traceable to their ability, as speakers of the language, to grasp the syntactic structure of utterances and to assign to them an "ideal" stress contour by the rules of the transformational cycle. Such an achievement may have little to do with any physical fact. This is, incidentally, a matter which should be subject to experimental investigation.[15]

To summarize this discussion of phonetic representation, we do not doubt that representations of stress contours and similar predictable phenomena correspond, up to a point, to some perceptual reality that can be brought to consciousness with training and care. That this must be true is shown by the fact that phoneticians trained in the same system of conventions can reach considerable agreement in transcribing novel utterances in languages that they know. These perceptual facts may be of interest only to the extent that they provide data for testing empirical hypotheses such as the principle of the transformational cycle. Accordingly, perceived stress contours are of very great linguistic interest since they offer evidence bearing on this hypothesis, whereas degree of aspiration will be of no linguistic interest if, as one might suspect, it is determined by principles of little depth or generality. Furthermore, the representation of the perceptual facts is likely to be governed in part by arbitrary convention or irrelevant cognitive limitations after a certain degree of complexity is reached. Thus, it is impossible to expect (and, for purposes of investigating linguistic structures, unnecessary to attain) a complete correspondence between the records of the impressionistic phonetician and what is predicted by a systematic theory that seeks to account for the perceptual facts that underlie these records.

3. The transformational cycle within the word

Let us return now to the problem of how the phonological component of a grammar is organized, and the more specific matter of the rules of English phonology. In the derivations given in Section 1, we did not provide rules for determining stress placement in the word *eraser* or, for that matter, in any word that is not a monosyllable (see rule (2)). In fact, it is evident that *eraser* is itself a complex form based on the verb *erase* and an agentive

---

[14] As noted, there is no acoustic evidence to support the view that perceived stress contours correspond to a physically definable property of utterances. However, even if such differentiations did exist along a single dimension of the acoustic signal, there would be some reason to doubt that they might be identified by phoneticians. There is evidence that even under experimental conditions, where complex stimuli are to be sorted along several dimensions, more than two or three distinctions along each dimension will overload the perceptual capacity. See Pollack and Ficks (1954) and Miller (1956).

[15] P. Lieberman (1965) has shown that a phonetician who is capable of describing a pitch contour with great accuracy in isolation may represent this very same contour quite differently when it is associated with an utterance of his language. This strongly suggests that what the phonetician "hears" in utterances depends very heavily on internalized rules that predict perceived phonetic shape. Similar results were obtained for stress.

affix. Thus, at the level where phonological rules of the kind we are now considering become applicable, the structure of this item is something like (20):[16]

$$\left(20\right) \qquad\qquad [_N \# \; [_V \# \textit{erase} \#]_V \; r \#]_N$$

If the principle of the transformational cycle is perfectly general, then this word too should have more than one cycle in its derivation. The rules should first apply to the underlying verb *erase* and then, in the next cycle, to the noun *eraser*. The verb *erase* is bisyllabic, and we see that stress is placed on the second syllable. As a first approximation to the rule of stress placement for lexical items, we can formulate the rule (21), which places primary stress on the final vowel of the string under consideration where this item is a noun, adjective, or verb. The symbol C_0, as before, stands for a string of zero or more consonants.

$$\left(21\right) \qquad\qquad V \;\rightarrow\; [1 \text{ stress}] \;/\; X \;\text{———}\; C_0]_{NAV}$$

Notice that rule (21) now includes, as a special case, rule (2), which placed primary stress on the only, hence final, vowel of a monosyllabic item. We can thus dispense with rule (2), and the rules of stress placement become rules (21), (10a) and (10b) (the Compound and Nuclear Stress Rules), and (7), which appears to be quite marginal.

There is a difficulty, however. If these rules apply in a cycle, rule (21) will be applicable to nouns such as *blackboard*, *blackboard eraser*, and so on, incorrectly assigning primary stress to the final vowel. We must therefore place some restriction on rule (21) to eliminate this possibility. The simplest way to do this is to require that the string to which (21) is applied must contain no occurrences of the boundary #. We therefore add to rule (21) the condition (22):

$$\left(22\right) \qquad\qquad X \text{ contains no internal occurrence of } \#.$$

With rule (21) replacing rule (2), we have provided sufficient information to complete the derivations that were given as examples of the operation of the transformational cycle. In the first stage, rule (21) applies to assign primary stress to the final vowel of each of the items *black*, *board*, *John*, *erase*. The second cycle will be vacuous in the case of *John's* or *eraser*, stress simply being reassigned to the stressed vowel.[17] Otherwise, the derivations proceed as before.

The transformational cycle operates within word boundaries in a much more far-reaching and extensive way than suggested by examples such as these. In complex derivational forms, for example, it seems quite natural to suppose that the phonetic shape of the full form is determined by general rule from the ideal representation of its parts in much the same way as in syntactic constructions. Investigation of English and other languages confirms this expectation and permits us to formulate the principle of the transformational cycle in full generality, applying to all surface structure whether internal or external to the word. The word is, as we shall see, a significant phonological unit, but its unique properties do not lead to violation of the general principle of the transformational cycle. We assume, then, that the cycle operates from the minimal units included in (or, in special cases, constituting) words up to the maximal domain of phonological processes, with no discontinuity.

---

[16] On the placement of # boundaries, see Chapter One, pages 12–14.

[17] We shall see that the reason for the inapplicability of any rules in the second cycle of these forms is actually quite different from what is suggested here. In both cases it is the # boundary preceding the affix which blocks all phonological rules that would otherwise be applicable.

4. The segmental phonology of English — a first approximation

We have described the phonological component as a system of rules, organized in accordance with the principle of the transformational cycle, which maps surface structures into phonetic representations, where a surface structure is a labeled bracketing of a string of formatives. Furthermore, we have been assuming that the formatives can themselves be regarded as strings, consisting of consonants and vowels. The lexicon, which is a part of the syntactic component of the grammar, determines the intrinsic structure of a formative in terms of phonological properties: in particular, the lexicon determines how a formative is represented as a string of consonants and vowels. We will refer to the consonants and vowels that constitute a formative as its "segments." The phonological rules modify the segmental structure of a string of formatives in accordance with the specified labeled bracketing. At the termination of the transformational cycle, all labeled bracketing has been erased, and we are left with a string of phonological elements which we will also refer to as segments, in this case "phonetic segments." These segments too can be analyzed as consonants and vowels of various types. We assume that linguistic theory includes a universal phonetic alphabet—of a sort that we will later describe in detail—which provides a uniform, language-independent system for the representation of phonetic segments. In brief, then, the phonological component maps a surface structure into a string of universal phonetic segments.

Let us for the moment assume a standard phonetic system for the representation of consonants and turn our attention to the system of English vowels.

For our immediate purposes, we may regard a formative as a string of consonants and "vocalic nuclei." The vocalic nuclei may be "simple," as in the boldface positions of *pit, pet, pat, put, putt, analyze*. We will use the phonetic symbols i, e, æ, u, ʌ, ə, respectively, for these simple vocalic nuclei, delaying a more detailed analysis until later. The segment represented as ə will be referred to as the "reduced vowel."

In addition to simple vocalic nuclei, there are "complex vocalic nuclei," such as those that appear in the boldface positions in *confide, feed, fade, feud, road*, and others. For the time being, we will use the symbols *I, E, A, U, O*, respectively, for the complex nuclei of the cited forms; that is, we use each capital letter with its conventional name as its phonetic value.

Following this convention, we will have quasi-phonetic spellings such as the following:

(23)

erase	ErÁs
irate	IrÁt
mutation	mUtÁšən
ecumenical	ekUmenikəl[18]
cupidity	kUpiditE
citation	sItÁšən
maintain	mAntÁn
collapse	kəlæps

[18] Or, perhaps, [ekUmenəkəl]. As indicated in the Preface, we will generally follow the phonetic representations of Kenyon and Knott, which agree quite well with our own normal speech in most respects. Although there are some differences which we will comment on later, none of them are very crucial, and for the moment we can ignore them.

The representation of other vocalic nuclei and a more detailed analysis of all of these elements will concern us in later chapters. We will discover, in fact, that the representations just proposed are somewhat more than a mere notational convenience.

In terms of the above notions, we can distinguish between "weak clusters" and "strong clusters" in the following way. A weak cluster is a string consisting of a simple vocalic nucleus followed by no more than one consonant; a strong cluster is a string consisting of either a vocalic nucleus followed by two or more consonants or a complex vocalic nucleus followed by any number of consonants. In either case, the cluster is assumed to be followed either by a vowel or by the boundary symbol # (with possible intrusions of the + boundary). These definitions will be emended and made more precise later on.

Using the symbol S for a strong cluster and W for a weak cluster, we can see that the items of (23) are phonetically of the following form in terms of clusters (with initial consonants omitted):

$$\left(24\right)$$

Er$\overset{1}{\text{A}}$s	SS
Ir$\overset{1}{\text{A}}$t	SS
mUt$\overset{1}{\text{A}}$šən	SSW
ek$\overset{3}{\text{U}}$m$\overset{1}{\text{e}}$nikəl	WSWWW
k$\overset{1}{\text{U}}$piditE	SWWS
sIt$\overset{1}{\text{A}}$šən	SSW
mAnt$\overset{1}{\text{A}}$n	SS
kəl$\overset{1}{\text{æ}}$ps	WS

5. More on the transformational cycle within the word

We can now proceed to deepen the account of stress placement within words. Rule (21), the only rule given so far that places stress within words, assigns primary stress to the final vowel of the string under consideration. Thus it assigns primary stress to the final syllable of words such as *evade, supreme, exist, absurd*. Observe, however, that all these examples have final strong clusters phonetically. In fact, if a verb or adjective has a final weak cluster, then stress is placed on the penultimate rather than the final syllable. Thus we have words such as $\overset{1}{re}lish, \overset{1}{co}vet, \overset{1}{de}velop, \overset{1}{sto}lid, \overset{1}{com}mon, clan\overset{1}{des}tine$, all with penultimate stress and final weak clusters.[19] These observations suggest that rule (21) should be divided into two cases, the first assigning primary stress to the vowel preceding a final weak cluster, the second assigning primary stress to the final vowel of the string under consideration. We can give this rule in the following form:

$$\left(25\right) \qquad \text{V} \;\rightarrow\; [1 \text{ stress}] \;\; / \; X\text{——}C_0(\text{W})]$$

where X contains no internal occurrences of # (see condition (22)) and W is a weak cluster. We interpret (25) as an abbreviation for two rules, in accordance with the general convention that a rule of the form (26), with a string in parentheses, is an abbreviation for the

---

[19] Exceptions to the rules we are now sketching will readily come to mind. To a considerable extent they will be taken care of by the more careful formulation given in the next chapter. Exceptions do remain, however. (See the Preface on the subject of exceptions.)
  Notice that the rule we are discussing here is, in effect, the familiar Latin stress rule.

sequence of rules (27) (where either Z or Q contains ——):

$$(26) \qquad\qquad X \;\rightarrow\; Y \;\mid Z(P)Q$$

$$(27) \qquad\qquad \begin{array}{ll} \text{(a)} & X \;\rightarrow\; Y \;\mid ZPQ \\ \text{(b)} & X \;\rightarrow\; Y \;\mid ZQ \end{array}$$

The order in (27) is crucial: in a sequence of rules abbreviated by the parenthesis notation, as in (26), the case (27a) that includes the string in parentheses is applicable before the case (27b) without the parenthesized string. In accordance with these conventions, rule (25) is an abbreviation for the two rules (28a) and (28b), in that order:

$$(28) \qquad\qquad \begin{array}{lll} \text{(a)} & V \;\rightarrow\; [\text{1 stress}] & / \; X \;\text{——}\; C_0 W] \\ \text{(b)} & V \;\rightarrow\; [\text{1 stress}] & / \; X \;\text{——}\; C_0] \end{array}$$

Words such as *relish*, *develop*, *common*, with final weak clusters, are subject to (28a) and receive penultimate stress. Words such as *evade*, *supreme*, *exist*, with final strong clusters, are not subject to (28a) and receive stress on the final syllable by (28b).

There is one additional condition to be noted in connection with rule (25). Suppose that we apply this rule to a word with a final weak cluster, such as *edit*. By case (28a), primary stress is placed on the penultimate syllable, giving *édit*. But then, by case (28b), primary stress will be shifted to the final syllable and the first syllable will be weakened to [2 stress], resulting in the incorrect form **èdít*. The simplest and most general way to avoid this is to establish a condition on the parenthesis convention itself. In fact, in all descriptive work in generative grammar with which we are familiar, it has been tacitly assumed that in the case of a rule such as (26), the two subcases (27a) and (27b) are ordered not only as shown, but are "disjunctively ordered," in the sense that if rule (27a) applies, then rule (27b) is not permitted to apply. Thus a sequence of rules abbreviated in terms of the parenthesis notation constitutes a disjunctively ordered block; as soon as one of these rules is applied, the remaining rules are skipped within any one cycle of a derivation. We now establish this as a general convention with regard to the parenthesis notation, to be extended and generalized as we proceed. We thus extend the general theory of the organization of a grammar expressed in the principle of the transformational cycle, by observing that certain subsequences of the linearly ordered rules may be disjunctively ordered. To return to the rules we have been discussing, the two cases (28a) and (28b) abbreviated by (25) will be disjunctively ordered, and the difficulty noted at the beginning of this paragraph will not arise; once case (28a) has applied to give the correct form *édit*, then case (28b) is prevented, by the principle of disjunctive ordering, from applying to that form.

Like other general conditions on the organization of a grammar, the convention just proposed constitutes an empirical hypothesis subject to refutation by linguistic fact. The hypothesis is, in this case, that if a sequence of rules is to be abbreviated by the parenthesis convention,[20] then this sequence forms a disjunctively ordered block. Obviously, this is not a necessary truth, by any means.

---

[20] The question of when a sequence of rules is to be abbreviated by the parenthesis convention is not a matter of choice but rather one of fact. That is, the convention regarding parentheses is just one part of an evaluation procedure to be applied to grammars. This procedure is perfectly general (language-independent) and performs the function of determining which of the grammars consistent with the data is to be selected as the grammar of the language for which the data provide a sample. For discussion, see Chomsky (1965) and many earlier references.

The matter of defining "optimal representation" is nontrivial. In the ensuing discussion we make certain tacit assumptions about "optimality" that will be explored further in Chapter Three, Section 1. See Chomsky (1967) for further discussion.

It is not to be expected that an absolutely crucial test case for this hypothesis will be very easy to come by. In any real case, there will presumably be other aspects of a grammatical description which, if modified, will allow this hypothesis to be retained in the face of superficially disconfirming evidence. This is the usual situation when an empirical hypothesis of such generality is at issue. Still, it is quite clear what sort of evidence is relevant to increasing or diminishing the plausibility of the hypothesis.

Returning now to the problem of stress assignment, we see at once that rule (25) requires refinement and elaboration if it is to account for the facts. Each of the examples given to illustrate the rule contains just a single formative. Where a word has an internal analysis in terms of formatives, rule (25) must apply in a slightly different way. To see this, consider the derived forms *person+al, theatr+ic+al, anecdot+al, dialect+al*. If rule (25) were to apply directly to these forms, it would assign primary stress to the penultimate syllable (the final cluster *-al* being weak), giving *personal, *theatrical, anecdótal, dialéctal, only the last two of which are correct. Notice that all four words would be assigned primary stress in the correct way by rule (25) if the affix *-al* were excluded from consideration at the point when the rule is applied. The residual forms *person-* and *theatric-*, with final weak clusters, would have primary stress assigned to their penultimate syllables by case (28a); the forms *anecdОt-* and *dialect-*, on the other hand, would be exempt from (28a) because of their strong final clusters and would instead have primary stress assigned to the final syllable by case (28b). This observation is in fact quite general for affixes, and we therefore replace rule (25) by the following sequence of rules:

$$\left(29\right) \quad \begin{array}{ll} \text{(a)} & V \;\rightarrow\; [1 \text{ stress}] \;\; / \; X \text{———} C_0(W)+\text{affix}] \\ \text{(b)} & V \;\rightarrow\; [1 \text{ stress}] \;\; / \; X \text{———} C_0(W)] \end{array}$$

Clearly there is a generalization being missed by the formulation (29), for the obvious similarity between the two cases is not expressed. To permit us to capture generalizations of this sort, we extend our notations to permit rules such as (30):

$$\left(30\right) \qquad\qquad X \;\rightarrow\; Y \;/\; Z \text{———} R \;/\; P \text{———} Q$$

In general, a rule of the form (31) can be regarded as an abbreviation for the rule (32), where Z and R are strings:[21]

$$\left(31\right) \qquad\qquad X \;\rightarrow\; Y \;/\; Z \text{———} R$$

$$\left(32\right) \qquad\qquad ZXR \;\rightarrow\; ZYR$$

Following this convention, we interpret (30) as an abbreviation for (33), where Z and R are strings:

$$\left(33\right) \qquad\qquad ZXR \;\rightarrow\; ZYR \;/\; P \text{———} Q$$

This is now a rule of a familiar form. Reapplying the convention that defines (31) in terms of (32), we interpret (33) as an abbreviation for (34):

$$\left(34\right) \qquad\qquad PZXRQ \;\rightarrow\; PZYRQ$$

[21] We will give more precise definitions of these notions in Chapter Eight. For the present, one can think of rule (31) (equivalently, (32)) as stating that a linguistic element of the form X is extended to contain the features Y (or is modified to contain Y, if Y differs in some respect from X) when this element of the form X appears in a context of the form Z ——— R. There are ambiguities in this account; they will be resolved later, and are not of the sort that should lead to misunderstanding in the present context.

Thus, when Z and R are strings, the notation (30) is well-defined. Suppose, however, that Z and R are not strings, but notations of any complexity, including braces, parentheses, and so on. Then it would not do to say that (31) is an abbreviation for (32); rather, (31) is an abbreviation for the sequence of rules (35), determined by the conventions for braces, parentheses, etc. The sequence (35) is then an abbreviation for the sequence (36), by the convention just stated.

$$(35) \qquad \begin{pmatrix} X & \to & Y & / & Z_1 \text{——} R_1 \\ X & \to & Y & / & Z_2 \text{——} R_2 \\ & & \vdots & & \\ X & \to & Y & / & Z_m \text{——} R_m \end{pmatrix}$$

$$(36) \qquad \begin{pmatrix} Z_1 X R_1 & \to & Z_1 Y R_1 \\ Z_2 X R_2 & \to & Z_2 Y R_2 \\ & \vdots & \\ Z_m X R_m & \to & Z_m Y R_m \end{pmatrix}$$

This leaves us with only the problem of explaining the meaning of (30) in the case when Z and R involve notations such as braces and parentheses. Since (31), in this case, is an abbreviation for (35) (ultimately, (36)), the conventions already given will interpret (30) as an abbreviation for (37):

$$(37) \qquad \begin{pmatrix} X & \to & Y & / & Z_1 \text{——} R_1 \\ X & \to & Y & / & Z_2 \text{——} R_2 \\ & & \vdots & & \\ X & \to & Y & / & Z_m \text{——} R_m \end{pmatrix} \quad / \; P \text{——} Q$$

The above can be seen to be (35) (or, equivalently, (36)) in the context $P\text{——}Q$. By the usual brace conventions, we can now interpret (37) as an abbreviation for (38):

$$(38) \qquad \begin{pmatrix} X & \to & Y & / & Z_1 \text{——} R_1 & / & P \text{——} Q \\ X & \to & Y & / & Z_2 \text{——} R_2 & / & P \text{——} Q \\ & & & \vdots & & & \\ X & \to & Y & / & Z_m \text{——} R_m & / & P \text{——} Q \end{pmatrix}$$

In (38), each Z_i and R_i is a string of symbols, so that (38) is itself interpretable by the convention that gives (30) as an abbreviation for (33).

We see, then, that there is a very natural way of interpreting familiar conventions so that a rule of the form (30) has, in effect, the following intuitive meaning: first, expand the context $P\text{——}Q$, in accordance with the brace and parenthesis conventions, into the sequence of its special cases $P_1\text{——}Q_1, \ldots, P_k\text{——}Q_k$; next, apply the rules abbreviated as $X \to Y/Z\text{——}R$ in the usual sequence, under the condition that the element ZXR under consideration is in the context $P_1\text{——}Q_1$; next, apply the same rules under the condition that the element ZXR is in the context $P_2\text{——}Q_2$; etc.

With these notational remarks, we can return to the generalization left unexpressed in rule (29) which can now be captured by the following rule:

$$(39) \qquad \text{V} \;\to\; [1 \text{ stress}] \;\; / \; X\text{——} C_0(\text{W}) \;\; / \text{——}(+\text{affix})\,]$$

where W is a weak cluster, C_0 is a string of zero or more consonants, and X does not contain an internal $\#$ boundary.[22] Our conventions interpret (39) as an abbreviation for

---

[22] Actually, the affix must be restricted to a glide or to a monosyllabic formative with a simple vocalic nucleus, for reasons that will be developed in the next chapter.

the following sequence of rules:

$$\left(40\right) \quad \begin{array}{llll}
\text{(a)} & V & \rightarrow & [1 \text{ stress}] & / & X\text{---}C_0W+\text{affix}] \\
\text{(b)} & V & \rightarrow & [1 \text{ stress}] & / & X\text{---}C_0+\text{affix}] \\
\text{(c)} & V & \rightarrow & [1 \text{ stress}] & / & X\text{---}C_0W] \\
\text{(d)} & V & \rightarrow & [1 \text{ stress}] & / & X\text{---}C_0]
\end{array}$$

The parenthesis convention proposed earlier imposes the following ordering conditions on (40a–d): (1) the order of application is (a), (b), (c), (d), as given; (2) if case (a) applies, then case (b) is inapplicable; (3) if case (c) applies, then case (d) is inapplicable; (4) if either case (a) or case (b) applies, then cases (c) and (d) are inapplicable. Summarizing, the convention implies that the ordering of (40) is totally disjunctive; if one case applies, then all later cases are skipped.

In forms such as *person+al* and *theatr+ic+al*, case (a) of rule (40) assigns primary stress in the antepenultimate syllable. Case (b) of (40) applies to words such as *dialect+al* and *anecdOt+al*, assigning primary stress in the penultimate position, which contains a strong cluster. Cases (c) and (d) are simply the two cases of rule (25); they apply to such words as *edit* and *develop*, assigning penultimate stress, and to words such as *evade* and *supreme*, assigning primary stress in the final syllable. Rule (39) thus expresses in a precise way the linguistically significant generalization that underlies this class of examples.

Notice that some of these examples involve more than one cycle. The word *theatrical*, for example, is clearly derived from *theater*, which will receive primary stress on the initial syllable in the first cycle (by a rule which will be given in the next chapter); thus, in isolation the stress will be in that position. But in the second cycle, the stress is shifted to the second (antepenultimate) syllable by rule (39). We thus have the derivation (41). (Recall that we assume all formatives to be automatically bounded by +, by convention. We therefore need not indicate all occurrences of this boundary in a derivation.)

$$\left(41\right) \quad \begin{array}{ll}
[_A \; [_N theatr]_N \; ic+al]_A & \\
\underline{\qquad 1 \qquad} & (\text{RULE TO BE GIVEN}) \\
\underline{\quad\; 21 \quad} & \text{RULE (39), CASE (40a)}
\end{array}$$

The stress on the first syllable is then weakened as a special case of rules that we will go into later.

Suppose that we have a still more complex form such as *theatricality*, for example. For this form, the same rules provide the following derivation:[23]

$$\left(42\right) \quad \begin{array}{ll}
[_N \; [_A \; [_N theatr]_N \; ic+al]_A \; i+ty]_N & \\
\underline{\qquad 1 \qquad} & (\text{RULE TO BE GIVEN}) \\
\underline{\quad\; 21 \quad} & \text{RULE (39), CASE (40a)} \\
\underline{\quad\; 32 \qquad 1 \quad} & \text{RULE (39), CASE (40a)}
\end{array}$$

---

[23] The analysis of *-ity* as *i+ty* might be disputed, but it seems well motivated on morphological grounds. There is, first of all, a noun-forming affix *-ty* (*loyalty*, *novelty*, etc.) Furthermore, the forms in *-ity* often have other derived forms with affixes beginning with *-i* (*sanctity–sanctify–sanctitude*, *clarity–clarify*, etc.), which suggests that *-i-* is a stem-forming augment. We shall see, in fact, that there are good reasons to suppose that no affixes are polysyllabic.

As rule (39) is stated, this analysis of *-ity* is necessary. From considerations presented in the next chapter, however, it can be shown that even if *-ity* were to be analyzed as a single formative, the rules would still provide the derivation (42). Therefore, in this instance at least, phonological considerations do not require the analysis into two formatives.

There is a generally accepted convention to the effect that secondary stress appears within a word only if it is the main stress within that word. Accordingly, we add the following rule:

$\left(43\right)$ Within a word, all non-main stresses are weakened by one.

The exact status of this rule, which we will call the Stress Adjustment Rule, is a matter to which we will return below. We will see, in fact, that it becomes a special case of the Nuclear Stress Rule (10b), when the latter is properly formulated. The Stress Adjustment Rule (43) converts *theatricality* to *theatricality*, which we can take to be the phonetic representation for this word up to the degree of detail we have discussed so far.

In the same manner, rule (39) assigns stress contours to many complex forms, in accordance with the principle of the transformational cycle. We can thus account for a substantial class of cases in a very simple and general way.

Actually, rule (39) may be extended somewhat further. Consider pairs of words such as:

$\left(44\right)$

phótograph	*photosýnthesis*
mónolith	*monománia*
télescope	*telekinésis*
prótoplasm	*protozóa*

Each of the forms consists of a prefix (*photo-*, *mono-*, *tele-*, *proto-*) followed by a stem (which may, in certain cases, function as an independent word). With minimal assumptions about surface structure, *photograph*, for example, will be represented $[_N photo\ [_{STEM} graph]_{STEM}\ ]_N$. In a case like *photosynthesis*, the bracketing will be the same, but *synthesis* will be labeled as a noun rather than a stem.

We note that primary stress falls on the prefix if the stem is monosyllabic,[24] and on the stem if the stem is polysyllabic. Though this observation will be modified slightly when a larger class of cases is considered, it can be accepted as a first approximation. We notice further that stress placement on the prefix is in accordance with rule (39); that is, by case (40c) (= (28a)), primary stress is assigned to the syllable preceding the final weak cluster of the prefix. (For reasons which appear below, the final vowel of *photo*, *mono*, etc., is lexically lax though in some positions it is phonetically tense.)

Using these observations and the assumed surface structure, we can account for the forms in (44) with a rule that accomplishes the following. After primary stress has been assigned to the stem (or inner noun) in the first cycle, it will be shifted left to the prefix if the stem (or inner noun) is a monosyllable, that is, if the form has a final stressed syllable when it enters the second cycle. For example, *photograph* will enter the second cycle as *photograph*, with a final stressed syllable, and our new rule will then shift the stress back to give *photograph*. The form *photosynthesis*, on the other hand, will enter the second cycle as *photosynthesis*; since the syllable that is stressed is not final, the new rule will not apply and the stress will remain on the inner noun. We can now proceed to formulate the rule as follows:

$\left(45\right)$ $\quad\quad\quad\quad$ V $\rightarrow$ [1 stress] $\ /\ X \text{———} C_0(W)\ /\ \text{———} \acute{\Sigma}]$

---

[24] We are using the term "monosyllabic" in a phonological, not a phonetic, sense in this context. Thus *plasm* is phonologically monosyllabic (cf. *plasma*) but phonetically bisyllabic, since postconsonantal nasals become syllabic in final position.

where W is a weak cluster and $\acute{\Sigma}$ a stressed syllable, that is, a string of the form $C_0\overset{1}{V}C_0$. Making minimal assumptions about surface structure, as before, this provides derivations such as (46):

$$\left(46\right)$$

$$[_N photo\ [_{STEM} graph]_{STEM}\ ]_N$$

	1	RULE (39), CASE (40d)
1	2	RULE (45)
1	3	RULE (43)

Where the stem (or inner noun) is polysyllabic, the stressed syllable will not be final and rule (45) will not apply. This accounts for the fact that in the examples in the right-hand column of (44), primary stress remains on the stem (or inner noun).[25]

Before proceeding to investigate other applications of rule (45), we can observe that it obviously falls together with rule (39). Combining (39) and (45), then, we have the following rule:

$$\left(47\right) \qquad V\ \rightarrow\ [1\ \text{stress}]\ /\ X\text{———}C_0\,(W)\ /\ \text{———}(\begin{Bmatrix} +\text{affix} \\ \acute{\Sigma} \end{Bmatrix})\,]$$

where W is a weak cluster, C_0 is a string of zero or more consonants, $\acute{\Sigma}$ is a syllable of the form $C_0\overset{1}{V}C_0$, and X does not contain $\#$ boundary internally. We will henceforth refer to this rule, with its various elaborations, as the Main Stress Rule, since it is the main rule applying to lexical categories. We return to this matter in Chapter Three.

In accordance with our notational conventions, rule (47) is an abbreviation for the sequence of rules:

$$\left(48\right)$$

(a)	V	$\rightarrow$	[1 stress]	/ X———C_0W+affix]
(b)	V	$\rightarrow$	[1 stress]	/ X———C_0+affix]
(c)	V	$\rightarrow$	[1 stress]	/ X———$C_0W\acute{\Sigma}$]
(d)	V	$\rightarrow$	[1 stress]	/ X———$C_0\acute{\Sigma}$]
(e)	V	$\rightarrow$	[1 stress]	/ X———C_0W]
(f)	V	$\rightarrow$	[1 stress]	/ X———C_0]

Cases (a), (b), (e), (f) are, respectively, cases (a)–(d) of (40). As before, they constitute a disjunctively ordered block; if one of the four cases of (40) applies, none of the later ones is applicable. Furthermore, the notational conventions that we have given imply that if case (48c) applies, then case (d) is inapplicable, and that if either case (c) or (d) applies, then cases (e) and (f) are inapplicable. There are no further disjunctive constraints. The only permitted sequences of applicable rules, then, are the following:

$$\left(49\right)$$

(a), (c)
(a), (d)
(b), (c)
(b), (d)

Apart from these possibilities, at most one of the rules of (48) can apply. The order in which they become applicable is, aside from this restriction, the linear order of (48). These empirical assumptions follow from the general hypothesis regarding notations and the fact that (47) is the optimal representation of the processes so far discussed (see note 20).

---

[25] We have not yet given the rules that assign primary stress to these stems and inner nouns in the first cycle.

Before we continue with the analysis of English stress placement, let us make quite clear the status and character of our assumptions concerning the organization of grammars and the conditions on the applicability of grammatical rules. We have, so far, placed the following conditions on the grammar. The grammar is a linear sequence of rules of the form illustrated in (48), applying in accordance with the principle of the transformational cycle (see (15)). The relation of disjunctive ordering is defined on certain pairs of rules of this sequence by virtue of their formal similarities. To determine disjunctive ordering, we apply to the fullest possible extent the notational conventions involving parenthesization, bracketing, and the slash-dash notation defined as in (30)–(34). In this way we form an underlying schema which represents this sequence of rules and which is expandable into this sequence by the successive application of conventions involving the notations. (When this process is formalized later in our discussion, we will guarantee that the order of expansion is unique.) If at some stage in the expansion we reach a schema of the form $Z(X)Y$, expandable into the sequence of schemata ZXY, ZY, then all rules derived by expanding ZXY (or ZXY itself, if it is a rule) are disjunctively ordered with respect to all rules derived by expanding ZY (or ZY itself, if it is a rule). In this way, disjunctive ordering is defined on the rules of the sequence constituting the grammar. Notice that rules may be disjunctively ordered with respect to one another even if they are not adjacent in the ordering; for example, in (48), rule (a) is disjunctively ordered with respect to rule (f), but not with respect to rule (c).

The conventions associated with disjunctive ordering make use of the notations for stating grammatical schemata in a way that is rather novel within the theory of generative grammar. In earlier work these notations have been regarded solely as part of the system for evaluating grammars. They have been proposed as an explication of the notion "linguistically significant generalization"; the degree of linguistically significant generalization attained by a grammar—its "simplicity," in a technical sense of the term—is measured by the number of symbols appearing in the underlying schema that expands to this grammar by the use of the notations. (See Chomsky (1965) and many earlier references for discussion.) But now we are also making use of the notations to determine how the rules apply, in particular, to determine disjunctive ordering. That is to say, we are proposing that certain formal relations among rules, statable in terms of the notations that are used for the evaluation of grammars, are significant in determining how the grammar generates derivations. If the empirical hypothesis embodied in the definition of "disjunctive ordering" is correct, then this fact offers a powerful argument in support of the empirical reality of the evaluation procedures that have been developed within the theory of generative grammar, as it has evolved in recent years.

We can now return to the role of the Stressed Syllable Rule, as we shall henceforth refer to it—namely, cases (c) and (d) of the Main Stress Rule. We will refer to cases (a) and (b) of (48) as the Affix Rule.

Consider now the following sets of words:

$$\left(50\right)$$

1	1　3	1
torment	*torment*	*torrent*
1	1　3	1
convict	*convict*	*verdict*
1	1　3	1
export	*export*	*effort*
1	1　3	1
progress	*progress*	*tigress*

The words in the left-hand column are verbs, with stress on the final syllable; those in the other two columns are nouns, with primary stress on the penultimate syllable. Comparing the words in the middle column with those in the right-hand column, we can see that they differ in the degree of stress on the final syllable and, concomitantly, in the quality of the final vocalic nucleus, which is reduced to [ə] in the right-hand column but not in the middle column.

We can account for the nouns in the middle column, that is, those with stress contour 13, by regarding them as derived from the corresponding verbs. Thus we view the relation between *tórmènt* and *tórmĕnt* as roughly analogous to the relation between *advertisement* and *advertise* or *impression* and *impress*. We then have derivations such as the following:

$$\left(51\right) \qquad [_N \; [_V torment]_V \;]_N$$

	1		RULE (47), CASE (48f)
1	2		RULE (47), CASE (48d)
1	3		RULE (43)

In the first cycle, the Main Stress Rule applies to the underlying verb, assigning primary stress in the final strong cluster. Since the verb undergoes no further applications of the Main Stress Rule, in isolation it retains primary stress in this position. But the derived noun must undergo a second application of the Main Stress Rule, in accordance with the principle of the transformational cycle. In this application, the Stressed Syllable Rule applies, shifting primary stress to the left. Secondary stress on the final syllable is then weakened to tertiary by the Stress Adjustment Rule, giving the contour 13. The distinction between the elements of the left and middle columns of (50) can thus be attributed to the extra cycle in the derivation of the nouns. The distinction between the elements of the middle and right columns can be attributed to the fact that the right-hand elements are not derived from associated verbs and therefore have never received primary stress on the final syllable.[26] In this way, the Stressed Syllable Rule accounts for a distinction between tertiary and zero stress in the final syllables of pairs such as *tórmĕnt–tórrĕnt, éxpŏrt–éffŏrt*.[27]

We have not yet explained why stress falls on the final syllable of the verb *progréss* in (50), even though this contains a weak cluster. As we will show in Chapter Three, Section 10, we must assume there to be a special boundary in such verbs—between *pro* and *gress* in this case—which blocks the application of (48e) in the first cycle but not of (48d) in the second cycle. Thus the derivation of the noun *prógress* from the underlying verb *progréss* will be identical to that of *tórment* in (51).

We have now seen two rather different effects of the Stressed Syllable Rule. In the case of *phótogràph* versus *photósynthesis*, it accounts for the distinction between a falling

[26] We have not yet given the rule that determines stress placement in nouns such as those of the right-hand column of (50). The fact is that in nouns, as distinct from verbs and adjectives, a final syllable with a simple vocalic nucleus is disregarded for purposes of stress placement, and the Main Stress Rule is then applied to the residue in the usual way. Thus, for nouns, a final syllable with a simple vocalic nucleus is treated in the same way as an affix and a stressed syllable by rule (47). We do not give this rule here because it involves certain assumptions with respect to notations and ordering that we prefer, for expository reasons, to leave for the next chapter. The facts are clear, however. By extending the Main Stress Rule in this way, we can account for the fact that primary stress appears in the penultimate syllable in the nouns of the right-most column of (50), as well as in words such as *phlOgíston* and *horÍzon*, which have a strong medial cluster; that it appears in the antepenultimate syllable in words such as *vénison, cánnibal, élephant*, with a weak medial cluster and simple vocalic nucleus in the final syllable; and that it falls on the final syllable (by rule (48f)) in words such as *machíne, careér*, which have a complex vocalic nucleus in the final syllable.

[27] Observe that in the case of *torrent*, we know that the vowel of the final syllable is *e* (cf. *torrential*). In the case of *effort* there is no way of determining the phonological quality of the underlying vowel, which need not, therefore, be specified in the lexical entry for this formative.

and a rising contour for the prefix-stem combination, exactly as in the case of the noun *export* versus the verb *export*; in the case of *export* versus *effort* or *torment* versus *torrent*, it accounts for the difference between tertiary and zero stress in the final syllables.

Consider now words such as:

$\binom{52}{}$ (a)   *relaxátion, annexátion, emendátion, connectívity, domestícity, authentícity*
            (b)   *devastátion, demonstrátion, contemplátion, opportúnity*

Observe that in each case the cluster preceding the primary stress is of the form VC_2 and is therefore a strong cluster, and that in each case this syllable has a weak stress.[28] However, the vowel quality is retained in the syllable preceding primary stress in the examples of (52a) but is lost in the same position in the examples of (52b). This distinction is clearly traceable to the fact that the examples of (52a) are derived from underlying forms in which this vowel has primary stress, whereas the examples of (52b) are derived from underlying forms in which this vowel is unstressed. Thus we have derivations such as the following:[29]

$\binom{53}{}$ (a) $[_N\ [_V relax]_V\ At + ion]_N$

1		RULE (47), CASE (48f)
2	1	(SEE NOTE 29)
2 3	1	(SEE NOTE 29)
3 4	1	RULE (43)

         (b) $[_N\ [_V devast At]_V\ ion]_N$

1	2	(SEE NOTE 29)
2	1	(SEE NOTE 29)
3	1	RULE (43)

Although certain details are not given in these derivations, there is still sufficient information to account for vowel quality in the weak-stressed syllable preceding primary stress. It is clear that the process of vowel reduction depends in a fundamental way on stress; in particular, a vowel that is sufficiently stressed, in some sense that we will make precise later, is protected from vowel reduction. Thus the degree of stress on the final syllable of *torment* (see derivation (51)) is sufficient to prevent vowel reduction, but that on the final syllable of *torrent* is not. Similarly, the second syllable of *relaxation*, having received primary stress in the first cycle, is immune to vowel reduction, but the second syllable of *devastation*, never having received any stress, does undergo the process of vowel reduction. In this way, we can account quite readily for the distinction between the examples of (52a) and (52b).

For some dialects (in particular, our own), we can find near minimal pairs to illustrate these far-reaching phonetic effects of the rules of the transformational cycle. Consider,

---

[28] Here, as elsewhere, we rely on the phonetic representations in Kenyon and Knott, which agree with our own pronunciation, with the provisos stated elsewhere. The stress on the syllable preceding primary stress cannot be stronger than [4 stress] in any of these cases, since the first syllable in each case has tertiary stress and the second (pre-main-stress) syllable is clearly weaker than the first. We would give the contour 3415 for (52a) and 3515 for (52b).

[29] These derivations involve various principles that will not be discussed until the next chapter. In particular, the affix -*ion* invariably places stress on the syllable immediately preceding it, and there is a rule changing a ˇ21 contour to 231, as a special case of more general processes that we will discuss. We also omit here the rules that assign the proper stress contour 1ˇ2 (which would become 1ˇ3 by the Stress Adjustment Rule) to *devastAt* in the first cycle. Filling in these omissions will lead to no change in the analysis of the facts under discussion here.

for example, the words *compensation–condensation*.[30] In *condensation*, the vowel in the second syllable has received stress in the first cycle of the derivation because of the underlying verb *condense*: therefore, it does not reduce, and we have the phonetic representation [kandénsÁšən]. The corresponding vowel of *compensation*, never having received stress, is subject to vowel reduction, resulting in the phonetic representation [kámpənsÁšən].

To conclude this preliminary discussion of the principles that determine stress contours and the related phenomenon of vowel reduction, let us turn to the set of words in English that have the noun-forming affix -*y* (not to be confused with the adjective-forming -*y* of such words as *stringy* and *brawny*, which has very different phonetic effects and a different underlying representation). This is the affix that we find in such words as *aristocrac+y*, *econom+y*, *galax+y*. Before turning to its effect on stress placement, let us consider its phonological representation.

Phonetically, this affix is either [i] or [E], depending on the dialect; that is, it is a high front vowel of dialectally varying degree of tenseness and diphthongization. The tenseness and diphthongization give no information about the underlying phonological representation since there are no relevant contrasts in this position. As we shall see in the next chapter, even phonologically nontense vowels (i.e., simple vocalic nuclei) become tense and diphthongized in final position in the dialects in question. But, in fact, we do know that phonologically the affix cannot consist of a complex vocalic nucleus [E] if it is to be subject to the Main Stress Rule (47), since the cases of this rule that involve affixes, as we shall see, are restricted to affixes with simple vocalic nuclei.

With this possibility eliminated, let us now ask whether the affix -*y* can be phonologically represented as the simple vocalic nucleus *i*. An argument against this analysis is provided by consideration of the stem-forming vowel [i], which, along with the parallel stem-forming vowel [u], appears in the derived forms of pairs such as *proverb–proverbial*, *professor–professorial*, *habit–habitual*, *tempest–tempestuous*. The underlying forms must be represented in the lexicon in such a way as to indicate that they take the stem-forming augment [i] or [u] in their derived forms. A natural, and apparently the simplest, proposal is to enter these words in the lexicon in the form *professor+i*, *habit+u*, etc., with the augment deleted in final position by rule (54):

$$\left(54\right) \qquad \begin{Bmatrix} i \\ u \end{Bmatrix} \rightarrow \phi \; / + \text{---} \#$$

But if this suggestion is followed, then words such as *economy* cannot be entered with the representation *econom+i* for the affix will be incorrectly deleted in final position by rule (54).

These considerations suggest that the representation of the affix -*y* in lexical entries should be +*y*. That is, it should be entered as a high front glide, which later becomes a

---

[30] The latter is the nominalized verb that means "act of condensing," not the noun that means "a condensed state or form" or "a condensed mass" and that, although in some way related to the verb *condense*, is not derived from it as is *condensation* in the first sense. Kenyon and Knott give only the form with unreduced second syllable for *condensation*, and give both reduced and unreduced variants for *compensation*, as well as for the underlying form *compensate*. There is well-known dialectal divergence in these positions. In general, with respect to phonetic minutiae of this sort, it is impossible to expect complete consistency between speakers or for one speaker at various times. Nor should it necessarily be assumed that the transcriptions suggested by phoneticians, at this level of detail, correspond in any very clear way to an acoustic reality. As pointed out in Section 2 of this chapter, we are concerned here with ideal forms that may undergo various modifications in performance and that may relate more closely to a perceptual than an acoustic reality.

vowel by an extremely simple rule. We shall see, in fact, that the required rule converting
y to *i* falls together with other rules that are needed on independent grounds. Thus, in terms
of its analysis into vowels and consonants, the word *economy* is of the phonological form
VCVCVCC, consistent, in fact, with the orthographic representation.

Adopting this quite well-motivated proposal, let us now turn to the effect of the affix
-*y* on stress placement. We have already provided one quite general rule describing the effect
of an affix on the assignment of primary stress, namely, cases (48a) and (48b) of the Main
Stress Rule (47). But the affix -*y* does not seem to fall under this generalization, as we can
see by considering data of the sort presented in (55), where the symbols W, S, and A stand
for syllables terminating in weak, strong, and arbitrary clusters, respectively, and where
the formula to the left of the colon describes the underlying form of the examples to the
right:

$\left(55\right)$ (a) ÁW+*y*: *economy, policy, aristocracy*
    (b) #ÁS+*y*: *industry, galaxy, modesty*
    (c) ÁWS+*y*: *orthodoxy, testimony, rhinoplasty, promissory, auditory*
    (d) AŚS+*y*: *advisory, compulsory, refractory, trajectory*[31]

The examples of case (a) are in fact consistent with the assumption that -*y* is simply
a regular affix subject to the Affix Rule that is part of the Main Stress Rule (47). Since the
syllable preceding the affix contains a weak cluster, case (48a) of (47) will assign primary
stress to the syllable preceding this cluster, in the usual way. The examples of (55b), however,
appear to be inconsistent with this assumption. If -*y* were subject to the Affix Rule, then
primary stress would be placed on the strong cluster immediately preceding the affix, in
accordance with case (48b) of rule (47), whereas in these examples primary stress is actually
on the syllable preceding this strong cluster. Examples such as these might lead one to
suggest another rule, unique to the suffix -*y*, namely, the rule that this suffix places primary
stress on the syllable preceding it by two. Under such a rule, the examples of (55a) and (55b)
would be accounted for.

The forms in (55c), however, show at once that this new proposal is incorrect. In
these examples, primary stress is three syllables removed from the affix -*y*, and there is an
unexplained tertiary stress on the syllable immediately preceding this affix (a syllable which,
we observe, contains a strong cluster). We cannot simply add a special case requiring that
stress be three syllables removed when -*y* is preceded by a strong cluster, for this possibility
is excluded by the examples of (55d).

With no further attempt at patchwork solutions, let us see how close we can come
to the facts by making the weakest and most general assumption, namely, that -*y* is simply
a regular affix obeying the Main Stress Rule as it now stands.

As we have already noted, the examples of (55a) are consistent with this analysis.
That is, the affix -*y* will now, like all affixes, assign stress to the syllable preceding a final
weak cluster.

Consider next the examples of (55b). Under the assumption that -*y* is a regular affix,
case (48b) of the Main Stress Rule (47) will place primary stress on the final syllable of
the string preceding -*y*, since this syllable contains a strong cluster. This gives, for example,
the form *industry*. Recall that according to the ordering constraints on the subcases (48a–f)

---

[31] We assume here that these words have the same affix -*Or*+*y* as *promissory, auditory*. Other analyses might
be suggested for many of these words, taken in isolation, but the analyses we are supposing are at least
as well motivated, on grounds independent of stress placement, as any others. We shall see directly that
considerations of stress placement strongly support the analyses proposed here.

of rule (47), after (48b) has applied, case (c) or (d) may still be applied (see (49)). Case (48d) applies to a string of the form $VC_0\acute{\Sigma}]$, where $\acute{\Sigma}$ is a stressed syllable, assigning primary stress to the vowel. But, as we have noted above, the affix -*y* is a glide in the underlying representation. Hence *indústry* is a string of the form $VC_0\overset{1}{V}C_0]$, which is a special case of $VC_0\acute{\Sigma}]$. Case (48d) thus applies to *industry*, giving the stress pattern *indŭstry*, after which the Stress Adjustment Rule applies to give *indŭstry*. Other rules, to which we return below, determine that a tertiary-stressed vowel in the context of the *ŭ* of *indŭstry* loses its stress and reduces. This gives the desired stress pattern. The examples of (55b), then, are quite consistent with the assumption that -*y* is a regular affix.

Consider now the forms of (55c), which, as we have noted, are inconsistent with the assumption that -*y* places primary stress two syllables back. Taking *orthodoxy* as a typical example, the Main Stress Rule, as it stands, provides the following derivation:

$$\left(56\right) \quad [_N [_A ortho [_{STEM} dox]_{STEM}]_A y]_N$$

	1	RULE (47), CASE (48f)
1	2	RULE (47), CASE (48c)
2	1	RULE (47), CASE (48b)
1	2	RULE (47), CASE (48c)
1	3	RULE (43)

In the first cycle, primary stress is placed on the monosyllabic stem *dox* (exactly as it is placed on the monosyllabic stem *graph* in the derivation (46) of *photograph*). In the next cycle we consider the adjective *orthodóx*. The Stressed Syllable Rule (48c) places primary stress on the syllable preceding the weak cluster, again exactly as in the case of *photograph*. Thus, in isolation, the adjective would have the stress contour *órthodòx* (the Stress Adjustment Rule weakening the final stress to tertiary). But in (56) there is still another cycle. In this third cycle, primary stress is assigned by the Affix Rule (48b) to the syllable with the strong cluster preceding the affix. The result is a string terminating with the stressed syllable *dóxy*, a syllable of the form $C\overset{1}{V}CCC$. Hence the Stressed Syllable Rule (48c) applies once again, as it did in the preceding cycle, reassigning primary stress to the first vowel. The Stress Adjustment Rule (43) now applies to give the desired form *órthodòxy*. The other examples of (55c) are similar. In sum, these forms are consistent with the assumption that -*y* is a regular affix. The examples in (55d) are derived in a manner parallel to that of (55b), with case (48d) of the Stressed Syllable Rule applying on the last pass through the transformational cycle.

We see, then, that by taking the affix -*y* to be nonvocalic phonologically, all of the cases of (55) are explained on the assumption that it is a perfectly regular and unexceptional affix subject to the general Main Stress Rule. This fact alone would motivate the representation of the affix -*y* as a glide in underlying forms, but, as we have seen, there is independent support for this conclusion. The peculiar arrangement of data noted in (55) follows from this assumption, with no modification of the general rules. Here, then, is a striking example of the effectiveness of the principle of the transformational cycle, in conjunction with the principle of disjunctive ordering, in explaining otherwise quite refractory data.

Other forms in -*y* support these conclusions. Before turning to them, however, let us consider the following:

$$\left(57\right) \quad \text{\textit{invéstigative, génerative, illústrative, demónstrative}}$$

Clearly these have the underlying forms:

$$\left(58\right) \qquad\qquad \textit{invéstigAt, génerAt, íllustrAt, démonstrAt}$$

But notice that the affix *-ive* should assign primary stress to the final strong syllable *-At*, in each case, giving the incorrect forms **investigátive, *generátive, *illustrátive, *demonstrátive*. What actually happens is that the affix *-ive* assigns primary stress to the syllable immediately preceding *-At* if that syllable has a strong cluster, or one syllable further back if the syllable preceding *-At* has a weak cluster. In other words, primary stress is assigned just as if the affix were not *-ive*, but rather *-Ative*. In fact, we shall see that in general the element *-At* is considered to be a part of the affix for the purposes of stress placement. We can achieve this effect by reformulating the Main Stress Rule (47) as:

$$\left(59\right) \qquad V \;\rightarrow\; [1\ \text{stress}]\ /\ X\!\rule[0.5ex]{1em}{0.4pt}C_0(W)\ /\ \rule[0.5ex]{1em}{0.4pt}((At)\left\{\begin{array}{c}+\text{affix}\\ \acute{\Sigma}\end{array}\right\})]^{32}$$

To resolve an ambiguity in the expansion of the schema (59), let us assume, as a general principle, that braces are expanded before parentheses. With this assumption, schema (59) expands to (60), which is then expanded to a sequence of rules in the usual way.

$$\left(60\right)\qquad V \;\rightarrow\; [1\ \text{stress}]\ /\ X\!\rule[0.5ex]{1em}{0.4pt}C_0(W)\ /\ \rule[0.5ex]{1em}{0.4pt}\left\{\begin{array}{l}At+\text{affix}\,]\\ +\text{affix}\,]\\ At\ \acute{\Sigma}\,]\\ \acute{\Sigma}\,]\\ \,]\end{array}\right\}\quad\begin{array}{l}\text{(a)}\\ \text{(b)}\\ \text{(c)}\\ \text{(d)}\\ \text{(e)}\end{array}$$

Disjunctive ordering holds between (60a) and (60b), between (60c) and (60d), and between each of (60a)–(60d) and (60e).

Let us consider the effect of this slight modification of the rule on examples with the affix *-y*. We will now have typical derivations such as (61) and (62), for *confíscatory* (similarly, *compénsatory, refórmatory*, etc.) and *antícipatory* (similarly, *revérberatory, concíliatory*, etc.), respectively:

$$\left(61\right)$$

[$_A$ [$_V$*confiscAt*]$_V$ *Or+y*]$_A$				
1	2			(RULES TO BE GIVEN)
2	3	1		AFFIX RULE (60b)
3	1	4	2	STRESSED SYLLABLE RULE (60c)
4	1	5	3	RULE (43)

$$\left(62\right)$$

[$_A$ [$_V$*anticipAt*]$_V$ *Or+y*]$_A$				
1	2			(RULES TO BE GIVEN)
2	3	1		AFFIX RULE (60b)
1	4	2		STRESSED SYLLABLE RULE (60c)
1	5	3		RULE (43)

The two derivations correspond point by point. In both cases the stress contour is assigned to the underlying verb by rules that we will give later on. The verbs, in isolation, would be *confiscate, anticipate*. In the second cycle, the Affix Rule shifts primary stress to the strong

---

[32] Notice that the ordering implied by the use of parentheses carries over to this case, as we would expect. Thus, if the Affix Rule applies in the context $\rule[0.5ex]{1.5em}{0.4pt}At+ive$ (giving, e.g., *illustrÁtive*), it is not permitted to reapply in the context $\rule[0.5ex]{1.5em}{0.4pt}ive$ (giving **illustrÁtive*).

syllable immediately preceding the affix -*y*, in the usual way. At this point the Stressed Syllable Rule applies, under the modification (59)-(60)—that is, with the element -*At* regarded as part of the context of application rather than as subject to the application of the rule. Excluding -*AtOry* from consideration in this way, the rule assigns primary stress to the final strong syllable of the residual string *confisc-* in (61), and to the syllable preceding the final weak syllable of the residual string *anticip-* in (62). Stress is then weakened and vowels reduced in accordance with fairly straightforward rules to which we will return. Here, again, the various cases of the Main Stress Rule interact to generate some rather complex phonetic structures, in accordance with the general principle of the transformational cycle and the general empirical assumptions regarding ordering that we have formulated.

6. *Particular and universal grammar*

In Section 2, on the basis of some preliminary observations about stress contours in English, we suggested that certain principles of organization of a grammar might serve as preconditions for language acquisition, and we discussed some questions of psychological and physical fact relating to this assumption. Now, after a more detailed account of English stress contours, the tentative conclusions of Section 2 have been strengthened.

We have seen that simple rules applying under very general conditions can explain data of a rich and varied sort. This fact raises interesting and important questions. To facilitate the discussion of these questions, we can invoke a traditional distinction between "particular grammar" and "universal grammar." A particular grammar for a single language is a compendium of specific and accidental (that is, nonessential) properties of this language. A universal grammar is a system of conditions that characterize any human language, a theory of essential properties of human language. It is reasonable to suppose that the principle of the transformational cycle and the principles of organization of grammar that we have formulated in terms of certain notational conventions are, if correct, a part of universal grammar rather than of the particular grammar of English. Specifically, it is difficult to imagine how such principles could be "learned" or "invented" in some way by each speaker of the language, on the basis of the data available to him.[33] It therefore seems necessary to assume that these principles constitute a part of the schema that serves as a precondition for language acquisition and that determines the general character of what is acquired. While the general principles of organization of a grammar that we have been discussing can most plausibly be regarded as part of universal grammar, it seems that such rules as the Main Stress Rule must, in large part at least, be a part of the particular grammar of English. A reasonable tentative assumption, then, is that the Nuclear Stress Rule, the Compound Rule, and the Main Stress Rule must be learned by the child acquiring the language, whereas the conditions on the form of rules, the principle of the transformational cycle, and the principles of organization embodied in the various notational conventions that we have established are simply a part of the conceptual apparatus that he applies to the data.

[33] Furthermore, insofar as phonetic transcription corresponds to a perceptual rather than an acoustic reality —see Section 2—departures from the rules are undetectable. Quite apart from this, it is difficult to imagine that adults, whose perceptual set is extremely strong and whose phonetic acuity is very limited, could note and correct deviations in low-level phonetic forms even where these do have a direct counterpart in the physical shape of the utterance.

The Nuclear Stress Rule, the Compound Rule, and the Main Stress Rule, in its various cases, assign primary stress in certain positions. A very small body of data concerning the position of primary stress in simple utterances is sufficient to justify these rules. Correspondingly, a small body of data of this sort might be sufficient to enable the language learner to postulate that these rules form part of the grammar of the language to which he is exposed. Having accepted these rules, the language learner can now apply the general principles of universal grammar to determine their effects in a wide variety of cases. As we have seen, very simple rules can have extremely complex effects when applied in accordance with these general principles. The effects in themselves might well be undetectable by the native speaker or the language learner. When they are determined by a framework of internalized general principles, they become quite accessible to him.

Phonetically untrained speakers of a language seem to find it quite easy to determine the position of main stress in simple utterances, but extremely difficult to trace complex stress contours in a detailed and consistent way. There is, furthermore, some doubt as to the physical reality of these contours, although there is no doubt that with phonetic training, a speaker of the language can identify stress contours and other phonetic details with reasonable consistency. These observations are just what we would expect, given the assumptions to which we have tentatively been led about universal and particular grammar. A small body of data relating to the position of main stress can lead to the formulation of the major stress placement rules. Their effects in complex utterances are determined by the universal unlearned principles of organization of a grammar. There is no need for the speaker or hearer to attend to these automatically determined aspects of an utterance, even where they are physically real; but with training, they can be brought to the level of awareness, whether or not they have acoustic reality. In particular, stress contours can be "heard" with a fair degree of consistency even though they may not correspond in detail to any physical property of utterances.

7. On the abstractness of lexical representation

The syntactic component of the grammar contains a lexicon which lists lexical items with their inherent properties, in particular, those phonological properties that are not determined by general rule. The considerations of the preceding sections suggest that these underlying forms will in general contain no indication of the stress contour of the items or of the distinction between reduced and unreduced vowels. In these respects the lexical representation of an underlying form will be very different from the phonetic representations of its variants in particular contexts. As we investigate further, we will find many more dramatic examples of this discrepancy between underlying forms and their phonetic realizations.

In note 26, we pointed out that the placement of primary stress in nouns is governed by the following rule (where V_s is a simple vocalic nucleus):

$$(63) \qquad V \;\rightarrow\; [1\ stress] \;/\; X\text{------}C_0(W) \;/\; \text{------}V_sC_0]_N$$

This rule clearly falls together with the general Main Stress Rule, in a way which we will examine in the next chapter. As pointed out in note 26, it accounts for the stress placement in words such as *vénison*, *horízon*, *élephant*. To assign primary stress in these words, we disregard the final simple vocalic nucleus with the consonants following it, and assign primary stress to the penultimate syllable of the residue if its final cluster is weak or to this final cluster itself if it is strong. Thus the rule is of precisely the sort with which we are now familiar. If the final syllable of a noun contains a complex vocalic nucleus, then rule (63) is inapplicable, and case (48f) of the Main Stress Rule applies in the usual way, placing primary stress in the final syllable of such words as *machíne, careér*.

Superficially, words ending in vowels seem to contradict this rule. Thus, in words such as *country, menu, window*, the final vocalic nucleus is complex (namely, *E, U, O*, respectively) in many dialects. Nevertheless, it does not receive stress. This seems difficult to explain within our present framework until we observe that there is no contrast between simple and complex vocalic nuclei in word-final position (see p. 39). Consequently, there is no barrier to representing words such as *country, menu, window* in the lexicon with simple vocalic nuclei in final position. This will then make the forms subject to rule (63), which excludes the final syllable from consideration and then assigns primary stress to the residue in the usual way. A later rule will then determine the quality of the word-final vocalic nucleus. This later rule is well motivated, apart from any question of stress placement. Hence these words do not contradict rule (63).

Further investigation of final unstressed vowels reveals that there is a peculiar gap in the pattern. We do not at this point in the exposition have the means to justify this remark, but we will be able to show that of the six simple vocalic nuclei that might appear in final position, only *i, æ, u, o*, and *ɔ* do in fact appear. There are no examples with *e* as the final vowel of the lexical representation.

With these observations as background, let us return to the problem of stress placement. Consider the words *ellipse, eclipse*. If the lexical representation were *elips, eklips*, then rule (63) would apply, eliminating the final syllable from consideration (since it contains a simple vocalic nucleus) and assigning primary stress to the first syllable, giving **Élips, *Éklips* as the phonetic forms. Recall, now, the remarks of the preceding paragraph. Suppose that we were to assign to these words the lexical representations *elipse, eklipse*, respectively. Rule (63) will exclude the final simple vocalic nucleus *e* from consideration and will assign primary stress to the strong cluster that precedes it, giving *elípse, eklípse*. To obtain the correct phonetic forms, we now add the *e*-Elision Rule (64) to the grammar:

$$\left(64\right) \qquad\qquad\qquad e \;\rightarrow\; \phi \;\; / \; \text{———} \, \#$$

This rule gives the correct final forms. It also explains the gap noted in the preceding paragraph. We see now that this gap is not in the underlying lexical representations but only in the phonetic output.

Rule (64), as we shall see, has independent motivation apart from the considerations just mentioned. As one further example, consider the word *Neptune* with the phonetic representation [néptUn].[34] The final cluster of the phonetic representation is strong and hence should receive primary stress by the Main Stress Rule. We cannot simply add a final *e* in the lexical representation here, as we did in the preceding examples, for if we were to enter *Neptune* in the lexicon as *neptUne*, primary stress would still be placed on the second syllable, this time by rule (63). The only apparent alternative is to enter *Neptune* with the lexical representation *neptune*, that is, with the simple vocalic nucleus *u* in the second syllable. Rule (63) will now assign primary stress in the first syllable since the

---

[34] We overlook dialectal variants for the time being.

second syllable contains a weak cluster. We now add the rule (65) (where C is a single consonant):

$$\left(65\right) \qquad\qquad u \;\rightarrow\; U \;\; / \;\; \text{——} CV$$

We thus have the following derivation:

$$\left(66\right)$$

	n e p t u n e	
	1	RULE (63)
	U	RULE (65)
	φ	RULE (64)

The final phonetic form is [néptUn], as required.

Rule (65) is, in fact, justified on independent grounds. Thus we find only phonetic [U], and not the other phonetic reflexes of underlying u,[35] in the context ——CV (e.g., *music, mutiny, mural*).

Here, as in the forms discussed previously in this section, we are again led to an underlying representation which is quite abstract (and which, once again, corresponds directly to conventional orthography).

Consider next verbs such as *caréss* and *haráss*.[36] The final syllable of the phonetic representations for these forms has a stressed weak cluster, which is contrary to what is asserted by the Main Stress Rule (47). Suppose, however, that we were to provide these words with the lexical representations *kVress, hVræss*, with V here standing for an un-specified simple vocalic nucleus.[37] The two final consonants now make the final cluster strong, and case (48f) of the Main Stress Rule will apply to assign primary stress on this final strong cluster. To obtain the correct forms, we need another rule, which we shall call the Cluster Simplification Rule, to delete one of the *s*'s:

$$\left(67\right) \qquad\qquad \text{The first of two identical consonants is deleted.[38]}$$

This gives us [kərés], [həræs] as the phonetic forms, eliminating another apparent exception to the stress placement rules.

Once again, we find that the rule that we postulate (in this case, rule (67)) is well motivated on independent grounds, as we see from considerations such as the following. Consider first words such as *cunning, currency*, and *mussel*, in which the phonetic reflex of underlying u in the first syllable is [ʌ] rather than [U] (see note 35). According to rule (65), underlying u should give phonetic [U] in the context ——CV, as in *punitive, mural, music*, and so on. We can prevent the application of this rule to forms like *cunning* by assuming double consonants in the underlying representations. These will then simplify by rule (67). Alternatively, we would have to assume a contrast between u and U in underlying representations. This is highly implausible, not only because of the examples already noted that motivate rule (65), but also because of the system of vowel alternations that we shall describe.

Observe next that in the near pair *music – mussel*, noted above, the form with phonetic [U] has a voiced medial consonant, whereas the form with phonetic [ʌ] has an unvoiced

---

[35] The simple vocalic nucleus u of underlying lexical representations generally becomes phonetic [ʌ] before consonants by general rules that we will describe later.

[36] The latter, with the phonetic representation [hərǽs]. An alternative form, [hǽrəs], will derive from the lexical representation *hærVs*.

[37] We return later to the precise content of this remark.

[38] Notice that this rule is not, strictly speaking, formulable within the framework that we have established up to this point. We will return to this matter.

medial consonant. Thus the contrast is between [Uz] and [ʌs] in intervocalic position. This correlation is general. We can account for it by postulating a rule that voices [s] medially, this rule applying prior to (67):

$$\left(68\right) \qquad\qquad s \;\rightarrow\; [+\text{voice}] \;/\; V\!\!-\!\!\!-\!\!V$$

Given the rule (68), which we will make more exact later on, we have the derivations (69):

$$\left(69\right)$$

	musik	*mussel*	
	U		RULE (65)
		ʌ	(SEE NOTE 35)
	z		RULE (68)
		φ	RULE (67)

The rule (68) is independently motivated by many considerations. Compare, for example, pairs such as *resent – consent*, *resist – consist*, in which the initial consonant of each of the stems *-sent* and *-sist* voices intervocalically but not postconsonantally. Such examples give even more direct justification for rule (67)—the rule deleting the first of two identical consonants. Thus consider words such as *dissemble*, *dissent*, with the prefix *dis-* (cf. *distrust*, *disturb*, etc.) and a stem beginning with *s*. Evidently, rule (67) is required to account for the fact that the medial cluster is phonetically a single consonant [s]; it is protected from voicing by (68) because of the final *s* of the prefix, in contrast with *resemble*, *resent*, etc. Similarly, we must rely on rule (67) to account for the fact that the prefix *ex-* is phonetically [ek] when the stem begins with an [s], as in *exceed* versus *extend*. Thus, several considerations converge to support the analysis proposed.

Consider next words such as *radium*, *medial* versus *radical*, *medical*. These examples have the complex nuclei [A], [E] in the context ——CiV, and the simple nuclei [æ], [e] in the context ——CiC. A great many examples of this sort, which we shall study in detail below, lead us to postulate rules which have the following effect (where C is a single consonant):

$$\left(70\right) \qquad\qquad \begin{Bmatrix} æ & \rightarrow & A \\ e & \rightarrow & E \end{Bmatrix} \;/\; \text{——CiV}$$

Notice that where the vowel in question is followed by a double consonant (*calcium*, *compendium*), it is not subject to rule (70) and therefore remains simple.

We now proceed to words such as *potassium, gymnasium, magnesium*. As in the case of *music – mussel*, we find that where we have unvoiced [s], here in the context ——*iV*, the vocalic nucleus preceding it is simple, but where we have voiced [z], the vocalic nucleus preceding it is complex. We can now account for this arrangement of data with underlying forms and derivations much like the following:

$$\left(71\right)$$

	potæssium	*gimnæsium*	
		A	RULE (70)
		z	RULE (68)
	φ		RULE (67)

Once again, we rely on rule (67), among others, in accounting for the relevant data.

Finally, notice that words such as *confetti*, *Mississippi*, *Kentucky* appear to violate rule (63), which assigns stress in the antepenultimate syllable of a noun that ends in a simple vocalic nucleus preceded by a weak cluster. We can avoid this violation of the rule by giving the lexical representations *kVnfetti*, *mississippi*, *kVntukki*, respectively. The penultimate syllable, being strong, will now take primary stress by rule (63). The double consonants prevent the voicing of [s] by rule (68) and the change of *u* to [U] by rule (65). Rule (67) then simplifies them, as before. In further support of this analysis, we observe that, quite generally, medial obstruent clusters are unvoiced in English; correspondingly, in the positions where a double consonant must be postulated to account for peculiarities in stress placement, consonant quality, and vowel quality, as in the examples of this paragraph, it is with rare exceptions an unvoiced obstruent that appears.

To recapitulate, the *e*-Elision Rule (64), the Cluster Simplification Rule (67), and the others that we have discussed here form a mutually supporting system of rules that can be justified in a variety of independent ways and that account for a fairly extensive array of data. These rules lead us to postulate underlying forms which are quite abstract. Furthermore, these abstract underlying representations are, in general, very close to conventional orthography.

We will conclude with two more examples. Consider the word *giraffe*, phonetically [jəræf]. Here we have a stress on the final weak cluster. We can explain this by postulating the underlying lexical representation *giræffe*. The rule (63) of stress placement assigns primary stress to the penultimate syllable. By *e*-Elision and Cluster Simplification (note again that an unvoiced cluster is involved) we derive [giræf]. Clearly ·we must have a rule that softens *g* to [j] (and *k* to [s]) before nonlow front vowels, with qualifications to be added later.

$$\left(72\right) \qquad\qquad \begin{Bmatrix} g & \rightarrow & \check{j} \\ k & \rightarrow & s \end{Bmatrix} \Big/ \text{———} \begin{Bmatrix} i \\ e \end{Bmatrix}$$

With rule (72) and the general rule of Vowel Reduction, we derive [jəræf], as required. Alternatively, we might take the underlying representation to be *jVræffe*; there are other possibilities for deriving the phonetic form by regular processes.

Finally, consider the words *courage* [kʌ́rəj] and *courageous* [kərÁjəs]. Superficially, these seem to contradict the rules of stress placement and vowel quality that we have presented in this chapter. Suppose, however, that we were to take the underlying form to be *koræge*.[39] On this assumption, we have the following derivations:

$$\left(73\right)$$

	koræge	*koræge*+əs	
	1		RULE (63)
		1	RULE (47), CASE (48a)
		A	RULE (70)[40]
	ǰ	ǰ	RULE (72)
	φ	φ	RULE (64)[41]
	ʌ		(SEE NOTE 39)
	ə	ə	ə	(VOWEL REDUCTION)

---

[39] In our discussion of the Rounding Adjustment Rule in Chapter Four, we shall show that lax back vowels become unrounded under certain conditions. A consequence of this rule is the shift *o* → ʌ, where [ʌ] is regarded as a lax unrounded back mid vowel, differing from [o] only in not being rounded.

Incidentally, a better representation would be *coræge*, where *c* stands for a symbol identical in its feature composition to *k* except that it appears in a lexically designated class of forms that undergo certain syntactic and phonological processes (i.e., they take derivational affixes of the Romance and Greek systems and undergo rules such as (72)). We return to this matter at the end of Chapter Four.

[40] Actually, we generalize (70) so that it applies in the context ——— CαV, where α is a nonlow front vowel or glide, that is, [i], [e], [ī], [ē], or the corresponding glides. This is a simplification of the rule, in our terms, as we shall see.

[41] We generalize rule (64) so that it elides final *e* not only before word boundary, but also before any formative boundary. This, too, is a simplification in our terms, as we shall see.

In the case of *courage*, in isolation, primary stress is placed by the Noun Rule (63); in the case of *courageous*, by the Affix Rule (47), in the familiar way. The second syllable of *courageous* becomes a complex nucleus by rule (70), before the nonlow front vowel followed by another vowel. The consonant *g* then softens to [ǰ] by rule (72), and the final *e* is elided. Vowel Reduction then gives the desired forms. Once again, a quite abstract underlying form, very similar to conventional orthography, accounts for the variant forms by rules of great generality and wide applicability.

There is, incidentally, nothing particularly surprising about the fact that conventional orthography is, as these examples suggest, a near optimal system for the lexical representation of English words. The fundamental principle of orthography is that phonetic variation is not indicated where it is predictable by general rule. Thus, stress placement and regular vowel or consonant alternations are generally not reflected. Orthography is a system designed for readers who know the language, who understand sentences and therefore know the surface structure of sentences. Such readers can produce the correct phonetic forms, given the orthographic representation and the surface structure, by means of the rules that they employ in producing and interpreting speech. It would be quite pointless for the orthography to indicate these predictable variants. Except for unpredictable variants (e.g., *man – men*, *buy – bought*), an optimal orthography would have one representation for each lexical entry. Up to ambiguity, then, such a system would maintain a close correspondence between semantic units and orthographic representations. A system of this sort is of little use for one who wishes to produce tolerable speech without knowing the language— for example, an actor reading lines in a language with which he is unfamiliar. For such purposes a phonetic alphabet, or the regularized phonetic representations called " phonemic " in modern linguistics, would be superior. This, however, is not the function of conventional orthographic systems. They are designed for the use of speakers of the language. It is therefore noteworthy, but not too surprising, that English orthography, despite its often cited inconsistencies, comes remarkably close to being an optimal orthographic system for English. Correspondingly, it would not be surprising to discover that an adequate theory of the production and perception of speech will find a place for a system of representation not unlike orthography, though there is, for the moment, little evidence that phonemic transcription is a " psychologically real " system in this sense.

It should also be observed that very different dialects may have the same or a very similar system of underlying representations. It is a widely confirmed empirical fact that underlying representations are fairly resistant to historical change, which tends, by and large, to involve late phonetic rules.[42] If this is true, then the same system of representation for underlying forms will be found over long stretches of space and time. Thus a conventional orthography may have a very long useful life, for a wide range of phonetically divergent dialects.

These observations suggest a description of the process of reading aloud that might, to first approximation, be described in the following way. We assume a reader who has internalized a grammar G of the language that he speaks natively. The reader is presented with a linear stretch *W* of written symbols, in a conventional orthography. He produces as an internal representation of this linear stretch *W* a string *S* of abstract symbols of the sort that we have been considering. Utilizing the syntactic and semantic information available to him, from a preliminary analysis of *S*, as well as much extra-linguistic information

---

[42] See Halle (1964), Kiparsky (1965), Postal (1968).

regarding the writer and the context, the reader understands the utterance, and, in particular, assigns to *S* a surface structure Σ.[43] With Σ available, he can then produce the phonetic representation of *S* and, finally, the physical signal corresponding to the visual input *W*. Clearly, reading will be facilitated to the extent that the orthography used for *W* corresponds to the underlying representations provided by the grammar G. To the extent that these correspond, the reader can rely on the familiar phonological processes to relate the visual input *W* to an acoustic signal. Thus one would expect that conventional orthography should, by and large, be superior to phonemic transcription, which is in general quite remote from underlying lexical or phonological representation and not related to it by any linguistically significant set of rules. On the other hand, for an actor reading lines in a language that he does not know, phonemic transcription should be much superior to conventional orthography, since it can be read without comprehension, whereas conventional orthography, being close to the linguistically significant system underlying ordinary speech, can be read only when the surface structure (including the internal structure of words) is known, that is, when the utterance is to some degree understood.

There are many interesting questions that can be raised about the development of systems of underlying representation during the period of language acquisition. It is possible that this might be fairly slow. There is, for example, some evidence that children tend to hear much more phonetically than adults. There is no reason to jump to the conclusion that this is simply a matter of training and experience; it may very well have a maturational basis. Furthermore, much of the evidence relevant to the construction of the underlying systems of representation may not be available in early stages of language acquisition. These are open questions, and it is pointless to speculate about them any further. They deserve careful empirical study, not only because of the fundamental importance of the question of "psychological reality" of linguistic constructs, but also for practical reasons; for example, with respect to the problem of the teaching of reading. These further topics, however, lie beyond the scope of this book.

8. *Vowel alternations*

We have already noted that simple and complex vocalic nuclei alternate in some way. Let us now consider these processes in more detail.

A comparison of words such as *profane – profanity, compare–comparative, grateful–gratitude, serene–serenity, appeal–appelative, plenum–plenitude, divine–divinity, derive–derivative, reconcile–conciliate*, and innumerable others suggests that the grammar must contain rules which have the following effect:

$$\left(74 \right) \qquad \begin{array}{ccc} \text{A} & \rightarrow & æ \\ \text{E} & \rightarrow & e \\ \text{I} & \rightarrow & i \end{array}$$

The vowel in boldface stands for a complex vocalic nucleus in the first member of each pair, and for a simple vocalic nucleus in the second member of each pair. Furthermore, both the vowel quality and the stress placement in the first member of each pair seem to

---

[43] Obviously, it is an oversimplification to assume that conversion of *W* to *S* precedes the interpretive processes that assign Σ to *S*. There is no reason for this having to be the case, and such commonplace phenomena as proofreading errors suggest that in fact it is not the case.

require that the underlying form have the complex rather than the simple vocalic nucleus, that is, that the rule be (74) rather than (75):

$$\left(75\right) \qquad\qquad \begin{aligned} æ &\rightarrow A \\ e &\rightarrow E \\ i &\rightarrow I \end{aligned}$$

Thus we postulate underlying forms such as *profAn, serEn, divIn*,[44] which are stressed on the final complex nucleus by the Main Stress Rule (case (48f)). To account for the second members of the pairs, we apply rule (74) in the context (76) (where $\breve{V}$ stands for an unstressed vocalic nucleus):

$$\left(76\right) \qquad\qquad\qquad — C_0\breve{V}C_0V$$

Superficially, the vowel alternations illustrated by (74) appear to be extremely complex and unsystematic. We have disguised this fact by our capitalization notation. Stated in terms of symbols that receive a direct phonetic interpretation, the rules in (74) appear as:

$$\left(77\right) \qquad\qquad \begin{aligned} \bar{e}y &\rightarrow æ \\ iy &\rightarrow e \\ \bar{a}y &\rightarrow i \end{aligned}$$

where the symbols $\bar{e}, \bar{\imath}, \bar{a}$ stand for phonetically tense counterparts to *e, i, æ*.[45] These rules are extraordinarily complex in terms of the otherwise well-motivated feature system that we will develop below and in terms of any concept of complexity that seems to have any merit at all.

Compounding the problem is the fact that it is not enough to postulate the rules (74)-(77); it is also necessary to postulate the rules (75), which have precisely the opposite effect. To see this, consider words such as *various–variety, German–Germanic–Germanium, manager–managerial*. The underlying form for *vary* must be *vAri*, with a final simple vocalic nucleus. Stress placement will then be determined correctly by rule (48e). The final vowel is converted from *i* to [E] finally or before another vowel by the rule discussed on page 45 in connection with words such as *country, window*. But notice that under stress, in *variety*, the vowel in question becomes not [E] but [I]. Therefore we must have a rule converting *i* to [I] in this position. Consider next the triple *German–Germanic–Germanium*. The position of stress on the first member of this triple shows that the vocalic nucleus of its final syllable must be weak. The second member shows that it must be æ. The third member shows that this underlying æ becomes [A] by a rule of the form æ → *A* in certain contexts (see rule (70) and the discussion of *courage–courageous* on p. 48). Consider now *manager–*

---

[44] If we were restricted to lowercase Latin letters and to a principle of absolute linearity of spelling, we could not use this device and would have to find an alternative notation. The proper choice is obvious, in the light of the rules given above. We can represent *profAn, serEn, divIn* in the form *profæne, serene, divine*; stress placement will now be determined correctly by the Main Stress Rule (case (48e)); the simple vocalic nuclei will become complex in the context ——*Ce* by a rule rather like (65); and the final *e* will be elided by rule (64), giving the correct phonetic forms.

One might inquire whether this proposal is not after all correct, for the underlying representations. We have considered this possibility quite seriously, and it has something to recommend it. We reject it, however, in favor of the analyses with final complex nuclei in the underlying representations, for two reasons which will become clearer later on: first, the solution with final *e* is less highly valued in terms of the general measure of evaluation (complexity measure) that we will develop; second, we have not been able to find a simple system of rules that gives the required results in detail under this assumption.

[45] The phonetics is straightforward except with respect to postulation of the [æ]-[āy] relation, which begs a few questions to which we shall return in Chapter Four.

managerial. Considerations of stress and vowel quality show that the final vowel of *manager* must be a simple vocalic nucleus. This vowel becomes [E] in the context ——CiV; it must therefore be the vowel *e* (since æ becomes [A] and *i* becomes [I]). Many examples of this sort show that we must, in fact, set up rules with the effect of (75), in addition to rules with the effect of (74).

We have now reached a conclusion which is quite unacceptable. The rules (74) (= (77)) and (75) are extremely complex in themselves. It is evident, furthermore, that there must be some underlying generalization that accounts for the fact that the rules (74) and the rules (75) are precisely opposite in their effects. If we give the rules in the form (74), (75), there is no way to express this generalization. In brief, we have two extremely complex processes which are surely related, but related in some way which is not statable if these processes are described in the form (74), (75).

These considerations suggest very strongly that something is seriously amiss in the analysis we have been tacitly assuming, with the symbols A, E, I, O, U taken simply as informal notational abbreviations for complex nuclei of underlying forms.

Notice that the processes (74) and (75) involve alternations of two kinds, from a phonetic point of view. We can see this by considering the formulation (77) of (74). Clearly these rules affect both the complexity and the quality of the vocalic nuclei in question; that is, the complex nuclei become simple, and the vowel of the vocalic nucleus changes in quality as well. Let us consider these processes individually.

To begin with, let us disregard the question of vowel quality and consider the matter of complexity of the vocalic nucleus. We note at once that the presence of the *y*-glide correlates with tenseness of the vowel. We need therefore account only for the tenseness. The presence of the glide will then be determined by the Diphthongization Rule (78):

$$\left(78\right) \qquad \phi \;\rightarrow\; y \;/\; \bar{V}\text{——}$$

where $\phi \rightarrow y$ stands for "insert *y*" and where $\bar{V}$ is a tense vowel. (We shall see that this rule is, in fact, more general.) We may now assume that there are no postvocalic glides in underlying forms.

The examples that we have already given illustrate fairly adequately the general scope of the rules governing tenseness. Summarizing what we have observed, we can formulate the following rules, as a first approximation:

$$\left(79\right) \qquad V \;\rightarrow\; [-\text{tense}] \;/\; \text{——}C\breve{V}CV$$

$$\left(80\right) \qquad V \;\rightarrow\; [+\text{tense}] \;/\; \text{——} \begin{cases} \# & \text{(a)} \\ V & \text{(b)} \\ C\left\{\begin{matrix} i \\ e \end{matrix}\right\}V & \text{(c)} \end{cases}$$

The Laxing Rule (79) converts the tense vowels in the boldface positions of *gratitude* (cf. *grAteful*), *serenity* (cf. *serEn*), *derivative*, (cf. *derIv*) to their lax counterparts. If the underlying forms are *græt*, *serēn*, *derīv*, respectively, rule (79) will give the forms *græt*(*itude*), *seren*(*ity*), *deriv*(*ative*), as required. On the other hand, the Tensing Rule (80) will apply in the following way: (a) in the context ——#, the final vowels of *country*, *window*, *vary*, etc., will become tense; (b) in the context ——V, the vowels in boldface in *various*, *variety*, *impious*, *piety*, etc., will become tense; (c) in the context ——CαV (where α is a nonlow nonback vowel), the vowels in boldface in *managerial*, *courageous*, *Canadian*, etc., become tense. In all three cases, the tense vowel is diphthongized by rule (78).

The rules (78)–(80), which are quite simple and straightforward, account for the complexity of the vocalic nuclei in all of the cases that we have considered. The problem of vowel quality still remains, however, for the tense vowels (the complex vocalic nuclei). At this stage of our analysis, the vowels in boldface in the words *grateful*, *serene*, *derive*, for example, will be [ǣy], [ēy], [īy], respectively, from underlying æ, e, i, by Tensing and Diphthongization. But the vocalic nuclei of these words should be [ēy], [īy], [āy], respectively. That is, we must add a Vowel Shift Rule which has the following effect on stressed vowels:

$$\left(81\right) \quad \begin{array}{ccl} \bar{\text{æ}} & \to & \bar{\text{e}} \\ \bar{\text{e}} & \to & \bar{\text{i}} \\ \bar{\text{i}} & \to & \bar{\text{a}} \ (= \bar{\text{æ}}\text{—see note 45}) \end{array}$$

In other words, the rule (81) effects the shifts:

$$\left(82\right) \quad \bar{\text{æ}} \ \to \ \bar{\text{e}} \ \to \ \bar{\text{i}} \ \to \ \bar{\text{æ}}$$

We shall see, in Chapter Four, that the Vowel Shift Rule can be stated in a very simple way, and, in fact, that it can be generalized beyond the class of examples that we have considered. With the Tensing and Laxing Rules, the Diphthongization Rule, and the Vowel Shift Rule, we have now fully accounted for the examples considered so far, as we can see by the following typical derivations:

$$\left(83\right)$$

profǽn (*profane*)	
profǽn	MAIN STRESS RULE (48f)
profǽyn	DIPHTHONGIZATION (78)
proféyn	VOWEL SHIFT (81)

$$\left(84\right)$$

profǽnity (*profanity*)[46]	
profǽnity	MAIN STRESS RULE (48a)
profǽnity	LAXING RULE (79)

$$\left(85\right)$$

mænVger (*manager*)	
mǽnVger	MAIN STRESS RULE (63)
mǽnVjer	RULE (72)
mǽnəjər	VOWEL REDUCTION

$$\left(86\right)$$

mænVgeriæl (*managerial*)	
mænVgériæl	MAIN STRESS RULE (48a)
mænVjériæl	RULE (72)
mænVjḗriæl	TENSING RULE (80c,b)
mænVjḗyrīyæl	DIPHTHONGIZATION (78)
mænVjíyrīyæl	VOWEL SHIFT (81)[47]
mænəjíyrīyəl	VOWEL REDUCTION

---

[46] In these derivations, we omit all cycles except the last.

[47] Note that the Vowel Shift Rule is restricted to vowels that carry stress, though not necessarily primary stress.

The points to be noted are the following. Instead of the extremely complicated rules (74), (75), we now have the quite simple rules (78)–(81).[48] More important, we have succeeded in expressing the generalization underlying the rules (74) and their inverses, the rules (75). By extracting the Vowel Shift Rule from these processes, we are left with only rules (79) and (80) (the Tensing and Laxing Rules) as inverses. This is a bare and irreducible minimum. We have, in other words, avoided the absurdity of assuming that the processes stated as (74) and (75) have no relation to each other. We now have abstract underlying representations such as *profæn*, *serēn*, *derīv*, *mænVger*. Observe that the device of capitalization used earlier corresponds to the phonological category of tenseness at the level of lexical representation. Note also that in the case of an underlying tense vowel, the corresponding phonetic element will invariably differ from the underlying vowel either in quality (if it remains tense) or in tenseness. For example, corresponding to the tense vowel in the boldface position in the underlying representation *serēn*, we have either [īy] (in the word *serene*) or [e] (in the word *serenity*). Once again, the postulated underlying forms are systematically related to conventional orthography (see note 44) and are, as is well known, related to the underlying forms of a much earlier historical stage of the language. There has, in other words, been little change in lexical representation since Middle English, and, consequently, we would expect (though we have not verified this in any detail) that lexical representation would differ very little from dialect to dialect in Modern English. If this assumption proves to be correct, it will follow that conventional orthography is probably fairly close to optimal for all modern English dialects, as well as for the attested dialects of the past several hundred years.

Bringing this discussion to a close, we will show that entirely independent considerations also support the postulation of the Vowel Shift Rule (81) for modern spoken English. In Section 7 we discussed the Velar Softening Rule that converts *g* to [ǰ] and *k* to [s] before nonlow front vowels, that is [i], [e], [ī], and [ē]. But consider words such as:

$$\left(87\right) \qquad \begin{array}{l} \textit{criticism–critical–criticize} \\ \textit{medicine–medical–medicate} \end{array}$$

Using the symbol *c* to represent unvoiced velars in lexical entries that are subject to the Velar Softening Rule (72) (see note 39), we have the underlying representations *critic-*, *medic-* for the base forms of (87). Evidently the Velar Softening Rule must precede the Vowel Reduction Rule, since we have softening in the boldface position in *medicine* (before underlying *i*) but not *medical* (before underlying *æ*), although in both cases the vowel following the consonant in question is reduced to [ə] by Vowel Reduction. Under this assumption, the words *criticism* and *critical* also cause no difficulty. But consider the words *criticize* and *medicate*. In the case of *criticize*, we have velar softening before a vocalic nucleus which is phonetically [I] (= [āy]); in the case of *medicate*, we do not have velar softening before a vocalic nucleus which is phonetically [A] (= [ēy]). In other words, we have softening before a low back vowel but not before a nonlow front vowel, which is precisely the opposite of what we would expect in terms of rules of otherwise great generality. The paradox is resolved, of course, by the Vowel Shift Rule. The underlying representation for *criticize* is *criticīz*, and the underlying representation for *medicate* is *medicǣt* (as indicated in both cases by the spelling—see note 44). If Velar Softening applies not only prior to Vowel Reduction but also prior to Vowel Shift, then we will have softening in the case of *criticize*

---

[48] The sense in which the latter rules are much simpler will be explained later. We shall argue that this is the only sense of "simplicity" that is relevant to the choice of a grammar.

(before an underlying high front vowel) but not *medicate* (with an underlying low vowel after the *c*). After Velar Softening applies, the Diphthongization and Vowel Shift Rules convert *ī* to [āy] (giving [kritisāyz]) and *ǣ* to [ēy] (giving [medikēyt]); in our alternative notation, the Velar Softening, Diphthongization, and Vowel Shift Rules convert underlying *criticīz*, *medicǣt* to phonetic [kritisIz], [medikAt], respectively.

There are many other examples of this sort, some of which we will discuss when we deal with vowel alternations more carefully in Chapter Four. For the present, we simply point out that these examples provide an independent justification for the Vowel Shift Rule, and show once again the necessity of postulating lexical representations of a quite abstract sort.

PART II
ENGLISH PHONOLOGY

Chapter three

THE TRANSFORMATIONAL CYCLE IN ENGLISH PHONOLOGY

1. Introductory remarks

One of the most complex aspects of the phonetics of English is its intricate system of stress contours, both within the word and within the phrase. It has long been known to phoneticians that stress contours in English have at least four (and probably five or more) perceptual levels, so that many degrees of stress must be recorded in an adequate phonetic transcription. Furthermore, it is well known that a vowel that is insufficiently stressed, in some sense, reduces to a mid or high central "neutral" vowel.[1]

For the most part, the study of English sound structure has been limited to the problem of developing an adequate notation,[2] but there have also been a few attempts to go beyond this and discover the underlying principles that determine these phenomena.[3] Several years ago we showed (Chomsky, Halle, Lukoff, 1956) that the major stress contours are determined by the operation of a transformational cycle. We assumed then that the position of main stress was an independent ("phonemic") feature, and we did not investigate the rules that determine this or the rules that determine vowel reduction. In the present chapter, we will discuss the rules of stress assignment and vowel reduction on a somewhat larger scale. We will see that both the placement of main stress and the stress contours within

---

[1] We will represent this "neutral" vowel with the symbol [ə], using the symbol [ʌ] for the vowel of *but*, *luck*, etc. Phonetically the vowel which we represent here as [ə] may often (or, in some dialects, always) be raised to the high central vowel [ɨ]. We will not consider at this point the question of how, in detail, this vowel is phonetically realized in various contexts and dialects. For expository purposes, we may accept the fiction that the vowel we are representing as [ə] is distinct from all other vowels.

[2] See, for example, Bloomfield (1933), Bloch and Trager (1942), Trager and Smith (1951), Hill (1958), Kenyon (1958), Kurath (1964), and, for general discussion, Gleason (1961, Chapter 3).

[3] For example, Newman (1946). In particular, there have been studies in which affixes are classified in terms of their effect on stress placement (e.g., Kingdon, 1958), and others in which some of the major rules are stated (e.g., Cooper, 1687, Elphinston, 1765, Marchand, 1960, all of whom noted that in many cases placement of primary stress in English follows the familiar Latin rules).

The distinction between the problem of devising an adequate (so-called "phonemic") notation and that of discovering the underlying principles that determine phonetic representations is not a sharp one. Thus, even a phonemic notation takes an initial step toward systematization in that it is concerned with low-level generalizations about phonetic variation that can be stated in terms of immediate phonetic contexts.

the word and the phrase are largely predictable from the syntactic and the nonprosodic phonological structure of an utterance by means of a transformational cycle.

1.1. THE RULES OF THE PHONOLOGICAL COMPONENT

The rules of the grammar operate in a mechanical fashion; one may think of them as instructions that might be given to a mindless robot, incapable of exercising any judgment or imagination in their application. Any ambiguity or inexplicitness in the statement of rules must in principle be eliminated, since the receiver of the instructions is assumed to be incapable of using intelligence to fill in gaps or to correct errors. To the extent that the rules do not meet this standard of explicitness and precision, they fail to express the linguistic facts.[4]

In Chapter Two we outlined our assumptions regarding the ordering of rules in the phonological component of a generative grammar. To repeat the main points briefly, we assume that the rules are linearly ordered and that they are applied in the given order in forming a derivation. Furthermore, this order is cyclical, in the following sense. The syntactic component generates a string with a surface structure that is represented by labeled bracketing. The sequence of phonological rules is first applied to all innermost constituents of this string. Innermost brackets are then deleted, and the sequence applies to the new innermost constituents. This cyclical application is repeated until the maximal domain of phonological processes is reached. (The maximal domain is the "phonological phrase," which we assume to be marked in the surface structure.)

We will see that certain rules are limited to the context $\# \# \ldots \text{——} \ldots \# \#$; that is, they apply only at word boundaries. These make up the "noncyclical phonology" that we will discuss in greater detail in the next chapter. Our attention here will be directed rather to the cyclical transformational rules that apply in contexts determined by major syntactic categories—rules that therefore reapply, in general, at successive stages of the transformational cycle.

We have also assumed that there may be a somewhat more complex principle of ordering within the linear sequence of rules. A certain subsequence may form a block of rules which are "disjunctively ordered" in the sense that if one of these rules applies to a certain substring, the other members of the block are not applicable to this substring in this stage of the cycle. Rules not subject to this restriction on their application are "conjunctively ordered." Disjunctive ordering must be indicated by an appropriate convention; we will show various examples and will suggest appropriate formal devices and generalizations as we proceed, extending the observations of Chapter Two. In Chapter Eight these notions will be further developed and sharpened.

In short, at this point in the exposition we suppose the phonology to consist of a linear sequence of rules, some subsequences of which form disjunctively ordered blocks. These rules apply in a cycle, as determined by the surface structure of the string to which they apply. In this way they convert a formal object generated by the syntactic component, that is, a string of formatives with surface structure marked, into a phonetic representation of the string. The sequence of representations formed in this process we call a "derivation" of the phonetic representation from the underlying phonological representation. Thus the

---

[4] It is a curious fact that this condition of preciseness of formulation for the rules of a generative grammar has led many linguists to conclude that the motivation for such grammars must be machine translation or some other use of computers, as if there could be no motive in clarity and completeness other than this.

phonological component specifies the relation between phonetic and phonological representation.

To be slightly more precise, the syntactic component generates a string of formatives, some of which are given in lexical representation, with surface structure marked. The readjustment rules, operating along the lines indicated in Chapter One (pp. 9–11), convert this formal object into a string in full phonological representation, with surface structure marked. The readjustment rules thus provide a link between the syntactic and the phonological components of the grammar. We presuppose, henceforth, that we are dealing with the formal objects provided by the readjustment rules which apply to the structures generated by the syntactic component. In Chapter Eight, we return to a brief consideration of readjustment rules.

1.2. *NOTATIONAL CONVENTIONS*

Let us now briefly review and extend the notational conventions introduced in the preceding chapters.

Where X, Y, Z, and W are strings of symbols of arbitrary complexity, an expression of the form (1) is an abbreviation for the sequence (1a), (1b), and an expression of the form (2) is an abbreviation for the sequence (2a), (2b), *in the order shown.*

$$(1) \qquad X \begin{Bmatrix} Y \\ Z \end{Bmatrix} W$$

  (a) XYW
  (b) XZW

$$(2) \qquad X(Y)Z$$

  (a) XYZ
  (b) XZ

In expression (1) there are two items enclosed by the braces; thus (1) abbreviates a sequence of two expressions, i.e., (1a), (1b). Similarly, (3) abbreviates the sequence (3a), (3b), (3c), and the same convention is extended to an arbitrary number of items in braces.

$$(3) \qquad X \begin{Bmatrix} Y \\ Z \\ W \end{Bmatrix} P$$

  (a) XYP
  (b) XZP
  (c) XWP

When notations such as (2) have been used in the construction of generative grammars, it has generally been tacitly assumed that *the ordering abbreviated by the use of parentheses is disjunctive* (in this case the ordering (2a), (2b)). In the case of braces, however, the ordering is assumed to be conjunctive. Thus the expressions (3a), (3b), (3c), abbreviated as (3), are conjunctively ordered; but the expressions (2a), (2b), abbreviated as (2), are disjunctively ordered.

For any feature complex X, the symbol X_m^n stands for a string of no less than m and no more than n occurrences of X. Thus C_0^1 stands for one occurrence or zero occurrences of C, and C_1^1 stands for exactly one occurrence of C (where C stands for a segment which is a nonvowel—see p. 68). The symbol X_m stands for a string of no less than m X's. Thus C_2 stands for a string of two or more occurrences of C. When no subscript or superscript is given, it is to be assumed that both the subscript and the superscript are "1." Thus CVC_0, for example, stands for a string of exactly one nonvowel followed by exactly one vowel followed by zero or more nonvowels; the notation $\begin{bmatrix} -\text{tense} \\ V \end{bmatrix}$ stands for exactly one occurrence of a lax (nontense) vowel; etc.

The notation X_m^n is definable in terms of the parenthesis notation. We will tentatively assume that it has the same formal conventions associated with it. Thus, a rule of the form $\ldots C_1^2 \ldots$, for example, abbreviates the two disjunctively ordered rules $\ldots CC\ldots, \ldots C\ldots$; we thus take $\ldots C_1^2 \ldots$ to be an abbreviation for $\ldots C(C)\ldots$. We will actually make little use of this property of the notation X_m^n (see, however, pp. 175–76, Chapter Four), and we mention it here only to clarify the meaning of the notation.

There is one ambiguity that must be resolved. The notation (4a), for example, is an abbreviation for (4b), which is ambiguously interpreted as either the sequence (5a) or the sequence (5b), depending on which parentheses are expanded first in (4b).

$$\left(4\right) \qquad \begin{array}{ll} \text{(a)} & \ldots C_0^1(X)\ldots \\ \text{(b)} & \ldots(C)(X)\ldots \end{array}$$

$$\left(5\right) \qquad \begin{array}{ll} \text{(a)} & \ldots CX\ldots \\ & \ldots X\ldots \\ & \ldots C\ldots \\ & \ldots\ldots\ldots \\ \\ \text{(b)} & \ldots CX\ldots \\ & \ldots C\ldots \\ & \ldots X\ldots \\ & \ldots\ldots\ldots \end{array}$$

We will assume henceforth, rather arbitrarily, that alternative (5a) is correct and that, in general, substrings abbreviated as Y_i^j are expanded *later* than substrings enclosed in parentheses.

There are several other ambiguities to be resolved in the meaning of these notations. One, of crucial importance in our material, is this. Suppose that we have the sequence of expressions (6):

$$\left(6\right) \qquad \begin{array}{ll} \text{(a)} & XY \\ \text{(b)} & XZ \\ \text{(c)} & X \end{array}$$

If we apply the brace notation to (6a), (6b), we derive (7):

$$\left(7\right) \qquad X\left\{\begin{matrix} Y \\ Z \end{matrix}\right\}$$

But now we can apply the parenthesis notation to the sequence (7), (6c), giving (8):

$$\left(8\right) \qquad X(\left\{\begin{matrix} Y \\ Z \end{matrix}\right\})$$

Alternatively, we might first have applied the parenthesis notation to (6b), (6c), giving (9), and then applied the brace notation to the sequence (6a), (9), giving (10):

$$\left(9\right) \qquad\qquad\qquad\qquad X(Z)$$

$$\left(10\right) \qquad\qquad\qquad\qquad X\begin{Bmatrix} Y \\ (Z) \end{Bmatrix}$$

The alternatives that lead to (8) and (10), respectively, differ in their empirical consequences, because of the conventions just stated regarding conjunctive and disjunctive ordering. If the sequence (6) is abbreviated as (8), it follows that (6a) and (6b) are each disjunctively ordered with respect to (6c). If the sequence (6) is abbreviated as (10), it follows that only (6b) is disjunctively ordered with respect to (6c). Therefore, it is clearly an empirical question whether one or the other alternative is correct.

We have one clear case to illustrate the empirical effects of this choice, namely, the case of stress placement with affixes, which was discussed in Chapter Two (pp. 31–36), and which will be discussed in more detail in Section 6 of this chapter. The correct choice, in this case, is (8). That is, when confronted with a sequence such as (6), we must first apply braces and then apply parentheses. This was the decision made, without comment, in Chapter Two.

It is conceivable that this decision is ad hoc and depends on the empirical facts in each case. If so, it follows that one cannot determine from the sequence of rules constituting the grammar what is the organization of the grammar in terms of disjunctive and conjunctive ordering. In other words, this organization is in part arbitrary, a feature of grammar that must be specified independently of the linear ordering of rules. Evidently, it would be quite interesting to determine whether there is a general principle governing this organization, given the sequence of rules. A natural principle that suggests itself at once is this: *abbreviatory notations must be selected in such a way as to maximize disjunctive ordering.* Given the sequence of rules (6), this principle would lead us to assign the organization of rule application defined by (8) rather than that defined by (10). The principle seems to us a natural one in that maximization of disjunctive ordering will, in general, minimize the length of derivations in the grammar. The question of how an internalized grammar is used in performance (speech production or perception) is of course quite open. Nevertheless, it seems reasonable to suppose that the grammar should be selected in such a way as to minimize the amount of "computation" that is necessary, and that "length of derivation" is one factor in determining "complexity of computation." Naturally, this principle must be regarded as quite tentative. We will adhere to it where a choice arises, but we have very little evidence for or against it. To find empirical evidence bearing on a principle of this degree of abstractness is not an easy matter, but the issue is important, and one should bear it in mind in a detailed investigation of phonological structure.

These remarks by no means exhaust the quite deep question of how disjunctive and conjunctive ordering are to be assigned to the sequence of rules constituting the phonological component and how ambiguities in the interpretation of the notations are to be resolved. We shall have a few more comments to make on this matter as we proceed. There is no difficulty, in principle, in resolving all ambiguities one way or another. However, our feeling is that premature formalization should be avoided, and that we should leave questions open where we have no empirical evidence and no considerations of plausibility, however vague, that would lead us to one or another of the possible decisions. Research in phonology is barely beginning to reach the depth where questions of this sort can be examined.

With these remarks, we merely wish to point to the fact that these problems can now be posed in a meaningful way and that one can search for empirical evidence to resolve them.

Proceeding now to other types of notation used here, we will follow the convention of marking the heaviest (main) stress as 1 stress, the next heaviest (secondary) stress as 2 stress, etc. This convention conforms to familiar usage but has the disadvantage that weaker stresses are indicated by larger numbers. The reader should take note of this to avoid possible confusion. We will also occasionally use the conventional notation V́, V̂, V̌ for primary, secondary, and tertiary stress, respectively.

In stating rules of the transformational cycle, we will, as in the first two chapters, use boldface square brackets **[ ]** to indicate the syntactic IC analysis of the surface structure. If the brackets are labeled by a sequence of (one or more) category symbols, the rule in question is restricted to strings belonging to one of the indicated categories. If the brackets are unlabeled, the rule is unrestricted as to category. The boldface square brackets that are used to mark syntactic structure are not to be confused with the brackets [ ] used to enclose feature sets.

The rules that determine stress contours are, for the most part, rules that assign primary stress in certain positions, at the same time weakening the stresses in all other positions by one. We might think of these as rules that assign [0 stress], with the convention that after every application of such a rule, all integral values for stress within the domain of this rule (which is a maximal string containing no internal brackets) are increased by one. Whenever primary stress is placed by a rule $V \rightarrow [1 \text{ stress}] / \ldots$, an interpretation of this sort is to be understood.

1.3. DISTINCTIVE FEATURES

We take "distinctive features" to be the minimal elements of which phonetic, lexical, and phonological transcriptions are composed, by combination and concatenation. The alphabetic symbols that we use freely in the discussion below are therefore to be regarded as nothing more than convenient ad hoc abbreviations for feature bundles, introduced for ease of printing and reading but without systematic import. Thus, for example, if the symbol /i/ appears in the discussion, it is to be understood as an abbreviation for a feature complex such as:

$$
(11) \qquad \begin{bmatrix} + \text{segment} \\ + \text{vocalic} \\ - \text{consonantal} \\ + \text{high} \\ - \text{low} \\ - \text{back} \\ - \text{round} \\ - \text{tense} \end{bmatrix}
$$

A feature complex of this sort we call a "unit" if it is fully specified in terms of features; otherwise, an "archi-unit." If the unit has the feature [+segment], we call it a "segment" (or, if not fully specified, an "archi-segment"). If it has the feature [−segment], we call it a "boundary." However, in discussing examples, we will not always make a consistent distinction between fully specified segments and archi-segments where this is not relevant to the point at issue, and we will often use the same alphabetic symbol for a segment and various archi-segments of this segment. We do this simply to limit the use of alphabetic symbols in expository passages to some reasonable number. Except for this proviso, we will generally use alphabetic symbols with their conventional phonetic interpretations as abbreviations for feature sets; but where possible ambiguity in the exposition might result, we will resort to the full use of features.

Our use of the concept "distinctive feature" differs from that of many others in a number of ways. On the one hand, we have made fairly extensive revisions in the catalog of features as well as in the terminology utilized in previous work. A detailed discussion of the revised framework is to be found in Chapter Seven. In addition, we distinguish sharply between the classificatory and the phonetic function of distinctive features. It is only in their classificatory function that all features are strictly binary, and only in their phonetic function that they receive a physical interpretation. As classificatory devices, the distinctive features play a role in the full specification of a lexical entry (along with syntactic and semantic features and idiosyncratic classifications of various sorts that determine the behavior of a lexical entry with respect to the rules of the grammar). As phonetic parameters, the distinctive features provide a representation of an utterance which can be interpreted as a set of instructions to the physical articulatory system, or as a refined level of perceptual representation. The major function of the phonological component is to derive the phonetic representation of an utterance from the surface structure assigned to it by the syntactic component, that is, from its representation in terms of classificatory features of the lexical items it contains, its other nonlexical formatives, and its analysis in terms of immediate constituents, all of this material having been modified in an appropriate way by readjustment rules.

As classificatory devices, features are binary. As a first approximation, we may assume that they are provided with a coefficient that can take one of two values: + (plus) or − (minus). On the other hand, since phonetic features are generally multivalued, we may think of them as having positive integers as coefficients. Thus, in the representations that constitute the surface structure (the output of the syntactic rules), specified features will be marked as plus or minus; but the phonological rules, as they apply to these representations, will gradually convert these specifications to integers. We will not actually give the rules that effect this conversion in most cases because our interest in sound structure, in this book, does not extend to matters such as degree of aspiration, degree of fronting of vowels, etc.; we will, however, give the rules that determine degree of stress. In principle, all rules should be given.[5]

It is conventional to enclose phonemic representations in diagonals (i.e., in the form /.../) and phonetic representations in square brackets (in the form [...]). We will follow a similar convention where it contributes to the clarity of the exposition, using diagonals for representations in which the features are functioning as classificatory devices (and are specified plus or minus) and square brackets for representations in which they function phonetically (and are specified with integers, in principle). But we cannot adhere to this convention rigidly. The diagonal vs. square-bracket convention was designed for a taxonomic theory that assumed two levels of representation, phonemic and phonetic, related by unordered taxonomic rules (e.g., phoneme A has the variant B in the context X——Y)[6] which apply simultaneously. However, a grammar consists of a long sequence of ordered rules

---

[5] See Sledd (1966) for a discussion of very detailed low-level phonetic rules for a Southeastern American dialect, within a general framework of the sort that we are discussing here.

[6] Whether phonetic or phonemic context is intended is not always made clear, and there is, in fact, some question as to how well the requirement of simultaneous application is met. For discussion, see Chomsky (1964).

that convert initial classificatory representations into final phonetic ones, and in the inter-mediate stages there will be representations of a highly mixed sort. We will therefore make no attempt to use the diagonal vs. square-bracket convention systematically, though we will use it when convenient.

It appears from our investigations that the optimal grammar of English is one in which stress is predicted by rule rather than one in which stress is inherent in the phonolo-gical matrix of a lexical entry. Thus we are assuming, in effect, that one of the earliest rules of the phonological component is a rule R which assigns to each segment and boundary (see Section 1.3.1) the feature specification [−stress]. Various rules will then replace [−stress] in vowel segments, but not in boundaries or consonants, by integral values of stress, in certain positions. We will assume, as a convention, that all integral values of stress are a subdivision of the category [+stress]. Thus, when a rule assigns the specified feature [$n$stress], for some integer n, in a certain segment, this segment now belongs to the category [+stress] rather than the category [−stress] to which it belonged after the application of rule R. The notation [+stress], then, serves as a "cover symbol" for all segments with integrally marked values of stress; a rule applying to a segment containing the specification [+stress] automatically applies to all segments which contain the specification [$n$stress], for some integer n, and which are not otherwise excluded by the formulation of the rule.

We expect that the same (or some similar) convention is needed for all features, but since we have not systematically investigated the problem of replacing categorial specifi-cation by phonetic degree in the case of features other than stress, we do not propose this now as a general convention but merely as a specific one for present purposes. We note, however, that some such convention is needed as part of general linguistic theory.

A detailed discussion of the phonetic correlates of the different features is given in Chapter Seven. For the present we will limit ourselves to a brief comment on the features that play a central role in determining stress contours. These are the features " segment," " vocalic," " consonantal," " tense."

1.3.1. BOUNDARY FEATURES

The feature "segment" distinguishes segments from boundaries. It seems to us that the appropriate way to exhibit the structure of a system of boundaries is by an explicit feature analysis. Thus each boundary will be a set of features, one of which is the feature [−segment].

Our tentative assumption is that the segmental features and the boundary features fall into distinct sets (with an exception noted on pages 67–68). Among the features of the boundary system, "formative boundary" (henceforth "FB") requires explicit mention. Only a single boundary is marked [+FB]. This boundary, which we will designate with the symbol +, appears between the final segment of one formative and the initial segment of the following formative. We can think of it as being inserted in this position in terminal strings by a general convention.[7] All other boundaries are marked [−FB]. One of the non-FB boundaries is the unit # that appears automatically before and after a word and in

---

[7] Alternatively, we could dispense with this element and permit reference in rules to formative-initial and formative-final position. Note that formative boundary is an actual symbol of the representation, with a feature structure, and is not to be confused with the concatenation operator that would be represented in a fully formalized version of linguistic theory.

     In our formulation, formative boundary *never is preceded or followed by a boundary* but must be bounded on both sides by segments.

sentence-initial and sentence-final position.[8] We will also have occasion to refer to another boundary, which we will denote by the symbol =. In our terms, the unit = must be distinguished from # by some feature, let us say the feature "WB" (word boundary). Thus the symbol + stands for the feature complex [−segment, +FB, −WB],[9] # stands for the feature complex [−segment, −FB, +WB], and = for the feature complex [−segment, −FB, −WB].

We assign a very special status to formative boundary, in the following way. We assume that the presence of + can be marked in a rule, but that the absence of + cannot be marked in a rule. This means that a rule such as (12), where X, Y, and Z are segments, applies to the three-unit string $X+Z$, converting it to $Y+Z$; but a rule such as (13) is an abbreviation for the sequence (14).

$$(12) \qquad X \;\rightarrow\; Y \;/\; \underline{\quad\quad} +Z$$

$$(13) \qquad X \;\rightarrow\; Y \;/\; AB\underline{\quad\quad}C$$

$$(14) \qquad X \;\rightarrow\; Y \;/\; \begin{cases} A+B+\underline{\quad}+C \\ AB+\underline{\quad}+C \\ A+B\underline{\quad}+C \\ A+B+\underline{\quad}C \\ AB\underline{\quad}+C \\ AB+\underline{\quad}C \\ A+B\underline{\quad}C \\ AB\underline{\quad}C \end{cases}$$

This assumption regarding the role of formative boundary in phonological rules is indispensable. The other boundaries do not behave in this manner. Thus rule (13) does not abbreviate a sequence of rules like (14) but with + replaced by #. A string containing # is not subject to a rule unless this rule explicitly mentions # in the proper position. Notice that this convention amounts to a fairly strong empirical assumption about the nature of rules. It implies that although we can frame phonological processes which are blocked by the presence of the boundary #, we cannot frame processes that are blocked by the presence of formative boundary.[10] If a process applies to a sequence without formative boundaries, it also applies to otherwise identical sequences containing these units. This condition is inoperative only in the case of the lexical redundancy rules, which refer exclusively to the internal structure of formatives and really belong to the system of readjustment rules rather than the phonology (see pp. 9–11, Chapter One).

As noted on page 66, one of the earliest rules of the phonological component will assign to all units—both segments and boundaries—the feature [−stress]. Since our

---

[8] Recall the discussion of # and word boundary in Chapter One, pages 12–14.

[9] Thus we are supposing that [−WB] is an automatic, redundant feature of formative boundary. The general basis for this remark will become clear in Chapter Nine.

[10] More precisely, in order to express the fact that a process is blocked by the presence of formative boundary, we must resort to certain auxiliary devices, described in the next chapter, thus adding to the complexity of the grammar. The most highly valued ("simplest") grammar, then, is one in which phonological processes that apply when there is no formative boundary apply also when this unit is present, though not conversely, and in which processes stated in terms of other boundaries apply where and only where these appear in strings.

rules assign stress only to vowels, a sequence of n units specified $[-\text{stress}]_n$ may include not only unstressed vowels and consonants, but all types of boundaries as well. This unique treatment of the feature "stress" reflects the fact that stress is a prosodic feature, i.e., a feature whose domain extends over sequences that are longer than a word.

1.3.2. SEGMENTAL FEATURES

Let us turn now to the features that classify segments, limiting our discussion here to features that are relevant to the functioning of the transformational cycle.

The features "vocalic" and "consonantal" give a four-way classification of segments, as follows:

$$\begin{pmatrix} 15 \end{pmatrix}$$

(a) $\begin{bmatrix} +\text{vocalic} \\ -\text{consonantal} \end{bmatrix} = \text{vowel} = V$

(b) $\begin{bmatrix} -\text{vocalic} \\ +\text{consonantal} \end{bmatrix} = \text{true consonant}$

(c) $\begin{bmatrix} +\text{vocalic} \\ +\text{consonantal} \end{bmatrix} = \text{liquid } (l, r)$ $\Bigg\} = C$

(d) $\begin{bmatrix} -\text{vocalic} \\ -\text{consonantal} \end{bmatrix} = \text{glide } (h, ?, y, w)$

As indicated in (15), we will use the cover symbol V as an (informal) abbreviation for the feature complex $\begin{bmatrix} +\text{vocalic} \\ -\text{consonantal} \end{bmatrix}$ and the cover symbol C as an abbreviation for nonvowel, that is, for the complex $\left\{ \begin{matrix} [-\text{vocalic}] \\ [+\text{consonantal}] \end{matrix} \right\}$.

Among vowels we will rely on a further classification provided by the feature "tenseness." Our use of tenseness, as a phonetic feature, can be clarified by an examination of the following typical cases:[11]

$$\begin{pmatrix} 16 \end{pmatrix}$$

APPRECIABLY TENSE	NEGLIGIBLY TENSE
bean	*bin*
bane	*Ben*
ban (in some dialects)[12]	*bat*
balm	*bun*[13]
pawn	*pot* (British RP)
bone	
boon	*put*

Phonetically the difference between tense and lax sounds can best be characterized as a difference in the manner in which the articulatory gesture is executed. A tense sound is executed deliberately so that the articulating organs actually attain their various target configurations; in producing a lax sound, on the other hand, the gesture is executed rapidly and with reduced

[11] There are certain dialects (western New England, for example) in which the gap in this chart, namely, the lax correlate of *bone*, is marginally filled.

[12] Namely, those in which (*tin*) *can* is distinct from the modal *can*. This distinction is fairly common, and almost completely predictable, in many American dialects, but the contexts in which it appears vary.

[13] The vowel of *bun* is higher as well as laxer than that of *balm*. Some dialects have another vowel corresponding more closely in quality to the vowel of *balm* but shorter, namely, the vowel of *bomb*. In general, of course, the tense vowels undergo many phonetic modifications.

amplitude. Tense vowels are, therefore, distinguished from the corresponding lax vowels by being more intense, of longer duration, and articulated with a greater deviation of the vocal cavity from its neutral (rest) position. These facts have led to the description of lax vowels as being "lazy" variants of the corresponding tense vowels.

It will often be convenient to use a special notation for the tense vocalic nuclei. As in Chapter Two, we will use capital Latin letters for this purpose, each letter being used for the sound which serves as its name.[14] Thus we will frequently make use of informal representations of the following kind:

$$
(17)
$$

bane	bAn	rebate	rEbAt
bean	bEn	violate	vIolAt
pine	pIn	denotation	dEnOtAtion
bone	bOn	mutation	mUtAtion
pure	pUr	hibernate	hIbernAt

Except for frequent use of this device, we will generally give examples in ordinary orthography (occasionally with internal morphological structure indicated and with occasional use of standard phonetic symbols). This slight deviation from ordinary orthography serves the present purpose of identifying certain vocalic nuclei as tense; but as we have already seen in Chapter Two, it has much other justification as well.

Our decision to use slightly modified conventional orthography in presenting examples instead of, let us say, familiar (taxonomic) phonemic notation is motivated in part by a desire to avoid burdening the reader with a new notation; but, much more importantly, it is justified by the fact that conventional orthography is remarkably close to the optimal phonological representation when letters are given a feature analysis—much closer, in most respects, than standard phonemic transcription. We have touched on this matter in Chapter Two, and we will return to it again in the next chapter where we will give a full analysis of the vowel system in terms of features.

2. Stress placement in verbs—a first approximation

Consider the stress assignment in the following list of verbs:

$$
(18)
$$

I	II	III
astónish	maintaín	collápse
édit	eráse	tormént
consíder	caroúse	exhaúst
imágine	appeár	eléct
intérpret	cajóle	convínce
prómise	surmíse	usúrp
embárrass	decíde	obsérve
elícit	devóte	cavórt
detérmine	achiéve	lamént
cáncel	careén	adápt

The verbs in column I have main stress on the penultimate vowel, whereas in columns II and III stress falls on the final vowel. A closer examination of the list shows that the verbs with penultimate stress end in a nontense vowel followed by a single consonant, while the verbs

---

[14] We are thus considering diphthongs (and the triphthong [yūw]) to be, phonologically, tense vowels.

with final stress have a tense vowel or a diphthong in the last syllable (column II) or they end in two consonants (column III). To account for the observed stress distribution, we propose, as a first approximation, the following rule:

(19) Assign main stress to
    (i) the penultimate vowel if the last vowel in the string under consideration is non-tense and is followed by no more than a single consonant;
    (ii) the last vowel in the string under consideration if this vowel is tense or if it is followed by more than one consonant.[15]

Using the customary formalism for the statement of phonological rules, we can restate (19) as (20):

$$(20) \quad V \rightarrow [1 \text{ stress}] \bigg/ \left\{ \begin{array}{ll} \left(\rule{0pt}{2.5em}\right. \underline{\quad} C_0 \left[\begin{array}{c} -\text{tense} \\ V \end{array} \right] C_0^1 \left.\rule{0pt}{2.5em}\right) & \text{(i)} \\ \left(\left\{ \begin{array}{c} \left[\underline{\quad} \\ +\text{tense} \end{array} \right] \\ \underline{\quad} C_2 \end{array} \right\} C_0 \right) & \text{(ii)} \end{array} \right] $$

As in Chapter Two, let us tentatively refer to a string of the form $\left[\begin{array}{c} -\text{tense} \\ V \end{array} \right] C_0^1$ as a "weak cluster," and a string of the form $\left[\begin{array}{c} +\text{tense} \\ V \end{array} \right] C_0$ or VC_2 as a "strong cluster." (We will later extend these notions slightly—see pp. 83, 103–104.) Thus case (i) asserts that primary stress is placed on the penultimate syllable if the final syllable terminates in a weak cluster; and case (ii) asserts that a final strong cluster receives primary stress.

As just formulated, rule (20) is unduly cumbersome, since the same condition is, in effect, stated twice, case (i) and case (ii) being mutually exclusive. Case (ii) can therefore be replaced by the condition that the rule applies in all contexts other than those specified in case (i). We can achieve this effect by making use of the notion of disjunctive ordering. Suppose that we replace rule (20) by (21), *specifying that the two rules abbreviated by (21) be a disjunctively ordered block.*

$$(21) \quad V \rightarrow [1 \text{ stress}] \bigg/ \underline{\quad} \left\{ \begin{array}{l} C_0 \left[\begin{array}{c} -\text{tense} \\ V \end{array} \right] C_0^1 \\ C_0 \end{array} \right\}] \quad \begin{array}{l} \text{(i)} \\ \\ \text{(ii)} \end{array}$$

Case (i) of rule (21) is identical to case (i) of (20). Case (ii) of (21) asserts that:

(22)   The last vowel in the string under consideration receives primary stress.

The requirement of disjunctive ordering guarantees that case (ii) (= (22)) will apply only where case (i) has not applied; that is, it allows us to express the notion "elsewhere."

The two parts of rule (21) apply in sequence, the first assigning primary stress to a penultimate vowel if the final syllable terminates in a weak cluster, and the second part assigning primary stress to the vowel of the final syllable if this syllable terminates in a

---

[15] We note without further comment the essential identity of (19) and the rule governing stress distribution in Latin. See Halle and Keyser (forthcoming) for discussion of how this rule was incorporated into the phonology of English.

    Recall that we regard diphthongs as tense vowels in underlying lexical representations, the glide being inserted (and the quality of the vowel determined) by phonological rules (see Chapter Two, Section 8).

strong cluster (i.e., elsewhere). Thus, (21), plus the condition of disjunctive ordering, restates (20) precisely.

However, our notations permit a somewhat more compact statement of (21), namely:

$$(23) \qquad V \rightarrow [1\ \text{stress}] \Big/ \underline{\quad} C_0 \left(\begin{bmatrix} -\text{tense} \\ V \end{bmatrix} C_0^1 \right)]$$

The fact that the rule must, in our terms, be stated in the form (23)[16] explains why the ordering is disjunctive, given our general conventions regarding the parenthesis notation (see Chapter Two, p. 30). We therefore need make no separate statement about the disjunctive ordering of cases (i) and (ii) of (21), since it follows as a consequence of the fact that (23) is the correct representation for these rules. Notice that the appropriateness of the abbreviation (23) depends on the convention regarding the order of expansion of parentheses discussed on pages 61–63.

For ease of exposition, we will continue to refer to the rule of stress placement in the form (21) rather than in the fully reduced form (23), keeping in mind that the two cases of (21) are disjunctively ordered.

Let us now return to the examples in (18), at the beginning of this section. The items in column I of (18) (e.g., *astonish*) are assigned primary stress on the penultimate vowel by case (i) of (21), since the final syllable terminates in a weak cluster. If the ordering of (21) were not disjunctive, case (ii) would now apply, assigning primary stress on the final syllable to give *astónish.[17] As matters stand, however, case (ii) is inapplicable and we derive *ástonish*, as required. The examples of column II (e.g., *maintain*) and column III (e.g., *collapse*) are not subject to (21i) because the final cluster is strong. Consequently case (ii) applies, assigning primary stress to the vowel of the final syllable. Notice that monosyllables (e.g., *eat, fit*) are also assigned primary stress by (21ii).

3. Stress placement in nouns—a first approximation

Consider now the stress pattern in the following nouns:

$$(24)$$

I	II	III
América	*aróma*	*veránda*
cínema	*balaláika*	*agénda*
aspáragus	*hiátus*	*consénsus*
metrópolis	*horízon*	*synópsis*
jávelin	*thrombósis*	*amálgam*
vénison	*coróna*	*uténsil*
ásterisk	*aréna*	*asbéstos*
ársenal	*Minnesóta*	*phlogíston*
lábyrinth	*angína*	*appéndix*
análysis	*factótum*	*placénta*

[16] To say that the rules may be given in a simpler form implies that they *must* be given in that form. More precisely, the notations that we use define a certain valuation measure for grammars; the value of a grammar is determined by the number of symbols that appear in it when notations are used in the optimal fashion. Rules are ordered by conventions associated with the parenthesis (or other) notation when the use of this notation is in fact optimal in the case in question. See Chapter Eight for more detailed discussion.

[17] Other conditions can be invented to prevent application of case (ii); for example, we might propose that stress is placed by (22) only in the context [−stress]₀ ——. Stronger evidence that it is the condition of disjunctive ordering that is actually involved here will be forthcoming in Section 6, where examples are presented that rule out the apparent alternatives.

We have here a stress pattern that is identical with that exemplified in (18) except for the final extra syllable, which, it will be observed, consists in each case of a nontense (lax) vowel followed by zero or more consonants. We can therefore apply rule (21) here too if we exclude the final lax vowel (with the consonants following it, if any) from the domain of application of the rule. It appears, then, that rule (21) operates in two separate contexts: first, it applies to nouns ending in a nontense vowel followed by zero or more consonants,[18] this last VC_0 string being omitted from consideration; secondly, it applies in an environment which we will provisionally describe simply as "elsewhere." More formally, we have the following rule:[19]

$$(25) \qquad V \rightarrow [1 \text{ stress}] \quad \Big/ \underline{\quad} \begin{cases} C_0 \begin{bmatrix} -\text{tense} \\ V \end{bmatrix} C_0^1 & \text{(i)} \\ C_0 & \text{(ii)} \end{cases}$$

$$\Big/ \underline{\quad} \begin{cases} \begin{bmatrix} -\text{tense} \\ V \end{bmatrix} C_0]_N & \text{(b)} \\ ] & \text{(e)} \end{cases}$$

Notice that we have here a rule of the form $A \rightarrow B/C \underline{\quad} D/E \underline{\quad} F$. Recall that the notation $A \rightarrow B/C \underline{\quad} D$ has the meaning $CAD \rightarrow CBD$. By a double application of this convention, the notation $A \rightarrow B/C \underline{\quad} D/E \underline{\quad} F$ has the meaning $ECADF \rightarrow ECBDF$. Thus our earlier conventions have already accounted for rules of the form (25). The order of the rules abbreviated in this way, which we will discuss below, is also strictly determined by the definition of the notation $A \rightarrow B/C \underline{\quad} D$ as an abbreviation for $CAD \rightarrow CBD$. (See pp. 31–33, Chapter Two.)

To apply rule (25) to a string φ, we ask first whether φ is a noun with a lax vowel in its final syllable, that is, whether it meets condition (b). If not, we turn to condition (e). Suppose, however, that the answer to the first question is yes, so that φ is of the form:

$$(26) \qquad \varphi = \psi \begin{bmatrix} -\text{tense} \\ V \end{bmatrix} C_0]_N$$

We now ask whether ψ falls under case (i). If it does, we assign primary stress as indicated by (25bi), and we skip (ii) since the order (i), (ii) is disjunctive. If ψ does not fall under case (i), we ask whether it falls under case (ii), and, since the answer to this question is always yes, we assign stress to the last vowel of ψ, as required by (25bii).

No matter what has happened so far to the string φ, we now ask whether it meets condition (e). The answer is always positive. We therefore apply case (i) if the final cluster of φ is weak (skipping case (ii) because of the disjunctive ordering), or we apply case (ii) if the final cluster of φ is strong.

As matters now stand, rule (25) abbreviates a sequence of four rules which apply in the order of (27):

$$(27) \qquad\qquad (25bi), (25bii), (25ei), (25eii)$$

---

[18] The stress pattern of nouns with a tense vowel in the final syllable does not follow the present rule; e.g., *anecdote, Palestine, magazine, attaché*. These cases are discussed in Sections 4 and 16.

[19] In order to preserve uniformity of reference in the various versions of the rules that we will consider, we will designate the subparts of these rules by the symbols that will identify them in the final formulation to be given in this chapter. Thus here we give only conditions (b) and (e); others will be added below.

The subsequence (25bi), (25bii) forms a disjunctively ordered block, as does the subsequence (25ei), (25eii). The block (25ei), (25eii) is simply the sequence represented as (21) and discussed in Section 2. In the case of the verbs of Section 2, condition (b) is never met and (25) has exactly the effect of (21).

Let us now turn to the examples of (24). Consider first *America*, as a prototype of column I. Condition (b) of (25) holds, since the last vowel of *America* is nontense and the word itself is lexically marked as a noun. Dropping from consideration the context indicated in condition (b), we are left with the string *Americ-*, to which we must apply rules (i) and (ii) of (25), in that order. Case (i) is applicable; it assigns primary stress to the penultimate vowel of *Americ-*, giving *Amérïca*. Case (ii) is skipped because of disjunctive ordering. We next turn to condition (e) of rule (25). Unfortunately, this is applicable, as it always is, and case (i) will give the form **Amérïca*. We must therefore prevent the application of condition (e) in this case. In fact, as we shall see, application of condition (e) must always be blocked when condition (b) has applied. In other words, the ordering of (b) and (e) must be disjunctive if the rules are to apply correctly.

We will return directly to the question of the disjunctive ordering of conditions (b) and (e). Let us now simply assume that the ordering of (27) is fully disjunctive; that is, if any one of the rules of (27) applies, the later ones in the sequence are skipped.[20] The examples of column I of (24) are now correctly handled.

Turning to column II, let us take *arOma* as a prototype. Condition (b) holds, giving *arOm-* as the string to which cases (i) and (ii) are to be applied. Case (i) is blocked by the tense vowel of the final syllable of *arOm-*. We can therefore go on to case (ii), which assigns primary stress to this tense vowel. Condition (e) is then skipped because of the disjunctive ordering, and we are left with *arÓma*. The example *veranda* of column III is treated in exactly the same way, except that application of case (i) under condition (b) is now blocked by the consonant cluster *-nd-* instead of by the tenseness of the penultimate vowel. The other examples of columns II and III are handled in exactly the same way.

Thus rule (25) correctly determines the placement of primary stress for the verbs of (18) and the nouns of (24). The only difference between the verbs and the nouns is that for the latter, a final string VC_0 (where V is lax) must be omitted from consideration before the application of the rule to either (i) the syllable preceding a weak cluster or (ii) the final vowel, that is, the strong final cluster of the string under consideration at this point.

This distinction between nouns and verbs with respect to stress placement can be illustrated with bisyllabic forms as well as with the longer examples of (24). Thus, nouns such as *lárynx, lántern, témpest, stípend, ínfant, ónyx, mállard* have penultimate rather than final stress, indicating that stress has not been assigned under condition (e) of rule (25).

Further support for the rule in the form given is provided by doublets such as *umbílicus–umbilícus, ábdomen–abdÓmen*. In accordance with (25), we have penultimate stress if the penultimate vowel is taken to be tense in the underlying representation, and antepenultimate stress if the penultimate vowel is taken to be lax.

Exceptions to rule (25) will readily come to mind, e.g., *cemént, giráffe, burlésque, Mississíppi, ellípse, umbrélla*. We will return to several classes of real and apparent exceptions in Section 16.[21]

---

[20] Since the ordering of cases (i) and (ii) is disjunctive, to achieve full disjunctive ordering in (27) it is necessary only to add the condition that the ordering of (b) and (e) is disjunctive.

[21] See also Chapter Two, Section 7.

The following nouns have the same stress pattern as those of (24):

$$\left(28\right)$$

I	II	III
búffalo	*albíno*	*commándo*
archipélago	*casíno*	*embárgo*
rádio	*volcáno*	*fiásco*
bróccoli	*macaróni*	*chiánti*
menágerie	*shillélagh*	*attórney*
Menómini	*Winnipesáukee*	*Ypsilánti*
kínkajou	*Kikúyu*	*jujítsu*

In the dialect of American English that is the basis for our description, these nouns end in tense vowels. Therefore they do not fall under rule (25), and their stress pattern is still unexplained.

We note, however, that in this dialect, there are peculiar gaps in the phonetic distribution of vowels in final position. Roughly speaking, we have the following vowel system in English:

$$\left(29\right)$$

	i	u	
			NONLOW
	e	o	
	æ	ɔ	LOW

For the purposes of this discussion, we distinguish only the low vowels from the non-low vowels, and we note that in each position in (29) there is a tense-lax pair (see discussion of (16), p. 68). Limiting ourselves to nonstressed (i.e., minus-stressed) vowels in final position, we find only tense nonlow vowels, as in (28), and the reduced vowel [ə] (see note 1). There are no lax nonlow vowels in this position,[22] and the low vowels of (29) do not appear at all, tense or lax (with apparent exceptions that we will note). Thus it would seem that unstressed low vowels reduce to [ə] in final position, while unstressed nonlow vowels become tense. Since there are no stressed lax vowels in final position, these must become tense as well. These observations suggest that we add to the grammar a rule tensing stressed vowels and nonlow nonstressed vowels in final position, and that we then formulate the Vowel Reduction Rule so that it does not apply to vowels that are tense. Further investigation of vowel reduction in Section 14 will support this suggestion, as we shall see.

Notice, furthermore, that the rule tensing vowels applies not only in final position, but also in prevocalic position. Thus, in words such as *society*, *neophyte*, *archaic*, the vowel in boldface position is tense [I], [E], [A], respectively.

Combining these observations, we might give the Tensing Rule in the form (30):

$$\left(30\right) \qquad V \;\rightarrow\; [+\text{tense}] \;/\; \begin{bmatrix} \overline{} \\ \alpha\text{low} \\ \beta\text{stress} \end{bmatrix} \begin{Bmatrix} V \\ \#, \text{ where } \beta = + \text{ if } \alpha = + \end{Bmatrix}$$

With rule (30) in the grammar, we can now allow all vowels to appear freely in final and

---

[22] There is apparently considerable dialectal variation here, as has been noted repeatedly in the literature, as, for example, the comments on final *-y* in Kenyon and Knott (1944): "When final, the unaccented vowel in *pity* . . . and similar words varies with different speakers in America from a sound like the ɪ in *bit* . . . or like the first ɪ in *pity* . . . to a sound that approaches the *i* in *bee*. . ." (p. xviii).

Notice that of the nonlow vowels, only [i], [o], and [u] appear in the examples of (28) ([u] only marginally). Thus there is an additional gap in phonetic distribution beyond that under discussion here, namely, in the case of final [e]. We return to this matter in Section 16.

prevocalic position in underlying forms. In particular, the final vowel of the items of (28) can be lax. Thus the examples of (28) are assigned stress by rule (25) in exactly the same way as those of (24). Then, after stress assignment, they become subject to rule (30) and the Vowel Reduction Rule. When the final vowel is phonologically low and lax, it will reduce, as in *Canada* (from /kænædæ/), *agenda* (from /ægendæ/). When it is nonlow, it will become tense by rule (30) and will remain unreduced, as in the examples of (28).

Notice that as rule (30) now stands, it tenses all vowels in prevocalic position, independent of lowness or stress. Thus we find unstressed tense vowels in the boldface positions of *various*, *arduous*, *archaism* ([árkAizm]), *Hébraism* ([hébrAizm]), etc. We shall see in the next chapter that the [A] of the last two examples derives from a phonologically low vowel. There is, however, another dialect in which the forms *archaism*, *Hebraism* are phonetically [arkəizm], [hebrəizm]. To derive these results, we assume that the affix *-ism* is preceded by #.

We shall observe, as we proceed, that there are quite a few examples of conditions such as that on α and β. Conditions of this sort are not, strictly speaking, formulable within the framework we have established up to this point. However, in Chapter Eight, where we give a careful analysis of the postulated notational system, it will be seen that such conditions can actually be accommodated in a rather natural way.

We will see in the next chapter that rule (30) is one of several tensing rules. Examples with phonologically tense vowels in final position will be considered at the conclusion of the next section.

Our decision to represent the underlying final vowel in words such as *fiásco*, *Chicágo* as nontense may raise some question, since a nontense /o/ (i.e., the lax counterpart to the vowel in *cone*) does not appear phonetically in the utterances of the dialect we are describing. But we specifically reject the assumption that there must be a one-one relationship between the underlying lexical or phonological representation and the phonetic output, and we see no reason to suppose that underlying representations will be restricted to segments that appear in phonetic representations. Such a requirement would, in fact, be quite artificial and ad hoc. Whatever motivation it might have had is lost once the classificatory and phonetic functions of distinctive features are distinguished. We will find other empirical examples which, like the example of /o/ just discussed, indicate that no strong one-one requirement on linguistically significant representations can be maintained; and we will, furthermore, find good evidence that underlying /o/ also appears nonfinally in lexical representations. Postulation of phonetically unrealized segments is no great departure from established practice. Thus, junctures (i.e., what we are calling "boundaries") of the sort that are freely used in all phonemic descriptions do not generally have uniquely identifiable direct reflexes in the utterance.[23]

---

[23] See Z. S. Harris (1951, Chapter 8); Hockett (1955); Chomsky, Halle, Lukoff (1956). It was once thought that a useful notion of juncture might be developed in purely phonetic terms, specifically, in terms of the tempo of the preceding segments. (See, for example, Stockwell, Bowen, Silva-Fuenzalida (1956, p. 643); Hill (1958, p. 24); and the discussion in Hill (1962).) This proposal was supported by the claim that such phonetic correlates are "clearly audible" and by reference to a few observations reported by Joos (in Hill, 1962), which were taken to show that the slowing down in tempo for the three postulated junctures was, respectively, "approximately two average phoneme lengths," "about one-half phoneme length less," and "about one average phoneme length" (Stockwell, et al., 1956). That anyone still retains this hope is doubtful, particularly in the light of the criticism in Lehiste (1964) and the results of Lieberman (1965).

(continued on page 76)

Summarizing the discussion so far, we have established the rule (25), which, as a first approximation, accounts for placement of primary stress in nouns with a lax vowel in the final syllable (condition (b)) and elsewhere (condition (e), which we have so far illustrated only with verbs). The rule has two cases which apply under each of these conditions: case (i) assigns primary stress in the syllable preceding a weak cluster and case (ii) assigns primary stress to the final vowel. The two cases are disjunctively ordered, so that case (ii) in fact applies to monosyllables and to strings with final strong clusters. The two conditions (b) and (e) are also disjunctively ordered, so that the parts of the rule (namely, (bi), (bii), (ei), (eii)) constitute a disjunctively ordered block. Rule (25), with its successive modifications, will henceforth be referred to as the Main Stress Rule.

Still to be accounted for is the requirement that conditions (b) and (e) are disjunctively ordered. We will naturally try to accomplish this on the basis of some general empirical assumption regarding the form of grammars, instead of leaving it as an ad hoc and particular constraint. Earlier, we proposed that when rules can be simplified by the parenthesis notation, they are disjunctively ordered. Suppose, in fact, that we were to modify slightly our notation for marking surface structure, using a string of symbols such as **N]** instead of labeled brackets such as **]ₙ**. The two conditions of rule (25) would, in this notation, be expressed as:

$$\left(31\right) \qquad\qquad \underline{\qquad} \left\{ \begin{array}{l} \left[\begin{array}{c} -\text{tense} \\ V \end{array} \right] C_0 \, N] \\[2mm]] \end{array} \right\} \quad \begin{array}{l} \text{(b)} \\[4mm] \text{(e)} \end{array}$$

Utilizing the parenthesis notation, we can simplify this to:

$$\left(32\right) \qquad\qquad \underline{\qquad} \left(\left[\begin{array}{c} -\text{tense} \\ V \end{array} \right] C_0 \, N \right)]$$

Hence, if we were to use the notation **N]** instead of **]ₙ** for representing surface structure, the conditions (b) and (e) would be assigned a disjunctive ordering automatically by our general empirical assumption about simplifiability with the parenthesis notation. But obviously there can be nothing of any significance that turns on the choice between these two notations for representing surface structure. We must therefore extend our system for expressing rules in such a way as to eliminate this particular discrepancy between the notations. This can be accomplished readily by generalizing the parenthesis notation so that it permits the expression of discontinuous dependencies. For this purpose, we will make use of angled brackets ⟨ ⟩ in the following way. An expression of the form (33) is to be an abbreviation for the

---

McCawley (1967b) gives evidence that Sapir, in his phonological analysis, accepted the convention that we are rejecting here, namely, that segments can appear in a phonological representation only if they also appear, somewhere, in phonetic representations. (Actually, due to other differences in the theoretical framework, the assumptions are not strictly identical.) We have remarked in various places that our approach to problems of phonological structure is in many respects very similar to that of Sapir, although quite different from that developed in both the United States and Europe since the mid-1930s. (In fact, the title of this book is intended to suggest just this.) If McCawley's observations are correct, this historical remark must be qualified, though it remains true that in many significant respects we are following in the general line of Sapir's approach to linguistic structure.

two expressions in (34), in the order given:[24]

$$\left(33\right) \qquad X_1\langle Y_1\rangle X_2\langle Y_2\rangle \ldots X_n\langle Y_n\rangle X_{n+1}$$

$$\left(34\right) \qquad \begin{array}{ll} \text{(a)} & X_1 Y_1 X_2 Y_2 \ldots X_n Y_n X_{n+1} \\ \text{(b)} & X_1 X_2 \ldots X_n X_{n+1} \end{array}$$

In other words, an expression with angled brackets abbreviates two expressions—one in which all angled elements appear and another in which none of these elements appear. This is a generalization of the use of parentheses to the case of discontinuous dependencies. It is therefore quite natural to stipulate as a general principle that when rules can be simplified by this notation, they are disjunctively ordered.

Returning to the two conditions of rule (25), we can now abbreviate them in the form:

$$\left(35\right) \qquad \underline{\quad\quad}\left\langle \begin{bmatrix} -\text{tense} \\ V \end{bmatrix} C_0 \right\rangle]_{\langle N\rangle}$$

Summarizing, the Main Stress Rule can now be given in its fully abbreviated form (36):

$$\left(36\right) \qquad V \rightarrow [1\ \text{stress}] \ / \ \underline{\quad\quad} C_0 \left(\begin{bmatrix} -\text{tense} \\ V \end{bmatrix} C_0^1 \right) \ / \ \underline{\quad\quad} \left\langle \begin{bmatrix} -\text{tense} \\ V \end{bmatrix} C_0 \right\rangle]_{\langle N\rangle}$$

The expression (36) abbreviates the four rules (27), and, furthermore, it assigns a fully disjunctive ordering to these four rules. For ease of exposition, we will continue to present the rules in the expanded form (25), bearing in mind, however, that they are disjunctively ordered.

As far as we know, the only cases of disjunctive ordering are those in which rules can be simplified in terms of parentheses and angled brackets, and in all such cases the rules are disjunctively ordered. If this is correct, we can tentatively propose the following quite strong empirical hypothesis: *where parentheses or angled brackets are required* (see note 16) *for the abbreviation of a sequence of rules, these rules are disjunctively ordered; in all other cases, rules are conjunctively ordered* (but see Chapter Eight, Sections 3 and 4). We have too little evidence to be able to assert this as a general hypothesis about linguistic structure with full confidence, but we will adhere to it, with some refinements and elaborations, in this study of English phonology.

4. Alternating Stress Rule

Let us now consider the effect of the Main Stress Rule on nouns with a tense vowel in the final syllable of the phonological representation, for example, the word *domain* (phonologically, /dOmAn/). Since the vowel in the final syllable is tense, condition (b) of rule (25) is not met, and case (i) is inapplicable under condition (e). Thus, by (eii), primary stress is

---

[24] We will use the angle notation in several closely related ways as we proceed, giving a precise and general account in Chapter Eight, where parentheses are also covered as a special case. We will interpret a string $X\langle Y\rangle Z$, where X and Z contain no angles, as the same in meaning as XZ.

We should point out that the angle notation is not invented ad hoc for the description of English. In fact, the angled bracket and parenthesis notations have been used in essentially the way we use them here in most of the work in generative grammar, particularly generative phonology, during the past fifteen years. As we have now noted several times, the choice of abbreviatory notations within our framework amounts to an empirical hypothesis regarding the notion "linguistically significant generalization" and, ultimately, regarding the basis for language acquisition. The fact that the same notations appear adequate in a wide variety of cases is therefore a matter of some interest.

placed on the final syllable, giving *dOmÁn*. In the same way, rule (25) accounts correctly for the position of primary stress in nouns such as:

$\left(37\right)$ *machíne, brassiére, regíme, careér, baróque, toupeé, canoé, cheroót, políce, bazaár, brocáde*

In searching for additional examples of nouns with final stress, we observe that there are few examples with three or more syllables. There are, of course, words such as *Tennesseé, attaché, chandeliér, kangaroó, chimpanzeé*, and almost all words ending in certain suffixes (e.g., *-eer, -ier, -ee, -ette*). However, the large majority of words of three or more syllables have primary stress on the antepenultimate vowel and tertiary stress on the final vowel, as in the examples in (38):

$\left(38\right)$ *húrricàne, ánecdòte, pédigrèe, níghtingàle, mártingàle, mátadòr, formáldehỳde, báritòne, gúillotìne, Árkansàs, ántelòpe, stévedòre, hypótenùse, cándidàte, cávalcàde, cántalòupe*

The Main Stress Rule will account for *Tennesseé, attaché*, etc., but not for the large mass of examples illustrated by (38), which would incorrectly receive final primary stress by case (ii), under condition (e). To account for forms such as those in (38), we must add a new rule that applies after the Main Stress Rule and assigns primary stress to the vowel of the antepenultimate syllable. We will call this rule, which we formulate as (39), the Alternating Stress Rule:

$\left(39\right)$ $\qquad\qquad V \;\rightarrow\; [1 \text{ stress}] \;\; / \;\; \underline{\hspace{2em}} C_0VC_0\overset{1}{V}C_0]$

Consider now a typical example with (39)—*hurricAn*, for instance. By rule (25eii), primary stress is assigned to the final vowel, giving *hurricÁn*. By the Alternating Stress Rule (39), primary stress is then assigned to the first vowel, and the stress on the final vowel is automatically reduced to secondary (see p. 64), giving *húrricÀn*. To obtain the conventional representation, we add the very late subsidiary rule (40), which limits secondary stress to constructions longer than the word:

$\left(40\right)$ $\qquad$ Within a word, all nonprimary stresses are weakened by one.[25]

We will refer to rule (40) as the Stress Adjustment Rule. In the case of *hurricane*, it gives, finally, *húrricÀn*, as required. The other examples of (38) are taken care of in exactly the same way. The few words like *Tennesseé* and *attaché*, on the other hand, must be lexically categorized in some way so as to prevent application of the Alternating Stress Rule (39). We thus put them, for the moment, in the class of exceptions. Notice, incidentally, that for some words (e.g., *refugee, magazine*), application of the Alternating Stress Rule is optional.[26]

Rule (39) produces alternations of stressed and unstressed vowels. It is thus one of the factors contributing to the frequently observed predominance of iambic rhythms in English.

---

[25] We will formulate this rule precisely later on. Notice that the rule is, in effect, a terminological convention regarding the designations "primary," "secondary," etc. It is a natural convention, since it retains integral values for the perceptual stress levels. Notice also that this rule does not apply until we reach the level of word boundary in the cycle.

[26] In the next chapter, we will discuss a method for marking exceptions to rules which will also make it possible to describe situations such as this.

Notice that the final stress of such words as *Tennessee* may shift in certain syntactic constructions (cf. *Tênnessèe Wílliams, Tênnessèe Válley*). We return to this phenomenon on page 117.

The examples of (38) are all nouns, but the Alternating Stress Rule applies to verbs as well. In columns II and III of (18) (that is, the verbs with final stress, p. 69) all the examples were bisyllabic. But consider verbs such as:

$$\begin{pmatrix} 41 \end{pmatrix}\quad \begin{array}{l} \textit{víolàte, extrápolàte, insínuàte, expériment, ímplement, gállivànt, cáterwàul, éxercìse,}\\ \textit{éxorcìse, órganìze, récognìze, solídifỳ, transmógrifỳ} \end{array}$$

In these cases the tense vowel of the final syllable receives tertiary rather than primary stress, and the primary stress is antepenultimate, exactly as in the case of the nouns of (38). The reason is identical. Thus, the final vowel of *vIolAt* receives primary stress under case (25eii) of the Main Stress Rule, and rule (39) shifts the primary stress to the first syllable, giving *vIolĀt*. Rule (40) then adjusts this representation to *vĪolĀt*. The other examples are derived in the same way.

In discussing the examples of (28) in Section 3, we concluded that all vowels can appear in word-final position in underlying representations, and the Tensing Rule (30) will combine with Vowel Reduction to convert the nonlow lax vowels to their tense counterparts and the unstressed low vowels to [ə] in this position. Now we are able to compare polysyllabic words having final lax vowels in their lexical representations (e.g., words such as *búffalo, albíno, commándo,* and the others of (28)) with words having final tense vowels in their lexical representations.

Consider, for example, the word *Arkansas.* Notice first of all that there are the alternative pronunciations [ārkənsɔ̄w], [ārkǽnzəs]. The latter is straightforward; it derives from /ǽrkænzVs/, with an unspecified lax vowel in the final syllable, by case (25bii) of the Main Stress Rule and other rules irrelevant here. The former derives from a lexical representation in which the final vowel is tense rather than lax, and in absolute final position rather than before /s/. Condition (b) of the Main Stress Rule (25) is therefore excluded, and by (25eii) we derive *arkansās*. This becomes *ārkansās* by the Alternating Stress Rule (39) and *ārkansās* (= [ārkənsɔ̄w]) by the Stress Adjustment Rule (40).

Similarly, consider such familiar pairs as *éffigy–refUgĒ* and *Kénnedy–chickadĒ.* Here we have a phonetic contrast of tertiary versus quaternary (zero) stress on the final [E]. We account for the distinction by giving the lexical representations /efVgi/–/refug+E/, /kenVdi/– /čikVdE/, respectively.[27] The stress pattern of *éffigy* and *Kénnedy* is, then, determined by rule (25bi), exactly as in the case of the examples of (28), column I. The stress pattern of *réfugèe* and *chíckadèe,* on the other hand, is determined by rules (25eii), (39), and (40), exactly as in the case of *hurricane, Arkansas,* etc. We have here the alternants *refUgée, chickadée* in the case where application of rule (39) is blocked (as in *Tennesseé, attaché*). The (fairly free) alternation in this case supports the decision to take the final vowel to be lexically tense. The variants are then determined by an optional lexical feature which blocks rule (39). Tensing and diphthongization of the final vowel are automatic, by the Tensing Rule (30) and other rules that we discuss in the next chapter, in all the cases in question here.

5. Stress placement in adjectives

We have so far considered only nouns and verbs, but the rules we have given apply to adjectives as well. Consider the examples of (42), in which columns I, II, III correspond to columns

---

[27] We are concerned here only with the final vowel, but, as we shall see in the next chapter, the lexical representations given here are essentially correct, *in toto.*

I, II, III of (18) and (24), and column IV corresponds to (38) and (41):

$\left(42\right)$

	I	II	III	IV
	sólid	*supréme*	*absúrd*	*mánifèst*
	frántic	*sincére*	*corrúpt*	*résolùte*
	hándsome	*secúre*	*imménse*	*dérelìct*
	clandéstine	*ináne*	*abstráct*	*dífficùlt*
	cértain	*obscéne*	*robúst*	*móribùnd*
	cómmon	*obscúre*	*ovért*	*cómatòse*
	vúlgar	*extréme*	*augúst*	*sáturnìne*
	wánton	*remóte*	*succínct*	*rétrogràde*
	shállow	*discre'et*	*occúlt*	*láchrymòse*
	stúrdy	*compléte*	*diréct*	*érudìte*

The placement of primary stress on the penult in column I is determined by rule (25ei). (The last two examples in column I involve an application of rule (30) as well, to tense the underlying lax vowel in word-final position.) In columns II and III, the final syllable is stressed by rule (25eii). In column IV, the final syllable is stressed by rule (25eii), exactly as in the case of columns II and III, but then the primary stress is shifted two syllables to the left by the Alternating Stress Rule (39) and the contour is adjusted by rule (40). Thus the four types of forms *sólid*, *supréme*, *absúrd*, *mánifèst* are all assigned their proper stress contours.

We find, as in the case of nouns, that the Alternating Stress Rule is optional for certain adjectives. Thus, alongside of *óbsolète* we have *òbsoléte*; alongside of *ábsolùte* we have *àbsolúte*. This option is restricted to certain adjectives with tense vowels in the final syllable. Another occasional doublet is *clandéstine* (with a final lax vowel and penultimate stress) versus *clàndestín* or *clàndestén* (with a tense vowel in the final syllable and antepenultimate primary stress). In this case it is the choice of the final vowel that is free. Once its tenseness is determined, the position of primary stress is automatic.

To the exceptions that we noted before, we must now add several others, e.g., *módern*, *hónest*, *hággard*.

6. Derivational affixes

Consider the following adjectives, all of which end in a suffix consisting of a lax vowel followed by one or more consonants:[28]

---

[28] Strong examples for column II in (43) are rare: there are few polysyllables with final tense vowels before these affixes, and some of them (e.g., *sonórous*, *decórous*) have variants with a lax vowel (in which case the examples will fall in column I). The reason for including *polyhédral* and *polyhédrous* in column II rather than column III will be given directly.

    Certain words that might seem appropriate for column II (e.g., *audácious*, *ferócious*) actually belong in column I, since the orthography is, in these cases, essentially correct as an underlying representation, for reasons which will become clear in the following chapter. Notice that if this were not so, certain examples (e.g., *judícious*, *auspícious*) would be exceptions.

$\left(43\right)$

	I	II	III
	pérsonal	*anecdótal*	*dialéctal*
	máximal	*adjectíval*	*incidéntal*
	medícinal	*sacerdótal*	*fratérnal*
	munícipal	*polyhédral*	*univérsal*
	ephémeral	*mediéval*	*abýsmal*
	magnánimous	*desírous*	*moméntous*
	polýgamous	*polyhédrous*	*amórphous*
	rígorous		*polyándrous*
	precípitous	*sonórous*	*treméndous*
	calámitous	*decórous*	*stupéndous*
	vígilant	*complaísant*	*repúgnant*
	méndicant	*defíant*	*relúctant*
	signíficant	*clairvóyant*	*obsérvant*
	árrogant	*obeísant*	*indígnant*
	díssonant	*adjácent*	*redúndant*
	ínnocent	*complácent*	*depéndent*
	díffident	*antecédent*	*contíngent*
	benévolent	*inhérent*	*recúmbent*

The similarity of these examples to those of (18), (24), and (42) is evident, and we therefore would naturally expect that the Main Stress Rule (25) would account for (43) with at most minor modifications. Notice, in fact, that rule (25) would account for these examples directly if we were to extend condition (b) of (25) to adjectives as well as nouns. We cannot simply do this, however, for consider the effect on the examples of (42), in particular those of column III. If these are assigned stress by the noun rule (25b), stress will fall on the first syllable.[29] Similarly, the examples of column IV of (42) with final double consonant require the verb rule (25e), rather than the noun rule (25b), to account for the tertiary stress on the final syllable.

　　We conclude, then, that the adjectives of (43) are subject to the noun rule, while those of (42) are not. The basis for the distinction of these two classes is evident; the examples of (42) are primary adjectives, unanalyzable into stem plus adjectival suffix, while those of (43) are secondary adjectives, formed by adding a suffix to a stem. Thus primary adjectives are assigned stress by the verb rule (25e), while secondary adjectives are assigned stress by the noun rule (25b).

　　We can express this fact by adding, alongside of condition (b), a new condition (a) which is exactly like (b) except that the sequence it specifies is a monosyllabic formative. Thus we have the two conditions (44a) and (44b) (where $+$ in (a) stands for formative boundary—see pp. 66–67):

---

[29] As it actually does in the case of the exceptions *hónest, módern, hággard*, etc., noted above. Thus an extension of condition (b) to adjectives would make these regular and the examples of (42), column III, exceptions. But the latter are much more numerous, and, furthermore, there are subregularities among the former that allow a still more succinct statement of exceptions in this case. There are also, as we will see, other reasons for distinguishing the adjective rule from the noun rule.

$$\left(44\right) \qquad +C_0 \begin{bmatrix} -\text{tense} \\ V \end{bmatrix} C_0]_A \quad \text{(a)}$$

$$\begin{bmatrix} -\text{tense} \\ V \end{bmatrix} C_0]_N \quad \text{(b)}$$

Using the angle convention discussed on pages 76–77, we can abbreviate the two cases of (44) as (45):

$$\left(45\right) \qquad \langle +C_0 \rangle \begin{bmatrix} -\text{tense} \\ V \end{bmatrix} C_0]_{N\langle A \rangle}$$

This abbreviates a disjunctively ordered sequence of two conditions: the first applies to a noun or an adjective with a final monosyllabic formative containing a lax vowel; the second applies to a noun with a lax vowel in its final syllable. Since the ordering is disjunctive, (45) truly abbreviates (44). (If the ordering were conjunctive, (45) would have a different effect from (44) in the case of nouns, since both of the rules abbreviated by (45) would apply.)[30]

The formula (45) is the appropriate way to present the facts that we have so far exhibited, but for ease of exposition, we will keep the two cases separate in this discussion and refer to the unabbreviated form (44). We will consider in the next section the question of compatibility between (45) and the abbreviation (36) for conditions (b) and (e) of the Main Stress Rule.

In sum, we allow the Main Stress Rule to apply under both of the conditions given in (44) (= (45)), that is, to a noun with a lax vowel in the final syllable or to an adjective with a monosyllabic suffix containing a lax vowel. We apply cases (i) and (ii) of (25) after omitting from consideration the final $+C_0\check{V}C_0$ string (or $\check{V}C_0$ string in the case of nouns).

Before restating the expanded Main Stress Rule, we take note of another qualification that must be added. Consider the adjectives:

$$\left(46\right) \qquad \textit{éloquent, recálcitrant, chívalrous, lúdicrous, vértebral}$$

These have stress on the antepenultimate vowel, indicating that they are treated by the Main Stress Rule as examples of column I rather than column III of (43). In other words, stress is assigned to these words by case (i) of (25) rather than by case (ii). But case (i) assigns stress to a syllable followed by a weak cluster, that is, followed by a lax vowel and no more than a single consonant, whereas in (46) the penultimate lax vowel is followed by two consonants. Evidently, we must extend the notion "weak cluster" to include a lax vowel followed by no more than a single consonant followed by an optional liquid or glide.

Closer examination reveals that clear examples of such clusters are restricted to those ending with [r] and [w]. Since the absence of clusters ending with [y] is due to the fact that [y] is generally not found in postconsonantal position, we need not restrict our rule so as to exclude such sequences explicitly. On the other hand, the absence of weak clusters ending in [l] suggests that we explore the possibility that clusters ending in a consonant followed by [l] are strong rather than weak. An immediate consequence of this is that the geminate

---

[30] There is a further difference between (44) and (45) for the case of nouns of the form $\ldots VC_0\check{V}C+C_1VC_0$ or $\ldots VC_0\check{V}+C_2VC_0$, where $\check{V}$ is a lax vowel. Rule (44) would assign primary stress to the penultimate syllable in such cases, whereas rule (45) would assign antepenultimate stress. We have no very clear examples one way or the other. We may, however, make use of (45) in describing such exceptions to the general rules as *mínister*, for example. The lexical representation cannot be /ministr/ (cf. *ministérial*), but must rather have /ster/ as its final syllable. By rule (44) the stress contour should then be *miníster. If we give the lexical representation as /mini+ster/, however, rule (45) will assign stress in the proper way.

sequence [ll] renders a cluster strong. There must be in the grammar a special rule that simplifies geminate sequences of consonants (see (156) below and rule (67) of Chapter Two). We can, then, account for the placement of primary stress in adjectives such as *cerebéllar, morbíllous, medúllar* by representing these with geminate /ll/, as opposed to *céphalous, périlous, scúrrilous,* etc., which have a single /l/ in the underlying representation, or *chívalrous,* which contains a weak cluster ending with /r/. Notice that [r] *followed by* a true consonant gives a strong rather than a weak cluster:[31]

$$(47) \qquad fratérnal, detérgent, univérsal, obsérvant, amórphous$$

The proposed extension of the concept "weak cluster" (and the corresponding modification of the Main Stress Rule) is needed also for nouns, that is, for the examples falling under condition (b). Thus we have *álgebra, vértebra,* with antepenultimate rather than penultimate stress, indicating that the penultimate syllable is treated as a weak cluster, as opposed to *armadíllo, vanílla, umbrélla,* with a strong cluster ending in a geminate /ll/.[32]

To express the concept of weak cluster properly in our rules, we refer to the feature analysis of liquids and glides given in (15) (p. 68). Liquids are consonantal and vocalic; glides are nonconsonantal and nonvocalic. Thus liquids and glides are the categories that are identical in specification with respect to the features "vocalic" and "consonantal." We will follow the practice of using small Greek letters as variables ranging over feature specifications (that is, over the symbols + and − and the integers). With this convention, we can characterize liquids and glides as the category:

$$(48) \qquad \begin{bmatrix} \alpha\text{vocalic} \\ \alpha\text{consonantal} \end{bmatrix}$$

However, we need to exclude [l] as the last segment in a weak cluster while allowing [r]. The difference between [l] and [r] in feature terms is that [l] is [+anterior], whereas [r] is [−anterior]. Glides, on the other hand, are [−anterior]. (See Section 3 of Chapter Four.) Thus, in the feature notation that we have adopted in this book, a cluster is weak if it ends in a consonantal segment followed by a segment which is [−anterior] and in which the coefficients of the features "vocalic" and "consonantal" assume the same value. A weak cluster will therefore be represented as:

$$(49) \qquad \begin{bmatrix} -\text{tense} \\ V \end{bmatrix} C_0^1 \begin{bmatrix} \alpha\text{voc} \\ \alpha\text{cons} \\ -\text{ant} \end{bmatrix}_0$$

7. Summary of stress placement rules

The stress rules we have discussed so far are the Main Stress Rule, the Alternating Stress Rule, and the Stress Adjustment Rule. These rules now have the following tentative form:

---

[31] At this stage of representation, there are no sequences VGC, where G is a glide, since diphthongs are still represented as single tense vowels. See note 15.

[32] We again make note of several apparent exceptions, e.g., *pellágra, candelábra, allégro* (in the dialectal variant with a phonetically lax penultimate vowel). We return to these in Section 16. There also seem to be some cases where the sequence V*Cl* acts as a weak cluster. See note 82 and pages 140 and 197.

We are indebted to J. Fidelholtz and J. R. Ross for the particular form of the concept of weak cluster that has been adopted here.

(50)   MAIN STRESS RULE

$$V \rightarrow [1\ \text{stress}] \Big/ [X\text{------} \begin{cases} C_0 \begin{bmatrix} -\text{tense} \\ V \end{bmatrix} C_0^1 \begin{bmatrix} \alpha \text{voc} \\ \alpha \text{cons} \\ -\text{ant} \end{bmatrix}_0 & \text{(i)} \\ C_0 & \text{(ii)} \end{cases}$$

$$\Big/ \text{------} \begin{cases} +C_0 \begin{bmatrix} -\text{tense} \\ V \end{bmatrix} C_0]_{NA} & \text{(a)} \\ \begin{bmatrix} -\text{tense} \\ V \end{bmatrix} C_0]_N & \text{(b)} \\ ] & \text{(e)} \end{cases}$$

(51)   ALTERNATING STRESS RULE

$$V \rightarrow [1\ \text{stress}] \ / \text{------} C_0 V C_0 \overset{1}{V} C_0]_{NAV}$$

(52)   STRESS ADJUSTMENT RULE
         Within a word, all nonprimary stresses are weakened by one.

Rule (52) is noncyclical, applying just at the level of word boundary in the cycle. Rule (50) is the central cyclic rule. Rule (51) will, in fact, apply only once in a derivation, for other reasons, but it is not restricted to the level of word boundary.

Within rule (50) the ordering is automatically determined as (ai), (aii), (bi), (bii), (ei), (eii). Furthermore, the ordering of cases (i) and (ii) is disjunctive, and the ordering of conditions (a), (b), and (e) is disjunctive. These facts are made explicit if we state the Main Stress Rule in its more abbreviated form (see (36), (45)) as follows:

(53)
$$V \rightarrow [1\ \text{stress}] \Big/ [X\text{------} C_0 \Big(\begin{bmatrix} -\text{tense} \\ V \end{bmatrix} C_0^1 \begin{bmatrix} \alpha \text{voc} \\ \alpha \text{cons} \\ -\text{ant} \end{bmatrix}_0 \Big)$$

$$\Big/ \text{------} \langle_1 \langle_2 + C_0 \rangle_2 \begin{bmatrix} -\text{tense} \\ V \end{bmatrix} C_0 \rangle_1]_{\langle_1 N \langle_2 A \rangle_2 \rangle_1} \quad \begin{matrix} \langle_2 (a) \rangle_2 \\ \langle_1 (b) \rangle_1 \\ (e) \end{matrix}$$

Angled brackets with the same numerical indices are expanded together. We number the angles here only to bring out the structure of (53) more clearly. The indices are actually superfluous in this case since there is only one way to expand the expression (53) in accordance with our conventions. Later we will make use of indexing of brackets to enrich our system for the formulation of phonological rules.

In accordance with the convention for angled brackets, the expression (53) states that the two rules (50i) and (50ii) are applied in the three contexts (50a), (50b), and (50e), obtained by reading (53) first with all angled material included (case (a)), then with the material enclosed in $\langle_2 \ \rangle_2$ excluded (case (b)), and finally with all angled material excluded (case (e)). Furthermore, the ordering of (a), (b), and (e) and of (i) and (ii) is disjunctive. The parenthesis and angle notations therefore characterize the ordering explicitly.

Before illustrating these rules with several examples, we will mention some additional limitations on the applicability of condition (a). Alongside of the affixes that affect stress placement and that are subject to condition (a), there are other "neutral affixes" which characteristically play no role in the placement of stress, for example, the adjective-forming affixes *-y*,[33] *-like, -able, -ish*, and affixes such as *-ing, -past tense, -hood, -ness, -ly, -wise*. We can indicate the fact that an affix is neutral by making use of the # boundary which is introduced, by a universal convention, before and after each string belonging to a lexical category, that is, each string dominated by N, A, or V in the surface structure (see Section 1.3.1 and Chapter One, Section 5.3). Thus, the word *soliloquizing*, for example, might be represented in surface structure as:

$$(54) \qquad [\, [_{V} \# \text{soliloquIz} \#]_{V} \text{ ing}]$$

where the word may be functioning as a verb (*he is soliloquizing*), as a noun (*soliloquizing is out of fashion*), or as a noun modifier (*the soliloquizing Dane*). On the first cycle, the innermost constituent receives the stress pattern $[_{V}\overset{1}{\text{soliloqu}}\overset{2}{\text{Iz}}]_{V}$ by rule (50eii) and rule (51). On the second cycle, condition (a) is ruled out since it is limited to affixes preceded by $+$. Condition (b) is also inapplicable, because of the presence of # in *soliloquiz # ing*. (Recall that #, as opposed to $+$, must be mentioned in a rule if that rule is to apply to a string containing #.) Condition (e), however, applies, and will shift primary stress, incorrectly, to the affix *-ing* because of the double consonant in the underlying form. To eliminate this possibility, we add to the Main Stress Rule (50), (53) the qualification:

$$(55) \qquad X \text{ contains no internal } \# \text{ boundary.}$$

This qualification guarantees that a word-internal cycle will be vacuous when it applies to a string of the form $\ldots \# C_{0}VC_{0}]$.

Notice that the presence of the # boundary is quite well motivated on different grounds in many of these cases. The inflectional affixes which are neutral with respect to stress also characteristically affect final clusters in the same way as word boundary does. For example, in many dialects /g/ drops after nasals in word-final position but remains in word-medial position, so that we have [siŋ] but [miŋgl] (from underlying /siNg/, /miNgl/, respectively, /N/ being the archi-segment "nasal consonant"). But before *-ing, -er* (agentive), *-ed, -ly*, etc., /g/ also drops, so that we have [siŋiŋ], [siŋr], contrasting with [fiŋgr]; [riŋd], [hɔltiŋly] (or, with a different *-ly* affix, [kiŋly]), contrasting with [siŋgly], the latter from phonological /siNgl # ly/, with the /l/ of / # ly/ dropping after /Cl/; or [kiŋlət], from /kiNg # lVt/, contrasting with [singlət], from /siNgl # lVt/.

Furthermore, we must have a rule:

$$(56) \qquad \text{sonorants become syllabic } / C\underline{\quad\quad} \#^{34}$$

This is needed to account for the fact that in words such as *hinder, cylinder, remember,*

---

[33] Not to be confused with the noun-forming *-y* of *democracy, presidency*, etc.

[34] The feature "sonorant" is redundant in English, though not in all languages. It distinguishes vowels, liquids, glides, and nasals from nonnasal (obstruent) consonants. A syllabic sonorant consonant will ultimately have the neutral vowel (which we are representing as [ə]—see note 1) inserted before it. Thus *hinder* is phonetically [hindr] = [hindər]. Notice that not all words with a final syllabic sonorant have a final consonant-sonorant cluster in the underlying representation. Thus *odor, danger, valor, titan, Homer*, for example, have final vowel-sonorant clusters in both underlying and phonetic representations, as we can see from the forms *odorous, dangerous, valorous, titanic, Homeric*.

    Notice that rule (56) is also needed to account for stress placement, and that it must follow the Main Stress Rule in the sequence of rules. Consider, for example, the forms *cýlinder, cárpenter*. Only rule (50bii) can assign primary stress in the first syllable to these words, but the application of (50bii) here requires that the final cluster be of the form /V̆ndr/, /V̆ntr/, respectively, where V̆ is a lax vowel.

carpenter, disaster, schism, burgle, twinkle, the sonorant is syllabic in word-final position although the underlying representations must be /hiNdr/, /siliNdr/, /rEmeNbr/, /kærpVNtr/, /disæstr/, /sizm/, /burgl/, /twiNkl/, as shown by the related forms where these sonorants are not syllabic: *hindrance, cylindric, remembrance, carpentry, disastrous, schismatic, burglar, twinkling* (in the sense of "instant," from /twiNkl+liNg/, the /l/ of /liNg/ dropping, as above, after /Cl/). However, the sonorant is also syllabic in forms such as *hindering, hindered, remembering, burgled, twinkling* (the participle),[35] indicating that these neutral affixes also carry the boundary #. Similarly, the noun-forming *-y* affix, which is not neutral with respect to stress placement, changes preceding /t/ to [s] (*democrat–democracy, president–presidency*), but the neutral, adjective-forming *-y* does not affect final /t/ (*chocolaty, bratty*, etc.),[36] indicating that it carries the boundary # that blocks this process.

The affixes that carry # are, to a certain extent, syntactically distinguished. For the most part, these are the affixes that are assigned to a word by a grammatical transformation, whereas the derivational affixes that affect stress placement are, largely, internal to the lexicon. In other words, if # is automatically associated with lexical items and automatically introduced to the right of a suffix (or the left of a prefix) attached to a member of a lexical category by a transformation, then the resulting distribution of boundaries is fairly close to what is required for the operation of the phonological component. This principle for assigning # is the same, in many cases, as the principle that # should be introduced at the boundary of strings dominated by a lexical category in the surface structure (see Chapter One, pp. 12–14). Thus the word *singing* is a verb containing the verb *sing*, and so on.

Notice that # may be deleted before affixes under certain circumstances. Consider, for example, the variants *análỳzable–ánalyzáble*. We can derive the former from the phonological representation $[_A [_V ana+lIz]_V \# abl]_A$, and the latter from the same representation with # deleted. When the word boundary # is present, the stress pattern is that of the underlying form *análìz* in isolation, since the second cycle is vacuous. When the boundary is dropped, as is not uncommon when *-able* is added to longer forms, the affix *-able* (represented /æbl/) is subject to condition (a) of the Main Stress Rule. Thus, in the second cycle, case (ii) of the rule shifts primary stress to the strong cluster immediately preceding the affix in this example.

So far, then, we have two classes of affixes, those that assign primary stress by the Main Stress Rule and those that carry # boundary and are therefore neutral. Superficial examination would suggest that it is necessary to distinguish two other classes of affixes (apart from those that take primary stress), namely, those of the -1 category, which place primary stress on the final syllable of the string to which they are affixed (e.g., *-ion, -ic, -ity, -ify*), and those of the -2 category, which generally place stress on the penultimate syllable of the string to which they are affixed (e.g., *-y, -ate, -ize*). Actually, most of these affixes are perfectly regular and require no special comment. In particular, the -2 category is superfluous. As far as *-y* is concerned, we will see in Section 15 that it is entirely regular. Examples such as *illustr-àte, antágon-ìze*, as we shall see, receive their stress contour by the Main Stress Rule, which places primary stress on the final strong cluster, and the Alternating Stress

---

[35] In more casual speech, the syllabicity of [l̩] (and sometimes even of [r̩]) may disappear as one of many optional modifications of the idealized phonetic form.

[36] Notice that not all cases of adjective-forming *-y* are to be assigned to this /#y/ formative. Thus we have *angry, hungry* with the lexical representations /æNgr+y/, /huNgr+y/ (where N represents the archisegment "nasal"). Here the affix is not /#y/, but a different affix, identical in its phonetic form but not in its phonetic effects; it does not carry # and is restricted to adjectives derived from abstract nouns. Clearly this distinction is in accord with the sense as well as the phonetics.

Rule (51), which then shifts primary stress two syllables to the left. In other examples (e.g., *cháracterize*, *rádicalize*), *-ize* is simply a neutral affix preceded by #.

As far as the -1 category is concerned, we see at once that most of its members simply fall under the Main Stress Rule. If we analyze *-ity*, for example, as *-i+ty*,[37] then the fact that stress falls on the syllable immediately preceding it is accounted for by case (ai) of the Main Stress Rule (50), since the "stem-forming" element *-i-* that precedes the final affix is lax.

In fact, aside from the two categories of neutral affixes and affixes that assign stress by the Main Stress Rule, we have only the exceptions *-ic* and *-ion* to deal with among lax affixes, and no further classification need be given. Furthermore, as we have noted, the distinction between neutral and nonneutral affixes is drawn fairly clearly on general grounds. It seems, then, that there is no significant classification of affixes with respect to stress placement; there is the mass of affixes that fall under the general Romance Rule, and, in addition, there is the margin of exceptions to be expected in the case of any phonological rule.

The best way to deal with exceptions is to modify their representations in some ad hoc way so as to enable them to fall under the regular rules, which can then remain unaltered in their simplest and most general form. Thus the fact that *-ion* always places primary stress on the syllable immediately preceding it is easily accounted for if we give *-ion* the underlying representation /iV̆n/, /V̆/ standing for the archi-segment "lax vowel." Words such as *prohibítion*, *inhibítion*, *nutrítion* will now be represented [prohibit+iV̆n]¹, etc., when we enter the second cycle. Condition (a) of the Main Stress Rule (50) does not apply, since the affix contains two vowels, but condition (b) does apply, excluding the final string /V̆n/ from consideration and assigning primary stress to the syllable preceding the weak cluster of the residue /prohibit+i/ by case (i). Thus we have [prohibitiV̆n]², which receives its full stress contour in the appropriate way by rules to which we shall turn later on. Primary stress, however, is now correctly placed. The forms in *-Ation* will receive primary stress on /At/, as required, in the same way. In the case of words such as *compúlsion*, *permíssion*, *invásion*, *profúsion*, primary stress will have been placed on the second syllable in the first cycle. (The final stress on verbs like *compél* and *permít* will be accounted for in Section 10 of this chapter.) The second cycle, then, is vacuous. Primary stress will also be placed properly by the same rule in words such as *pavílion*, *battálion*, *chámpion*, *compánion*, *domínion* if we give them the representations /pævil+iV̆n/, etc. Other reasons for treating *-ion* as bisyllabic in the underlying form will appear in Chapter Four, Section 4.1.

To complete the account of *-ion*, we must add the rule:

$$\begin{pmatrix}57\end{pmatrix} \qquad\qquad i \;\rightarrow\; y \;/\; \begin{bmatrix}\text{dental} \\ C\end{bmatrix} +\!\!-\!\!- V^{38}$$

Thus, rule (57) applies in words such as *battalion, pavilion, million, rebellion*,[39] *companion, dominion, union*, but it does not apply in *Albion, champion, clarion, criterion, oblivion*.

---

[37] This is well motivated. See note 23, Chapter Two.

[38] In terms of distinctive features, dental consonants are coronal and anterior. We regard [l] as dental, [r] as nondental (in this case, coronal and nonanterior), throughout. Thus the rule applies after [l] and [n] as well as the dental obstruents. We will return to a somewhat more careful formulation of this rule in Section 6 of the next chapter.

[39] In the case of *rebel* (and several other words), rule (57) also applies before *-ous*, giving *rebellious* [rEbelyəs], as opposed to *punctilious* [pʌŋktilEəs], for example. For more discussion of this matter, see Chapter Four, Section 6.

Notice that rule (57) must be in the cycle. Consider the form *convéntional*, for example. On the first application of the cycle we obtain the representation [convent+iV̆n]. If this representation is submitted to the second cycle with the affix -*al*, primary stress will be placed incorrectly on the /i/ of the affix string /iV̆n+al/ by case (i) of the Main Stress Rule (50) under condition (a). Hence (57) must apply, removing this vowel, before the application of the second cycle.[40] As we shall see rule (57) is actually somewhat more general.

In the case of the second exceptional suffix, namely, -*ic*, we must resort to some similar artifice to account for the fact that it places stress on the immediately preceding syllable. The simplest method is to represent -*ic* as the variant form /ik+æl/. We then add the ad hoc rule (58) after the Main Stress Rule:

$$\left(58\right) \qquad\qquad\qquad \text{æl} \;\rightarrow\; \phi \;\; / \; \text{ik}+\text{──}$$

Using certain devices that we will develop in Chapter Four, Section 2.2, we will associate with each lexical item taking -*ic*+*æl* an indication as to whether it may or may not undergo rule (58). Thus, in the words *basic, public, sulfuric*, rule (58) is obligatory; in *theatrical, neurological*, it is inapplicable; in *ironic*(*al*), *analytic*(*al*) the rule is optional. In some cases (e.g., *economic*(*al*), *historic*(*al*)) the applicability of rule (58) depends on the sense of the word, that is, its semantic features.

We shall see in the next chapter that we can make use of this underlying bisyllabic representation and rule (58) to account for other exceptional features of -*ic*, in particular, its effect on stressed vowel alternations. Notice that all forms undergo rule (58) when the affix -*ly* is added; thus the rule is needed even apart from the considerations mentioned here.[41]

A word such as *titánic* will now have the representation [ₐtItæn+ik+æl]ₐ as we enter the second cycle. The Main Stress Rule will assign primary stress to the antepenultimate syllable by case (i) under condition (a), and [æl] will then be deleted by rule (58).

We now give two examples—*theatricality* and *indemnification*—to illustrate the stress placement rules in the case of affixes. Consider first the word *theatricálity*, with the underlying representation indicated in the derivation (59):

$$\left(59\right)$$

[N [A [Nθeætr]N ik+æl]A i+ti]N		
1		RULE (50bii)
2 1		RULE (50ai)
3 2	1	RULE (50ai)
4 3	1	RULE (52)

---

[40] An apparent alternative to rule (57), in such cases, would be to introduce into the cycle the rules that convert /ti/ to [š], as in *convention*, so that on the final cycle we consider the full form *conventional* with the representation [convenšV̆n+æl]. This is impossible, however, as we shall see in Chapter Four, Section 6, because the reduction of the vowel is conditional upon the degree of stress on the following vowel (compare *cordial-cordiality*), and this is determined later in the cycle.

[41] The adjective-forming suffix -*ic*, which we are at this point representing as /ik+æl/, is not to be confused with the noun-forming ending -*ic*, which we represent simply as /ik/. The latter, then, will assign stress in the normal way in nouns such as *aríthmetic, Cátholic, ársenic, climácteric*. Notice that only -*al* and not -*ical* is affixed to forms ending in -*ic*. The effect is to shift the stress, giving such pairs as the noun *aríthmetic* versus the adjective *arithmétic* (from *arithmetical*, by rule (58)), as in *arithmetic progression*. There are a few well-known examples in which the adjective-forming affix assigns stress to a syllable preceding it by two (e.g., *Árabic, chóleric*); we might indicate this by a readjustment rule deleting -*al*. Presumably the adjectives *Catholic, politic* are derived from the corresponding nouns by an adjective-forming process that does not involve affixation of -*ic*.

We are indebted to G. Carden and G. H. Matthews for suggestions regarding the analysis of -*ic*.

The final line of (59) becomes a full phonetic representation by other rules that we have not discussed.

Reviewing the steps of this derivation briefly, we see that in the first cycle the innermost constituent $[_N \theta e \ae tr]_N$ falls under condition (b) since it is a noun with a lax vowel in the final syllable. Case (i) does not apply, since there is only the single syllable /θe/ under consideration when the final $\breve{V}C_0$ string /ætr/ is excluded. Thus case (ii) applies, assigning stress to /θe/. This completes the first cycle and we erase innermost brackets. If we were dealing with *theater* in isolation, we would now apply rule (56), to make the final *r* syllabic, and the Vowel Reduction Rule, giving, finally, [θÉətr̩]. (The change of [e] to [E] in this position results from rule (30), the quality change (Vowel Shift) being contingent on tensing for stressed vowels.)

In the second cycle we are dealing with an adjective with a lax vowel in the final monosyllabic affix. Thus condition (a) is applicable, and case (i) shifts primary stress one syllable to the right. We pass by case (ii) and conditions (b) and (e) because of the disjunctive ordering. If we were dealing with *theatrical* in isolation, we would derive the phonetic representation [θÉǽtrəkəl], by rule (52), rule (30), Vowel Shift, and Vowel Reduction.

In the third cycle, condition (a) holds and case (i) shifts stress to the right once again. The disjunctive ordering requires us to skip case (ii) and conditions (b) and (e). Finally, we apply the Stress Adjustment Rule (52), giving *theatricality*, as in the last line of (59). Rule (30), Vowel Shift, and Vowel Reduction give [θÉætrəkǽlətE].

Consider now the word *indemnificátion*:

$$
\left(60\right) \quad [_N \ [_V \text{indemn}+\text{i}+\text{f Ik}]_V \ \text{At}+\text{i}\breve{V}\text{n}]_N
$$

	1		RULE (50eii)
1	2		RULE (51)
2	3	1	RULE (50bi)
3	4	1	RULE (52)

In the first cycle conditions (a) and (b) are not met, and we turn to condition (e). Case (i) is inapplicable because of the final strong cluster, and case (ii) assigns primary stress to the final syllable. The Alternating Stress Rule (51) then shifts primary stress to the antepenultimate vowel. In isolation, therefore, we would have *indémnify*, by Stress Adjustment and a rule which deletes [k] in the position $+C_0 I \text{---}] \# \#$.

In the second cycle, we are dealing with a noun that falls under condition (b), which shifts stress to the right by case (i). Case (ii) and condition (e) are skipped because of the disjunctive ordering. The Stress Adjustment Rule (52) then gives us the desired stress pattern. Vowel Reduction, consonant softening, and other rules we will discuss give, finally, [indemnəfəkÁšən].

Innumerable other examples receive their stress patterns by these rules in similar ways.

8. Nuclear stress

The rules we have given so far apply only within the word; the condition (55) in the Main Stress Rule, that X must not contain the boundary # internally, is sufficient to guarantee this. In Chapter Two we described the operation of the transformational cycle above the level of the word, noting that two rules are involved, the Compound Rule and the Nuclear

Stress Rule. We must now incorporate these "higher level" processes into the formulation of the rules of stress placement.

The salient facts concerning nuclear stress were well summarized by S. S. Newman (1946), as follows: "When no expressive stress disturbs a sequence of heavy stresses, the last heavy stress in an intonational unit receives the nuclear heavy stress" (p. 176). Thus, in a noun phrase such as *absolute equality* or a verb phrase such as *demand capitulation*, the main stress of the second word is heavier than that of the first.

Suppose that we have the phrase *absolute equality*, with the phonological representation taken tentatively as (61) (with segments which will be justified later):

$$\left(61\right) \qquad [_{NP}\# \, [_A\# \text{æbsəlUt}\#]_A \, [_N\# \, [_A\text{Eku}+\text{æl}]_A \, \text{i}+\text{ti}\#]_N \, \#]_{NP}$$

In the first cycle, *absolute* becomes $\overset{1}{abso}\overset{3}{lute}$ by rules (50eii), (51), and (52); and *equal* becomes $\overset{1}{equal}$ by (50ai). Innermost brackets are now erased, and the second cycle applies to the noun *equality*, giving $\overset{3}{equa}\overset{1}{lity}$ by (50ai) and (52). Thus, at the end of the second cycle we have the representation (62) (after the nontransformational, word-level rules have also applied):

$$\left(62\right) \qquad [_{NP}\# \, \# \overset{1}{\text{æ}}\text{bsəl}\overset{3}{\text{U}}\text{t}\# \, \# \overset{3}{\text{E}}\text{kwāl}\overset{1}{\text{ə}}\text{tE}\# \, \#]_{NP}$$

As our rules now stand, the next cycle is vacuous and gives (62) as the final output.[42] We may take account of the phenomenon of nuclear stress by adding the new rule (63):

$$\left(63\right) \qquad V \rightarrow [\text{1 stress}] \; / \; [\# \, \# \, X \left[\dfrac{}{\text{1 stress}}\right] Y \# \, \#]$$

where Y contains no vowel with the feature [1 stress]

We will call this the Nuclear Stress Rule, as in Chapter Two. As formulated, it will not apply to units smaller than a word. Applying it to (62), we derive (64), as required:[43]

$$\left(64\right) \qquad [_{NP}\# \, \# \overset{2}{\text{æ}}\text{bsəl}\overset{4}{\text{U}}\text{t}\# \, \# \overset{4}{\text{E}}\text{kwāl}\overset{1}{\text{ə}}\text{tE}\# \, \#]_{NP}$$

Notice that we can now eliminate the Stress Adjustment Rule (52), since it is simply the special case of the Nuclear Stress Rule that applies at the level of word boundary (when X contains no primary-stressed vowel). However, we will generally continue to refer to the Nuclear Stress Rule as the Stress Adjustment Rule when it applies to the single primary-stressed vowel that appears at the level of words.

---

[42] One of the widely accepted conventions for representing stress levels is precisely this. See, e.g., Jones (1956b). We will, however, accept the position of Newman, Trager and Smith, and others regarding nuclear stress in such constructions, and will modify the rules so as to accommodate their descriptions of the impressionistic phonetics.

[43] Recall the discussion in Chapter Two, Section 2, regarding the accuracy of such transcriptions and the physical basis for them. If one makes the assumption (quite gratuitous, for the moment) that stress contours are physical as well as perceptual phenomena, then it would make sense to ask whether the internal relations of stress in the words *absolute* and *equality* are the same when these words are in isolation as when they appear in the phrase *absolute equality*. The familiar paired utterance test should provide an answer to this question. The representation (64) implies that the internal relations of *absolute* are the same in the phrase *absolute equality* as in isolation, while those of *equality* differ. Our conventions could be modified to permit other representations, but in the absence of any evidence bearing on the matter, it seems pointless to pursue such possibilities. See also the discussion in Chapter Two, Section 1, page 23.

Suppose that we were to define a scale of "sonority" in such a way that more heavily stressed vowels are greater in sonority than less heavily stressed vowels and that all vowels are greater in sonority than consonants or boundaries. Then the Nuclear Stress Rule states that primary stress is placed on the last sonority peak of a string that contains at least one word (the only sonority peak, in the case of Stress Adjustment). Similarly, in the first cycle case (ii) of the Main Stress Rule has the effect of placing primary stress on the last sonority peak of the string under consideration (the only sonority peak, where this string is a mono-syllable). In [ErAs], for example, the second vowel is the final sonority peak; in [rAn] (*rain*) there is only one sonority peak, namely, the vowel. This observation suggests that it might be possible to formulate the Main Stress Rule so as to include the Nuclear Stress Rule as a special case, combining it with case (ii). We have investigated this possibility in detail, but we are inclined to think that this is a spurious generalization since such a refor-mulation requires a network of otherwise unnecessary conditions in the statement of these rules. (See Chapter Five for some further discussion.)

The verb phrase *demand capitulation* will be derived in exactly the same way as the noun phrase *absolute equality*. Thus we have the following derivation:

$\left(65\right)$ $\quad$ $[_{VP}\# \ [_V \# dEmænd \#]_V \ [_N \# \ [_V kæpitUlAt]_V \ i\breve{V}n \#]_N \ \#]_{VP}$

	1			1	RULE (50eii)
			1	2	RULE (51)
			2	1	RULE (50bi)
			3	1	RULE (63)
	2		4	1	RULE (63)

In the first cycle, primary stress is placed on the final syllable of the two innermost constituents, both of which are verbs, and the Alternating Stress Rule (51) applies to the polysyllabic form *capitulate*. At the next stage we deal with the phrase *capitulation* and assign primary stress to the antepenultimate vowel /A/. The Stress Adjustment Rule then assigns primary stress to the last (and only) sonority peak, giving *capitulation* (with superscripts 3 and 1 over the final syllables). In the third cycle, we consider the verb phrase as a whole and assign primary stress to the last sonority peak by the Nuclear Stress Rule. (See note 43.)

The other examples of the Nuclear Stress Rule discussed in Chapter Two now fall into place in the same way.

9. Compounds

Our informal discussion of the transformational cycle in Chapter Two dealt with Nuclear Stress and Compound Stress. We have accounted for the former, and must now add a rule for compound nouns, adjectives, and verbs such as those of (66) (the nouns, of course, being by far the richest and most productive category):

$\left(66\right)$

chemistry laboratory	*hard-headed*	*hedge-hop*
Christmas party	*hot-blooded*	*trouble-shoot*
venture capital	*rose-colored*	*air-condition*
toy factory	*heart-rending*	*boot-lick*
sugar cane	*mealy-mouthed*	*horse-whip*

As in the case of the Nuclear Stress Rule, we deal here with two constituents, each of which has received a primary stress on the preceding cycle.[44] The Nuclear Stress Rule (63) assigns primary stress to the second sonority peak, reducing by one all other stress levels in the phrase under consideration; the Compound Rule, on the other hand, assigns primary stress to the first of the two peaks, reducing all other stress levels by one.

We can state the Compound Rule as (67):

$$(67) \qquad V \rightarrow [1 \text{ stress}] \ / \ [\#\#X\left[\overline{\atop 1 \text{ stress}}\right] Y\#\#Z\#\#]_{NAV}$$

This rule will apply to a string of the form $\#\#X\overset{1}{V}Y\#\#Z\#\#$ which is a noun, adjective, or verb with the two immediate constituents $X\overset{1}{V}Y$ and Z. Its effect will be to weaken all stresses in the construction under consideration except that of the primary-stressed vowel of $X\overset{1}{V}Y$. Thus $\#\#\overset{1}{chemistry}\#\#\overset{1}{laboratory}\#\#$ will become $\#\#\overset{1}{chemistry}\#\#\overset{3}{laboratory}\#\#$, etc. (See note 43.)

Clearly the Compound Rule (67) must apply prior to the Nuclear Stress Rule (63); furthermore, the ordering of these rules must be disjunctive or the Nuclear Stress Rule will reapply after the Compound Rule, weakening all but the primary stress. Now observe that our system of notations in fact requires (68) as the simplest formulation of the two rules (63) and (67):

$$(68) \qquad V \rightarrow [1 \text{ stress}] \ / \ [\#\#X\left[\overline{\atop 1 \text{ stress}}\right] Y\langle \#\#Z\rangle \#\#]_{\langle NAV\rangle}$$

where Y contains no vowel with the feature [1 stress][45]

The formulation (68) expresses the disjunctive ordering (67), (63) in precisely the desired way. The two rules abbreviated as (68) determine the stress contours discussed in Chapter Two exactly as outlined there. With the material in angles, (68) is the Compound Rule; when the material in angles is omitted, (68) is the Nuclear Stress Rule. We will, as usual, continue to refer to these rules in their unabbreviated forms (67) and (63).

There is an ambiguity in the formulation of the Compound Rule in (67) and (68) for one particular construction, namely, a compound whose second member is again a compound, that is, a construction of the form:

$$(69) \qquad [_N \#\#A\# \ [_N \#B\#\#C\#]_N \ \#]_N$$

Such constructions are rare. Possible examples are *chemistry research-laboratory* (in the

---

[44] This remark is not quite correct. Although it is true that compounds are strictly limited to two immediate constituents, this is not necessarily true of the phrases to which the Nuclear Stress Rule applies. Thus the rule may apply to a noun phrase such as *an old, tired, disconsolate, retired teacher*, in which there is no internal structure among the coordinated items. It will assign main stress to the last sonority peak (namely, *teacher*) and reduce the stress on each of the adjectives to secondary.

The operation of the transformational cycle is guided by the surface structure produced by the syntax. The syntactic component must assign to each generated string a labeled bracketing that determines appropriately the sequence of applications of the rules. In the example of the last paragraph, it must assign no internal structure to the coordinated items (consistently with the sense, in this case). It is possible, however, that certain adjective sequences must be internally organized in the surface structure in order for the correct phonetic output to be produced (e.g., *tired old man* as distinct from *old, tired man*), though there may be a different basis for this phenomenon—see page 117. Just what the syntactic rules are that determine these surface structures is not known, and we have arbitrarily placed this problem, along with other syntactic problems, outside the scope of our study. We simply note here that various types of surface structure must be submitted to the phonological component, in particular, coordinate structures of arbitrary length with no internal organization.

[45] The condition on Y is irrelevant for the Compound Rule.

sense of "research laboratory for chemistry," not "laboratory for chemistry research"), *kitchen towel-rack* (in the sense of "towel rack in the kitchen," not "rack for kitchen towels"), *evening mathematics-class* (meaning "mathematics class held in the evening"), etc. Notice that the phrases *chemistry laboratory*, *research laboratory*, *kitchen rack*, *towel rack*, *evening class*, *mathematics class* all have primary stress on the first element, and the full phrases are of the form (69).

The early applications of the transformational cycle will assign a single primary stress to A, B, and C in (69). In the cycle, we consider the now innermost phrase $[_{\mathbf{N}} \# \overset{1}{B} \# \# \overset{1}{C} \#]_{\mathbf{N}}$. Primary stress is placed on B by the Compound Rule. Erasing innermost brackets, we have $[_{\mathbf{N}} \# \# \overset{1}{A} \# \# \overset{1}{B} \# \# \overset{2}{C} \# \#]_{\mathbf{N}}$. But the Compound Rule, as it stands, is ambiguous in its application to this form. We can take Z of (67), (68) to be C, or we can take it to be $B \# \# C$. If we take Z to be C, the primary stress will be placed on B (the last sonority peak), and we will have the stress contour 213 for the examples given above. If we take Z to be $B \# \# C$, the primary stress will be placed on A (the only sonority peak), and we will have the stress contour 123 for these examples.

To guarantee the contour 213, we can add the following qualification to (67) and (68):

$$\left(70\right) \qquad\qquad Z \neq \ldots \# \# \ldots$$

To guarantee the contour 123, we can add to (67) and (68) the qualification:

$$\left(71\right) \qquad\qquad Z \text{ contains [1 stress]}$$

Our impression is that the normal stress contour in these cases is 213, and we will therefore give the Compound Rule with qualification (70) rather than (71) in subsequent formulations.[46]

Our formulation of the Compound Rule does not take account of a familiar convention for the representation of English stress contours, namely, that there is a distinction in stress contour between compounds such as $\overset{1}{elevator}\ \overset{3}{boy}$ or $\overset{1}{chemistry}\ \overset{3}{teacher}$, which are represented with tertiary stress on the second member of the compound, and those such as $\overset{1}{elevator}\ \overset{2}{operator}$ or $\overset{1}{chemistry}\ \overset{2}{laboratory}$, in which the second member of the compound retains secondary stress. With the system of rules that we have given so far, the second member of the compound will, in each case, have secondary stress. To account for this distinction, we must add an ad hoc rule providing that secondary stress in the rightmost member of a compound is reduced still further when this member has some property P. The property P might, for example, be the property of containing just a single vowel with the feature [+stress], or it might be formulated in a slightly different way, depending on how one wishes to assign a stress contour to compounds such as *soccer referee*, *UN attaché*, *land surveyor*, *pi-meson*, *car window*. It is not clear whether this is a question of fact or merely of convention. Whatever decision is made as to the appropriate property P (which might, for example, involve idiosyncratic features of particular lexical items, if we take the contours that have occasionally been described in the literature as factually accurate), the appropriate rule can be formulated in terms of it, with no effect on the rest of the system. We will therefore disregard this matter and tentatively assume that in all cases the stress contour is to appear as primary-secondary.

---

[46] We will also omit the string $\# \# X$ from the formulation of rules (68). This string plays no role; it was included only to bring out the domain of the rule more clearly.

To summarize, the rules that apply at the word level or beyond are the Compound and Nuclear Stress Rules, which apply in this order, disjunctively.[47] Each assigns primary stress to a vowel which already contains primary stress, weakening all other stresses in the string under consideration. Applying at the level of words, the Nuclear Stress Rule is what we called earlier the Stress Adjustment Rule; its effect is to reserve secondary stress for phrases that contain more than one word. The Nuclear Stress Rule assigns primary stress to the rightmost sonority peak in the string under consideration; with the possible exception of items of the form (69), the Compound Rule assigns primary stress to the leftmost sonority peak in the string under consideration.

10. Complex verbs

There are many verbs in English that are morphologically analyzable into one of the prefixes *trans-*, *per-*, *con-*, etc., followed by a stem such as *-fer*, *-mit*, *-cede*, *-cur*, or *-pel*. This analysis is strictly internal to the lexicon, playing no role in syntactic rules, so far as we know. The stress placement rules must assign primary stress to the final formative in these words, regardless of whether it contains a strong or weak cluster. Thus, even when such verbs end in a weak cluster, as in (72), stress is final:

$$\left(72\right) \qquad\qquad\qquad \textit{permít, concúr, compél, detér, transfér}$$

Clearly, then, we must prevent case (i) of the Main Stress Rule (under condition (e)) from applying to these forms while still allowing it to apply to *fúrnish*, *wórship*, *cóvet* and other examples of the sort illustrated in column I of (18). That is, we must identify the complex verbs in some manner that will account for their exceptional behavior. The simplest way to do this is by a readjustment rule which adds an identifying feature to the internal boundary in verbs of the prefix-stem type (72). (See Section 1.3.1 for a discussion of the feature analysis of boundaries.) Since these stems and prefixes are not, in general, independent words or even separate lexical items, we do not expect to find $\#$ in this position. Rather, we expect to find the boundary which, in terms of feature analysis, is $[-\text{FB}, -\text{WB}]$, that is, distinct from both $+$ and $\#$. We use the symbol $=$ as an informal abbreviatory notation for the feature set $[-\text{segment}, -\text{FB}, -\text{WB}]$. Thus we assign to the examples of (72) the underlying representations (73), where $/\text{N}/$ is the archi-segment "nasal" and $/\dote{I}/$ is the archi-segment "lax vowel" (which is, furthermore, back and high, at least in the case of *concur* in dialects which have the phonetic form [kənkʌ́rənt] for *concurrent*—see the next chapter for details). The features of the boundary are introduced into the representation by a readjustment rule.

$$\left(73\right) \qquad\qquad \text{pɪr=mit, kəN=kɪr, kəN=pel, de=tɪr, træns=fɪr}$$

When we now apply the Main Stress Rule to the forms in (73), conditions (a) and (b) are inapplicable and case (i) is blocked under condition (e) because of the $=$ boundary. Case (ii) then assigns primary stress to the vowel in the final syllable, under condition (e).

This analysis of morphologically complex verbs accounts for several other peculiarities of such forms. Notice, in the first place, that trisyllabic verbs with prefixes are generally not subject to the Alternating Stress Rule (51), which assigns antepenultimate primary stress in

---

[47] One additional rule that may apply beyond the word level will be mentioned in Section 14.

words such as *éxercise, ánalyze, cómplicate, clárify*. That is, the final stress assigned by (50eii) is retained in verbs such as *comprehénd, apprehénd, intervéne, introspéct, introdúce, contradíct, controvért*. Introduction of an automatic = boundary after these prefixes will block the application of rule (51), thus accounting for this apparent violation of the Alternating Stress Rule. We will refine this observation directly.

A second peculiar feature of these constructions relates to segmental phonology. There are various positions in which /s/ becomes voiced in English, in particular, intervocalically when the preceding vowel belongs to one of the verb-forming prefixes that we are now considering. Thus we have voicing of /s/ in *resist, resemble, resolve, design, presume* (compare *consist, semblance, solve, consign, consume*—some apparent exceptions will be discussed in Section 16). We can now describe this phenomenon by a rule such as (74) (which, as we shall see, can be somewhat generalized):

$$\left(74\right) \qquad\qquad \text{s} \;\rightarrow\; [+\text{voice}] \;/\; V = \underline{\qquad} V$$

Notice that voicing of /s/ does not take place intervocalically when there is no boundary preceding /s/ (e.g., *misogynist, asylum*) or when there is a boundary but the element in question is not a morphologically complex verb (e.g., *para+site, para+sitic, chromo+somal, philo+sophical, meta+soma*). Hence the complex verbs must be distinguished from other forms for the purpose of rule (74); the obligatory = boundary makes the required distinction.

In short, the device proposed for determining the stress placement in morphologically complex forms such as (73) is not only the simplest, given the framework of rules that we have so far developed, but it is also independently motivated. We shall find still further support for this analysis.

Notice, incidentally, that rule (74) must, as indicated, be limited to the boundary [−FB, −WB]. We have given several examples to show why it is limited to boundaries which are marked [−FB]. To see that the boundary [+WB] (namely, #) must also be excluded, consider *parasynthesis, photosynthesis, proto-Siouan, resell, resettle*. In all of these prefix-stem constructions, the stem, which begins with /s/, is an independent word, and we therefore expect it, on general syntactic grounds, to be preceded by the boundary #.[48] Observe that rule (74) does not apply to the stem-initial /s/ in these cases. Thus we have contrasts such as *resolve* (/rE=səlv/, [rEzᾱlv], "determine") versus *re-solve* (/rE#səlv/, [rEsᾱlv], "solve anew"), and *reserve* (/rE=sɨrv/, [rEzərv], "withhold") versus *re-serve* (/rE#sɨrv/, [rEsərv], "serve anew").

The decision to identify prefix-stem forms by a = boundary necessitates a slight revision of the Alternating Stress Rule (51). The readjustment rule that introduces = should give representations such as /kəN=kɨr/ for *concur*, /kəN=pre=heNd/ for *comprehend*, /iNtɨr=sekt/ for *intersect*, /kəN=teNplAt/ for *contemplate*, /kəN=stitUt/[49] for *constitute*, /kəN=peNsAt/ for *compensate*, etc. In the case of *concúr*, the Alternating Stress Rule is inapplicable; in the case of *comprehénd, interséct*, it is blocked by the boundary. But forms such as *cóntemplàte, cónstitùte, cómpensàte* show that it is the second, not the first, occurrence of = that blocks the rule in the case of *comprehend*. We must therefore reformulate the Alternating Stress Rule so as to permit an occurrence of = before the penultimate syllable

---

[48] Additional phonological justification for the syntactically expected analysis will appear in Section 13.
[49] Actually, as we shall see, [kəN=stitu+At].

because of forms like *cóntemplàte*. Accordingly we restate the rule as:

$$\left(75\right) \qquad V \;\rightarrow\; [\text{1 stress}] \;\;/\;\; \underline{\quad\quad} C_0 (=) C_0 V C_0 [\text{1 stress}] C_0]_{\mathbf{NAV}}$$

Formulated in this way, the Alternating Stress Rule will apply to representations such as $de=sign\overset{1}{A}t$, $re=plic\overset{1}{A}t$, $coN=plic\overset{1}{A}t$, $iN=plic\overset{1}{A}t$, $re=nov\overset{1}{A}t$, $de=ton\overset{1}{A}t$. It will not apply, however, to $coN=pre=he\overset{1}{N}d$, $iNter=se\overset{1}{c}t$, $coNtra=di\overset{1}{c}t$, and other forms with a boundary before the final syllable, and primary stress will therefore remain on the final syllable in these forms.

There remain certain words (e.g., $perseve\overset{1}{r}e$) which seem to be true exceptions and must therefore be excluded from the domain of rule (75) by other means (see Chapter Four, Section 2.2).

11. Nouns derived from verbs

The preceding discussion leads naturally to the topic of stress patterns in the nouns that are derived from verbs with primary stress on the final syllable. The general rule is that the primary stress is nonfinal in these nouns. Thus we have nouns such as those in (76), all with primary stress on the first syllable:

$$\left(76\right) \qquad \textit{tránsfèr, pérmìt, éxpòrt, súrvèy, prótèst, ínsèrt, prógrèss, cónvìct, súspèct, tórmènt, cómbìne}$$

It is important to note that the final syllable of these nouns has a tertiary stress. This is evident by comparison of noun pairs such as the following:

$$\left(77\right) \qquad \textit{tránsfèr–dóctŏr, pérmìt–hérmĭt, éxpòrt–éffŏrt, súrvèy–scúrvў, prótèst–déntĭst, ínsèrt–cóncĕrt, prógrèss–tígrĕss, cónvìct–vérdĭct, tórmènt–tórrĕnt, cómbìne–érmĭne}$$

The nouns of (76) have the stress pattern 13; the items paired with them in (77) have the stress pattern 1–. Clearly this distinction is related to the fact that verbs with final stress underlie the forms in (76) but do not underlie the forms paired with them in (77). We can therefore account for the stress difference by means of the transformational cycle. The nouns of (76) will be derived from underlying verbs on the second cycle by a rule which shifts primary stress to the left, weakening the stress on the final syllable to secondary. The final stress then becomes tertiary by the Stress Adjustment Rule. The new rule, which we will refer to as the Stressed Syllable Rule, will be given below (see (80)) as cases (c) and (d) of the Main Stress Rule. Thus we will have derivations such as (78) for the examples of (76), and (79) for the items paired with these in (77):

$$\left(78\right)$$

$[_N [_V p\dotlessi r = mit]_V]_N$	$[_N [_V t\partial rment]_V]_N$	$[_N [_V s\dotlessi rvA]_V]_N$	
1	1	1	RULE (50eii)
1 2	1 2	1 2	STRESSED SYLLABLE RULE
1 3	1 3	1 3	RULE (63)

$$\left(79\right)$$

$[_N h\dotlessi rm\dotlessi t]_N$	$[_N t\partial rent]_N$	$[_N sk\dotlessi rvi]_N$	
1	1	1	RULE (50bii)

The examples of (79) are straightforward. In each case the final syllable of the noun has a lax vowel so that condition (b) of the Main Stress Rule applies. Primary stress is therefore assigned to the vowel of the first syllable, the final cluster being excluded from consideration under condition (b). (Notice that the underlying vowel of the second syllable of *torrent* must be /e/—cf. *torrential*.) The final vowel of *scurvy* becomes tense in word-final position by rule (30), but only after the application of the Main Stress Rule. In each case the vowel of the second syllable retains [−stress] (and therefore reduces to [ə] nonfinally).

Consider now the derivations of (78), beginning with the noun *survey*. In the first cycle, primary stress is assigned to the final tense vowel under condition (e) of the Main Stress Rule by case (ii), case (i) being inapplicable because of the final strong cluster. This completes the cycle, and innermost brackets are erased. On the next cycle, conditions (a) and (b) are inapplicable because the final vowel is tense, and condition (e) will apply vacuously. Thus the Main Stress Rule as formulated above has no effect in this cycle. But we need a rule which will shift the stress to the left. This rule, which we formulate as (80), asserts that in a noun with primary stress on the last syllable, cases (i) and (ii) of the Main Stress Rule apply to the string preceding this final stressed syllable.

$$\left(80\right) \qquad V \;\rightarrow\; [1 \text{ stress}] \;\Big/\; \underline{\quad} \left\{ \begin{array}{ll} C_0 \begin{bmatrix} -\text{tense} \\ V \end{bmatrix} C_0^1 \begin{bmatrix} \alpha\text{voc} \\ \alpha\text{cons} \\ -\text{ant} \end{bmatrix} & \text{(i)} \\[3ex] C_0 & \text{(ii)} \end{array} \right.$$

$$\Big/ \;\underline{\quad}\, ([-\text{seg}])\, C_0 \overset{1}{V} C_0]_N \qquad\qquad \text{(c), (d)}$$

For reasons which will appear as we proceed, we stipulate that rule (80) constitutes conditions (c) and (d) of the Main Stress Rule; it applies after condition (b) and before condition (e). We will refine and extend this rule in several stages as we proceed. First, however, let us see how it applies to the examples given above and how it interrelates with the other parts of the Main Stress Rule.

Returning to the derivation of *survey* in (78), we see that the new rule (80) is applicable in the second cycle. (Neither condition (a) nor condition (b) of the Main Stress Rule applies.) Rule (80) specifies that we exclude from consideration the final string -rvA of [$_N$s$lrvA$]$_N$ and assign primary stress to the vowel that immediately precedes it by (80ii) (which is simply case (ii) of the Main Stress Rule), thus reducing the stress on the final syllable to secondary. The stress is then further reduced to tertiary by the Stress Adjustment Rule. This completes the derivation of *súrvey* given in (78). Notice that condition (e) must not be applied in the second cycle of this derivation or stress will again be shifted, incorrectly, to the final syllable. Hence the ordering of rule (80) and condition (e) of the Main Stress Rule must be disjunctive. An apparent alternative, at this point, would be to have condition (e) precede (80). We shall see directly that this is not possible, however.

Consider now the derivation of the noun *torment* in (78). Clearly this should be precisely parallel to the derivation of *survey*. In the first cycle primary stress is assigned to the final strong cluster under condition (e), case (ii), exactly as in the verb *survey*. In the second cycle, we expect the stress to be shifted left by rule (80), again as in the analogous case of *survey*. However, as we have formulated the Main Stress Rule, condition (b) is applicable since the vowel of the final syllable happens to be lax in this case. Clearly this is not a relevant distinction between *torment* and *survey*, and it indicates that the rules are in error.[50] Evidently we must prevent the application of condition (b) in this cycle. The simplest way to achieve this result is to require that under condition (b) (similarly, (a)) the vowel of the final syllable be not only lax but also nonstressed. This qualification admits all of the cases for which conditions (a) and (b) are appropriate and eliminates the unwanted applications.

With this modification of conditions (a) and (b), the derivation of *torment* proceeds in the second cycle in exact analogy to that of *survey*. In the very same way we also derive the noun *permit* from the underlying verb *permit*. Thus the contrasts *pérmìt–hérmĭt*, *tórmènt–tórrĕnt*, *súrvèy–scúrvy̆* are accounted for on the basis of the fact that the first member of each pair, but not the second, corresponds to a related verb.

Notice that the new rule (80) must precede condition (e), as we have assumed. If the order were reversed, a noun such as *machine*, which receives primary stress on the final syllable under condition (e), would have the stress shifted to the left under the subsequent rule (80), giving the incorrect form **machine*. Furthermore, we will see below that rule (80) must follow condition (a). Thus its position in the ordering is narrowly determined.

The examples of rule (80) given above all involved (80ii), that is, case (ii) of the Main Stress Rule. Case (i) is involved in the derivation of nouns such as *intercept* and *interlock* from the underlying verbs *intercept*, *interlock*. In the case of *interlock*, for example, we have the underlying representation (81):

$$\left(81\right) \qquad\qquad [_N \, [_V \text{iNter} = \text{lɔk}]_V \,]_N$$

In the first cycle case (ii) of the Main Stress Rule assigns final stress under condition (e) (case (i) being blocked by the = boundary, which also blocks an unwanted application of the Alternating Stress Rule). In the second cycle rule (80) is applicable and the string = *lóck* is omitted from consideration. Case (i) then assigns stress to the first syllable, giving finally the noun *interlóck* after application of the Stress Adjustment Rule.

12. *Revised version of the Main Stress Rule*

Let us now consider how the Stressed Syllable Rule (80) can be introduced into the Main Stress Rule. Cases (i) and (ii) of rule (80) are identical to cases (i) and (ii) of the Main Stress Rule, so amalgamation causes no difficulty in this respect. We must, however, find a way to incorporate the outermost condition in (80) in such a way as to meet the following requirements: the condition (80) follows condition (a) and precedes condition (e); the ordering (80), (e) is disjunctive. It will be recalled that in the Main Stress Rule, as it now stands, the ordering (a), (b), (e) is disjunctive. This fact was made explicit in the formulation (53), which is the optimal representation for the conditions (a), (b), and (e).

---

[50] In fact, as we shall see, the Stressed Syllable Rule (80) applies when the stress on the syllable in the outermost context has [2 stress] as well as [1 stress]. When the rule is extended in this way, the error in the rules which was just noted will lead to an incorrect stress assignment, since under condition (b) the representation $[_N \text{torment}]_N$ will be changed to $[_N \text{torment}]_N$, and by rule (80) it will then be changed to $[_N \text{torment}]_N$, becoming, finally, $[_N \text{torment}]_N$ by the Stress Adjustment Rule. This consequence could be avoided if the ordering of (b) and rule (80) were specified as disjunctive, but this is impossible, given the empirical hypotheses we have proposed, since condition (b) is not related to rule (80) in a way expressible by angles or parentheses.

Within our framework, the sequence (a), (b), (80), (e) can be generalized in one of several ways which are, for the present, quite equivalent. Looking ahead to later refinements, we choose one of these and give the rule in the following form:

$$
(82) \quad V \rightarrow [1\ \text{stress}] \ \Big/ \ [X \!-\!\!-\! C_0 \left(\begin{bmatrix} --\text{tense} \\ V \end{bmatrix} C_0^1 \begin{bmatrix} \alpha\text{voc} \\ \alpha\text{cons} \\ -\text{ant} \end{bmatrix}_0 \right)
$$

$$
\Big/ \!-\!\!- \left\langle \begin{cases} \langle +C_0 \rangle \begin{bmatrix} -\text{stress} \\ -\text{tense} \\ V \end{bmatrix} \\ \langle [-\text{seg}] \rangle C_0 \overset{1}{V} \end{cases} C_0 \right\rangle]_{\langle N \langle A \rangle \rangle}
$$

where X contains no internal occurrence of $\#$

Expanding (82), we have the following sequence of rules:

$$
(83) \quad V \rightarrow [1\ \text{stress}] \ \Big/ \ [X \!-\!\!-\! \begin{cases} C_0 \begin{bmatrix} -\text{tense} \\ V \end{bmatrix} C_0^1 \begin{bmatrix} \alpha\text{voc} \\ \alpha\text{cons} \\ -\text{ant} \end{bmatrix}_0 \quad \text{(i)} \\ C_0 \qquad\qquad\qquad\qquad \text{(ii)} \end{cases}
$$

$$
\Big/ \!-\!\!- \begin{cases} +C_0 \begin{bmatrix} --\text{stress} \\ --\text{tense} \\ V \end{bmatrix} C_0]_{\textbf{NA}} & \text{(a)} \\[4pt] \begin{bmatrix} -\text{stress} \\ -\text{tense} \\ V \end{bmatrix} C_0]_{\textbf{N}} & \text{(b)} \\[4pt] [-\text{seg}] C_0 \overset{1}{V} C_0]_{\textbf{NA}} & \text{(c)} \\[4pt] C_0 \overset{1}{V} C_0]_{\textbf{N}} & \text{(d)} \\[4pt]] & \text{(e)} \end{cases}
$$

where X contains no internal occurrence of $\#$

The sequence (83) is uniquely determined by (82). By our general conventions, it follows that in (83) cases (i) and (ii) are disjunctively ordered and apply under conditions (a)–(e), taken in that order. Among the conditions (a) through (e), the permitted sequences within a single cycle are: (a), (c); (a), (d); (b), (c); (b), (d). Apart from these possibilities of successive application, the ordering is fully disjunctive. Conditions (a), (b), and (e) are exactly as described in our earlier formulation of the Main Stress Rule (50), (53). Conditions (c) and (d) are the two cases of the Stressed Syllable Rule (80), with and without the unit [−segment], the rule being extended automatically to adjectives in the case where the boundary is present. As we shall see directly, this extension is necessary. Notice that it was condition (c) that was applied in the derivation of the noun *pérmìt*, and condition (d) in the derivation of the nouns *súrvèy* and *tórmènt*, where no internal boundary is present.

Summarizing, we have found evidence that the grammar contains the sequence of rules (83ai), (83aii), (83bi), (83bii), (83ci), (83cii), (83di), (83dii), (83ei), (83eii). Earlier we proposed an empirical hypothesis of a very general nature regarding disjunctive ordering. The hypothesis asserts that when certain formal relations hold between two rules of a linearly ordered sequence of rules—namely, the relations expressed by the parenthesis and angled bracket notations, applied and reapplied consistently along with the other notational devices in the most complete manner possible—then these rules are disjunctively ordered with respect to each other. This empirical hypothesis implies that in the case of the sequence just listed, the relation of disjunctive ordering holds between each of (83xi) and (83$x$ii) (x = a, b, c, d, e); (83ax) and (83by), (83ax) and (83ey), (83bx) and (83ey), (83cx) and (83dy), (83cx) and (83ey), (83dx) and (83ey) (x, y = i or ii). Thus the hypothesis concerning disjunctive ordering has precisely the effects required here on empirical grounds.

13. Complex nouns and adjectives

Many nouns consist of prefixes such as *mono-*, *tele-*, *photo-*, *bio-*, followed by stems or nouns. Thus the prefix *mono-* combines with the stem *-graph* to give *monograph*, and with the noun *genesis* to give *monogenesis*. The noun *genesis*, as distinct from the *-graph* of *telegraph*, happens to be an independent word with a specific semantic content that is carried over to the complex form. On syntactic grounds it is not clear what, if any, categorial structure should be assigned to the prefix. We will tentatively accept the weakest assumption and assign no categorization to it at all. Thus *monograph* will be represented [$_N$*mono* [$_S$*graph*]$_S$]$_N$ and *monogenesis* will be represented [$_N$*mono* [$_N$ # *genesis* #]$_N$]$_N$. This underlying representation identifies *-graph* as a stem and *genesis* as a noun which is an independent word, and assigns *mono-* to no category at all.[51] This is the analysis that is most appropriate for the phonological rules; it is, furthermore, at least as well motivated on syntactic-lexical grounds as any other, as far as we can see, in that it assigns no categorization beyond what is independently motivated.

It is also a fact that prefixes can be formed fairly freely from other words (e.g., *politico-*, *parallelo-*) and in this case we will assign them to the syntactic category "prefix" instead of (rather than in addition to) the category to which the underlying form belongs in isolation. The word *parallelogram* will be represented [$_N$ [$_P$*para* [$_S$*lel*]$_S$ *o*]$_P$ [$_S$*gram*]$_S$]$_N$, indicating that it is a noun of the form prefix-stem, where the prefix in turn consists of a stem with an uncategorized prefix *para-*, the latter being on a par with *mono-*, *tele-*, and so on. This analysis, once again, seems to be reasonably well motivated on syntactic-lexical grounds and is appropriate for the phonology.

Consideration of complex nouns and adjectives of this sort sheds additional light on the detailed form of the Main Stress Rule. Consider first the following examples:

$\left(84\right)$

$\overset{1}{monograph}$	$\overset{1}{monogenesis}$
$\overset{1}{monotone}$	$\overset{1}{monomania}$
$\overset{1}{monolith}$	$\overset{1}{mononucleosis}$
$\overset{1}{monosyllable}$	$\overset{1}{monometalism}$

The examples in the left-hand column of (84) have initial primary stress. Those in the right-hand column have primary stress on later syllables, as indicated.

We can account for most of these forms with our present rules. For example, the

---

[51] As Paul Postal has pointed out to us, the prefix might, in such cases, be regarded as a lexical feature of the stem or noun, syntactically on a par with other inherent features of a lexical entry.

items heading the two columns in (84) will have the following derivations:

$$\left(85\right)$$

	$[_N mono\ [_S graph]_S\ ]_N$	$[_N mono\ [_N \#\,genes + is\,\#\,]_N\ ]_N$	
		1	RULE (83ai)
			RULE (83eii)
	1		RULE (83ci)
1	2		
1	3		RULE (63)

In the first cycle, primary stress is assigned in the usual way. In the second cycle, condition (c) holds of *monográph*, which has a final stressed syllable, but not of *monogénesis*, which does not have a final stressed syllable. (The condition on *X* in (83) blocks (ai) in the second cycle of *monogenesis*.) In *monograph* the string *-graph* is omitted from consideration. Since the final vowel of the prefix is lax /ə/ phonologically (for reasons we shall discuss subsequently), case (i) then applies to the prefix. Thus the primary stress is shifted to the left under condition (c) in *monograph*, but not in *monogenesis*. The Stress Adjustment Rule (63) then gives the desired form. Except for *monosyllable*, the other examples of (84) are properly handled in exactly the same way.[52]

Putting aside the problem of *monosyllable* for the moment, we see that a great many words fall into the class illustrated in (84), such as the following:

$$\left(86\right)$$

télephòne	tèlemechánics
arístocràt	elèctrophorésis
áutogràph	àutohypnósis
áquaplàne	àquamaríne
bíoscòpe	bìophýsics
dodécagòn	dodècahédron
éndomòrph	èndothélium
thérmocòuple	thèrmodynámics
pàrallélogràm	pàrallèlepíped

To illustrate with a slightly more complex case than (85), consider the derivation of the final items in the two columns of (86), beginning with *parallelogram*:

$$\left(87\right)$$

	$[_N\ [_P pæræ\ [_S lel]_S\ ə]_P\ [_S græm]_S\ ]_N$		
	1	1	RULE (83eii)
	1	2	RULE (83ci)
	1	3	RULE (63)

In the first cycle the monosyllabic internal elements receive primary stress in the usual way. Innermost brackets are erased, and we turn to the next largest phrase, the prefix *parallelo-*. Conditions (a)–(d) have so far been limited to nouns and adjectives, so they are not applicable. Under condition (e), case (i), primary stress is reassigned to the syllable *-lel-*.[53] The second cycle is therefore vacuous. Erasing innermost brackets, we proceed to the full form *parallelogram* on the third cycle. Conditions (a) and (b) are ruled out because the final

---

[52] We have not yet given the rule that puts various secondary (ultimately, tertiary) stresses in the items of the right-hand column of (84) (and in certain of the forms of (86), which follows). These omissions will be taken care of subsequently.

[53] We will see later that the vacuous application of the Main Stress Rule actually falls under (aii) rather than (ei).

syllable is stressed. We therefore turn to condition (c). This case of the Stressed Syllable Rule applies, excluding the primary-stressed syllable -*gram* from consideration. Primary stress is then placed on the penultimate syllable -*lel*- of the residue *parallelo*- by case (i) of the Main Stress Rule, the final cluster of the residue being weak.[54] This weakens the stress on -*gram* to secondary. Conditions (d) and (e) do not apply because of the disjunctive ordering. We terminate this cycle with the Stress Adjustment Rule (63), giving the final form *parallelogram* (after we have presented the rule assigning secondary, ultimately tertiary, stress on the first syllable—see note 52).

The derivation of *parallelepiped* is similar, but it suggests a slight modification of the rules. (We assume that phonologically the prefix *parallelo*- appears also in *parallelepiped* in spite of the obvious violation of the true etymology of the word.)

$$\left(88\right) \qquad [_N\,[_P\text{pær}æ\,[_S\text{lel}]_S\,ɔ]_P\,[_S\text{pIped}]_S\,]_N$$

		1	RULE (83bii)
1			RULE (83eii)
2		1	RULE (83bii)
3		1	RULE (63)

The top line of (88) is the underlying representation. In the first cycle we assign primary stress to the monosyllable -*lel*- as before, by rule (83eii); but we must also assign primary stress to the first syllable of -*pIped*. This effect is achieved by rule (83ei). However, if we were to extend condition (b) to stems, it would be achieved by (83bii). Without any very compelling reason (relevant forms being few), we will assume that condition (b) is the appropriate rule and will extend it to stems. This completes the first cycle. As in the case of (87), the second cycle (applying to *parallele*-) is vacuous, and we proceed to the third cycle and the noun *parallelepiped*. Condition (b) applies since the string in question is a noun with an unstressed lax vowel in the final syllable. Exactly as in the first cycle, primary stress is then placed on the strong cluster preceding the syllable excluded from consideration in accordance with condition (b). The effect at this stage of the derivation is to weaken the stress on the first of the two primary-stressed syllables (namely, the syllable -*lel*-) to secondary. The Stress Adjustment Rule then weakens this to tertiary, giving the final line of the derivation (88). Other rules, to which we will turn later, give the desired phonetic representation.

Notice that the Stressed Syllable Rule does not apply in the derivation (88), as it does at the comparable stage in the derivation (87), by virtue of the fact that the stressed syllable is not final. Thus the difference in stress contour between *parallélogram* and *parallelepíped*, as in the case of *mónograph* and *monogénesis*, is determined by the position of primary stress in the underlying final element of the compound.

There is another possible interpretation of forms such as *parallelepiped* that should be mentioned here. We have observed that case (ii) of the Main Stress Rule can, in a certain sense, be regarded as a special case of the Nuclear Stress Rule (see p. 91). Both rules assign primary stress to the rightmost sonority peak of the string under consideration. If these two rules are amalgamated, then one might reformulate the Main Stress Rule so that condition (b) becomes inapplicable in the final cycle of the derivation (88), primary stress now being

---

[54] For reasons that will appear below (p. 104), it is really case (ii) rather than case (i) that applies under condition (c), the affix -*o* being assigned to the string excluded from consideration under this condition.

placed on the rightmost of the two sonority peaks by the Nuclear Stress Rule, appropriately revised. This would require the imposition of several conditions on the Main Stress Rule. We have no evidence to suggest either that such a restatement of the rules is necessary or that it is ruled out conclusively. The extra conditions that must be added seem to us to rule against such an attempted generalization, but the possibility of this analysis should be kept in mind.

Notice that *párallèl*, in isolation, is assigned a stress contour as in the left-hand column of (86). Hence condition (c) must clearly be extended to adjectives, as indicated in (83), though examples are rather sparse. (Other relevant forms are those with *-dox*, e.g., *órthodòx*.)

Complex nouns and adjectives necessitate other slight modifications in the Main Stress Rule. Consider, for example, the word *polìtico-económic*. The first element, *politico*, is a prefix, and it must receive a primary stress on its antepenultimate syllable in the first cycle, where this form is considered in isolation. Within our framework, this stress can be assigned only by condition (a) or condition (b), which must therefore be extended to cover prefixes as well as nouns and stems. Thus conditions (a) and (b), in their abbreviated form (see (82)), will be as follows:

$$
\left(89\right) \qquad \langle +C_0 \rangle \begin{bmatrix} -\text{stress} \\ -\text{tense} \\ V \end{bmatrix} C_0]_{\text{NSP}\langle A \rangle} \qquad \left\{ \begin{matrix} \langle (a) \rangle \\ (b) \end{matrix} \right\}
$$

However, this quite natural extension of the Main Stress Rule leads to a difficulty in the derivations (87) and (88). In these derivations the second cycle, applying to $[_\text{P}\text{pæræ}+\text{lel}+\text{ə}]_\text{P}$, was vacuous; but, with the extension to (89), condition (a) now holds of this form, and case (i) places primary stress in the syllable preceding the weak cluster *-lel-*. With condition (a) modified as indicated in note 54, the derivation will now result in the incorrect forms *parallèlogràm*, *parallèlepìped* as the final phonetic representations. To prevent this, we clearly must restrict the notion "weak cluster" so as to exclude syllables which have primary stress, as does *-lel-* in these cases. Thus, we must adjust the feature composition of the nontense vowel specified in case (i) of the Main Stress Rule so as to guarantee that it have a stress weaker than primary.

One possibility would be to add the feature [−stress] to the specification of this vowel, just as we added the feature [−stress] to lax vowels specified in conditions (a) and (b) of the Main Stress Rule. This is incorrect, however, as we can see by considering words such as *telegraphy*. This is derived from *telegraph*, and must therefore have the underlying representation (90):

$$
\left(90\right) \qquad [_\text{N} [_\text{N}\text{tele} [_\text{S}\text{græf}]_\text{S}]_\text{N} y]_\text{N}
$$

In the first cycle the stem *-graph* receives primary stress on its sonority peak. In the second cycle condition (c) applies, shifting stress to the left and giving $[_\text{N}\text{télè}+\text{græf}+y]_\text{N}$ as we enter the third cycle. But in this cycle we must apply case (i) of the Main Stress Rule, assigning primary stress to the syllable immediately preceding the weak cluster *-graph*.[55] However, if the lax vowel specified in case (i) of the Main Stress Rule must have the feature [−stress], as just suggested, case (i) will not apply to *télègraph+y*, and case (ii) will apply

---

[55] Clearly this application of case (i) must fall under condition (a). That is, we exclude from consideration the final unit *-y* of the noun *telegraphy* and then assign primary stress by case (i). We return to a discussion of the affix *-y* in Section 15.

to give the incorrect phonetic form *$\overset{3}{\text{tele}}\overset{1}{\text{graphy}}$. Clearly, then, we must require not that the lax vowel of the weak cluster of case (i) have the feature [− stress], but rather that it have a stress less than primary. Then case (ai) will apply, correctly, to $\overset{1}{\text{telegraph}}$ in $\text{telegraph}+\overset{2}{y}$, but it will not apply to $\overset{1}{\text{parallel}}$ in $\text{parallel}+o$.

In summary, we must define a weak cluster as one containing a lax vowel with less than primary stress followed by no more than a single consonant followed by an optional *r*, *w*, or *y*.

A minor modification of condition (c) is dictated by consideration of examples such as $\overset{1}{\text{pra}}\overset{3}{\text{xinoscope}}$, $\overset{1}{\text{si}}\overset{3}{\text{deroscope}}$, $\overset{1}{\text{ste}}\overset{3}{\text{reoscope}}$, $\overset{1}{\text{he}}\overset{3}{\text{lioscope}}$, $\overset{1}{\text{pla}}\overset{3}{\text{tinotype}}$, $\overset{1}{\text{he}}\overset{3}{\text{licograph}}$, $\overset{1}{\text{mi}}\overset{3}{\text{meograph}}$, $\overset{1}{\text{car}}\overset{3}{\text{diograph}}$, $\overset{1}{\text{hie}}\overset{3}{\text{roglyph}}$, $\overset{1}{\text{he}}\overset{3}{\text{teronym}}$. In all of these items the first element is of the form $C_0 \overset{1}{V} C_0 V^* C_0 o$, where the cluster $V^* C_0$ is weak in its underlying form and the stress on the first member of the compound is antepenultimate rather than penultimate, as required by our rule. Notice that if the cluster $V^* C_0$ is strong, the stress is penultimate, on V^*, as expected. Thus we have $\overset{1}{\text{kalei}}\overset{3}{\text{doscope}}$, $\overset{1}{\text{laryn}}\overset{3}{\text{goscope}}$, $\overset{1}{\text{ophthal}}\overset{3}{\text{moscope}}$, $\overset{1}{\text{elec}}\overset{3}{\text{troscope}}$, etc. Apparently the final *-o* of the first element of the complex form is acting as part of the context for cases (i) and (ii) of the rule, that is, as part of the string to be omitted from consideration in the application of cases (i) and (ii). Hence an optional *-o* (that is, /ə/, in the underlying representation) must be added to the statement of condition (c). We can therefore reformulate condition (c) as (91) and, correspondingly, abbreviate conditions (c) and (d) as (92):

$$\left(91\right) \qquad\qquad (+\text{ə})\,[-\text{seg}]\,C_0 \overset{1}{V} C_0]_{\mathbf{NA}} \qquad\qquad \text{(c)}$$

$$\left(92\right) \qquad\qquad \langle (+\text{ə})\,[-\text{seg}]\rangle\,C_0 \overset{1}{V} C_0]_{\mathbf{N}\langle\mathbf{A}\rangle} \qquad \left\{\begin{matrix} \langle(\text{c})\rangle \\ (\text{d}) \end{matrix}\right\}$$

Thus, if *helicograph*, for example, is represented after the first cycle in the form $[_{\mathbf{N}}\text{helic}+\text{ə}+\overset{1}{\text{græf}}]_{\mathbf{N}}$, then condition (c) will hold in the second cycle, excluding from consideration the sequence $[+\text{ə}+\overset{1}{\text{græf}}]$, which is of the required form $+\text{ə}\,[-\text{seg}]\,C_0 \overset{1}{V} C_0$. Case (i) of the Main Stress Rule will now apply to the remaining sequence *helic-*, assigning primary stress to the first vowel.

We therefore reformulate the Main Stress Rule, replacing conditions (a), (b), (c), and (d) with (89) and (92).[56]

---

[56] In discussing disjunctive ordering we stipulated that the ordering by the use of parentheses is always disjunctive and that the rule that contains the parenthesized element always *precedes* the rule that omits this element. Thus the sequences enumerated by (92) are, in order, the following: (I) $+\text{ə}\,[-\text{seg}]\,C_0 \overset{1}{V} C_0$; (II) $[-\text{seg}]\,C_0 \overset{1}{V} C_0$; (III) $C_0 \overset{1}{V} C_0$. Applying the Main Stress Rule to a hypothetical form *helic+o+scope*, on the second cycle we would find that condition (c) is applicable under interpretation (I), excluding from consideration the sequence $[+\text{ə}+\overset{1}{\text{skOp}}]$. Hence primary stress would be placed by case (i) on the first syllable, giving, ultimately, $\overset{1}{\text{helic}}\overset{3}{\text{oscOp}}$. Similarly, given *tele+scope*, in the second cycle we apply (II), excluding from consideration the sequence $[+\overset{1}{\text{skOp}}]$ and assigning primary stress to *tel-*.

Notice that there are some complex nouns with initial elements ending in *-o* which do not follow this rule. Thus, in $\overset{1}{\text{galva}}\overset{3}{\text{noscope}}$, $\overset{1}{\text{chroma}}\overset{3}{\text{toscope}}$, $\overset{1}{\text{daguer}}\overset{3}{\text{reotype}}$ ([dəgerətIp]), $\overset{1}{\text{hya}}\overset{3}{\text{lograph}}$, $\overset{1}{\text{cinema}}\overset{3}{\text{tograph}}$, etc., in order that primary stress be properly placed by case (i) of the rule, the *-o* must be regarded not as part of the context but as part of the string considered after the context of condition (c) is excluded. We can account for this simply by omitting the + boundary before *-o* in such cases. Thus *galvánoscope* will be represented $[\text{gælvæno}+\text{skOp}]$ when it enters the second cycle, and primary stress will be properly

We must now return to the problem of the stress pattern of *monosýllable*, which we had put aside temporarily above. According to our rules, as so far established, the primary stress of this word should be on *syl-* rather than *mon-*. Thus, at the beginning of the second cycle we have the representation [$_N$mono $\#$ silæbl]$_N$. Since this form does not have a final stressed syllable, it is not subject to condition (c); it should, therefore, fall into the same stress class as *monogénesis* and *parallelepíped*. There are other similar examples, e.g., *métalanguage*, *ántibody*, *métaphysics* (in one pronunciation), *páralanguage*. Apparently, under certain circumstances condition (c) applies even though there is an extra nonstressed syllable on the extreme right. The circumstances are easy to detect. Recall that the complex forms that have been occupying us in this section consist of a prefix followed by an item which is either a stem or an independent noun. In each case in which the extra nonstressed syllable on the right is disregarded, the element filling the second position in the complex form is a noun rather than a stem, and it is this fact that permits condition (c) to be relaxed to allow this extra nonstressed syllable. Where we have an independent noun as the second element of a complex form, we naturally expect it to carry with it a $\#$ boundary. Using the angle notation, we can express the fact that the extra permitted syllable on the right is conditional on the presence of the $\#$ boundary, this being automatically associated with the incorporated lexical item in representations such as *mono $\#$ syllable*, *meta $\#$ language*. Thus we replace (91) by (93), as a more fully adequate version of condition (c):[57]

$$\left(93\right) \qquad (+\mathrm{ə}) \begin{bmatrix} -\mathrm{seg} \\ \langle -\mathrm{FB}\rangle \end{bmatrix} C_0 \overset{1}{V} C_0 \langle V_0 C_0 \rangle]_{NA}$$

Following our conventions for the use of parentheses and angles, we can list the sequence of rules abbreviated by (93) as (94):

$$\left(94\right)$$

$$(I) \quad +\mathrm{ə} \begin{bmatrix} -\mathrm{seg} \\ -\mathrm{FB} \end{bmatrix} C_0 \overset{1}{V} C_0 V_0 C_0]_{NA}$$

$$(II) \quad +\mathrm{ə} \, [-\mathrm{seg}] \, C_0 \overset{1}{V} C_0]_{NA}$$

$$(III) \quad \begin{bmatrix} -\mathrm{seg} \\ -\mathrm{FB} \end{bmatrix} C_0 \overset{1}{V} C_0 V_0 C_0]_{NA}$$

$$(IV) \quad [-\mathrm{seg}] \, C_0 \overset{1}{V} C_0]_{NA}$$

Each of the above, of course, stands for a sequence of rules, one for each choice of allowed

---

placed under condition (cII) of the preceding paragraph (which omits from consideration the sequence [+skŌp] in this case) by case (i) of the Main Stress Rule.

Certain forms that seem to fall in the latter class actually may have $+o$, even though primary stress falls on a phonetically weak cluster. Thus, in *oscílloscòpe*, for example, the vowel with primary stress is phonetically lax but can be regarded as tense in the underlying representation, as we shall see in the next chapter; therefore the final -*o* of the prefix can be separated by a $+$ boundary. Another possibility would be to assume a double *l* in the underlying form (see p. 148).

[57] The examples we have given so far leave open the question of whether the feature within angles in this rule should be [+WB] or, more generally, [−FB] (which includes [+WB]). We shall see later (p. 159) that the choice of [−FB] is correct.

Conventions to be discussed below (note 78) will require minor formal modifications in the statement of the rules abbreviated by (93) (see (94)) but will not affect their empirical content.

consonant and vowel string.[58] The sequence (94) is, by convention, pairwise disjunctively ordered. Case (94II) applies to examples such as $helic+o+\overset{1}{graph}$, giving $\overset{1}{heli}co\overset{3}{graph}$. Case (94III) gives $\overset{1}{mono}\overset{3}{tone}$ from $\overset{1}{mono}\#t\overset{3}{On}$, $\overset{1}{mono}\overset{1}{syllable}$ from $\overset{1}{mono}\#\overset{3}{syllable}$, $\overset{1}{meta}\overset{1}{language}$ from $\overset{1}{meta}\#\overset{3}{language}$, as well as the nouns $\overset{1}{inter}\overset{3}{cept}$ from $\overset{1}{inter}=\overset{1}{cept}$, $\overset{1}{per}\overset{3}{mit}$ from $\overset{1}{per}=\overset{1}{mit}$, and $\overset{1}{com}\overset{3}{bat}$ from $\overset{1}{coN}=\overset{1}{bat}$. Case (IV) accounts for $\overset{1}{tele}\overset{3}{scope}$ from $\overset{1}{tele}+sk\overset{1}{Op}$ and $\overset{1}{galvano}\overset{3}{scope}$ from $\overset{1}{galvano}+sk\overset{1}{Op}$. Case (I) would, for example, account for words such as $\overset{1}{ornitho}\overset{3}{fauna}$ from $\overset{1}{ornith}+o\#\overset{1}{fauna}$.

In short, where the second element of a complex noun is itself a noun, stress is shifted to the left under condition (c) even if this incorporated noun is bisyllabic with initial stress.[59] We state this fact, in (93), by permitting an optional extra syllable in the second member of the complex form if this form is preceded by a boundary other than formative boundary, that is, if it is an independent noun instead of simply a stem.

We note, however, that there are many complex nouns with a bisyllabic second element which are not subject to condition (c) even though their second element exists as an independent word, e.g., $\overset{1}{biophysics}$, $\overset{1}{monoacid}$. In such a case we must drop the internal # boundary or primary stress will shift to the prefix. But there is no syntactic justification for dropping the boundary; it must be done ad hoc, simply to accommodate the phonetic facts. Such individual characteristics of particular formatives must be listed in the lexicon. They illustrate the marginally distinctive character of position of main stress placement in English.

Notice also that there are optional variants such as *meta(#)soma* or *meta(#)physics*, with initial or penultimate primary stress, depending on how the word is analyzed—that is, with or without the boundary, respectively. Here too the option is an idiosyncratic lexical matter.

The sharpening of the rules represented by (93) makes it necessary to extend slightly the system of notations that we have been presupposing. This becomes clear when we replace (91) by the revised form (93) in the more general frame (92). This replacement yields (95):

$$\left(95\right) \qquad \langle_1(+\partial)\left[\begin{matrix}-\text{seg}\\ \langle_2-\text{FB}\rangle_2\end{matrix}\right]\rangle_1 C_0\overset{1}{V}C_0\langle_2 V_0C_0\rangle_2]_{N\langle_1\mathbf{A}\rangle_1}$$

---

[58] We have not actually established a convention for the ordering of these subrules (see Chapter Eight). Furthermore, we have not given a convention to establish an ordering between (II) and (III) of (94). The ordering of (94) presupposes that parentheses are expanded before angles but we have no evidence for this arbitrary decision.

[59] Notice that *syllable* is phonologically bisyllabic, becoming phonetically trisyllabic by rule (56), so that *mono≠syllable* is subject to condition (c).

Notice also that in forms such as $\overset{1}{resell}$, $\overset{1}{mismanage}$, $\overset{1}{overprice}$, $\overset{1}{anti\text{-}tax}$, $\overset{1}{unwise}$, $\overset{1}{ultramodern}$, which consist of a prefix that is syntactically and semantically functional, combined with a full lexical form, the incorporated lexical form must not undergo a separate application of the cycle. The extra cycle would cause a shift of stress to the left under condition (c) (that is, by (94III)). When there is an extra cycle (as in the nouns $\overset{1}{mis}\overset{3}{match}$, $\overset{1}{re}\overset{3}{sale}$), a shift to the left is precisely what we find. If we want to adopt representations with assignment of *sell*, *tax*, *wise*, etc., to their categories, we must limit condition (c) to nouns. Although this is not totally ruled out as a possibility (as we have noted, condition (c) is rather marginal for adjectives), it leads to some difficulties and does not seem highly motivated.

This matter is one that cannot be settled within the framework of the phonology in isolation. What is at issue is the problem of how fairly productive prefixes are to be described within the syntactic component of the grammar (including, in particular, its lexical subcomponent). There is little known about this question today, and therefore any decision that can be made within the phonology is necessarily quite tentative. It is not at all clear how this matter can be accommodated within our framework.

In the formulation (95), we have indexed angles in such a way as to show how they are paired. If the indices are dropped, (95) will be expanded, incorrectly, as:

$$\left(96\right) \qquad \text{(I)} \quad (+\partial) \begin{bmatrix} -\text{seg} \\ \langle -\text{FB} \rangle \end{bmatrix} C_0 \overset{1}{V} C_0 V_0 C_0]_{NA}$$

$$\text{(II)} \quad C_0 \overset{1}{V} C_0]_N$$

In (96), (I) abbreviates two rules, both of which incorrectly omit [−FB] (see note 24). Clearly we must enrich our notational system to permit indices on angles, adding the convention that angles with the same indices are expanded together. Thus we must replace the notational convention for angled brackets (pp. 76–77) by the convention that (97) is an abbreviation for the two rules of (98), in that order, where $Y_1 \ldots Y_{n+1}$ contain no angles $\langle_j \rangle_j$ for $j \leq i$:

$$\left(97\right) \qquad Y_1 \langle_i X_1 \rangle_i Y_2 \langle_i X_2 \rangle_i \ldots Y_n \langle_i X_n \rangle_i Y_{n+1}$$

$$\left(98\right) \qquad \text{(a)} \quad Y_1 X_1 Y_2 X_2 \ldots Y_n X_n Y_{n+1}$$

$$\text{(b)} \quad Y_1 Y_2 \ldots Y_n Y_{n+1}$$

Considering the intuitive meaning of the angled bracket notation, this is a very natural extension. We have already used it as an expository device in the formulation (53) above. We will henceforth use indices explicitly where they are necessary for determining the correct order of expansion; we will continue to omit them, however, where they are superfluous.[60]

Returning now to the Stressed Syllable Rule, we see that we can extend it to account for another well-known fact, namely, that words such as *advocate*, *delegate*, *precipitate*, *regiment*, *compliment*, which can be nouns or verbs, characteristically differ in stress contour in their nominal and verbal functions. The verbs, in each case, have tertiary stress and a nonreduced vowel in the final syllable; the nouns have zero stress and a reduced vowel.[61] Thus we have verb-noun contrasts such as [ǽdvəkÀt]–[ǽdvəkət], [déləgÀt]–[déləgət], [réjəmènt]–[réjəmənt], [dákyəmènt]–[dákyəmənt].

These forms can be explained by deriving the noun in each case from an underlying verb[62] and by modifying the Stressed Syllable Rule so that it permits secondary as well as primary stress on the final syllable. We will now be able to derive the noun *delegate*, for example, in the following way:

$$\left(99\right)$$

$[_N [_V \text{deleg}+\text{At}]_V]_N$		
	1	RULE (83eii)
1	2	RULE (51), (75)
1	3	RULE (83ci)
1	4	RULE (63)

[60] In case $n = 1$ in (97), we expand it simply as the single rule $Y_1 Y_2$ (see note 24). This decision is crucial for the correct interpretation of (95).

As pointed out in note 24, it is important to show that a single set of notational devices underlies all descriptive grammar. In fact, the indexing of brackets has been utilized in earlier descriptive work in generative phonology, and such devices should be incorporated in a full and explicit account of linguistic theory. Specifications of a system of notational devices which require only slight modifications for our purposes have been presented in Chomsky (1951), (1955b); Postal (1962); Matthews (1964).

[61] At this level of phonetic detail, there is both stylistic and dialectal variation, particularly in the case of the forms with *-ment*. Here, as elsewhere, we adopt the phonetic representations of Kenyon and Knott, which agree with our own standard pronunciation. The derivation of nouns from such verbs is marginally productive, as is often the case in derivational systems of this sort.

[62] Notice that there are nouns of the form $C_0 V C_0 V C_0 At$ with tertiary stress on the final nonreduced vowel

In the first cycle, stress is placed on the final strong cluster of the underlying verb and then shifted two syllables to the left, in the usual way, by the Alternating Stress Rule (51), now modified as (75). Thus the verb in isolation would have the form [delegÅt], after the Stress Adjustment Rule (63). For the noun there is a second cycle, in which condition (c), modified in a way which we discuss directly, places primary stress by case (i), weakening all other stresses by one. The Stress Adjustment Rule next weakens the final vowel to stress 4, and Vowel Reduction is then automatic because of the weakened stress.

Application of condition (c) in the second cycle of the derivation (99) will be permitted if we modify the Stressed Syllable Rule (conditions (c) and (d) of the Main Stress Rule, in their latest formulation, rule (95)), replacing it by (100):

$$
(100) \qquad \langle_1 (+\partial) \left[\begin{array}{c} -\text{seg} \\ \langle_2 - FB \rangle_2 \end{array} \right] \rangle_1 C_0 \, [\beta\text{stress}] \, C_0 \, \langle_2 V_0 C_0 \rangle_2 \,]_{N \langle_1 A \rangle_1}
$$

$$
\beta = \begin{Bmatrix} 2 \\ 1 \end{Bmatrix}
$$

In formulating this rule, we must specify that the stressed syllable may have either secondary or primary stress and that the two cases must be taken *in this order.* Thus (100) abbreviates

---

A of *-At*; for example, *cáliphàte, bíllingsgàte, súrrogàte, cándidàte, mágistràte* (some of which have stylistic or dialectal variants with final reduced vowel, in which case we represent them lexically with a final lax instead of final tense vowel). This fact supports the analysis we are presenting, since none of the nouns with final *-Àt* are paired with verbs. Thus the nouns with underlying verbs have a reduced vowel in the final syllable; the nouns with nonreduced, tertiary-stressed vowel in the final syllable do not have associated verbs.

Adjectives paired with verbs (e.g., *animate, approximate, articulate*) also have reduced vowels with zero stress in the final syllable, in forms of the sort we are considering here. These can be accounted for by the same mechanism proposed for the nouns *advocate, regiment,* etc. On the other hand, in adjectives such as *delicate, desperate,* which have a final reduced vowel but no underlying verb, there is no reason not to assume an underlying lax vowel in the final syllable. Derived forms such as *desperation* may seem to contradict this assumption, but we will see in the next chapter that they in fact do not.

As we have formulated the Stressed Syllable Rule, only condition (c) applies to adjectives. Therefore the adjectives discussed in the preceding paragraph must have a + boundary before *-ate*. Alternatively, it may be that condition (d) should also be extended to adjectives, in which case the + boundary is unnecessary. As we have noted previously, there are very few relevant examples involving adjectives, and therefore we are uncertain as to the correct decision. Neither alternative seems to us to pose any particular difficulty, and we will not go into the matter any further here.

Notice that where adjectives and nouns are paired with verbs, there are, very commonly, some syntactic reasons for regarding the noun phrase in which the noun appears as a transform of the verb phrase in which the corresponding verb appears, so that the noun is derived from the verb on syntactic grounds. In the same connection, note that phrases such as . . . *is (all, fully) dressed,* . . . *is furnished,* . . . *is sanded,* . . . *is closed,* . . . *is broken* cannot strictly be regarded as passives (and, in fact, contrast with passives). The syntactic analysis of these constructions is, at present, not clear. They are similar to passives at least in the grammatical relation between the grammatical subject and the underlying verb. It may be that they are in some way derived from passives or derived from underlying actives in a manner analogous to the transformational derivation of passives. If so, it may also be the case that the relation of . . . *is elaborate* to . . . *is elaborated,* etc., parallels this relation, in which case the adjective *elaborate* will in fact derive from the verb on syntactic grounds, as required by the phonological rules. There are many open syntactic questions here that make a more complete formulation of the phonological rules impossible. These considerations illustrate quite nicely the dependence of phonological rules on assumptions about syntactic structure. (See also note 64.)

There are certain other nouns which have variants with final [At] instead of final [ət], as they should if derived from verbs (e.g., *precipitate, concentrate*). Perhaps, in this case, these words are to be analyzed as containing the suffix *-ate* of *phosphate, manganate,* rather than as derived from the corresponding verb. For discussion of tense affixes, see Section 16.

two rules in this respect, the first of which has $\beta = 2$ and the second $\beta = 1$. If the ordering were inverted, both cases of the rule would apply in a form like *telegraph*. In the second cycle of the derivation, rule (100) would apply to *tele+graph* with $\beta = 1$, giving *tele+graph*, and it would then reapply with $\beta = 2$, giving *tele+graph*, which would become, finally, *[teləgrəf] by the Stress Adjustment and Vowel Reduction Rules, instead of the required [teləgræf].

In discussing the Compound Rule in Section 9, we observed that in compounds such as *elevator boy, chemistry teacher*, it is customary to represent the second element with tertiary stress, rather than with the secondary stress that is retained in the second element of *elevator operator, chemistry laboratory*. The conditions under which this further weakening from secondary to tertiary is generally marked seem very much like the conditions under which the Stressed Syllable Rule applies. That is, when the second member of the compound is a monosyllable, with an optionally present extra syllable and perhaps some other slight modifications, primary stress is reassigned in the first element of the compound. This observation suggests that we seek a generalization that covers both the case of assignment of primary stress to the prefix in *mono # tOn* and *mono # syllable* and the case of reassignment of primary stress to the first element of *elevator # # boy, chemistry # # teacher*. Clearly all that is necessary is that (100) be modified to permit two successive boundaries where it is specified that a boundary may occur, and that a general convention be stated requiring that above the word level primary stress can be placed only on sonority peaks. We have observed several times that condition (e) of the Main Stress Rule can perhaps be amalgamated with the Nuclear Stress Rule, if a convention of this sort is established. With such modifications as these, we can explain the weakening of stress that is often noted in certain compounds. However, because of the marginal character of this problem and the dubious factual status of the observations in question, we will not develop this extension of the rules in any further detail.

With the various modifications that we have seen to be necessary, the Main Stress Rule (82) now takes the following form:

$$\left(101\right) \quad \text{MAIN STRESS RULE}$$

$$V \rightarrow [1\ \text{stress}] \quad \Big/ \quad [X\text{———}C_0\left(\begin{bmatrix} -\text{tense} \\ \gamma\text{stress} \\ V \end{bmatrix} C_0^1 \begin{bmatrix} \alpha\text{voc} \\ \alpha\text{cons} \\ -\text{ant} \end{bmatrix}_0 \right)$$

$$\Big/ \text{———} \left\langle \begin{cases} \langle_1 + C_0 \rangle_1 \begin{bmatrix} -\text{stress} \\ -\text{tense} \\ V \end{bmatrix} C_0 \\ (+\partial)\langle_1 \begin{bmatrix} -\text{seg} \\ \langle_2 -\text{FB}\rangle_2 \end{bmatrix} \rangle_1 C_0 [\beta\text{stress}] C_0 \langle_2 V_0 C_0 \rangle_2 \end{cases} \right\rangle]_{\langle \text{NSP} \langle_1 \text{VA} \rangle_1 \rangle}$$

where X contains no internal # boundary, $\gamma = 2$ or weaker, $\beta = \begin{Bmatrix} 2 \\ 1 \end{Bmatrix}$

Expanding the schema (101), we have the sequence of rules given in (102) (next page). The ordering conditions, once again, are the following: cases (i) and (ii) apply disjunctively, in that order, under the conditions (a)–(e); either (c) or (d) may follow either (a) or (b) within a single cycle; otherwise, the ordering is fully disjunctive.

We have slightly modified cases (c) and (d), shifting the position of the first occurrence of $\langle_1$ (compare (95) and (100)) for minor reasons that will be presented later.

$$
\left(102\right) \quad \text{V} \rightarrow [1 \text{ stress}] \Bigg/ \left[X \text{——} \begin{cases} C_0 \begin{bmatrix} -\text{tense} \\ \gamma\text{stress} \\ V \end{bmatrix} C_0^1 \begin{bmatrix} \alpha\text{voc} \\ \alpha\text{cons} \\ -\text{ant} \end{bmatrix}_0 & \text{(i)} \\[2em] C_0 & \text{(ii)} \end{cases} \right.
$$

$$
\Bigg/ \text{——} \begin{cases} +C_0 \begin{bmatrix} -\text{stress} \\ -\text{tense} \\ V \end{bmatrix} C_0]_{\textbf{NSPVA}} & \text{(a)} \\[1.5em] \begin{bmatrix} -\text{stress} \\ -\text{tense} \\ V \end{bmatrix} C_0]_{\textbf{NSP}} & \text{(b)} \\[1.5em] (+\mathrm{\partial}) \begin{bmatrix} -\text{seg} \\ \langle -\text{FB} \rangle \end{bmatrix} C_0 [\beta\text{stress}] C_0 \langle V_0 C_0 \rangle]_{\textbf{NSPVA}} & \text{(c)} \\[1.5em] (+\mathrm{\partial}) C_0 [\beta\text{stress}] C_0]_{\textbf{NSP}} & \text{(d)} \\[1em]] & \text{(e)} \end{cases}
$$

where X contains no internal $\#$ boundary, $\gamma = 2$ or weaker, $\beta = \begin{Bmatrix} 2 \\ 1 \end{Bmatrix}$

We have extended cases (a) and (c) to verbs for reasons that will appear in Sections 15 and 16. Actually, the only examples we have of verbs involve condition (c), but there is no harm in accepting the simplest solution, which extends condition (a) to verbs as well.

14. Vowel reduction

We have referred several times to the well-known fact that lax vowels reduce to a central, high, or mid unrounded "neutral" vowel in English when they are sufficiently weakly stressed, in some way that must be made explicit. We have been representing this neutral vowel as [ə]. The exact phonetic realization of [ə] does not concern us. For any particular dialect, the feature specifications and the appropriate phonetic rules can be established. For ease of exposition, we will simply make the assumption here that [ə] is distinguished from all other vocalic segments.

It is an open question to what extent vowel reduction is a matter of phonological rule. The distinction between a theory of competence (a grammar) and a performance model, which is crucial throughout, is particularly relevant in the discussion of vowel reduction.[63] In actual speech, the reduction of vowels is determined not only by the functioning of the underlying grammatical rules, but also by a variety of other factors (speed, casualness, frequency of use of the item, predictability in a particular context, etc.) These factors interact in complex and not very well-understood ways to determine the extent and place of vowel reduction, and they result, as well, in many other modifications of underlying grammatically determined forms (slurring, consonant elision, etc.) The grammar itself, here as always, generates only an idealized representation. A theory of performance will necessarily incorporate the grammar, but will also attempt to study the many other factors that determine the actual physical signal. Any investigation of grammar is, then, a contribution to the study of performance, but it does not exhaust this study.

[63] For discussion of the competence-performance distinction, see Chapter One, page 3, and Chomsky (1964, 1965), as well as many other references.

It must, incidentally, be borne in mind that the specific competence-performance delimitation provided by a grammar represents a hypothesis that might prove to be in error when other factors that play a role in performance and the interrelation of these various factors come under investigation. Although this is not usually a serious problem in grammatical study, it does become a real issue when we turn to low-level phonetic processes such as those we are now investigating. Since other aspects of performance have not been systematically studied, our attempt to delimit the boundary of underlying competence by providing specific rules for vowel reduction must be taken as quite tentative. When a theory of performance ultimately emerges, we may find that some of the facts we are attempting to explain do not really belong to grammar but instead fall under the theory of performance, and that certain facts that we neglect, believing them to be features of performance, should really have been incorporated in the system of grammatical rules.

In particular, we should like to point out that the distinction we draw between competence and performance is not invariably the same as that drawn implicitly by Kenyon and Knott in their choice of phonetic representation. That is, the output of our rules does not always agree with their phonetic notation with respect to the marking of reduced vowels, although it does agree for the mass of cases (in particular, for the examples that we cite here). In part the differences are systematic (for example, we mark reduced vowels in many positions where they retain an underlying /i/ as [i], and they mark lax [i] in certain positions where our representation is *E*—e.g., *rElax, dEnOt*); in part, the differences are idiosyncratic. Insofar as the differences are systematic, it is a fairly trivial matter to adjust the rules to give either phonetic output.

In short, we are formulating the rules so as to generate what we take to be the phonetic representation underlying our normal pronunciation, in agreement with Kenyon and Knott in crucial cases. Various modifications of these phonological rules would be needed to accommodate dialects differing in a systematic way from what we have here assumed. It should, incidentally, be expected that low-level phonetic rules such as those we are now considering will differ in detail across dialects.

Bearing these points in mind, we now turn to an examination of the set of processes that determine the reduction of vowels. We note, first, that nontense vowels specified as [−stress] reduce to [ə] fairly generally. Thus, as a first step, we can formulate the Vowel Reduction Rule as in (103):

$$(103) \qquad \begin{bmatrix} -\text{stress} \\ -\text{tense} \\ V \end{bmatrix} \rightarrow \ [\text{ə}]$$

In Section 3 it was noted that only unstressed low vowels reduce in final position; and it is clear that vowels never reduce prevocalically. Thus, the vowels in boldface in *fiasco, effigy, hindu, annual, radiate* do not reduce even though they are minus-stressed, but the final vowels of *algebra, formula* do reduce. Furthermore, the vowels which do not reduce even though nontense and minus-stressed are phonetically tense. Clearly, then, the rule that tenses vowels in prevocalic and, when they are nonlow, in final position must precede the general Vowel Reduction Rule (103), as we have already noted in Section 4. For the case of nonstressed vowels, rule (30) of Section 4 has exactly the effect of (104):

$$(104) \qquad \begin{bmatrix} V \\ -\text{stress} \end{bmatrix} \rightarrow \ [+\text{tense}] \ \Big/ \ \left\{ \begin{matrix} \underline{\qquad} V \\ \begin{bmatrix} \underline{\qquad} \\ -\text{low} \end{bmatrix} \# \end{matrix} \right\}$$

The vowels that undergo tensing by rule (104) are then immune from Vowel Reduction, despite their lack of stress.

An early rule of the phonology assigns to each vowel (in fact, to each unit, whether boundary, consonant, or vowel—see pp. 67–68) the feature [−stress]. A vowel belongs to the category [+stress], and thus is immune from Vowel Reduction, in the tentative formulation (103), only if it receives primary stress at some stage of the application of the cyclical rules. This stress may be weakened by successive applications of the stress placement rules in other positions of the utterance, but the vowel will still belong to the category [+stress] and hence will not be subject to Vowel Reduction.

Although (103), as we shall see, requires supplementation, it does express the central feature of the process of Vowel Reduction insofar as this is a grammatical phenomenon. We can give some idea of its wide range of applicability by a few selected examples.

Rule (103) accounts for the fact that the vowel reduces in the first syllable of *machíne*, but not the second, and in the second syllable of the verb *délegàte*, but not the first or third. In each case a vowel which has never received primary stress (and therefore retains the specification [−stress]) reduces, and a vowel which has at some point received primary stress (and thus belongs to the category [+stress]) is immune from phonological reduction. Similarly, consider the example *theatricality* analyzed in Section 7. The four vowels given in boldface do not reduce—the fourth because it has been tensed by rule (104), the second and third because they have at some stage of their derivation been assigned primary stress, and the first for both reasons. The other two vowels do reduce, never having been introduced into the category [+stress] in the course of the derivation.

As a further illustration, consider the nouns *torrent* and *torment* that were discussed in Section 11. The three vowels given in boldface in these examples are exempt from reduction, having been assigned primary stress at some stage of the derivation; but the final vowel of *torrent* does reduce, since it has the feature [−stress] when rule (103) applies.

As a last example, consider the *-ation* forms of bisyllabic final-stressed verbs such as *reláx, attést, depórt*, as compared with the superficially analogous forms *information*,[64] *illustration, demonstration, devastation*. The boldface vowel in *relaxation, attestation, deportation* is not subject to phonological reduction, whereas the antepenultimate vowel of the other *-ation* forms just given does reduce in each case. The reason is that the nominalized bisyllabic verbs have received stress in the antepenultimate syllable at an earlier stage of the cycle (namely, as verbs), whereas the other forms have never had stress assigned to this vowel. We will return to the details of the determination of stress contours in these cases. Although, as we shall see, the facts are not so clear-cut as these examples suggest, the general point does seem correct; that is, stress assignment in an early cycle can protect a vowel from phonological reduction, even when its actual stress, at the point when the Vowel Reduction Rule applies, is quite weak, and even though minus-stressed vowels in the same context do characteristically reduce. The important point is that rule (103) serves as a reasonably good tentative statement of the process of Vowel Reduction when this process is embedded within the general framework of the transformational cycle.

---

[64] Notice that *information* is not the nominalized form of *inform*, but rather a single noun presumably represented as /inform+At+iVn/. Thus we cannot have phrases such as **his information of my friend about the lecture* related to *he informed my friend about the lecture*, as we have *his relaxation of the conditions* related to *he relaxed the conditions*. Correspondingly, the meaning of *information* is not derivable from that of *inform* by any regular process.

We are not concerned here with the syntactic basis for these and other nominalized elements. For an approach that seems to us promising, see Chomsky (1965, pp. 219–20).

We see at once, incidentally, that the Vowel Reduction Rule cannot itself be cyclical. Once a vowel has been subject to rule (103), its original underlying form is unrecoverable. Therefore, if this rule were to apply at any point in the first cycle, for example, certain vowels will be reduced to [ə] even though in some later cycle they may receive primary stress. Evidently, rule (103) must apply only after the process of stress assignment within the word is complete. Within our framework, this means that the rule of Vowel Reduction is restricted to the level of word boundaries (see Section 1.1).

The tentative statement (103) is at best a first approximation to the description of vowel reduction; it does not specify the positions that are subject to this process with sufficient precision, although it is fundamental to such a specification. In fact, in certain positions a vowel will not reduce even though it has never received primary stress and thus remains in the category [−stress]; in certain other positions a stressed vowel will reduce if the stress is sufficiently weakened. Consequently, we must supplement the Vowel Reduction Rule (103) with certain auxiliary rules of the form (105a), (105b) which change the stress (and, sometimes, tenseness) category of vowels in certain positions before the application of (103).

$$\left(105\right) \qquad \begin{array}{lll} \text{(a)} & V \;\rightarrow\; [\text{2 stress}] & \text{in certain contexts} \\[2ex] \text{(b)} & V \;\rightarrow\; \begin{bmatrix} -\text{stress} \\ -\text{tense} \end{bmatrix} & \text{in certain contexts} \end{array}$$

Rule (105a) will apply to certain vowels that have never received primary stress and will assign them secondary stress, thus exempting them from reduction to [ə] by (103). The Stress Adjustment Rule will then weaken this stress to tertiary. (For reasons that are discussed on pages 118–19, we will not extend to rules of secondary stress placement the convention associated with placement of primary stress, namely, that other stresses in the domain under consideration are weakened by one.) Rule (105b) will apply to certain vowels which have received primary stress at some earlier stage of derivation and will switch them back to the category [−stress] so that they can undergo reduction by (103). Precise specification of the appropriate contexts for (105) is a complicated and, so it appears, relatively uninteresting matter,[65] and we will not attempt a detailed analysis. We will, however, give several cases of (105), illustrating some of the major conditions and accounting for examples discussed elsewhere in this chapter. We will continue to refer to (103) as the Vowel Reduction Rule and to the various cases of (105) as Auxiliary Reduction Rules.

Notice that rule (105b), like the Vowel Reduction Rule (103), cannot be permitted to apply cyclically beyond the level of word boundary. The reason is simple. As we proceed to apply the transformational cycle to more complex phrases, vowels are successively weakened in stress as more gradations and differentiations are introduced by successive applications of the cyclical rules. Above the word level even primary-stressed vowels may be weakened considerably in this process. However, this weakening of stress never leads to a shift of category with respect to stress or tenseness, nor does it lead to vowel reduction. In other words, although vowels that are weakened to stress 2 or stress 3 in certain positions within words may be subject to (105b), a vowel that is weakened to stress 2 or stress 3 in cycles beyond the word level will never, in these contexts, be subject to rule (105b); in

---

[65] In the sense that there are many details and special cases that do not seem to fall under any large-scale generalizations and that shed little light on general questions of phonological theory or on the structure of English.

particular, the sonority peak of a word will never be subject to this rule no matter how weak the stress on this word becomes by iteration of cyclic rules beyond the word level.

In short, neither rule (103) nor rule (105b) can be cyclical. Both must apply only once in the course of a derivation; within our framework this means that these must be noncyclical rules restricted to the level of word boundary.

To see the necessity for Auxiliary Reduction Rules of the form (105a), consider the following words:

$$\left(106\right)$$ *rhododéndron, Oklahóma, Kalamazoó, Tatamagóuchi, Coriolánus, Winnipesáukee, Monongahéla, Conestóga, mulligatáwny*

The vowels that are not subject to reduction are given in boldface. Of these, the ones that are in final or prevocalic position and the ones with primary stress pose no problem so far as Vowel Reduction is concerned; and our rules also account for the reduction of the vowels not cited in boldface. The other boldface vowels, however, all of which have tertiary stress, are still not accounted for, for they have never received primary stress at any stage of their derivation. In each case, in fact, there is only a single cycle and a single application of a stress placement rule.

It seems, then, that to account for the unreduced tertiary-stressed vowels of these words, we need an Auxiliary Reduction Rule which will be a special case of (105a). We state this as (107):

$$\left(107\right)$$

$$
\begin{bmatrix} -\text{stress} \\ V \end{bmatrix} \rightarrow [2\ \text{stress}] \Big/ \# \begin{cases} [-\text{stress}]_0 \underline{\hphantom{xx}} \begin{Bmatrix} C_0 \begin{bmatrix} -\text{tense} \\ V \end{bmatrix} C_0^1 \\ C_0 \end{Bmatrix} \overline{C}_0 \begin{bmatrix} \alpha\text{stress} \\ V \end{bmatrix} \overline{C}_0\, [1\ \text{stress}] & \text{(a)} \\ & \text{(b)} \\ C_0 \begin{Bmatrix} \underline{\hphantom{xx}} C_2 \\ \begin{bmatrix} \underline{\hphantom{xx}} \\ +\text{tense} \end{bmatrix} \end{Bmatrix} & \text{(c)} \\ & \text{(d)} \end{cases}
$$

where α is weaker than 2[66] and $\overline{C}$ is an informal abbreviation for a unit which is a consonant or a boundary

Notice that the first two parts of this rule are strikingly similar to the rules of primary stress placement, particularly to condition (c) of the Main Stress Rule (102). Cases (a) and (b) of (107) assert that secondary stress is placed on a vowel preceding a weak cluster (case (a)) or on a strong cluster (case (b)) when the string under consideration falls under the condition $\underline{\hphantom{xx}} V^* C_0 \overset{1}{V}$, V^* having stress weaker than two. The rule is closely analogous to the Main Stress Rule, the central difference being that secondary stress is assigned rather than primary stress. Thus, given the word *Monongah$\overset{1}{E}$la* (primary stress having been assigned by case (ii) of the Main Stress Rule (102) under condition (b)), rule (107) requires us to omit from consideration the final sequence *-ah$\overset{1}{E}$la* and to apply first case (a) and then, if case (a) is inapplicable, case (b) to the residual string *Monong-*.[67] Case (a) is inapplicable, since the

<hr />

[66] That is, where α is an integer greater than 2, or has the value "minus" ($-$), which, by convention, is weaker than any value that belongs to the category [+*stress*], i.e., weaker than [*n*stress] for any integer *n*.

     Notice that we cannot permit $\alpha = 2$ in this case, as we can see from words such as *ĕlectrónic, ĕlectrícity*, which at this stage have the stress contour $-21\ldots$, but do not, in the dialect in question, receive secondary stress in the first syllable by rule (107b).

[67] The ordering of cases (a) and (b) of (107) is disjunctive, just as the ordering of cases (i) and (ii) of the Main Stress Rule is disjunctive, and for exactly the same reason.

final cluster of this string is strong, so we turn to case (b) and assign secondary stress to the strong cluster, giving *MononḡahÉla*. The Vowel Reduction and Stress Adjustment Rules give, finally, [mənäŋgəhÉlə].

Consider now the word *Winnipesaúkee* (primary stress again having been assigned by case (ii) of the Main Stress Rule under condition (b)). As before, rule (107) tells us to omit from consideration the final string *-esaukee* and to consider the residue *Winnip-*. But now case (a) of (107) applies, the final cluster of *Winnip-* being weak, and we derive *Winnipesaukee*. The Vowel Reduction and Stress Adjustment Rules give, finally, [winəpəsɔ̀kE].

In the word *OklahÓma*, primary stress is again assigned by case (ii) of the Main Stress Rule under condition (b). In accordance with rule (107), we omit from consideration the string *-ahÓma* and consider the residual string *Okl-*. Case (b) assigns secondary stress to its only vowel. In the same way the other examples of (106) receive secondary stress in the appropriate place.

There are many other forms that are phonetically interpreted in this way, for example, verbs such as *òverthrów*, *èxtrapóse*, *ùnderstánd*, *còmprehénd*, all of which have tertiary-stressed nonreduced vowels in the first syllable. Since many of these forms contain = and # boundaries between the vowel that receives secondary stress and the following primary-stressed vowel, cases (a) and (b) of (107) must permit occurrences of [− segment], as indicated in (107). The word *comprehend*, for example, has the representation [kəN=pre=hend] at the point when rule (107) is to apply. Case (b) applies, with a boundary preceding and following the α-stressed vowel. The word *automobile* would have the representation *auto+mÓbEl*, and case (a) of (107), with the α-stressed vowel preceded by [− segment] C, assigns secondary stress to *au-*, so that we have the phonetic representation *automobile* ultimately. (Other variants require slightly different underlying representations.)

Notice, incidentally, that the similarity of cases (a) and (b) of (107) to cases (i) and (ii) of the Main Stress Rule is not a merit of this grammar but rather indicates a defect either in the analysis or in the underlying theory. As matters now stand, we are unable to formulate a generalization that covers both the rule of primary stress assignment and the rule of secondary stress assignment, despite the near identity of context in the two rules. We have, so far, been unable to find any way to overcome this defect without ad hoc extensions of the general framework for grammatical description or revisions of the rules which are unacceptable on other grounds. We are therefore forced to leave this as an open problem. In Chapter Five, note 3, we will come across another indication of this theoretical defect, in connection with a different sort of phenomenon.

Before turning to cases (c) and (d) of the Auxiliary Reduction Rule (107), let us consider a few more examples of the first two cases. Consider the nouns *relaxation, attestation, deportation*, etc., which we discussed above. Since these are derived from bisyllabic verbs with a final strong cluster, we enter the word-level cycle with representations such as [rElǽks+At+iVn]. Primary stress is placed on [At], weakening the stress on [æ] to secondary, i.e., [rElæ̀ks+Át+iVn]. We now turn to the phonological rules which are limited in applicability to the level of word boundary. Notice that the phonetic output must be [rElæ̀ksÁšən]. Of the rules we are now considering, the final one to apply in this derivation is the Stress Adjustment Rule. Prior to the application of this rule, we must, therefore, have the representation [rÉlæ̀ksÁšən]. Our problem, then, is to provide a rule that will carry the stress contour from −21−, which we now have, to 231−, which we need as the proper input to the Stress Adjustment Rule. If we weaken the stress from 2 to 3 in the second syllable, then rule (107b) will assign [2 stress] in the first syllable, as we require. Therefore we must add a new rule (108) which weakens stress in the position immediately preceding primary stress.

$$\left(108\right) \qquad \text{[2 stress]} \;\rightarrow\; \text{[3 stress]} \;/\; \text{——} \, C_0 \, \text{[1 stress]}$$

We now have the following derivation for *relaxation*:

$$\left(109\right)$$

$[_N [_V rElæks]_V At+i\breve{V}n]_N$			
1			RULE (102eii)
2	1		RULE (102bi)
3	1		RULE (108)
2 3	1		RULE (107b)
3 4	1		RULE (63)

In the first cycle primary stress is placed on the strong final cluster of the underlying verb. In the second cycle the primary stress is shifted to the syllable preceding *-ion* in the usual way (see p. 87). Rule (108) then weakens the pretonic stress, and the Auxiliary Reduction Rule (107) assigns secondary stress in the first syllable. The Stress Adjustment Rule (63) then weakens all of the nonprimary stresses in the word. The vowel [æ], although it now has stress 4, is immune from reduction as the rules are formulated.[68]

In a similar way we derive analogous representations in the case of *attestation, deportation*, etc., as well as in many other cases (e.g., *connectivity, conductivity, objectivity, elasticity*). In each case the stress contour of the first three syllables is 341 and the vowel with [4 stress] remains unreduced. In contrast, words such as *information, demonstration, adjectival* all have the stress contour 3–1– and a reduced vowel in the second syllable, since in these words the second syllable has never received stress in an earlier cycle. We can even account, in this way, for such a fine distinction as is exhibited by the pairs *compensation* [kămpənsÁsən], *condensation* [kăndensÁsən], from underlying $[_N [_V kɔN = peNsAt]_V + i\breve{V}n]_N$ (cf. *compensatory*), $[_N [_V kɔN = deNs]_V At+i\breve{V}n]_N$ in exactly the same way.[69]

If, for some reason, rule (108) does not apply to a word with the stress contour –21..., then cases (a) and (b) of the Auxiliary Reduction Rule (107) will not assign secondary stress to the initial minus-stressed vowel, since the rule (107), as formulated, requires that the pretonic vowel have a stress weaker than secondary. In fact, rule (108) is optional for certain classes of words, and when it does not apply, rule (107) is blocked. Thus, in the case of words such as *elasticity, electricity*, we may have either the contour –31–– or 341––. In the

---

[68] Because of these facts, it is easy to detect at least five degrees of stress in English. Thus, in forms such as *relaxation*, we have the stress contour 341–, [–stress] being numerically representable as [5 stress] in this case. Notice that we could not take the contour to be 2314, because of contrasts such as *either nation* (with 2–1–) versus *emendation* (with 341–).

[69] This is an accord with our pronunciation and also with a distinction between these forms noted in Kenyon and Knott. It is, however, unreasonable to expect cross-dialectal identity on a minute point such as this, particularly in the light of the problematic nature of phonetic representation at this level of fineness of detail.

　　Actually, to be even more precise, our grammar generates [kăndensÁsən] for the nominalized verb ("act of condensing") and [kăndənsÁsən] for the noun referring, e.g., to drops of water on the window pane (which, like *information*, does not have an underlying cycle for the contained verb).

　　The reason for assuming /kɔN/ (N being the archi-segment [+nasal]) in the phonological representation is that the point of articulation of the nasal is determined by the following consonant.

former case, neither rule (108) nor rule (107) has applied; in the latter, both have applied. As we have formulated the rules, the option is restricted to rule (108), the subsequent applicability of (107) being completely determined in all cases.

    As a further example of rule (107a, b), consider the nouns *instrumentality*, *complementarity*, *experimentation*, each of which has an unreduced vowel under [4 stress] immediately before a primary stress. Taking *instrumentality* as an example, we have the derivation (110), which is analogous to (109):[70]

$\left(110\right)$

$[_N [_A [_N\text{instrument}]_N æl]_A i+ti]_N$			RULE (102bi)
1			RULE (102bi)
2	1		RULE (102aii)
3	2	1	RULE (102ai)
3	3	1	RULE (108)
2	3	1	RULE (107a)
3	4	1	RULE (63)

In the first cycle we disregard the final lax syllable of the noun under condition (b) of the Main Stress Rule and assign primary stress by case (i). Thus in isolation we would have the phonetic representation [ínstrəmənt].[71] In the second cycle the affix *-al* causes primary stress to be assigned to the strong cluster that immediately precedes it. In the final, word-level cycle, the affix *-ty* causes primary stress to be placed on the syllable preceding the weak cluster that immediately precedes *-ty*, giving the third line of the derivation. Rule (108) then weakens the pretonic stress, and rule (107) raises the stress on the syllable before the weak cluster to secondary by case (a). The Stress Adjustment Rule next weakens the nonprimary stresses. The final affix becomes [tE] by rule (104), and the Vowel Reduction Rule gives, finally, [ìnstrəméntælətE]. Again we have a nonreduced vowel under stress 4.

    Before leaving this topic, we should make several further remarks about assignment of secondary stress by an Auxiliary Reduction Rule. First, it should be noted that this phonological process is considerably more general than we have indicated. The joint effect of rules (108) and (107a, b) is to convert a stress contour of the form $x21$ to 231 or $xy21$ to $2y31$. We have given rules for this process within the scope of word boundaries only, but it also operates above the level of the word. Thus, in isolation *fifteen* or *abstract* (the adjective) has main stress on the final syllable, but, as has often been noted, in the construction *fifteen men* or *abstract art*, we have the stress contour 231 (see also note 26). The reason for this is perhaps the following. In the manner described in Section 8, the Nuclear Stress Rule converts *fifteen men* and *abstract art* to *fifteen men* and *abstract art*, respectively. Now, by a phenomenon superficially similar to the one we have formalized in terms of rules (108) and (107), the resulting $x21$ contour is converted to 231. Similarly, in a sequence such as *tired old men*, the 221 contour produced by the Nuclear Stress Rule is generally converted to 231, perhaps by the same process. We do not know precisely what the domain of this process is, or how it should be described in detail. We merely note here that our description, which is limited in scope to the word, is insufficiently general.

[70] On the analysis of *–ity*, see page 87 and note 90. On the stress contour of *experimentation*, see note 72.
    We modify (107) below (see (120)) so that it applies to vowels with other than primary stress and hence to the first vowel in *instrumentality*.
[71] Alternatively, this could be regarded as derived from an underlying verb, like the examples of page 96.

Actually, even within a word the process we have now been discussing has slightly wider scope than we have indicated. Consider, for example, *artificiality*. We enter the final, word-level cycle with the representation $[_N \overset{2}{\text{æ}}\text{rtifiki}\overset{1}{\text{æ}}\text{l} + \text{i} + \text{ti}]_N$. Primary stress is then placed on the antepenultimate syllable, giving $[_N \overset{3}{\text{æ}}\text{rtifi}\overset{2}{\text{k}}\text{i}\overset{1}{\text{æ}}\text{liti}]_N$. Since the secondary-stressed vowel is not immediately followed by the primary-stressed vowel, the change of contour from 3–2–1 to 2–3–1 should not take place, as we have formulated rule (108), and the resulting contour should be 4–3–1; but, in fact, the correct contour is 3–4–1 rather than 4–3–1. Thus rule (108) must be slightly generalized to take account of this case and similar cases.[72]

Returning now to rule (107), we have still not given examples to illustrate cases (c) and (d). These cases of the rule assign secondary (ultimately, by the Stress Adjustment Rule, tertiary) stress to the vowel of a strong cluster in the initial syllable of a word. Thus, in *vòcátion, gèstátion, plàntátion, àsbéstos, àudácious*, etc., the vowel of the first syllable does not reduce and has [3 stress]. (Some would say [4 stress], in which case a slight revision of the rule becomes necessary.) Actually, the situation is a bit more complex in this position, but we omit any more precise specification of the relevant context here (see note 65).

Case (c) of rule (107) protects a vowel from reduction in the context —— CC, but not in the context C=C. Thus stress is introduced by (107c) in the first syllable of *Mòntána, pòntíficate, càntánkerous, làmpoón*, etc., but not in the verbs *com=bat, con=tend, con=vert, con=tinue*, and so on. This fact provides an additional justification for the decision to have a readjustment rule insert a boundary with the feature [–FB] in prefix-stem constructions (see Sections 10 and 13).

Given a stress contour of the form –21, rule (108) converts it to –31 and rule (107a) converts it to 231. A reasonable suggestion would be to drop rule (108) from the grammar altogether and to adopt a slightly different convention for assigning secondary stress. The convention for assignment of primary stress is as follows: when primary stress is assigned in a particular position, the stress value in every other position is weakened by one. Suppose that (following Kiparsky, 1966) we were to say, more generally, that when stress *n* is assigned in a particular position, then the stress value in any other position with stress not heavier than *n* is weakened by one. Under this convention, if rule (107a) applies to a contour –21, it assigns secondary stress to the minus-stressed vowel and automatically reduces the secondary stress already present to tertiary. Thus rule (107a) itself converts –21 to 231, and rule (108) is superfluous.

We do not accept this proposal, however, for several reasons. First, the suggested convention leads to technical difficulties. Consider, for example, the word *anticipate*. In the normal way, the stress assignment rules provide the stress contour $antici\overset{1}{p}\overset{2}{A}t$. As matters

---

[72] As an additional example, yet to be covered, consider the word *Ticonderoga*. The Main Stress Rule assigns primary stress to the penultimate syllable. Rule (107b) then assigns secondary stress to the strong cluster preceding the primary stress by two syllables, giving $Ticond\overset{2}{e}r\overset{1}{o}ga$. Case (c) of rule (107), which we discuss directly, assigns secondary stress to the strong cluster in the first syllable, giving $\overset{2}{T}icond\overset{2}{e}r\overset{1}{o}ga$. As our rules now stand, the Stress Adjustment Rule will give, finally, $\overset{3}{T}icond\overset{3}{e}r\overset{1}{o}ga$. Actually, this should be modified to either of the two optional variants $\overset{4}{T}ic\overset{3}{o}nd\overset{1}{e}roga$ or $\overset{3}{T}ic\overset{4}{o}nd\overset{1}{e}roga$. The first of these might be produced by a process similar to the one we have just been discussing. The second would require a subsidiary rule much like (108). Apparently what is needed is a variety of subsidiary rules to assign relative stress among weak stresses that are equal as our rules are now formulated. Such rules are needed, for example, to assign the contour 43–41– to *experimentation* (see p. 117). Rule (107c) should assign secondary stress in the first syllable, protecting the vowel from reduction. The Stress Adjustment Rule weakens this vowel to tertiary stress. A further weakening requires a rule of the sort just discussed.

now stand, rule (107c) will assign secondary stress in the first syllable and the Stress Adjustment Rule will then apply, giving *anticipAt*, as desired. But if we were to adopt the suggested convention, then when secondary stress is assigned in the first syllable, the secondary stress of the final syllable will reduce to tertiary, giving *anticipAt*. However, as we have seen in the discussion of verb-noun pairs such as [delǝgAt]–[delǝgǝt], [reȷ̌ǝment]–[reȷ̌ǝmǝnt], a tertiary-stressed vowel reduces in this position. Thus we derive the incorrect phonetic form *[æntisipǝt]. This fact seems to provide a compelling argument against the convention.

Apart from such technical considerations, there are others of a more general nature that lead us to question the proposed convention. It seems to us mistaken to regard the rules for assignment of secondary stress as forming a part of the system of stress assignment rules. Rather, they form a part of the system of vowel reduction. They are simply a device for preventing vowel reduction in certain positions, on a par with the other Auxiliary Reduction Rules that weaken stress as a device for permitting vowel reduction in other positions. If this conception of the role of the rules for assignment of secondary stress is correct, then the suggested generalization of the convention for stress assignment is a spurious one and inappropriate for the rules in question. There is, however, an interesting theoretical issue here, and we emphasize that our argument is far from conclusive. Thus, a generalization such as that proposed on page 117 for constructions beyond the word level would argue against our conclusion, as Kiparsky has correctly observed.

We have now given several examples of the first type of Auxiliary Reduction Rule, namely, the type (105a) that protects a vowel from reduction despite its lack of earlier stress. Let us now turn to the second type, that is, the type (105b) that makes a vowel subject to reduction despite its earlier stress. Such rules place a vowel in the category $\begin{bmatrix} -\text{stress} \\ -\text{tense} \end{bmatrix}$ in certain contexts, so that the Vowel Reduction Rule (103) will apply to them. Our problem now is to specify these contexts.

Consider first the words *solidity, telegraphy*. These are derived from the underlying forms *solid* and *telegraph*, and therefore enter the word-level cycle with the stress contours *solid+i+ty, telegraph+y*. Since the cluster preceding -(t)y is weak in both cases, primary stress is shifted to the antepenultimate syllable, giving *solidity* and *telegraphy*. However, the vowels in boldface must reduce, despite the fact that at this stage of derivation they belong to the category [+stress]. Therefore we must give an Auxiliary Reduction Rule of the form (105b) to shift them to the category [−stress] (all vowels in these examples are already lax) so that the Vowel Reduction Rule (103) can apply to them.

We have so far been assuming that all rules relating to Vowel Reduction precede the Stress Adjustment Rule (63), which, it will be recalled, is just a special case of the Nuclear Stress Rule. Continuing with this assumption, we must now formulate (105b) so as to convert the tertiary-stressed vowel of *-graph* and the secondary-stressed vowels of *tel-* and *sol-* to the category [−stress]. It seems that the relevant aspects of these contexts are essentially as given in (111):

$$\left(111\right) \qquad \text{(a)} \quad \left[\dfrac{}{3 \text{ stress}} \right] [-\text{stress}]_0 \ \#$$

$$\text{(b)} \quad \text{---} C_0^1 \,[1 \text{ stress}]$$

We shall have to revise and extend both cases slightly as we proceed. As (111) stands, it states that a tertiary-stressed vowel which is the final stressed segment in the word becomes lax and nonstressed (case (a)), and that any vowel becomes lax and nonstressed if it is followed by no more than a single consonant followed by a primary-stressed vowel (case (b)). Case (a) will apply to the tertiary-stressed vowel in $\overset{2\ 1\ 3}{telegraphy}$. Case (b) applies to the vowel in the first syllable of $\overset{2\ 1\ 3}{telegraphy}$ and $\overset{2\ 1}{solidity}$, assigning it, in each case, to the category [−stress]. Thus (111) accounts for the reduction of vowels in these words.

Notice that the Auxiliary Reduction Rule we are discussing does not apply to the pre-main-stress vowel of $\overset{2\ 1}{mentality}$, $\overset{2\ 1}{sensation}$, $\overset{2\ 1}{gestation}$, $\overset{2\ \ \ 3\ 1}{instrumentality}$, $\overset{2\ 3\ 1}{relaxation}$, etc.; it is blocked by the double consonant following the vowel. We have, however, formulated (111) so that it applies freely to tense vowels. We will see that certain restrictions are needed here.

Consider now the nouns *document, regiment, experiment, delegate, advocate*, etc., and adjectives such as *animate, elaborate*. As we have pointed out, these forms can be regarded as derived from underlying verbs. The additional cycle required for this derivation reduces the stress in the final syllable to tertiary, as compared with the corresponding verbs, which, with one less cycle in the derivation, have secondary stress in this position at this stage (see p. 107). In all cases the tertiary-stressed vowel in the final syllable becomes nonstressed and lax by the Auxiliary Reduction Rule (105b), applying in the context (111a), and then reduces to [ə] by (103). Thus we have now fully accounted for the contrast between the verbs $\overset{1\ \ \ 3}{document}$, $\overset{1\ \ \ 3}{delegate}$, $\overset{1\ \ \ \ 3}{elaborate}$, etc., with unreduced tertiary-stressed vowels in the final syllables, and the nouns and adjectives $\overset{1}{document}$, $\overset{1}{delegate}$, $\overset{1}{elaborate}$, with reduced minus-stressed vowels in the final syllable.

Notice that the Auxiliary Reduction Rule in question does not apply to a tertiary-stressed vowel followed by a double consonant if there is a stressed vowel later in the word. Thus consider the words *documentation, regimentation, experimentation*. Taking the first as an example, we derive the stress contour $\overset{1\ \ \ \ 2}{document}$ in the first cycle. In the next cycle primary stress is placed on *-At-*, giving $\overset{2\ \ \ 3\ 1}{documentation}$. But the tertiary-stressed vowel of this word does not fall under case (a) of (111) because it is followed by a later stressed segment; and it does not fall under case (b) because it is protected by a double consonant. Thus the Auxiliary Reduction Rule gives, finally, $\overset{3\ \ \ 4\ 1}{documentation}$, with a nonreduced vowel under stress 4, as required for the dialect we are considering.

Consider now forms such as *explanation, provocation, defamation, divination*, all of which have reduction of the pretonic vowel. Taking the first as an example, we have the following derivation:

$$\left(112\right)$$

$[_N \ [_V eksplAn]_V \ At+iVn]_N$			
1			RULE (102eii)
	2	1	RULE (102bi)
	3	1	RULE (108)
2	3	1	RULE (107b)
2	–	1	RULE (111b)
3	–	1	RULE (63)

In the first cycle, *explain* receives primary stress on its final syllable. In the next cycle, the affix *-ion* causes primary stress to be shifted to the right by (102bi). Rule (108) weakens the pretonic secondary stress to tertiary; and the first Auxiliary Reduction Rule (107b) assigns secondary stress in the initial syllable. But now the second Auxiliary Reduction Rule, operating in the context (111b), weakens the stress on the pretonic syllable to minus, at the same time specifying the vowel as [−tense] (see (105b)). The Vowel Reduction Rule (103) then reduces this segment to [ə], and the Stress Adjustment Rule (63) gives us the final phonetic representation [èksplənÀšən].

Notice that the forms *relaxation, attestation, connectivity,* etc., which we discussed above, are identical to forms such as *explanation* in their derivational history up to the point at which the word-level rules apply. But in the case of the former words, the Auxiliary Reduction Rule (105b) does not apply to the pretonic vowel, which is protected by the double consonant that follows it. Thus this vowel remains unreduced, with, finally, [4 stress].

The context (111b) is not formulated quite correctly, however. As given, it will lead to the reduction of any vowel, tense or lax, with or without stress, if this vowel is separated from a following primary stress by no more than a single consonant. As we have observed above, however, a strong cluster remains unreduced in pretonic position in word-initial syllables. Thus we have an unreduced vowel in the initial syllable of words such as *location, gradation, totality, iconic, baboon,* as well as in *asbestos, gestation, mentality,* etc. We must therefore restate the context (111b) so as to introduce this distinction between initial and noninitial positions in the case of tense vowels. We now replace (111b) by (113):

$$
(113) \qquad \left\{ \begin{array}{l} \left[\begin{array}{c} \overline{\quad\quad} \\ -\text{tense} \end{array} \right] \\[2ex] VC_0 \left[\begin{array}{c} \overline{\quad\quad} \\ +\text{tense} \end{array} \right] \end{array} \right\} C_0^1 \, [1 \text{ stress}]
$$

The necessity for still further emendation is clear from consideration of words such as *concéptual, contémplative.* These enter the word-level cycle with the representations $\overset{1}{con} = \overset{2}{cept} + u + al$, $\overset{1}{con} = templ\overset{2}{At} + iv$. The affix *-al* causes primary stress to be shifted to *-cept-,* and, for reasons which we shall go into shortly, the affix *-ive* also causes a stress shift to the right in *contemplative,* as one option. In each case, then, the initial sequence is $[\overset{2}{kəN} = \overset{1}{CV} \dots]$ after application of the Main Stress Rule in the word-level cycle. But now the pretonic vowel should reduce. Notice that in forms such as *conchólogy, cómptómeter, bòmbárd,* the secondary stress (deriving from a primary stress assigned in the first cycle or, alternatively, assigned by (107c) if the forms are analyzed without an internal cycle) is protected from weakening to minus by the following double consonant, whereas in *concéptual, contémplative,* reduction does take place despite the double consonant. The difference is evidently the presence of the = boundary in the latter forms. Thus we extend (113) to (114):

$$
(114) \qquad \left\{ \begin{array}{l} \left[\begin{array}{c} \overline{\quad\quad} \\ -\text{tense} \end{array} \right] \\[2ex] VC_0 \left[\begin{array}{c} \overline{\quad\quad} \\ +\text{tense} \end{array} \right] \end{array} \right\} C_0^1 \, (=C_0) \, [1 \text{ stress}]
$$

Summarizing these remarks, consider a vowel V* that appears in the context ——$C_m^n Ation$. If $m = n = 0$, V* will be tensed by rule (104) and therefore will not reduce to [ə] by (103) (e.g., the boldface vowels of *valuation* and *radiation*). Suppose that m ≠ 0. If V* has never received primary stress and the syllable is noninitial, then it will reduce (e.g., *information, demonstration*). Suppose that V* has received primary stress at an earlier stage. In this case, if $n = 1$ (hence $m = n = 1$), V* will nevertheless reduce if it is lax (e.g., *allegation*), or if it is tense and not in an initial syllable (e.g., *explanation, provocation, justification, multiplication*). If it is tense and the syllable is initial, it will not reduce (e.g., *rotation, location, elation*). If $m = 2$ (hence $n \geq 2$), V* will not reduce (e.g., *relaxation, deportation*), although its final phonetic stress, after later rules apply, will be [4 stress]. With the usual margin of exceptions, these remarks appear to cover the facts.

Further consideration of tense stressed vowels in the context ——C¹₁*Ation* sheds some additional light on vowel reduction. Such vowels will be reduced by (103) only if they are subject to the Auxiliary Reduction Rule (105b) that assigns them to the categories [−tense] and [−stress]. Thus reduction of a tense vowel is contingent on laxing. If, for some reason, a vowel is tense at the point where the Vowel Reduction Rule (103) applies, it will not be reduced. We have already made use of this fact to account for the nonreduction of unstressed nonlow vowels in prevocalic and final position. But there are two vocalic nuclei which are always tense in positions where others are lax, namely, [ɔy] and [yūw]. Thus, in words such as *exploîtative, commútative*, the stressed vowel is not lax, as it is in the parallel forms *compárative, provócative*,[73] *rélative, conspírator, derívative, explánatory*. As we shall see in the next chapter, a rule of great generality makes vowels lax in the position where the main stress falls in all of these examples, and a subsequent rule causes the segments that underlie [ɔy] and [yūw] to become tense.[74] (Other rules, not now relevant, account for the glides that appear in these vocalic nuclei.) Clearly the Auxiliary Reduction Rule (105b) should fall together with the other laxing rules. It will therefore precede the rule that tenses the segments underlying [ɔy] and [yūw], so that when the Vowel Reduction Rule applies, these elements will be tense, hence not subject to vowel reduction. For this reason, we have an unreduced pretonic syllable in words such as *exploitation* and *commutation*,[75] which are otherwise parallel in their derivational history to *explanation, provocation*, etc. For just the same reason, we do not have reduction in the final syllable of the noun *constitute*, which is related to the verb *constitute* in exactly the way the noun *advocate*, with

[73] In American English, the primary-stressed vowel of *provócative*, which is originally /O/ (cf. *provoke*), is tensed in most dialects to phonetic [ā] by a later rule, after having been laxed by the general laxing rule. Thus the analog to the tense-lax pairs [A]–[æ], [I]–[i], [E]–[e] is actually [O]–[ā], and alongside of *sAn–sanity, divIn–divinity, obscEn–obscenity*, we have *verbOs–verbosity*. That a later tensing rule is involved in these cases is evident not only from the symmetry, but also from the fact that an originally lax vowel becomes tense in this position. (Compare *cúrious–curiósity, frívolous–frivólity, recíprocal–reciprócity*, etc. We know that the vowel in boldface is phonologically lax in these cases because of the placement of primary stress in the first member of each pair.) Hence we see that despite the phonetic tenseness, the stressed vowel of words such as *provócative* has, in fact, undergone laxing along with the other examples just cited. We return to this matter in detail in the next chapter.

[74] Alternatively, the monophthong underlying [ɔy] may be exempted from the laxing rules, but this matter is not relevant to the point here at issue. The same two options are available in the case of the formative *-note*, discussed below. See page 176 for further discussion.

As we shall see in the next chapter, the tensing rules must, in general, follow the laxing rules. See also Chapter Two, (79) and (80) (p. 52).

[75] The vocalic nucleus [yūw] can optionally be reduced to [yə] in various contexts when it is unstressed. An accurate description of this process involves questions concerning the phonological analysis of the vowel system to which we will turn in the next chapter. For the present, it is enough to observe that what is involved here is not simply the process of vowel reduction.

reduced final syllable, is related to the verb *advocate*, with unreduced final syllable. Further-more, there are certain particular formatives which, as an idiosyncratic (lexically marked) feature, are exempt from laxing—for example, -*nOt*, as in *denOt*. Thus the word *denotative* is phonetically [dEnŌtətəv],[76] instead of the expected [dEnātətəv] (analogous to *provócative*). But since this vowel is not subject to laxing, in general, it does not undergo (105b) and therefore is also not subject to Vowel Reduction, since (103) applies only to nontense vowels. Thus we have [dĒnŌtĀšən], instead of the expected [dēnətĀšən], which would be parallel to [eksplənĀšən], [prāvəkĀšən], [derəvĀšən], etc.

Case (a) of (111) also must be somewhat extended. This is clear from a comparison of words such as *advisory–promissory* and variants such as [benəfišEerE]–[benəfišərE] (*beneficiary*—the basis for the alternation will be discussed in Chapter Four, Section 6). We will return below to the problem of how primary stress is assigned in words such as these. It is clear, however, that the secondary stress of -*Ory*, -*Ary* is weakened to minus in imme-diate poststress position, but it remains as secondary (ultimately being weakened to tertiary by the Stress Adjustment Rule) when it is separated from primary stress by a nonstressed syllable. The reduction, however, does not take place in word-final syllables, as in nouns such as *prótest*, *súrvey*, *tórment*. To account for this phenomenon, we extend (111a) to (115):

$$
(115) \qquad\qquad \left\{ \begin{array}{c} \left[\overline{} \\ 3\ \text{stress} \right] \\[4pt] [1\ \text{stress}]\,C_0 \underline{} C_0 V \end{array} \right\} [-\text{stress}]_0 \,\#
$$

Under this extended condition, then, a vowel will become lax and minus-stressed, subse-quently reducing to [ə] by the Vowel Reduction Rule.

One final emendation is needed in the Auxiliary Reduction Rules (105), now formu-lated tentatively as (107), (115), and (114). As we have formulated (107a, b) and (114), secondary stress is inserted by (107) and [−stress] is introduced by (114) in positions deter-mined by a subsequent primary stress. Recall, however, that these rules apply only at the level of word boundary. If the word is sufficiently complex in its internal structure, the stress that determines the positions in which the Auxiliary Reduction Rules apply may have itself been reduced from primary to secondary by the time the word-level stage of the trans-formational cycle is reached. In fact, what is required for the application of these rules is not an occurrence of primary stress (as in all the examples given above), but simply an occurrence of a stress greater than that of the position in which the rules apply; i.e., what is needed is a stress peak, regardless of its value. Thus we have relied on (114) to switch the first syllable of *solídity* to the category [−stress] before the primary-stressed vowel. The word *solídify* would undergo reduction of the first vowel in exactly the same way. But consider *solidification*. In this case, after the Main Stress Rule has applied in the word-level cycle, we have secondary, not primary, stress on the second syllable -*lid*, but this still causes reduction of the preceding vowel, exactly as in the case of *solidity*, *solidify*. Or, to take a slightly more complex example, consider the word *componentiality*, which has the following derivation:

[76] As we have pointed out on page 111, our conventions are systematically different from those of Kenyon and Knott in certain aspects. Thus their representation, in this case, is [dEnOtətiv]. As we have noted, in cases such as this only trivial modifications of the rules are needed to change the phonetic output to correspond to the Kenyon and Knott representations.

$$\left(116\right) \quad [_N [_A [_N k\mathfrak{d}N = pOn + eNt]_N i + æl]_A i + ti]_N$$

	1			RULE (102aii)
	2	1		RULE (102ai)
	3	2	1	RULE (102ai)
2	3	2	1	RULE (107b)
2	–	2	1	RULE (114)
3	–	3	1	RULE (63)

In the first cycle, the affix *-ent* places stress on the preceding strong cluster, and in isolation we would have *compónent*. In the second cycle, the affix *-al* causes stress to be placed in the syllable that precedes it by two, the immediately preceding cluster being weak. In isolation the adjective would therefore be *compònéntial*. The stress on the first syllable would be introduced by (107b) after (108) has weakened the second syllable to tertiary; the second syllable ultimately would reduce by (103) after application of the Auxiliary Reduction Rule (105b) in the context (114). But in the derivation of the noun *componentiality*, there is a third cycle, in which the stress is once again shifted to the right by the affix *-ty*. We must now introduce a secondary stress on the first syllable by rule (107b), exactly as in *componential* (or *explanation*, etc.), but the syllable that determines the position of stress placement now has not primary but secondary stress. Consequently (107) must be generalized to accommodate this case. After placement of the secondary stress by (107), suitably generalized, we next must weaken the stress on the second syllable to minus by (105b), applying in the context (114). Once again, the syllable that determines the position of reduction has not primary but secondary stress, and this is sufficient to allow the rule to apply. Finally, the Stress Adjustment and Vowel Reduction Rules (with others we have not yet discussed) give the phonetic form [kə̀mpə̀nenšiǽlətE].[77]

Let us now summarize the discussion of this section. We have discussed the Tensing Rule (104) which makes unstressed vowels tense before vowels or, when nonlow, before word boundary; rule (108) which converts a ... 21 ... contour to ... 31 ... ; Auxiliary Reduction Rules of the type (105a) which introduce secondary stress in certain positions; Auxiliary Reduction Rules of the type (105b) which place certain vowels in the category [−tense, −stress]; and the Vowel Reduction Rule (103) which converts lax unstressed vowels to [ə]. As far as ordering is concerned, it is clear that the Vowel Reduction Rule is the last of these, and that rule (108) must precede the Auxiliary Reduction Rules that introduce secondary stress, since it provides a relevant context for the latter. Furthermore, the Tensing Rule must follow the Auxiliary Reduction Rules of the type (105b), as we have noted in discussing words such as *exploitation, exploitative, commutation, commutative, denotation, denotative*. We will see in the next chapter (p. 183) that there is some reason to suppose that the Auxiliary Reduction Rules that assign secondary stress follow the Tensing Rules, since assignment of secondary stress to tense vowels applies also to vowels which are tensed only by the Tensing Rules. These facts suggest that we give the rules in the following order (adding slight qualifications that will be needed later on):

$$\left(117\right) \quad \text{(rule (108))}$$

$$[2 \text{ stress}] \quad \rightarrow \quad [3 \text{ stress}] \quad / \quad \underline{} C_0 [1 \text{ stress}]$$

---

[77] In this case, as in the case of *artificiality*, discussed on page 118, we have omitted an application of (108). Here (108) should apply to the vowel of *ent*, so that the final stress contour is 3–4–1– –.

(118) AUXILIARY REDUCTION RULE I (rules (105b), (114), (115))[78]

$$V \rightarrow \begin{bmatrix} -\text{stress} \\ -\text{tense} \end{bmatrix} \Bigg/ \left\{ \begin{matrix} \langle VC_0 \rangle \begin{bmatrix} \overline{} \\ \alpha\text{stress} \\ \langle +\text{tense} \rangle \end{bmatrix} C_0^1 (=C_0) \begin{bmatrix} \beta\text{stress} \\ V \end{bmatrix} & \begin{matrix} \langle (a) \rangle \\ (b) \end{matrix} \\[12pt] \left\{ \begin{matrix} \begin{bmatrix} \overline{} \\ \gamma\text{stress} \end{bmatrix} \\ [1 \text{ stress}] C_0 \!\!-\!\!-\!\! C_0 V \end{matrix} \right\} [-\text{stress}]_0 \, \# & \begin{matrix} (c) \\ (d) \end{matrix} \end{matrix} \right\}$$

where β is 1, 2, or 3, α is weaker than β, γ is weaker than 2

(119) TENSING (rule (104), special case of (30))

$$V \rightarrow [+\text{tense}] \Bigg/ \left\{ \begin{matrix} \overline{} V \\ \begin{bmatrix} \overline{} \\ -\text{low} \end{bmatrix} \# \end{matrix} \right\}$$

(120) AUXILIARY REDUCTION RULE II (rule (107))

$$\begin{bmatrix} \alpha\text{stress} \\ V \end{bmatrix} \rightarrow [2 \text{ stress}] \Bigg/ \# \left\{ \begin{matrix} [-\text{stress}]_0 \!\!-\!\!-\!\! C_0 (\begin{bmatrix} -\text{tense} \\ -\text{stress} \\ V \end{bmatrix} C_0^{\frac{1}{2}}) \overline{C}_0 \begin{bmatrix} \beta\text{stress} \\ V \end{bmatrix} \overline{C}_0 \begin{bmatrix} \gamma\text{stress} \\ V \end{bmatrix} \overline{C}_0 \left\{ \begin{matrix} \# \\ \begin{bmatrix} \delta\text{stress} \\ V \end{bmatrix} \end{matrix} \right\} \\[12pt] C_0 \left\{ \begin{matrix} \overline{} C_2 \\ \begin{bmatrix} \overline{} \\ +\text{tense} \end{bmatrix} \end{matrix} \right\} \end{matrix} \right\}$$

where $\overline{C}$ is a consonant or a boundary, $\alpha \neq 1$, β is weaker than 2, δ is weaker than γ.[79]

[78] We have reversed the ordering of cases (a) and (b) of (111) so as to account for forms such as the noun *correlate*, derived from the corresponding verb. In the manner described above, the vowel of the final syllable is subject to (118) and hence to Vowel Reduction in the noun (but not the verb). But the vowel of the medial syllable of *correlate* may be tense, as suggested by considerations raised on page 128. In this case, it, too, must be subject to (118), becoming lax and then reducing by (121). But only case (a) of (118) can apply to this vowel, and case (a) will not apply if the final vowel has already had its stress changed to minus.

We assume here that where F is a feature, the schema $Y\langle X \rangle Z \begin{bmatrix} W \\ \langle +F \rangle \end{bmatrix} Q$ is an abbreviation for the sequence $YXZ \begin{bmatrix} W \\ +F \end{bmatrix} Q$, $YZ \begin{bmatrix} W \\ -F \end{bmatrix} Q$. A generalization of the notations providing this interpretation will be presented in the Appendix to Chapter Eight.

We have changed $\gamma = 3$, as in (115), to $\gamma = 3$ or weaker, for reasons which will appear subsequently. Notice that this modification is entirely natural in this case.

Recall once again that a weaker stress is associated with a greater numerical value in our notation. Thus [2 stress] is weaker than [1 stress], [3 stress] is weaker than [2 stress], etc.

It is possible that we should have [δstress], $\delta \neq 1$, instead of [−stress] in (118c), (118d), but we have no crucial examples.

[79] The condition that δ is weaker than γ guarantees that the vowel with [γstress] is a stress peak in the required sense.

In most of the examples given so far, [αstress] has in fact been [−stress]. We give the slightly more general condition on α to accommodate such examples as *instrumentality* (see the derivation (110), p. 117) and *elementary* (derivation (143), p. 137).

$\left(121\right)$ VOWEL REDUCTION (rule (103))

$$\begin{bmatrix} -\text{stress} \\ -\text{tense} \\ V \end{bmatrix} \rightarrow [\textschwa]$$

Although these rules are not complete, they come sufficiently close to specifying the positions of vowel reduction for the purposes of our present discussion.

15. *Further investigation of derivational affixes*

We have now covered many of the major phonological processes that determine stress contours and vowel reduction, but there are still a number of refinements to be added. In this section we will sharpen and extend the rules of primary stress placement that involve derivational affixes.

Let us consider first the noun *ádvocacy*. This form has the underlying representation $[_N [_V \text{advocAt}]_V \text{ y}]_N$. In the first cycle it follows the pattern we have outlined in the previous sections, and it enters the word-level cycle in the form $[_N \overset{1}{\text{advoc}}\overset{2}{\text{At}}+\text{y}]_N$. As our rules now stand, condition (a) of the Main Stress Rule (102) is fulfilled, -*y* being the stress-determining affix,[80] and case (ii) will assign primary stress to -*At*-, giving $\overset{2}{a}\text{dvoc}\overset{1}{A}\text{ty}$, which becomes, finally, phonetic *$[\overset{3}{\text{æ}}\text{dvək}\overset{1}{A}\text{sE}]$. However, the correct phonetic representation is, rather, $[\overset{1}{\text{æ}}\text{dvəkəsE}]$.

To account for this example, we must modify condition (a) (and, as we shall see directly, condition (c)) of the Main Stress Rule in such a way that the sequence -*At*- is regarded as part of the context omitted from consideration. We thus reformulate condition (a) as follows:

$\left(122\right)$ $(At)+C_0 \begin{bmatrix} -\text{stress} \\ -\text{tense} \\ V \end{bmatrix} C_0]_{NSPVA}$

With this modification, we have the following derivation for *advocacy*:

$\left(123\right)$

$[_N [_V \text{advocAt}]_V \text{ y}]_N$			
		1	RULE (102eii)
	1	2	RULE (75)
	1	3	RULE (102ai), (122)
	1	–	RULE (118c)

In the first cycle primary stress is placed on the final strong cluster and is then shifted left two syllables by the Alternating Stress Rule (75). Thus, after application of the Stress Adjustment Rule, we would have the phonetic representation $[\overset{1}{\text{æ}}\text{dvək}\overset{3}{A}\text{t}]$ for the verb *advocate* in isolation. But for the noun *advocacy*, there is a second cycle, in which condition (a) of the Main Stress Rule holds in its new formulation (122), with -*At*+*y* functioning as

---

[80] We are assuming here that the affix -*y* will place stress under condition (a) of the Main Stress Rule along with other affixes. This, of course, requires that the lexical representation for -*y* be compatible with condition (a). It is not immediately obvious that this is the case, but the assumption is in fact correct, as we shall see directly.

the stress-determining element of the context. Omitting -*At*+*y* from consideration, we apply case (i) to the remaining sequence *advóc*-, reassigning primary stress on the first syllable and weakening stress on -*At*- to tertiary. The tertiary-stressed vowel then becomes minus-stressed and lax by the Auxiliary Reduction Rule (118) and, finally, reduces by the Vowel Reduction Rule (121). We thus derive [ǽdvəkəsE] as the phonetic representation for the nominalized form of *advocate*, as required.

The modification proposed in (122) also accounts for adjectives derived from verbs that end in -*ate*. Thus consider the words in (124):

$$\left(124\right)$$

demónstrative	génerative
illústrative	conféderative
contémplative	appréciative
altérnative	remúnerative

Several of these words have variant pronunciations to which we return directly. However, it is immediately obvious from these examples that the position of primary stress is governed by cases (i) and (ii) of the Main Stress Rule applying to the string preceding -*ative* in the now familiar fashion: primary stress is assigned to the penultimate vowel of this string if the string ends with a weak cluster; otherwise it is assigned to the terminal strong cluster. We thus have the following typical derivations:[81]

$$\left(125\right)$$

$[_A [_V \text{demonstrAt}]_V \text{ ive}]_A$			$[_A [_V \text{generAt}]_V \text{ ive}]_A$		
	1			1		RULE (102eii)
1		2	1	2		RULE (75)
2	1	3	1	3		RULE (102a), (122)
–	1	–	1	–		RULE (118b, c)

In the first cycle we derive *demonstrÁt*, *generÁt*, in the usual way. In the second cycle, condition (a) of the Main Stress Rule (102) holds in both cases, in its revised formulation (122), excluding the sequence -*Ative* from consideration. Case (i) of the Main Stress Rule applies in the case of *generative*, placing primary stress on the first syllable of *gener*- since the second syllable has a weak cluster. The effect here is not to shift the stress, which is already on this syllable, but to weaken the stress on -*At*- to tertiary. Case (ii) applies to *demonstrative*, shifting primary stress to the strong cluster. The Auxiliary Reduction Rule (118) then converts the tertiary-stressed vowels and the pretonic secondary-stressed vowel to [−stress] in the manner described in the preceding section. Finally the Vowel Reduction Rule (121) gives the phonetic representations [dəmǽnstrətəv], [jénərətəv].

It should be noted, incidentally, that the reformulation of condition (a) of the Main Stress Rule as (122) relies in an essential way on the general convention that parentheses imply disjunctive ordering. Thus (122) abbreviates two successive rules that assign primary

---

[81] As we shall see in the next chapter, the underlying representations for *demonstrate* and *generate* are actually /demɔNstrAt/ and /genVrAt/, respectively. The rules changing [ɔ] to [ā] and [g] to [j] will be discussed there, along with the phonological interpretation of the symbol *A*.

See note 76 on the divergence of our representation from Kenyon and Knott in the case of -*ive*. An obvious minor adjustment in the rules is needed to give the Kenyon and Knott representations.

stress in the contexts (126a) and (126b) (where $\breve{V}$ is a lax, minus-stressed vowel), taken in that order:

$$\left(126\right) \qquad \begin{array}{ll} \text{(a)} & \text{——}At + C_0\breve{V}C_0 \\ \text{(b)} & \text{——} + C_0\breve{V}C_0 \end{array}$$

Suppose that the ordering of (126a) and (126b) were not disjunctive. Taking the word *demonstrative* as an example, we would first assign primary stress under condition (126a), giving *demónstrative*, and we would then proceed to (126b), which, in this case, would assign primary stress to the strong cluster *-At-*, giving *demònstrÁtive*, ultimately **dèmonstratíve*. The disjunctive ordering of (126a) and (126b) prevents this incorrect derivation.

There are words, such as *indícative*, *corrélative*, that seem inconsistent with the analysis given, since the stress is shifted to a weak cluster. However, we have the means to deal with these forms. In fact, this can be done in either of two ways. One possibility is to represent these words phonologically as /iN=dikAt+iv/, /kəN=relAt+iv/, respectively, with the = boundary that appears in prefix-stem forms. This boundary will not block the correct derivation of the underlying verbs in the first cycle, since the Alternating Stress Rule (75), which shifts stress two syllables back from *-At-*, can apply to strings with = in this position. Case (i) of the Main Stress Rule, however, cannot. Thus, in the second cycle that is required for the derivation of the adjective, when the affix *-ative* places primary stress, this boundary will block case (i). Case (ii) will then apply, assigning primary stress to the syllable preceding *-ative*. Still another representation that would give the correct result is suggested by the laxing rule to which we have alluded several times, that is, the rule that converts A to æ, E to e, I to i, O to $\bar{a}$ (see note 73) in certain contexts, among which are the contexts *-ative*, *-itiv*. Thus we have *comparative*, *repetitive*, *derivative*, *provocative* from *compAr*, *repEt*, *derIv*, *provOk*. This rule permits us to derive *indicative*, *correlative* from underlying representations with a tense vowel in the syllable that takes primary stress:

$$\left(127\right)$$

$$[_A [_V indIkAt]_V iv]_A$$

		1	RULE (102eii)
	1	2	RULE (75)
2	1	3	RULE (102aii), (122)
2	1	–	RULE (118c)
3	1	–	RULE (63)

In the first cycle we derive the stress pattern *indÌkÁt* in the usual way. If we were dealing with the verb in isolation, the Auxiliary Reduction Rule (118a), with $\beta = 2$, would now apply to the medial vowel, making it lax. This vowel would then be reduced by (121), giving [indəkÁt] after application of the Stress Adjustment Rule. To derive the adjective, there is a second cycle, in which the Main Stress Rule applies under condition (a) in its formulation (122). The sequence *-ative* is thus omitted from consideration, and primary stress is placed on the strong cluster immediately preceding this sequence. The Laxing Rule, which applies in the context *-ative*, then converts [I] to [i]. The Auxiliary Reduction Rule (118), the Vowel Reduction Rule (121), and the Stress Adjustment Rule (63) now give the phonetic representation [indÌkətÁv].

We noted above that alongside of the examples of (124) there are, in several cases, variant phonetic forms. Thus we have the alternative forms [kəntɛ́mplətəv]–[kǎntəmplÁtəv] and [jɛ́nərətəv]–[jěnərÁtəv].[82] We have accounted in this section only for the first member of each pair. But it is clear that in the alternative form, -*ive* is simply acting as a neutral affix, leaving intact the phonetic representation of the underlying verb. We therefore provide for the option of affixing -*ive* with a # boundary that is not deleted by readjustment rules, for when an affix is preceded by #, the cycle in which it appears as a stress-determining element is vacuous (see p. 85). Summarizing, we see that where the underlying representation is as in the left-hand column in (128), the phonetic form will be the corresponding item of the right-hand column:

$$(128)$$

    (a) $[_A [_V kəN = teNplAt]_V iv]_A$ [kəntɛ́mplətəv]

          $[_A [_V kəN = teNplAt]_V \# iv]_A$ [kǎntəmplÁtəv]

    (b) $[_A [_V generAt]_V iv]_A$ [jɛ́nərətəv]

          $[_A [_V generAt]_V \# iv]_A$ [jěnərÁtəv]

These forms are of some interest since it is by no means obvious from superficial examination that the paired items are all related by the same system of phonological processes. However, as we have seen, it is precisely this pairing that is predicted by independently motivated phonological rules.

Let us turn next to a consideration of the derivational affix -*y* as in *aristocracy, telegraphy, synonymy, economy, galaxy, industry, melody,* etc. Notice that this is not to be confused with the -*y* variant of the nominalization element, as in *advocacy* (see p. 126) or with the affix #*y* of *shiny, stringy,* etc. (see p. 85). We review here some material presented in earlier sections, extending the scope and refining the content of our previous discussion.

Before considering the effect of -*y* on stress placement, let us investigate the question of its underlying representation. Since with regard to stress value it is phonetically identical with the final vowel of *éffigy, Kénnedy,* rather than the final vowel of *refugée, chickadée,* we see that it must be phonologically lax rather than tense, and subject to tensing by rule (119). Hence, at the stage of derivation prior to the application of (119), the affix -*y* is represented [i]. However, [i] cannot be the underlying representation. The reason is that the grammar must contain rule (129), which applies before the stress rules:

$$(129)$$

                        $i \; \rightarrow \; \phi \; / +\text{---}\#$

This rule is necessary to account for forms such as *bile–bilious, reptile–reptilian, Arab–Arabian, professor–professorial, manager–managerial, matter–material, president–presidential.* The question of whether an item takes the ending -*ial,* -*ious,* -*ian,* with an -*i*-, or -*al,* -*ous,* -*an* (as in *peripheral, general, oriental,* etc.), without an -*i*-, is determined by the item itself, as an inherent property. Consequently, forms such as *bile, reptile, professor, president*

---

[82] Notice that in a case such as *legislative,* we will have the variants [lɛ́jəslÁtəv]–[lɛ́jəslətəv], instead of [lɛ́jəslÁtəv]–[ləjíslətəv], provided that lax vowel followed by consonant followed by the liquid *l* constitutes a weak cluster. But see (49) and note 32 (p. 83).

must be represented as /bII+i/, /reptIl+i/, /prɔ=fes+Or+i/, /pre=sId+ent+i/,[83] and so on, just as *habit*, *tempest*, etc., must be represented in the lexicon as /hæbit+u/, /tempest+u/.[84] In short, there are "stem-forming" vowels /i/ and /u/ which are deleted in final position by rule (129) but which remain before certain affixes.

Since final *-y* is not subject to deletion by rule (129), it must be represented in such a way as to differentiate it from the stem-forming vowels, if this method of analyzing *-i* and *-u* augments is correct. There are several possible ways of achieving this result. The simplest and most straightforward is to distinguish *-y* from stem-forming /i/ and /u/ by a single feature, and the natural choice is the feature [vocalic]. Since /i/ and /u/ are represented as [+vocalic, −consonantal], let us represent *-y* as [−vocalic, −consonantal], that is, as the glide /y/ (see p. 68), the other features remaining unchanged. We then add rule (130) to convert /y/ to [i]:

$$\left(130\right) \qquad\qquad\qquad y \;\rightarrow\; i \;\; / \; C\!\!-\!\!-\!\![-\text{seg}]$$

The position of rule (130) in the sequence of rules is a question to which we will return directly.

Recall that we found earlier that there is a rule (rule (57), p. 87) that converts [i] to [y] in certain contexts. Clearly, the case for rule (130) will be strengthened if it falls together with rule (57). As we shall see in the next chapter (Section 6), this is precisely what happens.

In short, we may represent *-y* as the glide /y/, converting it to [i] by (130) and finally to [E] by the Tensing Rule (119). Thus *industry*, for example, will be entered in the lexicon as /industr+y/,[85] whereas *reptile* will be entered /reptIl+i/. (In the case of such variants as *doctoral–doctorial*, we will have the lexical representation /dɔktɔr(+i)/ for *doctor*, with optional stem-forming /i/.) The stem-forming vowel /+i/ will drop in final position, but the glide /y/ will remain, become a vowel, and, finally, become tense.

Having determined the underlying representation for the affix *-y*, let us now turn to the question of how this affix affects stress placement. At first glance it appears that the *-y* affix assigns stress to the syllable preceding it by two, as in the examples *aristócracy*, *telé-graphy*, *synónymy*, *ecónomy*, *gálaxy*, *índustry*, *mélody*, cited above. Notice, however, that many of these examples do not justify the assignment of any special status to *-y*. In any case in which the cluster immediately preceding the affix is weak, the placing of primary stress on the syllable preceding the affix by two can be perfectly well explained on the assumption that *-y* is a regular affix that assigns primary stress by the usual rule involving weak and strong clusters (i.e., cases (i) and (ii) of the Main Stress Rule). For example, the

---

[83] Notice that the representation could not be /bIli/, /reptIli/, etc. (or, in the cases we are considering, /industri/, etc.), without the + before the stem-forming vowel, since a vowel in the context C——# does not drop (cf. *pity*, *valley*, etc.) and, in the case of *industry*, would give the stress pattern *indústry, like *attórney*, *inférno*, and so on. (See Section 3.)

[84] The forms with +*u* indicate that rule (129) is actually somewhat more general than given here. It must state that any high vowel (i.e., /u/ as well as /i/) is deleted in this position.

[85] We have as yet given no justification for representing the medial vowel as /u/. This will be done in the next chapter.

derivation of *aristocracy* would be as follows:[86]

$$\left(131\right) \qquad [_N \ [_N \text{æristə} \ [_s \text{kræt}]_s \ ]_N \ y]_N$$

		1		RULE (102eii)
	1	2		RULE (102ci)
	2 1	3		RULE (102ai)
	3 1	3		RULE (117)
	3 1	–		RULE (118c)
2	3 1	–		RULE (120b)
3	4 1	–		RULE (63)

In the first cycle the stem *-crat* receives primary stress as a monosyllable. In the second cycle we are dealing with the noun *aristocråt*. Conditions (a) and (b) of the Main Stress Rule are inapplicable, but condition (c) holds, and case (i) assigns primary stress to the syllable two away from the primary-stressed syllable *-crat*. If we were dealing with the word *aristocrat* in isolation, the Stress Adjustment Rule would then apply, giving *aristocrat*, the minus-stressed vowels finally reducing to [ə]. In the case of (131), however, we proceed to an additional cycle. Condition (a) of the Main Stress Rule holds, the stress-determining affix being *-y*.[87] Since the cluster preceding the affix is weak, primary stress is assigned two syllables back by case (i). Rules (117) and (120) then convert the –21 contour to 231, in the manner described in the preceding section. The Auxiliary Reduction Rule (118c) weakens the tertiary-stressed vowel of *-crat* to minus stress since it is not followed by any stressed vowel. This vowel then reduces to [ə] by rule (121), and we derive the phonetic representation [æristäkrəsE] by the rules that tense the word-final vowel (that is, (119)), change [ə] to [ā], and change [t] to [s], under conditions that we describe in the next chapter.

Thus, most of the examples cited do not serve to show that *-y* is in any way distinct from the regular affixes *-ous*, *-al*, etc., which operate by the familiar rules. To demonstrate that *-y* actually belongs to an ad hoc category of affixes that assign stress to the syllable preceding the affix by two, it would be necessary to show that when the terminal cluster of the sequence preceding *-y* is strong, then it is still the case that *-y* always causes stress to be assigned to the syllable preceding this strong cluster. This assumption seems to be correct when we look at words such as *gálaxy*, *índustry*, *blásphEmy*. It no longer holds, however, when we come to other examples such as *órthodoxy*, *pólyandry*, *rhínoplasty*, *pédagOgy*, *állegOry*, *téstimOny*, *míscellAny*. All of these have a strong terminal cluster before *-y*, but primary stress is placed in the syllable preceding *-y* by three, not two.

Thus we have the following situation to account for. Along with the regular affixes such as *-al* and *-ous*, the affix *-y* assigns primary stress to the syllable two away when the immediately preceding cluster is weak (e.g., *polýgamous*, *polýgamy*). When the immediately preceding cluster is strong, then this syllable receives primary stress when the affix is *-ous*

---

[86] As has been becoming more and more obvious throughout this chapter, the underlying representations are in many cases very similar to conventional orthography, if we use the alphabetic symbols *a*, *o* for phonological /æ/, /ɔ/, respectively, as is quite natural for English. We shall see in the next chapter that there is a diacritic feature introduced by readjustment rules into segments of formatives that are subject to derivational processes. Using the alphabetical symbol *c* to represent /k/ with this redundant extra feature, the phonological representation of the word *aristocracy* will therefore be /aristo+crat+y/.

[87] This requires a slight modification (actually, simplification) of condition (a), to which we turn directly.

(e.g., *polyándrous*), but it receives only secondary (ultimately, tertiary) stress when the affix is -*y*, primary stress appearing on an earlier syllable (e.g., *polyandry*).

Actually, the facts are still more complex than this. Consider the ending -*Or*+*y*, as in the items of (132):

$\begin{pmatrix}132\end{pmatrix}$

prómissory	*compúlsory*	*mémory*
állegory	*illúsory*	*ármory*
cátegory	*refráctory*	*cúrsory*
térritory	*advísory*	*sénsory*
aúditory	*introdúctory*	*réctory*
inhíbitory	*contradíctory*	*hístory*

In each case, the cluster preceding -*y* is strong.[88] In the first column the primary stress precedes this strong cluster by two syllables (as in the case of *órthodoxy*, *téstimony*, etc.) In the second and third columns, however, the primary stress immediately precedes this strong cluster. Notice that in the second column the cluster which takes the primary stress is itself strong, whereas in column one the cluster preceding *Or*+*y* is weak in each case.

Summarizing these various observations, we seem to have the following stress contours with final -*y*, where S stands for a syllable with a strong cluster, W for a syllable with a weak cluster, and A for an arbitrary syllable:

$\begin{pmatrix}133\end{pmatrix}$

    (a)   ... ÁW+*y*   (*aristócracy*, *ecónomy*, *pólicy*)
    (b)   ÁWS+*y*   (*órthodoxy*, *téstimony*, *prómissory*, *aúditory*)
    (c)   AŚS+*y*   (*advísory*, *compúlsory*, *refráctory*)
    (d)   #ÁS+*y*   (*mémory*, *sénsory*, *índustry*, *gálaxy*)

Evidently, whatever the correct explanation may be for stress distribution before -*y*, it will not do simply to assign -*y* to a special category of affixes that place primary stress two syllables away from the affix in question.

Actually, a closer look shows that the apparently aberrant behavior of -*y* can be explained on the assumption that it is a perfectly regular affix. It is precisely this behavior that is predicted for -*y* by the system of rules we have developed on independent grounds.

To see why this is so, let us turn back to the Main Stress Rule and give a somewhat more precise and, in fact, simpler account of it. We have stated the determining context for conditions (a) and (b) of the Main Stress Rule as (134), and for conditions (c) and (d) as (135), repeating here only the parts essential for this discussion:

$\begin{pmatrix}134\end{pmatrix}$
$$\begin{bmatrix} -\text{stress} \\ -\text{tense} \\ V \end{bmatrix} C_0]$$

$\begin{pmatrix}135\end{pmatrix}$
$$[\beta\text{stress}] C_0] \qquad \beta = 2 \text{ or } 1$$

Recall that the symbol V is an informal abbreviation for the feature complex [+vocalic, −consonantal] and that the symbol C is an informal abbreviation for the feature complex $\left\{ \begin{matrix} [-\text{vocalic}] \\ [+\text{consonantal}] \end{matrix} \right\}$, that is, either [−vocalic] or [+consonantal]. Thus six features are

---

[88] The examples of the third column are not really crucial, since for most of them one might assume that the penultimate vowel is lax in the underlying forms. However, there are also more crucial examples illustrating the point now at issue, in particular, those of the form $\#C_0\acute{V}C_0VC_2+y$ listed in (133d).

actually mentioned in (134). We can simplify (134) to (136), eliminating two features:

$$
\left(136\right) \qquad
\begin{bmatrix}
-\,\text{stress} \\
-\,\text{tense} \\
-\,\text{cons}
\end{bmatrix}
[+\text{cons}]_0
$$

This revision has no effect on any of our earlier discussion,[89] and the simplified formulation (136) is obviously to be preferred to (134) in terms of any reasonable evaluation measure, in particular, the one that we adopt throughout and will discuss in greater detail in Chapter Eight. We retain the formulation (135) for conditions (c) and (d) without change, listing it here only for ease of reference.

In the case of a form ending in -*y*—for example, *telegraphy*—we see that it falls under condition (a), reformulated as (136), with /y/ taken as the segment [−stress, −tense, −consonantal] and no consonants preceding or following it in the affix. Furthermore, this is the only way of interpreting $\overset{1}{\text{tele}}\overset{2}{\text{gra}}\text{phy}$ as an instance of condition (a).[90]

To complete the derivation of *telegraphy*, we now apply rule (130), converting the final glide to the vowel [i], which the Tensing Rule (119) will convert finally to [E].

With this simplification of the Main Stress Rule, let us now return to the problem of accounting for the four types of stress contours with final -*y* that we have noted in (133).

Case (a) of (133), namely, ÁW+*y*, is handled exactly as before. In the case of *aristocracy*, for example, we have the underlying lexical form [N [N ærist∂ [s kræt]s]N y]N, and the derivation is as in (131). The other examples of case (133a) have analogous derivations.

Consider now the examples of (133b), which have the general form ÁWS+*y*. Taking *orthodoxy* as an example, we have the following derivation (using the notational conventions of note 86):

$$\left(137\right)$$

		[N [A orθo [s doks]s]A y]N	
		1	RULE (102eii)
1	2		RULE (102ci)
2	1		RULE (102aii)
1	2		RULE (102ci)
1	3		RULE (63)

The first two cycles are as described earlier. In isolation we would have the form $\overset{1}{\text{ortho}}\overset{3}{\text{dox}}$, after Stress Adjustment. In the third cycle, we first apply case (ii) of the Main Stress Rule under condition (a), now formalized as (136), taking /y/ as the stress-placing affix. According to the disjunctive ordering, we skip condition (b) and turn to condition (c), which is conjunctively ordered with respect to (a). This condition, which is repeated in its essentials

---

[89] A fact that we have not yet dealt with systematically but that is important throughout this discussion is that phonetic [E], [A], [U], [O], [ɔ̄w], as well as the vocalic nuclei with centering glides and the "true" diphthongs [I], [ɔ̄y], and [āw] (with their several dialectal variants), all derive from underlying monophthongs. Hence, at the stage of derivation when the Main Stress Rule applies, there are no terminal sequences of the form vowel-glide. We go into this matter in detail in the next chapter.

[90] Similarly, if we represent the affix -*ity* as /i+ty/ or /i+ti/, then a word of the form ——*ity* is uniquely interpretable under condition (a) with -*ty* taken as the affix. With this analysis, -*ity* behaves exactly like all regular affixes; without the assumption that it is morphologically complex, we would have to treat it as an exceptional element which always places stress on the final syllable of the item to which it is affixed. This assumption is independently well motivated, as noted earlier. For one thing, -*ty* is a common noun-forming affix (e.g., *royalty*, *loyalty*, *certainty*). Furthermore, forms with -*ity* frequently fall into a more general paradigm with -*ify* and -*itude* forms (e.g., *clarity–clarify*, *gratify–gratitude*, *infinity–infinitude*, *sanctity–sanctify–sanctitude*). Also, as we shall see in Section 6 of the next chapter, the analysis /it+y/ or /it+i/ is ruled out by the rules for spirantization. All these facts support the assumption that a stem-forming element -*i*- is involved.

as (135), excludes from consideration a stressed vowel followed by no vowels and then assigns primary stress to the residue in the usual way. In this example we do have a stressed vowel followed by no vowels, namely, the string -*dóxy*, represented as [dɔks+y] at this stage. Case (i) of the Main Stress Rule reassigns primary stress to the initial syllable, weakening the stress on -*dox*- to secondary. The Stress Adjustment Rule reduces the latter to tertiary, and other phonetic rules give, finally, [ɔ̄rθədǎksE]. The other examples of (133b) (including the examples of the first column of (132)) are derived in the same way.

We next turn to the examples of (133c), which have the structure AŚS+*y*. Taking *advisory* as an example, we have the following derivation:

$$\left(138\right)$$

[$_A$ [$_V$ad=vIs]$_V$ Or+y]$_A$		
1		RULE (102eii)
2	1	RULE (102aii)
1	2	RULE (102cii)
1	–	RULE (118d)

In the first cycle primary stress is assigned to the tense vowel of the final syllable of the verb in the usual way. In the second cycle the affix -*y*, under condition (a) of the Main Stress Rule, causes primary stress to be shifted to the tense vowel of the syllable immediately preceding the affix. Then condition (c) holds, with -*Óry* as the final stressed syllable of (135) that causes primary stress to be assigned. In this instance the stress is assigned by case (ii) of the Main Stress Rule, the final cluster of *advís*- (the string that remains after the exclusion of -*Óry*) being strong. If this cluster were weak, as in *prómissory*, case (i) would have applied, assigning primary stress to the penultimate syllable of the residual string. The Auxiliary Reduction Rule then applies, converting the vowel [O] to the category [−tense, −stress] so that the Vowel Reduction Rule (121) can then reduce it to [ə].[91] Notice that for (118d) to apply in (138), either rule (130), which converts [y] to [i], must precede (118) or else the final V of (118d) must be simplified to [−consonantal]. Actually, both of these conditions hold, and there is therefore no problem here. Once again, had we been dealing with the otherwise analogous form *promissory*, rule (118) would have been inapplicable and the secondary stress would have remained on O, ultimately being reduced to tertiary by the Stress Adjustment Rule.

Finally, we turn to the examples of (133d) and the third column of (132). Taking *industry* as a typical case, we have the following derivation:

$$\left(139\right)$$

[$_N$industr+y]$_N$		
1		RULE (102aii)
1	2	RULE (102dii)
1	–	RULE (118d)

---

[91] The initial vowel of *advise* and *advisory* reduces, despite the double consonant that follows it, because of the intervening = boundary. The underlying representation of *advisory*, dropping labeled brackets, should presumably be [æd =vIs≠Or+y]. However, the Main Stress Rule (102) will not apply as required in the second cycle of (138) unless ≠ is simplified to + (see the condition on X in (102)). We therefore assume that an ad hoc readjustment rule replaces ≠ by + before -*Ory* and -*Ary*. Alternatively, we might restrict the condition on X in rule (102) to condition (e) of the rule.

Notice, incidentally, that a rule replacing ≠ by + is needed to account for all cases where the distribution of ≠ does not accord with the syntactically derived surface structure. Thus, in the case of the affix -*ion*, the /y/ realization of the nominalization element in *advocacy*, and so on, we have + boundary instead of the ≠ which might be expected on syntactic grounds, the effect being that the affix in question is not neutral with respect to stress placement.

Primary stress is first assigned to the strong cluster by the affix rule. Then, under condition (d) of the Main Stress Rule, primary stress is assigned to the monosyllable preceding the sequence *-ústry*, which, being of the form $\overset{1}{V}C_0$] specified in (135), is omitted from consideration for the purposes of stress assignment by condition (d). The secondary stress on *u* resulting from this operation is further reduced to minus by the Auxiliary Reduction Rule (118d). The other phonetic rules give, finally, the phonetic form [indəstrÉ].

It is important to observe that no new machinery is needed to account for the apparently idiosyncratic behavior of *-y* with respect to stress placement. The only assumption we have made, beyond the assumptions that were independently motivated in earlier discussions, is that rule (130) follows the Main Stress Rule. (We already knew that it had to precede the Tensing Rule (119) and follow (129), which drops stem-forming /+i/ when final.) In short, given this ordering, the independently motivated rules predict that *-y* will assign stress in the manner indicated in (133). Thus *-y* is a perfectly regular affix; it belongs to no special category. The fact that it differs so markedly from the other affixes in the superficial form of the stress contours that it provides is simply a consequence of its unique segmental constitution, *-y* being the only derivational affix that consists solely of nonvowels. It is this fact that allows a stressed syllable terminating in *-y* to fall under condition (c) or (d), giving rise to the phenomena in (133). As we noted, there is motivation for this analysis of *-y* apart from considerations of stress, though the latter would, in any event, suffice as justification.

This is an interesting demonstration of how a system of rules can cause a small difference in underlying representation to have large-scale and otherwise quite inexplicable phonetic effects. As noted in Chapter Two, the empirical hypothesis regarding disjunctive and conjunctive ordering is playing a particularly crucial role here.

We have so far come across lexical items that are represented in the four forms (1) /*X*E/, (2) /*X*i/, (3) /*X*+i/, and (4) /*X*+y/. Words such as *pedigree, chickadee* are of type (1); *attorney, macaroni* are of type (2); *president, professor* are of type (3); *economy, testimony* are of type (4). Thus we have underlying representations such as (1) /čikVdE/; (2) /mækVrOni/; (3) /prɔ=fes+Or+i/; (4) /testVmOn+y/. We will see in Chapter Five (note 6) that there is some slight evidence that words such as *city, pity* have the underlying representations /citee/, /pitee/, giving another source for phonetic final [E]. There is, furthermore, some justification (see pp. 225–26) for an underlying representation /colony/, rather than /colon+y/, for *colony* (continuing to use the notational conventions of note 86). We will also see that /y/ is otherwise restricted in distribution in lexical items to initial position. Therefore the range of contrast between /i/ and /y/ is extremely limited. In general, glides play a very marginal role in underlying representations in English.

Consider next the stress patterns of words ending in *-ary*:

$\left(140\right)$

	(a) *apóthecary*	*annivérsary*
	subsídiary	*exémplary*
	áncillary	*infírmary*
	cápillary	*dispénsary*
	córollary	*placéntary*
	órdinary	*eleméntary*
		compliméntary
		documéntary

(continued)

$\left(140\right)$ *continued*

(b) *mómentary*
     légendary
     cómmentary

(c) *sédentary*
     vóluntary
     ádversary

(d) *véterinary*
     dísciplinary

Among these are nouns and adjectives of various kinds, some based on an underlying independent form, some not. The general similarity between *-ary* forms and *-ory* forms suggests that we analyze the examples of (140) as containing a final sequence /+Ar+y/ which will then be parallel in its behavior to the /+Or+y/ ending discussed previously. Thus *apothecary* and *anniversary* would have the following derivations:

$\left(141\right)$

apothec+Ar+y		annivers+Ar+y			
		1			RULE (102aii)
1	2				RULE (102ci)
		1	2		RULE (102cii)
		1	–		RULE (118d)
		2	1	–	RULE (120b)
1	3	3	1	–	RULE (63)

In both cases, the *-y* affix first places primary stress on the strong cluster that directly precedes it, under condition (a) of the Main Stress Rule (102), now simplified as (136). Under condition (c), the final stressed syllable *-Áry* is now omitted from consideration, and primary stress is shifted back two syllables in the case of *apothecary*, the final cluster of the residual sequence being weak, and shifted back one syllable in the case of *anniversary*, the final cluster of the sequence under consideration being strong. The Auxiliary Reduction Rule (118d) now weakens the stress on the immediately post-tonic syllable to minus, causing it to be reduced by the Vowel Reduction Rule. The second Auxiliary Reduction Rule (120) assigns secondary stress to the antepretonic syllable of *anniversary*. The Stress Adjustment Rule, rule (130), and the Tensing Rule give the final phonetic forms in both cases of (141), except that we must also add a subsidiary Laxing Rule to change [A] to [e] in *-ary*:

$\left(142\right)$ A → e / in the affix *-ary*

We will formulate this rule properly in Section 4.3.5 of Chapter Four, incorporating it into the sequence of rules in the appropriate place. The rule will apply only to the element *-ary*, thus distinguishing the phonetically lax boldface vowel of *secretary, secretarial, apothecary*, etc., from the phonetically tense boldface vowel of *area, various, malaria*, and so on.

We will see in the next chapter that rule (142) is quite straightforward. Also, there is independent evidence in favor of the rule, quite apart from the necessity to analyze the underlying vowel of *-ary* as tense so as to account for the stress contours in (140). Thus consider alternations such as *solidary–solidarity, capillary–capillarity*. We have noted several times that *A–æ* is a regular alternation. There is, however, no other instance of an *e–æ* alternation.[92] Hence, if we were not to accept (142) as a rule, we would have to add a new

---

[92] There is a marginal rule converting [æ] to [e] in certain exceptional forms, but not under the circumstances here noted (see p. 202).

rule to account for the *e–æ* alternation in these words. Instead rule (142) explains this as a special case of the general *A–æ* alternation before *-ity*.[93]

We see, then, that with the single addition of rule (142), the rules that we already have account for examples such as *apothecary* and *anniversary* and, in fact, for all of the examples of (140a).

For some varieties of British English, the example *corollary* should be in the second rather than the first column of (140a). Its underlying representation should then be /kɔrOl+Ar+y/, rather than /kɔrV̆l+Ar+y/ (with V̆ an unspecified lax vowel) as in American English.

Some of the examples in the second column of (140a) have two cycles in their derivations. The word *elementary*, for example, will be derived as follows:[94]

$$\left(143\right)$$

$[_A \, [_N \text{element}]_N \, \text{Ar}+\text{y}]_A$			
1			RULE (102bi)
2		1	RULE (102aii)
3	1	2	RULE (102cii)
3	1	–	RULE (118d)
2	1	–	RULE (120b)
3	1	–	RULE (63)

In the first cycle, primary stress is placed on the first syllable, the second having a weak cluster and the final one being excluded from consideration under condition (b). In the second cycle, the affix rule (a), with *-y* as the affix, places primary stress on the immediately preceding strong cluster, and condition (c) then causes primary stress to be shifted left to the strong cluster immediately preceding the final stressed syllable. The Auxiliary Reduction Rules readjust the nonprimary stresses, and Stress Adjustment gives the desired final form.

We observed earlier that the affix *-Ary* would be expected to be quite parallel to *-Ory* in its behavior, and derivation (143) illustrates that this is in fact the case. Thus the derivation of *elementary* in (143) is identical, in the second cycle, with the derivation of a word such as *supervisory*. The underlying representation for this form is $[_A \, [_V \, \text{supervIs}]_V$ Or+y]_A$. In the first cycle, primary stress is placed on the final strong cluster by (eii) of the Main Stress Rule, and is then shifted two syllables to the left by the Alternating Stress Rule (75). For the verb in isolation, then, we would have [sÚpərvĬz], when the Stress Adjustment Rule and other phonetic processes have applied. But in the case of the adjective *supervisory*, we have a second cycle exactly like (143). Primary stress is placed by (102aii) on the tense vowel of *-Or-* before the affix *-y*. Under condition (c), case (ii) of the Main Stress Rule (102) then shifts primary stress to the tense vowel of the syllable immediately preceding *-Óry*, giving [supervÍsŌry]. The Auxiliary Reduction and Stress Adjustment Rules then give the stress contour [supervÍsory], exactly as in the last three lines of (143).

Let us now turn to the other examples of (140), namely, those listed in (b), (c), and (d). Consider first the forms of (140b). Taking *momentary* as a typical example, we should

---

[93] It is interesting to note that Bloomfield took the phonological representation of *-ary* in *secretary* to be /ejri/, thus implicitly accepting (142) as a phonological rule. He is criticized for this by Kent (1934) and defended by Bolling (1934), in an exchange which is of some interest in the light of subsequent developments in phonological theory. For discussion see Chomsky (1964, Section 4.2, note 7).

[94] For reasons discussed in note 91, we assume that the # boundary which would be expected on syntactic grounds has been simplified to +.

expect the following derivation, in close analogy to (143):

$$\left(144\right) \quad \begin{array}{l} [_A\ [_N mOment]_N\ Ar+y]_A \\ \hline \end{array}$$

1			RULE (102bii)
2	1		RULE (102aii)
3	1	2	RULE (102cii)
3	1	–	RULE (118d)
2	1	–	RULE (120d)
3	1	–	RULE (63)

We thus derive *$\overset{3}{m}$omen$\overset{1}{t}$ary*, instead of *momen$\overset{1}{t}$ar$\overset{3}{y}$*, as required. Evidently, *momentary* and the other examples of (140b) are different in that they are not subject to condition (c) of the Main Stress Rule in the second cycle. In these forms, when the stressed syllable $+\overset{1}{A}ry$ is excluded from consideration under condition (c), primary stress is not placed on the strong cluster that terminates the residual string, as it is in the second column of (140a); rather, it is placed on the syllable immediately preceding this strong cluster. The strong cluster in question is thus excluded from consideration along with the stressed syllable in this application of condition (c). In other words this strong cluster is treated exactly like the element $/+\partial/$ discussed previously in connection with condition (c) (see p. 104). As far as we can see, the forms that behave in this way must be marked by some "diacritic" feature [D] that determines the appropriate application of condition (c). It seems that the most direct way to account for these facts is by assigning the diacritic marking [+D] to the final vowel of the underlying lexical items of (140b), then reformulating conditions (c) and (d) of the Main Stress Rule so that syllables marked [+D] are excluded from consideration, along with $/+\partial/$, when these conditions are applied. We therefore restate conditions (c) and (d) of (102) as in (145):

$$\left(145\right) \quad ([+D]C_0) \begin{bmatrix} -seg \\ \langle -FB\rangle \end{bmatrix} C_0\ [\beta stress]\ C_0\langle V_0 C_0\rangle\ ]_{NSP\ VA} \quad (c)$$

$$([+D]C_0)\ C_0\ [\beta stress]\ C_0]_{NSP} \quad (d)$$

$$\beta = \begin{Bmatrix} 2 \\ 1 \end{Bmatrix}$$

We stipulate that the prefix-forming element $/+\partial/$ and the second vowel of a lexical item of the form $\#C_0 V C_0 V$ [+sonorant][+consonantal] ... automatically have the feature specification [+D], all other units being redundantly marked [−D].[95] We therefore have

---

[95] The feature [+sonorant] distinguishes nasals, glides, and liquids from other consonants. See note 34.

In note 56 we observed that some prefixes ending in *-o* depart from the regular rule in that the final *-o* is not excluded from consideration under condition (c) (e.g., *galvanoscope*, *hyalograph*), and we suggested that the final *-o* in this case not be separated by a + boundary from the string that precedes it. An alternative would now be to distinguish these instances of *-o* from others by the feature [+D]. This is a minor matter, and it makes little difference how it is resolved.

We can use the same device to extend our account of nouns and adjectives derived from verbs of the form ...$C_0 \overset{1}{V} C_0 \overset{2}{V} C_0$ (see p. 107). We noted that in such cases the derived form undergoes vowel reduction in the final syllable, though the underlying verb does not; and we explained this on the basis of an application of conditions (c) and (d) in the second cycle, as in the case of derivation (99) for the noun *delegate* ([delǝgǝt]) from the verb *delegate* ([delǝgÄt]). But in the case of the derived forms *alternate*, *designate*, condition (c) should place primary stress on the penultimate syllable in the second cycle,

the derivation (146) instead of (144) for *momentary*:

$$\begin{pmatrix} 146 \end{pmatrix}$$

	[_A [_N mOment]_N Ar+y]_A		
	+D		(READJUSTMENT RULE)
	1		RULE (102bii)
	2	1	RULE (102aii)
	1	2	RULE (102cii), (145c)
	1	3	RULE (63)
		e	RULE (142)

There are analogous derivations for *legendary* and other similar examples of the form $\# X + Ary$, where X is a bisyllabic noun and terminates in a sonorant-consonant cluster. With this artifice, we now account for the examples of (140b). Notice that we have also accounted in this way for the examples of (140c), which differ from those of (140b) only in that *-Ary* is not added to an underlying noun. The readjustment rule of the preceding paragraph assigns [+D] in the second syllable of these forms as well, so that the derivations will be exactly like (146).

Once again we have closely analogous examples ending in *-Ory*. Thus consider the nouns *ínventòry, prómontòry, óffertòry, répertòry*. In these words we would expect primary stress to fall on the second rather than the first syllable, as it does in *refráctory, trajéctory, reféctory*, and so on, since the second syllable terminates with a strong cluster. However, the string preceding *-Ory* is of the form C_0VC_0V [+sonorant] [+consonantal], exactly as in the case of the exceptions with *-Ary*. Notice that the exceptions with *-Ory* just given differ from those of (140b) in that they have no boundary before the string *-Ory*. However the absence of a boundary has no phonetic consequences here. It simply causes condition (d) to be applied at the point in the derivation where condition (c) applies in (146). Otherwise the derivations will be exactly as in the second cycle of (146). Similarly, in the case of *dýsentery* (see note 95), with no boundary before *-Ary*, condition (d) will apply. But in the case of an adjective like *désultòry*, condition (d), being restricted to nouns, is inapplicable. We must therefore assume a formative boundary before *-Ory* in this case to make condition (c) applicable. Such words as *dysentery* and *inventory* provide the reason for the modification of conditions (c) and (d) noted in the last paragraph of Section 13. The effect of this modification, restated in (145), is simply to permit [+D] C_0 to appear in condition (d) so that the Stressed Syllable Rule can apply to these words even though they contain no internal boundary.

By a similar artifice, we can account for the fact that in the examples of (140d),

---

since this terminates in a strong cluster. To avoid this consequence, we can assign the feature [+D] to the second syllable so that it is excluded from consideration along with the stressed final syllable when condition (c) is applied. In the case of *alternate*, assignment of [+D] in this position would be a special case of the readjustment rule dealing with strings of the form C_0VC_0V [+sonorant] [+consonantal]. This will not preclude the assignment of primary stress to the second syllable by condition (a), as in *altérnative*. Notice that *sign*, as in *designate*, does not take primary stress, as expected, under other circumstances as well; thus there is no such form as **desígnative* (like *illústrative* or *altérnative*).

   The same readjustment rule explains the stress contour of *dysentery* from the underlying representation /disVntAr+y/. Incidentally, because of the extension (136) of conditions (a) and (b) of the Main Stress Rule, the stress assignment in nouns such as *promontory, dysentery* would be unaffected if these nouns were represented without a + boundary before *-y*. There are so few relevant forms in this case that it is useless to carry the discussion any further.

primary stress is on the initial syllable rather than on the second syllable, as we would otherwise expect. These are apparently the only forms with more than two syllables before *-Ary* with a final weak cluster. We extend the readjustment rule for [D] so that it assigns [+D] in the syllable preceding *-Ary* in these words, this extension being entirely ad hoc. We now have the following derivation for *veterinary*:

$$\left(147\right)$$

ₐ[veterin+Ar+y]ₐ			
+D			(READJUSTMENT RULE)
	1		RULE (102aii)
1	2		RULE (102ci), (145c)
1	3		RULE (63)

The derivation of *disciplinary* has an additional cycle but is the same as (147) in its second cycle. Under condition (c), in both cases, an extra syllable is excluded from consideration along with the following stressed syllable, and primary stress is placed by case (i) of the Main Stress Rule in the syllable preceding the weak cluster of the residue. (Note that in *disciplinary* we must regard *pl* as a weak cluster—see p. 83, p. 197, and note 82.)

The examples of (140) therefore appear to require a rather general readjustment rule and a slight revision of condition (c). Apart from this they are accommodated by independently motivated rules.

The example *commentary* in (140b) deserves some further discussion. Notice that in the underlying form *comment*, the second syllable is unreduced; whereas in *legend* and *moment*, the second syllable reduces as expected. A further peculiarity of the underlying form is that *comment* has the same phonetic shape as a noun and as a verb, whereas we would expect [kəment] as the verb and [káment] as the noun derived from it. Another example sharing this exceptional behavior of *comment* is *triumph*, which has the phonetic realization [trɪ́ʌmf] both as a noun and as a verb, whereas we would expect [trɪʌmf] as the verb and [trɪʌmf] as the noun derived from it.

The items *comment* and *triumph* clearly depart from the regular patterns, and we must enter them in the lexicon in such a way as to indicate this. One possible analysis, which does little violence to the grammar as already constituted, is to add an extra cycle, quite artificially, to the verb in each case, and to assume that the nouns *comment* and *triumph* and the corresponding verbs are independently derived from underlying stems of a new class S. With this artifice, we then have the following derivation for *commentary*:

$$\left(148\right)$$

[ɴ [ᵥ [ₛkəment]ₛ]ᵥ Ar+y]ɴ			
+D			(READJUSTMENT RULE)
1			RULE (102eii)
1 2			RULE (102dii), (145d)
2 3	1		RULE (102aii)
1 4	2		RULE (102cii), (145c)
1 –	2		RULE (118d)
1 –	3		RULE (63)

In the first cycle, the feature [+D] is introduced by the readjustment rule just discussed and primary stress is placed on the final strong cluster so that, were it not for the exceptional behavior of the verb in this case, we would have the isolated form [kəmȅnt]. In the second, artificially introduced cycle, condition (d) applies (or condition (c) if we take the form to derive from underlying /kəN = meNt/) and requires us to exclude the final stressed syllable from consideration, assigning primary stress by case (ii) to the remaining monosyllable. Thus in isolation we have the verb [kȁměnt] after the application of other familiar rules. (Notice that this application of condition (c) requires its extension to verbs, as provided in (102) and (145); if condition (d) is to be applied, then it too must be extended to verbs, a rather minor matter concerning which we have insufficient evidence to motivate a decision.) In the next cycle the affix -*y* causes primary stress to be shifted to the syllable preceding it. Condition (c) then holds, requiring us to omit from consideration the final stressed syllable and the syllable marked [+D] that precedes it, and to place primary stress on the mono-syllabic residue. The Auxiliary Reduction Rule (118d) weakens the occurrence of [4 stress] to [−stress] so that the Vowel Reduction Rule reduces the vowel to [ə]. The Stress Adjustment Rule (63) then weakens the secondary stress on -*Ary* to tertiary. Rules (142), (130), and (119), along with the rule that changes [ə] to [ā], give, finally, the phonetic representation [kȁmənterE]. The vowel of the syllable -*ment* does not reduce in *comment* but does reduce in *commentary* because of the extra cycle. Similarly, it would reduce in *commentator* (from /kəment+At+ər/), by a derivation analogous to (148).

There are a few other examples that do not appear to follow the general rules for items ending in -*ary* and -*ory*, namely, words such as *medúllary*, *centénary* (both of which, incidentally, have variants with the expected initial stress). We return to these on page 151.

We should also mention that throughout this discussion we have been assuming that the phonetic representation of -*Ory* is [*OrE*] when the vowel [O] is not reduced. Actually, in many dialects this vowel is phonetically low, as a result of phonetic rules that apply to [A] and [O] before liquids.

Summarizing, we have been led to modify conditions (c) and (d) slightly, reformulating them as (145), to add the marginal phonetic rule (142), and to postulate a readjustment rule that inserts the diacritic feature [+D] in various positions, in particular, in forms with sonorant-consonant clusters in the second syllable followed by -*Ary* or -*Ory* (and perhaps /At/—see note 95) and in trisyllabic forms terminating in a weak cluster followed by /Ary/. We stress that this readjustment rule is introduced ad hoc to account for what appears to be exceptional behavior. Perhaps there is a deeper explanation of the facts that can eliminate the rule; however, even as it stands there are clear subregularities that can be exploited to account for the exceptions in a fairly simple way.

Let us now turn our attention to complex forms ending in -*Ory*, such as the following:

$\left(149\right)$

(a)   *compénsatòry*   *antícipatòry*
           confíscatòry   *artículatòry*
           expúrgatòry   *revérberatòry*
           derógatòry   *hallúcinatòry*
           oscíllatòry   *manípulatòry*

(b)   *inflámmatòry*
           comméndatòry
           prepáratòry

For the examples of the first column of (149a), we must have derivations such as the following:

$$\left(150\right) \quad [_A [_V kəN = peNsAt]_V \; Or + y]_A$$

		1		RULE (102eii)
1		2		RULE (75)
2		3	1	RULE (102aii)
3	1	4	2	RULE (102cii)
–	1	–	2	RULE (118b, d)
–	1	–	3	RULE (63)

In the first cycle primary stress is placed on the final strong cluster and then shifted back two syllables by the Alternating Stress Rule (75). Thus in isolation we would have the verb *compénsàte*. In the second cycle the affix *-y* places primary stress on the preceding strong cluster in the usual way. We turn next to condition (c). As our rules are now formulated, condition (c) requires us to omit from consideration the final stressed syllable and to place stress in the residual string *compènsÁt-*. Since the final cluster of this residual string is strong, primary stress will fall on this final syllable by case (ii) of the Main Stress Rule, giving *còmpensÁtŏry* at this stage of the derivation. This is incorrect, however, for American English. Instead we want primary stress to be placed on the syllable *-pens-* at this point. Clearly what is required is that the sequence *-At* be omitted from consideration under condition (c), along with the sequence that follows it, precisely as in the case of condition (a). In other words we must extend condition (c) exactly as we extended condition (a) in (122). We therefore stipulate that the string *-At* be considered part of the omitted context, rather than part of the residual form, under conditions (a) and (c) (and, irrelevantly, (b) and (d)). Combining this with the modification of condition (c) given as (145c), we now replace condition (c) of (102) by (151).[96]

$$\left(151\right) \quad \left(\left\{ \begin{array}{c} At \\ [+D]\,C_0 \end{array} \right\}\right) \left[\begin{array}{c} -\text{seg} \\ \langle -\text{FB}\rangle \end{array} \right] C_0 [\beta\text{stress}] C_0 \langle V_0 C_0 \rangle]_{\text{NSPVA}}$$

$$\beta = \left\{ \begin{array}{c} 2 \\ 1 \end{array} \right\}$$

We have now replaced condition (a) of (102) by (122) and condition (c) of (102) by (151). In each case the modification assigns the string *-At* to the omitted context. When the rules

---

[96] Actually, our examples illustrating the assignment of *-At* to the external context all involve conditions (a), (c), and (d). In fact, under condition (b) the element *-At* is not treated in this way (cf. *ultimátum, potáto*). Precise statement of this fact requires the use of a generalization of the angled bracket notation, which we develop in Chapter Eight but have not made full use of in the body of the text.

    Not only /At/ but also /f Ik + At/ is treated in this way. This accounts for the fact that we have words such as *jústificàtory* and *clássificàtory*, with five syllables after the primary stress, as contrasted with *multiplícative* (with [I] becoming [i] for reasons that will be discussed in the next chapter).

    It should also be mentioned that there are apparently some marginal subsidiary rules that prevent long sequences of unstressed syllables after primary stress in many cases. Thus, on syntactic grounds we should expect the affix *-ly*, for example, to appear with a # boundary and to be neutral with respect to stress placement for this reason (see p. 85). Under certain conditions, however, the # boundary is simplified to +, so that *-ly* places stress by the affix rule (102a). We thus have forms such as *ordinárily, obligatórily*, and, as an optional variant, *evidéntly*, where stress is shifted to the right by *-ly* regarded as a regular affix. When affixed to words such as *satisfáctory* or *perfúnctory*, however, *-ly* does not cause stress to be shifted to the right and thus remains a neutral affix preceded by #. The conditions for replacement of # by + before *-ly* are fairly clear; the basic point seems to be that a barrier is placed against long strings of unstressed syllables following primary stress. (See also note 91, p. 134.)

are given in their optimal representation (cf. (101)), the condition involving *-At* need be stated only once. Thus the modification of condition (c) just proposed is actually a generalization of (122) to condition (c).

Assuming this modification of the Main Stress Rule, we can now return to the derivation (150). We have reached the second line of the second cycle. Applying condition (c), modified as (151), we omit from consideration the string *-At+Or+y* and use case (ii) of (102) to place primary stress on the final syllable of the residual string $\overset{2}{compens}$-, case (i) being blocked by the final strong cluster. The Auxiliary Reduction Rules (118b) and (118d) apply to the vowels of the first and third syllables, respectively, and these are then subject to Vowel Reduction. By other familiar rules, we derive, finally, the phonetic representation [$\overset{1}{k}$əmpens$\overset{3}{ə}$tOrE].

In a similar manner we derive the other examples of the left-hand column of (149a). Notice that in the case of *dérogate*, *óscillate*, we might postulate a tense vowel in the second syllable, just as suggested in the case of *indicate*, *correlate* (see p. 128).

The examples of the second column of (149a) are now straightforward. Thus *anticipatory* will have the derivation (152), and the other examples will be quite parallel.

$\left(152\right)$

```
       [A [V aNticipAt]V Or+y]A
                1                    RULE (102eii)
             1   2                   RULE (75)
       ─────────────────
           2   3   1                 RULE (102aii)
           1   4   2                 RULE (102ci), (151)
           1   -   2                 RULE (118d)
       2   1   -   2                 RULE (120c)
       3   1   -   3                 RULE (63)
       ─────────────────
```

The first cycle is much like that of (150), and the underlying verb in isolation would be $\overset{3}{a}$ntic$\overset{1}{i}$p$\overset{3}{A}$t. In the second cycle primary stress is placed by *-y* exactly as in (150). We turn next to condition (c), reformulated as (151). Excluding the string *-$\overset{3}{A}$t$\underset{2}{\overset{1}{O}}$ry* from consideration, we assign primary stress in the residual string *anticip-* by case (i), the final cluster of this string being weak. In other words, we reassign primary stress to the syllable that contained primary stress in the first cycle, weakening all other stresses in the word by one. The vowel [$\overset{4}{A}$] becomes [−tense] and [−stress] by the Auxiliary Reduction Rule (118d), then undergoing reduction to [ə] in the usual way, and secondary stress is placed on the first syllable by the Auxiliary Reduction Rule (120c). Other familiar rules give, finally, the phonetic representation [$\overset{3}{æ}$ntis$\overset{1}{ə}$p$\overset{3}{ə}$tOrE].

Notice the parallel between the examples of (149a) and the examples of (124), with the affix *-ive*. Thus $\overset{-}{dem}\overset{1}{on}\overset{-}{stra}\overset{-}{tive}$ is related to $\overset{-}{gen}\overset{-}{er}\overset{1}{a}\overset{-}{tive}$ exactly as $\overset{1}{compen}\overset{3}{satory}$ is related to $\overset{3}{an}\overset{1}{tic}\overset{-}{ipa}\overset{3}{tory}$. The only difference between the examples with *-ive* and those with *-ory* is that there are no forms such as *$\overset{1}{compen}\overset{3}{satory}$*, *$\overset{3}{an}\overset{1}{tic}\overset{3}{ipatory}$*, paralleling *$\overset{1}{contem}\overset{3}{plative}$*, *$\overset{1}{gener}\overset{3}{ative}$*, respectively. The reason is that the elements *-Ary*, *-Ory* take primary stress, at one stage of the derivation, by the Affix Rule, and then shift stress to the left by the Stressed Syllable Rule (102c) (now formulated as (151)). Syntactically *-ive* and *-ory* are quite parallel. The few differences between them in their phonetic effects are, we see, simply a reflection of the difference in their underlying representations. (See also note 91.)

Returning to (149), the examples of (149b) now raise no difficulties. The derivation (153) is typical.[97]

$$\begin{pmatrix}153\end{pmatrix}$$

[$_A$ [$_V$in = flAm]$_V$ At+Or+y]$_A$		
1		RULE (102eii)
2	1	RULE (102aii)
1	2	RULE (102cii), (151)
1	3	RULE (63)

In the first cycle primary stress falls on the final strong cluster. Matters then proceed exactly as before. (The *A–æ* alternation is automatic in this position, as we shall see in the next chapter.) Thus the difference in structure between the underlying verbs of (149a) and (149b) does not affect the phonetic forms.

Examples such as *prédatory*, *gústatory*, and *mígratory* are derived as required from the underlying representations [$_A$pred+At+Or+y]$_A$, [$_A$gust+At+Or+y]$_A$, [$_A$ [$_V$mIgr+At]$_V$ Or+y]$_A$, respectively.

We still have not given the rules for deriving the phonetic representation [mĬgrĂt] or for deriving the variants [rŎtĂt], [rŎtĂt], and so on. We return to this question on page 155. Notice, however, that whether primary stress is on the first or the second syllable in such words, the derived form with *-ory* has primary stress on the first syllable. Thus we have *mígratory*, *óratory*, *rótatory*, *rótatory* from *mígrate*, *oráte*, *rótate*, *rotáte*, respectively. This apparent anomaly is accounted for by the rules already given. For example, the word *rótatory* is derived either from *rótate* or *rotáte* by the derivations (154):

$$\begin{pmatrix}154\end{pmatrix}$$

[$_A$ [$_V$rOt+At]$_V$ Or+y]$_A$			[$_A$ [$_V$rOtAt]$_V$ Or+y]$_A$			
1			1			RULE (102cii)
1	2					(RULE TO BE GIVEN)
2	3	1	2	1		RULE (102aii)
1	4	2	1	3	2	RULE (102cii), (151)
1	–	2	1	–	2	RULE (118d)
1	–	3	1	–	3	RULE (63)

In the first cycle, primary stress is assigned to the final strong cluster in both cases, and, for reasons we have not yet discussed, it is then shifted left in the left-hand derivation of (154). The second cycle operates exactly as in the cases dealt with above, and, as we see, it gives the same final form in both cases despite the difference between them at the end of the first cycle.

In this section we have been concerned with the affixes *-y*, *-Ary*, *-(At)Ory*, and *-(At)ive* and their diverse phonetic effects. We have seen that these can be accounted for quite simply, largely on the basis of rules established independently. The only modification of any significance in the Main Stress Rule (102) is the requirement that *-At* be considered as part of the element omitted from consideration, along with the string that follows it, under conditions (a)–(d). This change and other minor modifications are expressed in (122) and

[97] In this case the element /At/ is lexically part of the underlying verb, just as the stem-forming elements /i/, /u/ of *componential*, *habitual* are lexically part of the underlying forms (see pp. 129–30). Thus *inflame* differs from *compel*, for example, in that the former takes an *-At-* augment before the affixes *-Ory* and *-ion*. However, as we have already noted (see p. 116), these augments are assigned to the exterior rather than the interior cycle.

(151), which replace conditions (a)–(d) of rule (102). At the same time, we have seen that conditions (a) and (b) can be simplified to (136). Beyond this, we have introduced only minor modifications. Thus we have seen how a collection of complex and superficially quite exceptional phonetic facts can be explained on the basis of a fairly simple system of rules which are, for the most part, independently motivated on other grounds.

The reader who has followed the exposition carefully will have noticed the crucial role played by the conditions on ordering determined by the relations among the successive parts of the Main Stress Rule (102). We have relied in an essential way on the fact that condition (c) or (d) can follow (a) or (b), whereas no other sequences are allowed within a single cycle. This is an important fact, for it provides evidence in support of the extremely strong hypothesis regarding conjunctive and disjunctive ordering tentatively suggested on page 30.

16. Stress as a lexical category

We have now described most of the processes known to us that determine stress contours and related phenomena. It may be useful at this point to reconsider briefly the general problem to which this investigation has been addressed.

We have presupposed a syntactic component of the grammar that generates a surface structure for each utterance. This surface structure is a string with labeled bracketing. The string consists of lexical and grammatical formatives represented in matrix form. Each string, then, consists of matrices with labeled bracketing, the columns of the matrices standing for segments and boundaries, the rows standing for various phonological categories. Everything in the surface structure except the representation of the formatives is determined by the nonlexical syntactic rules. The matrix representation of the lexical formatives is given in the lexicon as part of the entry for these formatives. Each lexical formative has a single entry in which is represented all information relevant to the item's phonetic form in various positions.

This syntactic surface structure is further modified by the readjustment rules, which, however, change only specific elements in the representation and do not affect its general character. It is this modified surface structure that is subject to the rules of the phonological component and is converted by them into a phonetic representation.

Corresponding to each surface structure there is a phonetic representation consisting of a matrix in which columns stand for phonetic segments and rows are labeled by distinctive features provided by a universal phonetic theory. This representation stands in a direct relationship with particular elements of the complex array of stress contours, reduced and nonreduced vowels, etc., that are found in the phonetic record. The rules of the phonological component of a grammar apply to the surface structure representation of an utterance as modified by the readjustment rules and convert it into a phonetic representation, using the information that is present in the surface structure representation and that ultimately derives, therefore, from the lexical entries and the syntactic rules.

In a phonetic representation, each square of the matrix is filled by an entry indicating the specification of a particular unit in terms of a particular feature. In their phonetic function, many of the features—in particular, the feature of stress—are scales, and the entries are integers indicating position along these scales in a conventional way. In the underlying lexical representation, only those specifications that are not determined by general rule are indicated. The entry in a particular square of the lexical matrix indicates membership of the unit in question in one or another of two disjoint categories which are, furthermore, exhaustive in the domain in which membership is not determined by rule.[98]

The feature composition of a particular lexical entry is not a matter of choice but rather one of fact. In the case of the examples we have discussed so far, the facts seem to be that stress is not a category that is specified in lexical entries. That is, lexical matrices are not distinguished from one another in terms of the categorial feature [±stress] in certain positions, as they are distinguished in terms of the categorial features [±vocalic], [±voice], [±strident], etc. Instead, the contours of stress and the arrangement of reduced and unreduced vowels are determined by general rule.

It is important to recognize that this conclusion would not be affected by the discovery (supposing this to be a fact, for the sake of illustration) that there is a class of items for which stress or reducibility is a category that is distinctive in their lexical entries. The situation here is quite analogous to the more familiar and far more trivial one of regular and irregular verbs. Monosyllabic verbs must be categorized as regular or nonregular in their lexical entries.[99] Only the nonregular verbs require further lexical specification; the inflected forms of the other verbs are determined by general rule. Among the verbs marked as nonregular, there are subgeneralizations involving rules that limit the extent of lexical specification; apart from these subregularities, each nonregular lexical entry must indicate exactly which rules do or do not apply to the item in question. The discovery of nonregular verbs, however, does not force us to provide such additional specification for the regular verbs, in particular, the polysyllabic verbs. Similarly, the discovery of lexical items that are irregular with respect to stress placement or vowel reduction would not, in itself, show that the mass of regular items need be specified in terms of a lexical feature of stress or reducibility.

We repeat this rather obvious point in preparation for an investigation of some cases in which stress might appear to be marginally distinctive on the lexical level. We will attempt to determine whether stress is, in fact, a distinctive lexical category for any of these items or whether, alternatively, their irregularity must be marked by a different sort of categorial feature or complex of features. But whatever the results of this investigation may be, it is important to realize that it may have no effect at all on what has been presented so far, just as an investigation of irregular verbs may have little or no effect on the rules for the regular paradigms. In either case, investigation of exceptions to rules will affect the statement of these rules only if it leads to the discovery of still deeper regularities that replace them.

In the course of the discussion of regular cases, we have several times made note of examples that do not fall under the general rules that were developed. One such case was on page 73, in connection with condition (b) of the Main Stress Rule (102), which determines the position of primary stress in nouns ending in a syllable with a nontense vowel. The general rule is to omit the final syllable from consideration and then to place primary stress in the residue by case (i) or case (ii) of the Main Stress Rule. Typical examples are *aspáragus, arÓma, uténsil, clÍmax.*[100] We also listed several examples that do not fall under this generalization, such as *cemént, giráffe, burlésque, Mississíppi, ellípse.*

[98] The exact meaning of this rather vague remark will be discussed in Chapter Eight.
[99] The few nonregular polysyllabic verbs can be identified by their internal structure. There is little doubt that within the category of monosyllables there are identifiable subcategories that need not be specified with respect to regularity. We have made no attempt to investigate the exact domain of the categorial feature in detail.
[100] The final vowel of *climax* is immune from reduction because of the tense vowel of the preceding syllable. Thus we find variants such as [ǽrəb], [Áræb] for *Arab.* This minor regularity was pointed out to us by J. Fidelholtz. There are further conditions and complications which we shall not elaborate.

In the face of such apparent exceptions, there are three paths open to us: (1) giving up the general rule for stress placement in nouns with a lax vowel in the final syllable and assigning to each such noun a lexical feature determining its category with respect to the position of primary stress; (2) specifying nouns of the lax final-syllable class as [±regular] in the lexicon and then further categorizing those that are [−regular] in terms of stress placement; (3) assigning a representation in terms of segments and boundaries to each apparently nonregular noun in such a way that the correct phonetic form is predicted by rules that are needed on independent grounds.

Of these alternatives, the first is ruled out at once. Condition (b) would have to be dropped from the grammar and each noun of the type to which condition (b) applied would have to have an additional feature specification in its lexical entry, thus greatly increasing the complexity of the lexicon. Furthermore, it is important to notice that by dropping condition (b) from the grammar we do not reduce the complexity of the grammar *at all*. To see this, consider the fully formalized grammar containing rule (101) (p. 109) as an abbreviation for conditions (a)–(e). Notice that to exclude condition (b) from (101) is simply to drop occurrences of angled brackets in this rule. Under any reasonable evaluation measure—in particular, that which we shall discuss—the notations used in abbreviating rules do not count in determining the value of the system of rules. These notations provide a measure of the extent to which a system of rules expresses generalizations that are, by hypothesis, linguistically significant. The measure that we propose is in terms of number of feature specifications after certain notational transformations of a well-defined class have applied. These notational transformations are part of the definition of simplicity, and therefore it would be senseless to "count them" in some way in measuring simplicity.

In short, even if the language contained no nouns of the sort we are now discussing, there would be no more highly valued grammar than the one that contains condition (b), as formulated above. Consequently, we gain nothing in simplicity by excluding condition (b). But we lose a great deal under the first alternative by having to complicate the lexicon, not to mention the new phonological rules needed to interpret this lexical categorization in terms of phonetic stress.

The only plausible alternatives, then, are the second and third. The second requires adding a new feature [+regular] to the lexical entry for each regular noun. The third alternative involves no such complication and is therefore preferable, if it can be realized. It is, then, interesting to observe that there are certain "phonological gaps" which, when filled, lead to just the phonetic representations that we require.

To begin with, notice that nouns such as *burlésque*, *ellípse*, *cemént* would receive the proper stress contour by case (bii) of the Main Stress Rule if the lexical representation in each case were to terminate in a lax vowel. In discussing lax final vowels, we noticed a certain phonological gap (see note 22). Of the six expected lax vowel segments, we found in final position examples only for underlying /i/, /u/, /o/, /æ/, /ɔ/; there was no example to illustrate final /e/. These observations suggest that we add to the grammar a rule of *e*-Elision such as (155):

$$\left(155\right) \qquad \qquad \text{e} \;\rightarrow\; \phi \;\; / \;\; \underline{\qquad} [-\text{seg}]$$

The exact position of this rule in the sequence of rules will concern us later. For the moment we note merely that it must apply after the Main Stress Rule.

We can now represent *burlesque*, *ellipse*, *cement* in the underlying forms /bVrleske/,

/Elipse/, /sEmente/, respectively.[101] Primary stress, in each case, will be placed on the penultimate vowel under condition (b) of the Main Stress Rule (102), by case (ii). The final vowel will then be elided by rule (155). Words such as *clímax, sérpent*, on the other hand, will be represented with no word-final vowel. In this way the "phonological gap" in the lexicon is filled; the class of lexical items is more symmetrical in that all possibilities are realized, and we need not provide a categorial specification, with respect to stress placement, for nouns terminating in syllables containing lax vowels.

We shall see that rule (155) plays a role in explaining many other phonetic facts and is therefore quite essential to English phonology. For the present, however, we simply observe that it allows us to make use of a phonological gap to avoid introducing a new and ad hoc lexical categorization and the new phonological rules of stress placement that would be required to interpret this ad hoc categorization in phonetic terms.

Consider now words such as *Mississíppi, Kentúcky, confétti, abscíssa, Philíppa*. In each item the final vowel is lax in the underlying form (see pp. 74–75). Thus condition (b) holds, omitting the final syllable from consideration. Case (i) of the Main Stress Rule will apply to the residual string, giving an incorrect antepenultimate stress in each case. To derive the correct stress contour, we must somehow block the application of case (i) so that case (ii) will assign primary stress to the final syllable of the residual string, that is, to the penultimate syllable of the word.

A simple device for blocking case (i) in each case would be to represent these words with a double consonant before the final vowel, as in conventional orthography. Thus the lexical representations would be /misisippi/, /kVntukki/, /kVnfetti/, /æb=cissæ/, /filippæ/.[102] This artifice accomplishes our purpose. Case (i) is blocked because of the double consonant, and case (ii) then correctly assigns primary stress to the penultimate syllable. We must then add to the grammar a rule of consonant simplification which we state informally as (156):

$$\left(156\right) \qquad\qquad C \;\to\; \phi \;\; / \text{ before an identical C}$$

Thus the word *Mississippi*, for example, terminating with the phonological segments / ... ippi/, will receive primary stress on the penultimate syllable because of the strong cluster, and the consonant string will then simplify to [... ípi].

There is quite a bit of empirical evidence supporting the postulation of rule (156). We noted in Section 10 that there are rules voicing the segment [s] in many positions. One such case is rule (74), which voices [s] in the context V = ―― V. Thus we have intervocalic [z] in *resist, resemble, design, presume*; but the corresponding segment remains nonvoiced in *consist, semblance, consign, consume*. Notice, however, that in *assist, assemble, assign, assume*, the segment [s] remains unvoiced, in apparent violation of rule (74). This contradiction can be avoided by the assumption that the prefix in these examples is not *a-* but rather *as-*, so that when rule (74) applies, the representations will be [æs=sist], [æs=sembl], etc. Further analysis of the prefix-stem construction shows that the prefix is not *as-* but is rather

---

[101] Notice that these apparently optimal lexical representations depart in an important way from conventional orthography only in the case of *cement*. If *cement* were represented as /sEment/, it would become [sÉment] in the phonetic representation. This is, in fact, a dialectal variant.

      The first vowel of *burlesque* is actually the archi-segment "lax vowel." The first vowel of *ellipse* is subject to dialectal variation in its phonetic form.

[102] On the interpretation of the symbol *c*, see notes 86 and 103.

of the form aC-, where C is a consonant which assimilates to the following consonant under conditions which we describe in more detail in the next chapter. In any event, this analysis requires postulation of a rule such as (156) to simplify the [ss] cluster that would otherwise appear in the phonetic representation.

Such pairs as *potassium–gymnasium* give further justification for the postulation of [ss] strings which are simplified phonetically by rule (156). We have discussed several cases of the tense-lax vowel alternations that involve the pairs *A–æ*, *E–e*, *O–ā*, etc. As we shall see in the next chapter, [æ] is replaced by [A], [e] by [E], and [ɔ] (which underlies [ā]) by [O] in the context ——C$_1^1$iV, as in *gymnasium, magnesium*. A double consonant blocks this rule, as in *calcium, compendium*, where the vowel given in boldface remains lax. But in *potassium* the boldface vowel is lax, indicating that it is followed by a double consonant in the underlying form, which then simplifies by rule (156). In further support of this assumption, notice that in the cases where the vowel tenses (e.g., *gymnasium, magnesium, cesium*), the [s] segment voices, obviously by a generalization of the rule (74) that voices [s] in intervocalic position. But in *potassium* we have phonetic [s], not phonetic [z], in this position, indicating that the rule voicing intervocalic [s] must somehow be blocked. Postulation of [ss] in the underlying phonological representation thus accounts for the fact that in the phonetic form [pɔtæsEəm] the antepenultimate vowel is lax and the following consonant is unvoiced, thereby eliminating two independent exceptions. Once again, this is possible only by virtue of rule (156).

Deeper analysis of English sound structure provides still further justification for these assumptions. Consider, for example, the words *music, Pusey, Russell, russet*. The first two have intervocalic [z] following [U] in the phonetic representation; the last two have intervocalic [s] following [ʌ] in the phonetic representation. In fact, these configurations are characteristic. There is no relevant case with the phonetic form [CÚsVC];[103] a form [mÚsək] or [pÚsE], for example, would deviate from the regular sound patterns of English. The explanation for this is provided by the rules of [ʌ]–[U] alternation that we shall discuss in detail in the next chapter. Of relevance to our present discussion is the fact that of the two segments [ʌ], [U], only [ʌ] appears freely in strong clusters, as in *musket, mustard*. On the other hand, the lax, high, back vowel which, as we shall see, underlies [ʌ] in strong clusters becomes [U] in underlying weak clusters followed by vowels, as in *futile, pewter, putrid, cutaneous, cupola*. In conformity with this rule, we must assume the medial cluster in *Russell, russet*, and so on to be [ss]. This assumption then automatically accounts for the fact that the cluster is not affected by the rule that voices the medial [s] of *music, Pusey*. Once again, two independent phonetic facts follow from the postulation of [ss], namely, the voiceless-voiced opposition in the consonant and the corresponding [ʌ]–[U] opposition in the preceding syllable. Again, this explanation presupposes that rule (156) is in the grammar.

Combining these observations with what we have discovered about *e*-Elision, we can now account for the stress pattern of otherwise exceptional forms such as *Neptune*, which is phonetically [néptUn] (or, in some dialects, [néptūwn], [néptšūwn], [néptšUn], etc., after the application of late phonetic rules that we will discuss in the next chapter). If we were to take the underlying vowel of the second syllable to be tense, it should have primary stress, as in *machine, career*, etc. (See (37), p. 78.) If we were to take it to be lax, we would have the

---

[103] A word such as *lucid* is only an apparent exception. We can derive this from the underlying representation /luc+id/, where /c/ (as the variant of /k/ in forms that undergo Romance derivational processes) becomes [s] when followed by a nonlow, nonback vowel, *after* the intervocalic [s]-voicing rule has applied. Actually, the remark in the text needs some qualification (cf. *fuselage, grue+some, dOs+age, Osage, Caruso*), but it is essentially correct. See page 228 for a somewhat more careful statement.

problem of accounting for its phonetic tenseness. We can now solve this by taking the underlying lexical representation to be /neptune/. Under condition (b) of the Main Stress Rule, the
final lax vowel is omitted from consideration and primary stress is placed, by case (i), on the
initial syllable of the residual string /neptun/, the final cluster of this string being weak. By
the rule just mentioned which determines the [ʌ] – [U] alternation, the underlying segment
/u/ of the medial syllable of [nep̍tune] then becomes [U]. Rule (155) then elides the final
vowel, giving [nep̍tUn]. The Vowel Reduction Rule does not apply to the vowel of the now
final syllable because of its tenseness. Furthermore, as we have noted, the Auxiliary Reduction Rule that makes segments nontense and nonstressed does not apply to [U] (see p. 122
and note 75).

From the considerations just outlined, we conclude that rule (156) is quite well

Notice, incidentally, that the rules determining the choice of [ʌ] or [U] as a reflex of
underlying /u/ provide additional justification for rule (156), quite apart from the question
of [s]-voicing. Thus, to preserve the general rule that determines the choice of [ʌ] in a strong
cluster and [U] in a weak cluster followed by a vowel, we must represent words such as
bucket, Kentucky, putty with doubled consonants that become simplified by rule (156).

With the postulation of doubled consonants, just as with the postulation of final /e/,
we fill a gap in underlying structures (a " phonological gap ") and extend the symmetry of the
system of lexical entries. Strings of consonants appear intervocalically with considerable
freedom. The restriction that they may not be doubled would be difficult to formulate within
our framework.[104] It is therefore interesting that we now have good reason to assume that
doubled consonants do in fact appear in underlying representations. Notice further that
obstruent clusters are, with rare exceptions, unvoiced in English. Correspondingly, almost
without exception, where a double consonant must be postulated to account for stress
placement or vowel quality, this cluster either involves a sonorant or is unvoiced.[105] Hence,
not only do double consonants fill a phonological gap in general but they do so in a way
which is in accord with the general rules of consonant combination in English.

From the considerations just outlined, we conclude that rule (156) is quite well
motivated, and another class of apparent irregularities disappears.

Rules (155) and (156) now permit us to derive the phonetic representation of *giraffe*
from the underlying representation /giræffe/ (or, as far as the phonetic evidence goes,
/jVræffe/). Primary stress is placed on the penultimate syllable under condition (b) of the
Main Stress Rule (102), by case (ii), the strong cluster /æff/ preventing case (i) from applying.
After the stress is placed, the final /e/ is elided by rule (155) and the cluster is simplified by
rule (156). By rules that we discuss in detail later, /g/ becomes [j] before certain vowels. By
the general Vowel Reduction Rule discussed previously, the vowel of the first syllable
becomes [ə]. We therefore derive, finally, the phonetic representation [jəræf]. In just the
same way we can derive the phonetic forms of words such as *coquette, marionette* from the
underlying representations /kOkette/, /mæriVnette/. Notice that in the latter case, the final
[e] also serves to block the application of the Alternating Stress Rule (75).

---

[104] To put the same thing in somewhat different terms, there would be no simple way, within our framework,
to explain the fact that forms with phonetically doubled true consonants depart in an extreme way from
the normal phonetic structure of English. We return to the problem of phonological admissibility and
lexical redundancy in Chapters Eight and Nine.

[105] There are a few marginal exceptions, such as *Passamaquoddy*, for which we must postulate the underlying
representation /pasVmVkwɔddi/, with /dd/. (We discuss the /kw/ string in Chapter Four, observing that
it is, perhaps, a new phonological segment /kʷ/.) This word will, therefore, be an exception to the devoicing
of obstruent clusters, along with exceptions such as *adze, smaragd, rugby, abdomen, afghan, anecdote,
asbestos, husband, Lisbon, Presbyterian, tidbit, lobster.*

These observations show one way in which a marginal phonetic opposition between stress contours may arise. For example, a person who is given the "segmental" phonetic representation for the name of the Massachusetts town *Assinippi* would not be able to determine whether the stress contour should be *Assínippi* or *Assiníppi*, although he would know that these are the only possibilities. The former presupposes the underlying representation /æsinipi/; the latter, the representation /æsinippi/.

The rule of cluster simplification accounts for several other apparent exceptions that we have noted in the course of this chapter. Consider the phonetic variants [sèntənerÉ], [sèntənərÉ] for *centenary*. The first form derives from the underlying representation /centen+Ar+y/ in the manner described in detail in Section 15; the latter can be derived from /centenn+Ar+y/ by the same rules along with the rule of cluster simplification. In support of the latter representation, we observe that double /n/ must be postulated in *centennial* (/centenn+i+æl/) to account for the fact that the $e \rightarrow E$ rule, which should apply in the context ——$C_1^1 iV$ (see p. 47), does not apply in this case.

Similarly, we can now account for verbs such as *caress*, *acquiesce*, and adjectives such as *remiss*, *quiescent*, and so on. We might derive *caress*, *remiss*, *quiescent* from the lexical representations /kVress/, /rEmiss/, /kwiess+ent/, respectively, in the familiar way, simplifying the cluster after it plays its role in stress placement.[106] The verb *acquiesce* requires both rules (155) and (156), since an underlying final *e* is needed to prevent application of the Alternating Stress Rule (75). We can derive it from /æckwiesse/, or, perhaps, /æckwiesce/, in which case the second occurrence of /c/ becomes [s] before [e], in the usual way, or even from /æC=kwiesce/, by the processes mentioned on page 149. Assuming the last as the underlying form, we would have the following derivation:

$$\left(157\right)$$

		æC = kwiesce				
			1			RULE (102ei)
	2					RULE (120b)
	3		1			RULE (63)
			E			RULE (119)
				s		($c \rightarrow s$ RULE)
					φ	RULE (155)
	k					ASSIMILATION (see p. 149)
	φ		φ			RULE (156)

Primary stress is placed on the penultimate syllable under condition (e) of the Main Stress Rule by case (i), the final cluster being weak. (As mentioned, the final [e] prevents application of the Alternating Stress Rule (75), which would incorrectly give *[æ̀kwÉes] as the final phonetic form. The Auxiliary Reduction Rule (120b) assigns secondary stress in the first syllable, this becoming tertiary by the Stress Adjustment Rule (63). The vowel of this syllable is barred from the $æ \rightarrow A$ rule that applies in the context ——$C_1^1 iV$ (see p. 47) by virtue of the fact that it is followed by the consonant cluster [Ckw]. The vowel [i] tenses prevocalically by rule (119); the occurrence of /c/ before [e] becomes [s]; the final [e] elides; and the [ss] cluster is simplified by rule (156). Similarly, the medial cluster assimilates to [kkw] and then simplifies to [kw] by rule (156). We derive, finally, the phonetic form [æ̀kwÉes].

Words such as *pellágra*, *candelábra* also appear to be exceptions to the rules of stress

---

[106] Some modifications of these representations are required by considerations developed in the next chapter.

placement since the weak cluster [æCr] receives primary stress.[107] Investigating the situation more closely, we note many other cases where a weak cluster containing the vowel [æ] is treated as strong. Furthermore, in these cases there is apparently no contrast between [æ] and [ā] within a single idiolect. This observation suggests that we represent these clusters as /āCr/, with a tense vowel, and add a rule converting [ā] to [æ] in certain positions. There are, as we shall see, other examples of [ā]–[æ] alternation. This rule would enable us to account for words such as *pellágra*, *Alabáma*, *Koála*, and *panoráma* with the phonological representations /pVlāgræ/, /ælVbāmæ/, /koālæ/, /pænVrāmæ/. A more extensive study would undoubtedly reveal much heavier constraints on the occurrence of /ā/ and /æ/. Notice, incidentally, that these observations suggest another analysis for the word *giraffe*, namely, as derived from /jVrāf/.

Consider now words such as *álabàster*, *sálamànder*, *póetàster*. The phonetically penultimate syllable contains a strong cluster and therefore receives primary stress in the usual way. But then stress is shifted back two syllables, presumably by the Alternating Stress Rule (75). For this rule to apply, however, the primary stress must fall on the final syllable, rather than on the penultimate syllable. It follows, then, that the underlying representation must be not /ælVbæstVr/ but /ælVbæstr/, etc., the final sonorant later becoming syllabic by rule (56) (p. 85).[108] This decision, however, faces the difficulty that condition (b) requires the final syllables /æstr/, /ændr/ to be omitted from consideration when primary stress is assigned. These syllables will therefore not be protected from vowel reduction, never having received stress. To avoid this consequence we may make use, once again, of the rule converting [ā] to [æ]. The words in question can be represented as /ælVbāstr/, /sælVmāndr/, /pǝVtāstr/. Primary stress is placed on the final syllable by case (ii) of the Main Stress Rule (102) under condition (e); condition (b) is now inapplicable because of the tense vowel in the final syllable. The Alternating Stress Rule assigns primary stress to the antepenultimate syllable, weakening the stress on the last syllable to secondary, ultimately, tertiary. The final [r] then becomes syllabic, and [ā] becomes [æ]. The word *tabernacle* is now analyzed in the same way, from underlying /tæbVrnākl/.

We have not yet accounted for words with tense affixes such as *-oid*, *-ine*, *-ize*. The vowels of these affixes have a tertiary stress and do not reduce; and, furthermore, these affixes sometimes determine the placement of stress by the rules involving strong clusters. These observations suggest that tense affixes receive a primary stress before the application of the Main Stress Rule (102) so that they place stress under condition (c).[109] One possibility, then, would be to add to the grammar the rule (158), which precedes the Main Stress Rule in the ordering.

$$(158) \qquad \begin{bmatrix} +\text{tense} \\ V \end{bmatrix} \rightarrow [1 \text{ stress}] \ / \ + \text{—} C_0 \#$$

---

[107] The word *allegro* is regular in the pronunciation [ǝlÁgrO] but deviant in the alternative form [ǝlégrO]. One might consider extending rule (142), which converts [A] to [e], to this context, the *A–e* opposition being very marginal here, but there are too few examples to allow the question to be decided in any satisfactory way.

[108] Support is provided for this analysis by the fact that the adjective derived from *alabaster* is *alabastrine* [ælǝbǽstrEn], rather than [ælǝbǽstǝrÈn].

[109] As we shall see in the next chapter, the affix *-oid* is of the underlying form /VC/, as are the others under discussion here. Recall that condition (c) of the Main Stress Rule has now been reformulated as (151), but the modifications are not pertinent to the examples we consider here. Notice that many of the examples with tense affixes are verbs. It is for this reason that we extended condition (c) to verbs. (See (102), p. 110.)

We will now have typical derivations such as the following:

$$(159)$$

	$[_A \; [_N mol022lusc]_N + oid]_A$		$[_A amygdal + oid]_A$		
	1				RULE (102bii)
	2	1		1	RULE (158)
			1	2	RULE (102ci)
	3 1	2			RULE (102cii)

In the case of *mollúscoid* (similarly, *aráchnoid*, *cylíndroid*, *salamándroid*, etc.), stress is assigned in the internal cycle in the usual way. In the word-level cycle, primary stress is first assigned to the affix by rule (158). Turning next to the Main Stress Rule, we see that conditions (a) and (b) are inapplicable because of the final tense stressed vowel, but condition (c) does apply since the final syllable of the form under consideration has primary stress. In the case of *amygdaloid*, primary stress is assigned to the penultimate syllable of the residual string *amygdal-* by case (i), since the final syllable of this string has a weak cluster. In the case of *molluscoid*, primary stress is assigned to the final syllable of the residual string *mollusc-* by case (ii) since this syllable has a strong cluster. The familiar rules of Stress Adjustment and Vowel Reduction now apply to give the phonetic representations.

There is, in fact, another approach that might be explored, namely, to extend the Alternating Stress Rule (75) so that it assigns stress to the immediately preceding syllable under certain circumstances, now permitting primary stress to fall on the affix in the usual way under condition (e) of the Main Stress Rule. The approach in terms of (158) seems to us preferable, and we will postulate this as the correct rule. (See, however, pp. 236–38.)

The exact role of rule (158) can be brought out clearly by a comparison of the two derivations of (160), for the variant pronunciations [rəkǎndǐt], [rèkəndǐt] for *recondite*:

$$(160)$$

	$[_A recɔnd + It]_A$		$[_A recɔndIt]_A$		
		1			RULE (158)
	1	2			RULE (102cii)
				1	RULE (102eii)
			1	2	RULE (75)
	1	3	1	3	RULE (63)

In the left-hand derivation, we analyze the adjective as containing the affix *-ite*, which, being tense, receives primary stress by rule (158) before application of the Main Stress Rule. Since the final syllable is now stressed, condition (c) of the Main Stress Rule is in force and stress is shifted to the preceding strong cluster by case (ii) of (102). Other rules that we have already discussed give, finally, [rəkǎndǐt]. In the right-hand derivation rule (158) does not apply since the form is not analyzed as containing an affix. Consequently, condition (c) of rule (102) is inapplicable and only condition (e) applies, assigning primary stress to the final syllable of the word by case (ii). At this point, the Alternating Stress Rule (75) shifts primary stress two syllables to the left. (Recall that for application of the Alternating Stress Rule, it is immaterial whether the cluster preceding the primary-stressed final syllable is strong or weak.) Other familiar rules give, finally, the phonetic representation [rèkəndǐt]. Thus the effect of rule (158) is to make condition (c) of the Main Stress Rule applicable so that primary stress is assigned by the rules involving strong and weak clusters.

The full range of possibilities allowed by rule (158) is evident from a consideration of polysyllabic words ending in *-ize* (or *-ise*). If the ending is not subject to rule (158), we have derivations analogous to the right-hand derivation of (160), as in the case of *éxorcise, éxercise, mérchandise, ádvertise, súpervise, jéopardize, stándardize, díphthongize, énergize, sólemnize, módernize, fráternize, wésternize, sólipsize.* Since in each case primary stress falls on the antepenultimate syllable despite the strong medial cluster, it must be that final primary stress is assigned under condition (e) of the Main Stress Rule and then shifted to the left by the Alternating Stress Rule. On the other hand, if the ending is subject to rule (158), then condition (c) of the Main Stress Rule will apply to the string preceding *-Iz*. If this residual string terminates in a strong cluster, then this will receive primary stress by case (ii), as in *enfránchise, anthropomórphize, etérnize, sycophántize, propagándize, metamórphize.* If this residual string terminates in a weak cluster, then its penultimate syllable will receive primary stress by case (i), as in *cathólicize, grammáticize, políticize, platitúdinize, gelátinize, diplómatize, démocratize, anésthetize.* Actually, however, in such cases with a weak cluster preceding *-Iz*, it makes no difference whether rule (158) is in effect or not. Certain words have variant forms, depending on whether or not rule (158) is in effect, as in the case of *recondite.* Thus we have the variants *aggrándize–ággrandize, amórtize–ámortize.*

There is another category of examples with *-ize*, illustrated by words such as *skéletonize, álphabetize, prótestantize.* In these cases *-ize* acts as a neutral affix, and we must therefore assume that it is preceded by #, like the inflectional affixes in general (see p. 85). As we have seen, in this case the cycle involving the affix will be vacuous.[110]

We find, in fact, several options for the ending *-Iz*. If the form to which it is added is an independent word, then we expect it, on syntactic grounds, to be preceded by # and to be neutral with respect to stress placement. We see, however, that the expected # boundary is sometimes replaced by +, as in *cathólicize, démocratize, gelátinize.* Where *-Iz* is preceded by + rather than #, there is the further option of applicability of rule (158), which assigns it primary stress. Rule (158) applies in the case of *propagándize, enfránchise,* and so on, but not in the case of *éxercise, jéopardize,* and the other forms with antepenultimate primary stress and a strong cluster in the penultimate syllable. It appears to be the case, then, that words containing the affix *-Iz* must be specified by two ad hoc features, the first determining whether or not # is replaced by +, the second determining whether or not rule (158) applies to *-Iz*. Though there are certain redundancies, the examples given above suggest that these two classificatory features are not entirely predictable. Here, then, is an example of a range of possible phonetic forms determined by two partially free lexical features.

The verbal affix *-At* provides another example, though a somewhat marginal one, of the optionality of rule (158). Among bisyllabic verbs terminating with *-At* we have such

---

[110] A slight problem arises here in connection with reduction of the vowel of the neutral affix *-Iz*. Since it is nonstressed, as matters now stand it is subject to the Auxiliary Reduction Rule (118c), which makes it lax and subjects it to the Vowel Reduction Rule. We can exclude it from the domain of (118) by modifying that rule slightly in one of two ways: we can add the requirement that γ is stronger than minus, or we can restrict the segment marked [γstress] to the context $[-WB]_0$ —— in various ways.

In either case, it should be noted that the vowels of neutral affixes (*-ing, -Iz*, etc.) are not subject to vowel reduction even if lax, and the formulation of the process of reduction must somehow take account of this fact.

In the case of the word *próselytize*, the affix *-Iz* is neutral with respect to stress, but leads to the reduction of the penultimate vowel, although with *-ism, -ist*, it seems that there is no reduction in this position in general. According to our rules, the penultimate vowel should not reduce. Thus the Auxiliary Reduction Rule (118) must be complicated slightly to permit reduction of this vowel where it does take place.

Notice also that in a word such as *systematize*, where the affix *-Iz* is preceded by *-At*, the segment *-AtIz* is excluded from consideration as a whole when the Stressed Syllable Rule (condition (c) of the Main Stress Rule) is applied, in accordance with formulation (151).

stress variants as *locáte – lócate*. We can derive the former from the representation /1OcAt/ and the latter from the representation /1Oc+At/. Rule (158) will be inapplicable in the first form, which will therefore receive primary stress under condition (e) of the Main Stress Rule by case (ii). Rule (158) will, however, apply automatically to the representation /1Oc+At/, assigning primary stress in the final syllable; under condition (c) of the Main Stress Rule, case (ii) will then assign primary stress to the first syllable, giving [1Òc+Át]. We then proceed, by the usual rules, to derive the phonetic representations [lÒkÁt], [lÓkÀt], respectively. The presence or absence of the + boundary is not otherwise motivated, however; it therefore plays the role of a classificatory feature in the lexicon, determining, in effect, whether or not rule (158) applies. If a bisyllabic form in *-At* has only the variant with initial stress, it will appear in the lexicon only with the + boundary (e.g., *vácate*, /vAc+At/); if such a form has only the variant with final stress, it will appear in the lexicon only without the + boundary (e.g., *creáte*, /creAt/). To some extent such an analysis is independently motivated, as in the case of *vácate – creáte*; but in part it is an arbitrary lexical classification, imposed so as to determine the phonetic form correctly and for this reason alone.

The same property can be observed in the case of trisyllabic verbs ending in *-At*. Thus consider such variants as *íllustràte – illústràte*, *ádumbràte – adúmbràte*. We can derive *íllustràte* from the phonological representation /ilustrAt/, primary stress being assigned to the final syllable by case (ii) of the Main Stress Rule under condition (e) and then shifted two syllables to the left by the Alternating Stress Rule. The form *illústràte*, on the other hand, will be derived from the phonological representation /ilustr+At/. In this case, rule (158) applies to assign primary stress to the affix. The stress is then shifted to the preceding strong cluster by case (ii) of the Main Stress Rule under condition (c). Again, the presence or absence of + boundary before *-At* in these polysyllabic forms is largely unmotivated on independent grounds and therefore functions as a classificatory principle in the lexicon. Notice that, as with forms in *-Iz*, where the penultimate syllable has a weak cluster (for example, in the verbs *ánimate*, *extrápolate*), there is no way to determine whether or not a + boundary appears before *-At*; either decision will lead to the same phonetic form.

This framework suffices to resolve most of the problems that arise in connection with final syllables with tense vowels. There are still a few minor points to be made, however. Consider words such as *ádjective*, *infínitive*. These have several peculiarities that require discussion. First, note that in the derived forms we have *adjectíval*, *infinitíval*, with tense primary-stressed [I]. This indicates that the underlying vowel of the final syllable must be tense /I/ rather than lax /i/; otherwise there is no way to account for the position of primary stress. Furthermore, the stress contour of *ádjective* is sufficient to show that in any event the final *-ive* of the underlying forms cannot be identified with the affix of *colléct+ive*, *prospéct+ive*, *detéct+ive* or the final syllable of *invéctive*. In fact, primary stress can fall on the antepenultimate syllable of *ádjective* only by an application of the Alternating Stress Rule to the form *adjectíve*; and the latter form can arise only from case (e) of the Main Stress Rule, the form being analyzed as a stem with a tense vowel in the final syllable. These observations show that the underlying forms must be *adjectIv*, *infinitIv*, and the grammar must contain the very special rule:

$$\left(161\right) \qquad\qquad I \rightarrow i \ / \ \acute{V}C_0VC_0\text{———}v\#$$

The form *adjectIv* now receives primary stress on the final syllable under condition (e), case (ii), of the Main Stress Rule (102), and the phonetic form [ǽjəktìv] results from the Alternating Stress Rule (75), the Stress Adjustment and Vowel Reduction Rules, and rule (161). The form *adjectíval* is derived in a second cycle in the usual way, rule (161) being inapplicable in nonfinal position.

Rule (161) is actually of somewhat greater generality, for the affixes *-ile* and *-ine* are subject to a similar process. Thus we find variant pronunciations for single words (e.g., *júvenĬl – júvenil, Býzantĭn – Byzántin*, in some dialects); or, within a single dialect, forms such as *quártĭl* in contrast to [hástəl] (*hostile*); or such dialectal variants as British *hóstĬl* and American [hástəl]; etc. Additional rules must be stated, depending on the facts of dialect and style, to account for the *-Ĕl, -Ĕn* variants of these affixes (e.g., *mercantĔl, ByzantĔn*).

Let us now turn to another matter. Primary stress tends to be shifted to the right in successive cycles, both within the word, as new affixes are taken into account, and within the phrase, by successive applications of the Nuclear Stress Rule. However, we have come across three processes that shift primary stress to the left: the Compound Rule (67) of Section 9, conditions (c) and (d) of the Main Stress Rule (102), and the Alternating Stress Rule (75). Of these, only the latter two operate within the word. All three processes are subject to certain exceptions, and we must now consider these briefly.

The exceptions to the Compound Rule are of various sorts. There is considerable dialectal variation in connection with the placement of primary stress in items such as *chocolate cake, apple pie*, and many others. There are also widely maintained but syntactically unmotivated contrasts such as *Fifth Ávenue*, with nuclear stress on the second element, versus *Fífth Street*, with compound stress on the first element. Furthermore, proper nouns (e.g., *John Smíth, John Paul Jónes*) and names with titles (*President X́, Senator Ý*, etc.) typically have the nuclear stress of phrases rather than the initial stress of compounds, as do also such noun-noun constructions as *stone flóor* and *iron bóx*. Many examples of such contrasts have been mentioned in the literature, in one connection or another, although there is, to our knowledge, no general treatment of the question.[111] The fact that a phrase is not subject to the Compound Rule might be formally indicated in various ways: for example, by a feature specification of the boundary between the constituents, in which case the rule can be limited to boundaries not containing this feature. This, obviously, does not solve the general problem, but serves only to eliminate it from the domain of phonology. The problem remains of determining under what syntactic conditions this feature is or is not present. Alternatively, we might provide for an ad hoc deletion of the node N dominating such compounds. In fact, the general problem certainly belongs in part to syntax, in part to the readjustment component, rather than to phonology proper, and it can be clarified and resolved only by an investigation of the conditions, syntactic and other, under which the Compound Rule is applicable. For this reason, we will make no attempt to go more deeply into the question here. We have throughout been limiting ourselves arbitrarily to problems of phonological interpretation, and are making no attempt in the present study to investigate the processes by which the syntactic component of the grammar forms the surface structures that are phonetically interpreted by the rules we have been discussing here. Because of this limitation of scope, we will simply leave this question in its present unsatisfactory state.

Conditions (c) and (d) of the Main Stress Rule (102) and the Alternating Stress Rule (75) also have certain exceptions, as we have noted in the course of the exposition. Consider

---

[111] A serious and extensive investigation of phrases that fall under the Compound Rule and their syntactic structure is presented in Lees (1960, Chapter 4).

first conditions (c) and (d), which we have been calling the Stressed Syllable Rule. One of the many roles of this aspect of the Main Stress Rule is to shift the final primary stress of bisyllabic prefix-stem verbs to the initial syllable in the related nouns (see Section 11). Thus we have the noun-verb pairs *pérmìt – permít, súrvèy – survéy*, and so on. There are, however, certain nouns of this form that do not undergo stress placement under condition (c) or (d) in the second cycle and retain stress on the second syllable. To some extent these exceptions are systematic; for example, nouns with the prefix *de-* (e.g., *demand, delay, desire, decay, defeat, despair*) fall into this class quite generally.[112] Such items must be lexically marked in a way that prevents condition (c) or (d) from applying to them in the second cycle. Within the present range of our formal means, we can represent lexical items that are not subject to the Stressed Syllable Rule with a special internal boundary or with a final /e/. The latter would have no effect on the first cycle but would block this rule on the second cycle, after which the *e*-Elision Rule (155) would eliminate the final vowel. Where there are subregularities among the exceptions, as in the case of the prefix *de-*, we can specify the boundary or add the final /e/ by a readjustment rule. A different method for expressing the fact that a certain class of items is excepted from a rule will be discussed in the next chapter. Formalism apart, any such device simply adds a new classification of lexical items, a classification analogous to the subdivision of verbs into strong and weak.

Consider now the Alternating Stress Rule (75). This places primary stress in the context $——C_0VC_0\overset{1}{V}C_0$, reducing the final stress to secondary. We have made note of certain exceptions to this rule, such as *Tennesseé, attaché, chandeliér, kangaroó, chimpanzeé*, all of which retain primary stress in the final syllable. Evidently, these items must be exempted from the Alternating Stress Rule by some sort of lexical classification. Again, there are several mechanisms by which such a classification can be expressed, and, without an exhaustive analysis of cases, it is not clear which is optimal. We have already observed that the Alternating Stress Rule does not apply if the final syllable is preceded by or contains a = boundary (see pp. 95–96). We might, then, insert this boundary before the final VC_0 sequence of these forms. This seems an appropriate device insofar as exemption from the Alternating Stress Rule is associated with certain specific endings, such as *-oo, -ee, -eer, -ier, -é, -ese*.[113] Such affixes can be supplied with a preceding = boundary as part of their feature composition; or, if the association is sufficiently general, the boundary can be inserted by a readjustment rule.[114] An alternative would be to provide the items that are exempt from

[112] If we take words such as *décoy* and the optional variant *détail* to be derived from the corresponding verbs, then to preserve this generalization these forms must be represented phonologically without =, that is, as monomorphemic rather than as of a prefix-stem construction.

[113] Notice, incidentally, that forms such as *Japanese* and *Siamese* are correctly derived in the second cycle from *Japán, Siám*, by rules (158), (117), (118b), (120b), and (121). The underlying representations are presumably /jæpān/, /siām/, the rule of *ā–æ* alternation discussed on page 152 applying when these forms are in isolation. The appearance of [I] in [sǐæm] is normal, as we shall see in the next chapter.

[114] If the affixes in question here are assigned a = boundary, they will be exempt from rule (158) and will receive primary stress under condition (e) of the Main Stress Rule. If they are supplied with a final /e/, to be elided later on, they will be assigned primary stress under condition (b). In either case, both the Stressed Syllable and Alternating Stress Rules will be inapplicable. If, on the other hand, an affix that retains primary stress is assigned this stress prior to the Main Stress Rule—for example, by rule (158)—then it cannot have been assigned = or final /e/. It must, then, be lexically specified as exempt not only from the Alternating Stress Rule (if the form to which it is affixed contains two or more syllables), but also from the Stressed Syllable Rule, that is, from conditions (c) and (d) of the Main Stress Rule.

There are other examples that are excepted from the Alternating Stress Rule beyond those that have characteristic endings such as those cited. For example, the word *Aléxánder*, as contrasted with *sálamànder*, does not undergo this rule. We might express this fact by entering *Alexander* in the lexicon

rule (75) with a final /e/ (to be elided by rule (155)), either as part of each lexical entry or, if the class of exceptions under consideration is specifiable, by rule. This would be necessary for nouns in -*esque* and -*ette*, for example, as this is the only way in which primary stress can be placed on these syllables. A third possibility, which we discuss in the next chapter, is to use a general device for specifying exceptions to rules. In any event, it is fairly clear, details aside, how to deal with these marginal contrasts within the lexicon.

Verbs ending in -*ute* have certain properties that deserve special mention. Consider first the verb *cónstitùte*, with the derived form *constítutive*. A natural phonological representation would be /kəN=stitUt/. This will give the phonetic representation [kå̇nstətÛt] in the usual way. But now consider the derived form *constítutive*.[115] As our rules now stand, primary stress should be shifted from the first syllable (which is the sonority peak at the end of the first cycle) to the strong cluster immediately preceding -*ive*, by case (ii) of the Main Stress Rule (102) under condition (a). But this is incorrect. Apparently, the ending -*Ut*, like -*At*, must be considered part of the string omitted from consideration under condition (a) rather than part of the residual string, and we must generalize the formulation of condition (a) in (122) (and of (c) in (145)) to permit this. With this modification, the string omitted from consideration under condition (a) in the second cycle is -*Ut+iv*, and the residual string is *kəN=stit-*. Case (i) of the rule is blocked by the = boundary, and case (ii) shifts primary stress to the second syllable. The representation [kənstitÛtəv] is then derived in the usual manner.

In just the same way we can derive forms such as *consecutive*, *execute – executive*, and so on. The word *execute*, for example, might receive the phonological representation /eks=secUt/.[116]

---

with the representation /ælVksændre/, with a final /e/. Primary stress will be placed on the penultimate strong cluster under condition (b), and the final /e/ will be elided by rule (155) after blocking application of the Alternating Stress Rule. In final position, the postconsonantal [r] becomes syllabic (see p. 85); if there is another cycle, as in *Alexandrian*, it remains nonsyllabic before the following vowel.

Several of the words that are exceptions to the Alternating Stress Rule are exceptional in other ways as well. For example, *chimpanzee* is in conflict with the Vowel Reduction Rule in that its medial vowel does not reduce. If we were to attempt to extend coverage to borrowed words and proper nouns more fully, the number of exceptions to be listed in the lexicon would, of course, mount considerably. Notice, however, that this extension of the lexicon would not affect the system of rules or lexical entries that account for the other, regular cases.

[115] Recall that the # boundary is generally optional before -*ive* (see p. 129). If it were present in this case, we would derive the form *constitutive*.

[116] The resulting [ss] sequence is simplified by rule (156). Notice that the modification of the prefix /eks/ to [ek] before stems beginning in [s] provides an additional reason for incorporating the Cluster Simplification Rule (156) in the grammar. Notice also that in *executive* the [ks] cluster voices, although it remains unvoiced in *exceed*, *excite*, etc. This matter will be discussed in the next chapter.

An argument might be made for extracting the morpheme /sEkʷ/ (see note 105) of *sequence*, *consequence* from words such as *consecutive* and *execute*. Thus we might enter these words with the representations /con=sEkʷ+At+iv/, /eks=sEkʷ+At/, respectively (dropping internal brackets). An early rule would convert /kʷ+At/ to /Ut/. The derivations would then proceed in the usual way. In the same manner, we could account for the relations between *locution*, *elocution*, *loquacious*, *interlocutor*, *eloquent*.

This analysis can be extended to the word *constitute*, which can be derived from the representation /cɔN=stitu+At/. The rule converting /kʷ+At/ to /Ut/ can be extended to /tu+At/. In favor of this proposal is the fact that it would account automatically for the derived form *constituent*.

A further advantage of the analysis suggested here is that it dovetails properly with the analysis of [U] presented in Chapter Four. As we will see there, [U] does not appear in the context ——Cₒ# in phonological representations. A verb such as *attribute* (see (162)) may be a unique, lexically marked exception to this generalization.

Consider now the somewhat different form *attríbute*, with the derived nominalized form *áttribute*. We have, for the latter, the derivation (162):

$$\begin{pmatrix}162\end{pmatrix}$$

		$[_N [_V æC = trib + Ut]_V]_N$	
		1	RULE (158)
	1	2	RULE (102cii)
1	2	3	RULE (102cii)
1	–	3	RULE (118d)
1	–	4	RULE (63)

In the first cycle, primary stress is first placed on the tense affix by rule (158). Under condition (c), it is then shifted back one syllable by case (ii), case (i) being inapplicable because of the = boundary separating the prefix from the stem. In isolation, then, we would derive the verb *attríbute* after the Stress Adjustment Rule (63).[117] In the second cycle, condition (c) entitles us to omit the string *-tríbUt* from consideration. Note that the = boundary after the prefix /æC/ permits a second syllable in this omitted form, as well as preventing application of (ci) in the first cycle. The residual string is now simply /æC=/, and this receives its primary stress under condition (c). The Auxiliary Reduction Rule (118) and the Vowel Reduction Rule (121) reduce the vowel of the medial syllable, and the Stress Adjustment Rule, along with the rules of assimilation and simplification of clusters, gives the form [ǽtrəbÙt].

Our rules therefore account for the verb *attríbute* and the noun *áttribùte* on the assumption that they are related in the same way as the verb *délegàte* and the noun *délegate*, or, for that matter, the verb *convért* and the noun *cónvert*. Once again, it is by no means obvious, on superficial examination of the phonetic facts, that these pairs are lexically related in exactly the same way. It is therefore interesting to discover that an independently motivated system of rules does account for the phonetic forms of lexically related items.

A similar pattern of explanation can be used to account for the well-known fact that stress is shifted to the left in words such as *réferent*, *cónfident*, *résident*, *éxcellent*, *pértinent*, *déferent*, *réverent*, which derive from underlying verbs with primary stress on the second syllable. In contrast, we have forms such as *depéndent*, *repéllent*, *inhérent*, *abhórrent*, *insístent*, *recúrrent*, in which the stress remains on the stress peak of the underlying verb. The second class is the more productive; members of the first class in many cases have a less simple semantic relation to the form that underlies them. This suggests that we distinguish these classes in terms of the presence or absence of the # boundary before the affix *-ent*. If this is freely added, by a syntactic process, we have forms such as /de=pend#ent/, /re=pel#ent/; if, on the other hand, the component formatives are more closely amalgamated and the # boundary is weakened to +, we have [re=fer+ent], [cəN=fÍd+ent], etc. In the productive class that retains #, the affix is neutral with respect to stress placement (see p. 85), and the stress contour of the underlying form remains in the derived word. Where # is weakened to +, we still derive forms with stress on the final syllable in the first cycle (e.g., [re=fér], [cən=fÍd]), but in the second cycle the stressed syllable followed by *-ent* is omitted from

---

[117] Recall that the vowel [U] is immune to laxing by the Auxiliary Reduction Rule (118) and, consequently, does not reduce (see p. 122). Notice that the proposal of the preceding footnote would explain the difference in the position of stress in *attríbute*, on the one hand, and *éxecùte*, *cónstitùte*, on the other, by the fact that there is no independent formative /tribu/ (though there is motivation for /stitu/ by virtue of the form *constituent*, and for /sEkʷ/ as noted above) and that there is no phonological segment /bʷ/ analogous to /kʷ/. Thus there is no basis for analyzing *attribute* as /æC=tribu+At/ and then dropping the + boundary, as in *execute*, *constitute*.

consideration under condition (c) (inclusion of the extra syllable *-ent* in this omitted string being permitted because of the = boundary between the prefix and the stem), and stress is placed on the residual string. This gives [re$\overset{1}{=}$fer$\overset{2}{+}$ent], [cɔN$\overset{1}{=}$fĭd$\overset{2}{+}$ent], etc. By the Auxiliary Reduction Rule (118d), the vowel of the medial syllable becomes nontense and nonstressed, so that it reduces to [ə] by the Vowel Reduction Rule. In this way the phonetic representations of all of these forms are derived.[118]

In precisely the same way, we can account for the position of primary stress in words such as *ádmirable*, *irrévocable*, *réparable*, *cómparable*, *préferable*, *réputable*, as opposed to *remóvable*, *enjóyable*, etc. The elements of the second class will either retain the # boundary before the freely added affix *-able* or, as in the case of *allówable*, *emplóyable*, they will contain no internal = boundary, so that condition (c) is inapplicable in the second cycle. Such words as *ádmirable*, *irrévocable* will be derived exactly along the lines of *réferent*, *cónfident*.[119] A few items will require ad hoc adjustments, but many fall directly into place under this analysis. Once again, it would be expected, and appears very largely to be the case, that the examples without # are the more ossified forms that have been reanalyzed, in effect, as single lexical items.[120]

Notice that examples such as *áttribute*, *cónfident*, *préferable* require that the extra syllable permitted in the Stressed Syllable Rule be contingent on the presence of a boundary with the feature [−FB], not simply the boundary [+WB] (see note 57).

Forms derived from words ending in *-ent* are more of a problem. Thus consider the words *présidency*, *mílitancy*. Our rules would predict the phonetic forms [prəzĭdənsE] and [milətænsE], respectively, analogous to *advísory*, *órthodòxy* (see Section 15). The simplest way to avoid this problem and to produce the correct phonetic output is to extend rules (122) and

---

[118] Other vowel alternations that are observed in these forms (e.g., *E–e*, as in *refer–referent*, and *ɔ–ā*, as in *confide–confident*, are automatic, as we shall see in the next chapter.

[119] The affix *-able* seems to pose a unique problem because of the following facts. Forms such as *ability*, *preferability*, etc., seem to indicate that the form is bisyllabic in its underlying representation, i.e., /Abil/. But the forms *ably*, *preferably* apparently require that the underlying form be monosyllabic, namely, /Abl/. Similarly, we presuppose a monosyllabic analysis in the interpretation of stress placement in words such as *preferable*, *ádmirable*; if the form is bisyllabic, condition (c) will not hold. However, as J. Ross has pointed out to us, the point at issue does not involve only *-able* but also forms such as *nobly–nobility*, *possibly–possibility*, *humbly–humility*; and the problem can be solved by accepting the monosyllabic analysis as /Abl/ and postulating a rule that converts [Blity] to [Bility], where B is a labial consonant. Thus *preferability* derives from /preferabl+ity/, *nobility* from /nobl+ity/, *humility* from /huml+ity/. To derive [hʌmbəl], we make use of an obvious rule of epenthesis. The [ʌ]–[U] alternation of *humbly–humility* is now explained in the normal way, as developed in the next chapter. Since *-able* is phonologically monosyllabic, the analysis of stress placement proceeds in the intended way.

[120] Deletion of # is to be expected as a word is intuitively reanalyzed from a syntactically generated member of a productive class to a derived element based on independent formatives that merge to form a single lexical item, the semantic content of which is no longer completely predictable by general rules from that of its parts. A similar phenomenon can be observed above the word level. Thus a noun phrase such as *mâin##lánd* can be reanalyzed as a single noun *máin##lànd*, and may even lose word boundaries completely, becoming *máinland*, with a reduced vowel in the second syllable. Similarly, a phrase such as *old##maid* or *Long##Island* may be reanalyzed as a single word *old+maid*, *Long+island*, in which case the secondary stress on the first element (assigned by the Auxiliary Reduction Rule (120)) is reduced to tertiary by the Stress Adjustment Rule (63). Thus we have $\overset{3}{old}$-$\overset{1}{maid}$ ("spinster") contrasting with $\overset{2}{old}$##$\overset{1}{maid}$ ("maid who is not young"); $\overset{3}{Long}$ $\overset{1}{Island}$ (the place name) contrasting with $\overset{2}{long}$ $\overset{1}{island}$ ("island that is long"), etc.

The problem of semantic representation in the lexicon for forms such as these, which preserve their underlying structure only partially and in an unsystematic way, is far from settled. But it seems clear that any solution must meet the conditions that we require here to explain the phonetic form.

(151) so that the affix *-ent* (along with *-At* and *-Ut*) is omitted from consideration under condition (a), along with an affix that follows it. This modification produces the desired effects.[121] Thus, in the final cycle, the string which acts as stress-placing affix under condition (a) is not *-y* but *-ent*+*y* and *-ant*+*y*, so that we derive [pre=sĺd+ent+y] and [milit+ánt+y], the former becoming [prē=sĺd+ent+y] under condition (c) (/ent+y/ being monosyllabic), and the final phonetic forms then resulting in the familiar way.

Notice that alongside of the *-ency* and *-ancy* forms, and often in free variation with them, we have *-ence* and *-ance* forms such as *residence, confidence, tolerance*. These forms are perfectly parallel to the *-ency, -ancy* forms in their behavior. What we clearly need, for these cases, is a noun-forming affix that will cause [t] to become [s], just as *-y* does, but that will differ from *-y* in that it is deleted after having had its effects on stress placement and consonant alternation. The $t \rightarrow s$ alternation is one of several that take place before nonlow front vowels and glides in certain positions, in particular, before [i] or [y] and [e]. Since we already have an *e*-Elision Rule (namely, rule (155)), it seems obvious that the final affix in the *-ence* forms must be the glide which is related to /e/ as /y/ is related to /i/, that is, the glide with the features "nonhigh," "nonlow," "nonback." Let us designate it as /ε/. Then *residence, tolerance* will be represented /rE=sĺd+ent+ε/, /tɔlVr+ænt+ε/[122] in the lexicon. The glide /ε/ will have precisely the same effects as /y/ with respect to stress placement and consonant alternations, and will then be deleted by a simplified version of the *e*-Elision Rule (155) which omits reference to the feature [+vocalic].

In Section 14 we showed that the distinction in patterns of stress and reduced vowels between forms such as *relaxation, deportation, condensation*, with unreduced 4-stressed vowels in the second syllable, and *demonstration, information, compensation*, etc., with reduced minus-stressed vowels in the analogous position, is directly determined by their syntactic structure. Matters are not always this straightforward, however, and the *-ation* forms of certain bisyllabic verbs undergo anomalous derivations. Consider, for example, the phonetic alternatives [prĒzèntÁšən] – [prèzəntÁšən] for *presentation*. The first is derived in the normal way from *présént*. The second must be derived without a first cycle for the underlying verb, or with an artificial analysis [N [V*present*+*At*]V *ion*]N.[123] The same artificiality is necessary for a word such as *transformation*, which, even as a nominalized verb, has a reduced vowel in the second syllable instead of the expected 4-stressed nonreduced vowel. In each such case an ad hoc lexical analysis must be given for the underlying forms, specifying that they undergo the necessary reanalysis before the application of the phonological rules. Such examples, then, are true exceptions.

Other apparent exceptions are forms such as *modern, honest, haggard*, mentioned above in the discussion of adjectives. Our rules predict that final stress should fall on the final syllable in these examples. We can provide the correct phonetic form only by analyzing these elements as *mod*+*ern, hon*+*est, hagg*+*ard*, so that stress is assigned under condition (a) to the penultimate syllable, instead of under condition (e) to the vowel of the final strong cluster. There is some justification for this (cf. *mode, Western, honor, lag – laggard*, etc.), but

---

[121] Notice that the question can be regarded as one of where to assign the diacritic feature [+D] discussed on page 138, once conditions (a) and (c) have been amalgamated as indicated on page 142. As we noted there, [+D] is quite generally assigned to the vowel of a vowel-sonorant-consonant cluster such as *-ent, -ant*.

[122] Notice that verbs in *-At* delete the ending *-At* before the affix *-ent* or *-ant*.

[123] As we shall see in the next chapter, the choice of [E] or [e] in the first syllable of *presentation* is determined by the stress on the following vowel, by a rule of great generality.

in some cases the analysis is ad hoc. A more serious exception is the adjective *pérfect*. In this case, not only the position of primary stress is contrary to rule but the reduction of the vowel of the final syllable as well.[124]

Although we have not yet exhausted the material, we have reached the point where no further insight into stress contours and vowel reduction can be achieved from application of the rules and phonological principles that we have so far been able to discover and formulate. There are still many examples that resist analysis and that must, so far as we can see, be treated by ad hoc lexical classification and special rules. So far as we can determine, these examples have no bearing on what we have presented so far; but one must keep in mind the fact that they might turn out to be relevant, if it can be shown that deeper generalizations or alternative principles can account for the remaining problems only by revising the analysis presented above.

Within the framework of this book, there would be no point in our going on to present ad hoc analyses of particular examples. As we stated in the Preface, we are interested in an analysis of the facts of English insofar as this analysis serves to reveal general principles of linguistic structure. Thus we have been concerned with details of stress contour and vowel reduction because of the way they bear on such general notions as the principle of the transformational cycle. We are not, in this book, interested in these details for their own sake. We have tried to show that quite a variety of phenomena can be explained on the basis of the general principles of phonological structure that we have been developing in the course of the exposition. Insofar as this attempt is successful, it provides empirical justification for these principles. Since the residue of unexplained phenomena do not, so far as we can see, bear on these principles one way or the other, we deal with them no further here.

---

[124] We might account for the position of primary stress by deriving the adjective from the underlying verb *perféct*, in the familiar way, but this would still leave unexplained the vowel reduction in the final syllable.

Chapter four

WORD-LEVEL PHONOLOGY

1. Introductory remarks

We have seen in the preceding chapter how a variety of stress contours and a complex interplay of stress level and vowel reduction are determined by a small number of transformational rules that apply in a cyclical manner, beginning with the smallest constituents of the surface structure and proceeding systematically to larger and larger constituents. In this chapter we turn our attention to the phonological rules that do not reapply in this cyclic fashion. Among these, the ones that concern us most directly are the rules of word phonology.

We have been assuming that each terminal string that enters the phonological component is uniquely and exhaustively analyzed as a sequence of words, and that each of these words is a constituent of the surface structure. Thus the surface structure specifies that each word constitutes a stage of the transformational cycle. By a word, we mean an element of the form # # ... # #, where ... contains no occurrence of # #. (See Chapter Eight, Section 6.2, for a more careful formulation.) A rule restricted in application to contexts meeting this condition is what we call a rule of word phonology. Evidently, such rules will not reapply at successive stages of the transformational cycle, even if interspersed freely among the cyclic transformational rules.

The surface structure that enters the phonological component is determined by three factors: syntactic rules, lexical representations, and readjustment rules. The syntactic rules generate a syntactic surface structure of strings of grammatical and lexical formatives, the latter appearing in what we have called "lexical representation." The readjustment rules, which provide a link between syntax and phonology, may slightly modify the syntactically generated surface structure, and they will, furthermore, convert the string of formatives into what we have called "phonological representation," introducing various modifications into the lexical representations and eliminating grammatical formatives in favor of phonological matrices, in the manner discussed briefly in Chapter One, Section 5.1. In this chapter the distinction between lexical and phonological representation will not be too crucial, although the conceptual distinction should be borne in mind to prevent confusion. We will be concerned in this discussion with only one aspect of the readjustment rules, namely, with their effect on lexical representations of lexical items, particularly in connection with the matter of redundancy. Those readjustment rules which have the effect of restricting the class of possible lexical entries by eliminating certain possibilities we shall sometimes designate as "lexical redundancy rules." We return to the discussion of readjustment rules in Chapter Eight.

2. *Phonological and phonetic representation*

The phonological component accepts as input a structurally analyzed string. As output it provides the "phonetic representation" of this string. The phonetic representation consists of a sequence of "phonetic segments," each of which is nothing other than a set of "phonetic feature specifications." A phonetic feature specification consists of a "phonetic scale" (called a "phonetic feature") and an integer indicating the position of the phonetic segment in question along this scale.[1] The phonetic scales form a predetermined universal set, namely, the "(phonetic) distinctive features." Thus a particular segment might be marked as "noncontinuant" (i.e., "minus" with respect to the phonetic feature "continuant"), "highly aspirated," "nonvoiced," etc. In short, a phonetic representation is a "phonetic matrix" in which the columns correspond to segments and the rows to features and in which each entry states the extent to which a given segment possesses the corresponding feature. We will discuss the phonetic distinctive features in more detail in Chapter Seven. Here we merely emphasize that they must be determined absolutely, within general linguistic theory, and independently of the grammar of any particular language.

Let us now consider the structurally analyzed string that the phonological component takes as input. Its minimal elements are formatives. These formatives are provided originally by the lexicon, which forms one part of the syntactic component of the grammar. They may then undergo slight modification by the readjustment rules. In the lexicon, each formative must be represented in such a way as to determine precisely how the rules of the phonological component will operate on it, in each context in which it may appear. Thus the representation of a formative must be sufficiently rich so as to specify the corresponding phonetic matrix in each environment, given the phonological rules and the structural analysis of the string. As we noted in Chapter One, each formative falls into many categories; in fact, each formative can be regarded as being constituted simply by a certain set of categories. For example, the formative *inn* belongs to the syntactic categories "noun," "common," "nonanimate," "count," etc.; to certain semantic categories which specify its meaning; and to the phonological categories "initial-vocalic," "initial-nontense," "second-consonantal," "second-nasal," etc. The lexical entry *inn* is simply the complex of these categories, and the terminal symbol *inn* in the terminal string *the+man+stop+past+ at+the+inn* (underlying *the man stopped at the inn*) is nothing other than the complex symbol consisting of this set of category specifications.

It is clear that many of the phonological categories can be represented in a natural way in terms of a "phonological matrix," in which the rows are associated with features such as "nasality" and "tenseness" and the columns are called "phonological segments." Thus, assignment of the morpheme *inn* to the categories "initial-vocalic" and "initial-nontense" can be indicated by entering + in the first column in the row labeled "vocalic" and − in the first column in the row labeled "tense"; its assignment to the category

---

[1] Often we restrict ourselves to two positions along a phonetic scale, in which case we may use the symbols + and − instead of integers to indicate phonetic values. We emphasize that the value in a phonetic specification is not an absolute physical property but is relative to the context of phonetic segments. (See Chapter Seven for further discussion.) Thus, the phonetic distinctive features are absolute in one sense, namely, they are universals, independent of any particular language and providing the basis for phonetic representation in every language; and they are relative in another, namely, the actual physical event represented will depend on the integral value of the phonetic specification, interpreted relative to the context in which the given segment occurs. Criticism of distinctive feature theory has occasionally confused these two entirely different notions of absoluteness.

"second-nasal" can be indicated by entering + in the second column in the row associated with "nasality," and so on. Details aside, it is clear that this is an appropriate means for presenting much of the categorial composition (the assignment to categories) of a complex symbol representing a formative, and it is reasonable, therefore, to propose that a lexical entry will, in general, consist of a phonological matrix of the kind just described, along with a set of other categories (syntactic, semantic, and phonological) to which the morpheme given by this lexical entry belongs. To a first approximation, then, we may think of this phonological matrix as the lexical representation, abstracting away from possible effects of readjustment rules.

The distinction between the phonological and phonetic matrices must be kept clearly in mind. In the case of the phonetic matrix, each row corresponds to a phonetic feature, physically defined, from a predetermined initial set. The entry occupying a particular square of the matrix will be an integer specifying the degree to which the segment in question is characterized by the corresponding property. In the case of the phonological matrix, each square represents simply a pair of opposed categories, to at most one of which the formative in question may belong. A + in this square indicates membership of the formative in one of these categories; a −, membership in the other, complementary category; a 0 indicates simply that no information is given for the formative in question concerning membership in these two categories. Thus the second column of the phonological matrix for *inn* would contain a + in the square associated with the feature "nasal," a − in the row associated with the feature "vocalic," and a 0 in the row associated with the feature "tense." This is a way of representing the fact that in the lexicon *inn* is assigned to the two categories "second-nasal," "second-nonvocalic," but is not assigned to either of the categories "second-tense" or "second-nontense." It is unnecessary for the tenseness of the nasal consonant in *inn* to be indicated in the lexicon since this information is redundant—it is provided by a general rule and is not an idiosyncratic property of the particular formative in question. It is this fact that is indicated by the zero entry in the phonological matrix. We will return later (Chapter Eight, Section 8, and Chapter Nine) to a more careful consideration of redundant information and how it is supplied. For the time being, we will continue to use the entry 0, along with + and −, as an expository device.

The categories of the phonological matrix for some formative may correspond in part to the feature specifications of the corresponding phonetic matrix, but this need not be the case in general. To illustrate some of the possibilities that may arise, let us consider in a bit more detail the phonological and phonetic matrices for the formative *inn* (in the context *the man stopped at the*——) and the formative *algebra* (in *he likes*——). The phonetic matrices, omitting irrelevant details, might contain the following submatrices:

$$\left(1\right)$$

	(a)	*inn*		(b)	*algebra*						
		i	n		æ	l	g	e	b	r	æ
consonantal		−	+		−	+	+	−	+	+	−
vocalic		+	−		+	+	−	+	−	+	+
nasal[2]		2	+		−	−	−	−	−	−	−
tense		−	−		−	−	−	−	−	−	−
stress		1	−		1	−	−	4	−	−	4
voice		+	+		+	+	+	+	+	+	+
continuant		+	−		+	+	−	+	−	+	+

[2] By giving the entry 2 for the vowel of *inn*, we indicate that its degree of nasalization is partial. For a discussion of the physical correlates of the phonetic features, see Chapter Seven.

Recalling now that the lexicon specifies only idiosyncratic features of lexical entries, omitting all those that can be determined by general rules, we might propose the following as the corresponding subparts of the phonological matrices:

$\begin{pmatrix}2\end{pmatrix}$

	(a)	*inn*		(b)	*algebra*					
		i	n		æ	l	g	e	b	r	æ
consonantal		−	+		−	+	+	−	+	+	−
vocalic		0	0		0	+	−	0	−	+	0
nasal		0	+		0	0	−	0	−	0	0
tense		−	0		−	0	0	−	0	0	−
stress		0	0		0	0	0	0	0	0	0
voice		0	0		0	0	+	0	+	0	0
continuant		0	0		0	0	−	0	−	0	0

There are general rules that convert the representations of (2) into those of (1); consequently, the redundant specifications in (1) need not appear in the lexical entries themselves. A segment which is not fully specified may be called an "archi-segment." Phonological matrices typically consist of archi-segments. Thus, an important difference between phonological and phonetic matrices is that the latter are fully specified while the former are not. In fact, one major function of the phonological rules is to extend phonological matrices to full phonetic matrices. Notice that (2a) is a proper submatrix of (1a) and that (2b) is a proper submatrix of (1b). Thus, the only function of the phonological rules as so far discussed is to convert archi-segments to fully specified phonetic segments.

Suppose that a certain formative meets the following condition: the phonological matrix given in its lexical entry is a submatrix of the phonetic matrix corresponding to it, in each context in which it occurs.[3] In this case, we may say that the formative in question meets the condition of "invariance." (We can also extend the definition of invariance, in the obvious way, to the case of a particular segment of a formative.) Thus the formative *inn* meets the invariance condition, but the formative *algebra* does not, as we see if we carry the discussion a few steps further.

The lexical entry (2b) for *algebra* must specify that the final vowel is nontense; otherwise, it will not be stressless, nor will it reduce to [ə] (see Chapter Three, Section 14). But consider the form *algebraic*. In this case the final vowel of *algebra* is marked [+tense] in the phonetic matrix because of the rule that vowels become tense before vowels:

$\begin{pmatrix}3\end{pmatrix}$　　　　　　　　　　V　→　[+tense]　/ ──V

This is the rule that we have stated as part of (30) in Chapter Three (p. 74). The phonetic matrix for *algebra* in *algebraic* will thus differ from that in #*algebra*# not only with respect to redundant features (e.g., degree of stress), but also with respect to the inherent feature of

---

[3] Technically this condition is never satisfied since the entries of phonological matrices are the symbols +, −, and 0 while the entries of phonetic matrices are positive integers. What we mean, of course, is that if the integral values for a particular feature are divided into two classes, one of which (1 to *n*, for some *n*) represents a refinement of the category + and the other of which (*n*+1 to *m*, where *m* is the minimal value along this dimension) represents a refinement of the category −, then the phonological matrix is a submatrix of the phonetic matrix when the integers 1, . . . , *n* are replaced by + and the integers *n*+1, . . . , *m* by −.

tenseness. This illustrates the fact that phonological rules not only fill in redundant entries of matrices but also may change inherent features marked in the lexical entry.

Suppose that we now extend the description to the features that determine vowel quality. We have already noted that there is a rule determining that nonstressed, nontense vowels in final position become tense if they are nonlow (that is, [i], [e], [u], [o]), but reduce to [ə] if they are low (see Chapter Three, p. 74). Since the final vowel of *algebra* reduces, it must be marked in the lexicon as [+low]. Since it is also [−tense], the stress assignment rules of the preceding chapter assign stress only to the first syllable. But in *algebraic* this vowel is phonetically both [+tense] and [−low]. Consequently not only the inherent tenseness but also the inherent lowness of the lexical entry may be altered by the phonological rules. In fact, it is often the case that phonological rules change inherent properties, and it is not to be expected that the invariance condition will be met in general.

Occasionally the factors that determine what the underlying lexical entry must be are quite complex. To illustrate the range of considerations that may be involved, consider the words *reciprocal–reciprocity, frivolous–frivolity, demon–demonic*, etc. In each case we have a formative ending with a vowel followed by a single consonant, to which is added a suffix (*-al, -ity, -ous, -ic*). The final vowel of each formative appears in one of two phonetic forms—either [ə] (*reciprocal, frivolous, demon*) or [ā] (*reciprocity, frivolity, demonic*).[4] The problem is to determine the underlying phonological shape. We see at once that the vowel in question must be nontense in the phonological matrix to account for the stress placement in *recíprocal, frívolous, démon*. In each case, if the boldface vowel were tense, it would receive stress by the rules discussed in Chapter Three. Since, however, it is nontense and therefore nonstressed, the vowel instead reduces to [ə] by the Vowel Reduction Rule (rule (121) of Chapter Three). But we now have to account for the fact that when the vowel does receive stress, as when it is followed by the affix *-ity* or *-ic*, it becomes tense. Thus there must be a rule such as (4) (where V* is some nontense vowel):

$$\left(4\right) \qquad\qquad V^* \;\;\rightarrow\;\; [+\text{tense}]$$

If this rule follows the Vowel Reduction Rule, no further context need be given. Thus when V* is unstressed, it will reduce; when stressed, it will become tense by rule (4).

What, then, is the feature composition of V* beyond its nontenseness? The simplest solution would be to take V* as the nontense cognate of [ā], that is, as the low, back, nonround vowel [a]. In this case, rule (4) will suffice to determine the quality of V* when it does not reduce. We will see, however, that there are strong reasons for regarding [a] as itself being derived, by obligatory unrounding, from its round cognate [ɔ], which does not appear in phonetic matrices although considerations of symmetry would lead us to expect it.[5] But if we are to take V* as [ɔ], we must formulate rule (4) in terms that have the effect of (5) (where ˘ stands for "lax," that is, "nontense"):

$$\left(5\right) \qquad\qquad \breve{\mathfrak{o}} \;\;\rightarrow\;\; \begin{bmatrix} +\text{tense} \\ -\text{round} \end{bmatrix}$$

---

[4] This is true of one major dialect. In other dialects the vowel in the second case may be [ɔ], [ɔ̄], or [ă] contrasting with [ā]. We return to the question of this dialectal variation later. It does not affect the point at issue here.

On our use of diagonals versus square brackets (i.e., / / vs. [ ]), see Chapter Three, page 65.

[5] We return to this matter later. Actually invariance is violated whether [a] or [ɔ] is chosen for V*, although the example is more striking, of course, in the latter case.

Moreover, if the boldface vowel in *reciprocal, frivolous, demon* is [ɔ] in the underlying matrix, then the vowel of the phonological matrix *never* appears in a phonetic matrix without a change in quality, so that the invariance condition is violated in an extreme way. However, the actual forms are determined by quite simple rules, and the choice of the underlying vowel is determined by a variety of systematic considerations.

Notice that in the case of the pair *reciprocal–reciprocity*, there is still another violation of invariance, namely, with respect to the final consonant of the formative *reciproc-*. This segment appears in one case as [k], in another as [s]. Other familiar facts of English force us to the conclusion that the underlying consonant is /k/ and that we have rules with the effect of (6):

$$
(6) \qquad\qquad k \;\rightarrow\; s \;/\;\underline{}\left\{\begin{matrix} i \\ e \end{matrix}\right\}
$$

We will see that rule (6) can be generalized considerably and analyzed into several independently motivated steps. For the moment we record it simply as another case of the violation of invariance of lexical entries.

Even though we cannot impose the condition of invariance on phonological matrices, we might still inquire whether some weaker condition is not satisfied. Can we, for example, require that the underlying phonological segment and the phonetic segment that corresponds to it not differ "too greatly," in some sense? Rule (6) suggests that this is unlikely, since [k] and [s] differ in the features "anterior," "coronal," "continuant," "strident." Later we will find an even more extreme violation of the invariance condition, in the vowel system. We shall see that in a sequence of steps, each well motivated and involving a change of just one feature, the underlying segment /ū/ becomes phonetic [æ] in certain dialects. This is a maximal change within the vowel system, for these two segments differ in the features "high," "low," "back," "round," "tense," that is, in all features that differentiate vowels.

Thus it seems that there is no hope for any condition of invariance that will relate phonological and phonetic matrices. No doubt there are certain conditions on "possible phonological rules," and these will, derivatively, impose certain conditions on the relation of phonological and phonetic matrices. But it seems that there is no general condition that can be established apart from whatever effects these conditions on rules may have.

Notice that although the invariance condition is not necessarily met by a grammar, there is often a cost attached to violating it, in terms of complexity of rules. Thus, in general, a grammar will contain fewer and simpler rules to the extent that the invariance condition is met; the condition will be violated, therefore, only when the corresponding gains more than compensate for the loss in simplicity. As we have indicated previously, an important part of linguistic theory is an evaluation measure for grammars that specifies those formal properties that play a role in the selection of one grammar (one theory of a language) over another, both by the learner of the language and the linguist analyzing it. A clear and precise formulation of such a measure (for discussion, see Chapter Eight) will determine exactly in what way violation of invariance will, *ceteris paribus*, reduce the valuation of a grammar. It will thus express a certain empirical hypothesis concerning the extent to which invariance is an important feature of language.

To summarize, we see that there are several respects in which phonological and phonetic matrices differ. First, the entries in the phonetic matrices may indicate degree along a physically defined scale, whereas the entries in the phonological matrices simply indicate membership of a segment in a category or in its complement (or give no information about membership). Secondly, the phonetic matrices are fully specified, whereas the phonological matrices in general are not. Thirdly, the phonetic matrices may differ from the underlying phonological matrices in the values which are inherent in the latter, as we have just noted. Finally, it is clear that a phonetic matrix may differ in number of segments from the underlying phonological matrix, as, for example, in the case of epenthesis or elision.

We have used the term "phonetic distinctive features" for the universal physical scales that determine the rows of the phonetic matrices. Correspondingly, we may use the term "phonological distinctive features" to refer to the categories that label the rows of the phonological matrices. Unfortunately, the discussion and development of the theory of distinctive features has been confused by the use of the term "distinctive feature" in both senses. This is appropriate only insofar as the invariance condition is met—that is, insofar as the phonological rules simply add redundant features to lexical matrices, giving additional specification of archi-segments. As we have seen, however, this is not the case in general. In fact, we do not believe that there is *any* significant intermediate level of linguistic representation between phonetic and phonological at which representations are strictly in terms of submatrices of the full phonetic representation.[6] In any event, the phonological and phonetic functions of distinctive features must be clearly distinguished.

It might be proposed, in the light of the distinction between phonological and phonetic distinctive features, that the two sets be absolutely unrelated—that in cases such as (1) and (2) above, for example, the rows be labeled entirely differently in the phonological and phonetic matrices. Thus in (1) we would have the phonetic features "consonantal," "vocalic," etc., as before, but in (2) we would have the phonological features A, B, and so on. Only the phonetic features would now be "substantive"; the phonological features would be without physical content and would provide an arbitrary categorization.

Adoption of this proposal would have two effects. For one thing, since all phonological rules would operate on the "empty" categories A, B, etc., gradually filling them in and revising their entries, the grammar would now have to be supplemented with a set of rules operating at the point at which all matrices are fully specified and providing that phonetic features be associated with the categories; for example, we would have rules providing that $[\alpha A] \rightarrow [\alpha \text{vocalic}]$, $[\alpha B] \rightarrow [\alpha \text{consonantal}]$ (where α is a variable ranging over the values of feature specifications, as in Chapter Three, p. 83). But every grammar will have to have exactly these rules; hence they do not contribute in any way to the choice among grammars and can just as well be eliminated from all grammars. To eliminate them means, simply, to use the names of the phonetic features to label the categories in the first place.

The second effect of this proposal would be nonvacuous, however. Recall that the phonetic features constitute a fixed and restricted set, independent of any particular language. Thus, our decision to restrict phonological categories to those that can be labeled by phonetic features amounts to an empirical hypothesis concerning the number of possible

---

[6] In other words, we believe untenable the view (characteristic of post-Sapirian linguistics, both in the United States and in Europe) that there is a level of representation meeting such conditions as invariance and biuniqueness. For discussion, see Halle (1959), Chomsky (1964), Chomsky and Halle (1965).

categories of a phonological matrix.[7] It reflects the hypothesis that beyond the categorization given by the features which are associated, ultimately, with phonetic values, all categorization applies to the formative as a whole and not to its separate (successive) parts. For example, a formative may belong to the category of items which are exceptions to a certain phonological rule, but we cannot state, in the lexical representation, that one but not another of its segments belongs to the category of exceptions to this rule. To achieve the latter effect, a special rule would have to be given, increasing the complexity of the grammar. We expect, to put it loosely, that there will be rules applying to segments specified in terms of categories very closely tied to phonetic features and rules applying to full lexical items; but rules of other sorts will necessarily be more complex, given the framework we are adopting. This becomes a significant claim as soon as an evaluation measure is fixed. If true, it is a formal property of language that would be missed if phonetic and phonological features were strictly dissociated.

We think, then, that there may be good reason to limit the class of phonological matrices in terms of the set of universal phonetic features. For the linguist or the child learning the language, the set of phonetic representations of utterances is a given empirical fact.[8] His problem is to assign a lexical representation to each word, and to develop a set of grammatical (in particular, phonological) rules which account for the given facts. The performance of this task is limited by the set of constraints on the form of grammars. Without such constraints, the task is obviously impossible; and the narrower such constraints, the more feasible the task becomes. Among the formal conditions is the one that we have just outlined, namely, that each lexical entry consists of a phonological matrix in which the rows are labeled by names of phonetic features along with a set of categories to which the formative in question belongs. The conditions on the form and application of rules and the evaluation measure for grammars set further constraints. The task, then, is to select the most highly valued grammar (including, in particular, a lexicon) that meets these conditions and is compatible with the particular data on which it is based.

---

[7] To further restrict the use of phonological features as mere "diacritics," we might add other conditions, for example, the condition that if a feature is totally redundant (as, for example, glottalization in English, which is always completely predictable from context), then it must not be used distinctively in lexical matrices. This would eliminate various techniques for escaping some of the force of the decision to limit phonological features to those with an absolute phonetic interpretation. We do not take this step here, however, since we are unable to formulate such a condition in a way which will still permit a wide class of familiar cases in which a distinctive feature is lost phonetically though it remains functional in phonological rules. Thus, to take just one of innumerable examples, in Modern Hebrew the feature of pharyngealization (which in Arabic distinguishes the class of "emphatic" consonants) is phonetically lost in stops, but it (or some other nonphonetic feature) must still be marked in lexical matrices, to prevent postvocalic spirantization in what is historically an emphatic [k], for example. Thus we have [kavar], [lixbor] contrasting with [kavar], [likbor], and we may account for the contrast by representing the former with a nonpharyngealized [k] and the latter with pharyngealized [k].

Presumably, the way to distinguish permissible from impermissible uses of diacritics is in terms of certain universal conditions on the kinds of rules in which a given feature can play a role. However, we are not in a position to say very much about this interesting question. For some discussion see Chapter Nine.

[8] But qualifications are necessary. Thus both the linguist and the child must determine which of the phenomena presented to them are legitimate examples on which to base their theory of the language of which these examples are a sample, and in part this decision must itself be made on grounds of systematic complexity. Furthermore, it must be borne in mind that the speaker of a language may assign to a physical signal a phonetic representation determined in part by grammatical rule rather than by overt properties of the signal.

2.1. LEXICAL REDUNDANCY RULES

To the rules that apply strictly within a single lexical entry and that simply fill in unspecified squares of phonological matrices, without violating invariance, we will give the special name of "lexical redundancy rules."[9] We will see that they have many special properties and interesting empirical correlates. Strictly speaking, they belong to the system of readjustment rules rather than to phonology, in our terms. Thus representations such as (2) are actually lexical rather than phonological representations. They become phonological representations when lexical redundancy rules (and perhaps other readjustment rules) apply, converting some—perhaps all—of the zero entries to plus or minus.

As an illustration of a lexical redundancy rule, we cite a familiar restriction on initial consonant clusters:

$$
\begin{pmatrix} 7 \end{pmatrix} \qquad [+\text{consonantal}] \quad \rightarrow \quad \begin{bmatrix} -\text{vocalic} \\ +\text{anterior} \\ +\text{coronal} \\ +\text{strident} \\ +\text{continuant} \\ -\text{voice} \end{bmatrix} \Big/ + \underline{} \begin{bmatrix} +\text{consonantal} \\ -\text{vocalic} \end{bmatrix}
$$

This rule asserts that the first segment of an initial consonant cluster must be [s] if the second segment is a true consonant (i.e., neither a liquid nor a glide). It rules out sequences such as [ps], [θm], but not [pl], [θr], in formative-initial position.

We cannot in all cases determine from the form of a rule whether it is a lexical redundancy rule or a rule of the phonology. If, for example, a rule such as (7) were to apply across formative boundary, it could not be a lexical redundancy rule. Thus consider the rule, dating back to Old English, that vowels are nontense in position before certain consonant clusters. Before clusters such as [kt] and [pt], we always find lax vowels, not only when the cluster occurs within a formative, as in *evict, apt, crypt*, but also when it occurs across formative boundary, as in *descrip+tion, satisfac+tion*. There are no tense vowels or diphthongs in this environment, that is, no morphemes such as *[dūwkt], *[dāwkt], *[ēypt], or *[krāypt] and no polymorphemic forms such as *[dāwk+tiv], *[skrāyp+tyūwr].[10] Thus this laxing rule, as opposed to rule (7), is a rule of the phonology rather than a lexical redundancy rule.

---

[9] These are rules which express regularities of lexical classification. In addition to the phonological redundancy rules, there are redundancy rules that deal with syntactic and semantic categories that appear in the lexicon, and that relate these several kinds of categories (see Chomsky, 1965, Chapter Four). In this book, however, we will consider only phonological redundancy rules. These are the "morpheme structure rules" of Halle (1959), where the notion is introduced.

[10] We find *opt* and *concoct* with tense [ā] before [pt] and [kt], but, as we have seen, this [ā] is the reflex of an originally nontense vowel by rule (5). The past tense [t] (e.g., *aped; liked*) must, of course, be marked as being excluded from the domain of this rule, as well as that of many other rules, in regular verbs. As we have already noted, it is regularly preceded by the boundary #. Some other apparent exceptions are dealt with below. The basic regularities discussed here were pointed out to us by P. Kiparsky.

    Notice, incidentally, that [ŋ] acts as a cluster of the form C_2, rather than as a single consonant like [m] or [n]. Thus we have words such as *lime–line, loam–loan, lame–lane, town*, etc., with [āy], [ōw], [ēy], [āw], respectively, but forms such as *[lāyŋ], *[lōwŋ], *[lēyŋ], *[tāwŋ] are impossible in English. This is one of many factors contributing to the conclusion that the phonological matrix [+nasal] [g] underlies [ŋ].

2.2. TREATMENT OF EXCEPTIONS

As mentioned directly above, vowels in English are generally laxed before consonant clusters. Excluded from the domain of this laxing rule, however, are vowels preceding certain clusters within a single lexical item, in particular, vowels preceding dental clusters. For example, we have words such as *pint, count, plaint,* in which a diphthong precedes the cluster [nt], and words such as *hoist, toast, wild, field,* with diphthongs before other dental clusters. But a dental cluster with an intervening formative boundary has no special status, and we do have laxing in the boldface position in words such as *conven+tion, interven+tion, deten+tion, absten+tion, reten+tive, conten+t, wid+th, los+t.* (Note that laxing does not occur in *plaint+ive,* from the lexical entry *plaint,* or in *restrain#t, complain#t*—contrasting with *cóntènt* from *contain+t*—which have word boundary rather than formative boundary in the dental cluster, as seen from the fact that stress is not shifted to the left in the noun cycle.) Thus the laxing rule (see rule (20III) and note 2 in Chapter Five for a refined version of this rule) states that, with the exception of vowels occurring before dental clusters within formatives:

$$\left(8\right) \qquad\qquad V \;\rightarrow\; [-\text{tense}] \;\; / \;\; \underline{\quad\quad} C_2$$

Exceptions of the type just noted cannot be easily incorporated into the grammar as developed up to this point. We therefore consider next an extension of the available descriptive devices which would enable us to treat such exceptions in a straightforward manner.

Each phonological rule of the language applies to certain formatives and, in general, not to others, the domain of its application being determined by the feature composition of the phonological matrices. If a certain rule does not apply to a certain formative, this fact must somehow be indicated in the feature composition of the formative at the stage of derivation at which the rule is applicable. It is quite obvious that many of the phonological rules of the language will have certain exceptions which, from the point of view of the synchronic description, will be quite arbitrary. This is no more surprising than the fact that there exist strong verbs or irregular plurals. Phonology, being essentially a finite system, can tolerate some lack of regularity (exceptions can be memorized); being a highly intricate system, resulting (very strikingly, in a language like English) from diverse and interwoven historical processes, it is to be expected that a margin of irregularity will persist in almost every aspect of the phonological description. Clearly, we must design our linguistic theory in such a way that the existence of exceptions does not prevent the systematic formulation of those regularities that remain.[11] Furthermore, we must provide means for expressing those regularities that hold within the class of exceptions, however limited they may be. Finally, an overriding consideration is that the evaluation measure must be designed in such a way that the wider and more varied the class of exceptions to a rule, the less highly valued is the grammar.

In short, the most highly valued (simplest) grammar will be that in which the phonological rule $X \rightarrow Y$ (where X and Y are matrices) applies to any string containing X as a submatrix. We are certain to find, however, that in many cases formatives will have to be differentiated with respect to the applicability of the rule in question. Some formatives containing the submatrix X will undergo the rule, and others will not. The wider and more

---

[11] This obvious point is always taken for granted in morphological studies—e.g., no one would think of refusing to incorporate the rule for regular plurals in an English grammar because of *children, oxen, fish,* etc.

varied the class of cases that do not undergo the rule, the more complex must be the grammar in terms of the evaluation procedure that must constitute part of a significant linguistic theory.

We will deal with this problem in the following way. Each rule of the phonology has a certain identifying number. We associate with each number n a new "distinctive feature" $[\pm n]$. Suppose that the rule numbered n is $A \rightarrow B / C \underline{\quad\quad} D$. Then we stipulate that A must be marked $[+n]$ if the rule numbered n is to apply to it. Furthermore, we establish the following general convention:

Convention 1: Every segment of a lexical matrix is automatically marked $[+n]$ for every rule n.

Since the various decisions just formulated contribute equally to the complexity of all grammars, we may regard their total contribution to the evaluation of a grammar as nil. This is to say that we need not even present these conditions explicitly in a grammar but may regard them merely as conventions for interpreting a grammar. They do, however, play a role in determining whether or not two matrices are distinct.

If a certain formative is not subject to rule n, its segments must be marked $[-n]$. In the light of the decisions on the form of grammars that we have so far adopted, we must conclude that this fact is not a feature of any segment of the formative but of the formative as a whole. That is, the formative as such must be marked in the lexicon as belonging to the category of exceptions to rule n, and, consequently, the feature $[-n]$ must be marked in each of its segments. But in accordance with Convention 1, each of its segments is marked $[+n]$. Thus we must add a new convention, to be applied after Convention 1 and having the following effect:

Convention 2: Every segment of a lexical matrix μ is marked $[\alpha K]$ for each category $[\alpha K]$ to which μ belongs.

Thus, in particular, if a formative belongs to the lexical category $[-n]$, each of its segments will be marked $[-n]$ by Convention 2, after automatically having been marked $[+n]$ by Convention 1. Thus every time a certain formative is an exception to a rule, there is a certain "cost" associated with this fact, namely, a certain category assignment must be given the lexical entry. But an item that does undergo a rule need not be specially marked. Thus only exceptions to a rule contribute to the complexity of the grammar in this connection.

Furthermore, notice that the less "predictable" the class of exceptions, the greater the contribution to complexity. For example, if the class of formatives belonging to the category $[-n]$ is totally idiosyncratic, then each such category assignment must be given in the lexicon. But if this class plays some other role in the grammar, in whole or in part, then the category assignment need not be given as an independent lexical property. Thus in English, for example, there are many items that must be marked in the lexicon for the fact that they do not enter into the Romance derivational system. We shall designate such formatives as belonging to the category $[-\text{deriv}]$. A phonological property connected with the independently motivated category "subject to derivational processes" will contribute less to the complexity of the grammar than one that is entirely idiosyncratic, since its occurrence in lexical entries can in part be stated by redundancy rules. Consider rule (6), for example, which, when appropriately generalized, will have the effect of changing [k] to [s] and [g] to [j] (in a series of steps) when these segments appear before a high or mid front vowel ([i], [e], [ĭ], [ē]). This rule applies to the boldface segments of *reciproc-*, *receive*, *general*, etc., but not to the boldface positions of *kill*, *kennel*, *lackey*, *gill*, and so on. Yet there is good reason to mark all these items as velar stops in the lexicon. Thus the items *kill, kennel, gill* (but not *reciproc-, -ceive, general*) will be marked in the lexicon as belonging to the category [−rule (6)].[12] However, this is not an entirely idiosyncratic classification since it is, in part, an automatic consequence (therefore statable by a redundancy rule instead of having to be independently marked in each case) of membership in the category [−deriv], characteristic of a formative which must anyway be specially marked in its lexical entry.[13] The lexical category [−rule (6)] will, by Convention 2, be marked as a segmental feature of each segment of the items belonging to this category, and these items will thereby be automatically excluded from the application of rule (6). This is a rather typical example of a characteristic aspect of English grammar to which we shall make reference again below.

Alongside of the partially systematic class of exceptions to rule (6), we also find purely idiosyncratic exceptions. For example, consider the rule that makes vowels nontense before certain affixes (e.g., compare *serene* and *serenity*, *obscene* and *obscenity*). There are exceptions to this rule (e.g., *obese–obesity*, in most dialects) which must simply be categorized as such in the lexicon, these lexical features becoming segmental features by Convention 2. Each such example contributes to the complexity of the grammar, but there is obviously no question of rejecting the rule. Doing so would amount to treating *each* item as an exception, in the manner of item-and-arrangement grammars (see Chapter Three, Section 16), and there is surely no point to such a decision.

Convention 2 asserts that each lexical category of a formative automatically becomes a distinctive feature of each of its segments. This will be true, then, even of the syntactic and semantic features ("animate," "proper," particular semantic properties, etc.) which ordinarily have no phonetic effects. No harm is done, however, by allowing Convention 2 to apply quite generally. In fact these lexical categorizations may indeed have phonetic effects occasionally. (See Chapter Eight, Section 7, for some examples.)

Let us be somewhat more precise about Convention 2. Suppose that a formative belongs to the syntactic categories [animate], [nonhuman], [exception to rule *n*]. Alternatively, we might represent these categories as [+animate], [−human], [−rule *n*] within the syntactic component of the grammar. From the point of view of the phonology, each of the categories [animate] (= [+animate]), [nonhuman] (= [−human]), [exception to rule *n*] (= [−rule *n*]) is simply a feature, which may be positively or negatively specified. Convention 2 asserts that each segment of the formative in question receives the specifications [+[animate]], [+[nonhuman]], [+[exception to rule *n*]], that is, the specifications [+[+animate]], [+[−human]], [+[−rule *n*]. To simplify the theory of rule application, we may assume that each segment of any formative is, by convention, specified as [−*X*] for any syntactic category *X* that appears anywhere in the lexicon for which it is not specified

---

[12] Notice that in the case of the unvoiced velar stop [k], the orthographic distinction of *k–c* comes close to marking the distinction [−rule (6)] vs. [+rule (6)], for obvious historical reasons.

[13] Notice that the items subject to derivational processes are further subdivided (ultimately, with respect to Greek or Latin origin) in terms of the categorization provided by rule (6). Thus we have *hierarch* (*-ic, -y*), *psych* (*-ic, -o-*), and a small number of other formatives which do not undergo softening of velars before *-ic*, etc., in contrast to the large class of regular cases which do. In short, we would certainly expect to find, in a complete grammar of English, that categories corresponding rather closely to Greek, Latin, and Germanic origin appear in lexical entries and that membership in these categories has phonetic effects. English is perhaps unusual in the intricate and complex way in which these categories and their effects have been worked into the grammar, but it is quite generally the case that the lexicon of a language is subdivided, in terms of phonological and morphological processes, into "native" and "foreign," or something of this sort. See, for example, Lees (1961) and the interesting discussion in Postal (1968).

$[+X]$. Thus the segments of the formative being considered in our example are specified $[-[-\text{animate}]]$, $[-[+\text{human}]]$. We now specify, again by a general interpretive convention, that $[+[-\text{rule } n]] = [-\text{rule } n]$. Thus the feature [exception to rule n] as introduced by a lexical feature and as introduced by a rule are indistinguishable from the point of view of the rules of the phonological component. With these interpretive conventions, exceptions are handled in the intended way.

The formal devices just developed seem to be appropriate for dealing with exceptions to phonological rules. As we have noted, the grammar becomes more complex as exceptions increase in number, variety, and unpredictability. The complication is less severe if a class of exceptions can be characterized by a redundancy rule rather than by listing each example, that is, rather than by idiosyncratic lexical marking.

We are now in a position to return to the problem of the laxing rule (8). As noted, this applies to vowels that appear in the context —— C_2 unless, among other exceptional cases, the consonant cluster in question is a dental cluster and is internal to a formative. In our framework dentals are marked [+anterior, +coronal]. We must therefore incorporate into the grammar the lexical redundancy rule (9):

$$\left(9\right) \qquad V \;\rightarrow\; [-\text{rule (8)}] \quad \Big/ \quad \underline{\qquad} \begin{bmatrix} +\text{consonantal} \\ +\text{anterior} \\ +\text{coronal} \end{bmatrix} \begin{bmatrix} +\text{consonantal} \\ +\text{coronal} \end{bmatrix}$$

Being a lexical redundancy rule, rule (9) applies only within a single lexical entry. It specifies that a vowel in the context —— C_2 will not undergo the laxing rule (8) if the following cluster is dental. Thus, the effect of the combination of the lexical redundancy rule (9) and the phonological rule (8) is precisely as indicated in the informal description of page 172.

Another possible sort of exception involves "negative contexts." Thus, when the rule n, $X \rightarrow Y$, applies everywhere except in the context Z —— W, we might state this fact in the following form:

$$\left(10\right) \qquad \begin{array}{ll} (n-1) & X \;\rightarrow\; [-\text{rule } n] \;\; / \; Z \underline{\qquad} W \\ (n) & X \;\rightarrow\; Y \end{array}$$

We have so far mentioned three kinds of exceptions: those indicated by lexical categorization, those given by lexical redundancy rules such as (9), and those that involve negative contexts for rules, as in (10). If we were to use the device of (10) more generally— if, in other words, we were to allow reference in a rule not only to the next rule, as in $(10n-1)$, but to any rule—then we would increase the power and flexibility of the system greatly.

We have no examples that suggest the necessity for negative contexts or for any extension of the device of (10). Therefore, we will make the tentative assumption that the only kinds of exceptions to rules are those given by lexical categorization or by lexical redundancy rules such as (9), and we will restrict the formalism of the theory accordingly.

Although this approach to the problem of exceptions seems to us correct as far as it goes, it is far from definitive. There is, first of all, a certain ambiguity of reference when we specify an item as $[-\text{rule } n]$. Consider, once again, the laxing of vowels in English. Rule (8) is really an abbreviation for several rules, one of which applies to a vowel in the context —— C^m (where m is the maximum length of a consonant cluster in English), another in the context —— C^{m-1}, etc., and the last of which applies in the context C^2. We must decide, then, upon general conventions that determine whether an item marked as an

TABLE 1. *Distinctive feature composition of English segments*

	ɨ	ī	ū	ē	ō	ǣ	ā	ǣ	ɔ̄	i	u	e	ʌ	o	æ	ɔ	y	w	ɛ
vocalic	+	+	+	+	+	+	+	+	+	+	+	+	+	+	+	+	−	−	−
consonantal	−	−	−	−	−	−	−	−	−	−	−	−	−	−	−	−	−	−	−
high	+	+	+	−	−	−	−	−	−	+	+	−	−	−	−	−	+	+	−
back	+	−	+	−	+	−	+	−	+	−	+	−	+	+	−	+	−	+	−
low	−	−	−	−	−	+	+	+	+	+	−	−	−	−	−	+	+	−	−
anterior	−	−	−	−	−	−	−	−	−	−	−	−	−	−	−	−	−	−	−
coronal	−	−	−	−	−	−	−	−	−	−	−	−	−	−	−	−	−	−	−
round	−	−	+	−	+	−	−	+	+	−	+	−	−	+	−	+	−	+	−
tense	+	+	+	+	+	+	+	+	+	−	−	−	−	−	−	−	−	−	−
voice																			
continuant																			
nasal																			
strident																			

exception to rule (8) is an exception to all of the rules abbreviated by (8) or only to a specific one. From some points of view it seems natural to adopt the convention that a specification of [−rule *n*] refers to the rule numbered *n* in the completely expanded system of rules which involves no abbreviatory notations. Items will then have to be categorized as exceptions to one or another rule abbreviated by (8). An item which is an exception to rule (8) applying in the context ——CC will not necessarily be an exception to the rule applying in the context ——CCC (the consonant cluster being followed by a vowel or a nonsegment in both cases). In the case in question, this seems the correct interpretation. The vowels that are marked as exceptions to the rule laxing vowels in the context ——CC are not, apparently, excluded from laxing in the context ——CCC (cf. *children, Christmas,* in which the tense vowel becomes lax even before a dental cluster—in the word *Christmas,* the [t] later drops). Examples are so sparse, however, that this observation cannot be taken very seriously. And there is very little doubt that items which are exceptions to certain subcases of a rule will also, under some circumstances, be exceptions to other subcases. What these circumstances may be, however, we do not know, and we therefore leave the problem in this unsatisfactory state.

There are other aspects of the problem of exceptions not taken care of in the system presented above. Occasionally items must be specified not as exceptions to some specific rule but as exceptions to all rules of some general sort. For example, in Hebrew there are several rules deleting vowels, but none of them apply to the high vowels [i] and [u]; and there are several rules modifying vowel quality, but none of them apply to [u]. Thus we want to mark underlying /u/ as immune to all rules affecting quality, and to mark underlying high vowels as immune to all deletion rules. We came across a similar but more marginal problem in English in studying Auxiliary Reduction Rules in Section 14 of Chapter Three. In discussing the immunity to reduction of [ɔ̄y] and such exceptional cases as the vowel of =*nOt,* we pointed out that such vocalic nuclei are also tense where they would be expected to be lax (e.g., *exploitative, denotative*), and we observed in note 74 (p. 122) that they might be lexically marked as exempt from laxing—that is, exempt from several separate but related rules that make vowels nontense under various circumstances. Here, once again, a principled solution to the problem requires insights into rule classification that go beyond our present understanding.

r	l	p	b	f	v	m	t	d	θ	ð	n	s	z	c	č	ǰ	š	ž	k	g	x	ŋ	h	kʷ	gʷ	xʷ
+	+	−	−	−	−	−	−	−	−	−	−	−	−	−	−	−	−	−	−	−	−	−	−	−	−	−
+	+	+	+	+	+	+	+	+	+	+	+	+	+	+	+	+	+	+	+	+	+	+	−	+	+	+
−	−	−	−	−	−	−	−	−	−	−	−	−	−	−	+	+	+	+	+	+	+	+	−	+	+	+
−	−	−	−	−	−	−	−	−	−	−	−	−	−	−	−	−	−	−	+	+	+	+	−	+	+	+
−	+	+	+	+	+	+	+	+	+	+	+	+	+	+	−	−	−	−	−	−	−	−	−	−	−	−
+	+	−	−	−	−	−	+	+	+	+	+	+	+	+	+	+	+	+	−	−	−	−	−	−	−	−
																			−	−	−			+	+	+
+	+	−	+	−	+	+	−	+	−	+	+	−	+	−	−	+	−	+	−	+	−	+	−	−	+	−
+	+	−	−	+	+	−	−	−	+	+	−	+	+	−	−	−	+	+	−	−	+	−	+	−	−	+
−	−	−	−	−	−	+	−	−	−	−	+	−	−	−	−	−	−	−	−	−	−	+	−	−	−	−
−	−	−	−	+	+	−	−	−	−	−	−	+	+	+	+	+	+	+	−	−	−	−	−	−	−	−

3. The features

In our discussion of the stress rules of English, we have had occasion to analyze the segments as [±vocalic], [±consonantal], and [±tense]. The universal phonetic theory which we accept presents further possibilities for the categorization of segments. Those categorizations which play a role in the discussion of the present chapter are summarized in Table 1. (For a more detailed discussion see Chapter Seven and the literature cited there.)

In the vowel system the essential features are "high," "back," "low," "round," and "tense." For the consonants, the traditional points of articulation are supplanted in the present system by the features "anterior" and "coronal" as in Table 2:

TABLE 2.

	labial	dental	palato-alveolar	velar
anterior	+	+	−	−
coronal	−	+	+	−

These categorizations suffice for the examination of English consonants presented in this chapter, and in general the features "high," "back," and "low" will play no role in the discussion of consonants here. (See Chapter Seven and Chapter Nine, Section 4, for a more detailed treatment.)

The phonological rules specify coefficients associated with different features. Thus, rule (8) supplies the coefficient "minus" to the feature "tense" in a vowel before two consonants; the stress rules of the preceding chapter supply coefficients represented by positive integers to the feature "stress" in vowels in various contexts.

We extend the notation to allow variables—for which we use letters of the Greek alphabet—to function as coefficients of features in the formulation of rules. This extension allows us to handle many phenomena that would otherwise not be expressible. We have already made use of this notation in formulating the rules of stress assignment in the

preceding chapter. The familiar rule of voicing assimilation in consonant clusters provides
another simple example of the use of variables:

$$(11) \qquad \begin{bmatrix} +\text{cons} \\ -\text{voc} \\ -\text{nasal} \end{bmatrix} \rightarrow [\alpha\text{voice}] \; / \underline{\hspace{1cm}} \begin{bmatrix} +\text{cons} \\ -\text{voc} \\ -\text{nasal} \\ \alpha\text{voice} \end{bmatrix}$$

In other words, a nonnasal consonant becomes voiced before a voiced nonnasal (true)
consonant and unvoiced before an unvoiced nonnasal (true) consonant.

Dissimilation can also be expressed by the use of variables. For example, in (11) if we
replace [αvoice] by [−αvoice] in the segment to which the rule applies, then the rule will
state a process of dissimilation, the first of two nonnasal true consonants becoming voiced
where the second is unvoiced, and unvoiced where the second is voiced. To take a real
example, consider a dialect of English in which diphthongs can take only low back vowels
before the nonback glide [y] (i.e., [ɔ̄y], [āy]) and only nonback vowels before the back
glide [w] (i.e., [æw]). To account for the phonetic quality of the vowels, we postulate the
dissimilation rule (12):

$$(12) \qquad \begin{bmatrix} +\text{voc} \\ -\text{cons} \\ +\text{low} \end{bmatrix} \rightarrow [-\alpha\text{back}] \; / \underline{\hspace{1cm}} \begin{bmatrix} -\text{voc} \\ -\text{cons} \\ \alpha\text{back} \end{bmatrix}$$

Observe that by permitting variables in the formulation of rules, we in effect commit
ourselves to the view that assimilation and dissimilation are not merely a matter of fortuitous
coincidence of almost identical rules, but are, rather, linguistic universals—that is, processes
available to all languages though not necessarily used in all.

As we proceed, we will come across other examples which call for the use of variables
in rules.

4. *Vowel alternations*

We are now in a position to deal with the central problem in the noncyclic phonology of
English, that is, the problem of accounting for the intricate system of vowel alternations
that are found primarily, but not solely, in the subpart of the vocabulary that is of Romance
origin. We will consider first the nonback vowels and will work out the rules governing their
alternations. We will then apply these results to the apparently still more complex system of
back vowels and to the question of back-nonback alternations.

4.1. *ALTERNATIONS OF NONBACK VOWELS*

Consider first forms such as *divine–divinity, serene–serenity, profane–profanity.*
Returning now to the notation of the preceding chapter (see p. 69), we give these in the
representation *divIn–divinity, serEn–serenity, profAn–profænity.*[14] There are many other
cases of the same system of alternations—*satIr–satiric, derIv–derivative, lIn–linear–
delineate, mEtr–metric, appEl–appelative, dElicious–delicacy, compAr–compærative, explAn–
explænatory, grAteful–grætitude,* and so on. It is clear that in the case of *divIn–divinity,
serEn–serenity, profAn–profænity,* the underlying representation must have a tense vowel

---

[14] As in Chapter Three, we will preserve conventional spelling in expository passages as much as possible,
using a fairly precise representation only for the elements explicitly under discussion.

in the second syllable so that in isolation the word will receive final stress by the strong cluster rule of Chapter Three; that is, these forms must be entered in the lexicon as *divIn*, *serEn*, *profAn*, where [I], [E], [A] (whatever their quality may be otherwise) are phonologically tense. In order to account for the lax vowels in the derivative nouns, however, we must incorporate in the grammar rules that have the effect of (13):

$$\left(13\right) \qquad \left\{\begin{array}{ccc} I & \rightarrow & i \\ E & \rightarrow & e \\ A & \rightarrow & æ \end{array}\right\} \quad \text{in certain contexts}$$

Apart from tenseness, we have not yet settled the phonological distinctive feature composition of the segments that we are representing by capital letters. Phonetically the segments represented as [I], [E], [A] will appear as [āy], [īy], [ēy], respectively, that is, as a tense vowel followed by a *y*-glide. Suppose that *divine*, *serene*, *profane* are entered in the lexicon with [āy], [īy], [ēy] (or, perhaps, archi-forms of these) in the position of the second vowel. Then rule (13) would have the form:

$$\left(14\right) \qquad \left\{\begin{array}{ccc} āy & \rightarrow & i \\ īy & \rightarrow & e \\ ēy & \rightarrow & æ \end{array}\right\} \quad \text{in certain contexts}$$

If we replace the informal notations of (14) by their precise representations in terms of features, we find that the rule is quite complex, expressing no underlying generalization. This suggests that the operation of the rule be subdivided into several stages, each of which can perhaps be expressed in some fairly general form. Instead of pursuing this possibility directly, however, let us turn to some other evidence that strongly brings into question the decision to accept the phonological feature analysis of [I], [E], [A] as [āy], [īy], [ēy], respectively.

Alongside of the rules (14), we must also have rules that produce effects precisely opposite to those of (14). To see this, consider the forms *various–varIety*, *impious–pIety*, *funeral–funEreal*, *manager–managErial*, *Abel–AbElian*, *Canada–CanAdian*, *marginal–marginAlia*, *algebra–algebrAic*, etc. We have already noted that there are rules applying to nontense vowels in final position, causing those that are nonlow (that is [i], [e], [u], [o]) to become tense and those that are low to reduce to [ə] (see (30), p. 74). Since the final vowel of *algebra* reduces, it must be marked in the lexicon as [+low]. Moreover, it must also be [−tense], for otherwise the stress assignment rules of the preceding chapter would have assigned stress to it. But in *algebraic* this vowel is both [+tense] and [−low]; it is, in fact, [A]. The vowel is also nonback and nonround in *algebraic*, and the simplest assumption with respect to these features is, clearly, that the same is true of the underlying representation of the vowel in *algebra*-. In sum, the segment underlying the final vowel of *algebra* must be nontense, low, nonback, and nonround; i.e., it must be /æ/. To give the proper vowel in *algebrAic*, then, the grammar must contain rule (15):

$$\left(15\right) \qquad\qquad æ \quad \rightarrow \quad A \quad \text{in certain contexts}$$

Consider now *various–variety*. Clearly the underlying form of *vary* must have a lax final vowel or the stress would be on the last syllable. The phonetic tenseness of this vowel in *vary* and in *various* is an automatic consequence of rules applying to vowels in final and in prevocalic position; its diphthongal quality is a consequence of its tenseness, as we shall see directly. Furthermore, it is clear from the word *vary* in isolation that the underlying vowel must be /i/. Since in *variety* this vowel appears as [I], we see that the grammar must contain, along with the rule æ → *A*, the rule *i* → *I*.

Consider, finally, *manager–managerial*. Again, considerations of stress placement and vowel reduction tell us that in *manager* the final vowel is lax. Considerations analogous to those cited in the preceding paragraph tell us that it is nonback. It can be neither /i/ nor /æ/ for it would then become [I] or [A] by the rules just discussed. Therefore it is /e/, and the grammar contains the rule *e* → *E*.

In short, the grammar must contain rules that have the effect of (16):

$$(16) \qquad \begin{Bmatrix} i & \to & I \\ e & \to & E \\ æ & \to & A \end{Bmatrix} \quad \text{in certain contexts}$$

If, as in (14), we take the phonological composition of [I], [E], [A] to be essentially the same as the phonetic composition, then (16) becomes:

$$(17) \qquad \begin{Bmatrix} i & \to & \bar{a}y \\ e & \to & \bar{i}y \\ æ & \to & \bar{e}y \end{Bmatrix} \quad \text{in certain contexts}$$

As we have noted above in connection with (14), this is an extremely complex rule.

For a grammar to contain a rule of the complexity of (14) or a rule of the complexity of (17) is implausible enough. For it to contain both of these rules is quite intolerable, not only because of the doubling of complexity, but, more importantly, because it is clear that such a grammar is missing a significant generalization. Thus the fact that (17) simply reverses (14) does not contribute to the simplicity of this grammar, i.e., the generalization that similar processes are involved is unexpressed. The grammar would be no more complex if (14) were retained and (17) were replaced by (18), for example:

$$(18) \qquad \begin{Bmatrix} i & \to & \bar{i}y \\ e & \to & \bar{e}y \\ æ & \to & \bar{a}y \end{Bmatrix} \quad \text{in certain contexts}$$

In fact, the grammar would actually be simplified in this particular case, contrary to obvious conditions of adequacy.

These considerations are sufficient to show that a theory of English (an English grammar) is surely in error if it attempts to account for the *I–i*, *E–e*, *A–æ* alternations by assigning to [I], [E], [A] a phonological feature analysis that corresponds to the phonetic feature analysis and relating the variants by the rules (14) and (17).

Let us therefore approach the problem of alternations of nonback vowels in a rather different way. It is clear that these alternations involve both a change of tenseness and a change of vowel quality. Let us put aside for the moment the question of the quality and concentrate on the tenseness. Rule (13) asserts that vowels become lax in certain contexts, and rule (16) asserts that they become tense in certain other contexts. Consideration of the examples given above, and many others, shows that the contexts in question are those in rules (19) (corresponding to (13)) and (20) (corresponding to (16)):

$$(19) \qquad V \to [-\text{tense}] \Big/ \underline{\quad} C \begin{cases} C_0 + i \begin{Bmatrix} k \\ d \\ \check{s} \end{Bmatrix} & \text{(a)} \\ (C_1 +) \begin{bmatrix} -\text{stress} \\ V \end{bmatrix} C_0 V & \text{(b)} \end{cases}$$

By rule (19) a stressed vowel becomes lax before the affix *-ic*, *-id*, or *-ish* (though not *-iv* or *-is*) and before an unstressed nonfinal syllable. In particular, then, bisyllabic affixes such as *-ity*, *-ify* will have the effect of laxing the immediately preceding vowel, and the same will be true in a variety of other cases.[15]

In case (b) we have the two subcases ——$CC + VC_0V$ and ——CVC_0V. The first subcase causes laxing in the boldface position in *profund+ity*, *pronunc+iation*, **wild***+erness* (if derived from *wIld*); but neither case applies in the boldface position of *mountainous*, *countenance*, *counterfeit*, *mountebank*, *bountiful*, etc., since in these words the consonant sequence after the stressed vowel is not followed by a formative boundary ($+$). Examples of laxing still unaccounted for in this analysis are *abundant*, *contrapuntal*.

Like many other phonological rules, the laxing rule (19) does not apply to a number of categorially marked exceptions (see Section 2.2). In monosyllables, in particular, we simply have two categories of formatives with respect to case (a)—those to which the rule applies and those to which it does not. Some examples that do not undergo laxing are *scEnic*, *bAsic*, *cIclic*. For case (b), there are exceptions such as *obEsity*, *hIbernate*, *Isolate*, *prObity*, and many before ——$CVC_0 \begin{bmatrix} -\text{low} \\ -\text{consonantal} \end{bmatrix}$ (e.g., *rotary*, *notary*, *rosary*, *decency*, *primary*, *papacy*, *vagary*, *vacancy*, *ivory*, *irony*, *regency*, *potency*, *credence*, *nature*—these examples from Luick (1898)).[16]

The tensing rule required by the facts examined above has the form:

$$(20) \quad V \rightarrow [+\text{tense}] \; / \; \left\{ \begin{array}{ll} \begin{bmatrix} \alpha\text{low} \\ \beta\text{stress} \end{bmatrix} \left\{ \begin{array}{l} V \\ \#, \text{ where } \beta = + \text{ if } \alpha = + \end{array} \right\} & \text{(a)} \\ \\ \begin{bmatrix} - \\ -\text{high} \end{bmatrix} C_1^1 \begin{bmatrix} -\text{low} \\ -\text{back} \\ -\text{cons} \\ -\text{stress} \end{bmatrix} V & \text{(b)} \end{array} \right\}$$

---

[15] The second part of the rule is the modern reflex of the Middle English "sound law," whose effects were characterized by Jespersen (1909, Section 4.33): "When a stressed syllable is followed by two (or more) weak ones, there is a strong tendency to shorten it." The rule itself was apparently discovered by Luick (1898).

Many writers on this subject (see, e.g., Jordan, 1934; Wyld, 1927; Dobson, 1957) give the impression that this development affected only a small part of the vocabulary. Luick (1898, pp. 349-50), however, specifically noted that "die englischen quantitaetsgesetze treten ferner zu tage in den vielen romanischen sowie auch in den spaeteren lateinisch-griechischen lehnwoertern." And Jespersen (1909, Section 4.71) gives an extensive list of examples from the non-Germanic component of the language.

[16] As implied here, part (b) of rule (19) should actually be generalized so that the last segment mentioned is [−consonantal] rather than V; that is, the segment in this position may be a glide as well as a vowel. Recall in this regard that the last two forms—*credence* and *nature*—like the other forms mentioned, have a final glide in their underlying representations. In the case of these two forms the glide is [ɛ], which is deleted by a simplified version of the e-Elision Rule (155) of Chapter Three. (See p. 161 for discussion.)

We may note that if we analyze *-ic* as /ik + al/, as suggested in Chapter Three, Section 7, the first part of case (a) disappears, falling under case (b). The motive for this analysis in Chapter Three was that it accounted for the exceptional behavior of *-ic* with respect to stress placement. The same artifice will, we now see, account for its exceptional behavior with respect to laxing.

In fact, there are other phenomena relevant here. Thus there are certain VC strings that permit only nontense vowels in the preceding syllable even though there is no reason to assign a formative boundary before VC $\#$; for example, *-id* (as in *acid*, *rapid*—the sole exception is *hybrid*), *-ish* (as in *radish*, *abolish*, *establish*, *relish*), and *-it* (as in *credit*, *limit*, *visit*). This may be a matter for a lexical redundancy rule. Notice that *-it* permits tense vowels when it can be regarded as an affix (*plaud+it*, *aud+it*).

Examples such as *lucid*, *stupid*, *cubic* are not exceptions to laxing before *-id*, *-ic*. We have already

Case (a) of (20) is simply rule (3) extended to final position and sharpened along the lines indicated in Chapter Three (see rule (30) there). Case (b) is the rule that is involved in all of the other examples given above in connection with the discussion of rules (16)–(17). It asserts that a nonhigh vowel becomes tense before a single consonant followed by [i] or [e] or the corresponding glides, which must in turn be followed by another vowel. Thus $e \rightarrow E$ in this position (*Abel–Abelian, manager–managerial*),[17] and $æ \rightarrow A$ (*Canada–Canadian, simultaneous, Arab–Arabian*), but *i* does not convert to *I* (*punctilious, Darwinian, reptilian, vicious*, etc.)

These observations support the decision to analyze the affix *-ion* as /iVn/. As we have already observed (p. 87), this decision is motivated by the placement of primary stress. But if we consider the syllables that precede *-ion*, we can give independent support for this conclusion. Examples such as *decision, revision* suggest that the trisyllabic laxing rule (19b) must have applied; thus *-ion* must be bisyllabic at this point. The high vowel in the context —— C+*ion* does not then become tense by rule (20b) since this context is restricted to nonhigh vowels; thus we have a lax vowel in this position in *decision, inhibition*, etc. But the first vowel of *-ation*, being nonhigh, does become tense by (20b), giving [At+iVn], which becomes [Ašən] by processes that we discuss in Section 6. (Certain formatives with nonhigh vowels are lexically marked as excluded from this tensing rule; e.g., *-cede*, as in *recede–recession, succeed–succession*.) Such configurations of nontense high vowels and tense nonhigh vowels are characteristic of the context ——C*i*V, as is clear from an inspection of rules (19b) and (20b).[18]

We must require in rule (19b) that the vowel following the vowel to which the rule applies be specified as [−stress], not just as having some weak stress. This is clear from consideration of the variants of *presentation*, for example, discussed in Chapter Three (p. 161). If the vowel in the second syllable has the specification [−stress], so that it eventually reduces, then rule (19b) applies to the vowel in the first syllable and we derive

---

seen (Chapter Three, pp. 149–50) that there is a subsequent rule that tenses underlying /u/ in the context ——CV. (Notice, however, that this tensing of /u/ does not take place before *-ish*. *Punish, flourish, nourish* are the only relevant examples.) Similarly, *abolish, stolid* are not exceptions because the phonetic [ā] in the penultimate syllable derives from underlying /ɔ/ (see rule (5)). Furthermore, *squalid* is not an exception, as we shall see in Section 4.3.7. The adjective-forming affix *-ish*, as in *swinish, loutish*, is irrelevant here, being preceded by #.

[17] Recall again that formatives may fall into two categories with respect to these rules, according to whether or not the rules apply. Thus, alongside of *Abelian* we have *Maxwellian*, and alongside of *managerial* we have *perennial*, etc. Nonapplication of the rule can just as well be marked, as in orthography, by a double consonant. (Recall that clusters of two identical consonants simplify—see (156), p. 148, Chapter Three.)

  Case (20b) often does not apply when the consonant following the vowel to be tensed is a liquid. Thus we have *valiant, batallion, clarion, Marion, secretarial*, etc. (The reason that [l] is followed by [y] and [r] by [E] in these forms will be discussed in Section 6; for *secretarial* see p. 202.)

[18] Comparison of *simultaneity* [sIməltənEətE] with *variety* [vərIətE] indicates that the underlying vowel following the [n] in *simultan-* must be /e/, not /i/, so that the rule $e \rightarrow E$ will apply. (The occasionally heard variant [sIməltənAətE] is apparently a hypercorrect form.) We might account for the appearance of phonetic [E] in forms such as *simultaneous* (but not in *courageous*) by postulating an ad hoc rule which raises unstressed /e/ to [i] under certain conditions. The vowel so raised, being high, will be subject to the Tensing Rule (20b) and then to Diphthongization (see rule (21)) but not to Vowel Shift (see rule (43) and the comments there). Formative-final /e/ that does not undergo raising is elided by the *e*-Elision Rule of Chapter Three.

[prez$\overset{3}{\text{ə}}$ntÁšən]; if the vowel in the second syllable has the specification [+stress], so that it is protected from reduction and eventually is marked [4 stress], then rule (19b) does not apply to the first vowel and we derive [pr$\overset{3}{\text{E}}$zent$\overset{4}{\text{Á}}$šən].

We must also require that the penultimate segment in the environment of (20b) be specified as [−stress], for otherwise tensing would take place in the nonprimary-stressed vowel of forms such as *variety*, with the result that the vowel would incorrectly be prevented from undergoing Vowel Reduction.

Notice that rules (19) and (20) must apply in the order given. Otherwise the forms that meet the contextual conditions of both rules (e.g., *simultaneous, emaciate*) will have lax rather than tense vowels in the phonetic representation. Notice also that rule (19) can be combined with rule (8), which makes a vowel lax before a double consonant.

In discussing Auxiliary Reduction Rules in Section 14 of the preceding chapter, we observed that the rule stated finally as (118), which makes a vowel lax and unstressed under certain conditions, must precede various tensing rules, in particular, those that determine that the vowels in the boldface position of words such as *commutation, commutative* have tense vowels (see p. 124). The Auxiliary Reduction Rule in question will fall together naturally with the Laxing Rule (19), and the rule that tenses the boldface vowel in these words will fall together with the Tensing Rule (20). Thus the observations of the preceding chapter confirm the conclusion that the order is Laxing Rules first and then Tensing Rules.

Clearly rules (19) and (20), which have opposite effects, are both needed in the grammar. This is a minimum of reversibility that is inescapable. Since, however, each of these rules is very simple in feature composition, this is not a disturbing or surprising fact.

Rules (19) and (20) allow us to account for the tenseness of the vowels that take part in the alternations of nonback vowels. As we have seen, the quality of the underlying lax vowel must be given in the lexicon. Still to be accounted for is the quality of the tense vowel and its diphthongization. We are now proposing that [I], [E], [A] be represented simply as the tense vowels corresponding to [i], [e], [æ] and that the specific quality of these tense vowels result from special rules, which in fact turn out to be rather simple.

It is a well-known fact that English tense vowels are diphthongized or have off-glides. For the nonback vowels [ī] and [ē], the glide is [y] (that is, high, nonback, nonround); for the back vowels [ū] and [ō], it is [w] (that is, high, back, round). Generalizing these phonetic observations somewhat, let us simply give a rule of diphthongization to the effect that after *any* tense vowel, a high glide is inserted which agrees in backness with the vowel in question and is, furthermore, nonround if nonback and round if back. Thus [y] is introduced after nonback vowels, and [w] after back vowels.

$\left(21\right)$ DIPHTHONGIZATION

$$\phi \;\rightarrow\; \begin{bmatrix} -\text{voc} \\ -\text{cons} \\ +\text{high} \\ \alpha\text{back} \\ \alpha\text{round} \end{bmatrix} \;\Big/\; \begin{bmatrix} +\text{tense} \\ \alpha\text{back} \end{bmatrix} \underline{}$$

We now have rules giving the alternations *i–īy, e–ēy, æ–ǣy*, and we must add a rule which changes [ī] to [ā], [ē] to [ī], and [ǣ] to [ē]. Taking [ā] of [āy] to be [ǣ] for the moment, we see that we need a rule which has the effect of (22):

$$\left(22\right) \quad \begin{array}{ccc} \bar{\text{\i}} & \bar{\text{e}} & \bar{\text{æ}} \\ \downarrow & \downarrow & \downarrow \\ \bar{\text{æ}} & \bar{\text{\i}} & \bar{\text{e}} \end{array}$$

We will then have to add a rule converting [ǣ] to [ā]. The rule sketched in (22) we will call the Vowel Shift Rule (it is, in fact, a synchronic residue of the Great Vowel Shift of Early Modern English), and we will discuss it in detail in Section 4.3.

We return now to our original examples in order to see how these are handled by the rules that have already been established here. Consider first the alternations *divīn–divinity*, *serēn–serenity*, *profĀn–profanity*. The underlying forms in the lexicon, as we have already noted, must be *divīn, serēn, profĀn*, with a tense vowel in the second syllable. We are now taking each capital letter to represent the tense vowel corresponding to the lower-case letter; that is, /I/ = /ī/, /E/ = /ē/, /A/ = /ǣ/, in terms of phonological features. Thus capitalization simply expresses tenseness, and this expository device used in the preceding chapters turns out to have systematic significance.[19] To derive the· forms *divine, serene, profane* in isolation, we apply the Diphthongization Rule (21) to the underlying forms that head the derivations of (23), giving the forms of the second line, to which we apply the Vowel Shift Rule, thus giving the forms of the third line:

$$\left(23\right) \quad \begin{array}{lll} \text{divīn} & \text{serēn} & \text{profǣn} \\ \text{divīyn} & \text{serēyn} & \text{profǣyn} & \text{RULE (21)} \\ \text{divǣyn} & \text{serīyn} & \text{profēyn} & \text{RULE (22)} \end{array}$$

The forms of (23) then receive their final phonetic interpretation by the application of other phonetic rules which, except for the change of [ǣy] to [āy], will not be considered here.

Suppose now that we wish to derive *divinity, serenity, profanity*. In this case we have the derivations of (24):

$$\left(24\right) \quad \begin{array}{lll} \text{divīn}+\text{i}+\text{ty} & \text{serēn}+\text{i}+\text{ty} & \text{profǣn}+\text{i}+\text{ty} \\ \text{divin}+\text{i}+\text{ty} & \text{seren}+\text{i}+\text{ty} & \text{profæn}+\text{i}+\text{ty} & \text{RULE (19b)} \end{array}$$

The initial forms are again from the lexicon. The second line derives from the first line by the rule that makes stressed vowels lax when they are followed by a nonfinal unstressed syllable. The full phonetic detail again follows by other rules that do not concern us now.

All of the cases that exemplify the $I \rightarrow i$, $E \rightarrow e$, $A \rightarrow æ$ alternations are handled in the same way.

Let us now turn to the cases that motivated the $i \rightarrow I$, $ė \rightarrow E$, $æ \rightarrow A$ alternations discussed in connection with rules (16)–(17). Consider the forms *vary, manager, algebra*. The vowel in the final syllable of these words in isolation is derived directly from the lexical

---

[19] Notice, incidentally, how well the problem of representing the sound pattern of English is solved in this case by conventional orthography. Corresponding to our device of capitalization of a graphic symbol, conventional orthography places the symbol *e* after the single consonant following this symbol ([e] being the only vowel which does not appear in final position phonetically—see Chapter Three, note 22). In this case, as in many other cases, English orthography turns out to be rather close to an optimal system for spelling English. In other words, it turns out to be rather close to the true phonological representation, given the nonlinguistic constraints that must be met by a spelling system, namely, that it utilize a unidimensional linear representation instead of the linguistically appropriate feature representation and that it limit itself essentially to the letters of the Latin alphabet. (See also note 44, Chapter Two.)

representations in (25) without application of any of the rules we are now considering:[20]

$$\left(25\right) \qquad\qquad \text{vǣri} \quad \text{mænǣger} \quad \text{ælgebræ}$$

To derive the forms *variety, managerial, algebraic*, we proceed as follows:

$$\left(26\right)$$

vǣri+i+ty	mænǣger+i+æl	ælgebræ+ic	
vǣrī+i+ty	mænǣgēr+i+æl	ælgebrǣ+ic	RULE (20)
vǣrīyity	mænǣgēyrīyæl	ælgebrǣyic	RULE (21)
vǣrǣyity	mænǣgīyrīyæl	ælgebrēyic	RULE (22)

By other familiar rules, not here relevant, we derive the full phonetic forms.

To appreciate further the scope and interplay of these rules, consider the class of polysyllabic words ending in *-ate*, with the antepenultimate syllable receiving main stress (see Chapter Three, Section 4). Consider, in particular, the character of this stressed vowel, which appears in the context:

$$\left(27\right) \qquad\qquad \underline{\qquad} C_j^i V C_m^n \bar{æ} t \#$$

Suppose first that $m \geq 1$; i.e., there is at least one consonant before *-ate*. Suppose also that $i = j = 0$; that is, the stressed vowel appears prevocalically. Then rule (20a) will tense this vowel and the Diphthongization and Vowel Shift Rules will apply to it, giving forms such as *violate, annihilate, aerate*.

Suppose now that $j = 1$; that is, at least one consonant appears directly after the stressed vowel. Then rule (19b) will make the stressed vowel lax, and we will have, typically, words such as *elaborate, prevaricate, medicate, mitigate*.

Finally, suppose that $m = n = 0$ and $i = j = 1$; that is, there is a vowel directly before *-ate*, and the stressed vowel appears in the context:

$$\left(28\right) \qquad\qquad \underline{\qquad} C_i^1 V \bar{æ} t \#$$

If, now, the stressed vowel is nonhigh and the following vowel is [i] or [e], the stressed vowel will become tense by rule (20b); hence it will be diphthongized and subject to the Vowel Shift Rule. Thus we have tense vowels in the boldface position in words such as *mediate, radiate, ingratiate* (compare *gratify, gratitude*). If, however, the stressed vowel in the context (28) is high or the vowel following it is not [i] or [e], then rule (20) will not apply, and the stressed vowel will remain lax and hence unaffected by Diphthongization or Vowel Shift. Thus we have *conciliate, officiate, attenuate, insinuate, superannuate*, etc.

These examples illustrate how a variety of forms can be generated by quite simple and general rules. It is particularly important to note that by breaking the alternation rules (13), (16) into several steps and by accepting underlying representations in which invariance is violated (e.g., the second vowel in *divIn, serEn, profAn*), we have been able to avoid the intolerable consequence of stating (14) and (17) as entirely independent and precisely opposed rules. In fact, the Vowel Shift Rule expresses just what is common to these two complex phonological processes, and the rules (19) and (20) express what differentiates them. We

---

[20] Actually, rule (20a) is applied to make the final vowel of *vary* tense, and rule (21) is applied to diphthongize it. As we have noted, these rules are needed quite apart from anything we are discussing here. The reason for nonapplication of the Vowel Shift Rule in this case and others (see (26)) will be given directly.

We disregard here the problem of determining the tenseness of the vowel in the first syllable of *vary–various–variety* (see also (26)).

have thus, in effect, extracted the Vowel Shift Rule as the generalization underlying both (13)-(14) and (16)-(17).

4.2. ALTERNATIONS OF BACK VOWELS

As we shall see in Section 4.3, the effect of the Vowel Shift Rule on back vowels is precisely parallel to its effect on the nonback vowels (cf. (22)):

$$
\left(29\right) \qquad
\begin{array}{ccc}
\bar{u} & \bar{o} & \bar{\mathrm{\sigma}} \\
\downarrow & \downarrow & \downarrow \\
\bar{\mathrm{\sigma}} & \bar{u} & \bar{o}
\end{array}
$$

Hence, from the lexical entries /pōl/, *pool*, and /gɔ̄l/, *goal*, we obtain [pūwl] and [gōwl], respectively, by Diphthongization (21) and Vowel Shift. From the entry /lūd /, *loud*, on the other hand, we obtain [lɔ̄wd] instead of the required [læwd] or [lāwd]. The latter forms will be obtained by special rules adjusting rounding (and, for some dialects, backness and tenseness) of vowels. We postpone discussion of these adjustments until the next section; in the present section our aim is to extend to the back vowels the results of our survey of the effects of tenseness alternations (resulting from rules (19) and (20)).

Among the back vowels we find the following major types of alternations:

$$\left(30\right)$$
    (a) ə–ōw: *Newton–Newtonian, custody–custodian*
    (b) ā–ōw: *verbosity–verbose, conic–cone*
    (c) ʌ–æw: *profundity–profound, abundant–abound*

Types (a) and (b) are both found in the case of forms such as *harmony–harmonious–harmonic*.

In fact, the rules as given above largely accommodate these vowel alternations. Consider the case of the formative *harmon-*. If we enter this in the lexicon in the form /harmən+/ (but see p. 193), we then have the following derivations:

$$\left(31\right)$$

harmən+y	harmən+i+ous	harmən+ic	
hármən+y	harmón+i+ous	harmón+ic	STRESS ASSIGNMENT RULES
	harmɔ́n+i+ous		RULE (20b)
	harmɔ́wn+i+ous		RULE (21)
	harmówn+i+ous		VOWEL SHIFT (29)

The first line represents the lexical forms. The rules of the transformational cycle assign stress in the manner indicated on the second line. Rule (19) applies vacuously. Rule (20b) tenses the boldface vowel of *harmonious*, which occurs before a single consonant followed by [iV]. The Diphthongization and Vowel Shift Rules then convert this tense vowel to its phonetic form [ōw].

The derived form [harmón+ik] deviates from the actually attested pronunciation in the dialect under description. In place of the lax [ə], the dialect has a tense [ā], a fact which we have already provided for with rule (5). We saw in Section 2 that this rule was needed to account for the position of stress and the vowel quality in words such as *recíprocal–reciprócity, frívolous–frivólity, démon–demónic*. We now see that there is independent motivation for this rule, namely, to account for ōw–ā vowel alternations, as in *harmonious–harmonic*, for Vowel Shift (29) turns [ɔ̄] in *harmonious*, which derives from lax /ə/ by (20b), into the required [ō].

Consider now the case of the alternation *verbose–verbosity*, for example. The word *verbose* will have the lexical entry given in the top line of (32) (with an underlying tense vowel to account for the stress on the final syllable in the isolated form), and the derivations will proceed in a straightforward manner, as shown:

$$\left(32\right)$$

verb+ōs	verb+ōs+i+ty	
verb+ő́s	verb+ő́s+i+ty	STRESS ASSIGNMENT RULES
	verb+ő́s+i+ty	RULE (19b)
verb+ő́ws		RULE (21)
verbő́ws		VOWEL SHIFT (29)
	verbásity	RULE (5)

Finally, consider case (30c), which illustrates the alternation [æw]–[ʌ]. Clearly the underlying form of *profound* must contain a tense /ū/ in stressed position, which by Vowel Shift and adjustment rules becomes [æw] or [āw], exactly as in the case of [læwd] from underlying /lūd/. In the word *profundity*, the tense /ū/ is laxed by rule (19b), but instead of the expected [u] we have phonetic [ʌ] in this position. The grammar must therefore contain a rule turning [u] into [ʌ]. We return to this rule on page 203.

Thus, we see that the major class of alternations of back vowels poses no problems and is already accounted for by the rules we have given for nonback vowels. Superficially, the nonback and back vowel alternations seem to differ, because in one case we have ē–æ, while in the other we have ō–ā, instead of what would be the parallel form, ō–ɔ; but this is simply a consequence of the independently motivated rule (5).

4.3. THE VOWEL SHIFT RULE

In (22) and (29) above, we have summarized the effects of what is without doubt the pivotal process of Modern English phonology, the Vowel Shift. We must now give a formal statement of this process.

It will be recalled that Vowel Shift operates after the tense vowels have been diphthongized by rule (21), which supplies the appropriate glides. As a result, it is necessary for the rule to account only for changes in the quality of tense vowels. For convenience of reference, we summarize these changes once again:[21]

$$\left(33\right)$$

ī	ū	ē	ō	ǽ	ɔ̄
↓	↓	↓	↓	↓	↓
ǽ	ɔ̄	ī	ū	ē	ō

The simplest account of these alternations is given by the following two-part rule:[22]

$$\left(34\right)$$

$$
\begin{bmatrix} +\text{tense} \\ V \end{bmatrix} \rightarrow
\begin{cases}
[-\alpha\text{high}] & / \begin{bmatrix} \overline{\alpha\text{high}} \\ -\text{low} \end{bmatrix} \quad (a) \\[2ex]
[-\beta\text{low}] & / \begin{bmatrix} \overline{\beta\text{low}} \\ -\text{high} \end{bmatrix} \quad (b)
\end{cases}
$$

The first part of the rule applies to nonlow vowels only, with the result that originally high

---

[21] As noted above, the reflexes [ǽ] and [ɔ̄] of original [ī] and [ū] are subject to further rules (see (37), (39), and (40) below) which adjust backness and rounding (and possibly tenseness) and result in the required [āy] and [āw] or [æw].

[22] The rule as stated applies to tense vowels only; it will later be extended to certain nontense vowels (see Section 4.3.5).

vowels become nonhigh while originally nonhigh vowels become high. In tabular form the effects of part (a) are represented as follows:

$$\left(35\right)$$

ī	ū	ē	ō	æ	ɔ̄	
↓	↓	↓	↓			(not applicable)
ē	ō	ī	ū	æ	ɔ̄	

An exchange rule also constitutes the second part of the Vowel Shift Rule (34); it affects the nonhigh vowels in the bottom row of (35) and causes them to exchange the values assigned to the feature "low." In (36) we summarize the modifications in the tense vowels that are produced by Diphthongization (21) and Vowel Shift (34) jointly:

$$\left(36\right)$$

ī	ū	ē	ō	æ	ɔ̄	
↓	↓	↓	↓	↓	↓	
īy	ūw	ēy	ōw	æy	ɔ̄w	DIPHTHONGIZATION
↓	↓	↓	↓	↓	↓	
ēy	ōw	īy	ūw	(not applicable)		VOWEL SHIFT (a)
↓	↓			↓	↓	
æy	ɔ̄w	(not applicable)		ēy	ōw	VOWEL SHIFT (b)

4.3.1. REFINEMENTS AND EXTENSIONS OF THE VOWEL SHIFT RULE

In our presentation of the Vowel Shift Rule, we made a number of tacit assumptions which must now be stated explicitly and properly justified. Several of these questions are of rather narrow scope; nevertheless, they must be dealt with. Furthermore, some fairly complex phenomena will fall into place rather naturally as we proceed.

4.3.1.1. ROUNDING AND BACKNESS ADJUSTMENTS. We have observed that low vowels before glides are subject to a great deal of dialectal variation which we will not attempt to deal with in any detail.[23] In the dialect that we are taking as a prototype, *ride* is phonetically [rāyd] and *loud* is phonetically [læwd]. As noted above, the Diphthongization and Vowel Shift Rules give [æy] and [ɔ̄w] as the reflexes of the high vowels [ī] and [ū]. Further rules are then called for to give, finally, [āy] and [æw] for the dialect in question. Thus, in *ride*, the low vowel [æ] resulting from Vowel Shift must subsequently become back, while the resulting low vowel [ɔ̄] of *loud* must go from back to nonback, at the same time also becoming nonround and nontense.

The unrounding of the segment [ɔ̄] resulting from Vowel Shift is quite general and cross-dialectal:[24]

$$\left(37\right) \qquad \begin{bmatrix} +\text{back} \\ +\text{low} \\ V \end{bmatrix} \rightarrow [-\text{round}]$$

[23] For some discussion of the matter, see Kurath and McDavid (1961) and Keyser's review (1963).

[24] It might be proposed that rule (37), because of its generality, be directly incorporated in the Vowel Shift Rule. This could be done easily if we were to restate the rule as follows, using the angle notation of Chapter Three, Section 3:

$$V \rightarrow \left\{ \begin{matrix} \begin{bmatrix} -\alpha\text{high} \\ \langle -\alpha\text{round} \rangle \end{bmatrix} \Big/ \begin{bmatrix} \overline{\alpha\text{high}} \\ -\text{low} \\ \langle +\text{back} \rangle \end{bmatrix} \\ \\ [-\beta\text{low}] \Big/ \begin{bmatrix} \overline{\beta\text{low}} \\ -\text{high} \end{bmatrix} \end{matrix} \right\} \Big/ \begin{bmatrix} \overline{} \\ +\text{tense} \end{bmatrix}$$

The first part of this rule now states not only that a nonlow tense vowel changes the value of the feature

The second modification undergone by low vowels, as mentioned above, is that those which at this stage of the derivation are nonback appear as back in the output, whereas those that are back at this point in the derivation end up as nonback; that is:

$$\left(38\right) \qquad [\bar{æ}y] \rightarrow [\bar{ɔ}y]^{25} \qquad [\bar{æ}y] \rightarrow [\bar{a}y] \qquad [\bar{a}w] \rightarrow [æw]$$

In discussing these facts in Section 3, we treated them as an instance of backness dissimilation contingent upon the backness of the glide. For reasons that will become clear later (see rule (88) on page 215 and the discussion there), it is more appropriate to treat this phenomenon as a shift in backness independent of the backness of the glide. We therefore replace rule (12) with (39):

$$\left(39\right) \qquad \begin{bmatrix} +\text{low} \\ \alpha\text{back} \\ V \end{bmatrix} \rightarrow [-\alpha\text{back}] \Big/ \underline{\quad} \begin{bmatrix} -\text{voc} \\ -\text{cons} \end{bmatrix}$$

For dialects which have phonetic [āw] in *loud, cow*, etc., instead of [æw], we can simplify rule (39) by dropping the specification [αback] on the left-hand side of the arrow and replacing the [−αback] on the right-hand side of the arrow with [+back]. For dialects such as we are discussing, which have phonetic [æw] in such words, α is free in (39), and we must add a rule converting [æw] to [ǽw]. This process is actually somewhat more general. Thus in many dialects we also find laxing of [āy] to [ăy] (and, in some, raising of [ăy] to [ʌy]) before nonvoiced segments (e.g., [răyt] or [rʌyt] vs. [rāyd], [lăyf] or [lʌyf] vs. [lāyv]). These two cases of laxing can be accounted for by the supplementary rule (40) (where G stands for a glide):

$$\left(40\right) \qquad \begin{bmatrix} +\text{low} \\ V \end{bmatrix} \rightarrow [-\text{tense}] \Big/ \underline{\quad} G \Big/ \left\{\begin{matrix} \underline{\quad}[-\text{voice}] & \text{(a)} \\ \begin{bmatrix} \underline{\quad} \\ -\text{round} \end{bmatrix} & \text{(b)} \end{matrix}\right\}$$

The central core of rules consists of rules (19) and (20), which determine tenseness, the Diphthongization Rule (21), and the Vowel Shift Rule (34) adjusted by rule (37). The Vowel Shift Rule and rule (37) are quite general; the supplementary rules (39) and (40) are subject to much dialectal variation. It is only the "true diphthongs" (that is, the low vowels followed by glides) that are subject to these adjustments.

Notice that underlying /ū/ becomes phonetic [æw] in the dialect we have discussed. Thus every feature of underlying /ū/, aside from [+vocalic] and [−consonantal], is modified by the phonological rules. This is an example of maximal violation of invariance, as noted above on page 168.

In Chapter Three (p. 152) we discussed another example of backness adjustment that converts [ā] to [æ], namely, in the boldface position of words such as *Alabama, koala*. This should presumably fall together with the process described by rules (39), (40b).

"high," but also that if the vowel in question is back, it becomes nonround if it was high (and remains round if it was nonhigh). Thus, underlying /ō/ will remain round, but underlying /ū/ will be unrounded as well as lowered.

Although this formulation has some plausibility, we prefer, rather, to separate the unrounding as a distinct process. The reason is that in many cases unrounding takes place quite apart from Vowel Shift, and we will see below that rule (37) generalizes considerably in ways which are incompatible with this formulation.

[25] The diphthong [ɔ̄y], which is the result of the diphthongization of an underlying tense vowel [ǣ], is discussed in detail in Section 4.3.3.

4.3.1.2. ROUNDING AND STRESS. As formulated above, the Vowel Shift Rule (34) applies to all tense vowels, but there are certain restrictions that must be imposed.

First, the Vowel Shift Rule must not apply to [ā] in *father*, *Chicago*, etc., for this vowel is not converted into the corresponding nonlow vowel. The rule must therefore be restricted to the nonback vowels [ī], [ē], [ǣ] and the back vowels [ū], [ō], [ɔ̄], that is, to the nonback vowels that are, furthermore, nonround, and to the back vowels that are round ([ā] being back and nonround); i.e., the Vowel Shift Rule must be restricted so as to apply only to vowels in the context (41):

$$
\left(41\right) \qquad\qquad \begin{bmatrix} \overline{\gamma\text{back}} \\ \gamma\text{round} \end{bmatrix}
$$

A second adjustment necessary in the Vowel Shift Rule is motivated by examples such as *various*, *variety*, which we considered above. In both of these forms, we have occurrences of the tense vowel [ī] at the stage of derivation at which the Vowel Shift Rule applies. That is, we have at this stage the forms of (42) for *various*, *variety*, respectively:

$$
\left(42\right) \qquad\qquad
$$

        (a) [vǣrī+əs]
        (b) [vǣrí+i+tī]

Of the three occurrences of [ī] in these forms, only the one which is stressed undergoes Vowel Shift. In general, we must limit the Vowel Shift Rule to tense segments which have the feature [+stress]. Tense vowels with the feature [−stress] will be reduced to [ə], except when they are prevocalic or final (see rule (20)); and in these positions they must be excluded from the application of the Vowel Shift Rule.

Summarizing these adjustments, we can now give the Vowel Shift Rule in the nearly final form (43):

$$
\left(43\right) \qquad \begin{bmatrix} \gamma\text{back} \\ \gamma\text{round} \end{bmatrix} \rightarrow \left\{ \begin{matrix} [-\alpha\text{high}] & / & \begin{bmatrix} \overline{\alpha\text{high}} \\ -\text{low} \end{bmatrix} \\ [-\beta\text{low}] & / & \begin{bmatrix} \overline{\beta\text{low}} \\ -\text{high} \end{bmatrix} \end{matrix} \right\} \Big/ \begin{bmatrix} \overline{+\text{tense}} \\ +\text{stress} \end{bmatrix}
$$

Notice that even weak-stressed tense vowels will undergo Vowel Shift since they are in the category [+stress]. For example, tense vowels in the context $\#C_0 \text{------} C_0 \overset{1}{V}$ receive secondary (ultimately, tertiary) stress by the Auxiliary Reduction Rule discussed in Chapter Three, Section 14, and formulated finally as (120d) of that chapter. The Auxiliary Reduction Rules precede the Vowel Shift Rule. Therefore, we have Vowel Shift in the first syllable of words such as *Crimea*, *Siam*, *reality*, *gradation*. Examples such as *Siam*, *reality*, incidentally, indicate that the Auxiliary Reduction Rule assigning secondary stress must apply after the Tensing Rule (20), as noted on page 124 of Chapter Three.

4.3.2. FINAL WEAK-STRESSED [o]

The fact that the Vowel Shift Rule applies only to those tense vowels that are stressed enables us to give a very simple account of a well-known and otherwise quite mystifying phenomenon of English phonetics, namely, that there is, in many dialects, a contrast between final zero-stressed phonetic [ōw], as in *mótto*, and final tertiary-stressed phonetic [ōw], as in *vétò*. A consequence of the stress difference in these dialects is a contrast between the aspirated [t] of *veto* and the alveolar flap [D] of *motto*—thus we have the phonetic contrast [vi̯yt^{h}ō̯w] vs. [mā̯Dōw]. Given the general predictability of stress, it would be very curious if a tertiary–zero stress contrast were phonologically distinct in this one position. Consequently, it seems likely that the phonetic contrast in stress can be attributed to some phonological distinction of vowel quality. The question arises, then, as to whether there is some vowel V* that does not appear phonetically in final position and that is similar in feature composition to [ō] so that a simple rule will convert it to [ō] when stressed. If such a vowel is found, we can provide the grammar with the following rules:

$$\left(44\right)\quad \begin{array}{ll} \text{(a)} & \text{V*} \rightarrow \text{[3 stress]} \; / \; ——\# \\ \text{(b)} & \text{V*} \rightarrow \grave{\text{o}} \end{array}$$

Then *veto* can be given the underlying representation /vētV*/, and *motto* the representation /moto/. Rules (44), together with the rule (20a) tensing final vowels, the Diphthongization Rule (21), and a rule that turns /t/ into the flap [D] intervocalically before unstressed vowels will give the correct contrasting phonetic forms.

Rules (44), however, are quite ad hoc and hardly preferable to a recognition of tertiary stress as phonologically distinctive in this position, strange as this conclusion would be. One is naturally led, therefore, to try to select V* in such a way that rules (44) are independently motivated. Suppose, in fact, that we were to take V* as phonological /ə/, so that *veto* is represented /vētə/. Then the final vowel of *veto* receives tertiary stress by rule (44a), is tensed by rule (20a), diphthongized by rule (21), and raised to [ȯw] by the Vowel Shift Rule. Vowel Shift, as we observed, applies to vowels only if they have the feature [+stress]; thus, it will apply to the final vowel of *veto* but not to that of *motto*, given the above analysis. Hence rule (44b) is superfluous and can be dropped from the grammar, leaving only the following rule:

$$\left(45\right)\quad\quad\quad \text{ɔ} \; \rightarrow \; \text{[3 stress]} \; / \; ——\#$$

This improves matters. However, we may still ask whether there is any independent justification for (45). In fact, there is. Notice, first of all, that final phonetic [ɔ] does not appear, for it would be reduced to [ə] by the Vowel Reduction Rule, which applies to lax low vowels. If [ɔ] were treated like [æ] by the Tensing Rule (20a), we would expect to find back alternations analogous to *algebra–algebraic*; that is, we would expect to find pairs of the form [...Cə]–[...Cōwik]. There are no such pairs (although we do have *hero–heroic, echo–echoic*, etc., with final [ō]). To explain this gap, we would need some rule that excludes final [ɔ] from the domain of the Vowel Reduction Rule. But (45) does precisely this, and thus has some independent motivation. Hence there is a quite simple and independently justified explanation for the [ȯw#]–[ōw#] contrast.

Notice that rule (45) must precede the Tensing Rule (20a), so that the final vowel will be tensed.

4.3.3. THE DIPHTHONG [ōy]

English has three "true" diphthongs phonetically, namely, [āy] (*ride*), [æw] (*loud*), and [ōy] (*coin*) (with their variants and several dialectal forms). Of these, we have so far accounted only for the first two. We now turn our attention to the phonological representation of phonetic [ōy].

Notice first that we have no vowel-glide sequences in the lexicon so far since [æw] and [āy] derive from /ū/ and /ī/, respectively. Hence the lexical redundancy rules will be much simplified if we can represent [ōy], too, as a monophthong V* on the lexical level. The optimal solution would be to take V* as some vowel which fills a gap in the phonological system and which is converted to phonetic [ōy] by independently motivated rules. In fact, this optimal solution can be attained in this case.

To see this, observe that we do have the Diphthongization Rule (21) which inserts a glide after a tense vowel. To account for the glide of [ōy], we must, therefore, take V* to be some tense vowel to which the *y*-glide can be attached by rule (21). Since a *y*-glide is inserted by this rule only after a nonback vowel, we must take V* to be nonback, which means it cannot be [ə]. The vowel of phonetic [ōy] is low and round; therefore, if we are to avoid adding new rules to the grammar, we must take the underlying vowel V* to be low and round as well. We are thus led to the conclusion that V* should be the tense, nonback, low, round vowel, that is, [ǣ]. In further support of this conclusion is the observation that [ǣ] in fact constitutes an otherwise unexplained gap in the phonological pattern, since the other three tense low vowels (namely, [ǣ], [ā], [ō]) do appear in lexical matrices.

Suppose, then, that we take the form /kǣn/ as the underlying lexical entry for *coin*, thus filling this gap in the phonological pattern. By the Diphthongization Rule (21), /kǣn/ → [kǣyn]. The Vowel Shift Rule, amended above as (43), applies only to vowels which are the same in backness and rounding. Consequently, it does not apply to [ǣ], which is round but nonback, just as it does not apply to [ā], which is back but nonround. We now require a rule which will convert [ǣ] to [ō], that is, a rule which makes this vowel back. But we already have such a rule in the grammar, namely, rule (39), which, in effect, makes a tense low vowel back before a nonback glide; hence it converts [ǣ] to [ō], just as it converts [ǣ] to [ā], before [y]. Thus it turns out that the grammar already contains rules that account for [ōy] from an underlying monophthongal segment [ǣ], which, furthermore, fills a gap in the phonological pattern.[26]

As we have noted several times, the segment [ǣ] which underlies [ōy] is not subject to laxing (e.g., in *exploitative*). Thus we must either restrict the Laxing Rule, like the Vowel Shift Rule, to segments which are the same in rounding and backness, or add a special adjustment to the Tensing Rule so that it always tenses [æ].

4.3.4. PREVOCALIC *y*-GLIDES

We have not yet accounted for the "vocalic nucleus" [yūw] that appears phonetically in words such as *pure*, *cutaneous*, *accuse* in the boldface position. As in the case of phonetic [ōy], which we discussed above, there is strong motivation for regarding this as phonologically unitary. We need not concern ourselves about the final [w] of [yūw]; this will be introduced by the Diphthongization Rule. The problem, rather, concerns the [y] preceding the vowel. If this is not introduced by some phonological rule, then the underlying representations of words such as *pure*, *cube* must be of the form CGVC. This conclusion would force us to give up several otherwise valid generalizations concerning consonant-glide-vowel sequences in underlying representations; for example, the following:

$$\begin{pmatrix} 46 \end{pmatrix}$$
　　　　　　(a) G → w / C——V
　　　　　　(b) C → [−nasal] / ——G
　　　　　　(c) [+ant] → [+cor] / ——G
　　　　　　(d) C → [−ant] / s——G

---

[26] Since contemporary English differs from its sixteenth or seventeenth century ancestor in the fact that it no longer admits phonological diphthongs—i.e., sequences of tense low vowels followed by lax high vowels—in its lexical formatives, [ǣ] is the proper representation for what historically was the diphthongal sequence [ōy]. For further discussion of this point, see Section 5 of Chapter Six.

$$(e) \quad \begin{bmatrix} +\text{voc} \\ -\text{cons} \\ -\text{low} \end{bmatrix} \rightarrow [-\text{back}] \ / \ [-\text{cont}] \, G \text{---}$$

Case (a) permits *twist, dwell, twang, quote, quarry,* etc., but excludes [y] in the position of the [w] of these words. However, we have [y] in phonetic [Cyūw]. Case (b) excludes forms such as **nwist, *nwell* (alongside of *twist, dwell*); but we have *new* ([nyūw])[27] and so on regularly with [+nasal] [y]. Case (c) explains the inadmissibility of **pwin, *bwell, *mwist* (compare also case (b)), and so on, but would be falsified by *pure, muse, abuse*. (We shall see that case (c) need not be restricted to anterior consonants when we turn to a more careful study of glides.) Case (d) permits forms such as *square, squint, squall,* but not **stware, *stwint*. On the other hand, we have *stew, fistula,* and so on. Case (e) excludes phonological forms such as /kwōt/, /kwūt/, which would eventuate as phonetic **[kwūwt], *[kwæwt]* (or **[kwāwt]*), respectively, by the Diphthongization and Vowel Shift Rules, while permitting phonological /kwēr/, /kwīt/, which become [kwīyr] (*queer*), [kwāyt] (*quite*), respectively. But it would be contradicted by *cube, accuse,* and numerous other such forms.

In short, consideration of lexical redundancy rules provides strong motivation for regarding phonetic [yūw] as a reflex of some unitary phonological segment, and we shall see directly that there are other, independent sources for this conclusion.

Let us consider, then, the question of whether there is some reason, apart from lexical redundancy rules, for adding to the grammar at some point the rule:

$$(47) \qquad \varphi \rightarrow y \ / \ \text{---} \begin{bmatrix} \alpha \psi \\ +\text{high} \\ +\text{back} \\ V \end{bmatrix}$$

where ψ is some feature that differentiates the cases of high back vowels before which [y] will be inserted from those before which it will not be inserted. Notice that whether (47) precedes or follows the Vowel Shift, some such discrimination must be made.

There are certain lexical items that have high vowels, either back or nonback, as "stem-forming augments" (see Chapter Three, pp. 129–30). Such items might be introduced into the lexicon as in (48):[28]

$$(48) \qquad \begin{array}{l} /\text{hæbit}+\text{u}/ \\ /\text{perpet}+\text{u}/ \\ /\text{prə}+\text{verb}+\text{i}/ \\ /\text{pre}=\text{sīd}+\text{ent}+\text{i}/ \end{array}$$

The stem-forming augment drops except before certain affixes (*-al, -ous, -ate, -ity*) by an early rule (possibly a lexical rule). Thus we have *president–presidential* (with [ti+V] going

---

[27] In some dialects, the effect of this and several other rules that we will mention is masked in certain forms by the fact that a later rule deletes [y] in certain positions after dentals and palatals, so that *new* would be [nūw]. Such dialects may also contain pairs such as *constitutive* ([kənstíčətiv], with [č] from [ty]) vs. *constitute* ([kǎnstətūt]), *residual* ([rəzíjūwəl], with [j] from [dy]) vs. *residue* ([rézədūw]), and so on. For simplicity of exposition, we dismiss this possibility from consideration here, returning to a discussion of it in Section 6.

Observe that the different cases of (46), as usual, have marginal exceptions, e.g., *ennui* (case (b)), *pueblo* (case (c)). Our formulation of redundancy rules will not include the rules of (46) as given, but these do remain as valid generalizations about formatives, and this is all that is necessary for the present argument.

[28] Notice that there are many obvious generalizations—e.g., the suffixes *-ent, -or,* and others are automatically followed by the augment [+i].

to [š+V] by rules that we describe in Section 6), *proverb–proverbial, habit–habitual– habituate, perpetual–perpetuity–perpetuate*, etc.

Our concern here is with the stem-forming augment [+u]. But consider first its nonback analog [+i]. When unstressed, this vowel is tensed by rule (20) and appears as phonetic [īy], as in *proverbial*. When stressed, it undergoes Vowel Shift after being tensed by rule (20) and appears as phonetic [āy], as in *sobriety, propriety*. This is straightforward in terms of the processes that we have already discussed.

Consider now the stem-forming augment [+u]. We would expect it to behave exactly as its counterpart does, that is, to become phonetic [ū] when unstressed and phonetic [æw] when stressed. But this is not what we find; rather, in both stressed and unstressed positions we have [yūw] (*ambiguous, ambiguity*). Thus stem-forming [+u] is peculiar in two respects: it has a *y*-glide inserted before it, and it does not undergo Vowel Shift where it would be expected to do so.

How are these two facts related? If they are to be related, there must be some segmental feature that is automatically assigned to stem-forming [+u] (but not to certain other occurrences of [u] or [ū]) that exempts it from the Vowel Shift while at the same time requiring rule (47) to apply to it, prefixing to it a *y*-glide. Notice that the augment [+u] is always prevocalic and therefore tensed by rule (20). Rule (47) thus inserts a [y] before some tense vowel that differs from [ū] in the feature ψ. Apparently, then, the stem-forming augment [+u] must be specified as [αψ], whereas [ū] is [−αψ]. We are then faced with the problem of determining ψ in such a way that when a high back vowel is [αψ], it is exempt from the Vowel Shift Rule. If this is possible, then stem-forming [+u] will not only be supplied with a preceding *y*-glide by rule (47), but will also be excluded from the Vowel Shift, as required.

We have already observed that for a tense stressed vowel to be exempt from Vowel Shift, it must not be the same in rounding and backness. Since stem-forming [+u] is tense and stressed in forms such as *ambiguity* (which are the crucial ones in this connection), we see that to be exempt from Vowel Shift it must be not [ū] phonologically but rather the corresponding unrounded vowel [ï] or the corresponding nonback vowel [ü]. But we know that the vowel in question receives a postvocalic *w*-glide, which is inserted by the Diphthongization Rule (21) only after back vowels. Therefore the vowel must be back, namely, [ï]. We see, then, that the feature ψ must be "round," and that the augment [+u] must receive the feature [−round] which differentiates it from ordinary [ū] and prevents it from undergoing Vowel Shift when stressed and tensed. Thus αψ in (47) must be [−round].

Summarizing, then, we have the following rules:

$$\left(49\right) \qquad\qquad u \;\rightarrow\; [-\text{round}] \quad \text{in some context}$$

$$\left(50\right) \qquad\qquad \phi \;\rightarrow\; y \;\Big/\; \underline{\qquad} \begin{bmatrix} +\text{tense} \\ -\text{round} \\ +\text{high} \\ +\text{back} \\ V \end{bmatrix}$$

$$\left(51\right) \qquad\qquad \ddot{\imath} \;\rightarrow\; [+\text{round}]$$

Rule (49) must precede the Vowel Shift Rule; rule (51) must follow the Vowel Shift Rule. We will determine the position of rule (50) directly.

It remains to establish the context for rule (49). Recall that we have already discussed a rule that converts /u/ to [yūw] in words such as *Neptune* (see Chapter Three, Section 16). This rule tenses /u/, inserts a *y*-glide in front of it and a *w*-glide after it, and prevents it from undergoing Vowel Shift (as in *neptunian*, for example, which does not become *[neptǽwnEən]). As we have already noted, this process applies in the context —— CV. If we now generalize it to the context —— C_0^1V, it will apply to the stem-forming augment [+u], which is always prevocalic. We therefore restate rule (49) as (52):

$$\left(52\right) \qquad\qquad u \;\rightarrow\; \begin{bmatrix} +\text{tense} \\ -\text{round} \end{bmatrix} \;/\; \underline{\qquad} C_0^1V$$

Rules (52), (50), Diphthongization, and (51) now convert underlying /u/ to phonetic [yūw] in the boldface position of words such as *cube, annual, Neptune, ambiguity*. Rule (52) belongs together with the Tensing Rules (20). Words such as *menu, value, cue, fuel* will be represented lexically as /menue/, /vælue/, /kue/, /fuel/. We thus, incidentally, account for the fact that the first syllable in words such as *menu, value, tissue, issue, nephew, sinew* has a lax vowel. Laxing here results from the application of rule (19b), the trisyllabic laxing rule (the only exception being *Hebrew*). Phonetic contrasts such as *cow–cue*, or *foul–fuel–mule* ([fæwl] – [fyūwəl], [myūwl]) do not require new phonological segments; rather, they result from the lexical contrasts /ku/ – /kue/, /fūl/ – /fuel/ – /mule/. Words such as *immune, commute, inure, cutaneous* will be derived from the underlying forms /imune/, /kəN=mute/, /inure/, /kutæni+əs/, respectively.

The stem-forming augments [+i] and [+u] may be represented phonologically simply as [−back] and [+back], respectively. Augments are redundantly vocalic, high, and lax. Rounding redundantly corresponds to backness for lax vowels. The augments are tensed by rule (52) or (20a) and achieve their final phonetic forms (as [īy] or [āy], or [yūw]) by other rules that we have already discussed. Thus for a word such as *ambiguity* we will have the following derivation:

$$\left(53\right)$$

æmbig+[+back]+ity	
æmbig+u+ity	READJUSTMENT RULES
æmbig+ɨ+ity	RULE (52)
æmbig+ɨw+ity	DIPHTHONGIZATION (21)
æmbig+yɨw+ity	RULE (50)
æmbig+yūw+ity	RULE (51)

Rule (52) is restricted to lax [u]. This is, in fact, a necessary restriction. It prevents *espousal* /espūs+æl/, *avowal* /ævū+æl/ from becoming *[espyūwzəl], *[əvyūwəl], for example.

Notice that phonetic [yūw] cannot occur before a double consonant, since it can arise only by rule (52) (but see Chapter Five, note 3). This excludes forms such as *[myūwnt] or *[pyūwnd]; rather, the reflex of underlying /ū/ in this position will always be [æw] (or [āw]), as in *mount, pound*.

There are certain redundancies involving phonological /u/ that deserve mention. As is well known, labials do not occur after phonetic [æw]; that is, we have *cube, dupe, fume*, but no such words as *[kæwb], *[dæwp], *[fæwm].[29] Actually, the restriction is more general: velars do not occur in this position either. That is, we do not have such forms as

---

[29] This rule has long been familiar to students of the historical phonology of English; see, e.g., Jespersen (1909, Section 8.23): "Before lip consonants we do not get the [[au]—NC/MH] diphthong."

*[dæwk] or *[hæwg] alongside of *duke* or *huge* (from underlying /huge/). We might account for these observations with a redundancy rule to the effect that:

$$\left(54\right) \qquad \text{C} \;\rightarrow\; [+\text{cor}] \;/\; \bar{\text{u}} \text{——} [-\text{seg}]$$

Thus noncoronal consonants will occur after /ū/ only before vowels (in which case $u \rightarrow U$); they cannot occur before consonants because of the restriction on tense vowels before clusters (see rule (8) and the related discussion on page 172).

Another phenomenon relevant at this point is illustrated by a comparison of forms such as *table–tabular–tabulate, constable–constabulary, angle–angular–triangulate, fable–fabulous, title–titular, miracle–miraculous, circle–circulate.* Evidently, in nouns and stems that are subject to derivational processes (see pp. 173–74), phonetic [yūw] appears in a final stop-[l] cluster when certain affixes follow. Thus we must have rules with the effect of (55):

$$\left(55\right) \qquad \phi \;\rightarrow\; \text{yūw} \;/\; \begin{bmatrix} -\text{cont} \\ -\text{voc} \\ +\text{cons} \end{bmatrix} \text{——} l + VC\,[-\text{seg}]$$

For the moment, let us simply take (55) as the required rule. We see, then, that it will convert [tæbl+ær] to [tæbyūwl+ær]. The segment [æ] of the latter form will be made lax by rule (19b) (which, as a result of the required ordering of the rules—see (57) below—will apply when the representation is [tæbul+ær]). We will have, then, [tæbyūwlər] (*tabular*), contrasting with [tēybl̩] (*table*), in which the segment [æ] has become [ēy] by Diphthongization and Vowel Shift, and the liquid has become syllabic by processes described in Chapter Three, pages 85–86. The other examples of this sort cited above can be taken care of in the same way.

We already have a rule that inserts [y] before [i] (originally [u]), namely, (50). Therefore we may simplify (55) to (56):[30]

$$\left(56\right) \qquad \phi \;\rightarrow\; \text{u} \;/\; \begin{bmatrix} -\text{cont} \\ -\text{voc} \\ +\text{cons} \end{bmatrix} \text{——} l + VC\,[-\text{seg}]$$

We assume the following ordering:

$$\left(57\right) \qquad \begin{array}{ll} \text{(a)} & \text{Rule (56)} \\ \text{(b)} & \text{Laxing Rule (19)} \\ \text{(c)} & \text{Tensing Rule (52)} \;(u \rightarrow i) \end{array}$$

---

[30] Note that (56) does not insert a vowel before the [l] in words such as *legislate* because a continuant rather than a stop precedes the [l]. It also will not apply when [l] precedes suffixes such as: *-age* (as in *assemblage*), which is phonologically [æge]; *-ify* (as in *amplify*), which is phonologically [i+fîk] (see Section 4.3.5, p. 201); the comparative and superlative (*nobler, noblest*) if we regard these as having the characteristic ≠ boundary of elements adjoined by transformation at the stage when (56) applies; *-ance, -ly*, etc. (*resemblance, capably*) because of their phonological shape. It does apply before the major affixes *-ate, -al, -ous*, etc. (Note that *-ar* is, with rare exceptions, simply the variant of *-al* after [l].)

As noted above, however, it is only the nouns and stems subject to derivational processes to which this rule applies. Thus it does not apply to agentive *-er* (*gambler, peddler, angler*, contrasting with *angular*).

Notice that rule (56) might also be used to account for the occurrence of [yə] in nouns ending in [l] followed by *-a, -us, -um* (e.g., *formula, modulus, curriculum*) as an alternative to considering this to be an inherent vowel. This is plausible since it would account for the overwhelming predominance of [U] over other vocalic nuclei in this position.

Another possibility, for all such cases, is to regard the [u] as an inherent vowel in the lexical entry, dropping rule (56). We see little to choose between these alternatives, and will simply continue, arbitrarily, with the assumption in the text.

(d) *y*-Glide Insertion (50)
(e) Diphthongization (21)
(f) Vowel Shift (43)
(g) Rounding Rule (51)

This will give the following derivation for *tabular*, for example:

$$\left(58\right)$$

tǽbl+ær	FIRST CYCLE
tǽbul+ær	RULE (57a)
tǽbul+ær	RULE (57b)
tǽbɨl+ær	RULE (57c)
tǽbyɨl+ær	RULE (57d)
tǽbyɨwl+ær	RULE (57e)
tǽbyūwl+ær	RULE (57g)
tǽbyūwlər	VOWEL REDUCTION

This derivation seems accurate for fairly careful speech, in which the medial vowel is rounded. Suppose, however, that we wish to account for the variant [tæbyələr]. We might add a special ad hoc laxing rule such as (59), which would apply only to this vocalic nucleus and would follow (57d) and precede (57e):

$$\left(59\right) \qquad \text{ɨ} \;\rightarrow\; [-\text{tense}] \;/\; \left[\begin{array}{c} \underline{\hspace{2cm}} \\ -\text{stress} \end{array}\right]$$

This rule would subject the medial vowel of *tabular* to the Vowel Reduction Rule, which applies to minus-stressed lax vowels (see Chapter Three, rule (121), p. 126), so that the derivation (58) would terminate with [tæbyələr]. The same rule would apply in forms such as *commutation, accusation*, where [U] derives from an original /u/, giving [kāmyətAšən], [ækyəzAšən] as possible variants. Recall that in these words we have *commute, accuse* at the termination of the first cycle, but in the second, word-level cycle the vowel in the second syllable becomes [−stress] by the Auxiliary Reduction Rule (118) of Chapter Three (which falls together with (57b) above) after the various stress placement rules have applied. Rule (57c) makes this vowel [+tense], permitting *y*-glide insertion by (57d). The application or nonapplication of (59) will therefore determine whether the phonetic form is [kāmyətAšən] or [kāmyūwtAšən], and so on.

There is more to the matter of reduction of [U] than these remarks indicate. Thus we have reduction in the boldface position of *nature, fortune, cómmunal*, as well as (optionally) in the examples given above, but not in *Neptune, commune*, for example. However, we have not been able to determine precisely what the correct form of (59) should be.

Of the rules listed in (57), all are rules of word-level phonology. In view of the uncertain status of VC*l* as a strong cluster (see Chapter Three, pp. 83, 140, and note 82), we have placed (57a) (= (56)) before the stress rules. We know that the underlying form of *miraculous*, for example, must be /mirækl+əs/. The position of main stress in the noun *míracle* indicates that the second vowel is phonologically lax. Thus, if /Vkl/ is a weak cluster, the vowel [u] must be inserted in the second cycle prior to the application of the stress rules, or we would derive **miráculous*. If /Vkl/ is a strong cluster, there is no such compelling need to impose this ordering, but it does not result in any incorrect forms. Since the Laxing Rule (57b) (= (19)) depends on the position of stress, it must follow the stress assignment rules. Rule (57c), which tenses the inserted segment [u], must also follow the stress assignment rules or we will derive *miracúlous*. Therefore the ordering of the rules is determined by several considerations to be as in (57), with the rules of stress assignment following (57a) and preceding the other rules of (57).

Summarizing, we see that there is good evidence to support the conclusion that all of the English vocalic nuclei that we have so far considered are phonologically monophthongal. Phonetic [īy], [ēy], [āy], [ūw], [ōw], [æw] (with their various dialectal and stylistic variants) derive from underlying /ē/, /æ/, /ī/, /ō/, /ɔ/, /ū/, respectively, by Diphthongization, Vowel Shift, Rounding Adjustment, and Backness Adjustment. Phonetic [ā] (which may have an off-glide which we discuss in Section 4.3.6) derives from underlying /ā/, which does not undergo Vowel Shift. Phonetic [ɔy] derives from underlying /æ/, the fourth possible low vowel, by Diphthongization and Backness Adjustment (Vowel Shift being inapplicable). Phonetic [yūw] (or [yə]) derives from underlying /u/ in the context ——C₀¹V. We can then preserve the generalizations regarding consonant-glide strings illustrated in (46). The rules of this section account for alternations such as *table–tabular*; the occurrences of phonetic [yūw] in forms such as *ambiguous, ambiguity*, instead of phonetic [ūw] (paralleling the [īy] of *proverbial*) or phonetic [æw] or [āw] (paralleling the [āy] of *sobriety*); the occurrence of phonetic [yūw] as a reflex of phonological /u/ in *fume, cutaneous*, and so on; the occurrence of phonetic [æw] or [āw] as a reflex of underlying /ū/ in *profound, mountain, pound*, and the impossibility of phonetic [yūw] in these positions; the impossibility of phonetic [æw] or [āw] before noncoronal consonants.

The rules summarized in (57) account for a few other apparently exceptional phenomena. For example, Jespersen remarks (1909, Section 4.73): "the three syllable rule [our rule (19b)—NC/MH] does not apply to [iu] = F *u* (or Latin *u*)"; and cites, among other examples: *credulity, community, obscurity, lunacy, scrutiny*. These examples now fall together with such apparent counterexamples to trisyllabic laxing as *mediate, radiate, ingratiate* (see p. 185). In all cases we have laxing by rule (19b) and subsequent tensing (by (52) in the case of [u]; by (20b) in the other cases). In the same way we account for the tenseness of the first vowel in words such as *mutual, usual, uvula*. Similarly, the fact that [U] does not reduce to [ə] in *commutation, communism*, etc., as noted in Section 14 of Chapter Three (see p. 122), is a consequence of the Tensing Rule that applies after the Auxiliary Reduction Rule which falls together with the Laxing Rule.

Consider, next, pairs such as *sulfur–sulfuric, talmud–talmudic, cherub–cherubic*. The vowel of the second syllable must be lax in the phonological representation, as we can see from the position of main stress in the simple form. The fact that we have a tense vowel in this position in the derived forms is explained by rule (52).

There is one problem in this analysis of [yūw] that must still be dealt with, however. Consider words such as *avenue, revenue, residue, continue*, which terminate with [yūw] (or, in the case of *residue*, with [dūw], in some dialects, for reasons that we will discuss in Section 6). As matters now stand, the underlying lexical representation must be /ævVnue/, /revVnue/, /re=sidue/, /kəN=tinue/. (In the case of *residue*, the medial vowel might be tense; the = boundary is required to account for the voicing of [s], as we shall see in Section 5.) But the stress placement rules, as given in the last chapter, will assign to these words the stress contours *avénue, *revénue, *resídue, *continúe. That is, in the case of the three nouns, the Main Stress Rule (Chapter Three, rule (102), p. 110) will exclude from consideration the final lax vowel /e/ and assign primary stress under case (i) to the syllable before the weak cluster /u/; and in the verb *continue*, the primary stress will be placed by case (i) of the Main Stress Rule on the vowel immediately preceding the weak cluster /e/.

Within the framework so far developed, we can account for this arrangement of facts only by treating the source of final [yūw] in these words as a weak cluster, that is, as a string of the form VC$_0^1$; if the words *avenue, revenue, residue, continue* are represented as /ævenφ/, /revenφ/, /re=sidφ/, /kəN=tinφ/, where φ is a weak cluster, then the stress contours will be assigned in the correct way. In the case of *avenue, revenue*, the final weak cluster φ will then be omitted from consideration under condition (b) of the Main Stress Rule, and primary stress will be placed on the first syllable of the residual string, its second syllable being weak. In the case of *residue*, the final cluster φ will be omitted from consideration in the same way, and primary stress will be placed on /sid/, the = boundary preventing stress assignment to /re/ under case (i). Under condition (c), the Stressed Syllable Rule, primary stress is shifted to the left, giving [re$\overset{1}{=}$sid$\overset{2}{φ}$], the string [$\overset{1}{=}$sidφ] being omitted from consideration, as is permitted by this rule. The other rules then give the form [rez$\overset{1}{ə}$d(y)ūw], as required. The verb *continue* will receive primary stress on the second syllable in the usual way, under condition (e) of the Main Stress Rule, by case (i), which places stress before the weak cluster φ.

The analysis presented earlier failed because φ was not a weak cluster, but was rather the phonologically bisyllabic element /ue/. We must therefore revise this analysis in such a way as to assign the words in question a weak cluster in the position of φ. There are two ways to achieve this result. The first would be to take φ to be not /ue/, as before, but rather /uε/, where [ε] is the glide corresponding to [e], that is, the segment with the features [−vocalic], [−consonantal], [−back], [−high], [−low]. This decision requires only one change in the rules given earlier: we must rephrase rule (52) so that [u] becomes [ɨ] in the context ——C$_0^1$[−consonantal], that is, before a vowel or a glide. Since this is a simplification of the rule, we would make the modification in any event. Furthermore, we have already had occasion to make use of /ε/ in the lexicon (see Chapter Three, Section 16, p. 161).

The second alternative is to take φ to be /u/, and to modify rule (52) so that it converts [u] to [ɨ] either in the context ——C$_0^1$[−consonantal] or in the context —— #. Under this modification, φ will be a weak cluster and stress will be assigned properly.

We see little to choose between these alternatives. Rather arbitrarily, we will accept the assumption that /uε/ is correct, for expository purposes, leaving a more principled resolution of the problem to a deeper study.

Notice that we can regard all instances of final /ue/ as /uε/. We have made use of the bisyllabic character of /ue/ for only one purpose, namely, laxing of the first vowel in *value, tissue*, etc. But quite apart from the analysis of [yūw], we would have to give the context for trisyllabic laxing in the simplest form: $C(C+)\begin{bmatrix} +\text{stress} \\ V \end{bmatrix}C_0[-\text{consonantal}]$; and in this form, it applies to the first vowel of [væluε], etc. Notice also that the choice of /uε/ requires a complication of condition (b) of the Main Stress Rule, which omits from consideration a final string of the form φ[+consonantal]$_0$, where φ is an unstressed lax vowel or glide (see p. 133). To cover the case [uε], we must replace φ[+consonantal]$_0$ by $φ\begin{Bmatrix} [+\text{consonantal}]_0 \\ [-\text{vocalic}]_0^1 \end{Bmatrix}$.

A form such as [re=siduε] falls under the second of these conditions in two ways, first with the omitted string being [uε] and second with the omitted string being [ε]. If the rules are to apply properly, these two cases must be disjunctively ordered and the first must apply before the second. This is provided for by our present system of notations. Notice that φ[−vocalic]$_0^1$ is an abbreviation for two cases, φ[−vocalic] and φ, applying in that order. Since [uε] falls under the first of these, the second will never apply to the forms in question.

Notice also that in a derived form such as *residual*, no further rules are needed. Thus we begin the second cycle with the representation [rē=siduɛ+æl]. Primary stress is placed before the weak cluster [uɛ] under condition (a) of the Main Stress Rule (the Affix Rule), giving [rē=siduɛ+æl]. The string [uɛ] becomes [yūw] in the usual way, and [ɛ] elides before a boundary by the *e*-Elision Rule. By other familiar processes, we derive [rəzijūwəl].

In short, by simplifying rule (52) (dropping one feature) and replacing final /ue/ by /uɛ/ (either in lexical representations or by a redundancy rule), we derive just the required forms in these examples.

We might mention a few other minor tensing rules that belong together with rule (52). There is some evidence that we should add the rules in (60) at this point:

$$\left(60\right) \quad \text{(a)} \quad \begin{Bmatrix} æ \\ u \end{Bmatrix} \rightarrow [+\text{tense}] \ / \ \left[\underline{}\atop{+\text{stress}}\right] nge$$

$$\text{(b)} \quad ɔ \rightarrow ɔ̄ \ / \ \underline{} CV[-\text{seg}]$$

Rule (60a) accounts for the appearance of a tense vowel in forms such as *angel* and *lounge*, which would otherwise contradict rule (8). Notice that *lunge*, *sponge* cannot be derived from underlying /lunge/, /spunge/, respectively. We shall see below in Section 4.3.7 that they can be derived from an underlying representation containing lax /o/ in stressed position.

Rule (60a) will also account for contrasts such as *angel–angelic* from underlying /æŋgel/. In *angel* in isolation, stress is placed on the first syllable, which is tensed by rule (60a) and then undergoes Diphthongization and Vowel Shift in the usual way. In *angelic*, (60a) does not apply, and we derive [æn̆jelik]. The same rule explains the tense vowel in *range*, *strange*, etc. (from underlying /ræŋge/, /stræŋge/, respectively). Tense vowels are not, in general, to be expected before this cluster. Notice, incidentally, that formatives with phonetic [...æn̆j...] are extremely rare (examples being *flange*, *gange*, and, with formative boundary, *tang+ent*). This fact is explained by rule (60a). The cluster [n̆j] will arise only from /nge/ by Velar Softening (see Section 6), and, when /æ/ precedes this cluster under stress, it will be tensed by rule (60a), with the exceptions noted.

Rule (60b) is needed to account for alternations such as *telescope–telescopic–telescopy*. Consider the underlying vowel of *scope*. From the position of stress in *teléscopy*, we know that this vowel must be lax. From the form *telescopic*, we know that the underlying vowel of *scope* must be either /ɔ/ or /ō/, since our study of back vowel alternations has shown that these are the only vowels that give rise to phonetic [ā] before *-ic*. Since the underlying vowel has already been determined to be lax, it must therefore be /ɔ/. But this leaves the problem of accounting for the form *telescope*, where the phonetic reflex of this vowel is [ōw]. This phonetic form can derive only from [ɔ̄], by Diphthongization and Vowel Shift. Therefore we need a rule tensing /ɔ/ in some position. It cannot be that /ɔ/ is tensed to [ɔ̄] in the context ——C#, as we can see from words such as *cot*, *stop*, where the /ɔ/ remains, to become [ā] in a manner we have already discussed. The only possibility, then, is to make use once again of the rule of *e*-Elision in final position, and to take the underlying representation to be /tele+skɔpe/, tensing being determined by rule (60b).

The same rule might also be used to account for contrasts such as *photograph* (with [ōw] in the first syllable) versus *monotone* (with [ā] in this syllable). In both cases it seems that the underlying vowel can only be /ɔ/. The distinction, then, can be in terms of a lexical opposition [±rule (60b)], which appears to be quite idiosyncratic from a synchronic point of view.

4.3.5. VOWEL SHIFT FOR LAX VOWELS

We have so far restricted the Vowel Shift Rule to tense vowels. By extending it to certain lax vowels, we can account for several other phenomena, some marginal, some perfectly regular.

Consider first the nonback high vowel [i]. If this were to undergo Vowel Shift, it would become [æ], just as [ī] becomes [ǣ]. (We continue to restrict Diphthongization and Backness Adjustment to tense vowels, so that the alternation [i]–[æ] for lax vowels is parallel to the alternation [ī]–[āy] for tense vowels.) The alternation [i]–[æ] is, in fact, found in a certain class of irregular verbs in English, e.g., *sit–sat, sing–sang.* These verbs will be marked in the lexicon as belonging to a special lexical category, and by Convention 2, page 173, this lexical category will be distributed as a feature of each segment of these verbs, in the appropriate context. Thus, in particular, the vowel of *sit* will have a certain feature [+F] when it is in the syntactic context ——*past.* (*Past* is deleted after determining the category of the lexical item and, in consequence, the distinctive feature composition of its segments.) We can then account for the alternation that gives the past tense form by permitting the Vowel Shift Rule to apply also to vowels in the following specially marked context:[31]

$$\left(61\right) \qquad \qquad \left[\frac{\quad}{+F}\right]$$

Thus we can find a small "subregularity" in the class of irregular verbs by generalization of the Vowel Shift Rule to certain lax nonback vowels.

Extension of the Vowel Shift Rule to the context (61) also enables us to account for the alternation *satisfy–satisfaction.* The form underlying *satisfy* clearly contains the formative *-fy* which we also find in *ramify, clarify,* etc., and, presumably, it also contains the formative *sate,* which has the underlying representation /sæt/. The underlying representation of *-fy* must be /fīk/. In forms such as *clarification,* the vowel of this formative will be reduced to [ə] by the processes described in Chapter Three, Section 14. In final position, the [k] is dropped by the ad hoc rule (62), which also applies to *multiply,* etc.

$$\left(62\right) \qquad \qquad k \;\rightarrow\; \phi \;\; / \;\; +C_1 \bar{\imath}\text{———}\#$$

When the vowel of *-fy* remains tense, it becomes phonetic [āy] by the Diphthongization and Vowel Shift Rules discussed above.

These remarks are quite general. We apply them now to the special case of *satisfy,* with the underlying representation /sæt+is+fīk/.

In isolation, this form emerges from the stress cycle with the representation [sǽt+is+fìk]. By rule (19b), the trisyllabic case of the Laxing Rule, the vowel [æ] becomes [æ]. The Diphthongization and Vowel Shift Rules convert [ī] to [āy], and rule (62) drops the final [k], giving [sǽtisfày].

Consider now *satisfaction,* with the underlying representation /sæt+is+fīk+ æt+iVn/. The lexical item *satisfy* belongs to the large class of irregular verbs that drop the /æ/ of /+æt+/ in the derived forms (*receive–reception, reduce–reduction, describe–descriptive,* etc.) This gives the form [sæt+is+fīk+t+iVn]. The stress cycle now yields [sæ̀t+is+fík+t+iVn]. In Section 2 we observed that English phonology contains

---

[31] Recall that by Convention 2, every segment of the lexical items that do not belong to the category [+F] is automatically marked [−F], so that the extended Vowel Shift Rule will apply only to the appropriate irregular forms.

rule (8), which makes vowels lax before consonant clusters, as a special case of the general Laxing Rule. As noted there, this rule is not a lexical redundancy rule which applies only within formative boundaries, but rather a phonological rule which applies to *any* tense vowel followed by a consonant cluster, in particular, to the vowel [ī] of [sæt+is+fīk+ t+iVn]. Furthermore, [æ] becomes lax by rule (19), as in *satisfy* in isolation. If, now, we assign *satisfy* (or, perhaps, the formative *-fy*) to the category [+F], along with *sit*, *sing*, etc., in their past tense forms, then the Vowel Shift Rule, now extended to the context (61), will apply, giving [sæ̀t+is+fǽk+t+iVn], which becomes [sæ̀tisfǽkšən] by rules to be discussed later.

In short, to account for the superficially unique [āy]–[æ] alternation of *satisfy–satisfaction*, we need only assign *satisfy* to a certain subclass of irregular verbs that receive the feature [+F]. Once again, we can extract a subregularity from what appears to be a totally exceptional case.[32]

Certain other irregular phenomena can also be brought into the scope of the Vowel Shift Rule in the same way. Consider, first, forms such as *retentive*, *retention*, *content*, *exemplary*, *biennial*. In each case the vowel in boldface has undergone an exceptional change from expected [æ] to phonetic [e]. Thus the vowel of *-tain*, for example, becomes lax by rule (8) before the double consonant in the derived forms. But the underlying vowel is /ǣ/ (which, when it remains tense, becomes [ēy] by Diphthongization and Vowel Shift, as in *retain*, *contain*); hence the corresponding lax vowel should be [æ]. To account for the fact that we have [e] in place of [æ] in these words, we can assign the formative *-tain* to the category [+F]. It will thus fall under the Vowel Shift Rule, extended to the context (61), after the vowel becomes lax by rule (8). Since the Vowel Shift Rule converts [æ] to [e], we derive the desired form. The other cases are similar.

We can use the same device to take care of the *A–e* alternation noted in the preceding chapter. As we observed there (see (142), page 136), underlying /ǣ/ becomes [e] in the affix *-ary* in words such as *secretary*, *secretarial*. Since a form of laxing is involved, it is reasonable to combine this with the Laxing Rule (19), as a special case. Thus the Laxing Rule, appropriately extended to *-ary*, will convert this /ǣ/ to [æ]. If we now assign to *-ary* the feature [+F], the Vowel Shift Rule will convert [æ] to [e]. Notice that Tensing will not apply to the laxed [æ] of *secretarial* (see note 17).

According to (43), Vowel Shift applies to vowels that are [+stress] and [+tense]. In (61) we extended Vowel Shift to vowels marked with the diacritic feature [+F]. By our conventions, these two contexts must be conjunctively ordered. Consequently, if a vowel satisfies both (43) and (61), it will undergo Vowel Shift twice. Thus, for instance, a tense stressed [æ] which is also marked [+F] would first be turned into [ē] by virtue of (43) and subsequently into [ī] by virtue of (61). The cases we have examined up to this point have all contained nontense vowels and were hence subject to only a single application of the Vowel Shift Rule. There are, however, instances where Vowel Shift does appear to apply twice; for example, double application of Vowel Shift gives *clear* [klīyr] from underlying /klǣr/ (cf. *clarity*). Similarly, verbs such as *rise–rose* and *take–took* require double application of the Vowel Shift Rule in their past tense forms. If we take the present tense form as the underlying form, we must assign the lexical representations /rīz/, /tǣk/, respectively, which give [rāyz], [tēyk] in the usual way. To derive the past tense forms, we first apply a rule shifting backness and rounding, which is widely applicable to irregular verbs and other

---

[32] Observe that extension of the Vowel Shift Rule to certain occurrences of lax [i] amalgamates entirely unrelated historical processes which have fallen together synchronically in English (see (36), Chapter Six).

irregular forms and which we shall discuss later. This gives [rūz], [tōk]. Diphthongization and Vowel Shift give [rōwz], [tōwk]. Finally, reapplication of the Vowel Shift Rule gives the forms [rōwz], [tūwk].[33] We can readily account for this double application of Vowel Shift by marking all such forms as [+F]. If the stressed vowels so marked are also tense, the Vowel Shift Rule will apply twice.

Let us turn now to the case of the lax, high, back vowel [u]. Suppose that we were to add (63) as a context for the Vowel Shift Rule:

$$\begin{pmatrix} 63 \end{pmatrix} \qquad \begin{bmatrix} \underline{} \\ -\text{tense} \\ +\text{high} \\ +\text{back} \end{bmatrix}$$

In this context, the first part of the Vowel Shift Rule would apply, with the result that [u] would be converted to [o]. The second part of the Vowel Shift Rule would not apply to this newly formed segment, however; [o], not being [+tense], [+F], or [+high], does not meet the conditions for application of the Vowel Shift Rule. We have seen that the Rounding Adjustment Rule (37) applies to the vowel [ō] which results from underlying /ū/ by Vowel Shift, so that original /ū/ becomes phonetic [āw]. If we extend this rule to [o] arising by Vowel Shift from /u/, then the rule will convert [o] to its nonround counterpart [ʌ] (i.e., to the lax vowel which is [−high], [−low], [−round]). We will see, in fact, that the Rounding Adjustment Rule is even more general than this. With this extension, underlying /u/ will become phonetic [ʌ] by Vowel Shift and Rounding Adjustment, whereas underlying /ū/, which undergoes *both* stages of the Vowel Shift, as well as Diphthongization and Rounding Adjustment, becomes phonetic [āw] (or [æw], with further Backness Adjustment and Laxing).

Thus, extension of the Vowel Shift Rule to the context (63), and a corresponding extension of Rounding Adjustment, will convert /u/ to [ʌ]. In fact, as we have already noted in connection with the alternation *profound–profundity* (30c), there is good evidence that this process exists as a part of English phonology. Notice further that phonetic [u] – [ʌ] contrasts are very rare in English, and in many contexts they are not found at all. Thus, for example, although we have words such as *fund, duct, lung, bunt* (phonetically, [fʌnd], [dʌkt], [lʌŋ], [bʌnt]), we could not have words with the phonetic forms *[fund], *[dukt], *[luŋ], *[bunt]. These forms are inadmissible in the English dialects that we are studying and must be excluded by appropriate rules. The Vowel Shift Rule and the extensions just mentioned have just the required effect, converting /fund/ to [fʌnd], etc. We can thus account for the lack of contrast and, at the same time, preserve the symmetry and simplicity of the system of lexical representations, which will contain, among lax vowels, only those which are [−back], [−round] (/i/, /e/, /æ/) or [+back], [+round] (/u/, /o/, /ɔ/).

The Vowel Shift Rule, as just formulated, will convert *all* cases of phonological /u/ to phonetic [ʌ]. But clearly there are cases of phonetic [u] in the language (e.g., *push, pull, bushel, bull*); that is, there are residual cases of contrast or near contrast involving phonetic [u] and [ʌ]. Phonological /u/ thus gives rise to phonetic [ʌ] by the Vowel Shift Rule, and to phonetic [u] when the Vowel Shift Rule does not apply.

---

[33] The representation [tūwk] becomes [tuk] by a fairly general rule that applies to [ūw] in various contexts, in particular ——*k*, before rule (62). Apart from the word *spook* and various slang forms, which often break low-level rules, all of the forms with phonetic [ūwk] derive from underlying /ŭ/.

On page 168, we noted that it is possible for the values of *all* of the features of an underlying vowel to be changed in its phonetic representation. The example given was underlying /ū/, which becomes [æ] in some dialects. Now we have another example, namely, underlying /æ/, which becomes [u] in *take–took*

In Section 4.3.4 we dealt with a very similar problem. There we wanted to find a tense, high, back vowel which did not undergo Vowel Shift and could serve as the source for [yūw]. We saw that the proper choice was the unrounded vowel corresponding to [ū], that is, the vowel [ɨ], which is immune to Vowel Shift because it is not the same in backness and rounding. This vowel itself derives from underlying /u/ by rule (52), which tenses and unrounds [u] in the context ——C_0^1V. The vowel [ɨ] finally becomes [ū] by the late rule (51).

The analysis of [yūw] suggests a way of providing for phonetic [u]. Suppose that we add an early rule with the effect of (64):

$$\left(64\right) \qquad\qquad u \;\rightarrow\; [-\text{round}] \quad \text{in certain contexts}$$

If we then generalize rule (51) so that it rounds [ɨ] as well as [ɨ], we will have the derivations of (65) for *push, pun*, for example:

$$\left(65\right)$$

	puš	pun	
	pɨš		RULE (64)
		pon	VOWEL SHIFT, EXTENDED TO (63)
		pʌn	EXTENSION OF ROUNDING ADJUSTMENT
	puš		GENERALIZATION OF (51)

All that is necessary, then, is to specify the contexts for rule (64) in such a way that it covers all words with phonetic [u]. Investigation of the examples suggests the following formulation:

$$\left(66\right)\qquad \begin{bmatrix} -\text{tense} \\ +\text{high} \end{bmatrix} \;\rightarrow\; [-\text{round}] \;\Big/\; \begin{bmatrix} -\text{nasal} \\ +\text{ant} \\ -\text{cor} \end{bmatrix} ——\; \begin{Bmatrix} 1 \begin{Bmatrix} 1 \\ \# \end{Bmatrix} & \text{(a)} \\[4pt] \begin{bmatrix} -\text{ant} \\ +\text{cor} \end{bmatrix} & \text{(b)} \end{Bmatrix}$$

Rule (66) unrounds /u/ when it is preceded by a nonnasal labial segment and followed either by [ll] or final [l] or by [š] or [č]. Case (a) applies in the boldface position in such words as *pullet, pulley, bullet, bullock, pull, full*. We know, in the first four cases, that the medial cluster is double [l] by the fact that /u/ does not become [ɨ] by rule (52) (and, finally, [yūw]), as would happen in the context ——CV. Case (b) of the rule applies in words such as *bush, push, bushel, butcher*. Notice that the occurrences of phonological /u/ that are unrounded by rule (66) (or rule (52)) will be phonetically round, and those that remain round because rule (66) (or rule (52)) does not apply will be phonetically nonround, that is, [ʌ].

Rule (66) is a lexical redundancy rule; it precedes all phonological rules. It does not cover several exceptional cases of unrounding; for example, *put, pudding, puss, cushion*. These must be listed in the lexicon, either as purely idiosyncratic or by an extension of rule (66). Thus, insofar as there is a marginal phonetic [u]–[ʌ] contrast, there is a marginal phonological /ɨ/–/u/ opposition in the lexicon.

There are various other problems connected with these cases; for example, the absence of tensing of /u/ in *budget, butcher*, and *bushel* (which suggest that the stressed vowel is followed by a double consonant) and the inapplicability of (66) to words such as *budge, budget*, and *fudge*, which can be accounted for either by limiting (66) to segments preceding voiceless palato-alveolars only, or by assuming that the lexical representation corresponds to the spelling, in which case (66) will be automatically blocked.

Summarizing the phonetic variety of underlying high back vowels, we have the following situation. The tense phonological segment /ū/ always undergoes Vowel Shift. In the cases so far considered (there will be a slight extension below), this gives phonetic [āw] or [æw], depending on dialect. The lax phonological segment /u/ becomes phonetic [yūw] when it is in the context —— C_0^1V; it remains phonetic [u] (after unrounding and compensating rounding) when it is in the contexts of (66); elsewhere it undergoes the first stage of Vowel Shift and becomes phonetic [ʌ].

4.3.6. FURTHER REMARKS ON DIPHTHONGIZATION

We are now in a position to account for a defect in the Diphthongization Rule, formulated as (21) in Section 4.1. This rule introduces a glide after a tense vowel, the glide being [w] if the vowel is back and [y] if the vowel is nonback. Thus, [ī], [ē], [ǣ], [ǣ] receive a *y*-glide, and [ū], [ō], [ɔ̄], [ā] receive a *w*-glide. This assignment is appropriate for all cases except [ā], where it is clearly incorrect. For example, *father* and *Chicago* do not become phonetic *[fāwðər], *[šəkāwgōw], respectively; rather, [ā] receives a centering glide of some sort or a feature of extra length (with various dialectal differences that do not concern us here).

We may account for this phenomenon by adding the following supplement to the Diphthongization Rule:

$$
\left(67\right) \qquad [-\text{cons}] \;\;\rightarrow\;\; [+\text{voc}] \;\; / \;\; \bar{a} \text{——}
$$

Thus Diphthongization will convert [ā] to [āw], and rule (67) will convert [āw] to [āu]. The first part of the Vowel Shift Rule, followed by the Rounding Adjustment Rule discussed in the preceding section, will then convert [āu] to [āʌ], just as /pun/ is converted to [pʌn]. Thus *father, Chicago*, which are lexically represented as /fāðVr/, /šVkāgo/, are converted ultimately to [fāʌðər], [šəkāʌgōw]. The phonetic interpretation of [āʌ] varies with the dialect, as does the phonetic interpretation of the other complex vocalic nuclei. Thus [āʌ] may represent [ā] followed by a centralizing glide (a mid central vowel) or simply extra-long [ā]; or the off-glide may be dropped and [āʌ] will not be distinguished phonetically from [ā].

In Section 2 we presented rule (5), which converts underlying /ɔ/ to phonetic [ā], as in *cot, stop*. This rule falls together with the Rounding Adjustment Rule and therefore comes after Vowel Shift in the ordering of the rules. The segment [ā] formed by rule (5) will not be diphthongized and will contrast with the phonetic [āʌ] that comes from original /ā/. Thus we have such contrasts as *father–bother* ([fāʌðər]–[bāðər]), from underlying /fāðVr/–/bɔðVr/, and *rajah–Roger*. For essentially the same reasons, we will have length contrasts as in *balm–bomb, starry–sorry*, with the shorter of the two paired vowels deriving from /ɔ/ by rule (5). (The source of [āʌ] in these items will be discussed in the next section.) In dialects in which [āʌ] is interpreted phonetically as [ā], the contrast will not appear.

4.3.7. FURTHER REMARKS ON PHONETICALLY LOW VOWELS

To complete the discussion of the system of English vocalic nuclei, we must account for the phonetically low tense vowels: [ɔ̄] as in *lawn, audacious*; [ā] as in *spa, balm*; and, for some dialects, [ǣ], as in *can*, meaning "receptacle" (as opposed to *can* meaning "be able," which has lax [æ] phonetically).

The distribution of [ǣ] varies from dialect to dialect, but in each dialect almost all cases are predictable from underlying /æ/, which tenses in positions determined by lexical category or by the following consonant. The few cases that cannot be predicted[34] must be listed in the lexicon as involving a highly marginal subclassification of [æ] in certain monosyllabic morphemes.

The case of [ɔ̄] is less marginal and more important. In words such as *laud, brawl*, it appears that [ɔ̄] must come from some tense vowel that does not undergo Vowel Shift. We must therefore find a vowel V* which is not subject to Vowel Shift and is later converted to [ɔ̄] by rules which are, as far as possible, independently motivated. The obvious proposal is to take V* to be [ā]; since this vowel is different in backness and rounding, it does not undergo Vowel Shift, and it can be converted to [ɔ̄] by a late rule of Rounding Adjustment of which we have already found many examples. This proposal is strengthened by the observation that [ā] has, otherwise, an extremely restricted distribution in lexical entries. In particular, it is excluded from monosyllables. Thus there are no such forms as *[lāʌn] contrasting with [lɔ̄ʌn] (*lawn*),[35] or *[brāʌl] contrasting with [brɔ̄ʌl] (*brawl*). This fact permits us to derive phonetic [ɔ̄] in monosyllables from underlying /ā/. We therefore add rule (68), which will fall together with the other Rounding Adjustment Rules, as we shall see.

$$\left(68\right) \qquad\qquad \bar{a} \;\rightarrow\; [+\text{round}] \;\; / \;\; [-\text{seg}]\,C_0\text{——}VC_0\,[-\text{seg}]$$

Thus the word *laud*, for example, will have the following derivation:

$$\left(69\right)$$
lād	
lāwd	DIPHTHONGIZATION (21)
lāud	RULE (67)
lāod	VOWEL SHIFT, EXTENDED TO (63)
lɔ̄ʌd	ROUNDING ADJUSTMENT

Rounding Adjustment applies twice to give the final line of (69), once to [ā] by case (68), rounding the tense vowel, and once in the manner described in the preceding section, unrounding the lax [o] that derives from [u] by Vowel Shift.

We thus are assuming that the vowel of *laud, brawl* has a centering glide, like the boldface vowel of *father, Chicago*. Again, we are limiting ourselves to the phonetics of a single, prototype dialect, passing over much phonetic detail and dialectal variation that are beyond the scope of this study.

We have already noted quite a few cases of Rounding Adjustment following the Vowel Shift Rule. We will summarize the various cases in Section 4.3.8. In order to achieve maximal generalization in the formulation of this rule, we will want to extract from the rule the particular contexts that restrict its various special cases. In particular, we will want to eliminate from (68) the restriction to monosyllables, which will be unique to this case. The obvious way to achieve this result is by a lexical redundancy rule that exempts /ā/ from rounding adjustment in polysyllables (e.g., *father, Chicago, restaurant*). We therefore add the rule (70) (where *n* is the number of the rule that rounds /ā/ after the Vowel Shift Rule as a special case of Rounding Adjustment, i.e., the rule temporarily formulated as (68)):

$$\left(70\right) \qquad\qquad\qquad \bar{a} \;\rightarrow\; [-\text{rule } n] \;\;\text{in polysyllables}$$

---

[34] For example, in our prototype dialect, the vowel in monosyllabic adjectives ending in [d], e.g., [sæd] (*sad*) versus [bǽd] (*bad*).

[35] Of course, we may have such forms from phonological /ɔ/, which goes to [ā] by rule (5). Thus words such as *conch, fond, pot* must be given the representations /kɔnč/, /fɔnd/, /pɔt/ in their lexical entries. Forms such as *spark, spar, spa* have underlying [æ], as we shall see directly.

We have now accounted for the cases of phonetic [ɔ̄] in monosyllables, but we must still find a source for the vowel in the boldface position of *audacious, claustrophobia, mulligatawny*, etc. An interesting fact regarding this vowel is that in polysyllables it is in complementary distribution with phonetic [āw] or [æw], that is, with the reflex of phonological /ū/. The latter appears only in the context ——[+nasal] C, as in *council, countenance, mountain, scoundrel, mountebank*, and in the context —— V in some dialects, as in *Howell, dowel* (contrasting with *howl, foul*). Typically, [ɔ̄] does not appear in these contexts and [āw] or [æw] does not appear elsewhere in polysyllabic formatives.[36] This fact suggests that in polysyllables phonetic [ɔ̄] may derive from underlying /ū/, just as [āw] or [æw] derives from /ū/. This is quite plausible on other grounds, since [ɔ̄] is, in fact, an intermediate stage in the derivation of [āw] (or [æw]) from /ū/. Recall that after it is diphthongized, /ū/ becomes [ɔ̄] by Vowel Shift and then becomes [ā] by Rounding Adjustment. To derive [ɔ̄] from underlying [ū], then, it is necessary only to arrest the /ū/ → [ɔ̄] → [ā] transition at its middle stage, permitting Vowel Shift to apply but not Rounding Adjustment. Since phonetic [ɔ̄] and phonetic [āw] are, as just noted, in complementary distribution in polysyllables, the cases in which only Vowel Shift applies to underlying /ū/ can be distinguished from the cases in which both Vowel Shift and Rounding Adjustment apply to underlying /ū/.

In short, there is good reason to suppose that phonetic [ɔ̄] derives from underlying /ā/ in monosyllables and from underlying /ū/ in polysyllables.[37]

Clearly the segment [ɔ̄] appearing in polysyllables is not to be distinguished on phonetic grounds from the segment [ɔ̄] in monosyllables, although they have different phonological sources. In particular, the following glide, if any, must be the same. In the dialect we are taking as our prototype, this is a centering glide, which we are representing as [ʌ]. In the case of the [ɔ̄] deriving from /ā/, we have already accounted for this glide by rule (67), which converts [w] to [u] after [ā], [u] then going automatically to [ʌ] by Vowel Shift and Rounding Adjustment. Clearly, then, we must extend (67) to the occurrences of [w] which follow those cases of /ū/ which are going to become phonetic [ɔ̄] rather than phonetic [āw]. That is, we must revise rule (67) so that it converts [w] to [u] not only after all cases of [ā] but also after [ū] everywhere except in final syllables, before nasal clusters, and before vowels. The simplest way to express these facts is by the rule (71), the exceptions to (71) being marked by the lexical redundancy rule (72):

$$\left(71\right) \qquad\qquad w \;\rightarrow\; u \;\; / \left\{\begin{matrix}\bar{u}\\\bar{a}\end{matrix}\right\}\underline{\qquad}$$

$$\left(72\right) \qquad\qquad \bar{u} \;\rightarrow\; [-\text{rule } (71)] \;\; / \underline{\qquad}\left\{\begin{matrix}C_0\#\\ [+\text{nasal}]\,C\\ V\end{matrix}\right\}$$

(The fact that (72) applies to the vowel whereas (71) applies to the glide will be dealt with shortly.) The phonological rule (71) will now convert [w] to [u] not only in words such as *father* and *laud*, as before, but also in *maudlin, aug*=*ment*, etc. The lexical redundancy rule

---

[36] This formulation requires that words such as *saunter, launder, trousers* be treated as phonologically monosyllabic. (Note that *laundry* is [lɔ̄ndrīy] phonetically, not [lɔ̄ndərīy].) There are, incidentally, other sources of phonetic [ɔ] (e.g., before liquids, in certain contexts), as we shall see directly.

[37] We have observed (see p. 195) that [āw] (or [æw]) does not occur before labials or velars, and we have suggested that this is a result of the lexical redundancy rule (54) that makes consonants coronal in the context *ū*——[−segment]. But this redundancy rule does not affect noncoronal consonants following /ū/ in medial position, and we have forms such as *awkward, auburn, augur, traumatic*, in which underlying /ū/ appears before a labial or a velar.

(72) will block the application of (71) in words such as *renown, frown, allow, rowdy; mountain, fountain; tower, dowel*. In these cases, it will leave a labializing glide after the tense vowel. For rule (72) to apply correctly, it is necessary to make a few otherwise unmotivated decisions about the placement of formative boundary, and there still will remain marginal contrasts in the lexicon; but we will not press the investigation of this point any further.

Let us now compare the derivations of *mountain* and *maudlin*:

$$\left(73\right)$$

mūntən	mūdlin	
mūwntən	mūwdlin	DIPHTHONGIZATION
	mūudlin	RULE (71)
mɔ̄wntən	mɔ̄odlin	VOWEL SHIFT
māwntən	mɔ̄ʌdlin	ROUNDING ADJUSTMENT

In the third line of (73), rule (71) applies to *maudlin*, changing [w] to [u]; but it is prevented by rule (72) from applying to *mountain*, which has a nasal cluster following /ū/. To form the final line of (73), Rounding Adjustment applies to the lax vowel [o], giving [ʌ], and changes the segment [ɔ̄] in the context ——w but not in the context ——V. The exact mechanics of the Rounding Adjustment Rule will be presented in Section 4.3.8. For the present it is only necessary to observe that the cases in which the rule effects a change are distinguishable from the cases where it does not, the relevant distinction here being the specification of the feature "vocalic" in the following segment.

Rule (71) makes the glide [w] vocalic when it follows [ā] or [ū] but not when it follows other vowels. Since the segments [ā] and [ū] are the only vowel segments followed by [w] that have the same coefficients for the features "round" and "high," we can reformulate rule (71) as follows:

$$\left(74\right) \qquad \begin{bmatrix} -\text{cons} \\ +\text{back} \end{bmatrix} \rightarrow [+\text{voc}] \Big/ \begin{bmatrix} \alpha\text{round} \\ \alpha\text{high} \\ V \end{bmatrix} ———$$

We will henceforth refer to this as the Glide Vocalization Rule.

There is a discrepancy in the formulation of rules (72) and (74) that must be eliminated. Notice that the lexical redundancy rule (72) assigns the feature [−Glide Vocalization Rule] (=[−rule (74)]) to the vowel /ū/ in certain contexts in lexical formatives. But the Glide Vocalization Rule (74) refers to a glide following the vowel [ū], not to this vowel itself. Therefore the fact that the vowel is marked [−rule (74)] will not prevent rule (74) from applying to the glide which follows this vowel, a glide which is inserted only by the Diphthongization Rule. Clearly this glide must also be assigned the feature [−rule (74)]. Recall that the Diphthongization Rule (21) inserts after a tense vowel a glide agreeing in backness and rounding with the backness of the vowel. Evidently, we must also require that the glide agree with the vowel in the feature [αrule (74)], and the Diphthongization Rule (21) must be modified to include this specification. The rule will then insert a glide which undergoes rule (74) just in case the vowel it diphthongizes is not excepted from Glide Vocalization by the lexical redundancy rule (72).

There is clearly a more general way to state the Diphthongization Rule, thus expressing an aspect of this rule missed in our formalization. The Diphthongization Rule inserts a glide which accepts from the vowel preceding it *all* feature specifications that are possible for a glide. The Diphthongization Rule is, in other words, the simplest sort of "assimilation rule," in a very general sense of this notion. This is clearly a linguistically significant fact, a generalization not captured in our formalization. We will return, inconclusively, to a discussion of this and several other related inadequacies in Chapter Nine.

The next problem involving phonetically low vowels has to do with the realization of underlying /ɔ/ as [ā], noted several times in our discussion. The rule (5) which converts /ɔ/ to [ā] can be analyzed into two steps, the first of which unrounds /ɔ/ and the second of which tenses the resulting [a]. The first step can then be formulated as a special case of the Rounding Adjustment Rule which follows Vowel Shift in the ordering. We will discuss some of the dialectal variation involving underlying /ɔ/ below.

Still to be accounted for are the occurrences of phonetic [ɔ̄ʌ]—the same phonetic segment as in *laud, audible,* etc.—in words such as *long, soft, cost, toss, cloth,* and before liquids. We will put aside the case of liquids for the moment and consider the other cases. Since the words cited are monosyllables, the vowel cannot derive from underlying /ū/ in the manner just outlined. The other alternative is underlying /ā/, as in *lawn* and *fraud.* This is ruled out in words such as *long* and *soft,* however, since tense vowels do not occur before such clusters, as we have noted (see p. 171 and note 19).

The case we are now discussing can be incorporated into the grammar as so far constructed in several different ways, and we have not found any entirely compelling argument for one or another approach. We therefore sketch one possibility, which seems to us to involve the fewest ad hoc rules and to leave the smallest number of exceptions, observing, however, that there are other plausible hypotheses.

In discussing double applications of the Vowel Shift Rule (p. 202), we noted that there is a phenomenon of backness adjustment that applies to many irregular lexical items. For example, if we take present tense forms of verbs to be the underlying forms, then we have nonback vowels becoming back and round in the case of alternations such as *cling–clung, tell–told, bind–bound, break–broke,* and back vowels becoming nonback and nonround in the case of alternations such as *run–ran, hold–held.* Similarly, in irregular plurals we have back vowels becoming nonback and nonround, as in *mouse–mice, foot–feet.* These phenomena suggest that there must be a pre-cyclic readjustment rule switching backness in certain lexical items in certain contexts:

$$
(75) \qquad V \;\rightarrow\; \begin{bmatrix} -\alpha\text{back} \\ -\alpha\text{round} \end{bmatrix} \Big/ \begin{bmatrix} \underline{\hphantom{xxxx}} \\ \alpha\text{back} \end{bmatrix} \quad \text{in certain irregular forms}
$$

Given the readjustment rule (75), we can account for the derived forms in the examples of the preceding paragraph by assuming the underlying representations /kliNg/, /tel/, /bīnd/, /bræk/, /run/, /hold/, /mūs/, /fōt/. Rule (75) will, in the appropriate contexts, convert: /kliNg/ to [kluNg], which becomes [klʌNg] by Vowel Shift and Rounding Adjustment, in the manner described above, and, finally, [klʌŋ] by Nasal Assimilation and the dropping of final [g] after a nasal; /tel/ to [tol] before [d] (the vowel then becoming [ōw] by processes discussed on page 214); /bind/, which by Diphthongization, Vowel Shift, and other rules becomes [bāynd], to [bünd], which in parallel fashion ultimately is turned into [bæwnd]; /bræk/, which becomes [brēyk] by Diphthongization and Vowel Shift, to [brōk], which becomes [brōwk] in the same way; /run/, which becomes [rʌn] by Vowel Shift under condition (63) and by Rounding Adjustment, to [rin], which must be marked [+F] in the past tense so that it becomes [ræn] by Vowel Shift under condition (61); /hold/ to [held]; /mūs/ to [mīs] (these being realized as [māws] or [mæws], [māys], respectively, in the usual way); /fōt/, which becomes [fūwt] by Diphthongization and Vowel Shift, then [fut] in the manner described in note 33, to [fēt], which then undergoes Diphthongization and Vowel Shift in the usual way.

But notice that we have the alternations *long–length*, *strong–strength*, which also clearly illustrate the backness switch stated by rule (75). This fact strongly suggests that the underlying forms should be /long/, /strong/, and that to account for the phonetic forms [lɔ̄ʌŋ], [strɔ̄ʌŋ], we consider some process that has the effect of (76):

$$\left(76\right) \qquad\qquad\qquad o \;\rightarrow\; ɔ̄ʌ^{38}$$

Further support for this assumption comes from the observation that we clearly cannot derive *long* from underlying /lɔng/, since /ɔ/ in this context becomes phonetic [ā] in the usual way, as we can see from words such as *congress*, *thong* (which is [θāʌŋ] in the dialect that is being described here). Additional evidence is provided by the example *lose–lost*. The simplest analysis of *lose* (phonetically [lūwz]) is from underlying /lōz/ by Diphthongization and Vowel Shift. Then *lost* must be represented /lōz+d/, the irregularity of this verb being that the usual # boundary before the past tense affix is replaced by formative boundary (i.e., # → [−word boundary]; see pp. 13, 67). There is a general rule devoicing clusters which will convert /lōz+d/ to [lōs+t]. (Cluster devoicing here must be a case of "linkage" in the sense of Chapter Nine.) The Laxing Rule (8), which applies to a vowel followed by a double consonant, will then convert [lōs+t] to [los+t]. (Recall that dental clusters are excluded from this rule only if they appear within a formative—see page 172.) Now the processes summarized as (76) will convert [lost] to the desired phonetic form [lɔ̄ʌst].

There are, then, fairly good reasons for assuming that there must be rules with the effect of (76). If we can convert /o/ to [ā], we will have succeeded in accounting for (76), since [ā] becomes [ɔ̄ʌ] by Diphthongization, vocalization of [w] by rule (74), Vowel Shift, and Rounding Adjustment.[39] The questions we must consider, then, are how much the grammar must be complicated to convert /o/ to [ā] before the application of the Diphthongization Rule and in what contexts this change takes place.

A change of [o] to [ā] involves three features, namely, "round," "tense," and "low." Notice that we already have a rule making [u] tense and unrounded, namely, rule (52), which is part of the system of Tensing Rules. We can therefore generalize rule (52) by extending it to [o]. If, then, we restate (52) as (77) and add rule (78) as a final addendum to the

---

[38] Consider, however, the alternation *broad–breadth*. As mentioned, *long* and *strong* cannot have an underlying /ā/ because of their final clusters. The word *broad*, on the other hand, has no such cluster and must derive from underlying /brād/ in the manner described previously (p. 206). Rule (75) will then convert /brād+θ/ to [brǣd+θ]. Cluster devoicing will convert the latter to [brǣt+θ], which will become [brǣt+θ] by the Laxing Rule (8). If we now assign the feature [+F] to *broad*, then [brǣt+θ] will become [bret+θ], just as [retǣntiv] becomes [retentiv], by Vowel Shift under condition (61). Thus the only irregularity of *broad*, other than its being subject to rule (75), will be its assignment to the ad hoc category [+F].

[39] Recall that Rounding Adjustment applies to all cases of [ā] except those specified by the lexical redundancy rule (70) as excluded from the rounding rule because they appear in polysyllabic formatives. Suppose, then, that the word *Boston* is represented as /boston/, and becomes [bāston] by the rules that we are now discussing, which convert /o/ to [ā]. By Diphthongization, Glide Vocalization, and Vowel Shift, we derive [bāʌstɔn]. But Rounding Adjustment now applies, despite the fact that this is polysyllabic, since the vowel [ā] in question is not an underlying vowel and hence is not excluded from Rounding Adjustment by the lexical redundancy rule (70). Therefore we derive [bɔ̄ʌstɔn], as required.

   Once again, we are not concerned here with the exact phonetic details of [ɔ̄ʌ], which will vary with dialect, phonetic context, and style. What is crucial at this point is that this vowel not be distinguished phonetically from the other cases of [ɔ̄ʌ], which undergo the same phonetic modifications.

system of Tensing Rules, we achieve the desired conversion of [o] to [ā].

$$
(77) \qquad
\begin{bmatrix} -\text{tense} \\ +\text{back} \\ V \end{bmatrix}
\rightarrow
\begin{bmatrix} +\text{tense} \\ -\text{round} \end{bmatrix}
\Bigg/
\begin{cases}
\left[\begin{bmatrix} \rule{1em}{0.4pt} \\ +\text{high} \end{bmatrix} C_0^1 \, [-\text{cons}] \right] & \text{(a)} \\[2em]
\begin{bmatrix} \rule{1em}{0.4pt} \\ -\text{high} \\ -\text{low} \end{bmatrix} \ldots & \text{(b)}
\end{cases}
$$

$$
(78) \qquad \overline{\Lambda} \rightarrow [+\text{low}]
$$

Rule (77a) is rule (52). Rule (77b) is the new rule applying to underlying /o/ in some yet-to-be-determined context, indicated in (77b) by .... Rule (78) is the only quite ad hoc modification that is necessary to account for the processes summarized in (76).

From the examples we have so far considered, it appears that the relevant context for rule (77b) is the following:

$$
(79) \qquad \rule{3em}{0.4pt}
\begin{cases}
\begin{bmatrix} -\text{voice} \\ +\text{cont} \\ +\text{ant} \end{bmatrix} \\
[+\text{nasal}] \, C
\end{cases}
$$

That is, the processes summarized in (76) apply, so far, before [f], [s], [θ], and nasal clusters. There are, in fact, many other restrictions, which can be stated as lexical redundancy rules.[40] These processes are, of course, the synchronic reflexes of the well-known tensing of ME /ā/ and /ɔ̄/ which is attested in our records from the sixteenth century onward. (See Horn and Lehnert, 1954, pp. 667–92.)

Given these rules, we will have the following derivation for *long*, for example:

$$
(80) \qquad
\begin{array}{ll}
\text{long} \\
\text{lÃng} & \text{RULE (77b), IN THE CONTEXT (79)} \\
\text{lāng} & \text{RULE (78)} \\
\text{lāwng} & \text{DIPHTHONGIZATION} \\
\text{lāung} & \text{RULE (74)} \\
\text{lāong} & \text{VOWEL SHIFT} \\
\text{lɔ̄ʌng} & \text{ROUNDING ADJUSTMENT} \\
\text{lɔ̄ʌŋ} & \text{NASAL ASSIMILATION; DROPPING OF FINAL POSTNASAL [g]}
\end{array}
$$

In the same way, we can derive *moss, often, cost, cloth* from the underlying forms /mos/, /ofn/ (or /oftVn/), /cost/, /kloθ/, respectively.

In the light of these extensions, we can return to the dialectal variation of the segment /ɔ/, as in *stop, cot, conic*. The rules that we have given so far assign to this segment the phonetic form [ā], which, as we have noted, may contrast with [āʌ] resulting from underlying /ā/ (*Roger–rajah, bother–father,* etc.—see p. 205). In another American dialect (Eastern New England), phonological /ɔ/ becomes not phonetic [ā] but what according to workers on the American Linguistic Atlas is "a weakly rounded low-back vowel."[41] If we disregard the fact that rounding is somewhat weaker here than in other rounded vowels, we can designate the segment under discussion as [ɔ̄ʌ], that is, as the same (at this level of representation) as

---

[40] For example, for many dialects we have only /o/, not /ɔ/, before /st/, /f/, and /θ/; only /ɔ/, not /o/, before /n[t, d]/.

[41] Wetmore (1959).

the vowel of *lawn, cost* in the dialect we have been taking as our prototype. To obtain this phonetic realization of the segment /ɔ/, we need only extend rule (77) to low vowels, as a third case. Then underlying /kɔt/ (*cot*), for example, will become [kāt] by the new (77c) and, finally, [kɔ̄ʌt] by Diphthongization, Rounding Adjustment, and the subsidiary processes that we have discussed. Notice that this modification of rule (77) can be stated without adding any features to the rule if we use the angled bracket notation of Chapter Three (see pp. 76–77). Thus we can reformulate rule (77) as (81):

$$
(81) \quad
\begin{bmatrix} -\text{tense} \\ +\text{back} \\ V \end{bmatrix}
\rightarrow
\begin{bmatrix} +\text{tense} \\ -\text{round} \end{bmatrix}
\Big/
\left\{
\begin{matrix}
\left[\overline{}\atop{+\text{high}}\right] C_0^1\,[-\text{cons}] & \quad\text{(a)} \\[2ex]
\left[\begin{matrix}\overline{} \\ -\text{high} \\ \langle -\text{low}\rangle \end{matrix}\right]\langle\ldots\rangle & \quad\langle\text{(b)}\rangle,\ \text{(c)}
\end{matrix}
\right.
$$

By the conventions that we have already established, this schema abbreviates three rules, each carrying out the process described in (81) in the contexts (82a), (82b), (82c), in that order:[42]

$$
(82)
$$

$$
\left[\overline{}\atop{+\text{high}}\right] C_0^1\,[-\text{cons}] \qquad \text{(a)}
$$

$$
\left[\begin{matrix}\overline{} \\ -\text{high} \\ -\text{low}\end{matrix}\right]\ldots \qquad \text{(b)}
$$

$$
\left[\begin{matrix}\overline{} \\ -\text{high} \\ +\text{low}\end{matrix}\right] \qquad \text{(c)}
$$

Consider next the situation in British Received Pronunciation, in which phonetic [ɔ] appears in *cot, stop, conic*, etc. We can account for this dialect by adding one further set of angled brackets to (81), as in (83):[43]

---

[42] Where . . . is as specified in (79). Recall that the angled bracket convention interprets a schema of the form $X\langle[\alpha F]\rangle Y\langle Z\rangle W$ as an abbreviation for the two successive, disjunctively ordered rules $X[\alpha F]\,YZW$, $X[-\alpha F]\,YW$, where F is a feature and Z some string other than a single specified feature. (See Chapter Three, note 78.) We give a precise statement of these conventions in the Appendix to Chapter Eight.

[43] The schema (83) (p. 213) expands to:

(I) $\qquad \begin{bmatrix} -\text{tense} \\ +\text{back} \\ V \end{bmatrix} \rightarrow \begin{bmatrix} \langle +\text{tense}\rangle \\ -\text{round} \end{bmatrix} \Big/ \left[\overline{}\atop{+\text{high}}\right] C_0^1\,[-\text{cons}]$

(II) $\qquad \begin{bmatrix} -\text{tense} \\ +\text{back} \\ V \end{bmatrix} \rightarrow \begin{bmatrix} \langle +\text{tense}\rangle \\ -\text{round} \end{bmatrix} \Big/ \left[\begin{matrix}\overline{} \\ -\text{high} \\ \langle -\text{low}\rangle\end{matrix}\right]\langle\ldots\rangle$

Schema (I) expands to two disjunctively ordered rules, the first with the element in angled brackets and the second without it. But notice that the second of the two will never apply, since it is disjunctively ordered with respect to the first and has the same context as the first. Therefore schema (I) is identical to case (a) of (81). Notice that we are here assuming a different convention than in Chapter Three for rules of the form $X\langle Y\rangle Z$. (See note 24 in Chapter Three.) At a later point we will incorporate these conventions into a more general framework which will permit both alternatives.

    Schema (II) expands to two disjunctively ordered rules, the first of which tenses and unrounds the nonhigh nonlow vowel in the context represented by . . . , and the second of which unrounds the nonhigh low vowel everywhere.

$$
\left(83\right) \qquad \begin{bmatrix} -\text{tense} \\ +\text{back} \\ V \end{bmatrix} \rightarrow \begin{bmatrix} \langle +\text{tense} \rangle \\ -\text{round} \end{bmatrix} \Bigg/ \left\{ \begin{matrix} \left[\begin{array}{c} \overline{} \\ +\text{high} \end{array} \right] C_0^1 \,[-\text{cons}] & \text{(a)} \\ \\ \left[\begin{array}{c} \overline{} \\ -\text{high} \\ \langle -\text{low} \rangle \end{array} \right] \langle \dots \rangle & \langle \text{(b)} \rangle, \text{(c)} \end{matrix} \right.
$$

With this modification, the rule converts [u] to [ɨ] and [o] to [ʌ̄] in the stated contexts, as in cases (a) and (b) of (77) and (81); but it converts [ɔ] to [a], the corresponding nonround, nontense vowel. Thus underlying /kɔt/ will become [kat] by (83c) and, finally, [kɔt] by Rounding Adjustment.

Thus all three dialects, namely, General American, Eastern New England, and British Received Pronunciation, have the same lexical representations for the words in question and differ only in trivial modifications of rule (77).[44] In our terms, the three variants of this rule (namely, (77), (81), and (83)) are equally complex (see Chapter Eight, Section 1).

Let us return now to the vowel /o/. Consider such words as *courage*, *oven*, *covey*, *honey*, *money*, with phonetic [ʌ] as the vowel of the first syllable. Notice that in each case we can derive the vowel of the first syllable from underlying /o/; furthermore, this is the simplest (and for *courage*, *oven*, the only) source for these forms.[45] In the case of *courage*, we know that the first syllable terminates in a weak cluster since it reduces in *courageous*; the vowel, however, cannot be /u/ or it would become [yūw] in *courage*. There is no other possibility, apart from /o/, that will not require new, ad hoc rules. Therefore we must take the underlying representation to be /korǣge/. The only rule that applies to the first syllable, then, is Rounding Adjustment, which converts the vowel to [ʌ]. Since the underlying /o/ does not appear in the context (79), it does not undergo the processes summarized in (76). Velar Softening, Vowel Reduction, and *e*-Elision give the phonetic form [kʌrəj] (see p. 235, (133)). In the word *oven*, once again we cannot have an underlying /u/ since rule (77a) would apply, changing the vowel ultimately to /yūw/. If we take the underlying form to be /ovVn/, we will derive phonetic [ʌvən] by Rounding Adjustment. Notice that *oven*, with a voiced medial consonant, does not fit the context (79) and therefore does not undergo the processes of (76), as contrasted with *often*, with an unvoiced consonant following /o/, which does undergo these processes.[46]

Proceeding now with the discussion of phonetic [ɔ̄ʌ], we must still account for its occurrence before [rC] in *port*, *chord*, *force*. One possibility is that the underlying vowel is /o/ and that the second context of (79) should be extended to all sonorants (that is, to nasals and

---

[44] A further differentiation, into dialects which do and those which do not contrast *Roger* with *rajah*, *bother* with *father*, etc., in the first syllable, depends on a late phonetic rule involving [ā̄ʌ]. (See p. 205.)

[45] In the case of *honey*, *money*, a possible lexical representation is /hunni/, /munni/ (the double consonant being necessary to prevent application of rule (77a), which would result finally in phonetic [yūw]. The representations /honi/, /moni/ are more economical, however, in terms of features. Furthermore, in the case of *money* the latter representation has the advantage that only one feature change is then necessary to account for the alternation *money* (/moni/) – *monetary* (/monitAry/).

[46] It is possible that the underlying representation of *oven* is /ofVn/ and that the medial consonant is voiced intervocalically. There are cases of intervocalic voicing of [s], and of [θ] as well, but we have not been able to arrive at a satisfactory formulation of these processes. (See Section 5.)

A similar observation is relevant in the case of the alternation *cloth–clothe*. Speculating beyond what we have worked out in detail, one might suppose that *cloth* has the underlying form /klɔθ/, and *clothe* the underlying form /klɔθe/. Intervocalic voicing converts the latter to [klɔðe], and the rule mentioned in note 40 converts the former to [kloθ], which then becomes phonetic [klɔ̄ʌθ] in the manner just indicated. The form [klɔðe] becomes [klōðe] by rule (60b), which tenses [ɔ] before final CV, and then [klōwð] by the regular processes of Diphthongization, Vowel Shift, and *e*-Elision.

liquids, there being no vowels in this context). Suppose, then, that we replace (79) by (84):

$$\left(84\right) \qquad \underline{\hspace{1.5cm}} \left\{ \begin{array}{c} \left[\begin{array}{c} -\text{voice} \\ +\text{cont} \\ +\text{ant} \end{array} \right] \\ [+\text{sonor}]\,\text{C} \end{array} \right\}$$

The examples so far discussed are unchanged. But underlying /port/ will undergo a derivation exactly like that of (80), becoming, finally, [pɔ̄ʌrt].[47]

Consider now the words *told*, *hold*, etc., in which [o] occurs before [lC]. (See the discussion of Backness Adjustment (75)). The phonetic reflex of [o] in such cases is not to be distinguished from [ōw] resulting from underlying /ɔ̄/; thus *told* is phonetically identical to *tolled*, from /tɔ̄l#d/. We thus must account for the modification in (85):

$$\left(85\right) \qquad\qquad\qquad \text{o} \;\rightarrow\; \text{ōw} \;/ \underline{\hspace{1cm}}\text{l}$$

This is fairly simple within the present framework of rules. The segment [o] in the context ——*l*C will become [ʌ] by rule (77b) in the context (84). If we now block application of both rule (78), which converts [ʌ] to [ā], and the Glide Vocalization Rule, then the vowel [ʌ] will be assigned the glide [w] by the Diphthongization Rule, will be unaffected by Glide Vocalization and Vowel Shift, and will become [ō] by Rounding Adjustment. Thus [told] (which results from the application of rule (75) to underlying /tel/ before [d]) and underlying /hold/ will become phonetic [tōwld] and [hōwld], as required. The only modification of our rules is that rule (78) and Glide Vocalization must be blocked before [l]. We might provide for this by a lexical redundancy rule adding the feature specifications [−rule (78)] and [−Glide Vocalization] to lax vowels followed by [l] (thus, to the vowels of *tell*, *hold*, etc.) The fact that two exceptional properties must be noted raises doubts about the analysis. Observe that if we were not to block Glide Vocalization, the phonetic reflex of /ol/ would be [ōʌl], which would be acceptable if [ōwl] and [ōʌl] are not distinguished on phonetic grounds.

Still to be accounted for are occurrences of phonetic [āʌ] in final position and before [r], as in *spa*, *spar*, *spark*, *start*, and in words such as *balm*, *palm*, *calm*. The latter might be derived from underlying /ɔ/ in dialects which do not contrast the reflexes of /ɔ/ and /ā/, i.e., which do not contrast *bother–father*, *comet–calmer*, *bomb–balm*, etc. The situation is more interesting where these contrasts are retained, and underlying /ɔ/ is therefore excluded as a source. We cannot derive these words from underlying /bām/, etc., because /ā/ undergoes Rounding Adjustment in monosyllables, as we have seen (rule (68)). Conventional orthography suggests what is probably the optimal phonological solution. Notice, in fact, that although there are words such as *film*, *helm*, *culm* (from underlying /film/, /helm/, /kulm/), there are no cases of low vowels in the phonetic context ——*lm*. This suggests that words such as *balm* derive from underlying /bV*lm/, etc., where V* is some lax low vowel, by rules that convert /V*l/ to [āʌ]. Before turning to the choice of V* and the position

---

[47] The redundancy rule implied in note 40 will then have to be extended to the context ——*r*C for dialects in which only /...orC.../ appears and not /...ɔrC.../. This rule will state that lax back vowels become nonlow in the context ——*r*C. Notice that this extended rule, however, must be a rule of the phonology rather than a lexical redundancy rule, and must, in fact, follow the Laxing Rule (8). Thus, consider words such as *tear*, *swear*, *bear*, from underlying /tær/, /swær/, /bær/. With past and perfect inflection, these forms undergo Backness Adjustment (75) and become [tōr], etc. In the perfect, furthermore, /+Vn/ becomes [+n], and we have [tōr+n], etc. The Laxing Rule (8) converts this to [tɔrn], which must undergo the rule making lax vowels nonlow in the context ——*r*C, so that it will eventually become [tōʌrn] (like [pɔ̄ʌrt], etc.)

and form of these rules, let us consider the other examples of phonetic [āʌ] mentioned at the outset of this paragraph.

Words such as *spa* seem rather difficult to account for. Clearly the underlying vowel cannot be /ā/, for Rounding Adjustment would give [spɔ̄ʌ] (like *law*, *flaw*). It cannot be any other tense vowel, for Vowel Shift would give a form from which [āʌ] cannot be derived; and even if the underlying vowel is lax, it will be tensed in final position by rule (20) and, being stressed, will undergo Vowel Shift, again giving a form which cannot become final [āʌ]. In fact, all of the tense vowels do appear in final position under stress (e.g., *fly*, *flee*, *flay*, *cow*, *coo*, *mow*, *boy*, *law*, from underlying /flī/, /flē/, /flǣ/, /kū/, /kō/, /mō/, /bǣ/, /lā/, respectively). Evidently, the only possibility is to represent *spa* with a lax vowel which is somehow prevented from being tensed by rule (20). We can block this rule, which tenses final vowels, by assigning some segment in the position after the vowel. This segment cannot be a vowel for the vowel of *spa* will become tense in prevocalic position. It cannot be a true consonant or a liquid since, in general, these segments do not drop when postvocalic in final position. It is, therefore, best to assume that these words end with a glide. We must, then, add a rule inserting some glide after the vowel of *spa* before the Tensing Rule (20) applies. Furthermore, consideration of the framework of already established rules indicates that the inserted glide must be [w], which will become [u] by the Glide Vocalization Rule (74) and will then undergo Vowel Shift to [ʌ], providing the centering off-glide needed in the phonetic representation [spāʌ]. We must therefore select as the underlying vowel of *spa* some lax vowel V* which will permit vocalization of the glide to take place and will ultimately become phonetic [ā]. In fact, we can achieve this result, adding only one rule, if we take V* to be /æ/.

Suppose, then, we represent *spa* as /spæ/ and add to the grammar a rule of *w*-Insertion, rule (86), to precede the Tensing Rule (20):

$$\left(86\right) \qquad \phi \;\rightarrow\; w \;/\; æ\!\rule{1.2em}{0.4pt}\!\#$$

We will then have the following derivation for *spa*:

$$\left(87\right)$$

spæ	
spæw	RULE (86)
spæu	RULE (74)
spæʌ	VOWEL SHIFT; ROUNDING ADJUSTMENT
spaʌ	BACKNESS ADJUSTMENT (39)
spāʌ	RULE (5)

The rule of *w*-Insertion, which is entirely new, precedes the Tensing Rule (20) and permits the preceding vowel to remain lax, as required. The Glide Vocalization Rule (74) converts [w] to [u] when [w] follows a vowel that has the same value for the features "round" and "high." In previous examples this rule applied after [ū] and [ā]; since [æ] is [−round] and [−high], the rule applies after this vowel as well, and gives the third line of derivation (87). Vowel Shift and Rounding Adjustment apply in the usual way to give the fourth line of the derivation. To derive the next line, we apply the Backness Adjustment Rule (39), modified so as to yield [āw] as the reflex of /ū/. In this form, the rule is:

$$\left(88\right) \qquad \begin{bmatrix} +\text{low} \\ V \end{bmatrix} \;\rightarrow\; [+\text{back}] \;/\; \rule{1.2em}{0.4pt}[-\text{cons}]$$

We have simplified rule (39) by dropping the feature [−vocalic] from the context (see p. 189). In the form (88), the Backness Adjustment Rule converts [ǣy], which results by Vowel Shift from underlying /ī/, to [āy]; it converts [ǣy] to [ɔ̄y] (see Section 4.3.3); and it converts [æʌ] to [aʌ] to yield the fifth line of the derivation (87). Recall that this form of the rule is designed for the dialect in which the phonetic reflex of /ū/ is [āw]. The rule must be slightly complicated, now, for the dialect in which the phonetic reflex is [æw].[48] The final line of the derivation results from the application of (89), which we have already presupposed, although we have not actually stated it:

$$\left(89\right) \qquad\qquad a \;\rightarrow\; [+\text{tense}]$$

This rule is presupposed by rule (5), which converts [ɔ] to [ā] (as in *cot, stop, conic*, etc.) Rule (5) involves unrounding and tensing. The unrounding will, of course, be a special case of Rounding Adjustment. Therefore (5) can be simplified to (89), which will apply in the derivation (87) to give the phonetic representation.

In summary, the only new rule is (86), the rule of *w*-Insertion.[49] Furthermore, there are several considerations that determine the underlying vowel of *spa* to be /æ/, as in the orthography.

Consider now phonetic [āʌ] in the words *spar, spark*, etc. We can account for these by extending rule (86) to (90):

$$\left(90\right) \qquad\qquad \phi \;\rightarrow\; w \;/\; æ\!\underline{}\!\begin{Bmatrix} rC \\ (r)\# \end{Bmatrix}$$

If we now take the underlying vowel to be /æ/, we derive the desired phonetic representations by derivations that are parallel to (87). Alternations such as *bar–barrier, bar–barrister, par–parity, car–carriage* lend some slight additional plausibility to the derivation of [ā] from /æ/ before [r].

Having outlined a possible solution to the problem of *spa, spar, spark*, etc., let us return to the forms *balm, calm*, and so on. We saw that these must apparently be derived from underlying /bV*lm/, /kV*lm/, where V* is some lax low vowel that we have not yet fully specified. Given the framework already established, the simplest solution seems to be to extend rule (90) to the context ——*lm* and to add a rule dropping [l] after the insertion

[48] For the dialect in which Backness Adjustment also applies to [āw], to give [æw], as in (39), we must further restrict the rule so that it applies to back vowels only in preglide position; otherwise [āʌ] (as in *father*) and [ɔ̄ʌ] (as in *law*) will become nonback. This modification is straightforward, but it complicates the rule.

[49] We have very little to say, unfortunately, about the interesting question of how complexity of the lexicon should be measured against complication of the phonology in evaluating a grammar. Examples of the sort just considered are relevant to this, although the obviously tentative nature of the analysis we have just offered prevents us from relying on such evidence too heavily. It seems fairly clear that words such as *spa, pa* are not exceptions that must be independently memorized but, rather, follow from general rules. If true, this means that the phonetic form of these words should not be accounted for by idiosyncratic lexical specification. Notice that we could have accounted for the phonetic forms of *spa, pa* by deriving them from underlying /spā/, /pā/, which are differentiated from *paw* /pā/, which becomes [pɔ̄ʌ] in the usual way, by the single feature [−Rounding Adjustment Rule]. Thus the alternatives seem to be these: (1) mark words such as *spa, pa* as exceptions with the single feature [−Rounding Adjustment Rule]; (2) incorporate rule (86) in the grammar. If it is correct that these words are "regular," not "exceptional," then (2) must be the correct alternative, and the evaluation measure must be so designed as to meet the empirical condition that having rule (86) in the phonology is less complex than adding the features in question to the lexicon.

of [w]. We can then take V* to be /æ/. We therefore extend rule (90) to (91) and derive *balm, calm*, etc., along the lines of (87).[50]

$$\left(91\right) \qquad \phi \;\rightarrow\; w \;\Big/\; æ \underline{\quad} \begin{Bmatrix} rC \\ (\begin{Bmatrix} r \\ lm \end{Bmatrix}) \# \end{Bmatrix}$$

It might be that (91) should be simplified by allowing *w*-Insertion after [ə] as well as [æ]. In this case we might account for the *horse–hoarse* contrast in certain dialects by representing *horse* as /hɔrs/, as before, and representing *hoarse* as /hɔrs/. *Horse* becomes phonetic [hɔʌrs] in the manner described earlier (see (84)). According to Kenyon and Knott, the vowel of *hoarse* in such dialects is [ōw]. To account for this pronunciation, we add a rule tensing [ɔ] before [w], after the Diphthongization Rule and before the Vowel Shift Rule. Then /hɔrs/ becomes [hɔwrs] by the proposed simplification of (91), and the new tensing rule converts this to [hōwrs]. Finally Vowel Shift gives [hōwrs], as required.

Notice that phonetic [ɔʌ] in *salt, fault, somersault, scald*, etc., can be derived by the usual method for this vocalic nucleus, namely, from underlying /ā/ in monosyllables and /ū/ elsewhere, since /lt/ and /ld/, being dental clusters, may be preceded by tense vowels in formatives. There are, in fact, phonetic [ælC] clusters, as in *alp, scalp, formaldehyde, altitude*, so that we would not want to derive phonetic [ɔʌlC] from underlying /ælC/ in general.

There are a few other obvious remarks about tense low vowels. For example, Backness Adjustment applies to [æ] after [w], giving [ā] instead of the expected [æ] in *squalid, equality, wallet, want*, etc.; and there is a further step of Rounding Adjustment after [w] before liquids, as in *warn, squall*, and so on. It should also be noted that the vowels of words such as *tear, tore, pale* are phonetically low in many dialects, necessitating either a restriction on the Vowel Shift Rule before liquids or a late rule affecting mid tense vowels before liquids. In general, there is much more to say about vowel-liquid clusters beyond the few remarks that we have made, but we have not investigated this in any detail and will drop the matter here.

4.3.8. ROUNDING ADJUSTMENT

We have so far come across the following cases of Rounding Adjustment following Vowel Shift:

$$\left(92\right) \qquad \begin{array}{lll} \text{(a)} & \mathrm{ï} & \rightarrow & [+\mathrm{round}] \\ \text{(b)} & \bar{\Lambda} & \rightarrow & [+\mathrm{round}] \\ \text{(c)} & \bar{a} & \rightarrow & [+\mathrm{round}] \\ \text{(d)} & \bar{\mathrm{ɔ}} & \rightarrow & [-\mathrm{round}] \\ \text{(e)} & \mathrm{ï} & \rightarrow & [+\mathrm{round}] \\ \text{(f)} & a & \rightarrow & [+\mathrm{round}] \\ \text{(g)} & o & \rightarrow & [-\mathrm{round}] \\ \text{(h)} & ɔ & \rightarrow & [-\mathrm{round}] \end{array}$$

The first case is the rule that applies to give phonetic [yūw] (p. 194). Case (b) gives phonetic [ōw] as in *told, sold* (p. 214). Case (c) gives phonetic [ɔʌ] as in *law, fraud* (p. 206). Case (d) gives phonetic [āw] or [æw] (p. 189). Case (e) gives phonetic [u] as in *pull, bush* (p. 204). Case (f) gives phonetic [ɔ] as in *cot, conic*, in British Received Pronunciation (pp. 212–13).

---

[50] We do not give (91) in the most compact possible form since it is quite likely that a deeper investigation of vowels before liquids will lead to a modification of the rules that we are suggesting here as a first approximation.

Case (g) gives phonetic [ʌ] in *courage, money* (p. 213). Case (h) gives [a] which becomes phonetic [ā] by rule (89) in General American *cot, conic* (p. 167).

Summarizing these facts, we can formulate the Rounding Adjustment Rule as (93):

$$
(93) \quad \begin{bmatrix} \alpha\text{round} \\ +\text{back} \end{bmatrix} \rightarrow [-\alpha\text{round}] \;\Big/\; \begin{cases} \begin{bmatrix} \underline{\quad\quad} \\ -\text{tense} \end{bmatrix} & \text{(a)} \\[1.5em] \begin{bmatrix} \underline{\quad\quad} \\ \beta\text{low} \\ \beta\text{round} \\ +\text{tense} \end{bmatrix} & \text{(b)} \\[2em] \underline{\quad\quad}\,V & \text{(c)} \end{cases}
$$

Case (a) of (93) accommodates (92e–h), which are the only lax back vowels that appear in derivations at the stage when the Rounding Adjustment Rule applies. Case (b) of (93) applies to the tense back vowels which have the same values for the features "low" and "round," that is, to the low round vowel [ɔ̄] and the two nonlow nonround vowels [ɨ] and [ʌ̄]. It thus accommodates cases (a), (b), and (d) of (92). Case (c) of (93) corresponds to case (c) of (92). The vowel [ā] is, in fact, the only one that is followed by a vowel at this stage so that the simplification of (92c) to (93c) is appropriate. To see why this is so, notice first that the only back vowels that can be followed by vowels at this stage are the low vowels [ā] and [ɔ̄].[51] But note further that the ordering of the three cases of (93) is conjunctive. Therefore, there will be no cases of [ɔ̄V] at the point where case (c) applies, since all cases of [ɔ̄] will have been unrounded by case (b). Therefore, (93c) has precisely the effect of (92c).

Although the three cases of (93) are conjunctively ordered, it is impossible for case (b) to apply to a segment to which case (a) has applied since the contexts are disjoint, and it is impossible for both case (c) and case (a) to apply since there are no nontense back vowels followed by vowels. It is possible, however, for case (c) to apply to a segment formed by case (b). This possibility is illustrated by the derivation of the vocalic nucleus [ɔ̄ʌ] from underlying /ū/. To clarify what is involved, we repeat (73), the derivations of *mountain* and *maudlin*, with the final step of Rounding Adjustment now made explicit in terms of rule (93):

(94)			
	mūntən	mūdlin	
	mūwntən	mūwdlin	DIPHTHONGIZATION
		mūudlin	GLIDE VOCALIZATION (74)
	mɔ̄wntən	mɔ̄odlin	VOWEL SHIFT
		mɔ̄ʌdlin	RULE (93a)
	māwntən	māʌdlin	RULE (93b)
		mɔ̄ʌdlin	RULE (93c)

We see, then, that the Rounding Adjustment Rule (93) has just the desired effects, covering the cases summarized in (92) in such a way as to account for the fact that [ɔ̄] remains rounded before a centering glide but not before a labializing glide.

The joint effect of the Rounding Adjustment and Backness Adjustment Rules is to centralize the vowels originating from underlying /ɨ/ and /ū/. Our analysis postulates that

---

[51] Recall that lax vowels have been tensed in prevocalic position by rule (20) and that glides have been inserted after all tense vowels by the Diphthongization Rule. Consequently, the only cases of VV are those in which the second V results from a [w] glide by rule (74), the rule of Glide Vocalization. As we have seen, Glide Vocalization applies only after the vowels [æ], [ā], and [ū]. The first of these is irrelevant, being nonback at this stage of derivation. The vowel [ū] has become [ɔ̄] by Vowel Shift. Consequently, only [ā] and [ɔ̄] can fall under (93c).

these processes of centralization follow Vowel Shift. An alternative analysis that deserves consideration would be to place the centralization rules before the Vowel Shift Rule in the ordering. We have investigated this possibility in some detail (following a suggestion by R. Stockwell) and have come to the tentative conclusion that it is not workable. The reasons are of some interest. The major phenomena for which the Vowel Shift and centralization rules are designed (namely, alternations such as *divine–divinity*, *profound–profundity*) can, in fact, be handled about as well with either analysis. But the subsidiary phenomena that we have discussed in the last few sections—specifically, the irregular verbs that can be explained in terms of double application of Vowel Shift (e.g., *drive–drove*; see p. 202), the various minor back vowel alternations, etc.—cannot, so far as we can see, be subsumed under even partial generalizations if the alternative ordering is accepted. These observations would tend to suggest that the ordering is determined not by the basic class of examples but by the subsidiary and marginal cases that can be brought under partial generalizations with one ordering but not the other.

Considerations involving general conditions on plausible phonological rules which we discuss in Chapter Nine suggest that there is a principled reason for the ordering of processes that we propose. Historical aspects of this problem are discussed in Chapter Six.

5. *Further consequences of the Vowel Shift Rule*

We have so far discussed the Vowel Shift Rule only in connection with vowel alternations. However, since consonant alternations are determined in part by vocalic context, we might expect to find effects of the Vowel Shift Rule in the consonant system, and this is in fact the case.

Consider alternations such as those illustrated below:

$$(95)$$
(a) *criticism–criticize–critical*
(b) *medicine–medical–medicate*
(c) *allege–allegation*
(d) *rigid–rigor*
(e) *regal–regicide*
(f) *analogous–analogize*

In each of the words *criticism*, *medicine*, *rigid*, the consonant in boldface undergoes softening before a nonlow nonback vowel (which may be [e] as well as [i]). This process of Velar Softening, one case of which we gave earlier as (6), we now restate as (96):

$$(96) \qquad \begin{Bmatrix} g & \to & \check{j} \\ k & \to & s \end{Bmatrix} \Big/ \underline{\qquad} \begin{bmatrix} -\text{low} \\ -\text{back} \\ V \end{bmatrix}$$

We observe, once again, that (96) can be analyzed into several steps and that it applies only to certain lexically marked elements.

Notice that Velar Softening must precede the Vowel Reduction Rule. After Vowel Reduction the boldface elements of *critical*, *medicine*, *medical*, *rigid*, *rigor* are all followed by the same vowel (which is, furthermore, back). Before the application of the Vowel Reduction Rule, on the other hand, the appropriate context for (96) is still in evidence: the phonological segments which do soften are followed by [i], and those that do not are followed by [æ] or the vowel of the affix *-or*.

Additional information bearing on the position of (96) in the sequence of rules is provided by the words *criticize, regicide, analogize, medicate, allegation* in (95). In these examples we have the [s], [ǰ] variants of /k/, /g/ in the phonetic context —— [āy] and the [k], [g] variants in the phonetic context —— [ēy]. Both cases seem to contradict the Velar Softening Rule (96). However, we observe that in these examples the underlying forms are [kritikīz], [rēgikīd], [ænæləgīz], [medikæt], [ælegætiVn], respectively. Thus, in the underlying forms, the velars that soften are followed by nonback nonlow vowels, and those that do not soften are followed by vowels that are back or low. We conclude, then, that rule (96) must also precede the Vowel Shift Rule, which changes the nonlow vowel [ī] to low [æ], and low [æ] to nonlow [ē]. Thus we have derivations such as (97) for the examples of (95):

$$\left(97\right)$$

	(a) rég+æl	(b) rég+i+kìd	
		réǰ+i+sìd	RULE (96)
		réǰ+i+sìd	LAXING RULE (19b)
	réyg+æl	réǰ+i+sìyd	DIPHTHONGIZATION (21)
	ríygəl	réǰəsàyd	VOWEL SHIFT (43), VOWEL REDUCTION

All three occurrences of phonological velars in (97) appear in the context of a following vowel which, in its phonetic quality, does not permit softening (namely, back [ə] or [ā]). Nevertheless, both velars of (97b) soften by rule (96) because the *underlying* vowel following them is nonback and nonlow, while the velar of (97a) does not soften because the underlying vowel following it is low. Here, then, is new justification for the Vowel Shift Rule, entirely independent of that adduced in Section 4.

Only one further comment is needed concerning the examples of (95). We must account for the softening of the phonological /g/ of *allege*. To soften, this segment must be followed by a nonback nonlow vowel, which drops in final position. Evidently, this must be the vowel [e], which has the appropriate features and which is dropped, when final, by the *e*-Elision Rule (Chapter Three, rule (155)). We conclude, then, that *allege* must have the phonological representation /ælege/.[52] These observations give independent support for the rule of *e*-Elision.

Along the same lines, we can now provide an explanation for the alternation [yūw]–[ʌ], as in *reduce-reduction*.[53] If we take the underlying form to be /re=duke/, where = is the boundary symbol discussed in Chapter Three (p. 94), and the stem is assigned to the category of elements that undergo derivational processes and Velar Softening, then we will have the following derivations:

$$\left(98\right)$$

	re=duke	re=duke+ǣt+iVn	
		re=duk+t+iVn	READJUSTMENT RULES
	re=duse		RULE (96)
	re=dīse		RULE (77a)
	re=dyīse		RULE (50)
	re=dyīwse		DIPHTHONGIZATION (21)
		re=dok+t+iVn	VOWEL SHIFT (43), CASE (63)
	re=dyūwse	re=dʌk+t+iVn	ROUNDING ADJUSTMENT (93)
	rədyūws	rədʌkšən	(RULES TO BE GIVEN LATER)

---

[52] Alternatively, /ad=lege/ (see p. 222). Either choice will lead to the correct stress assignment by the rules of Chapter Three. Notice that [e] drops here before *-ation*, exactly as in *reduction* (in which case [æ] of *-ation* also drops—see p. 201) and many other forms.

[53] In some dialects the alternation is [ūw]–[ʌ] because of the rule deleting [y] which was mentioned in note 27. We return to this matter in Section 6.

The only special feature of *reduce* is that, along with quite a few other verbs, it drops [(V)+æ] when suffixed with *-ation*, giving the second line of (98). To obtain the alternants [rīydyūws] and [rīydʌkšən], the prefix might be represented with tense /ē/; alternatively, the Tensing Rule might be slightly revised.

To conclude this discussion, we discuss one additional example illustrating the Velar Softening Rule (96). We had occasion in Chapter Three (p. 95) to refer to a rule that we restate for now as (99):

$$\left(99 \right) \qquad\qquad s \;\rightarrow\; [+\text{voice}] \;/\; V = \underline{\quad} V$$

Thus, in prefix-stem verbs, for example, we find pairs such as those of (100), where the /s/ of the stems *-sume, -serve, -sist, -sign* is unvoiced in the first column, since the prefix ends in a consonant, but voiced in the second, where the prefix ends in a vowel:

$$\left(100 \right)$$

consume	*resume*
conserve	*preserve, deserve*
consist, insist, persist	*resist*
consign	*resign, design*

Notice, however, that among the prefix-stem verbs there are certain pairs, such as *incite–recite, concede–recede*, which seem to contradict rule (99) since phonetic [s] rather than [z] occurs intervocalically following =. We now have an explanation for this. We give the stems *-cite, -cede* the underlying representations /kīt/, /kēd/, respectively, assigning them to the category of elements subject to derivational processes and Velar Softening. As we have just observed, Velar Softening precedes Vowel Shift. Thus, after Velar Softening yields [re = sīt], [re = sēd] for *recite, recede*, these become [re = sāyt] and [re = sīyd], respectively, by regular processes that we have already discussed. To prevent the voicing of [s] to [z] in these forms, it is necessary only to have rule (99) precede rule (96) (more properly, the last stage of (96), which gives [s]). In these and similar cases, the required phonetic output will be obtained if we enter the forms in the lexicon in the manner suggested by conventional orthography, which here, once again, turns out to be quite close to the correct underlying representation.

Consider next the following forms:

$$\left(101 \right)$$

extend	*contend*
expel	*compel*
exclude	*conclude*
exceed	*concede*
excite	*incite*

It is clear, from the first three pairs, that one of the prefixes of the paradigm we are concerned with is [eks]. We have just seen, furthermore, that the underlying stems in *concede, incite*— and, therefore, in *exceed, excite*—are /kēd/, /kīt/, with /k/ becoming [s] by Velar Softening. Thus *exceed* and *excite* must, at an intermediate stage of derivation, have the form [eks = sīyd], [eks = sāyt], respectively (after Vowel Shift). These words, however, do not have [ss] sequences phonetically, showing that there must be a rule that simplifies [s = s] clusters to [s]. As we have already seen (cf. rule (156) in Chapter Three, p. 148), this is simply a special case of the general rule of Cluster Simplification that replaces or deletes one C of a CC sequence where the two consonants are identical. Along with the rule (99) of *s*-Voicing, then, there is the rule of Cluster Simplification. In words such as *exceed, excel*, we have an unvoiced phonetic [ks] cluster produced by Cluster Simplification applied to [ks=s] (originally from [ks=k]). A rule voicing prestress [ks] clusters (compare *examine, exalt,* etc.—see (119), p. 228) is blocked by the cluster of three consonants.

Among the prefixes are also *ad-, ab-, sus-, sub-,* as in *adhere, admire, abhor, abduce, suspect, sustain, subdue, subsist.* Consider now, alongside of the examples of (100), such words as:

$$\left(102\right) \qquad\qquad\qquad\qquad \textit{assume, assist, assign}$$

In these forms we have phonetic [s] in intervocalic post-boundary position, in apparent contradiction to rule (99). Notice, however, that there are no forms **adsume, *adsist, *adsign,* just as there are no **adtest, *abpear* alongside of *attest, appear.* This arrangement of occurring forms indicates that the prefixes *ab-* and *ad-* undergo assimilation of the final consonant under certain conditions, with the resulting clusters later simplifying by the general Cluster Simplification Rule. Thus we have the rule:

$$\left(103\right) \qquad\qquad\qquad C \;\rightarrow\; C^* \;\; / \; \text{æ} \rule{2em}{0.4pt} = C^*$$

where C and C* are both noncoronal (i.e., labial or velar) or both coronal (i.e., dental or palato-alveolar). Thus [æd=test]→[æt=test]→[ætest] (by Cluster Simplification); [æb=pēr]→[æp=pēr]→[æpīyr] (*appear*); [æd=sist]→[æs=sist]→[æsist] (*assist*); and so on. The [s] in the forms of (102) thus remains unvoiced because the [s=s] sequence blocks (99) and only later simplifies to [s] by Cluster Simplification. In a similar way we can account for sets such as *resemble–dissemble–assemble,* with [z] in the first form, rule (99) having applied, and [s] in the other two forms, rule (99) having been blocked by the cluster which later simplifies.

Quite similar remarks apply to the prefixes *sus-, sub-.* Again, we have assimilation (analogous to (103)) and simplification, giving forms such as *suffice, support, succumb.*

Notice, incidentally, that rule (103) is actually somewhat more general, since we also have partial assimilation of the final nasal of a prefix, as in the words *compel, combat* versus *conceive, contend.*

Finally, consider the following words:

$$\left(104\right) \qquad\qquad\qquad\qquad \textit{accede, succeed, suggest}$$

By the symmetry of the paradigms we are considering, these must have the underlying representations of (105), although they have the phonetic representations of (106) (with, possibly, reduction of the vowel in the prefix):

$$\left(105\right) \qquad\qquad\qquad \text{/ab=kēd/, /sub=kēd/, /sub=gest/}$$

$$\left(106\right) \qquad\qquad\qquad \text{[æksīyd], [sʌksīyd], [sʌgǰest]}$$

The phonetic forms of (106) result from the underlying representations of (105) in the following way. First, the Assimilation Rule (103) (with the generalization to *sub-* mentioned above) applies to give the forms of (107):

$$\left(107\right) \qquad\qquad\qquad \text{[æk=kēd], [suk=kēd], [sug=gest]}$$

Next, Velar Softening applies, followed by Diphthongization and Vowel Shift in the usual way, giving, finally, (106). Hence the forms of (106) result from perfectly regular phonological processes and are quite analogous to those of (100), (101), (102), despite superficial differences.

The examples we have discussed in this chapter by no means exhaust the phonology of the English vowel system. However, they do cover what seem to us some of the most difficult and crucial aspects of vocalic phonology, and they illustrate the form that this aspect of a phonological description must apparently assume.

6. *The consonant system of English*

Although it is not without its problems, the consonant system seems less interesting than the vowel system, and we will not treat it in anything like the same detail. We have already discussed the analysis of consonants into true consonants, glides, and liquids, and have pointed out that there is a cross-classification into obstruents and sonorants, the latter category containing nasals, liquids, and glides (along with the vowels). We will be concerned here only with obstruents and their relation to glides.

The obstruents may be analyzed in terms of the features [±coronal] and [±anterior] in a way that corresponds roughly with the traditional analysis into dentals, palato-alveolars, labials, and velars. (See Chapter Seven for further discussion of our conception of the phonetic framework.)

$\left(108\right)$

	+coronal	−coronal
+anterior	dental	labial
−anterior	palato-alveolar	velar

We assume that of the segments listed in Table I, Section 3, the lexicon of English contains the following examples in the four categories of (108):

$\left(109\right)$

dental	t, d		s, z	θ, ð
palato-alveolar	č, ǰ		š, ž	
labial	p, b	f, v		
velar	k, g	kʷ, gʷ		x (xʷ)

Thus each category has stops and continuants, the dental continuants being further divided into [±strident]. Among the velars, the stops are subdivided into [±round]; the labialized (rounded) consonants are interpreted as the sequences [kw], [gw], and [xw], respectively. The velar continuant /x/ becomes phonetic [h]. The palato-alveolars (particularly when voiced), the rounded velars, and the velar continuant have limited distributions in the lexicon, but we will not go into the readjustment rules needed to describe these facts. Recall that there is a further lexical classification of velar stops in terms of the feature [±deriv], specifically, in terms of susceptibility to Velar Softening. We will represent the velar stops that belong to the "derivable" category and undergo Velar Softening as /kᵈ/, /gᵈ/, contrasting with /k/ and /g/. Among the readjustment rules, there are many that apply to specific derivable formatives; for example, the rule (110):

$\left(110\right)$

$$t \;\rightarrow\; d \;\; / = \begin{cases} mi \rule{1cm}{0.4pt} +ive \\ ver \rule{1cm}{0.4pt} +ion \end{cases}$$

This will account for the spirantization of /t/ in *submissive* (by rule (120a) below, with subsequent devoicing) and the voicing of /t/ in *subversion* (which then becomes [ž] by later rules). There will be no further discussion of these readjustment rules.

We will present here what seems to be the core of the system of rules involving consonants, listing the rules in the order in which they appear, with a few comments about each. Several illustrative derivations will follow the presentation of the rules.

If it is correct to take /x/ and /xʷ/ as the segments underlying [h] and [hw], as might be suggested on grounds of lexical simplicity (see also p. 234), then we must add a rule converting the velar fricative into a glide:

$$\left(111\right) \qquad \begin{bmatrix} -\text{cor} \\ -\text{ant} \\ +\text{cont} \end{bmatrix} \;\rightarrow\; h$$

We must now give a rule inserting [w] after rounded velars, that is, after /kʷ/, /gʷ/, and [hʷ] (resulting from (111)):

$$\left(112\right) \qquad \phi \;\rightarrow\; w \;/\; \begin{bmatrix} +\text{round} \\ C \end{bmatrix}\!\!\underline{\quad}$$

Rule (112) inserts [w] after the velar in words such as *square*, *language*, and (in some dialects) *when* [hwen]. This rule might be combined with (91), which also inserts [w].

We turn next to the Velar Softening Rule, which has been discussed several times (see (96)). This rule converts /g/ to [j] and /k/ to [s]. To convert /g/ to [j], we must modify /g/ with respect to the features "coronal" and "strident." Thus the rule affecting /g/ is (113):

$$\left(113\right) \qquad g^d \;\rightarrow\; \begin{bmatrix} +\text{cor} \\ +\text{strid} \end{bmatrix} \;/\; \underline{\quad} \begin{bmatrix} -\text{back} \\ -\text{low} \\ -\text{cons} \end{bmatrix}$$

If we were to generalize rule (113) simply by extending it to /kᵈ/, then it would convert /kᵈ/ to [č], which would fall together with the original /č/ of *chair*, *chastity*, *church*, etc. We therefore instead amend rule (113) so that it assigns to /kᵈ/, but not to /gᵈ/, the feature [+anterior] as well as the features [+strident], [+coronal]. (As mentioned in Section 3, the features "high," "back," and "low" play no crucial role in the consonant system of English, within the present framework, and will in general not appear in the rules of this section. See however, Chapter 9, Section 4, for a reformulation of the Velar Softening Rule in a revised framework.)

$$\left(114\right) \quad \text{VELAR SOFTENING}$$

$$\begin{bmatrix} -\text{cont} \\ -\text{ant} \\ +\text{deriv} \\ \langle -\text{voice} \rangle \end{bmatrix} \;\rightarrow\; \begin{bmatrix} +\text{cor} \\ +\text{strid} \\ \langle +\text{ant} \rangle \end{bmatrix} \;/\; \underline{\quad} \begin{bmatrix} -\text{back} \\ -\text{low} \\ -\text{cons} \end{bmatrix}$$

Rule (114) abbreviates two rules, the first of which changes /kᵈ/ to [c] (i.e., the dental affricate) and the second of which converts /gᵈ/ to [j]. The change of [c] to [s], which will complete the process of velar softening for /kᵈ/, will be effected by a later rule. Observe that rule (114) converts /kᵈ/ into a segment which is distinct from every other segment.

The rules mentioned so far must be quite early in the ordering. As we shall see later, they must precede the rules of Tensing and *e*-Elision, among others. We may, in fact, place them either before or immediately after the rules of stress assignment. Notice, however, that these are rules of word phonology, not cyclic rules.

At this point in the ordering, then, we reach the rules of the stress cycle discussed in the preceding chapter. Of particular relevance here are two rules that were dealt with in Chapter Three, one of which (rule (130), p. 130) converts [y] to [i] and the other of which (rule (57), p. 87) converts [i] to [y]. We restate these two rules as (115) and (116), respectively:

$$\left(115\right) \qquad\qquad y \;\rightarrow\; i \;\; / \; C\text{——}[-\text{seg}]$$

$$\left(116\right) \qquad\qquad i \;\rightarrow\; y \;\; / \; \begin{bmatrix} +\text{cor} \\ C \end{bmatrix} + \text{——} V$$

Rule (115) converts formative-final /y/ to [i] (ultimately, [īy]) in words such as *industry*, *oligarchy*, *industrial*, *industrous*. As we noted in Chapter Three, rule (115) must be in the cycle (and must clearly follow the rules of stress assignment if *-y* is to assign stress in the appropriate way). Thus the word *felonious*, for example, will have the underlying representation $[_A[_N\text{felən}+y]_N \text{əs}]_A$. In the first cycle, primary stress is assigned to the first syllable and /y/ becomes [i] by rule (115). Thus we begin the second cycle with the form $[_A\overset{1}{\text{felən}}+i+\text{əs}]_A$, and the rules of stress assignment, together with those discussed earlier in this chapter, give the phonetic representation [fəlównīyəs].

Now consider rule (116). As noted in Chapter Three, this rule too must be in the cycle, to account for the placement of primary stress in words such as *convéntional*. Therefore both rule (115) and rule (116) must be in the cycle, after the rules of stress assignment.

Rule (115) seems correct as it stands, but rule (116) requires somewhat closer study. As given it converts [i] to [y] in the context $C+\text{——}V$, where C is a dental or palato-alveolar. It does not apply where C is a labial (cf. *oblivion*, *champion*, *marsupial*, etc.)[54] or a velar (*Kentuckian*, *tracheal*—recall that velars of the phonological category [+deriv] have, at this point, become dentals if unvoiced or palato-alveolars if voiced). But when the consonant is dental or palato-alveolar, the situation is fairly complex. Thus the rule converting [i] to [y] applies to the words in Column I of (117) but not to those in Column II:

$$\left(117\right)$$

	I	II
(a)	*rebellious*	*punctilious*
	bilious	*familial*
	Pennsylvania	*Lithuania*
(b)	*pavilion*	*quaternion*
	battalion	*accordion*
	onion	*enchiridion*
	companion	*collodion*
		ganglion
(c)		*colonial*
		testimonial
		felonious
		ignominious
(d)	*religious*	*criterion*
	admonition	*clarion*

(continued)

---

[54] The word *savior* is an exception, if pronounced [sʌvyər].

$\left(117\right)$ *continued*   (e) *partial*   *cardial*
                                          officious   *invidious*
                                          Russian   *lithium*

                                      (f) *invasion*
                                           confession

Furthermore, there is nearly free variation in forms such as *mammalian, marginalia, Mendelian* and near contrasts such as *ingenious* versus *genial*.

Such facts suggest that the applicability of rule (116) is rather idiosyncratic and that there must be a feature [±rule (116)] that categorizes certain formatives containing [i]. The worst possible case would be that this feature is entirely free. However, closer inspection of examples such as those in (117) suggests that there are redundancies that can be exploited.

Consider first the examples under case (a). It seems that in the items of Column I there is some motivation for a formative boundary before the segment [i] that is subject to the rule, while in the items of Column II there is no reason to place a formative boundary in this position. These cases, therefore, are already taken care of by rule (116), which applies only to items with + in the appropriate position, and we can limit the feature [±rule (116)] to formatives that begin with [i]. It will then follow that rule (116) will not apply to words such as those of Column II, case (a), if the underlying forms are /puNktili+əs/, /fæmily+æl/,[55] /liθuæniæ/. If correct, this is a considerable improvement.

Consider now case (b) of (117). Notice first that there is good motivation for assuming that all of these words are phonologically represented in the form / . . . iVn/ rather than / . . . yVn/. There are two reasons for this: first, the representation / . . . yVn/ would violate otherwise valid restrictions on the distribution of /y/ in the lexicon; second, the placement of stress requires the analysis with /iVn/. Furthermore, except for the words *quaternion* and *ganglion*, all words with terminal *-ion*, where this is not a nominalization element, fall into Column II when the consonant is [d] and into Column I when it is any other consonant. Therefore, continuing with the assumption made in connection with case (a), we can add a readjustment rule assigning formative boundary in the context C——*iVn*, when C ≠ [d]. The only exceptions, then, are *quaternion* and *ganglion*. These are also the only examples in which the segment [i] which is subject to the rule follows a CS cluster (where S is a sonorant). We therefore restrict the readjustment rule that inserts formative boundary to the context φC——*iVn*, where φ is a vowel if C is a sonorant. With this rule, no classification with respect to rule (116) is necessary for the examples of case (b).

The examples of case (c), which are representative, indicate that the formative [i] or [y] takes the categorial feature [−rule (116)] when it follows [n]. The right-hand column of case (d) illustrates the fact that after [r], [i] is always assigned [−rule (116)]. Alternatively, we could modify the readjustment rule introducing + in the context C——*iVn* to exclude [r] as well as [d]. The reason for assuming that rule (116) applies in the examples of (d) of Column I is that there must be a later rule that deletes [y] after nonliquid palato-alveolars (rule (122)), as in the boldface positions of words such as *religious, admonition* (presumably

---

[55] Supporting evidence comes from comparing *familial* [fəmiliyəl] with *familiar* [fəmilyər]. The underlying form of the latter is /fæmil+i+æl/. A very general rule converts *-al* to *-ar* in the context *l*(+*i*)—— (cf. *similar, molecular*, etc.) Rule (116) then gives the cited phonetic form for *familiar*. If there is no formative boundary after /l/ in *familial*, the rule converting *-al* to *-ar* will not apply, and rule (116) will not apply. Thus both of the phonetic differences between *familiar* and *familial* are determined by the presence or absence of formative boundary.

from /ædmənis̆/, although such examples as *punish–punitive* might suggest a close relation between [s̆] and [t] in these forms). Case (e) demonstrates that the formative [i] is assigned [−rule (116)] after [d] (cf. case (b)) and also after nonstrident continuants. Case (f) shows that the nominalization affix *-ion* always undergoes rule (116), so that no categorization is necessary in this case.

It seems, then, that the feature [±rule (116)] can be predicted for the formatives /i/ and /iVn/ and that the position of formative boundary will otherwise determine its applicability in accordance with rule (116), with only a few ad hoc rules (e.g., case (b)) and marginal exceptions.[56]

With these observations, we can return to the problem of how to formulate rules (115) and (116). Since these are rather similar in form and since both must be in the cycle, it is clear that they fall together as indicated in (118):

$$(118) \qquad \begin{bmatrix} -\text{back} \\ +\text{high} \\ -\text{cons} \end{bmatrix} \rightarrow \begin{cases} [+\text{voc}] \quad / \ \text{C} \text{---} [-\text{seg}] & \text{(a)} \\[2ex] [-\text{voc}] \quad / \ \begin{bmatrix} +\text{cor} \\ \text{C} \end{bmatrix} + \text{---} \begin{bmatrix} \alpha\text{stress} \\ \text{V} \end{bmatrix} \end{cases} \quad \begin{matrix} \\ \\ \text{(b)} \end{matrix}$$

Case (a) restates (115); case (b), (116). The redundancy rules sketched above determine the correct applicability of (118b).

Let us now consider how rule (118) is ordered with respect to the other rules of the cycle, and, in particular, what the condition is on α in (118b). In the examples we have given so far, it was always the case that $\alpha = -$. Furthermore, it is quite clear that when $\alpha = 1$, rule (118b) does not apply. Thus consider the words *peculiar, familiar*. Since they terminate in phonetic [... lyər], the underlying forms must be /pekul+i+æl/, /fæmil+i+æl/, respectively. The rule mentioned in note 55 converts the final /l/ of *-al* to [r]. Rule (118b) then converts [i] to [y] in the expected way. But consider the forms *familiarity, peculiarity*. In one major dialect these terminate in phonetic [... lÉærətÉ]. Therefore it must be that in the final cycle, after stress is assigned to *-ar* and [y] becomes [i] before *-ár* by rule (118a), rule (118b) is blocked by the primary stress on the following vowel. Thus the segment [i] remains, and becomes [E] by familiar processes.

These facts show that rule (118) must follow the rules of stress assignment and that α must meet the condition $\alpha \neq 1$ in rule (118b). We see so far, then, that when $\alpha = -$, the rule is applicable, and when $\alpha = 1$, the rule is inapplicable.

Now consider the case in which the segment [i] is followed by a vowel in the [+stress] category with stress weaker than 1. Examples of this are *auxiliary, beneficiary*. The former will have the form [ūksil+i+ǽr+i] at the point when (118b) is to apply, as we shall see directly. If this rule does not apply, we will derive, finally, the form [ɔ̄gzilÉerÉ], by application of the other rules of this and the preceding chapter. If (118b) does apply, we derive [ɔ̄gzilyərÉ], the penultimate vowel reducing in immediate poststress position by the Auxiliary Reduction Rule (118d) of Chapter Three. In precisely the same way, we will derive for *beneficiary* the phonetic form [benəfis̆ÉerÉ] (from underlying /benefik+i+ǽr+y/) if (118b) does not apply, and [benəfis̆ərÉ] if (118b) does apply.

---

[56] It may be noted, moreover, that such words as *órientate, álienate, améliorate, detériorate* are apparent exceptions to the Alternating Stress Rule if they are pronounced with [iy] rather than [y] in the position V́C——. Notice that the exceptional behavior could be accounted for by extending (116) to cover these cases, with a later rule, following the Alternating Stress Rule, converting [y] once again to [i].

The applicability of rule (118b) in these cases depends on the condition on α. If the condition is α = −, then rule (118b) will not apply; if the condition is α ≠ 1, then rule (118b) will apply. As we have noted in Chapter Three (p. 123), both cases are possible. The dialectal variation, then, depends on how the condition on α is given in rule (118b). We note, incidentally, that in the dialect with the condition α ≠ 1 in rule (118b), this rule must precede the Auxiliary Reduction Rule that assigns to an immediately post-tonic vowel the features [−tense], [−stress] in certain contexts so that it becomes subject to reduction.

The position of rule (118) in the ordering is still more narrowly constrained than this, as we can see by considering forms such as *emaciate*. The only phonetic realization in this case is [EmĂšEĂt]. But consider the dialect with the condition α ≠ 1 in rule (118b). Since this rule does not apply to *emaciate*, it must be that [At] in *emaciate* has primary stress at the point in the derivation when we reach (118b); that is to say, it must be that the form is [emac+i+Át]. Evidently rule (118b) must precede the Alternating Stress Rule, which converts the preceding form to [emác+i+Àt]. Therefore rule (118b) must follow the Main Stress Rule and precede the Alternating Stress Rule (and, therefore, the Auxiliary Reduction Rules).

Summarizing, then, rule (118b) is in the cycle, following the Main Stress Rule and preceding the Alternating Stress Rule, and the condition on α is α ≠ 1 for one dialect (in which this ordering is determined) and α = − for another dialect.

At this point we reach the main rules of word phonology discussed earlier in this chapter, in particular, the Laxing and Tensing Rules. After the Tensing Rules, we come to the rule of *s*-Voicing that was mentioned earlier in this chapter (rule (99)) and in the preceding chapter. Rule (119) is a somewhat more accurate version of this rule:

$$\left(119\right) \qquad \begin{bmatrix} +\text{cor} \\ +\text{strid} \\ +\text{cont} \end{bmatrix} \rightarrow [+\text{voice}] \ / \ \left\{ \begin{array}{ll} V = \underline{\qquad} V & \text{(a)} \\ \begin{bmatrix} +\text{tense} \\ V \end{bmatrix} \underline{\qquad} V & \text{(b)} \\ Vk\underline{\qquad}\acute{V} & \text{(c)} \end{array} \right.$$

As it stands, rule (119) slightly extends rule (99) of Section 5. Case (a) applies in words such as *resume, reside, resident, design, resolute*. Case (b) applies in words such as *music, rosary, miser, gymnasium, Cartesian, Asia, usual*, from underlying /musik/, /rōsVry/, /misVr/, /gimnǣsi+Vm/, /kærtes+i+æn/, /æs+iæ/, /usuæl/ (with a further rule of palatalization for the last three forms). Notice that voicing does not take place in *issue* (from underlying /isue/), *asylum, misogyny, philosoph(-y, -ical)*, etc., because the preceding vowel is lax. However, as the rule now stands, there are quite a few exceptions (e.g., *basic, isolate, masonite, gruesome, awesome*).[57] Case (c) applies where the orthography has *x* in such words

---

[57] Many apparent exceptions to rule (119) can be accounted for by taking the source of [s] to be /kᵈ/ rather than /s/. Recall that original /kᵈ/ before [i], [e], [y], [ε] is now [c], at this stage of derivation (by Velar Softening (114)) and therefore is not voiced by rule (119). The last two examples listed—*gruesome* and *awesome*—suggest a readjustment rule exempting /s/ from rule (119) after formative boundary. Notice that the first three examples given as exceptions are also exceptions to the Laxing Rule (19b). Perhaps, then, we should say that these words undergo laxing and are therefore exempt from *s*-Voicing, and that their irregularity consists in the fact that they undergo subsequent idiosyncratic tensing. Certain other exceptions to (119), particularly to case (b), can be accounted for by lexical redundancy; for example, /s/ is exempt from this rule in the few words of the lexical form / ... VsV/ (e.g., *virtuoso, Caruso, Medusa*). Others will be accounted for by rule (124a), which devoices [z] in certain positions.

Notice that rule (118b), which converts the [i] in *Cartesian* to [y], applies before (119). The rightmost V in the context of (119b) should therefore be generalized to [−consonantal]. As the present discussion is rather informal, however, we shall not incorporate this consequence into the rule.

as *exist, examine, auxiliary, exasperate*. In poststress position, as in *axis* and *maxillary*, the cluster remains unvoiced. Notice, however, that the rule does not apply in *hexameter, toxicity, annexation*, and, in general, whenever the [ks] cluster is final in the formative. This exception requires a readjustment rule which assigns the feature [−rule (119)] to /s/ in the context *k*——+.[58] Perhaps case (c) should be extended to other C*s* clusters, as in *absolve, absorb, observe*. Notice that the voicing of [k] in the context ——*z* is by a later rule of voicing assimilation. Clearly there is a great deal more to the matter of voicing of [s] (and probably [f] and [θ] as well—see p. 232) that deserves more careful investigation.

Underlying stops and [c] which derives from /k^d/ become strident continuants before [i] or [y] under circumstances that we state as rule (120):

$$\left(120\right) \quad \text{SPIRANTIZATION}$$

$$\begin{bmatrix} +\text{cor} \\ +\text{ant} \\ -\text{sonor} \end{bmatrix} \rightarrow \begin{bmatrix} +\text{cont} \\ +\text{strid} \end{bmatrix} \Bigg/ \left\{ \begin{array}{ll} \left(\begin{bmatrix} \\ +\text{voice} \end{bmatrix} + ive \right) & \text{(a)} \\[1em] \left(\begin{bmatrix} \\ -\text{voice} \end{bmatrix} + \begin{bmatrix} -\text{cons} \\ -\text{back} \\ -\text{stress} \end{bmatrix} [-\text{seg}] \right) & \text{(b)} \\[1em] \left(+ y \right) & \text{(c)} \\[1em] \left(\begin{bmatrix} \\ +\text{strid} \end{bmatrix} \right) & \text{(d)} \end{array} \right.$$

Rule (120) converts dental stops to [s] if unvoiced or to [z] if voiced. Case (a) applies in words such as *corrode+ive, evade+ive*, giving, ultimately, *corrosive, evasive* by a later devoicing rule (see (124)). Case (b) applies in words such as *partiality, ingratiate*, in the boldface positions; in *democracy, controversy, residency* (from underlying forms in /...t+y/, with /y/ becoming [i] by rule (118a) and [ī] by the Tensing Rule); and to the parallel forms *confidence, residence*, etc., with final /+ɛ/ (see Chapter Three, p. 161), which, in contrast to final /y/, does not become [+vocalic] by rule (118a). Rule (120b) does not apply to *remedy* (where the dental is voiced) or to *difficulty, modesty* if we derive these from /difikult+ty/, /mɔd+est+ty/, as seems natural for nominalized adjectives (cf. *loyalty, royalty*, etc.) It does apply, however, to the /t/ in words such as *partial, Egyptian, expeditious*, the augment /i/ having become [y] by rule (118b). (The continuant formed by rule (120), in these cases, will palatalize by rule (121).) Rule (120c) applies in words such as *contrition*, from underlying /kɔntrit+iVn/, and *division*, from underlying /divīd+iVn/, the /i/ of /iVn/ having become [y] by rule (118b). Notice that the Spirantization Rule will not apply in *cardial, Canadian, invidious*, etc., in which the augment remains [i]. Case (d) applies to the segment [c] produced by the Velar Softening Rule (114). It constitutes the last stage of velar softening for the unvoiced segment /k^d/.

Notice that where [t] is not followed by formative boundary (e.g., all forms in *-ity*, which we have represented as /i+ty/—see p. 33—and words such as *patio, piteous, Antioch, Pontiac*), it does not become [s] (ultimately, [š]) by rule (120).

The Spirantization Rule must follow the rule of *s*-Voicing, since the [s] formed by rule (120) does not voice. It must precede the rule of *e*-Elision so as to account for the spirantization of [t] in *residence* (from underlying /re=sīd+ent+ɛ/), *confidence*, etc. It must also precede rule (50), which inserts the [y] glide of [yūw]. Therefore, we do not have spirantization of [t] in *fact+ual*, etc., by rule (120c). Clearly some further generalization is possible in the statement of (120), but we will leave it in this form.

---

[58] As in the context +——; see note 57. Notice that case (b) is also inapplicable before certain affixes (e.g., *dosage, usage*).

We are now at the point in the cycle where rule (50) inserts the [y] glide of [yūw]. This, in turn, is followed by a series of vowel adjustment rules which includes Dipthongization, Vowel Shift, and Rounding Adjustment. We then have a rule that changes dentals to palato-alveolars before [y]. Thus *division* has the form [diviz+yVn] at this stage of the derivation, the underlying /d/ having become [z] by the Spirantization Rule (120). This occurrence of [z] must now become palatal so that we derive, ultimately, [dəvižən], the glide after [ž] dropping by a later rule. Similarly, [s] deriving from underlying /kᵈ/ will become [š] in the boldface positions of words such as *logician, musician* (the post-palatal glide again dropping by a later rule), and the same is true of [s] from underlying /t/, as in *controversial, partial, prohibition*. And [t], [d], [s], and [z] will become [č], [ĵ], [š], and [ž], respectively, before [yūw] in words such as *actual, gradual, sensual, visual*. The process is blocked, however, if the dental consonant in question is followed by a vowel, as in the word *satiety*, which at this stage is represented as [sæt+áy+i+tīy], or if it is followed by [yV́], as in *fortuitous, endure, ensue, resume* (cf., for example, *perpetual* [pərpéčūwəl] versus *perpetuity* (pərpətyúwətīy]). To describe these and several other facts, we give the Palatalization Rule in the following form:

$$\left(121\right) \quad \text{PALATALIZATION} \quad \begin{bmatrix} -\text{sonor} \\ +\text{cor} \end{bmatrix} \rightarrow \begin{bmatrix} -\text{ant} \\ +\text{strid} \end{bmatrix} / \underline{\quad\quad} \begin{bmatrix} -\text{back} \\ -\text{voc} \\ -\text{cons} \end{bmatrix} \begin{bmatrix} -\text{cons} \\ -\text{stress} \end{bmatrix}$$

In the form given above, the Palatalization Rule applies to a dental obstruent followed by *y*V̆, where V̆ is a stressless vowel. Thus the rule will not apply to the segments in the boldface positions in *society, perpetuity*, or the verb *associate*, which are represented as [səsáyitīy], [pVrpetyúwitīy], and [æsówsīyèyt], respectively, at this stage of derivation.

The last example, *associate*, points to an inadequacy in the analysis presented. Although the phonetic segment [s] is fairly common in the boldface position, we also commonly find [š]; and, in certain forms (for example, *emaciate, beneficiary*), it seems that the phonetic realization of underlying /kᵈ/ is [š] in all dialects. The facts are unclear. Thus Kenyon and Knott give only [š] for *emaciate* and *associate*, and both [s] and [š] for *emaciation, association, sociology*. To account for [š] in this position, we must extend the rule to the context $\begin{bmatrix} \underline{\quad\quad} \\ +\text{continuant} \end{bmatrix} \bar{\imath}y \begin{bmatrix} \alpha\,\text{stress} \\ -\text{consonantal} \end{bmatrix}$, requiring that $\alpha \neq 1$ in dialects that have [š] in *associate* and [s] in *association*. Since these variants seem to coexist or to be distributed in various ways in many styles of speech, we must assume a considerable degree of arbitrary lexical categorization or of dialect mixture. Pending further analysis, we leave the question in this state.[59]

Since palatalization in dentals takes place by rule (121) only before glides, we do not have palatalization of the stops in the boldface positions of *primordial, remedial, medium, piteous, Pontiac*, etc. In all of these words, the segment following the dental consonant in question is the vowel [ī], not the glide [y], at the point when the Palatalization Rule (121) applies.

---

[59] We have made no systematic attempt to investigate the *s–š* alternation in these positions or to collect other exceptions to these rules. However, the following are among those that come to mind: *mature* [məčúr] in many dialects, instead of expected [mətūwr] or [mətyúwr]; *luxurious* [lʌgžúrīyəs] instead of expected [lʌgz(y)úriəs] (cf. *exude, exuberant*, in which palatalization does not take place).

One additional complication must be noted. Although the processes just described that convert [Di] to [Py] (where D is a dental and P the corresponding palato-alveolar) apply in the boldface positions in words such as *Cartesian, Russian,*[60] *prejudicial,* they do not apply in the boldface positions of *potassium, magnesium, gymnasium.* Thus we have phonetic contrasts such as [kārtEžən]–[jimnAzEəm]. The dropping of the glide is contingent on Palatalization, as we shall see directly. Palatalization depends on the change of [i] to [y] by rule (118b). Therefore it is sufficient to distinguish pairs such as *Cartesian–gymnasium* in terms of the applicability of rule (118b), as in the examples of (117). Notice that rule (118b) must be blocked only in certain cases of underlying /s/, but not in the case of underlying /k^d/, which is represented as [c] at the point in a derivation at which (118b) applies. Therefore, at worst a categorization of underlying /s/ is involved. However, notice that rule (118b) applies to [i] only when it is preceded by formative boundary. This suggests that we instead distinguish the cases in question by the presence or absence of formative boundary, with lexical representations such as /kærtes+i+æn/, /gimnæsi+Vm/. In many cases, the formative boundary seems reasonably well motivated. Alternatively, we could add [±rule (118b)] as a new classification of /i/ after /s/.

Next, we must delete glides after palato-alveolars, by rule (122):

$$
(122) \qquad \begin{bmatrix} -\text{cons} \\ -\text{voc} \end{bmatrix} \rightarrow \phi \ / \begin{bmatrix} +\text{cor} \\ -\text{ant} \\ -\text{sonor} \end{bmatrix}\underline{\qquad}
$$

This rule applies, in particular, to the [y]-glide inserted by rule (50) before [U], giving phonetic [ækčūwæl] from [ækčyūwæl] (*actual*), [išūw] from [išyūwe] (*issue*), etc. Similarly, the segment [y] from underlying /i/ drops in the boldface position in words such as *religion, decision, artificial.* Rule (122) is restricted to the position following obstruents. Thus it does not apply after the palatal liquid [r], and we have forms such as *virulent* with [ry], alongside of *pavilion* with [ly] where the liquid is not palatal. There are no glides in this position.

Notice that rule (122) will delete the element in the boldface position in *religion, artificial,* but not in *religiosity, artificiality, emaciate.* The reason is that the following vowel is stressed in the latter group, preventing the boldface segment from becoming a glide. Thus consider the final cycle in the derivation of words such as *religiosity.* The stress assignment rules assign [+stress] in the position following the boldface segment [i]. Rule (118a) converts this segment to [i] (if it was converted to [y] in an earlier cycle). But case (b) of (118) does not apply since the following vowel is stressed. Therefore this segment is not a glide and is not subject to rule (122).

We have observed (see note 27) that in some dialects [y] also drops after dentals and palato-alveolars in certain other positions, as in *residue, constitute, tune, rule, rejuvenate.* In such dialects [y] drops in all contexts in which rule (121) has not applied. Thus we have contrasts such as *residue* [rézədùw] – *residual* [rəzíjūwəl], *constitute* [kǎnstətùwt] – *constitutive* [kənstíčūwtiv]. Hence, if only dental obstruents were involved, we could state

---

[60] The fact that the Palatalization Rule applies in *Russian* indicates that rule (121) must follow the rule of Cluster Simplification discussed in Section 5. The underlying form for *Russian* must be /russ+i+æn/; if it were /rus+i+æn/, we would derive *[rUšən] instead of [rʌšən]. Thus, if Palatalization preceded Cluster Simplification, we would derive *[rʌššən], incorrectly. Furthermore, the rule of Cluster Simplification must follow the rule of Spirantization, since underlying /eks=kēd/, which becomes [eks=sēd] by Velar Softening and Spirantization, must then become [eksēd] by Cluster Simplification. The correct order, therefore, is: Spirantization, Cluster Simplification, Palatalization.

simply that [y] drops after dental obstruents, giving no further contextual information. But additional information is needed for instances of [y] following dental and palatal sonorants. Thus [y] never drops after these segments in words such as *virulent, annual, valuable*. The relevant fact is the stress on the following vowel. Where the stress is other than minus, the glide drops. Thus it drops after such dental obstruents as have not become palatal by rule (121) and after liquids before stressed vowels.

$$\left(123\right) \qquad\qquad y \;\rightarrow\; \phi \quad / \quad \begin{bmatrix} +\text{cor} \\ +\text{cons} \end{bmatrix}\!\!-\!\!-\,[+\text{stress}]$$

In addition to these rules, there are several other minor modifications needed; for example, that of (124):

$$\left(124\right) \qquad\qquad z \;\rightarrow\; [-\text{voice}] \quad / \;-\!\!-\!\!+ive$$

Rule (124) accounts for the devoicing in *abusive, evasive*. Notice that in the case of *evade, corrode, divide*, etc., we have a [d]–[ž]–[s] alternation ([EvAd]–[EvA̯žən]–[EvAsiv]) by a combination of regular processes.

Rule (124) should no doubt be extended to other cases. For example, we pointed out (note 58) that we have [s] rather than [z] in ——+*age*, a fact which can be accounted for by adding -*age* to (124) instead of by a readjustment rule as suggested in note 58. Examples such as *sausage* suggest that devoicing in this position may be more general, not requiring formative boundary. Words such as *kinesis, osmosis* suggest either that -*is* be added to (124) or that the underlying forms are *kinet-, osmot-*, etc., and that the Spirantization Rule (120) has an additional case involving -*is*. There are, however, questions about the [s]–[t] alternations in pairs such as *galaxy–galactic, climax–climactic, osmosis–osmotic* that we have not answered. Also relevant here are the well-known morphological processes that determine the voicing of final [f], [s], [θ] in noun-verb pairs and adjective-verb pairs. Thus we have devoicing in the nouns *choice*,[61] *advice, breath, abuse*, formed from the corresponding verbs, and voicing in the verbs *house, clothe*, etc., which are presumably formed from the underlying nouns. Similarly, we have pairs such as *safe–save, life–live*, with devoicing in the adjective and noun and voicing in the verb. Whatever the correct analysis of these forms may be, we should have no difficulty incorporating it within the framework so far established, For example, the rule that devoices the final continuant of a noun or adjective derived from a verb can be formulated in terms of a lexical category associated with such derived forms, which becomes a segmental feature [+φ] by the conventions discussed in Section 2.2. We can then add to rule (124) the context $\begin{bmatrix} - \\ +\varphi \end{bmatrix}$. If, alternatively, the suggestion of note 46 can be realized and the voicing of [f], [s], [θ] can be determined by the context $\begin{bmatrix} +\text{tense} \\ V \end{bmatrix}\!\!-\!\!-\,CV$ (where tenseness and thus voicing are

---

[61] If the verb is the underlying form, then we will presumably have to give it the lexical representation /čɔ̄z/. The past tense form will be determined correctly as [čōwz] by regular processes. To derive the present tense form [čūwz], we must mark the verb *choose* with the feature that permits double application of the Vowel Shift Rule in its present tense form, in the manner discussed in Section 4.3.5. To derive *choice*, we must subject the underlying form /čɔ̄z/ to a unique case of lexical backness adjustment which does not carry with it the automatic rounding adjustment that makes rounding coincide with backness. Thus /čɔ̄z/ will, by this process, become [čǣz], which becomes [čɔ̄yz] in the regular way, and then [čɔ̄ys] by the devoicing associated with the derivational process of nominalization.

presumably determined by the final /e/, which is later elided), we can omit any consideration of this matter from rule (124), since voicing will be accounted for by the *s*-Voicing Rule (119), extended to the other continuants by dropping the feature [+strident].

A further modification is required in the Spirantization Rule (120). If the rule remains in its present form, words such as *question* and *bastion* will appear in the output as *[kwesšən] and *[basšən], rather than as [kwesčən] and [basčən]. The reason is that (120) spirantizes occurrences of /t/ before the suffix *-ion*. The [s] resulting from (120) is then subject to the Palatalization Rule (121), which yields [š] in the output.⁶²

We recall in this regard that Spirantization does not apply in words such as *factual* (see p. 229). In these words the underlying /t/ is reflected in the output as [č], which is precisely what is needed in the case of *question, bastion*. Thus, if the Spirantization Rule can be modified so that it does not apply to the /t/ in *question, bastion*, the correct output will be obtained: the /t/ will be unaffected by Spirantization and will subsequently be changed to [č] by the Palatalization Rule (121), just as in the case of *factual*. The simplest way to achieve this result seems to be to block the application of cases (b) and (c) of the Spirantization Rule in obstruents that are preceded by [s]. In other words, we require that the segment undergoing the relevant cases of Spirantization be preceded by $\begin{Bmatrix} [+\text{sonorant}] \\ [-\text{continuant}] \end{Bmatrix}$, that is, by a segment which is either a sonorant or a noncontinuant. The rule will then not apply to the /t/ in *question, bastion*, which is preceded by a continuant obstruent, and the derivations will proceed correctly.

As matters now stand, the examples where Spirantization is blocked involve only the position following [s]. Note, however, that the above modification as stated will prevent the rule from applying after other continuant obstruents as well. This fact has an interesting consequence for a case not yet analyzed. Consider the word *righteous*, which is clearly derived from *right*. If the underlying form for *right* is /rīt/, then *righteous* would be represented as /rīt+i+əs/ on the lexical level. By the Laxing Rule, we derive [rit+i+əs]; and the rules of this section give, finally, *[rišəs]. Thus the correct form, [rāyčəs], deviates from what is expected in two ways: first, in that the first vowel is tense rather than lax; second, in that it has [č] instead of expected [š]. These observations lead us to seek a different analysis for the underlying form for *right*.

Suppose that we represent *right* as /riφt/, where φ is a continuant. Suppose then that we add the ad hoc rules (125) and (126):

$$\left(125\right) \qquad\qquad V \;\rightarrow\; [+\text{tense}] \;\; / \;\;\text{——}\;\varphi$$

$$\left(126\right) \qquad\qquad \varphi \;\rightarrow\; \phi \;\; / \;\;\text{——}\;C$$

Rule (125) must follow Laxing and precede Vowel Shift: it can therefore be part of the general Tensing Rule. Rule (126) will be one of the late rules of deletion, following (124). With these rules, we derive [riφt] from underlying /riφt/ by rule (125), and then [rāyt] by Diphthongization, Vowel Shift, Backness Adjustment, and rule (126). But now consider *righteous*, represented /riφt+i+əs/. Considering just the final cycle, we have the derivation shown in (127).

---

⁶² We are grateful to P. Schachter for drawing our attention to certain aspects of this problem.

$$\left(127\right) \quad \begin{array}{ll} \text{ri}\varphi\text{t}+\text{i}+\text{əs} & \\ \text{rī}\varphi\text{t}+\text{i}+\text{əs} & \text{RULE (125)} \\ \text{rī}\varphi\text{t}+\text{y}+\text{əs} & \text{RULE (118b)} \\ \text{rāy}\varphi\text{t}+\text{y}+\text{əs} & \text{DIPHTHONGIZATION, VOWEL SHIFT, BACKNESS ADJUSTMENT} \\ \text{rāy}\varphi\check{\text{c}}+\text{y}+\text{əs} & \text{RULE (121)} \\ \text{rāy}\varphi\check{\text{c}}+\text{əs} & \text{RULE (122)} \\ \text{rāy}\check{\text{c}}+\text{əs} & \text{RULE (126)} \\ \text{rāy}\check{\text{c}}\text{əs} & \text{VOWEL REDUCTION} \end{array}$$

Thus rules (125) and (126) will account for both of the unexpected features of *righteous*, if we can make an appropriate choice of a continuant for /φ/. Notice that Spirantization, rule (120), is blocked by the continuant preceding [t].

Note that as matters now stand, dental, palato-alveolar, and labial continuants can appear in postvocalic position (e.g., *miss*, *wrist*, *if*, *rift*, *swish*), but the velar continuant /x/ cannot. Filling this phonological gap, we can represent *right* as /rixt/, taking /x/ to be /φ/ in the analysis just suggested. We then replace (125) by (128) and coalesce the rephrased version of (126) with rule (111), which is now placed much later in the ordering, in fact, after (124):

$$\left(128\right) \qquad \text{V} \quad \rightarrow \quad [+\text{tense}] \ / \ \text{———}x$$

$$\left(129\right) \qquad \begin{bmatrix} -\text{cor} \\ -\text{ant} \\ +\text{cont} \end{bmatrix} \rightarrow \begin{Bmatrix} \phi \ / \ \text{———}C \\ [-\text{cons}] \end{Bmatrix}$$

We then form *righteous* from underlying /rixt+i+əs/ by derivation (127) with /x/ replacing /φ/. Both of the rules (125) and (126) fall together with other already motivated rules (see also (130) below).

The same device might be used to explain various other exceptions to trisyllabic laxing, as in the boldface positions of *nightingale* and *mightily*. Furthermore, we can use it to explain alternations such as *resign–resignation*, *paradigm–paradigmatic*. Suppose that we add a rule converting [g] to a continuant in the context ———[+nasal] #. Then underlying /re=sign/, /pæræ+digm/ will become [rezign], [pærədigm] before *-Ation*, *-atic*, respectively, but in the forms in isolation, [g] will become [γ] before [+nasal]#. If we simplify rule (128) to the context ———[x γ], then that rule will convert [re=siγn] and [pæræ+diγm] to [re=sīγn], [pæræ+dīγm], respectively. The tensed vowel becomes [āy] in the familiar way. Rule (129) will delete [γ], giving the forms [rīyzāyn], [pærədāym].

Finally, it has been suggested to us by S. Anderson that the apparently irregular occurrence of [ŋ] instead of [ŋg] in word-medial position, as in *dinghy*, *hangar*, *gingham*, *Birmingham*, may be readily accounted for if the forms are assumed to have underlying representations such as /dinxi/, /xænxr/, etc. The nasal will assimilate the point of articulation of the following velar by a rule that is independently motivated (cf. *think*, *finger*, etc.) Next, (129) deletes [x] by an extension which requires deletion of this segment in the context C———.

These alternations support the choice of [x] over other possibilities for φ in example (127).

The tensing of vowels before velar continuants is apparently restricted to high vowels. Although examples are far from plentiful, cases such as *phlegm–phlegmatic*, *diaphragm–diaphragmatic* seem to suggest that nonhigh vowels do not undergo tensing here.

Moreover, if cases such as *pugnacious–impugn* are also to be handled by this rule, (128) should be reformulated as

$$(130) \qquad \begin{bmatrix} +\text{high} \\ V \end{bmatrix} \rightarrow \begin{bmatrix} +\text{tense} \\ -\text{round} \end{bmatrix} / \underline{\quad\quad} [x, \gamma]$$

We can illustrate the rules we have discussed with derivations such as the following. We restrict ourselves to the rules of this section, for the most part.

(131)

logician	*logicism*	*religious*	
l ɔ g^d + i k^d + i + æ n	l ɔ g^d + i k^d + i z m	r e l i g^d + i + ɔ s	
ǰ c	ǰ c	ǰ	RULE (114)
y		y	RULE (118b)
s			RULE (120b)
	s		RULE (120d)
š			RULE (121)
φ		φ	RULE (122)
ləǰíšən	lắǰəsìzm^{63}	rəlíǰəs	

(132)

decision	*artificiality*	
d e = k^d ī d + i V n	æ r t i f i k^d + i + æ l + i + t y	
$\overset{1}{i}$	$\overset{1}{i}$	FIRST CYCLE RULE (114)
c	c	
	$\overset{2}{i}$ $\quad$ $\overset{1}{æ}$	STRESS RULES, SECOND CYCLE
y		RULE (118b)
	s	RULE (120b)^{64}
ż		RULE (120c)
s		RULE (120d)^{64}
ž	š	RULE (121)^{65}
φ		RULE (122)
dəsížən	ằrtəfìšīyǽlətīy	

(133)

courage	*courageous*^{66}	
k^d o r æ g^d e	k^d o r æ g^d e + ɔ s	
	$\overset{1}{o}$	FIRST CYCLE, FOR *courage*
ǰ	$\overset{1}{ǰ}$	RULE (114)
$\overset{1}{o}$	$\overset{2}{o}$ $\overset{1}{æ}$	STRESS RULES
	ǣ	TENSING RULE
φ	φ	*e*-ELISION
kʌ́rəǰ	kərέyǰəs	

---

[63] The pronunciation [lówjəsizm] requires the underlying form /lóg+ik/, an exception to laxing before -*ic*.

[64] Notice that the segment [i] following [c] in *artificiality* has already been tensed by the Tensing Rule, and the segment [ī] following [c] in *decision* has already been laxed by the Laxing Rule.

[65] Recall the discussion (p. 231) of the [s]–[š] alternation in such forms.

[66] See note 18.

Chapter five

SUMMARY OF RULES

In this chapter we restate the major rules of the phonology as given in the preceding chapters, ordered in the way that is required by the facts cited in the discussion.

In the previous chapters the assumption has been made that the vowels appearing in the abstract underlying representations of English lexical items are monophthongs. Diphthongs—i.e., sequences of a vowel followed by a glide—are the result of phonological rules that insert glides in certain positions.[1] There are six lax vowels in the underlying representations, namely:

	$-$back $-$round	$+$back $+$round
$+$high $-$low	i	u
$-$high $-$low	e	o
$-$high $+$low	æ	ɔ

In some dialects there is an additional marginal subcategorization of /æ/ (see p. 205).

The tense vowels include the tense correlates of the lax vowels; and there is distinctive rounding for the low tense vowels, so that we have the full set: /ǣ/ /ǣ/ /ā/ /ɔ̄/. The distinctive feature complexes of the individual segments mentioned in the discussion appear in Table 1 of Chapter Four (p. 176).

The rules that we have given fall into two general classes: the rules of the readjustment component and the phonological rules. The former apply before any of the phonological rules. They express properties of lexical formatives in certain restricted syntactic contexts, and they modify syntactically generated surface structures in a variety of ways. The phonological rules are organized in a transformational cycle. A considerable number of phonological rules, however, are limited so that they apply in the cycle only when the level of word boundary has been reached. We have called the latter "rules of word-level phonology."

---

[1] There are, of course, sequences of vowels in the underlying representations. These may occur across a formative boundary, as in *scient-*, which is phonologically /ski+ent/ (giving *science, scientific* by regular processes); or they may occur, marginally, within certain formatives, such as *neo-, dia-, dial, fuel, via*.

The cyclic rules fall together in the ordering, and all but rule (16) (which changes *i* to *y* and *y* to *i*) are rules of primary stress assignment. If the ordering were revised so that (17) (the Alternating Stress Rule) and (18) (the Compound, Nuclear Stress, and Stress Adjustment Rules) preceded (16), then the rules that assign primary stress would be consecutive and would collapse into a single schema of the form:

$$V \rightarrow [1 \text{ stress}] \ / \ ...$$

We noted that the justification for ordering (16) before (17) is not overwhelming, and there is no relation between (16) and (18). If, furthermore, the analysis is revised in such a way as to drop rule (16) from the cycle, then the cycle would be restricted to a single elaborate schema abbreviating a complex set of rules, with intricate relations of ordering among them, all assigning primary stress in certain positions. In Chapter Three we explained why we were unable to accept this analysis, but it seems sufficiently attractive for more thought to be given to its consequences.

Among the processes of primary stress assignment, there are three that shift stress to the left: the others shift stress to the right, in general. The three processes that shift stress left are the Stressed Syllable Rule (condition (c) of the Main Stress Rule (15)), the Alternating Stress Rule (17), and the Compound Rule of (18). As we have noted several times, it is not impossible that the Compound Rule can be amalgamated with the Stressed Syllable Rule (as the Nuclear Stress Rule can be amalgamated with condition (e) of the Main Stress Rule) in terms of a general notion of "sonority" (see p. 91). Although we rejected this analysis, for reasons indicated earlier, we feel that it still merits attention. It is also worth mentioning the possibility of amalgamating the Stressed Syllable and Alternating Stress Rules, each of which shifts stress to the left within a word before a final stressed syllable (with the modifications presented in the detailed exposition earlier). Such an amalgamation, like the others just noted, has more than a superficial plausibility, but we have rejected it for several reasons. First, there are certain technical difficulties, within our framework, in formulating the schema that would incorporate both these processes. More seriously, a careful analysis of the cases suggests that there really is a fundamental distinction between them. The matter is important, both for synchronic and diachronic study of English, and some additional comment may be useful.

Reducing the Stressed Syllable Rule and the Alternating Stress Rule to their essentials, we see that each defines a context containing a stressed syllable, and each assigns primary stress in a domain that is to the left of this context. The Stressed Syllable Rule interprets this domain in terms of the Romance Stress Rule; thus it assigns primary stress to a final strong cluster or to the syllable preceding a final weak cluster, in this domain. The Alternating Stress Rule, on the other hand, assigns primary stress to the penultimate syllable of the domain, independently of the form of the final syllable of the domain. Thus the Stressed Syllable Rule is responsible for placement of primary stress in the boldface position in *anticip–atory* and *confisc–atory* (where the dash separates the domain from the context); and the Alternating Stress Rule is responsible for the position of primary stress in *anecd–ote*. *confisc–ate, philist–ine*.

It might be supposed that these processes can be amalgamated by assigning the feature [+D], which excludes a syllable from the domain of stress assignment (see p. 138), in the case of the Alternating Stress Rule, just as [+D] was assigned for the Stressed Syllable and Affix Rules in certain instances. At best, this would be unfortunate, since assignment of [+D] is by general rule in the latter cases, whereas in this case it would be entirely idiosyncratic and ad hoc. Still worse, the proposal will fail because of such words as *extrapol–ate*, in which the penultimate syllable of the domain is weak and noninitial.

There is, however, a still more serious reason for suspecting that the two processes under discussion do not fall together. There is an interesting generalization that must somehow be captured by the rules in question: namely, the Alternating Stress Rule, which does not make use of the strong cluster principle, applies in a given cycle if and only if stress has been assigned to the final syllable in this cycle under one of the conditions (a)–(e) of the Main Stress Rule; whereas the Stressed Syllable Rule, which does make use of the strong cluster principle, applies in a given cycle if and only if stress has been assigned to the final syllable either in an earlier cycle under condition (e) of the Main Stress Rule or in the cycle in question under condition (a) of the Main Stress Rule. This is an important correlation between reliance on the strong cluster principle, on the one hand, and a complex interconnection of rules, on the other. It is precisely this generalization that is expressed by the ordering of condition (c) of the Main Stress Rule between conditions (a) and (e), along with the principles of cyclic application and of disjunctive and conjunctive ordering. This conclusion appears to us to be significant. It leads us to believe that the attempt to amalgamate the Stressed Syllable Rule and Alternating Stress Rule would be misguided, quite apart from any technical considerations, despite the similarity between the two processes.

We turn now to a summary of the rules.

In the list below a few readjustment rules are given first ((1)–(9)), merely as an illustrative sample. They are followed by the phonological rules ((10)–(43)). The rules that are not restricted to the level of word boundary are starred; all rules not starred in this list are rules of word-level phonology. We will give each rule with a citation of the chapter (Roman numeral) and example number of the most recent reference to it; where there are several citations, these refer to relevant comments about the form of the rule. The rules are not necessarily given in the most reduced form.

1. Readjustment rules

(1)
$$V \rightarrow \begin{bmatrix} -\alpha\text{back} \\ -\alpha\text{round} \end{bmatrix} \Big/ \begin{bmatrix} \underline{} \\ \alpha\text{back} \end{bmatrix} \begin{array}{l} \text{in a number of irregular} \\ \text{verbs, nouns, and adjectives} \\ \text{in certain contexts} \end{array} \qquad \text{IV (75)}$$

(2)
$$t \rightarrow [+\text{voice}] \Big/ = \begin{cases} mi\text{——}+ive \\ ver\text{——}+iVn \end{cases} \qquad \text{IV (110)}$$

(3)
$$C \rightarrow C^* \Big/ \begin{cases} \textit{æ} \\ \textit{su} \end{cases} \text{——} = C^* \qquad \text{IV (103)}$$

where C and C* are both
coronal or both noncoronal

(4)
$$V \rightarrow [-\text{rule (20 III)}] \Big/ \text{——} \begin{bmatrix} +\text{cons} \\ +\text{ant} \\ +\text{cor} \end{bmatrix} \begin{bmatrix} +\text{cons} \\ +\text{cor} \end{bmatrix} \begin{Bmatrix} [-\text{cons}] \\ [-\text{seg}] \end{Bmatrix} \qquad \text{IV (9)}$$

(5) $\quad$ $\bar{u} \rightarrow [-\text{rule (32)}] \;/\; \underline{\quad} \left\{ \begin{matrix} C_0\# \\ [+\text{nasal}]\,C \\ V \end{matrix} \right\}$ $\qquad$ IV (72)

(6) $\quad$ $\bar{a} \rightarrow [-\text{rule (34)}]$ in polysyllables $\qquad$ IV (70)

(7) $\quad$ $V \rightarrow \begin{bmatrix} -\text{rule (30)} \\ -\text{rule (32)} \end{bmatrix} \;/\; \underline{\quad} 1$ $\qquad$ IV p. 214

(8) $\quad$ $u \rightarrow [-\text{round}] \;/\; \begin{bmatrix} -\text{nasal} \\ +\text{ant} \\ -\text{cor} \end{bmatrix} \underline{\quad} \left\{ \begin{matrix} 1\left\{\begin{matrix}1\\\#\end{matrix}\right\} \\ \begin{bmatrix} -\text{ant} \\ +\text{cor} \\ -\text{voc} \end{bmatrix} \end{matrix} \right\}$ $\qquad$ IV (66)

(9) $\quad$ $C \rightarrow [+\text{cor}] \;/\; \bar{u} \underline{\quad} [-\text{seg}]$ $\qquad$ IV (54)

2. *Phonological rules*

(10) $\quad$ $[u, i] \rightarrow \phi \;/\; + \underline{\quad} \#$ $\qquad$ III (129) and note 84

(11) $\quad$ $\phi \rightarrow u \;/\; \begin{bmatrix} -\text{cont} \\ -\text{voc} \\ +\text{cons} \end{bmatrix} \underline{\quad} 1 + VC\,[-\text{seg}]$ $\qquad$ IV (56)

(12) $\quad$ $\phi \rightarrow w \;/\; \left\{ \begin{matrix} \text{æ} \underline{\quad} \left\{ \begin{matrix} rC \\ (\left(\begin{matrix}r\\lm\end{matrix}\right))\,\# \end{matrix} \right\} \\ \begin{bmatrix} +\text{round} \\ -\text{voc} \\ +\text{cons} \end{bmatrix} \underline{\quad} \end{matrix} \right\}$ $\qquad$ IV (91), (112)

(13) VELAR SOFTENING

$\begin{bmatrix} -\text{cont} \\ -\text{ant} \\ +\text{deriv} \\ \langle -\text{voice}\rangle \end{bmatrix} \rightarrow \begin{bmatrix} +\text{cor} \\ +\text{strid} \\ \langle +\text{ant}\rangle \end{bmatrix} \;/\; \underline{\quad} \begin{bmatrix} -\text{back} \\ -\text{low} \\ -\text{cons} \end{bmatrix}$ $\qquad$ IV (114)

$^*(14)$ $\quad$ $\begin{bmatrix} +\text{tense} \\ V \end{bmatrix} \rightarrow [1 \text{ stress}] \;/\; + \underline{\quad} C_0\#$ $\qquad$ III (158)

$^*\left(15\right)$ MAIN STRESS

$$V \rightarrow [1\ stress] \bigg/ \left[X\text{——}C_0 \left(\begin{bmatrix} -tense \\ \gamma stress \\ V \end{bmatrix} C_0^1 \left(\begin{bmatrix} \alpha voc \\ \alpha cons \\ -ant \end{bmatrix} \right) \right) \right.$$

III (101), (122)
(136), (151)

$$\bigg/ \text{——} \Bigg\langle \Bigg(\left\{ \begin{matrix} ((fik)At \\ \\ [+D]C_0 \end{matrix} \right\} \Bigg) \left\{ \begin{matrix} \langle_1 + C_0 \rangle_1 \begin{bmatrix} -stress \\ -tense \\ -cons \end{bmatrix} [+cons]_0 \\ \langle_1 \begin{bmatrix} -seg \\ \langle_2 -FB \rangle_2 \end{bmatrix} \rangle_1 C_0 \ [\beta stress] \ C_0 \langle_2 V_0 C_0 \rangle_2 \end{matrix} \right\} \Bigg\rangle \Bigg]_{\langle NSP \langle_1 VA \rangle_1 \rangle}$$

Conditions: $\beta = \left\{ \begin{matrix} 2 \\ 1 \end{matrix} \right\}$

$\gamma \leq 2$

X contains no internal #

$^*\left(16\right)$

$$\begin{bmatrix} -back \\ +high \\ -cons \end{bmatrix} \rightarrow \left\{ \begin{matrix} [+voc] & / \ C\text{——}[-seg] \\ [-voc] & / \begin{bmatrix} +cor \\ C \end{bmatrix} + \text{——} \begin{bmatrix} \alpha stress \\ V \end{bmatrix} X \end{matrix} \right]$$

IV (118)

Conditions: $\alpha = -$, or $\alpha \neq 1$

X contains no internal #

$^*\left(17\right)$ ALTERNATING STRESS

$$V \rightarrow [1\ stress] \ / \ \text{——} C_0 (=) C_0 V C_0 \ [1\ stress] \ C_0]_{NAV}$$

III (75)

$^*\left(18\right)$ COMPOUND, NUCLEAR STRESS, STRESS ADJUSTMENT

$$V \rightarrow [1\ stress] \ / \ [\#\#X \begin{bmatrix} \overline{\quad\quad} \\ 1\ stress \end{bmatrix} Y \langle \#\#Z \rangle \#\#]_{\langle NAV \rangle}$$

III (52),
(68), (70)

where $Y \neq \ldots [1\ stress] \ldots ; Z \neq \ldots \#\# \ldots$

$\left(19\right)$

$$[2\ stress] \rightarrow [3\ stress] \ / \ \text{——} C_0 [1\ stress]$$

III (117)

$\left(20\right)$ LAXING

(I) AUXILIARY REDUCTION—I

$$V \rightarrow \begin{bmatrix} -stress \\ -tense \end{bmatrix} \bigg/ \left\{ \begin{matrix} \langle VC_0 \rangle \begin{bmatrix} \overline{\quad\quad} \\ \alpha stress \\ \langle +tense \rangle \end{bmatrix} C_0^1 (=C_0) \begin{bmatrix} \beta stress \\ V \end{bmatrix} \\ \left\{ \begin{matrix} \begin{bmatrix} \overline{\quad\quad} \\ \gamma stress \end{bmatrix} \\ [1\ stress] C_0 \text{——} C_0 [-cons] \end{matrix} \right\} [-stress]_0 \# \end{matrix} \right\}$$

III (118)

Conditions: $\beta = 1, 2, 3$

α is weaker than β

γ is weaker than 2

(II) $\qquad$ V $\rightarrow$ [−tense] / +——·r+i[−seg] $\qquad$ III (142); IV p. 202

(III)[2] $\qquad$ V $\rightarrow$ [−tense] / ——[+cons]$\begin{bmatrix} +\text{cons} \\ -\text{voc} \end{bmatrix}$ $\qquad$ IV (8)

(IV) $\begin{bmatrix} \text{V} \\ \alpha\text{round} \\ \alpha\text{back} \end{bmatrix} \rightarrow$ [−tense] / ——C$\left\{ \begin{array}{l} \text{C}_0+ic,+id,+ish \\ (\text{C}_1+)\begin{bmatrix} -\text{stress} \\ \text{V} \end{bmatrix}\text{C}_0[-\text{cons}] \end{array} \right\}$ $\qquad$ IV (19), note 16, and p. 192

$\left(21\right)$ $\qquad$ ɔ $\rightarrow$ [3 stress] / ——# $\qquad$ IV (45)

$\left(22\right)$ $\qquad$ g $\rightarrow$ [+cont] / ——[+nasal]# $\qquad$ IV p. 234

$\left(23\right)$ TENSING

(I) $\qquad$ $\left\{ \begin{array}{l} \text{æ} \\ \text{u} \end{array} \right\} \rightarrow$ [+tense] / $\begin{bmatrix} \overline{\quad\quad} \\ \text{1 stress} \end{bmatrix}$nge $\qquad$ IV (60a)

(II) $\qquad$ ɔ $\rightarrow$ [+tense] / ——CV[−seg] $\qquad$ IV (60b)

(III)[3]

$\begin{bmatrix} -\text{tense} \\ +\text{back} \\ \text{V} \end{bmatrix} \rightarrow \begin{bmatrix} +\text{tense} \\ -\text{round} \end{bmatrix} / \left\{ \begin{array}{l} \begin{bmatrix} \overline{\quad\quad} \\ +\text{high} \end{bmatrix}\text{C}_0^1 \left(\begin{bmatrix} \alpha\text{voc} \\ \alpha\text{cons} \\ -\text{ant} \end{bmatrix} \right)[-\text{cons}] \\ \begin{bmatrix} \overline{\quad\quad} \\ -\text{high} \\ -\text{low} \end{bmatrix} \left\{ \begin{array}{l} \begin{bmatrix} -\text{voice} \\ +\text{cont} \\ +\text{ant} \end{bmatrix} \\ [+\text{sonor}]\text{C} \end{array} \right\} \end{array} \right\}$ $\qquad$ IV (77), (79), (84)

---

[2] The preconsonantal laxing rule as given here incorporates a refinement over the formulation in Chapter Four (rule (8)). Laxing does not take place in consonant clusters ending with a liquid. Thus, when a true consonant precedes a liquid, we find both tense and lax vowels: there is *supple, bubble, calibre, massacre*, in which the vowel is lax, as well as *maple, noble, Cyprus, migrate, meter* (cf. *metric*), *acre*, in which the vowel is tense.

[3] We have modified this rule and the tensing rule (23IV) that follows it by introducing an optional $\begin{bmatrix} \alpha\text{voc} \\ \alpha\text{cons} \\ -\text{ant} \end{bmatrix}$, just as we did in defining "weak cluster" for purposes of stress placement (cf. Chapter Three, (49)). This was done in order to account for the fact that here, too, a consonant followed by [r] or a glide behaves like a single consonant. With this extension we can account for tensing in the boldface position in words such as *cupric, putrify, Ukraine, inebriate, appropriate, opprobrium, repatriate, colloquial, obsequious*.

Clearly, we are leaving unexpressed an important generalization, namely, that in many different respects, consonant-liquid and consonant-glide strings function as single consonants. Actually, the situation is still more complex. We recall that we were forced to include the "weak cluster" option not only in the Main Stress Rule and Tensing Rules, but also in the Auxiliary Reduction Rule (120) of Chapter Three (see (24) here). As noted, this repetition indicates that we have failed to capture important properties of strong and weak clusters and thus points to a defect in our theory that merits further attention.

(IV)[4]

$$\text{V} \rightarrow [+\text{tense}] \; / \; \left\{ \begin{array}{l} \begin{bmatrix} \underline{} \\ \alpha\text{low} \\ \beta\text{stress} \end{bmatrix} \left\{ \begin{matrix} \text{V} \\ \begin{bmatrix} -\text{seg} \\ -\text{FB} \end{bmatrix} \begin{array}{l} \text{where } \beta = + \\ \text{if } \alpha = + \end{array} \end{matrix} \right\} \\[2em] \begin{bmatrix} \underline{} \\ -\text{high} \end{bmatrix} C_1^1 \left(\begin{bmatrix} \alpha\text{voc} \\ \alpha\text{cons} \\ -\text{ant} \end{bmatrix} \right) \begin{bmatrix} -\text{low} \\ -\text{back} \\ -\text{cons} \\ -\text{stress} \end{bmatrix} \text{V} \end{array} \right\} \qquad \text{IV (20)}$$

(V)

$$\begin{bmatrix} +\text{high} \\ \text{V} \end{bmatrix} \rightarrow \begin{bmatrix} +\text{tense} \\ -\text{round} \end{bmatrix} \; / \; \underline{} \, [x, \gamma] \qquad \text{IV (130)}$$

$\left(24\right)$ AUXILIARY REDUCTION—II

$$\begin{bmatrix} \alpha\text{stress} \\ \text{V} \end{bmatrix} \rightarrow [2\,\text{stress}] \; / \; \# \left\{ \begin{array}{l} [-\text{stress}]_0 \underline{} C_0 \left(\begin{bmatrix} -\text{tense} \\ -\text{stress} \\ \text{V} \end{bmatrix} C_0^1 \right) \bar{C}_0 \begin{bmatrix} \beta\text{stress} \\ \text{V} \end{bmatrix} \bar{C}_0 \begin{bmatrix} \gamma\text{stress} \\ \text{V} \end{bmatrix} \bar{C}_0 \left\{ \begin{matrix} \# \\ \begin{bmatrix} \delta\text{stress} \\ \text{V} \end{bmatrix} \end{matrix} \right\} \\[2em] C_0 \left\{ \begin{matrix} \underline{} C_2 \\ \begin{bmatrix} \underline{} \\ +\text{tense} \end{bmatrix} \end{matrix} \right\} \end{array} \right\}$$

where $\bar{C}$ is a consonant or a boundary   III (120)

$\alpha \neq 1$

β is weaker than 2

δ is weaker than γ

$\left(25\right)$

$$\begin{bmatrix} +\text{cor} \\ +\text{strid} \\ +\text{cont} \end{bmatrix} \rightarrow [+\text{voice}] \; / \; \left\{ \begin{array}{l} \text{V} = \underline{} \text{V} \\ \begin{bmatrix} +\text{tense} \\ \text{V} \end{bmatrix} \underline{} [-\text{cons}] \\ \text{Vk} \underline{} \hat{\text{V}} \end{array} \right\} \qquad \text{IV (119)}$$

$\left(26\right)$ SPIRANTIZATION

$$\begin{bmatrix} +\text{cor} \\ +\text{ant} \\ -\text{sonor} \end{bmatrix} \rightarrow \begin{bmatrix} +\text{cont} \\ +\text{strid} \end{bmatrix} \; / \; \left\{ \begin{array}{l} \begin{bmatrix} \underline{} \\ +\text{voice} \end{bmatrix} + ive \\[1em] \left\{ \begin{matrix} [+\text{sonor}] \\ [-\text{cont}] \end{matrix} \right\} \underline{} \; / \left\{ \begin{matrix} \begin{bmatrix} \underline{} \\ -\text{voice} \end{bmatrix} + \begin{bmatrix} -\text{cons} \\ -\text{back} \\ -\text{stress} \end{bmatrix} [-\text{seg}] \\ \underline{} + y \end{matrix} \right\} \\[1em] \begin{bmatrix} \underline{} \\ +\text{strid} \end{bmatrix} \end{array} \right\}$$

IV (120)
and p. 233

[4] We have extended this rule over (20) of Chapter Four by generalizing the pre-boundary case of tensing to all boundaries other than formative boundary, thus to = as well as #. Recall that = appears in forms such as /pre=tend/, /re=sist/ (cf. Chapter Three, Section 10), where tensing would otherwise not take place in the prefix. See also note 6 below.

$$\left(27\right) \qquad \qquad k \ \rightarrow \ \phi \ / +C_1 i \underline{\quad} \# \qquad \qquad \text{IV (62)}$$

$\left(28\right)$ CLUSTER SIMPLIFICATION

$$C \ \rightarrow \ \phi \ / \underline{\qquad} \textit{identical consonant}$$

III (156); IV p. 222 and note 60

$$\left(29\right) \qquad \phi \ \rightarrow \ y \ / \underline{\qquad} \begin{bmatrix} +\text{tense} \\ -\text{round} \\ +\text{high} \\ +\text{back} \\ V \end{bmatrix}$$

IV (50) and p. 196

$$\left(30\right) \qquad \qquad \bar{\Lambda} \ \rightarrow \ [+\text{low}] \qquad \qquad \text{IV (78)}$$

$\left(31\right)$ DIPHTHONGIZATION

$$\phi \ \rightarrow \ \begin{bmatrix} -\text{voc} \\ -\text{cons} \\ +\text{high} \\ \alpha\text{back} \\ \alpha\text{round} \\ \beta\text{rule 32} \end{bmatrix} \Bigg/ \begin{bmatrix} +\text{tense} \\ \alpha\text{back} \\ \beta\text{rule 32} \\ V \end{bmatrix} \underline{\qquad}$$

IV (21) and p. 208

$\left(32\right)$ GLIDE VOCALIZATION

$$\begin{bmatrix} -\text{cons} \\ +\text{back} \end{bmatrix} \ \rightarrow \ [+\text{voc}] \ / \begin{bmatrix} \alpha\text{round} \\ \alpha\text{high} \\ V \end{bmatrix} \underline{\qquad}$$

IV (74)

$\left(33\right)$ VOWEL SHIFT

$$\begin{bmatrix} \gamma\text{back} \\ \gamma\text{round} \\ V \end{bmatrix} \rightarrow \left\{ \begin{matrix} [-\alpha\text{high}] \ / \begin{bmatrix} \overline{\alpha\text{high}} \\ -\text{low} \end{bmatrix} \\[2em] [-\beta\text{low}] \ / \begin{bmatrix} \overline{\beta\text{low}} \\ -\text{high} \end{bmatrix} \end{matrix} \right\} \Bigg/ \left\{ \begin{matrix} \begin{bmatrix} \overline{\begin{matrix} +\text{tense} \\ +\text{stress} \end{matrix}} \end{bmatrix} \\[1.5em] \begin{bmatrix} \overline{} \\ +F \end{bmatrix} \\[1.5em] \begin{bmatrix} \overline{\begin{matrix} -\text{tense} \\ +\text{high} \\ +\text{back} \end{matrix}} \end{bmatrix} \end{matrix} \right\}$$

IV (43)

IV (61)

IV (63)

$\left(34\right)$ ROUNDING ADJUSTMENT

$$\begin{bmatrix} \alpha\text{round} \\ +\text{back} \\ V \end{bmatrix} \rightarrow [-\alpha\text{round}] \quad / \quad \left\{ \begin{bmatrix} \overline{} \\ -\text{tense} \end{bmatrix} \atop \begin{bmatrix} \overline{} \\ \beta\text{low} \\ \beta\text{round} \\ +\text{tense} \\ \overline{} V \end{bmatrix} \right\}$$

IV (93)

$\left(35\right)$ BACKNESS ADJUSTMENT[5]

$$\begin{bmatrix} +\text{low} \\ V \end{bmatrix} \rightarrow [+\text{back}] \quad / \quad \overline{}[-\text{cons}]$$

IV (88)

$\left(36\right)$

$$a \rightarrow [+\text{tense}]$$

IV (89)

$\left(37\right)$ PALATALIZATION

$$\begin{bmatrix} -\text{sonor} \\ +\text{cor} \end{bmatrix} \rightarrow \begin{bmatrix} -\text{ant} \\ +\text{strid} \end{bmatrix} \quad / \quad \overline{} \begin{bmatrix} -\text{back} \\ -\text{cons} \\ -\text{voc} \end{bmatrix} \begin{bmatrix} -\text{cons} \\ -\text{stress} \end{bmatrix}$$

IV (121)

$\left(38\right)$

$$\begin{bmatrix} -\text{cons} \\ -\text{voc} \end{bmatrix} \rightarrow \phi \quad / \quad \left\{ \begin{matrix} \begin{bmatrix} +\text{cor} \\ -\text{ant} \\ -\text{sonor} \end{bmatrix} \overline{} \\ \begin{bmatrix} +\text{cor} \\ +\text{cons} \end{bmatrix} \begin{bmatrix} \overline{} \\ -\text{back} \end{bmatrix} [+\text{stress}] \end{matrix} \right\}$$

IV (122)

IV (123)

$\left(39\right)$

$$z \rightarrow [-\text{voice}] \quad / \quad \overline{} +ive$$

IV (124)

$\left(40\right)$

$$\begin{bmatrix} -\text{cor} \\ -\text{ant} \\ +\text{cont} \\ -\text{voc} \end{bmatrix} \rightarrow \left\{ \begin{matrix} \phi \ / \ \left\{ \begin{matrix} C\ \overline{} \\ \overline{}\ C \end{matrix} \right\} \\ h \end{matrix} \right\}$$

IV (129)
and p. 234

---

[5] Note that this formulation of Backness Adjustment is for the dialect with [āw] rather than [æw] as the reflex of underlying /ū/. (See rule (39) and note 48 in Chapter Four.) This rule when stated in its fully general form should incorporate the rule that converts stressed [ā] into [æ] in forms such as *Alabama*, *alabaster* (see Chapter Three, p. 152). We omit rule (40) of Chapter Four, which, in dialects that have [æw] from [āw], laxes [ǣ] produced by Backness Adjustment.

$\left(41\right)$ *e*-ELISION[6]

$$\begin{bmatrix} -\text{back} \\ -\text{high} \\ -\text{low} \\ -\text{cons} \end{bmatrix} \rightarrow \quad \phi \quad / \text{——} [-\text{seg}] \qquad\qquad \text{III (155)}$$

$\left(42\right)$

$$\phi \quad \rightarrow \quad \vartheta \quad / \ C\text{——}[+\text{sonor}]\# \qquad\qquad \text{III p. 85}$$

$\left(43\right)$ VOWEL REDUCTION[7]

$$\begin{bmatrix} -\text{stress} \\ -\text{tense} \\ V \end{bmatrix} \rightarrow \quad \vartheta \qquad\qquad \text{III (121)}$$

---

[6] This rule deserves a more extensive study than we have given it. In particular, its position in the ordering is open to some question. Our only justification for placing it here is that, for reasons mentioned in note 18 of Chapter Four, it may follow Vowel Shift so as to account for nonelision in the boldface position in words such as *simultaneous*. The rule of *e*-Elision should be distinguished from a rule that drops both /e/ and the glides /y/ and /ɛ/ before various affixes, as in *telescopic, telescopy, harmonic,* and *harmonize*. The latter is, presumably, a lexical rule.

    We have noted (see p. 195 of Chapter Four) that the rule of *e*-Elision can be used to account for the fact that the first syllable is short in words such as *issue, tissue, value, menu*. As pointed out to us by S. J. Keyser, it can be used to explain the lax vowel in the first syllable in words such as *pity, city,* if we derive these from /pitɛ/, /sitɛ/. Stress will be placed on the first syllable by the usual rule for nouns, and the trisyllabic laxing rule will guarantee that the stressed vowel is lax. The [e]'s will tense, and the glide [ɛ] will elide. By the rule mentioned in note 18, Chapter Four, final [ĕy] will become [ĭy]. This idea has further consequences that might be explored.

[7] We leave open the question of just how the reduced vowel is actualized phonetically in various contexts.

PART III
HISTORY

Chapter six

THE EVOLUTION OF THE MODERN ENGLISH VOWEL SYSTEM

1. Introductory remarks

In this chapter we review the vowel systems of four English dialects spoken in earlier centuries. Our purpose is to trace the evolution of the pivotal rules of the modern English vowel system—Diphthongization, Vowel Shift, and Rounding Adjustment—and to provide some explanation for the remarkable stability of the underlying system of representations. The four dialects examined below were chosen because they illustrate the main steps in the evolution. They do not, of course, constitute a single line of descent from the earliest to the latest; nor is any of them necessarily the lineal ancestor of the dialect of modern English that is described in the main part of this book. The dialects are, however, sufficiently closely related so as to provide us with a reasonably clear picture of the main lines of development.

1.1. ON LINGUISTIC CHANGE

In our view, a grammar of a language represents the linguistic competence of a speaker. In acquiring a language, a child does not memorize the utterances he hears; rather, he somehow utilizes these utterances to construct for himself a grammar, that is, a collection of rules in accordance with which he can produce and understand an unlimited number of utterances, many of them new to him and not similar in any significant sense to those previously encountered. The rules that constitute the grammar of a particular speaker determine in detail the form of the sentences that the speaker will produce and understand. If two speakers differ in the phonetic (or semantic) interpretation they assign to sentences, this difference can only be due to some difference in the character or organization of the rules that make up their respective grammars. Consequently an observed linguistic change can have only one source—a change in the grammar that underlies the observed utterances.

A straightforward way of effecting changes in a grammar is to add new rules. The addition of a rule to the phonological component may be regarded as the most rudimentary type of sound change. When such a change takes place, the added rule will satisfy the same formal constraints as the other rules of the phonological component. Many sound changes known in diachronic phonology are of this type. By and large the familiar "sound laws" are, in fact, rules added to the phonological component, although one can easily imagine possible cases that could not be properly described in this way.

The conception of linguistic change as a change in the grammar is also implicit in the traditional views of sound change. One of the crucial facts that linguists have tried to explain is that speakers are by and large unaware of the changes that their language is undergoing. The reason for this, it has been claimed, is that changes affect only the phonetic actualization of particular sounds—and, moreover, in so slight a measure that the changes appear to be gradual. In other words, in this view, which we might call the "gradual" view of sound change, phonetic changes are restricted—with a few notable exceptions such as epenthesis, elision, and metathesis—to changes in the low-level phonetic rules that assign the precise numerical value to the different features in different contexts. Thus, vowels may be articulated somewhat farther back than before, or consonants may be actualized in some environment with aspiration of degree 4 whereas earlier they were actualized in that environment with degree 2. While there is no logical reason to reject this view of sound change, there is certainly no reason to give it special status. With the exception of the fact that speakers are unaware of an ongoing change—a fact which is easily explainable on the ground that speakers are, in general, unaware of the contents of their grammar—there is very little factual data to bear out this view. This embarrassing situation has not passed unnoticed. For example, Hoenigswald (1964) has written:

> . . . since it is surely difficult to imagine a speaker discoursing about an ongoing sound change, it was by no means unreasonable to think of sound change as gradual and hence imperceptible. The "sounds," the ranges of articulation, the statistical "maxima" of these ranges become more and more similar to each other in a nondistinctive way until, presumably, the harm is done, and the speakers (who would never have dreamed of dropping a given phonetic contrast of their own free will) are insidiously trapped—this seems to be the picture. So far as I know it has always been an entirely speculative picture whose best feature is a surface plausibility which it once possessed but does not possess any more. Are there any data that would bear it out? (p. 207)

The lack of evidence, however, has not prevented scholars from continuing to espouse the gradual view of sound change. Thus Hockett (1965) proposes to explain sound change precisely in the terms just sketched, without citing any actual instances. However, Hockett's exposition is notable for the fact that, unlike many writers on this subject, he explicitly recognizes the role that the rules of the grammar play in determining the physical shape of utterances. Thus the possibility arises immediately in Hockett's "stratificational" grammar, as it does in the grammar discussed here, that sound change—i.e., systematic changes in the phonetic actualization of particular utterances or parts of utterances—may be due to changes in the grammar other than in the low-level phonetic rules. For example, a change such as the Germanic spirantization of voiceless stops could readily arise if a rule were added to the component that in Hockett's grammar "maps strings of morphons into successions of bundles of distinctive features" (p. 200). Surprisingly, this possibility is not considered anywhere in Hockett's paper.[1]

In the traditional approach to sound change, a "sound law" is an observed correspondence between two stages of a language, a formula expressing the relationship between the phonological representation of formatives before and after the change. The effects of a

---

[1] For further discussion of Hockett's treatment of sound change, see Postal (1968, Chapter 14).

change, therefore, are incorporated directly into the lexical representations of individual formatives. In our approach, on the other hand, a rule that is added to the grammar may continue to function for many generations without causing changes in the lexical representations. Our view of sound change thus permits an explanation of the observations made by Bloomfield (1939) when he found, in a synchronic description of Menomini, that:

> our basic forms do bear some resemblance to those which would be set up for a description of Proto-Algonquian, some of our statements of alternation ... resemble those which would appear in a description of Proto-Algonquian, and the rest ... as to content and order, approximate the historical development from Proto-Algonquian to present-day Menomini (p. 106).

In the light of the preceding statements, the conclusion might be drawn that a grammar of a language contains nothing but rules that at one time or another were introduced into the language by the " operation " of a " sound law."[2] This does not happen to be the case: in synchronic grammars one finds numerous rules that cannot be traced directly to any sound change. Before we turn to actual examples, let us consider why this is so.

An essential feature of our theory of language is that it includes an evaluation measure which makes it possible to assign values to alternative grammars. It is on the basis of this evaluation measure that a child learning a language chooses one of the grammars (of which there are, in principle, infinitely many) compatible with the fairly restricted body of linguistic data to which he has been exposed. The grammar that a child constructs in learning his native tongue will therefore always be the one that ranks highest in terms of this evaluation measure.

It is easy to see that the addition of a given rule to a grammar G_1 may result in a grammar G_2 that produces the same linguistic forms as some other grammar G_3 yet is ranked lower than G_3 by the evaluation measure. We shall assume that when the language of adults undergoes such a change, their grammar is modified only by the addition of the rule in question.[3] When the children of these adults learn their native language from their parents, they will construct for themselves the highest ranking grammar G_3, which in principle may be quite different from G_2, the grammar of the parents. The fact that children and parents may have quite different grammars though speaking all but identical idiolects should hardly occasion surprise. When children learn their mother tongue, they are exposed not to its grammar directly but rather to the output of this grammar as it is actualized in the utterances of the parents, and it is on the basis of these utterances that children construct the grammar of the language. The children's grammar will contain a given phonological rule which corresponds to a historically attested change and is present in the grammar of their parents only if the grammar containing this rule is the most highly valued grammar in terms of the evaluation measure. In our discussion of the history of the English vowel system, we shall encounter changes such as the trisyllabic laxing rule (rule (19), Chapter Four), which has been carried over intact from the eleventh century into the contemporary language, and we shall also find changes where the particular rule that was added vanished

---

[2] Garde (1965), for example, reached this conclusion: "Nous arrivons donc à ce dilemme: ou bien les règles synchroniques sont une nouvelle formulation des lois diachroniques, ou bien elles sont fausses" (p. 145).
[3] One might speculate that the adult's inability to modify his grammar except by the addition or elimination of a few rules is one aspect of the well-known deterioration in the adult's capacity to acquire a new language.

from the contemporary language after having left appropriate traces in other parts of the grammar, in particular, in the representation of items in the lexicon and in new phonological rules.[4]

1.2. GENERAL COMMENTS ON THE EARLY HISTORY OF MODERN ENGLISH

Late Middle English is commonly assumed to have possessed the following simple vowels:

$\begin{pmatrix}1\end{pmatrix}$

TENSE				LAX		
ī	*time*	ū	*town*	i	*ship*	u	*cut*
ē	*meet*	ō	*goose*	e	*bed*	o	*dog*
ǣ	*mean*	ɔ̄	*boat*				
	ā	*hate*				a	*man*

In addition the language possessed a number of diphthongs which we shall assume were all made up of a tense vowel followed by a glide:

$\begin{pmatrix}2\end{pmatrix}$

	DIPHTHONGS		
ǣy	*day, maid*	ɔ̄y	*point*	ēw	*new*
ǣw	*dew*	ɔ̄w	*blow, know*	āw	*law, draw*

The diphthong represented here as /ēw/ derives historically from a number of sources (see Jespersen, 1909, pp. 101–102), among which are early ME *iw* and French *u*.[5] We shall assume that in late ME, i.e., at the stage of the language with which we are concerned here, this entity was represented as /ēw/, for this underlying representation results in the simplest grammar. If it is assumed that the underlying representation is /iw/, it would be necessary to add an ad hoc rule exempting this diphthong from an otherwise general tensing rule (see rule (4) below). In any event, we adopt the position of Jespersen and others who have held that in ME there were two, not three, diphthongs composed of front vowel and /w/. Some handbooks indicate that there was also a diphthong /uy/, but its status is quite unclear since sources differ as to the words that are supposed to exemplify /uy/.[6] We shall make the assumption that this diphthong occupied a marginal position in the language. Thus a few words, specifically marked in the dictionary, were allowed to contain /uy/, but otherwise the appropriate diphthong was /ɔ̄y/.

---

[4] It is obvious that the same development may take place when, instead of adding a rule, the language eliminates or changes an already existing rule. For further discussion of this question, see Kiparsky (1965).

[5] We shall not enter here into the involved question of whether Middle English had the sound [ü], but shall assume that this was not the case and that all English reflexes of foreign [ü] coincided with the contemporary reflexes of ME /ēw/. Our views in this matter have been decisively influenced by Zachrisson's study (1913). His conclusion that the diphthong /ēw/ and the French /y/ were both "pronounced *iu* or (ju.) . . . [and that] there is no conclusive evidence for the pronounciation (y)" (p. 223) seems to us correct. (See the survey of more recent literature in Danielsson (1963, pp. 113 f.))

[6] Jespersen (1909): "the early history of the diphthongs [ɔi and ui—NC/MH] is obscure: Luick's attempt to separate them is not successful" (p. 100). See also Dobson (1957), pages 910 f., and, especially, the last paragraph on page 823, where much evidence is presented showing that sixteenth century sources made no clear distinction between the two diphthongs. In view of this evidence it is somewhat surprising that Dobson draws from it the conclusion that "in the sixteenth and seventeenth centuries ME *ui* was still a falling diphthong [ui]."

The language had two phonological processes that affected the tenseness (tradition-ally the "quantity") of vowels. These processes, which are still productive in contemporary English (see (8), (19), (20), Chapter Four), are represented by the following rules:

$\left(3\right)$ LAXING

$$V \rightarrow [-\text{tense}] \quad / \underline{\quad} [+\text{cons}] \left\{ \begin{array}{ll} \begin{bmatrix} -\text{voc} \\ +\text{cons} \end{bmatrix} & \text{(a)} \\ \begin{bmatrix} -\text{stress} \\ V \end{bmatrix} C_0 V & \text{(b)} \end{array} \right.$$

$\left(4\right)$ TENSING

$$V \rightarrow [+\text{tense}] \quad / \underline{\quad} [-\text{cons}]$$

The Laxing Rule, essentially in the form given in (3), is quite old. According to Jordan (1934), laxing before double consonants is attested about the year 1000 (p. 41), and laxing in trisyllabic words before 1100 (p. 43). Rule (3) is not meant to exhaust all histori-cally attested instances of laxing but is specifically restricted to those that are still operative in the contemporary language. For similar reasons we have given only one environment for tensing, although at different stages of the evolution of the language there were numer-ous other environments in which tensing took place (see Excursus 2 below). The environ-ment in rule (4) is a special case of tensing in open syllable, a phenomenon well attested in English since at least the thirteenth century (Horn and Lehnert, 1954, p. 662).

Excursus 1.   In his discussion of tenseness (length) of vowels in Romance borrowings, Luick (1907) observes that in bisyllabic words great variation is apparent. While some of the words, such as *banner, barrel, bottle, button, gallon, mutton,* show a lax vowel, others such as *basin, mason, label, bacon* show a tense vowel, and still others such as *lever* vacillate between a tense and a lax vowel. We should like to propose the following to account for this phenomenon. In borrowed words stressed vowels were tense in open syllables; for example, *chace, vile, close* (see Luick, 1907). It has been shown by Halle and Keyser (forth-coming) that as a result of the laxing of vowels in a final syllable that was either open or closed by a single consonant, stress was shifted in trisyllabic and longer words, from the final syllable to the antepenult if the penultimate syllable ended with a weak cluster; other-wise, stress shifted from the final syllable to the penult. Examples of the latter shift are provided by words such as *condition* in Chaucer. In certain lines this word has final stress, as indicated by the rime, e.g., with *resoun* (A. P. 39); on the other hand, in lines such as

O hateful harm! condicion of poverte   (B. ML. 99)

the word must be stressed on the antepenult for the line to be metrically regular.

To account for these stress alternants, it must be assumed that in Chaucer's time the rule laxing vowels in final syllables was optional and, moreover, applied before the Stress Rule, whereas the rule tensing stressed vowels in Romance words, as well as the Laxing Rules (3a, b), must be assumed to have applied (synchronically) after the Stress Rule. The Laxing Rules (3a, b) are thus distinct and separate from the rule laxing vowels in final syllables.

Many ME inflected forms, e.g., plural forms, had an additional syllable (*baron–barones*). As a consequence, bisyllabic forms alternated with trisyllabic forms; i.e., a given word had case forms that were subject to the Laxing Rule (3b) as well as case forms that were not subject to laxing. Hence, at that stage of the language, tense-lax alternations sometimes served as supplementary signals for the difference between singular and plural. Schematically the situation might be represented as follows:

$$\begin{pmatrix} 5 \end{pmatrix}$$
galūn	galūn+es		bakūn	bakūn+es	
galun	galun+es		bakun	bakun+es	FINAL-SYLLABLE LAXING
gálun	gálun+es		bákun	bákun+es	STRESS RULE
gắlun	gắlun+es		bắkun	bắkun+es	STRESSED-VOWEL TENSING
gắlun	gắlun+es		bắkun	bắkun+es	LAXING RULE (3b)

When in the course of the further evolution of the language the /e/ of the plural suffix was lost, there were two types of bisyllabic words: those like (5), which had accompanying alternations between tense and lax vowels, and others which did not show such alternations. These tenseness alternations soon vanished, with the result that certain of the words were entered in the lexicon with tense vowels and others with lax vowels. Thus *gallon* now has a lax vowel, *bacon* a tense vowel, and *lever* (and perhaps a few other forms) vacillates between a tense and a lax vowel.

Excursus 2.   In modern English tensing also takes place in the environment (6) (see rule (20b), Chapter Four):

$$\begin{pmatrix} 6 \end{pmatrix} \qquad \left[\begin{array}{c} \underline{} \\ -\text{high} \end{array} \right] C_1^1 \left[\begin{array}{c} -\text{cons} \\ -\text{back} \\ -\text{low} \\ -\text{stress} \end{array} \right] \left[\begin{array}{c} +\text{voc} \\ -\text{cons} \end{array} \right]$$

It is interesting to observe that the sixteenth century orthoepist Hart (see Section 2) does not have tensing in this environment. Thus he gives *grīk* with a tense /ē/ actualized as [ī], but *gresian* with lax [e]. Furthermore, Hart shows lax vowels in his transcriptions of *period, nasions, experience, komodiuzlei*, in the boldface positions, where in modern English, because of the extension of tensing to environment (6), we get tense vowels. By 1644 Hodges (see Kauter, 1930b) does have tensing in this environment, as shown by his transcriptions *përiod, Säviour, convënient*[7] (although *experience* is listed twice without any indication of tenseness).

In the fifteenth century English underwent what is traditionally known as the Great Vowel Shift. We have clear evidence of this from the early sixteenth century. "The long /i/ must ... have become /ei/ about 1500; it is transcribed *ei* in the Welsh hymn written about that time" (Jespersen, 1909, p. 234). At about the same time tense /ē/ and /ō/ become [ī] and [ū], respectively. Jespersen (1909) notes that the development of special spellings for /ɔ̄/ and /ǣ/ distinct from those for /ō/ and /ē/ dates from this time only:

> ... in ME each of the letters *e* and *o* denoted two long vowels, /e· ɛ·/ and /o· ɔ·/. This was not felt to be singular any more than it is in many other languages, and no effort was made to give graphical expression to the distinction. But in the middle of the 16th century we find the spelling *ie* coming into use for the close variety of *e*, and *ea* for the open, and at the same time *oa* becomes usual for the open o-sound... If we assume the values /i·/ in *field* and /u·/ in *too* coexisting with /ɛ·/ in *beast* and /ɔ·/ in *road*, we can easily see why people should have adopted distinct notations for sounds which had become thus widely separated from one another (pp. 233 f.)

---

[7] The diaeresis is Hodges' device for indicating tenseness.

There has been a certain amount of discussion concerning the nature of the earliest (pre-seventeenth century) products of the Vowel Shift. In particular, Dobson, in his encyclopedic *English Pronunciation 1500–1700* (1957), concluded that the reflexes [ēy] and [ōw] of ME tense /ī/ and /ū/ could not have existed. He writes:

> The usual theory ... is that ME *ī* developed through the stages [ei] [ɛi] [æi] to [ai]. This view is altogether impossible. If the development had been that suggested, ME *ī* would have crossed the path of ME *ai* developing to [æi] and [ɛi] ... Yet the two sounds are always kept distinct, as they are still. ME *ī* can never have been [ɛi], and we must therefore admit that the orthoepists' transcription of ME *ī* as *ei* and their comparison of it with foreign [ɛi] sounds were not exact ... (p. 660).

> It is often argued, on the basis of some of these identifications with foreign sounds and some of the analyses and transcriptions, that ME *ū* was diphthongized in the first instance to [ou], as it is similarly argued that ME *ī* was diphthongized to [ei] ... But in this event ME *ū* would have become identical with ME *ou*, which remained as a diphthong long after ME *ū* had become one. It is obvious that they did not become identical; alleged rhymes between the two sounds are to be otherwise explained ... (p. 684).

It is important to note that Dobson's conclusions concerning the pronunciation of these sounds in the sixteenth century are not based on evidence from the sources, but are rather inferences drawn on the assumption that sound change is a gradual process. Since what Dobson terms "the usual view" concerning the facts of sixteenth century pronunciation of ME tense /ī/ and /ū/ cannot be reconciled with a view of sound change as a gradual process, Dobson feels justified in interpreting away the statements and transcriptions to be found in sixteenth century sources. (Cf. Zachrisson (1913, p. 205, p. 207); Dobson (1957, pp. 659–60, p. 684); and see Section 2 for quotations from one of these sources, John Hart.) We have seen, however (Section 1.1), that the existence of gradual sound change is far from solidly established in spite of its very general acceptance. Therefore it does not in itself provide sufficient reason for rejecting explicit statements made by an observer such as Hart, whom Dobson himself ranks "among the greatest English phoneticians" (p. 62), and whose statements there is no other reason to doubt. Incidentally, in Hart's speech the ME nonhigh nonlow (mid) vowels were high monophthongs, whereas the ME high vowels had become nonhigh nonlow (mid) diphthongs which were distinct from the reflexes of the ME diphthongs. This simultaneous lowering and raising process—which is to be distinguished from the one referred to by Dobson—could be accounted for without difficulty even if one were to adopt the gradual view of sound change: the environments where /ī/ and /ū/ are lowered to [ē] and [ō] are distinct from those where /ē/ and /ō/ are raised to [ī] and [ū] since only reflexes of ME /ī/ and /ū/ were diphthongized in Hart. Finally, as will be shown, the appearance in the seventeenth century of [ʌy] and [ʌw] as reflexes of ME tense /ī/ and /ū/ is correlated with the appearance at the same time of [ʌ] as the reflex of lax /u/ and with a host of other phenomena which were unknown in the sixteenth century.

At this point in time, then, the nonlow tense vowels of Middle English had undergone the following changes:

$$
\begin{pmatrix} 7 \end{pmatrix} \qquad
\begin{array}{ccccc}
\text{ME} & \bar{\imath} & \bar{u} & \bar{e} & \bar{o} \\
& \downarrow & \downarrow & \downarrow & \downarrow \\
& \bar{e}y & \bar{o}w^8 & \bar{\imath} & \bar{u}
\end{array}
$$

---

[8] In the absence of evidence either for or against, we shall assume that the diphthongized vowels were not laxed at first.

To account for these changes, we propose that the following two ordered rules were added to the grammar of English in the fifteenth century:

(8) DIPHTHONGIZATION

$$\phi \;\rightarrow\; \begin{bmatrix} -\text{voc} \\ -\text{cons} \\ \alpha\text{back} \end{bmatrix} \;/\; \begin{bmatrix} +\text{voc} \\ -\text{cons} \\ +\text{tense} \\ +\text{high} \\ \alpha\text{back} \end{bmatrix}\underline{\qquad}$$

(9) VOWEL SHIFT

$$\begin{bmatrix} \alpha\text{high} \\ -\text{low} \end{bmatrix} \;\rightarrow\; [-\alpha\text{high}] \;/\; \begin{bmatrix} \underline{\qquad} \\ +\text{tense} \\ +\text{stress} \end{bmatrix}$$

That is, we assume that high tense vowels were diphthongized and that subsequently tense nonlow vowels under stress were subject to an exchange rule that turned high vowels into nonhigh vowels and nonhigh vowels into high vowels.

Although the two rules have to apply in the order indicated, we do not claim that they were added to the language in this order. It is possible that in this case the synchronic order coincides with the history of the language, but it is equally possible that rule (9) was added first and that subsequently rule (8) was introduced before rule (9) in the synchronic order of the rules. Since there appears to be no factual evidence that would allow us to decide what actually transpired, this question must remain open.

1.3. CONCERNING EXCHANGE RULES[9]

The proposed solution raises a number of issues that require comment. In particular, the role of exchange rules such as (9) in phonological change has been questioned on the basis that the addition of such rules to a grammar would result in a serious impairment of intelligibility between speakers who had adopted the change and those who had not. It might be claimed that it would be confusing if an exchange rule such as the Vowel Shift were added to a grammar since this would result, for example, in former [pūl] being pronounced [pōl], while former [pōl] would be pronounced [pūl]. One may reasonably doubt, however, that intelligibility between dialects would be impaired, for it is well known that intelligibility is only moderately affected in normal everyday speech even when all vowel contrasts are eliminated and a single vowel is made to stand in their place. A change like the one described would have very striking effects if subjects speaking a dialect that had not undergone the change in question had to identify correctly words in a randomly selected list. But word identification tests of this type, though valuable for testing the quality of telephone lines, are of only marginal value in determining the effects of a phonological change on intelligibility. It might be noted that a subject's performance on such a test would

---

[9] The comments in this section, as well as some in the preceding section, are in response to questions raised primarily by R. P. Stockwell, in particular in his "Realism in Historical English Phonology," presented at the Winter 1964 meeting of the Linguistic Society of America, and "Problems in the Interpretation of the Great English Vowel Shift," presented at Austin, Texas, January 1966. Since these papers have remained unpublished, we deal with the issues raised without attributing specific views to Stockwell or to any other person.

be even worse if the change undergone by the language had been a phonetic merger, a possible change about which there surely can be no question. We conclude, then, that intelligibility considerations cannot be advanced as reasons for excluding exchange rules as vehicles of phonological change.

It may also be observed that it is easy to construct situations in which exchange rules would not result in any conceivable impairment in either intelligibility or word identification. Consider a language with an ordinary five-vowel pattern /u o a e i/. If this language were subject to a rounding shift, the following correspondences would be established:

$$\left(10\right) \qquad u \rightarrow i \qquad o \rightarrow \Lambda \qquad a \rightarrow \mathfrak{d} \qquad e \rightarrow \ddot{o} \qquad i \rightarrow \ddot{u}$$

All five of the vowels are kept distinct and there is a change only in the phonetic actualization. In such a situation there is likely to be no greater impairment of intelligibility than if each of the vowels had been slightly fronted or diphthongized. Consequently, if, as proposed above, intelligibility were the controlling factor, there would be no reason for excluding a rounding exchange rule. If, however, the language had also been subject to an umlauting rule which fronted back vowels in certain environments, then the addition of the exchange rule would result in the sort of phonetic switch that, according to the view under examination, is harmful to intelligibility, and the addition of the exchange rule could not be allowed.

This example brings out a further difficulty in the objection to exchange rules. Since it is impossible to tell from the form of a rule in isolation whether or not the addition of this rule would result in the type of phonetic switch that supposedly affects intelligibility, it may be necessary to check the derivations of all possible phonological phrases in order to determine this matter. This is a finite task, since an upper bound can realistically be imposed on the length of the phonological phrase. However, we feel that "global" conditions of this sort on the well-formedness of grammars should be excluded in principle. To allow such conditions would be to assert, in effect, that a check through all possible derivations must be performed by the speaker who is about to add a rule to his grammar, a supposition that is implausible in the extreme.

It should be noted, moreover, that, as we have just seen, the same impairment in a subject's performance on a word identification test would result if the language had originally contained the (by itself "harmless") rounding exchange rule and had added the umlaut rule later. In fact, if word identification were a factor in determining whether or not a rule could be added to a grammar, it would be necessary to check all possible derivations of the grammar before adding any rule at all, since phonetic shift ($a \rightarrow b$ while $b \rightarrow a$) can be produced by the addition of almost any type of rule. We describe a few such cases below.

A language may possess a pair of rules which have opposite effects in two distinct environments, and the two rules in question may, moreover, be adjacent in the synchronic order of the rules. This is by no means an unusual situation. It is found, for instance, in the phonology of English, where, as shown in rule (118) of Chapter Four, the glide [y] is replaced by the vowel [i] in one environment and the vowel [i] is replaced by the glide [y] in another environment. It can readily be imagined that subsequent changes in the grammar might result in a coalescence of the two environments, making the net effect of the two rules equivalent to a regular exchange rule which shifts the feature "vocalic" in some environment.

An exchange rule might also result from the addition of a rule to the grammar of a language which already contains a rule with precisely the opposite effect. For instance, consider a language that is subject to a rule assigning the feature [−low] to (i.e., raising) tense vowels which agree in backness and rounding. This rule, however, does not result in a merger with other nonhigh vowels, since by a (synchronically) prior rule, the latter nonhigh vowels become unrounded and back. More formally, we may say that the language has the following two ordered rules:

$$\left(11\right) \qquad (a) \quad \begin{bmatrix} -\text{high} \\ -\text{low} \end{bmatrix} \quad \rightarrow \quad \begin{bmatrix} -\text{round} \\ +\text{back} \end{bmatrix}$$

$$(b) \quad \begin{bmatrix} \alpha\text{back} \\ \alpha\text{round} \end{bmatrix} \quad \rightarrow \quad [-\text{low}]$$

Suppose that subsequently the language adds a rule lowering nonhigh vowels that do not agree in backness and rounding:

$$\left(12\right) \qquad \begin{bmatrix} -\text{round} \\ +\text{back} \end{bmatrix} \quad \rightarrow \quad [+\text{low}]$$

Once this happens, a simpler grammar is possible, namely, one including the exchange rule (13):

$$\left(13\right) \qquad [\beta\text{low}] \quad \rightarrow \quad [-\beta\text{low}] \quad / \quad \begin{bmatrix} \rule{1cm}{0.4pt} \\ \alpha\text{back} \\ \alpha\text{round} \\ -\text{high} \end{bmatrix}$$

followed by a rule turning the resulting low vowels into [a]:

$$\left(14\right) \qquad [+\text{low}] \quad \rightarrow \quad \begin{bmatrix} -\text{round} \\ +\text{back} \end{bmatrix}$$

In this case the exchange rule results from the restructuring of a grammar that did not contain rules involving feature shift. Something quite similar to this might have happened in the evolution of the second part of the Vowel Shift in the dialect from which the variety of English described here is derived. (See Section 5.2 of this chapter.)

It is possible that the first stage of the Vowel Shift—i.e., rule (9)—is also the result of this type of restructuring. Subsequent to Diphthongization, tense nonlow monophthongs may have been made high (raised), and then the vowels that had previously been diphthongized—i.e., the originally high vowels—were made nonhigh (lowered). More formally, instead of rule (9) the language added rule (15):

$$\left(15\right) \qquad \begin{bmatrix} -\text{low} \\ +\text{tense} \\ +\text{stress} \end{bmatrix} \quad \rightarrow \quad \left\{ \begin{array}{l} [+\text{high}] \\ [-\text{high}] \quad / \quad \rule{0.6cm}{0.4pt} \begin{bmatrix} -\text{voc} \\ -\text{cons} \end{bmatrix} \end{array} \right\}$$

Some of the dialectal evidence makes such an account quite plausible. At present, however, this is still far from established, and the possibility that (9) was added to the grammar directly cannot be ruled out. Moreover, even if research should ultimately determine that the first stage of the Vowel Shift is the result of restructuring, this would still not dispose of the possibility of exchange rules being added to a grammar directly.

As noted above, when phonological change is the result of the addition of a rule to a grammar, the added rule must satisfy the constraints that are placed on grammatical rules in general. It is conceivable that the constraints on rules that can be added to a grammar may be more severe than those on rules that can figure in a grammar. At the present time, however, we do not know of any reason why these additional constraints (if there are such) should rule out exchange rules. In fact, we have just seen that the attempts to impose constraints ruling out certain types of exchange rules are without foundation. These attempts were based on the mistaken assumption that intelligibility is necessarily impaired when a few distinctive cues are obliterated; they lead not only to the imposition of inappropriate "global" conditions on phonological change but also to the formal exclusion of phonemic merger, i.e., the exclusion of a type of change that has been observed on numerous occasions. In sum, it seems to us that exchange rules, which are implicit in a notation that allows variables as coefficients of distinctive features, should be no more restricted than other types of phonological rules and, in particular, that exchange rules may be added to a grammar to produce phonological change.

The fact that the Laxing and Tensing Rules (3) and (4) in one form or another have figured continuously in the language from the eleventh century to the present is one of the reasons for the great stability of the underlying vowel system. It has been argued in Chapter Four that because of the presence of these two rules, Diphthongization and Vowel Shift must also be phonological rules of the language. The alternative would be to incorporate the effects of Diphthongization and Vowel Shift directly into the lexical representations of the formatives. This alternative, however, is not really open to us, since these effects would have to be included in both the Laxing Rule and the Tensing Rule as well; that is, the complicated facts of Diphthongization and Vowel Shift would have to be stated repeatedly in the grammar. On the other hand, by representing the tense vowels that have undergone Diphthongization and Vowel Shift as monophthongs—i.e., by assuming an underlying vowel system that approximates that of an earlier stage of the language—it is possible to give the Tensing and Laxing Rules in essentially the same simple form as in (3) and (4) and to state the complicated Diphthongization and Vowel Shift Rules only once. Since the ME diphthongs, unlike the tense vowels, did not generally participate in tenseness alternations, the historical changes to which they were subject were directly reflected in the underlying representations, with the result that diphthongs were ultimately eliminated from the underlying system altogether.

The preceding argument, which is basically a recapitulation of an argument presented in Chapter Four with regard to the facts of modern English, holds for earlier stages of the language as well, since both the Laxing and Tensing Rules have figured in the language for close to a thousand years. In the discussion that follows, we shall therefore assume that Diphthongization and Vowel Shift are an integral part of the phonological components of the various dialects examined and that the underlying vowel system in large measure resembles that of ME.

2. John Hart (1551–1579)

The first of the dialects to be examined is that of John Hart, who was a court official during the third quarter of the sixteenth century. His complete works on English spelling have been published in a careful edition by Bror Danielsson (1955 and 1963), and it is this edition that serves as the basis for our exposition.

2.1. THE EVIDENCE

Hart recognized five distinct pairs of tense and lax (in his terminology, long and short) vowel sounds, and he represented these by the letters *a e i o u.* According to Hart (Danielsson, 1955, p. 190) *a* is produced "with a wyde opening of the mouth as when a man yauneth." *e* is produced "with somewhat more closing the mouth [than *a*—NC/MH], thrusting softlye the inner part of the tongue to the inner and upper great teeth (or gummes for want of teeth)," and *i* "by pressing the tongue in like manner [as *e*—NC/MH] yet somewhat more forward and bringing the iawe somewhat more near." We shall therefore regard [a] as low, back, nonround; [e] as nonlow, nonhigh, nonback, nonround; and [i] as high, nonback, and nonround.

At first sight, Hart's description of the sound symbolized by the letter *o* may make it appear that he is referring to a low [ɔ] rather than to a nonlow [o], for he characterizes the sound of *o* as being formed "by taking awaye all the tongue from the teeth or gummes, as is sayde for the a, and turning the lippes round as a ring." This, however, cannot be taken to mean that the sound in question had the same low tongue position as [a], but only that it was "back," i.e., "awaye from all the teeth or gummes," for Hart characterizes *u* as being formed "by holding in *lyke manner* the tongue from touching the teeth or gummes (as is said of the a, and o)" [our italics—NC/MH]. In other words, Hart neglects (or is unable) to indicate differences in tongue height for back vowels. Since Hart's statements cannot be used to establish whether his *o* is low or nonlow, we shall assume that he meant nonlow [o] everywhere, since this assumption not only provides a more symmetrical vowel system but also leads to a somewhat simpler set of rules.

In addition Hart recognized a number of diphthongs. Of these there are several distinct types:

(a) Sequences consisting of a glide—[y] or [w]—followed by a vowel, e.g., *iē*, "yea"; *uī*, "we."
(b) Sequences of low vowel followed by a centralizing glide, e.g., *ōer*, "oar."
(c) Rising diphthongs consisting of a vowel followed by a glide. It is this class that requires some further comment.

Hart does not have special symbols for the glides [y] and [w] but represents them by the letters *i* and *u*, respectively. This is a direct consequence of Hart's general theory of spelling, which leads him to economize on symbols and use the same symbol to represent phonetically similar sounds in complementary distribution.

In the last of his works, Hart draws a distinction between the reflexes of ME tense /ū/, which he transcribes *ou* (i.e., with a lax vowel followed by *u*), and the reflexes of ME /ōw/, which he transcribes *ọu* (i.e., with a tense vowel followed by *u*). We assume, therefore, that for Hart the reflex of ME tense /ū/ was [ow], whereas the reflex of ME /ōw/ was [ōw]. As might be expected, Hart transcribes the reflex of ME tense /ī/ by *ei*, which we shall take as representing the pronunciation [ey].

As noted above (p. 255), a number of scholars, notably, Dobson (1957), have suggested that when Hart (as well as other sixteenth century sources) wrote *ou* and *ei*, he is to be understood as having meant [ʌw] and [ɣy] as reflexes of ME tense /ū/ and /ī/. There is no evidence in Hart's writings for such pronunciations, and it would seem unlikely that Hart would fail to record the absence of lip rounding in his reflex of ME /ū/, as is explicitly assumed by Dobson's transcription [ʌw]. We have seen above that Dobson's refusal to take Hart's evidence at face value stems from his conception of sound change as a gradual process.

As has already been indicated, this conception of sound change is without factual support. We have little reason, therefore, to impose extreme interpretations on Hart's perfectly plain statements and transcriptions in this case.

As further evidence against the view that Hart pronounced [ʌw] and [ɣy], we analyze briefly a comment by Gil (1621), who wrote fifty years after Hart, since this comment has been cited as tending to cast doubt on Hart's transcriptions and to support the alternative interpretation advanced by Dobson and others. The passage in question notes that Smith, a contemporary of Hart's, had been criticized "quod noui eius characteres nec aspectu grati sunt, nec scriptu faciles." This shortcoming, according to Gil, had been rectified by Hart to the best of his ability, but "ille, praeterquam quod nonnullas literas ad vsum pernecessarias omisit, sermonem nostrum characteribus suis non sequi, sed ducere meditabatur." Gil thus appears to feel that Hart's choice of symbols was a result of his wish to impose a particular pronunciation, which Gil did not approve of; and after citing a series of what he regards to be mistaken symbolizations in Hart, including in particular "ei pro I," Gil adds, "Non nostras his voces habes, sed Mopsarum fictitias." It should be noted, however, that regardless of whether one accepts Gil's criticism of Hart, it is clear from Gil's words that Hart's transcriptions represent an actual dialect, which Gil disapprovingly terms "Mopsarum fictitias." Gil's remarks were therefore intended to question the social acceptability of the pronunciation recorded by Hart, not its existence, which is the point at issue here.

We have already mentioned that in his last work Hart represented the reflex of the ME diphthong /ɔ̄w/ as [ōw]. This, however, is not the only reflex of this diphthong in Hart. In his earlier works, as well as in several places in the last work, the diphthong in question is transcribed by *o̧*, i.e., by the same letter as the reflex of ME tense /ɔ̄/. We take this to represent the sound [ō].[10] (See (16), p. 263.) Against one's expectations, there is no similar vacillation with regard to the nonback partner of /ɔ̄w/: the reflex of ME /ǣy/ in Hart is uniformly transcribed *ȩ* and thus coalesces everywhere with the reflex of ME tense /ǣ/.

We are now faced with the question of whether the vacillations in Hart's transcriptions of ME /ɔ̄w/ represent actual vacillations in his speech or instead result only from certain inadequacies in his observations. We shall take the position that the latter was the case—that early in Hart's career he was unable to tell whether or not a tense [ō] was followed by a homorganic glide, whereas later he was able to distinguish between [ō] and [ōw]. A parallel question arises with regard to the absence of any distinction between the reflexes of ME /ǣy/ and /ǣ/. Here, too, we shall assume that Hart's evidence cannot be taken at face value and that in his speech the diphthongs had not been monophthongized.

(If, incidentally, Hart's transcriptions did accurately reflect his speech, we would have to modify the proposed set of rules (pp. 264–65) in the following way. We would have to add a rule monophthongizing low diphthongs except for /āw/. This rule would be obligatory for the reflex of /ǣy/ but optional for the reflex of /ɔ̄w/. We could generalize the Diphthong Laxing Rule (see rule (21)) to all vowels, provided that the optional diphthongal reflex of ME /ɔ̄w/

---

[10] Actually the vacillations are even more varied than indicated above. Thus Hart writes *ōu* for the words *own*, *bow*, *ho* (exclamation), *sew*, *sow*, *sole*, *mow* (Danielsson, 1955, p. 244), but he writes short *o* for *know* (seven times, though once *knōu*), *show* (three times), *bestowed*. Danielsson (1963, p. 154) believes that these spellings were a result of the fact that "Hart apparently considered the length mark superfluous in this case, but his pronunciation must have been *kno̧ ro̧ ʃo̧*." In any case, it is difficult to accept the spellings at face value, as was done by Dobson (1957, pp. 513–16), for as Danielsson and also Dobson himself note, English vowels are normally tensed in open syllables, and there is no evidence that vowels in open syllables were ever laxed.

were somehow exempted from laxing. These modifications, however, do not shed any new light on the evolution of the English vowel system. We have therefore adopted here the somewhat radical interpretation noted above. Our main purpose is as well served by the simpler facts as by the more complex facts that face us if we take Hart's transcriptions at face value.)

The reflex of the ME diphthong /ɔ̄y/ is normally represented with a lax first vowel. In the last of his works, however, Hart seems to make a distinction between two [oy] diphthongs, one with a lax vowel and the other with a tense vowel, although the diphthong with the tense vowel appears only in the one word *ǫister*. The rarity of the appearance of a tense vowel in [oy] seems to us to be connected with Hart's inability, except at the very end of his career, to distinguish tenseness of vowels in diphthongs. As long as he regarded [ōw] as a monophthong, he had no contrasts in tenseness for vowels in diphthongs, and he quite naturally transcribed all diphthongal vowels without any indication of tenseness, that is, as lax. When in 1569 or 1570 Hart discovered that in addition to [ō] he also had [ōw], he realized that he had diphthongs that contrasted in the tenseness of the vowel, i.e., [ōw] from ME /ɔ̄w/ and [ow] from ME /ū/. His attempts to determine which diphthongs had tense vowels and which had lax vowels were apparently not successful. We shall therefore not rely on Hart's indications completely but shall assume that only the reflexes of ME nonlow vowels were laxed before glides. Thus the reflex of ME /ɔ̄y/, with a *low* vowel, is taken to be [ōy], with a tense vowel, throughout. In line with this decision, we shall interpret Hart's *au* in *lau* or *because*, which is a reflex of the ME diphthong /āw/, as representing [āw] phonetically.

The word *join* is transcribed twice in Hart as *dʒiuïn*, where the diaeresis above the *ï* indicates that this is *not* a diphthongal pronunciation. Since this is a totally isolated instance, we shall not attempt to offer an explanation for it, but shall regard it as a special idiosyncracy without systematic significance. It is worth stressing that this exhausts the evidence in Hart for the existence of a distinction between the diphthongs /uy/ and /ɔ̄y/.

The ME diphthong /ǣw/ appears in Hart's transcriptions as *eu* or *ieu*, which we interpret phonetically as [ēw] and [yēw], respectively. The transcription *eau* which appears in Hart's renderings of the words *beautify* and *ewer* will be regarded as an error (cf. Dobson, 1957, p. 803) or, at any rate, as being without systematic import. The occasional appearance of the [y] before this diphthong will be accounted for by a rule which inserts a glide before certain diphthongs (see rule (19a)). In this case the rule will be optional.

The reflexes of /ǣw/—that is, [ēw] and [yēw]—are kept distinct by Hart from those of ME /ēw, īw/ or Romance /ū/. Danielsson (1963) observes with regard to the latter reflexes:

> In this case it is evident that Hart did not use [ju] but [iu], as is also shown by his transcriptions ð'*ius* "the use" ... and *t'iuz* "to use" ... which indicate that the words begin with a vocalic element, i.e., most probably the first element of the falling diphthong *iu* (p. 133).

While we accept Danielsson's interpretations in general, it seems to us that his arguments here are not conclusive. The elision of the final weak-stressed vowel in ð'*ius* and *t'iuz* cannot be taken as evidence that the following word begins with a vowel. Hart's transcription ð'*ualʃ*, "the Welsh" (Danielsson, 1955, p. 212), shows that weak-stressed vowels were elided before glides as well as before vowels. The transcription *iu* cannot represent a vowel sequence since in such cases Hart uses a diaeresis on the second of the two vowels.[11] It would appear, therefore, that Hart's *iu* is either [yu] or [iw]. However, Hart (Danielsson, 1955) himself states:

> Lett us then ... use the diphthong *iu* alwais for the sound of *you* and *u* in *suer*, *shut*, and *bruer*, and souch lyke, writing theim thus *siuer*, *shiut*, *briuer* (p. 131).

We conclude from this that Hart's *iu* stands for [yu] everywhere.

2.2. *HART'S PATTERN*

We have found in Hart's speech the following vowels and diphthongs (with optional variants enclosed in parentheses), exhibiting the indicated correspondences with ME vowels and diphthongs:

$$\begin{pmatrix} 16 \end{pmatrix}$$

ME	ī	ē	ǣ	ā	ɔ̄	ō	ū
	↓	↓	↓	↓	↓	↓	↓
Hart	ey	ī	ē	ā	ō	ū	ow

ME	ēw	ǣw	ǣy	āw	ɔ̄w	ɔ̄y
	↓	↓	↓	↓	↓	↓
Hart	yu	(y)ēw	ēy	āw	ōw	ōy

ME	i	e	a	o	u
	↓	↓	↓	↓	↓
Hart	i	e	a	o	u

Hart gives numerous examples of the operation of the Laxing Rule. Thus we find alternations such as the following (see the index in Danielsson (1955)):

$$\begin{pmatrix} 17 \end{pmatrix}$$

[ey]–[i]	*afein–afinite*
[ow]–[u]	*pronouns–pronunsiasion*
[ī]–[e]	*grīk–gresian, kīp–kept*
[ē]–[e]	*mēneθ–ment, lēv–left*
[ā]–[a]	*kompār–komparison* (also *komparizon*)

Examples of the alternations [ū]–[o] (e.g., *lose–lost*) and [ō]–[o] (e.g., *cone–conic*) are lacking. There can, however, be little doubt that such alternations were present in Hart's speech. Moreover, the rules to be postulated for his speech would in no way be simplified but would in fact have to be complicated if the absence of these examples were regarded as systematic rather than as fortuitous.

As already noted Hart's dialect did not have tensing in the environment (6), as shown by his transcriptions *period*, *gresian*, and *nasion*, with stressed vowels that are lax. Tensing of vowels before vowels was, however, characteristic of Hart's speech, as indicated by his transcriptions *leiön*, "lion," and *pouër*, "power," where the diaeresis is Hart's device for showing "2 voels (ioined in a word) being no diphthong" (Danielsson, 1955,

---

[11] "The last of the accents is the sondrer (which the latines cal divisio, and the grekes dyæresis).. for yt sheweth what voels are sundred in pronunciation, which in writing are ioyned together even as ar the diphthongs: as in voël, goïng, Poët, and souch lyke" (Danielsson, 1955, p. 155).

p. 147).[12] Unfortunately, word pairs such as *social–society, algebra–algebraic,* which would establish the Tensing Rule as productive in Hart's speech, are not found in his writing, although they are attested for the sixteenth century. In view of the fact that tensing is known to have been productive both before and after Hart, the absence of such examples will not be taken as proof that the Tensing Rule was not operative in Hart's dialect.

We are now ready to characterize Hart's vowel system more formally. We shall assume that in the lexical representations of Hart's grammar the following vowels and diphthongs were found:

$$\left(18\right)$$

	TENSE		DIPHTHONGS					LAX	
ī	ū							i	u
ē	ō	ēw						e	o
ǣ	ā	ɔ̄	ǣw	ǣy	āw	ɔ̄w	ɔ̄y	a	

These segments were subject to the rules of the phonological component, which included the Laxing Rule (3) and the Tensing Rule (4). The other rules needed to derive Hart's vowel system from (18) will be presented directly, after a brief comment on the first of these rules (see (19) below).

Hart's dialect requires a Glide Insertion Rule which is obligatory before /ēw/ and optional before /ǣw/ since in the latter environment [y] appears only sporadically in Hart's transcriptions. Since the Glide Insertion Rule has certain terms in common with the Diphthongization Rule (8), we shall incorporate both into a single rule with two separate environments. As these environments are totally disjoint, there is actually no reason for ordering them as in (19) below. We use this order here only because it is the order in which the contemporary analogs of these rules appear in a grammar of modern English.

$$\left(19\right)$$ GLIDE INSERTION (a), DIPHTHONGIZATION (b)

$$\phi \rightarrow \begin{bmatrix} -\text{voc} \\ -\text{cons} \\ \alpha\text{back} \end{bmatrix} / \left\{ \begin{array}{l} \underline{\quad} \begin{bmatrix} +\text{voc} \\ -\text{cons} \\ -\text{round} \\ \alpha\text{back} \end{bmatrix} \begin{bmatrix} -\text{voc} \\ -\text{cons} \\ -\alpha\text{back} \end{bmatrix} \quad (a) \\ \\ \begin{bmatrix} +\text{voc} \\ -\text{cons} \\ +\text{tense} \\ +\text{high} \\ \alpha\text{back} \end{bmatrix} \underline{\quad} \quad (b) \end{array} \right.$$

(a) *(optional in the context* ——— [+low])

---

[12] The transcriptions *poët* and *voël,* "vowel," lack the expected indication of tenseness. The former is probably not relevant since it appears only once, and in the earliest of Hart's writings, where vowel tenseness was not consistently indicated. The transcription *voël* is more serious since it appears forty-seven times in various parts of Hart's works. Danielsson (1963, p. 164) believes that Hart's transcription can be explained on the grounds that to Hart "the diaresis was sufficient indication that the first vowel was long and the second short." Unfortunately this leaves unexplained the fact that Hart has the vowel [ō] here, a pronunciation which according to Danielsson is not attested in other sources. We should like to propose that Hart's *voël* stands for [vowel] i.e., for the pronunciation that is to be expected on historical grounds. The omission of the *w* in this position is not too surprising. This explanation, however, cannot be considered fully convincing either, since, as we have seen above, Hart did not always fail to observe the [w], as his transcription of the word *pouër,* "power," clearly indicates.

$\left(20\right)$ VOWEL SHIFT (9)

$$\begin{bmatrix} \alpha\text{high} \\ -\text{low} \end{bmatrix} \quad \rightarrow \quad [-\alpha\text{high}] \quad / \quad \begin{bmatrix} \rule{1cm}{0pt} \\ +\text{tense} \\ +\text{stress} \end{bmatrix}$$

$\left(21\right)$ DIPHTHONG LAXING

$$[-\text{low}] \quad \rightarrow \quad [-\text{tense}] \quad / \quad \rule{1cm}{0pt} \begin{bmatrix} -\text{voc} \\ -\text{cons} \end{bmatrix}$$

$\left(22\right)$ VOWEL RAISING

$$\begin{bmatrix} \alpha\text{back} \\ \alpha\text{round} \end{bmatrix} \quad \rightarrow \quad [-\text{low}]$$

Rule (22) states, in effect, that vowels agreeing in rounding and backness are nonlow. Note, incidentally, that (22) is not restricted to tense vowels; it applies to the lax vowels nonvacuously, as in *meant* ([ment]) from underlying /mǣn+t/.

As can be seen from Table 1 (p. 266), the rules that have been stated up to this point yield [yiw] as the reflex of underlying /ēw/, whereas Hart's transcription is *iu* (= [yu]). It is a relatively straightforward matter to add a rule which would insure the required phonetic output:

$\left(23\right)$

$$[+\text{high}] \quad \rightarrow \quad \begin{bmatrix} +\text{back} \\ +\text{round} \end{bmatrix} \quad / \quad \rule{1cm}{0pt} \begin{bmatrix} -\text{voc} \\ -\text{cons} \\ +\text{back} \end{bmatrix}$$

To derive [yu], we must follow (23) by a rule deleting the postvocalic [w]. We shall not do so, however, since it seems rather dubious to us that Hart was able to distinguish [yuw] from [yu] when he failed in most of his writings to make the equally obvious distinction between [ōw] and [ō].

Rules applying to vowels characteristically come in blocks consisting of several rules. It is therefore possible to factor out the feature complex $\begin{bmatrix} +\text{voc} \\ -\text{cons} \end{bmatrix}$ and count it only once in evaluating the complexity of the entire block. To reflect this fact, we have omitted these two features to the left of the arrow in the above rules.

The order in which the rules have been given can be justified only in part. We have already noted that there is no reason for ordering the two parts of rule (19). Most of the other rules are, however, fully ordered. The relative order of Diphthongization and Vowel Shift can be justified on the grounds that in the distinctive feature system the class [i, u] can be referred to by fewer features than the class [e, o]. Diphthong Laxing must obviously follow Diphthongization, but it must precede Vowel Raising since otherwise vowels will be laxed in the reflexes of the low diphthongs. Vowel Raising must also follow Vowel Shift since the vowels raised are not subject to Vowel Shift. Finally the $i \rightarrow u$ Rule (23) must follow Vowel Shift but need not be ordered after any later rules.

In Table 1 (p. 266) we illustrate the derivation of the phonetic reflexes from the postulated underlying representations.

TABLE 1. *The derivation of the phonetic reflexes from their underlying representations in Hart's dialect*[a]

	ī	ē	æ	ā	ɔ̄	ō	ū	ēw	æw	æy	āw	ōw	ōy	i	e	a	o	u
GLIDE INSERTION (19a)								yēw	(y)æw									
DIPHTHONGIZATION (19b)	īy						ūw											
VOWEL SHIFT (9)	ēy	ī					ū	ōw	yīw									
DIPHTHONG LAXING (21)	ey							ow	yiw									
VOWEL RAISING (22)			ē		ō				(y)ēw	ēy		ōw	ōy					
i → u (23)									yuw									
	ey	ī	ē	ā	ō	ū	ow	yuw	(y)ēw	ēy	āw˙	ōw	ōy	i	e	a	o	u

[a] Optional elements have been enclosed in parentheses.

3. John Wallis (1653–1699)

John Wallis' *Grammatica Linguae Anglicanae*, which he published in several editions between the years 1653 and 1699, was one of the most influential books on the English language. Wallis' phonetic writings have been reviewed by Lehnert (1936) and by Dobson (1957), who devotes an entire section to Wallis (pp. 218–43) and discusses many details of Wallis' pronunciation in various places in his book. The present discussion is based on these secondary sources as we have had only limited access to the original.

3.1. THE EVIDENCE

Wallis presents his vowels in a two-dimensional array, as shown in Table 2. The horizontal dimension, "aperture," reflects the degree of constriction with which a vowel is articulated and corresponds roughly to the traditional phonetician's "tongue height."

TABLE 2. *Wallis' vowel system*[a]

	Majori	Media	Minori
Gutterales	â } ŏ } aperta long: *fall* short: *folly*	long: —— e foemininum short: *vertue*	ŭ } ŏ } obscurum long: —— short: *turn come*
Palatinae	à exile long: *same* short: *Sam*	é masculinum long: *seat* short: *set*	ee } ĭ } exile long: *feet* short: *fit*
Labiales	ô rotundum long: *those boat* short: ——	oo } û } pingue long: *fool* short: *full*	ú exile long: *new* short: ——

[a] Adapted from Lehnert (1936).

The other dimension reflects the location in the mouth of the major constriction. Wallis recognizes three discrete values along each dimension so that his vowel scheme allows for nine distinct vowels. This number is further increased by Wallis' recognition that most vowels may appear in two lengths. We quote from Dobson's (1957) detailed summary of Wallis' description of his vowel system:

> Gutturals are formed in the throat or with the back part of the tongue and the palate; the breath is moderately compressed. With the major opening is formed a vowel which when long is the German *â*; the French and others often use this sound in pronouncing *a*. We spell the long sound *au*, *aw*, and more rarely *a*, the short sound we spell *o*; thus *fall* and *folly*, between which there is no difference except in quantity. With the medium opening is formed French *e* feminine, which differs from *â* only in the jaws being more closed; it is heard in English only when *e* precedes *r*, thus *vertue*. With the minor opening is formed " obscure *ò* or *ŭ*," which is nearly the sound of French *eur* in *serviteur*, and is heard in English in *dull*, *turn*, *come*, *country*, etc. The palatal vowels are formed by the breath being moderately compressed between the palate and the middle of the tongue; since the middle of the tongue is raised, the vault of the palate resounds less than in the case of the gutturals. With the major opening is formed the English "*à* exile," which is either short (as in *bat*) or long (as in *bate*). With the medium opening is formed the French *é* masculine; in English this sound is represented by *e*, and also (when long) by *ea* and occasionally *ei*. With the minor opening is formed the vowel *i*; in English it is spelt *ee* when long, or (less frequently) *ie* or even *ea*. The labials are formed in the lips, which are gathered into a round shape, with the breath moderately compressed there. With the major opening is formed round *ô* ("*ô* rotundum"), which some people use for Greek *ω*; with it are pronounced French *au* and English long *o* and *oa*. With the medium opening is formed German "*û* pingue," which is spelt *ou* in French, *w* in Welsh, and *oo* in English. With the minor opening is formed "*ú* exile," which is used in French and in English ... Of these nine vowels two, "*ŭ* obscurum" and "*e* foemininum," are "seldom" long, while two, "*ô* rotundum" and "*ú* exile," are "seldom" short, "at least amongst us"; the rest are both long and short (pp. 225–26).

From this description we conclude that Wallis' palatal series contained the vowels [æ], [e], [i].

The labial series apparently contained the mid vowel [o] and the high vowel [u]. The third vowel in that series seems to be [ü], i.e., the fronted counterpart of [u]. However, other statements of Wallis' make it appear that he was not able to distinguish this vowel from the diphthong [iw].

The vowels of Wallis' gutteral series present more serious difficulties. It is probable that the most open of these sounds is [ɔ], but the value of *ŭ* or *ò obscurum* and of *e foemininum* cannot be directly determined. We shall follow Dobson and other scholars who identified *ŭ* or *ò obscurum* with its present-day reflex [ʌ], a vowel that is nonround, back, nonhigh, nonlow, and nontense. We have been unable to determine what sound Wallis meant by *e foemininum*. It seems reasonably clear that the sound was nonround and nontense; but the phonetic description given by Wallis and the discussions in secondary sources have not enabled us to determine its other features. Wallis finds the *e foemininum* in two environments only—before [r] and in the diphthongal reflex of tense /ī/; in the diphthongal reflex of tense /ū/, he observes *ò obscurum*. This distinction is not noted by

Wallis' contemporaries.[13] A parallel contrast in the vowel of the diphthongs is noted by Batchelor (see Section 5 of this chapter) a century and a half after Wallis. But Batchelor clearly has [ʌy] (i.e., Wallis' *ò obscurum*) in the reflex of tense /ī/, and [ɔw] (Wallis' *â*) as the reflex of tense /ū/. We therefore adopt a conservative position and treat *e foemininum* as a distinct sound in Wallis' speech whose precise phonetic value we are unable to determine (see pp. 272–73). We will represent it by the noncommittal symbol *¢*.

According to Wallis, diphthongs "consist of 'preposed' vowels and either of the consonants *y* and *w*" (Dobson, 1957, p. 233). In the reflexes of tense /ī/ and /ū/, the preposed vowels are, as already noted, *e foemininum* and *ò obscurum*, respectively. The diphthongs "*oi* and *ou* are said to have two pronunciations: one begins with *ŏ apertum* ... the other with *ò obscurum*" (*ibid.*) These two diphthongs are therefore actualized either as [ɔy] and [ɔw] or as [ʌy] and [ʌw]. In the latter pronunciation, the reflex of the diphthong /ɔ̄w/ merges with that of the tense vowel /ū/; the reflex of the diphthong /ɔ̄y/, however, remains distinct from that of the tense vowel /ī/. Both Lehnert and Dobson attempt to connect the two pronunciations of /ɔ̄y/ with different historical antecedents ([ɔ̄y] versus [uy]). In view of the fact that the same alternation occurs in the reflexes of /ɔ̄w/, where only a single historical source can be postulated, and in view of the general lability of this distinction in English (see Jespersen, 1909, p. 100), the relatively few (three or four) examples that are cited by Lehnert and Dobson in support of the existence of this distinction do not appear convincing to us. It must be noted, finally, that Wallis also knew of the pronunciation of /ɔ̄w/ as the monophthong *ô rotundum* [ō]; "sed et haec omnia ab aliis efferuntur simpliciter per ô rotundum, acsi scripta essent *sole, sold, sno*, etc." (Lehnert, 1936, p. 126).

The reflex of the diphthong /āw/ in Wallis is regularly the long monophthong represented by the letter *â aperta*, which we have identified above with tense [ɔ̄].

The reflex of the diphthong /æy/ is described by Wallis as composed "ex à Anglico (hoc est, exili) correpto, et y" (Lehnert, 1936, p. 112); this would imply the pronunciation [æy], with a lax vowel. Wallis makes no reference to the well-attested contemporary pronunciation of the diphthong as the monophthong [ē].

Like Hart, Wallis distinguishes the reflex of the ME diphthong /æw/ from that of ME /ēw/. The former is described by Wallis as being composed of "é clarum et *w*"; whereas the latter is "sonus quasi compositus ex *ī* et *w*," which is the pronunciation that shall be assumed here as basic for Wallis. In Hart's dialect, it will be recalled, the reflex of ME /ēw/ was [yuw] and was kept distinct everywhere from the reflex of ME /æw/. Wallis notes frequent coalescences of these two diphthongs:

> quidam tamen paulo acutius efferunt acsi scribantur *niewter, fiew, bieuty*, vel *niwter, fiw, biwty*; praesertim in vocibus *new* novus, *knew* sciebam, *snew* ningebat. At prior pronunciatio rectior est (Dobson, 1957, p. 239).

3.2. WALLIS' PATTERN

The main phonetic reflexes of the ME vowels and diphthongs in Wallis' speech are given in (24). (Secondary and optional variants have been enclosed in parentheses. The symbol *¢* represents Wallis' *e foemininum*.)

---

[13] In his *Defence of the Royal Society*, Wallis commented on his disagreement with Wilkins concerning this issue: "In some others, he continued to differ from me, as in the French feminine *e* and the English short *u*. Which letters he accounts to be the same: but I take to be different, (that of *u* being a broader sound than the other;) differing as *e* and *u* in our English pronunciation of *fer, fur; iter, itur; terris, turris; terter, turtur; perperam, purpuram*, etc." (Quoted in McIntosh, 1956, p. 172).

$$\left(24\right)$$

ME	ī	ē	ǣ	ā	ɔ̄	ō	ū
	↓	↓	↓	↓	↓	↓	↓
Wallis	ǿy	ī	ē	ǣ	ō	ū	ʌw

ME	ēw		ǣw		ǣy	āw	ōw			ōy	
	↓	↙	↓	↘	↓	↓	↙	↓	↘	↙	↘
Wallis	iw	(iw)	ēw	(yēw)	æy	ɔ̄	ɔw	(ʌw)	(ō)	ɔy	(ʌy)

ME	i	e	a	o	u
	↓	↓	↓	↓	↙ ↘
Wallis	i	e	æ	ɔ	ʌ u

With the exception of the reflexes of ME lax /u/, which basically paralleled those of the standard dialect (see Table 2 under *û pingue* and Lehnert (1936, pp. 107–108)), the number of phonetically distinct entities in Wallis' speech is the same as in ME, for all coalescences that have taken place are optional pronunciations. Since Wallis' dialect was subject to the Laxing and Tensing Rules (3) and (4), we shall assume that its underlying system of representation was identical with that postulated for ME and, thus, with Hart's underlying system as well. The reflexes of lax /u/ will be accounted for below by special rules.

An important difference that emerges from a comparison of Hart's dialect with that of Wallis (cf. (16) and (24)) is that there are many fewer instances of tense or lax [o] in Wallis' speech than in Hart's. Thus, the normal reflex of the lax monophthong /o/ is [o] for Hart, but [ɔ] for Wallis; the reflex of tense /ū/ is [ow] for Hart, but [ʌw] for Wallis. To account for the fact that tense /ū/ is actualized as [ʌw] rather than as [ow], we assume as a first approximation that after Vowel Shift and Diphthong Laxing, but before Vowel Raising, Wallis' grammar contained the Unrounding Rule (25):

$$\left(25\right) \qquad \begin{bmatrix} +\text{back} \\ -\text{tense} \\ -\text{low} \\ -\text{high} \end{bmatrix} \rightarrow [-\text{round}]$$

This rule unrounds the vowel in the diphthongal reflex of tense /ū/, resulting in [ʌw].

This diphthong is not the only instance of [ʌ] in Wallis' speech; the sound also appears as a reflex of lax /u/ in words such as *dull, country*, that is, in words which essentially coincide with those in which [ʌ] appears in modern English.[14] Since the Unrounding Rule (25) is independently motivated for Wallis' speech, it is natural to attempt to take advantage of this rule in accounting for the appearance of [ʌ] as a reflex of lax /u/. In other words, one would naturally wish to connect the appearance of [ʌ] in these two environments, rather than regard them, as is usual in the handbooks, as two unrelated phenomena. But if this is to be done, rule (25) must be preceded by some rule which lowers the appropriate lax /u/ to [o]. The machinery for achieving this already exists, in part, for the Vowel Shift Rule, which is known to be in Wallis' grammar, lowers tense /ū/. All we need to do, then, is to

---

[14] Wallis is one of the earliest orthoepists to note the appearance of this reflex of lax /u/. To the best of our knowledge, this reflex is first attested by an orthoepist about a decade before Wallis, in the works of R. Hodges.

extend this rule so that it will apply to lax /u/ as well:[15]

$$(26) \qquad \begin{bmatrix} \alpha high \\ -low \\ +stress \end{bmatrix} \rightarrow [-\alpha high] \Big/ \left\{ \begin{array}{l} \begin{bmatrix} \overline{} \\ \begin{bmatrix} -tense \\ +round \end{bmatrix} \end{bmatrix} \quad (a) \\ \begin{bmatrix} \overline{} \\ [+tense] \end{bmatrix} \quad (b) \end{array} \right.$$

It must be noted that the order in which the two parts of the Vowel Shift Rule are presented here is quite arbitrary, since the two environments are totally disjoint. The choice of the feature "round" in part (a), on the other hand, is not arbitrary, though it may appear so at this stage of our discussion since lax /u/ could also, at this point in the grammar, be uniquely identified by the features $\begin{bmatrix} +back \\ -tense \\ -low \end{bmatrix}$.

The rules given up to this point would not allow any lax [u] in Wallis' speech. Lax [u] does occur, however, in many of the same environments as in modern English. Wallis' grammar must therefore be assumed to contain a rule exempting certain cases of /u/ from Vowel Shift. Since we have formulated the Vowel Shift Rule so that it applies only to round lax vowels, it would be blocked if /u/ were unrounded in the relevant environments, that is, if the grammar contained a rule such as (27):

$$(27) \qquad \begin{bmatrix} +back \\ -tense \\ +high \end{bmatrix} \rightarrow [-round] \quad \text{in certain contexts}$$

However, rule (27) turns lax /u/ into [ɨ], which is not attested in Wallis' speech. Thus we now need a rule to undo the effects of (27) and reround precisely those instances of /u/ which rule (27) unrounded. This is hardly an attractive solution and indicates that the proposed rules may stand in need of revision.

To remedy these inadequacies, we suggest that rule (27) be retained as a readjustment rule but that the Unrounding Rule (25) be replaced by (28):

$$(28) \qquad \text{ROUNDING ADJUSTMENT (VERSION 1)}$$
$$\begin{bmatrix} +back \\ \alpha round \end{bmatrix} \rightarrow [-\alpha round] \Big/ \begin{bmatrix} \overline{} \\ -tense \\ -low \end{bmatrix}$$

Rule (28) unrounds [o] while simultaneously rounding [ɨ]. We observe that (28) requires exactly the same number of features as (25). This proposal gains additional plausibility from the fact that Rounding Adjustment accounts for another peculiarity of Wallis' speech, as we shall now see.

A further difference between the speech of Wallis and that of Hart is in the actualization of the diphthong /āw/. Whereas for Hart this diphthong is [āw], for Wallis the reflex

---

[15] The lowering of /u/ without accompanying unrounding is attested in a large area of England. Wright (1905) represents this reflex by the letter *ù* and characterizes it as (§15) "a sound formed with the lips more open than for *u*. Acoustically it somewhat resembles an *o* sound." According to Wright, it is found in the counties of Antrim, Lancashire, Isle of Man, Cheshire, Flint, Denbigh, Staffordshire, Derby, Nottingham, Leicester, Northampton, Warwick, Worcester, Shropshire, Hereford, Gloucester, and Oxford (§98). This indicates that the addition of environment (a) to the Vowel Shift Rule (26) is not an ad hoc device invented solely to account for the facts under discussion here.

of the diphthong is [ɔ̄]. It is readily seen that in order to get [ɔ̄] from /āw/, we require rules of monophthongization and rounding adjustment. The latter must apply here to a vowel that is both tense and low, whereas in (28) it applied to vowels that were nontense and non-low. We therefore extend Rounding Adjustment to apply in both cases:

$$\left(29\right) \quad \text{ROUNDING ADJUSTMENT (VERSION 2)}$$

$$\begin{bmatrix} +\text{back} \\ \alpha\text{round} \end{bmatrix} \rightarrow [-\alpha\text{round}] \ / \ \begin{bmatrix} \underline{} \\ \beta\text{tense} \\ \beta\text{low} \end{bmatrix}$$

Rule (29) now applies to back vowels that agree in tenseness and lowness: lax [u], [ɨ], [o], [ʌ] and tense [ā], [ɔ̄]. Its applicability to [u] and [ʌ] has no effect, however, since there are no such segments at this point in the grammar. (See Table 3, p. 274.)

It is necessary to insure that Rounding Adjustment does not apply to the reflexes of the diphthongs /ɔ̄y/ and /ɔ̄w/, for these diphthongs are actualized, in the dialect that we regard as basic for Wallis, with the lax round [ɔ]. (The secondary dialect is discussed below.) Rounding Adjustment will not apply to these diphthongs if the Diphthong Laxing Rule is allowed to precede Rounding Adjustment. In this case, however, it is necessary to exempt /āw/ from Diphthong Laxing, for the /ā/ of this diphthong is both tense and subject to Rounding Adjustment. We achieve this by imposing on Diphthong Laxing the condition that it applies only to vowels that agree in backness and rounding. We observe that this restriction appeared in Hart's dialect, where the Vowel Raising Rule (22) had to be similarly constrained. Furthermore, the Vowel Raising Rule must figure in Wallis' dialect in precisely the same contexts as in that of Hart. Since Vowel Raising may immediately follow Diphthong Laxing, the condition that these two rules require need not be stated twice but can be factored out by the usual notational conventions. The Vowel Raising Rule, however, must be slightly more constrained for Wallis than for Hart, since it must specifically exempt lax [ɔ]. The two rules will therefore be coalesced as follows:

$$\left(30\right) \quad \begin{bmatrix} \alpha\text{back} \\ \alpha\text{round} \end{bmatrix} \rightarrow \begin{cases} [-\text{tense}] \ / \ \underline{} \begin{bmatrix} -\text{voc} \\ -\text{cons} \end{bmatrix} & \text{(a)} \\[2ex] [-\text{low}] \ / \ \begin{bmatrix} \underline{} \\ +\text{tense} \end{bmatrix} & \text{(b)} \end{cases}$$

Rule (30a) is Wallis' Diphthong Laxing Rule, and (30b) is Wallis' Vowel Raising Rule.

In Wallis' grammar the possibility of coalescing Diphthong Laxing and Vowel Raising provides a justification for placing Diphthong Laxing after Vowel Shift and directly before Vowel Raising.

We note that a further modification is needed to account fully for the facts. In the dialect that Wallis considers basic, the diphthong /æw/ is actualized as [ēw], with a tense vowel that is also raised. In other words, in this dialect Diphthong Laxing does not apply to the diphthong /æw/, and, as opposed to Hart's dialect, this is the only diphthong to which it does not apply. To block Diphthong Laxing here, we assume that Wallis' grammar had a special readjustment rule which exempted /æw/ from the Diphthong Laxing Rule. But once Diphthong Laxing is blocked here, Wallis' Vowel Raising Rule automatically applies. This result is a further justification for ordering Vowel Raising after Diphthong Laxing.

This order does not hold in the second dialect described by Wallis—the one in which /ɔ̄w/ and /ɔ̄y/ are actualized as [ʌw] and [ʌy], respectively. Here it is necessary to invert the order of Diphthong Laxing and Vowel Raising. If Vowel Raising applies before Diphthong Laxing, the two diphthongs will be turned, respectively, into [ow] and [oy]. They will then be subject to Rounding Adjustment, which will result in the correct output. In this case, however, an additional readjustment rule will be required in order to block Vowel Raising in the diphthong /æy/, which in Wallis' dialect is actualized as [æy] rather than as [ey].[16]

To obtain the secondary pronunciation of /æw/, which Wallis characterizes as "compositum ex *i* et *w*," we shall assume that Wallis had a special readjustment rule that raised /æw/ to [ēw]. The subsequent derivation of this diphthong then proceeds exactly like that of the diphthong /ēw/.

Two facts must still be accounted for. In Wallis' speech tense and lax /a/ are fronted in monophthongs, whereas in the diphthong /āw/ the vowel is rounded by the Rounding Adjustment Rule. Moreover, the glide of the diphthong is not present in the output. To account for these facts, we postulate the two rules (31) and (32):

$\left(31\right)$ FRONTING RULE

$$\begin{bmatrix} +\text{low} \\ -\text{round} \end{bmatrix} \rightarrow [-\text{back}] \Big/ \underline{} \begin{cases} \# & \text{(a)} \\ [+\text{cons}] & \text{(b)} \\ [+\text{voc}] & \text{(c)} \end{cases}$$

Rule (31) applies only in monophthongs.

$\left(32\right)$ MONOPHTHONGIZATION

$$\begin{bmatrix} -\text{voc} \\ -\text{cons} \end{bmatrix} \rightarrow \phi \Big/ \begin{bmatrix} +\text{voc} \\ -\text{cons} \\ +\text{low} \\ +\text{tense} \end{bmatrix} \underline{}$$

Rule (32) deletes the glide after [ā].

The preceding accounts for the major features of Wallis' speech except for *e foemininum*. There is no difficulty in principle in accounting for *e foemininum* since its antecedents, [ey] and nonback vowel before /r/, remain distinct. Once it is determined what *e foemininum* represents phonetically, it is a trivial matter to add a rule assigning the appropriate

---

[16] It has been proposed by Kiparsky (1965) that differences in naturalness (markedness—see Chapter Nine) are to be recognized also with regard to the order in which a pair of rules appears in a grammar. Given a pair of rules such as

(I) $[\alpha F] \rightarrow X$ in the context Z

(II) $Y \rightarrow [-\alpha F]$ in the context W

where Z is not distinct from W, X is not distinct from Y, Kiparsky suggests that the order (I), (II) be regarded as less marked (more natural) than the order (II), (I) since in the former order the two rules are utilized more fully than in the latter: if the rules are applied in the order (II), (I), any part of the string subject to (II) is no longer subject to (I).

Kiparsky presents evidence in support of the view that languages tend to change from a more marked to a less marked order of rules. The two alternative treatments of the diphthongs /ɔy/ and /ɔw/ reported by Wallis exemplify such a change. In the first dialect Diphthong Laxing precedes Vowel Raising. Since Vowel Raising applies only to tense vowels, any vowel subject to Diphthong Laxing is automatically excluded from Vowel Raising. Similar exclusions do not apply if the order is reversed, as it is in the second dialect described by Wallis. The latter dialect exhibits, therefore, a less marked order of rules than the former. It is significant that the former dialect is also the more conservative, more archaic form of speech favored by Wallis.

features to the segments in question. In a parallel ad hoc fashion, it is possible to account for the alternative pronunciation of the diphthong /ɔ̄w/ as [ō]. We shall not do this, since it is clear that nothing can be learned from such rules.

To summarize the above discussion, we list the rules that have been postulated for Wallis' dialect. (Note the *o*-Lowering Rule (33IV) which is presented here without discussion since the need for such a rule is self-evident.) We shall give the rules only for the basic dialect reported by Wallis and omit the modifications required to obtain the other pronunciations.

$\left(33\right)$ WALLIS' DIALECT

(I)   SPECIAL READJUSTMENT RULES
   (a)   Unround lax /u/ after labials and in certain other environments (27).
   (b)   Mark /ǣw/ as exempt from Diphthong Laxing (30a).

(II)   LAXING (3)

(III)   TENSING (4)

(IV)   *o*-LOWERING $\qquad o \rightarrow ɔ$

(V)   GLIDE INSERTION (a), DIPHTHONGIZATION (b)   (19)

$$\phi \rightarrow \begin{bmatrix} -voc \\ -cons \\ \alpha back \end{bmatrix} \Bigg/ \left\{ \begin{array}{l} \underline{\quad} \begin{bmatrix} +voc \\ -cons \\ -round \\ \alpha back \\ +low \end{bmatrix} \begin{bmatrix} -voc \\ -cons \\ -\alpha back \end{bmatrix} \quad \text{(a) } (optional) \\[3em] \begin{bmatrix} +voc \\ -cons \\ +tense \\ +high \\ \alpha back \end{bmatrix} \underline{\quad} \qquad\qquad \text{(b)} \end{array} \right\}$$

(VI)   VOWEL SHIFT (26)

$$\begin{bmatrix} \alpha high \\ -low \\ +stress \end{bmatrix} \rightarrow [-\alpha high] \Bigg/ \left\{ \begin{array}{l} \begin{bmatrix} \underline{\quad} \\ \begin{bmatrix} -tense \\ +round \end{bmatrix} \end{bmatrix} \quad \text{(a)} \\[2em] \begin{bmatrix} \underline{\quad} \\ +tense \end{bmatrix} \quad \text{(b)} \end{array} \right.$$

(VII)   DIPHTHONG LAXING (a), VOWEL RAISING (b)   (30)

$$\begin{bmatrix} \alpha back \\ \alpha round \end{bmatrix} \rightarrow \left\{ \begin{array}{l} [-tense] \;/\; \underline{\quad} \begin{bmatrix} -voc \\ -cons \end{bmatrix} \quad \text{(a)} \\[2em] [-low] \;/\; \begin{bmatrix} \underline{\quad} \\ +tense \end{bmatrix} \qquad \text{(b)} \end{array} \right.$$

(VIII)   FRONTING (31)

$$\begin{bmatrix} +low \\ -round \end{bmatrix} \rightarrow [-back] \;/\; \underline{\quad} \left\{ \begin{array}{ll} \# & \text{(a)} \\ [+cons] & \text{(b)} \\ [+voc] & \text{(c)} \end{array} \right.$$

(IX)   MONOPHTHONGIZATION (32)

$$\begin{bmatrix} -\text{voc} \\ -\text{cons} \end{bmatrix} \rightarrow \phi \ \Big/ \begin{bmatrix} +\text{voc} \\ -\text{cons} \\ +\text{low} \\ +\text{tense} \end{bmatrix} \text{---}$$

(X)   ROUNDING ADJUSTMENT (29)

$$\begin{bmatrix} +\text{back} \\ \alpha\text{round} \end{bmatrix} \rightarrow [-\alpha\text{round}] \ \Big/ \begin{bmatrix} \overline{} \\ \beta\text{tense} \\ \beta\text{low} \end{bmatrix}$$

TABLE 3. *The derivation of the phonetic reflexes from their underlying representations in Wallis' dialect*[a]

	ī	ē	æ	ā	ɔ	ō	ū	ēw	æw*	æy	āw	ɔw	ɔy	i	e	a	o	u	ɨ
o-LOWERING (33IV)																	ɔ		
GLIDE INSERTION (19a)									(y)æw										
DIPHTHONGIZATION (19b)	īy						ūw												
VOWEL SHIFT (26)	ēy	ī				ū	ōw	īw										o	
DIPHTHONG LAXING (30a)	ey						ow	iw	—	æy	ɔw	ɔy							
VOWEL RAISING (30b)			ē		ō				(y)ēw										
FRONTING (31)			æ													æ			
MONOPHTHONGIZA-TION (32)											ā								
ROUNDING ADJUSTMENT (29)							ʌw				ɔ							ʌ	u
	ey ↓ ȼy	ī	ē	æ	ō	ū	ʌw	iw	(y)ēw	æy	ɔ	ɔw	ɔy	i	e	æ	ə	ʌ	u

[a] Optional elements have been enclosed in parentheses. The rule accounting for *e foemininum* is not included. The starred item is an exception to Diphthong Laxing. The effects of (33Ia) are shown in the last two columns of the top row.

Comparing the dialects of Hart and Wallis, we observe that with certain unsystematic exceptions the two dialects have underlying systems that are essentially identical with that of ME and with each other. The differences observed between the dialects would therefore seem to be the result of the addition of rules. This fact is further brought out by the parallel listing of the respective sets of rules shown in (34) (in which rules not identical in the two dialects are starred):

(34)

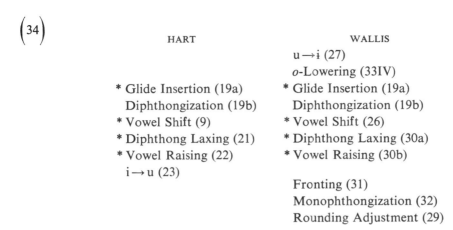

	HART	WALLIS
		u → i (27)
		o-Lowering (33IV)
	* Glide Insertion (19a)	* Glide Insertion (19a)
	Diphthongization (19b)	Diphthongization (19b)
	* Vowel Shift (9)	* Vowel Shift (26)
	* Diphthong Laxing (21)	* Diphthong Laxing (30a)
	* Vowel Raising (22)	* Vowel Raising (30b)
	i → u (23)	
		Fronting (31)
		Monophthongization (32)
		Rounding Adjustment (29)

The differences are of two kinds. Wallis' dialect is subject to certain rules that are not present in Hart's speech; moreover, several of Hart's rules appear in Wallis' dialect in somewhat modified form. In particular, Wallis' speech is subject to Rounding Adjustment (29), which is absent in Hart, and in Wallis' dialect the Vowel Shift is generalized to include the lax vowel /u/. It seems worth repeating here that the major phonetic developments in Wallis' speech—the change /u/ → [ʌ] and the modifications in the pronunciation of certain of the diphthongs—have been shown to be connected: they are largely due to the addition of Rounding Adjustment to Wallis' grammar.

It can be observed from (34) that the development up to this point does not show any discontinuities. Discontinuities due to restructuring are found in the next dialect to be examined—that of Wallis' younger contemporary Christopher Cooper.

4. Christopher Cooper (1687)

A comparison of the speech of John Wallis with that of Cooper, who was a younger contemporary of Wallis', reveals considerable differences. It has often been remarked that Wallis represented a strongly archaistic and conservative tendency. Cooper's speech would therefore seem to be much closer to the normal speech of the educated classes of the time. In our discussion of his dialect, we base ourselves on Cooper's book *The English Teacher* (1687), which is now available in the convenient reprint prepared by Sundby (1954), from which we have drawn all our citations unless otherwise indicated. We have consulted J. D. Jones' (1912) reprint of Cooper's Latin book *Grammatica Linguae Anglicanae* (1685) and have profited from the discussions of Cooper's work in Dobson (1957) and in Zachrisson (1913).

4.1. THE EVIDENCE

In Cooper's phonetic system a distinction is made between vowel quality or "essence" and vowel quantity or "measure of time. Every one of the vowels is pronounced short and long in their proper sound, except *u* guttural, whereby the number is doubled not in Essence, but only in the measure of time" (p. 9).

Cooper recognizes the following eight vowel qualities.

a lingual is formed "by the middle of the Tongue a little rais'd to the hollow of the Pallate. In *these can, pass by, a* is short; in *cast, past* for *passed*, it is long" (p. 4).

This suggests that *a lingual* is a nonback low vowel, [æ]. It is the reflex of ME lax /a/ and is apparently tensed before a voiceless continuant followed by [t].

e lingual "is form'd by the Tongue more rais'd toward the end and extended than in *a* foregoing; whereby the passage for the breath between the Tongue and the Pallate is made narrower, and the sound more acute; as in *ken, men* . . . The true lengthning of this sound is written by *a* and is falsly called *a* long; as in *cane, wane*; and before *ge* as in *age*; and *nge*, as in *strange*; but in all other words (unless I mistake) where *e* silent is added to the end of a syllable, *u* guttural . . . is put after *a*; as in *name* as if it was writ *na-um*, a disyllable. This sound, when it is purely pronounced, is written *ai* or *ay* as *pain, day*; which are commonly thus sounded in almost all words; so *ey* in *convey, obey, purvey, survey, they, trey, whey*; sometimes but rarely *ea, pearl*.

$$\text{It is short in} \begin{cases} Sell \\ Sent \\ Tell \\ Tent \end{cases} \qquad \text{And long in} \begin{cases} Sail \\ Saint \\ Jail \\ Taint \end{cases}$$

but in *sale, tale* it is sounded as if it was writ *sa-ul, ta-ul* (as before)" (p. 5).

This phonetic description argues that *e lingual* has the phonetic value of tense and lax [e]. Its lax variant represents ME lax /e/, and the tense variant, ME /æy/. ME tense /ā/, on the other hand, seems in Cooper's dialect to be reflected by a diphthong with a centering glide, [ēʌ], if the quoted passage is taken at face value. There is no particular difficulty in incorporating this fact into a grammar by setting up two entities in the under-lying representations. It appears, however, that the insertion of a centering glide after nonhigh tense vowels is a rather common feature of many dialects. Cooper notes a centering glide (p. 16) as following [ɔ] in a list of fifteen learned words, but remarks that "those that speak more carelessly, sound as α [= [ɔ], NC/MH]; in all others we pronounce *au* and *aw* as α onely." We shall assume, therefore, that this is an instance of dialect mixture and shall take as basic the variant without the centering glide.

i lingual is formed "by the Tongue nearer to the end, higher raised and more expanded, whereby the passage for the breath is rendered narrower, and the sound more subtle than in *ken* and *cane*; as in *win, priviledge* . . ." (p. 6).

This is the lax vowel [i]. According to Cooper the tense variant of this sound is found in words such as *wean* (see, e.g., pp. 7 and 13). However, this is not to be taken as proof that Cooper had four high [i] sounds, as we shall see.

ee lingual is formed "by the end of the Tongue fixed to the lower Teeth, both expanded and raised to the highest degree, whereby the passage of the Air is most of all straightened, and the sound made the closest of all vowels, and coming nearest to the nature of consonants; as in *feet, feed*; and therefore there is the least difference between the shortening or lengthening thereof because there is so little space between the Tongue and the Pallate in forming it" (p. 6).

This sound is evidently the tense, high, nonback [ī]. *ee lingual* represents the reflex of ME tense /ē/ in Cooper's speech, and the differences in length noted are, of course, due to the presence or absence of a following voiceless consonant. Thus, Cooper had correctly observed length distinction between the vowels in *feed* and *feet*. He had also observed that there were distinctions in quality (as well as in length) between the vowels in *win* and *feet* and had decided quite naturally that there must therefore also be a long vowel correspond-ing to the vowel in *win*. He assumed that this vowel was the vowel in *wean*, i.e., the reflex of ME /æ/. However, not all reflexes of ME /æ/ are treated by Cooper in this fashion; before [r] they are all said to be pronounced with *ee lingual*, i.e., [ī]. The simplest explanation for this choice is to assume that Cooper pronounced the vowel [ī] here but knew, of course, that in the writings of his predecessors the reflex of ME tense /æ/ did not coalesce with that of ME tense /ē/. He may therefore, as suggested by Zachrisson (1913):

> have felt obliged to keep up the old distinction ... even if this distinction merely consisted in giving the same sound two different names. This assumption may help us to explain the peculiar way in which Cooper treated ę, ę in front of *r*. Here neither the spelling nor earlier orthopoetical works gave any clue to the etymology. Hence Cooper confused ę and ę in this position, by placing *all* words in which he pronounced *ea* in front of *r* as *ī* under *ee lingualis* (p. 204).

We shall assume, therefore, that in Cooper's speech ME /æ/ and /ē/ coalesced into [ī], whereas ME lax /i/ remained a lax, high, nonback vowel.

   o labial is formed "by the lips a little contracted, while the breath is emitted circular; as in *hope*. Thus the *English* always pronounce this when long; (except in a few, where it is sounded *oo*, as *move*, or *ou* labial before *l*, as *bold*) which some times they express by *oa*, as *Coach*; it is seldom short in its own sound, unless in a few, which begin with a labial consonant, as after *w* in *wolf*, *wonder*, and such like, ... and in the syllable *wor-*; more I do not remember. In some *u* is pronounced thus, where the foregoing consonant is labial; as *pull*, *full*, not because this is the truest, but the easiest pronunciation: And *oo* in *good*, *hood*, *stood*, *wood*" (pp. 7–8).

   oo labial is formed "by the lips very much contracted; as *book*, *boot*; there is very little difference between the short and long sound, for the reason aforesaid under *ee*. We always pronounce it thus, except in those words which are excepted in the foregoing and following Sections" (p. 8).

   o guttural is formed "by the root of the Tongue moved to the inner part of the Pallat, while the middle of the Tongue is depressed, which causes the greatest space between the fore part of the Tongue and Pallat; and there it hath the most open and full sound of all the vowels, as in *loss*" (p. 8).

   From the foregoing it would appear that *o guttural* represents [ɔ]; *o labial*, [o]; and *oo labial*, [u]. However, the fact that, just as in the nonback vowels, the high lax vowel differed in quality rather obviously from the high tense vowel led Cooper to pair the former not with the high tense [ū] as in *boot* but rather with the nonhigh nonlow tense [ō] as in *hope*. In the back vowels, however, the situation is somewhat simpler than in the nonback vowels since in Cooper's speech there was no back counterpart to lax [e].

   In Cooper's speech, then, tense [ū] is the major reflex of ME tense /ō/; lax [u] represents ME lax /u/ after labials and ME tense /ō/ before velars and in certain morphemes. Cooper's tense [ō] mirrors ME low tense /ɔ̄/ and no lax [o] seems to be attested. The low tense [ɔ̄] is the reflex of the ME diphthong /āw/ (see p. 280) as well as of ME /ā/ in certain environments, e.g., before /l/, and of lax ME /o/ tensed before /f/, /θ/, /s/, +/t/; whereas the low lax [ɔ] is the reflex primarily of ME lax /o/.

   The ME lax /u/ is represented in Cooper's speech in most environments by *u guttural*.

   u guttural is formed "only in the throat, by the Larynx striking the Air, causing a naked murmur, which is the same with the groaning of a man that is sick or in pain; and which Infants also (before they are able to speak) first utter: And it is the principle, of which all the other Vowels are made by the various fashionings of the breath ... The *English* scarce ever pronounce this sound, when short, otherwise than in *nut*; (*as also in the Latine*) unless where the foregoing consonant is labial and shapes the lips to give it a fuller sound as in *pull*; between these there is very little, yet a specifical difference; such as is between the *English cup* and *French copy*; for the former sound is thinner, this latter fuller; that is formed onely by the Larynx in the Throat, this by the Lips contracted; therefore while *o* is formed by the Lips in a continued sound, if the Lips fall into an Oblong figure, *u* guttural is form'd" (p. 9).

In Cooper's description *u guttural* is thus the unrounded congener of lax [o], i.e., [ʌ].

ME tense /ī/ and /ū/ are represented in Cooper's speech by [ʌy] and [ʌw], respectively. "*u* in *cut* and *i* most easily make a diphthong, which we call *i* long; as *wine* (p. 15); "*u* guttural before the German *u*, that is the English *oo*, we always write *ou*; as in *out*, *about* " (p. 16).

The ME diphthong /æy/ is rarely actualized as [æy] or [ey]. " For the most part in common Discourse we speak *ai* as *a* simple in *cane*" (p. 15).

The ME diphthong /ɔy/ is actualized as [ɔy]. "*o* in *loss*, *lost* set before *i* is pronounced in *joy*, *coy*, *coif*; which is thus sounded in almost all words" (p. 15).

The ME /æw/ and /ēw/ have both become [yu] in Cooper's speech (p. 16).

The ME /āw/ is actualized in careful discourse as [ɔw] (p. 16); in less careful speech, as [ɔ].

"Cooper makes no distinction between Me *ǫ* in *hope* and *ou* in *know*... Both had acquired the value [o:] in his pronunciation" (Sundby, 1954, p. XLIII).

4.2. COOPER'S PATTERN

In (35) we give the main phonetic reflexes of the ME vowels and diphthongs as they appear in Cooper's speech.

(35)

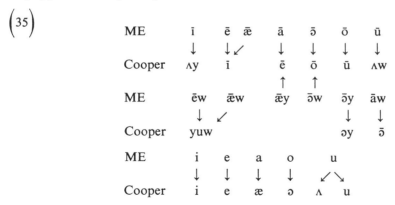

It will be recalled that in the dialects of Hart and Wallis we found that the ME contrasts were essentially intact and only their phonetic actualizations had undergone changes. In Cooper's dialect, on the other hand, this is no longer the case; as can be seen in (35), quite a number of the ME contrasts have been eliminated. We shall first assume that these mergers have not affected the underlying representations and develop a set of rules consistent with this assumption. We shall then show that a simpler grammar can account for all the data and that in this simpler grammar fewer contrasting vowel types are required in the underlying representation. This fact, however, will not deprive the former grammar of all interest, for it will provide some insight into the historical evolution of

Cooper's dialect, which must, of course, have descended from a dialect having the contrasts found in ME, in Hart, and in Wallis.

Since Cooper's dialect, like all other dialects of modern English, was subject to the Laxing and Tensing Rules, we shall assume that it was also subject to Diphthongization and Vowel Shift in the form in which these appeared in Wallis' speech, i.e., (19b) and (26). As we have seen, Cooper showed the same reflexes ([u] and [ʌ]) of lax /u/ as Wallis. Moreover, like Wallis, Cooper actualizes tense /ū/ as [ʌw]. These facts indicate that Cooper's speech must be assumed to have been subject to Rounding Adjustment (29) as well as to the other rules connected with this phenomenon, such as the readjustment rule unrounding certain occurrences of lax /u/ and the rule lowering lax /o/.

A difference between Cooper's and Wallis' dialects concerns ME /æ/, which in Cooper's but not in Wallis' speech merges with tense /ē/, except in the diphthong /æy/. To account for this, we postulate a special æ-Raising Rule which applies before Vowel Shift.

$$\left(36\right) \quad \text{æ-RAISING}$$
$$[-\text{back}] \;\rightarrow\; [-\text{low}] \;/\; except \text{——}y$$

Since, like all dialects reviewed in this chapter, Cooper's speech was subject to the Laxing Rule (3), the æ-Raising Rule (36) was not restricted to tense vowels but applied to lax vowels as well.

There is a certain amount of evidence to show that a rule much like (36) was optional in sixteenth and seventeenth century English. In the rhymes of the poets of the period, we find vacillations that could readily be accounted for if it were assumed that (36) was optional for them. Thus Wyld (1927) cites the following rhymes pointing to the absence of rule (36):

> Surrey, *please–days*;... Spenser, *uncleane–mayntayne*; Drayton, *dreams–Thames, mead–braid, maids–beads*;... Cowley, *play–sea*; Dryden, *dream–shame, obey–sea, seas–sways*; Pope, *weak–take, eat–gate, eat–state, speak–take, great–state, shade–dead*, etc. (pp. 171–72).

In the same period he also finds the following rhymes pointing to the presence of (36):

> Surrey, *reach–beseech*,... Spenser, *seas–these, streame–seeme, uncleane–weene*;... Waller, *sea–she–be*;... Cowley, *sea–be–he–thee*; Dryden, *sea–free, meat–seat, bread–feed*;... Pope, *seat–fleet, queens–means, sea–flee*...

We now observe that Cooper's reflex of /ī/ is [ʌy]. It will be recalled that in our discussion of Wallis' dialect we provided rules that yielded the reflex [ey] (see Table 3, p. 274). In order to obtain the correct result for Cooper, we shall modify Wallis' Diphthong Laxing Rule (30a) as follows:

$$\left(37\right) \quad \text{DIPHTHONG LAXING}$$
$$\begin{bmatrix} \alpha\text{back} \\ \alpha\text{round} \end{bmatrix} \;\rightarrow\; \begin{bmatrix} -\text{tense} \\ +\text{back} \\ -\beta\text{round} \end{bmatrix} \;/\; \begin{bmatrix} \text{——} \\ \beta\text{high} \end{bmatrix} \begin{bmatrix} -\text{voc} \\ -\text{cons} \end{bmatrix}$$

This rule will affect precisely the same diphthongs as before, but in addition to laxing their vowels, it will make the vowels [+back] and bring about dissimilation between the features "round" and "high."

As now formulated rule (37) would affect the diphthongs [ēy], [ōw], [yīw], [ǣy], [ɔ̄w], [ɔ̄y] (see Table 3) and convert them into [oy], [ow], [yɨw], [ɔy], [ow], [ɔy], respectively. The first three of these would then be subject to Rounding Adjustment, which would yield the phonetically correct reflexes. The last three must be subject to additional rules, since the reflex of /ǣy/ never merges with that of /ɔ̄y/, but is monophthongized instead. A further difficulty becomes apparent when we recall that the reflex of /ɔ̄w/, like that of /ǣy/, is monophthongized rather than laxed. These difficulties disappear if we assume that in Cooper's dialect Monophthongization preceded Diphthong Laxing. But if Monophthongization is to precede Diphthong Laxing, it cannot apply to all low diphthongs as in Wallis' dialect (see (32)), but rather must apply to glides that agree with the preceding vowel in the coefficient of the feature "back," that is, it must apply to [ǣy], [āw], [ɔ̄w].

(38)   MONOPHTHONGIZATION

$$\begin{bmatrix} -\text{voc} \\ -\text{cons} \\ \alpha\text{back} \end{bmatrix} \rightarrow \phi \ \Big/ \ \begin{bmatrix} +\text{voc} \\ -\text{cons} \\ +\text{low} \\ \alpha\text{back} \end{bmatrix} \underline{\qquad}$$

As already observed in our discussion of Wallis, the Fronting Rule (31) must precede Monophthongization, since otherwise the reflex of tense /ā/ would merge with that of the diphthong /āw/.

In Table 4 we illustrate the derivations of the phonetic reflexes attested in Cooper's speech from underlying representations that are identical with those of ME and hence with those of Hart and Wallis.

A comparison of Table 4 with Tables 1 and 3 reveals important similarities which reflect the close genetic relationship of Cooper's dialect with that of Hart and of Wallis.

TABLE 4.   *Derivation of the phonetic reflexes in Cooper's dialect from underlying representations essentially identical with those of ME*

	ī	ē	ǣ	ā	ɔ̄	ō	ū	ēw	æw	æy	āw	ɔw	ɔy	i	e	a	o	u	
u-UNROUNDING (33Ia)																		u	ɨ
o-LOWERING (33IV)																	ɔ		
æ-RAISING (36)			ē						ēw	—									
GLIDE INSERTION (19a)								yēw	yēw										
DIPHTHONGIZA- TION (19b)	īy						ūw												
VOWEL SHIFT (26)	ēy	ī	ī			ū	ōw	yīw	yīw									o	
FRONTING (31)				ǣ												æ			
MONOPHTHONGIZA- TION (38)										ǣ	ā	ɔ̄							
DIPHTHONG LAXING (37)	oy						ow	yɨw	yɨw				ɔy						
VOWEL RAISING (30b)				ē	ō					ē		ō							
ROUNDING ADJUSTMENT (29)	ʌy						ʌw	yuw	yuw		ɔ̄							ʌ	u
	ʌy	ī	ī	ē	ō	ū	ʌw	yuw	yuw	ē	ɔ̄	ō	ɔy	i	e	æ	ɔ	ʌ	u

If it can be supposed that the three dialects reviewed up to this point represent parallel but distinct developments from the same underlying base, then the set of rules underlying the derivations in Table 4 may be taken as showing the traces of this development. A comparison of Table 4 with Hart's dialect (Table 1, p. 266), which represents an earlier stage in the same general development, would then indicate that during the century and a quarter that intervened between Hart and Cooper the changes under discussion in this chapter were brought about mainly by the addition to the grammar of the following rules: *u*-Unrounding, *o*-Lowering (331V), æ-Raising (36), Fronting (31), Monophthongization (38), and Rounding Adjustment (29).

The order in which these rules are mentioned here does not correspond to their relative chronology, for as noted above there is no reason to suppose that rules are always added at a fixed point in a grammar. In fact, we have seen that the æ-Raising Rule (36) and *u*-Unrounding Rule, which must precede the Vowel Shift in the synchronic order of the rules, are historically later than the Vowel Shift.

The set of rules developed above and illustrated in the derivations of Table 4 presupposes that the underlying representations for Cooper's dialect were substantially identical with those for Wallis' and Hart's. This assumption, however, is not correct, for the same phonetic facts can be produced by an alternative grammar that requires fewer features and must therefore be preferred over Table 4. This alternative grammar must now be examined.

In Cooper's speech the following four pairs of entities, distinct in ME, were merged: /æ/ and /ē/, /æy/ and /ā/, /æw/ and /ēw/, /ɔ̄w/ and /ɔ̄/. There were in the language no phonological processes that would require that the merged entities be assigned distinct underlying representations. This is easily seen with regard to the tense /æ/ and /ē/, for well before the sixteenth century these two vowels merged into a single lax vowel when subjected to the Laxing Rule. Thus we found in Hart such alternations as [kīp] (from underlying /kēp/) and [kept] and [mēn] (from underlying /mæn/) and [ment]. The Laxing Rule therefore provides no motivation for keeping the distinction between the two tense vowels in the underlying representations once the vowels had merged phonetically.

A similar situation prevailed with regard to /æy/ and /ā/. In the environment where tense vowels were laxed, the diphthong /æy/ was replaced by the reflex of lax /a/, as shown clearly in the spellings *vain–vanity*. As far as we are able to tell, the language did not possess any other alternations that might require keeping these entities distinct in lexical representations. Hence, in place of /æy/ and /ā/ the lexical representations contained a single entity.

The low diphthongs /æw/ and /ɔ̄w/ did not participate in tenseness alternations either. They did, however, play a role in alternations of back and front vowels that are of some consequence in the verbal inflections; e.g., *know–knew*, *draw–drew*, *blow–blew* could be accounted for quite naturally by the set of rules in Table 4 if it is assumed that the diphthongs are distinct from the tense vowels with which they merged phonetically. However, the role of these alternations is so marginal in the language at this point that they alone could hardly justify maintaining the underlying entities as distinct after the phonetic reflexes of the diphthongs had merged.

If, then, the four pairs above are to be assumed to have merged, we must next ask what their respective underlying representations ought to be. If in place of /æ/ and /ē/ we postulate /ē/, and, analogously, in place of /æw/ and /ēw/ we assume /ēw/, we can immediately dispense with the æ-Raising Rule (36). This move, moreover, allows us to represent the pair /æy/ and /ā/ by /æ/. A consequence of the latter decision is that we no longer have need for the Fronting Rule (31), for there is nothing to prevent us from postulating an underlying lax /æ/ in place of /a/. If, finally, we represent /ɔw/ and /ɔ/ by /ɔ/, we need no longer include the Monophthongization Rule (38) in the grammar, provided that we represent /āw/ as /ā/. The latter is clearly desirable since it fills a hole in the pattern, as it were, created by the merger of original /ā/ with /ǣy/, and since, moreover, it reduces further the number of diphthongs in the underlying representations.

With these modifications, Cooper's dialect emerges with the underlying system as in (39):

$$\left(39\right)$$

ī		ū	i	u		
ē		ō	e	o		ēw
ǣ	ā	ɔ̄	æ			ɔ̄y

The appropriate phonetic reflexes can then be derived with the help of the following rules:

$$\left(40\right)$$

o-Lowering (33IV)
Glide Insertion (19a)
Diphthongization (19b)
Vowel Shift (26)
Diphthong Laxing (37)
Vowel Raising (30b)
Rounding Adjustment (29)

The derivation of these reflexes thus proceeds as shown in Table 5.

TABLE 5. *Derivation of the phonetic reflexes in Cooper's dialect from underlying representations that have undergone restructuring*

	ī	ē	æ	ā	ɔ	ō	ū	ēw	ɔy	i	e	æ	o	u	ɨ
o-LOWERING (33IV)													ɔ		
GLIDE INSERTION (19a)								yēw							
DIPHTHONGIZATION (19b)	īy						ūw								
VOWEL SHIFT (26)	ēy	ī				ū	ōw	yīw					o		
DIPHTHONG LAXING (37)	oy						ow	yɨw	ɔy						
VOWEL RAISING (30b)			ē	ō											
ROUNDING ADJUSTMENT (29)	ʌy		ɔ				ʌw	yuw						ʌ	u
	ʌy	ī	ē	ɔ	ō	ū	ʌw	yuw	ɔy	i	e	æ	ə	ʌ	u

5. *T. Batchelor (1809)*

The *Orthoëpical Analysis of the English Language*,[17] which T. Batchelor published in 1809, is apparently the earliest work in which the diphthongal quality of all English tense vowels is specifically recognized. In Batchelor's work reference is made to "a grammar of the

[17] We express our gratitude to Mr. W. M. Whitehill, director of the Boston Atheneum, for the loan of a copy of this book.

English Tongue which was published anonymously by J. Roberts, Warwick-Lane, in 1721, and contained (among many correct and some erroneous observations), almost the whole of the theory which makes the subject of the following pages" (p. vi). Since this book apparently has not been located (see Jespersen, 1909, p. 327), and since the comments in Batchelor are not clear on this point, we are unable to determine whether diphthongization of tense vowels was attested in English before the nineteenth century. Jespersen is inclined to believe that it was in the language long before Batchelor. His arguments, however, have failed to convince many scholars (see, e.g., Horn, 1912) and do not appear especially compelling to us, either. It seems to us safest, therefore, to assume that the reason for the absence of earlier testimony to the diphthongization of English tense vowels is not the lack of acuity of pre-nineteenth-century phoneticians and orthoepists, but rather the absence of the phenomenon.

5.1. THE EVIDENCE

Batchelor recognizes "eight vowels in English which possess a specific difference of character" (p. 21). These are:

$$\left(41\right)$$

i as in *swim, wit*
e as in *met, den*
u as in *pull, bull*
u as in *but, run*
$ụ$ as in *rostrum, honour* (unaccented)
a as in *pat, man* and *bard, task*[18]
o as in *not, top* and *order, offer, owl*[19]
c as in *rogue, broke*[20]

The phonetic descriptions given by Batchelor are unfortunately not models of clarity so that questions may well be raised concerning some of the identifications proposed below. There is no problem about the first five sounds; they obviously must be [i], [e], [u], and stressed and unstressed [ʌ]. If we assume that Batchelor's o represents [ɔ] and his a represents [æ], then his c, which is of very restricted distribution, should be identified with [o]. Batchelor's comments on c support this interpretation:

> To pronounce this sound, the tongue is more elevated in the middle than in the o in *hot awl*, &c; its highest part is also farther from the throat, though the tip of it is retracted farther from the teeth. The tone of this *short provincial o* has some degree of similarity with the o in *hot*, &c.; yet it is perceptibly softer, possesses less strength and distinctness, and seems rather more easy to pronounce (p. 9).

In describing the reflexes of the tense vowels in his speech, Batchelor observes:

> In the preceding table, the vowels which are heard in *tree, hey, buy, boy*, and *ay* are represented as diphthongs, which are formed by the junction of (y) consonant with the simple vowel sounds.
>   The errors which modern grammarians have promulgated, with respect

---

[18] "These sounds are justly considered by modern grammarians to differ only in length" (p. 8).
[19] "These two sounds are also specifically the same, the latter being only the lengthened sound of the former" (p. 8).
[20] "The sound which is here intended, is not similar to that heard in the words *tone, moan*, &c. The latter will be found to be true diphthongs; but the simple sound is heard only in the instances which are given, and a few others, when pronounced short, in the provincial manner" (p. 9).

to these diphthongs, have originated in great measure, from the difficulties which attend the subject, but principally in the absurd suppositions, that sounds cannot be described by words, and that it is of little consequence whether they can or not. [An opinion which, as Batchelor notes (p. v), his contemporaries owe to the redoubtable Dr. Samuel Johnson—NC/MH.] The distinction between *y* and short *i* has been sufficiently pointed out; and those who attentively examine the articulation of the long and slender sound which is represented by *ee* in *tree*, will find that the tongue makes a nearer approach towards the palate in the termination of that diphthong, than happens in the beginning of it. The ear may also distinguish a slender sound, followed by one still more slender, which is consequently the *y* consonant, and proves that *y* ought to be sounded exactly the same, as to the quality of the tone, whether it precedes or follows a vowel, though the strength of it will naturally be diminished at the end of a syllable (p. 52).

The radical vowels of the diphthongs which end in *y* consonant, as it is termed, are heard in the syllables *sin, bel, wed, but* and *hol*; and the insertion of a *y* between the vowels and the last consonant produces the sounds heard in *seen* (siyn), *bail* (beyl), *wade* (weyd), *bite* (buyt), and *hoyle* (hoyl) (p. 53).

We conclude from this that Batchelor had the following diphthongs in [y]: [iy], [ey], [ʌy] (which are the reflexes of /ē/, /ǣ/, /ī/, respectively, in his grammar), and [ɔy]. In addition, Batchelor had the diphthong [ay] in one word only:

The word (ay) signifying *yes*, is, I believe, the only diphthong of that kind in the English language. The radical sound of this diphthong is unquestionably the *a* in *father*; and it forms a combination very unlike the *i* in *mind, pint*, &c. (p. 54).

We shall not include this diphthong in our analysis as it clearly is an idiosyncracy of Batchelor's dialect without systematic significance.

The diphthongs which are formed by a final (w) are only three: the radical vowels on which they are founded, are heard in *pond, pull*, and the short provincial *o* in *broke* (brck); the insertion of (w) between the vowel and last consonant, changes *pond* into *pound* (pownd), *pull* (pul) into *pool* (puwl), and *brŏke* into *broke* (brcwk) (p. 55).

Batchelor thus recognizes three diphthongs in [w]: [ɔw], which is the reflex of tense /ū/; [uw], reflex of tense /ō/; and [ow], reflex of tense /ɔ̄/. It is to be noted that there is a curious asymmetry in his diphthongal system: the reflex of tense /ū/ is [ɔw], whereas that of tense /ī/ is, as we have seen above, [ʌy]. To account for this asymmetry, special rules will be required.

Finally, like Cooper, Batchelor has a triphthong in his speech:

The long *u* of the English alphabet may be termed a triphthong, as it consists of the *u* in *pull*, followed by *w* and preceded by *y* (p. 57).

5.2. *BATCHELOR'S PATTERN*

Batchelor's speech thus contained seven diphthongs: [iy], [ey], [ʌy], [ɔy], [uw], [ow], [ɔw]; one triphthong: [yuw]; six lax monophthongs: [i], [e], [æ], [ɔ], [ʌ], [u]; and two tense monophthongs: [ǣ] or [ā] found in *hard, task, father*, and [ɔ̄] found in *awe, order, offer*. In (42) we show the major ME antecedents of these sounds.

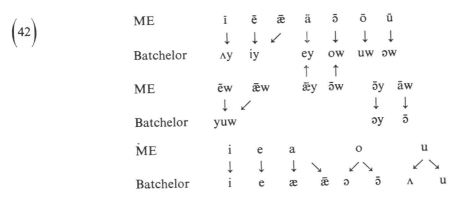

The similarity between (35), which represents Cooper's speech, and (42) is so striking that it is clear that both dialects must be derived from very similar underlying representations. Further examination of (35) and (42) reveals that the essential difference between the two dialects lies in the fact that in Batchelor's dialect the reflexes of all tense vowels are diphthongized, whereas they are mostly monophthongal for Cooper. In other words, if we can assume that Batchelor's dialect evolved from a dialect that was like Cooper's in having both diphthongs and monophthongs as reflexes of tense vowels, we must suppose that the change was effected by means of generalizing the Diphthongization Rule (19b). Generalizations of this kind constitute one common type of phonological change. In this case the generalization consists of dropping the feature specification [+high] in rule (19b). It is necessary to exempt the vowel /ā/ from Diphthongization (see Table 6 and the accompanying discussion, p. 286). There are several alternatives available to accomplish this. A motivated choice among them could only be made on the basis of a much deeper study of Batchelor's dialect than we are at the moment able to undertake. We therefore assume quite arbitrarily that Diphthongization of /ā/ is blocked by a readjustment rule.

The proposed generalization, however, would incorrectly turn the two diphthongs that were still found in Cooper's dialect into sequences of tense vowel followed by two glides. The most direct way of preventing this is by representing the diphthongs by tense vowels of appropriate feature composition. The generalized Diphthongization Rule will then insert the requisite glides without further difficulty. As noted in Chapter Four, the choice of the monophthongs to represent the diphthongs in question is limited by two facts: they must be distinct from all other tense vowels, and they must be [+back] if they have the glide [w] in the output, and [−back] if the glide in the output is [y]. Consequently the monophthong underlying [əy] will have to be [−back], whereas the one underlying [yuw] will have to be [+back]. The obvious candidates in view of these considerations are /ǣ/ for [əy] and /ɨ/ for [yuw]. This choice, however, has further consequences, for the machinery to turn these vowels into [ə] and [yu], respectively, is still lacking.

It is obvious that the Glide Insertion Rule (19a) must now be modified, because we shall want to insert [y] before tense [ɨ], that is, in the environment:

$$(43) \qquad \underline{\qquad} \begin{bmatrix} +\text{voc} \\ -\text{cons} \\ +\text{tense} \\ +\text{high} \\ +\text{back} \\ -\text{round} \end{bmatrix}$$

Next we must modify the Vowel Shift Rule, for in the form given in (26) it would apply to /i̵/ and turn it into [ʌ]. We therefore impose the condition on Vowel Shift that it applies only to tense vowels that agree in backness and rounding.

At this point in our exposition, it is helpful to stop and survey the results of the changes introduced so far. These are presented in Table 6.

TABLE 6.

	ī	ē	ǣ	ā	æ̿	ɔ̄	ō	ū	i̵	i	e	æ	o	u	i̵
								ū (→i̵)						u (→i̵)	
GLIDE INSERTION (43)									yi̵						
DIPHTHONGIZATION (19b)	īy	ēy	ǣy	—	æ̿y	ɔ̄w	ōw	ūw	yi̵w						
VOWEL SHIFT (26)	ēy	īy				ūw	ōw						o		
BATCHELOR'S OUTPUT	ʌy	iy	ey	ɔ̄	ɔy	ow	uw	ɔw	yuw	i	e	æ(ǣ)	ɔ(ɔ̄)	ʌ	u

Examination of Table 6 shows that tense /ā/ is unique in that it eventuates in a monophthong rather than in a diphthong. We recall that in the dialect of modern English described in Chapters One through Five, the tense low vowels have centering glides, and it is not unlikely that Batchelor's dialect was similar to modern English in this respect. Since he specifically states, however, that he had monophthongs in these positions, we have formulated the rules here so that monophthongs will be produced in the appropriate environments. We have done this by assuming that the dialect was subject to a special readjustment rule which exempted /ā/ from the Diphthongization Rule. We note, however, that this rule may reflect nothing other than a difference between the phonetic notation of Batchelor and that of modern phoneticians.

We now observe a curious set of correspondences between the representations derived by the three rules discussed in the preceding paragraphs and the phonetic output (see Table 6). What appears in the output as [ey], [ow], [ɔw] is represented in this stage of the derivation as [æ̿y], [ɔ̄w], [ōw], respectively. Omitting from consideration for the moment the difference in tenseness between the two sets of forms, the three diphthongs appear to have undergone a second Vowel Shift, one that affects only nonhigh vowels and that exchanges their coefficients for the feature "low." We observe, moreover, that the tense vowels involved in this second Vowel Shift, like those involved in the first Vowel Shift, agree in backness and rounding. The two Vowel Shifts can therefore readily be incorporated into one rule:

(44)   VOWEL SHIFT

$$[+\text{stress}] \rightarrow \begin{cases} [-\beta\text{high}] & / \begin{bmatrix} \underline{\quad} \\ \beta\text{high} \\ -\text{low} \end{bmatrix} \\ [-\gamma\text{low}] & / \begin{bmatrix} \underline{\quad} \\ \gamma\text{low} \\ -\text{high} \end{bmatrix} \end{cases} \Big/ \left(\begin{bmatrix} \underline{\quad} \\ +\text{high} \\ +\text{back} \\ -\text{tense} \end{bmatrix} \middle/ \begin{bmatrix} \alpha\text{back} \\ \alpha\text{round} \\ +\text{tense} \end{bmatrix} \right)$$

(a)

(b)

The effect of this extension of the Vowel Shift is to convert the vowels /ī/, /æ/, /ɔ̄/, /ū/, respectively, into [æy], [ēy], [ōw], [ɔw], leaving the reflexes of /ē/, /ō/ intact, as shown in Table 7.

TABLE 7.

	ī	ē	æ	ā	æ̃	ɔ	ō	ū	ï	i	e	æ	o	u	ï
GLIDE INSERTION (43)									yï						
DIPHTHONGIZATION (19b, modified)	īy	ēy	æy	—	æy	ɔw	ōw	ūw	yïw						
VOWEL SHIFT (44a)	ēy	īy						ūw	ōw				o		
VOWEL SHIFT (44b)	æy		ēy			ōw		ɔw							
BATCHELOR'S OUTPUT	ʌy	iy	ey	ɔ	ɔy	ow	uw	ɔw	yuw	i	e	æ(æ̃)	ɔ(ɔ̄)	ʌ	u

Before continuing our discussion of Batchelor's vowel pattern, we comment briefly on the possible historical steps whereby this evolution of the Vowel Shift Rule took place. We recall that most of the work done by the second part of the Vowel Shift Rule was performed in Cooper's grammar by the Vowel Raising Rule (30b). It seems likely, therefore, that what triggered the restructuring observed in Batchelor's grammar was the addition, to the end of a grammar like that of Cooper, of a special Vowel Lowering Rule such as (45) to lower [ʌw] to [ɔw]:

$$(45) \qquad \begin{bmatrix} -\text{high} \\ +\text{back} \\ -\text{round} \end{bmatrix} \rightarrow \begin{bmatrix} +\text{low} \\ +\text{round} \end{bmatrix} \Big/ \underline{\quad\quad} \begin{bmatrix} -\text{voc} \\ -\text{cons} \\ +\text{back} \end{bmatrix}$$

The addition of such a rule, however, resulted in a highly unstable situation, since the same phonetic effects can be produced with a simpler set of rules where the Vowel Raising and Vowel Lowering Rules are replaced by the second part of the Vowel Shift.

As can be seen from Table 7, to obtain the correct results for Batchelor's speech, we need adjustments in rounding. In particular, the lax [ï] which is a reflex of /u/, the tense [ï] in the triphthong [yïw], and the tense /ā/ must be rounded, whereas what appears at this stage in the derivation as lax [o] (from /u/) must be unrounded. As before we shall use Rounding Adjustment for this purpose, but we shall have to change the environment in which it applies, as follows:

$$(46) \qquad \text{ROUNDING ADJUSTMENT}$$

$$\begin{bmatrix} +\text{back} \\ \alpha\text{round} \end{bmatrix} \rightarrow [-\alpha\text{round}] \Big/ \begin{cases} \begin{bmatrix} \overline{} \\ -\text{low} \\ -\alpha\text{high} \end{bmatrix} & (a) \\[2ex] \begin{bmatrix} \overline{} \\ +\text{tense} \\ -\text{round} \end{bmatrix} & (b) \end{cases}$$

Part (a) of the Rounding Adjustment Rule affects tense and lax [ï] and [o], whereas part (b) affects only tense [ā] and [Λ], of which the latter is the result of unrounding of [ōw] < /ɔ̄/ by part (a) of Rounding Adjustment. It is to be noted that not all instances of /ā/ will be subject to Rounding Adjustment. Those that are exempt from it, e.g., /ā/ in polysyllables such as *father*, will be so marked either in the lexicon or by a special readjustment rule. Moreover, not all instances of tense [ɔ̄] are to be derived from an underlying tense /ā/. As indicated by Batchelor's examples, other sources for this vowel must be /ɔ/ before /r/ and before voiceless fricatives. The rule required here is in fact more general, for it also accounts for the tense monophthong [æ] in such words as *bard* and *task* (see p. 283). There are no doubt other such phenomena in Batchelor's dialect, but they do not appear clearly from the limited number of examples under consideration here. We shall not attempt to state any of these additional rules.

At this stage only two major discrepancies remain between the representations produced by our rules and the phonetically attested output. The diphthongs must be laxed, and it is necessary to make the vowels back in the diphthongs [æy] and [ǣy]. The latter can readily be effected by the following rule:

$$(47) \quad \text{BACKNESS ADJUSTMENT}$$
$$\begin{bmatrix} +\text{low} \\ +\text{tense} \end{bmatrix} \rightarrow [+\text{back}]$$

Rule (47) assures that all tense low vowels are back. This rule is followed by a generalized and simplified version of the Diphthong Laxing Rule (37).

TABLE 8. *The derivation of the vowels and diphthongs in Batchelor's dialect*

	ī	ē	æ	ā	ǣ	ɔ̄	ō	ū	ɨ	i	e	æ	o	u	ɨ
								ū						u	
o-LOWERING (33IV)													ɔ		
GLIDE INSERTION (43)									yɨ						
DIPHTHONGIZATION (19b, modified)	īy	ēy	ǣy	—	ǣy	ɔ̄w	ōw	ūw	yɨw						
VOWEL SHIFT (44a)	ēy	īy					ūw	ōw						o	
VOWEL SHIFT (44b)	ǣy		ēy			ōw		ɔ̄w							
ROUNDING ADJUSTMENT (46a)						Λ̄w			yūw					Λ	u
ROUNDING ADJUSTMENT (46b)					ɔ̄	ōw									
BACKNESS ADJUSTMENT (47)	āy				ɔ̄y										
DIPHTHONG LAXING (48)	ay	iy	ey		ɔy	ow	uw	ɔw	yuw						
ay-RAISING (49)	Λy														
	Λy	iy	ey	ɔ̄	ɔy	ow	uw	ɔw	yuw	i	e	æ(ǣ)	ɔ(ɔ̄)	Λ	u

$\left(48\right)$ DIPHTHONG LAXING

$$V \rightarrow [-\text{tense}] \ / \ \underline{\qquad} \begin{bmatrix} -\text{voc} \\ -\text{cons} \end{bmatrix}$$

It yields the correct results in all but one case: the reflex of /ī/ produced by these rules is [ay], whereas according to Batchelor's testimony the correct reflex is [ʌy]. This discrepancy can readily be repaired by a rule raising [ay] to [ʌy]:

$$\left(49\right) \qquad \begin{bmatrix} -\text{high} \\ +\text{back} \\ -\text{round} \end{bmatrix} \rightarrow [-\text{low}]$$

It is likely that Batchelor's dialect was somewhat unusual in this regard, for, as Batchelor himself notes, his near contemporary John Walker recommends a pronunciation with "*a* as in *father*" (p. 54), that is, [æy] or [ay].

In Table 8 we illustrate the derivation of the attested phonetic reflexes from the postulated underlying representations. The striking similarity of the rules employed here with those discussed in Chapter Four is, of course, not surprising, for only a century and a half separate us from the time of T. Batchelor.

PART IV
PHONOLOGICAL
THEORY

Chapter seven

THE PHONETIC
FRAMEWORK

1. *Phonetic representation*

1.1. *PHONETIC TRANSCRIPTION AND THE SPEECH SIGNAL*

The phonological component expresses the relationship between the surface structure of a sentence and its physical actualization insofar as this relationship is determined by grammatical rule, in the very general sense which we will elucidate below. The surface structure may be represented as a string of formatives, properly bracketed with labeled brackets (see Chapter One, Section 5). Given the surface structure of a sentence, the phonological rules of the language interact with certain universal phonetic constraints to derive all grammatically determined facts about the production and perception of this sentence. These facts are embodied in the "phonetic transcription." Therefore, as P. Postal has remarked, this transcription represents:

> the derivative knowledge a speaker has about the pronunciation by virtue of his knowledge of the superficial syntactic structure of the sentence, the lexical items or formatives it contains and the rules of phonology . . . The phonetic transcription . . . is the most gross and superficial aspect of linguistic structure . . . It is the most important but far from the only parameter determining the actual acoustic shape of the tokens of the sentence.

Our conception thus differs from an alternative view that the phonetic transcription is primarily a device for recording facts observed in actual utterances. That the latter view is not tenable, in any very strict sense, has been known at least since mechanical and electrical recordings of utterances have revealed that even the most skillful transcriber is unable to note certain aspects of the signal, while commonly recording in his transcriptions items for which there seems to be no direct warrant in the physical record. But even if the phonetic transcription were as faithful a record of speech as one could desire, there is still some question whether such a record would be of much interest to linguists, who are primarily concerned with the structure of language rather than with the acoustics and physiology of speech. It is because of this question that many structural linguists have felt that phonetics has very little to offer them and have therefore assigned to it a secondary, peripheral role.[1]

---

[1] As an illustration of this lack of interest in phonetics we may cite the numerous articles on phonological subjects that have appeared in the last thirty years in journals such as the *International Journal of American Linguistics* in which information concerning the phonetic properties of the phonemes of a language is often restricted to a simple listing of alphabetic symbols.
See also comments in Chomsky (1964, page 69n and pages 76 f).

These problems do not arise when phonetic transcription is understood in the terms outlined above, that is, not as a direct record of the speech signal, but rather as a representation of what the speaker of a language takes to be the phonetic properties of an utterance, given his hypothesis as to its surface structure and his knowledge of the rules of the phonological component. Since in this view phonetics is concerned with grammatically determined aspects of the signal, there can be no question about the relevance of phonetics to the study of language.   Moreover, since the phonetic transcription, in this sense, represents the speaker-hearer's interpretation rather than directly observable properties of the signal, the existence of certain discrepancies between the transcription and the signal can be understood. Thus it is no longer a problem that the transcription is composed of discrete symbols whereas the signal is quasi-continuous, or that the transcription provides information only about some properties of the signal and not about others, or, finally, that physically identical signals may have distinct phonetic transcriptions. Clearly, a person's interpretation of a particular speech event is not determined merely by the physical properties constituting the event. A person will normally not be aware of many properties manifest in the signal, and, at the same time, his interpretation may involve elements which have no direct physical correlates,[2] since what is perceived depends not only on the physical constitution of the signal but also on the hearer's knowledge of the language as well as on a host of extragrammatical factors.

Implicit in this approach is the view that speech perception is an active process, a process in which the physical stimulus that strikes the hearer's ear is utilized to form hypotheses about the deep structure of the sentence. Given the deep structure and the rules of the grammar, all other representations of the sentence can be derived, including in particular the phonetic transcription, which is the terminal representation generated by the grammar.[3] These derived representations are used by the speaker to check his hypothesis against the external stimulus, which provides the data that stand in the most direct (though not necessarily a point-by-point) relationship with the phonetic transcription. Since the hypotheses made in speech perception are highly specific—that is, we understand our interlocutor to have said a particular sentence—they are highly improbable. Consequently even crude agreement between the external stimulus and the internally generated hypothesis suffices to confirm the latter. In other words the dependence of perception on properties physically present in the signal is less than total. What is more, there are many extragrammatical factors that determine how close a fit between data and hypothesis is required for confirmation.

In the phonetic transcription an utterance is represented as a sequence of discrete units, each of which is a complex of phonetic features such as voicing, nasality, tongue height, etc. The phonetic transcription can therefore be taken to be a two-dimensional matrix in which the columns stand for consecutive units and the rows stand for different features. At this level of representation each feature is to be thought of as a scale. A particular entry in the matrix, then, indicates the position of the unit in question on the given scale. The total set of features is identical with the set of phonetic properties that can in principle

---

[2] In fact, we do not wish to exclude the possibility that under certain conditions distinctions that might be implied by the phonological rules of the language may not actually be realizable. This seems particularly to be true in the case of the different degrees of stress predicted by the stress subordination rules discussed in Chapter Three.

[3] It is not necessarily the case that each deep structure determines a single phonetic representation; if the grammar contains optional rules or analyses, a given deep structure can underlie two or more phonetic transcriptions.

be controlled in speech; they represent the phonetic capabilities of man and, we would assume, are therefore the same for all languages.

As already noted, phonetic transcriptions consistently disregard many overt physical properties of speech. Among these are phonetic effects that are not locatable in particular segments but rather extend over entire utterances, such as the voice pitch and quality of the speaker and also such socially determined aspects of speech as the normal rate of utterance and what has been called by some writers the "articulation base":

> the system of characteristic articulatory movements of a given language
> that confer upon it its general phonetic aspect; in French the mobility of the
> lips and forward position of the tongue (Marouzeau, 1943, p. 38).

In addition, phonetic transcriptions omit properties of the signal that are supplied by universal rules. These properties include, for example, the different articulatory gestures and various coarticulation effects—the transition between a vowel and an adjacent consonant, the adjustments in the vocal tract shape made in anticipation of subsequent motions, etc.

1.2. PHONETIC AND PHONOLOGICAL REPRESENTATION

As mentioned above, the phonetic transcription is related by the rules of the phonological component to a string of formatives with labeled bracketing which represents the surface syntactic structure of the sentence. We will now examine in some detail the manner in which these formatives are represented in a linguistic description. Many of the formatives are lexical items, the "roots" or "stems" of traditional grammar. A grammar must include a list of these items, for part of a speaker's knowledge of his language consists of knowing the lexical items of the language. It is by virtue of this knowledge that the native speaker is able to distinguish an utterance in normal English from an utterance such as Carnap's "Pirots karulized elatically" or from Carroll's jabberwocky, which conform to all rules of English but are made up of items that happen not to be included in the lexicon of the language.

The representations of the individual items in the lexicon must incorporate the knowledge which makes it possible for the speaker to utilize each lexical item in grammatically correct sentences. This includes certain syntactic information which the speaker must have. For example, he must know that a particular item is a noun and that it belongs to a large number of intersecting categories such as "animate" or "inanimate," "human" or "non-human," "feminine" or "masculine." Since the only question of interest here is whether or not a given item belongs to the category in question, it is natural to represent this information by means of a binary notation: *cow*, for example, would be specified as [+ animate, − human, + feminine]. In addition to these syntactic features, each lexical entry must contain specified features which determine the phonetic form of the item in all contexts. We shall call these the "phonological features." The phonological features cannot be chosen arbitrarily, for the phonological component would then have to include a huge number of ad hoc rules of the type

$$[+A, -B, -C, +D] \rightarrow [\text{h\'{a}t}]$$
$$[-A, -B, -C, +D] \rightarrow [\text{r\'{a}t}]$$
$$[-A, +B, -C, +D] \rightarrow [\text{əl\'{i}ps}]$$

Moreover, if we represented lexical items by means of an arbitrary feature notation, we would be effectively prevented from expressing in the grammar the crucial fact that items which have similar phonetic shapes are subject to many of the same rules.

We might consider overcoming these difficulties by representing each lexical item in its phonetic representation. However, this solution is not open to us either, for a lexical item frequently has several phonetic shapes, depending on the context in which the item appears. If we chose to represent each lexical item by the set of its phonetic representations, we would be treating all phonetic variations as exceptions and would, in principle, be unable to express within our grammar the phonetic regularities and general phonological processes that determine phonetic form. If, on the other hand, we chose to allow only a single phonetic representation for each item, then we would have to provide some rationale for our selection. Furthermore, it is easily shown that many of the most general and deep-seated phonological processes cannot be formulated as rules that directly relate phonetic representations; rather, these processes presuppose underlying abstract forms.

We therefore can represent lexical items neither in phonetic transcription nor in an arbitrary notation totally unrelated to the elements of the phonetic transcription. What is needed is a representation that falls between these two extremes. Accordingly we propose that each item in the lexicon be represented as a two-dimensional matrix in which the columns stand for the successive units and the rows are labeled by the names of the individual phonetic features. We specifically allow the rules of the grammar to alter the matrix, by deleting or adding columns (units), by changing the specifications assigned to particular rows (features) in particular columns, or by interchanging the positions of columns. Consequently, the matrix that constitutes the phonetic transcription may differ quite radically from the representation that appeared in the lexicon. There is, however, a cost attached to such alterations, for they require the postulation of rules in the phonological component. Such rules are unnecessary in cases where the lexical representation can be accepted as the phonetic representation. In general, the more abstract the lexical representation, the greater will be the number and complexity of the phonological rules required to map it into a phonetic transcription. We therefore postulate abstract lexical entries only where this cost is more than compensated for by greater overall simplification—for example, in cases where the combination of abstract lexical entries and a set of rules permits the formulation of phonological processes of great generality that would otherwise be inexpressible.

Thus, lexical representations and a system of phonological rules are chosen in such a way as to maximize a certain property that we may call the " value " of the grammar, a property that is sometimes called " simplicity." As has been emphasized repeatedly in the literature, the concept of " simplicity " or " value " is an empirical one. There is some correct answer to the question of how lexical items are represented and what the phonological rules are. A particular notion of " value " or " simplicity " will lead to an assumption about lexical items and phonological rules which is either right or wrong, and therefore the validity of the notion must be determined on empirical grounds, exactly as in the case of every other concept of linguistic theory. It may be difficult to obtain crucial empirical evidence bearing on proposed definitions of " simplicity," but this cannot obscure the fact that it is an empirical concept that is involved, and that one can no more employ a priori arguments in determining how " value " should be defined than in determining how to define " set of distinctive features " or " grammatical transformation " or any other concept of linguistic theory.

A specific proposal as to the definition of " value " will make certain assumptions as to what constitutes a linguistically significant generalization, as to what constitutes a " regularity " of the sort that a child will use as a way of organizing the data he is confronted with in the course of language acquisition. The child is presented with certain data; he arrives at a specific grammar, with a specific representation of lexical items and a certain system of phonological rules. The relation between data and grammar is, we naturally assume, language-independent: there is no basis for supposing that individuals differ genetically in their ability to learn one rather than another natural language. Consequently, the relationship is determined by a principle of universal grammar. Specifically, the definition of "value" or "simplicity" must be part of universal grammar, and a specific proposal will be right or wrong as it does or does not play its part in accounting for the actually existing relation between data and grammar.

Summarizing, we postulate a set of lexical matrices and a system of phonological rules which jointly maximize value, in some sense which will be defined. Phonological representation in terms of lexical matrices (as modified through readjustment rules—see Chapter One, Section 5.1, and Chapter Eight, Section 6.5) is abstract in the sense that the phonological representation is not necessarily a submatrix of the phonetic representation. We do not, in other words, impose the conditions of linearity and invariance (see Chomsky, 1964) on the relation between phonological and phonetic representation. The indirectness of this relation must be purchased at the cost of adding rules to the grammar. Given a definition of "value," we can therefore say that the facts of pronunciation induce the representation of items in the lexicon.[4]

Notice that the phonetic features appear in lexical entries as abstract classificatory markers with a status rather similar to that of the classificatory features that assign formatives to such categories as "noun," "verb," "transitive." Like the latter, the phonological features indicate whether or not a given lexical item belongs to a given category. In the case of the phonological matrices, these categories have the meaning "begins with a voiced stop," "contains a vowel," "ends with a strident nonback obstruent," and so on. In view of the fact that phonological features are classificatory devices, they are binary, as are all other classificatory features in the lexicon, for the natural way of indicating whether or not an item belongs to a particular category is by means of binary features. This does not mean that the phonetic features into which the phonological features are mapped must also be binary. In fact, the phonetic features are physical scales and may thus assume numerous coefficients, as determined by the rules of the phonological component. However, this fact clearly has no bearing on the binary structure of the phonological features, which, as noted, are abstract but not arbitrary categorial markers.[5]

As already noted, the phonetic representation can be thought of formally as a two-dimensional matrix in which the columns stand for consecutive units and the rows stand for individual phonetic features. The phonetic features can be characterized as physical scales describing independently controllable aspects of the speech event, such as vocalicness, nasality, voicing, glottalization. There are, therefore, as many phonetic features as there are aspects under partially independent control. It is in this sense that the totality of phonetic features can be said to represent the speech-producing capabilities of the human vocal apparatus. We shall say that the phonetic representations of two units are distinct if they differ in the coefficient assigned to at least one feature; phonetic representations of sequences of units are distinct if they contain distinct units or if they differ in the number or order of units.

At the level of phonetic representation, utterances are comparable across languages; it thus makes sense to ask whether the phonetic representation of an utterance of language L_1 is distinct from a phonetic representation of an utterance of a different language L_2. For

---

[4] For additional discussion see Chapter Four, Section 2.
[5] Failure to differentiate sharply between abstract phonological features and concrete phonetic scales has been one of the main reasons for the protracted and essentially fruitless debate concerning the binary character of the Jakobsonian distinctive features.

example, an utterance containing an apical dental stop must have a different phonetic representation from an utterance that is identical except for containing a laminal dental stop in place of the apical dental stop. The representation must differ since the distinction is determined in part by language-specific rules; it is not a case of universal free variation. An interesting example of cross-language contrasts that require a special phonetic feature is provided by the labiovelar consonants found in many African languages. In some languages, such as Yoruba, these consonants are produced with a special clicklike suction, whereas in other languages, such as Late, they are produced without this suction (Ladefoged, 1964, p. 9). Since clicklike suction is clearly an independently controllable aspect of the speech event, the data just cited establish suction as a separate phonetic feature, regardless of the fact that apparently in no language are there contrasting pairs of utterances that differ solely in this feature.

The situation is not always straightforward, however. Since phonetic features are scales which may in principle assume numerous discrete coefficients, the question may arise, under certain circumstances, whether a certain phonetic contrast is to be represented by means of a new phonetic feature or by increasing the number of coefficients that some already extant phonetic feature may be allowed to assume. The latter solution may appear especially attractive in cases where a slight redefinition of some phonetic feature would readily accommodate the proposed solution.

To summarize, the features have a phonetic function and a classificatory function. In their phonetic function, they are scales that admit a fixed number of values, and they relate to independently controllable aspects of the speech event or independent elements of perceptual representation. In their classificatory function they admit only two coefficients, and they fall together with other categories that specify the idiosyncratic properties of lexical items. The only condition that we have so far imposed on the features in their lexical, classificatory function is that lexical representations be chosen in such a way as to maximize the " value " of the lexicon and grammar, where the notion " value " is still to be defined precisely, though its general properties are clear. Apart from this, the representation of a lexical item as a feature complex may be perfectly abstract.

In a later discussion (see Chapter Nine), we will consider significantly heavier conditions on lexical representation. There we will turn to the question of " plausible phonological rules " and, more generally, to ways in which a particular feature may or may not function in the lexicon and in the phonology. These considerations will differentiate features from one another with respect to the role that they can play in the system of rules and in lexical representation. At that point in the development of our theory, considerations beyond maximization of value will enter into the determination of lexical representations.

2. *The phonetic features*

In the remainder of this chapter we attempt to sketch the universal set of phonetic features. Our aim is to cover every inherent phonetic feature regardless of whether it plays a role in the phonetics of English. We are well aware of the many gaps in our knowledge that make the success of this undertaking somewhat problematical, but we feel that general phonetics has been neglected for so long that agreement on even the most elementary propositions of phonetic theory cannot be taken for granted at present.

In the succeeding pages we shall list the individual features that together represent the phonetic capabilities of man. Each feature is a physical scale defined by two points, which are designated by antonymous adjectives: high-nonhigh, voiced-nonvoiced (voiceless), tense-nontense (lax). We shall describe the articulatory correlate of every feature and illustrate the feature by citing examples of its occurrence in different languages of the world. We shall speak of the acoustical and perceptual correlates of a feature only occasionally, not because we regard these aspects as either less interesting or less important, but rather because such discussions would make this section, which is itself a digression from the main theme of our book, much too long. We shall consider the phonetic features under the headings given below. (The numbers in parentheses refer to the section in which the feature is discussed.)

Major class features (3)
    Sonorant (3.1)
    Vocalic (3.2)
    Consonantal (3.3)

Cavity features (4)
    Coronal (4.1.1)
    Anterior (4.1.2)
    Tongue-body features (4.2)
        High
        Low
        Back
    Round (4.3)
    Distributed (4.4)
    Covered (4.5)
    Glottal constrictions (4.6)
    Secondary apertures (4.7)
        Nasal (4.7.1)
        Lateral (4.7.2)

Manner of articulation features (5)
    Continuant (5.1)
    Release features: instantaneous and delayed (5.2)
        Primary release (5.2.1)
        Secondary release (5.2.2)
    Supplementary movements (5.3)
        Suction (5.3.1)
            Velaric suction (clicks)
            Implosion
        Pressure (5.3.2)
            Velaric pressure
            Ejectives
    Tense (5.4)

Source features (6)
    Heightened subglottal pressure (6.1)
    Voice (6.2)
    Strident (6.3)

Prosodic features (7)
Stress
Pitch
High
Low
Elevated
Rising
Falling
Concave
Length

This subdivision of features is made primarily for purposes of exposition and has little theoretical basis at present. It seems likely, however, that ultimately the features themselves will be seen to be organized in a hierarchical structure which may resemble the structure that we have imposed on them for purely expository reasons.

2.1. THE NEUTRAL POSITION

In most X-ray motion pictures of speech, it can readily be observed that just prior to speaking the subject positions his vocal tract in a certain characteristic manner. We shall call this configuration the " neutral position " and shall describe some of the ways in which it differs from the configuration of the vocal tract during quiet breathing. In the latter state the velum is lowered, thereby allowing air to pass through the nose; in the neutral position, on the other hand, the velum is raised, and the air flow through the nose is shut off. The body of the tongue, which in quiet breathing lies in a relaxed state on the floor of the mouth, is raised in the neutral position to about the level that it occupies in the articulation of the English vowel [e] in the word *bed;* but the blade of the tongue remains in about the same position as in quiet breathing.[6] Since speech is generally produced on exhalation, the air pressure in the lungs just prior to speaking must be higher than the atmospheric pressure. During quiet breathing, the vocal cords must be widely spread apart since practically no sound is emitted. On the other hand, there is good reason to believe that prior to speaking the subject normally narrows his glottis and positions his vocal cords so that in the neutral position they will vibrate spontaneously in response to the normal, unimpeded air flow. Since this spontaneous vocal cord vibration has been almost totally ignored in the literature, we digress here in order to examine it in somewhat greater detail.

2.2. VOCAL CORD VIBRATION—SPONTANEOUS AND OTHERWISE

The two major factors controlling vocal cord vibration are the difference in air pressure below and above the glottis and the configuration of the vocal cords themselves—their tension, shape, and relative position. The subglottal pressure is that maintained in the trachea by the respiratory muscles. In the absence of a significant constriction in the oral cavity, the supraglottal pressure will be about equal to atmospheric pressure and will, of course, be lower than the subglottal pressure. If, on the other hand, there are significant constrictions in the oral cavity, the supraglottal pressure will rise above the atmospheric pressure since the air being exhaled from the lungs will not be allowed to flow out freely. Part or all of this air will be trapped in the supraglottal cavity, building up the pressure there and thus reducing the

---

[6] We follow here Bell, Sweet, D. Jones and other phoneticians in drawing a distinction between the body and the blade of the tongue. See D. Jones (1956, p. 15): ". . . the part which normally lies opposite the teeth ridge is called the *blade*. The extremity of the tongue is called the *tip* or *point*, and is included in the blade." An almost identical description is given by Westermann and Ward (1933, p. 17).

pressure difference below and above the glottis. This is of importance to us here since, all other things being equal, this pressure difference determines the rate at which the air will flow from the lungs through the glottis, and it is the flow rate which determines whether or not the glottis will vibrate.

In order to initiate vocal cord vibration, it is not necessary that the glottis be totally closed. If the velocity of the air flow through the glottis is high enough, it may reduce the pressure inside the glottis opening (the Bernoulli effect) to the point where the pressure is insufficient to prevent the elastic tissue forces from pulling the vocal cords together and closing the glottis. As soon as the glottis is closed, the subglottal pressure begins to build up and ultimately becomes large enough to overcome the elastic tissue forces pulling the glottis shut. At this point the glottis is opened, and air flows through it again. The air flow is subsequently cut off again since it once more produces a critical pressure drop inside the glottis opening. Obviously the Bernoulli effect can take place only if the vocal cords are appropriately positioned. If they are spread too far apart, as they are in quiet breathing, the pressure drop inside the glottis will not be great enough to pull the vocal cords together and thus initiate vibration.

We have already postulated that in the neutral position the vocal cords are placed so as to vibrate spontaneously in response to the unimpeded air flow. It is, however, a well-known fact that vocal cord vibrations also occur when there is a radical constriction, or even total closure, in the oral cavity. Although direct observations have not as yet been made, there is reason to suppose that the positioning of the vocal cords and their manner of vibration in the presence of a significant constriction in the oral cavity differ in important ways from the position and vibration observed during unimpeded air flow. It thus appears that voicing in obstruents is a rather different matter from that observed in sonorants.

Theoretical investigations by Halle and Stevens (1967) have shown that for sounds with low first formants—i.e., for sounds other than vowels—periodic vocal cord vibrations can be maintained only if the width of the glottal pulse is increased by lengthening the open phase during each glottal vibration over that normally found in vowels and/or if the damping of the first formant is substantially increased by creating a larger average glottal opening. The increased glottal opening would also help to maintain the vibration in the face of the reduced pressure drop across the glottis resulting from the buildup of pressure behind the consonantal constriction in the supraglottal cavity.

Certain well-known observations seem to support the theoretical conclusion that nonspontaneous voicing involves quite different adjustments than does spontaneous voicing. Thus, the air flow in voiced obstruents is noticeably faster than that in sonorants (vowels, glides, liquids, nasals). This fact is readily explained on the assumption that the average glottal opening is larger in obstruents than in vowels. Moreover, studies now in progress indicate that at least in the production of some voiced obstruents, the glottis is partially open during the phonation period. Finally, the very common lengthening of vowels before voiced obstruents can be explained on the grounds that it requires time to shift from the glottis configuration appropriate for vowels to that appropriate for obstruents.

3. Major class features

Reduced to the most rudimentary terms, the behavior of the vocal tract in speech can be described as an alternation of closing and opening. During the closed phase the flow of air from the lungs is either impeded or stopped, and pressure is built up in the vocal tract; during the open phase the air flows out freely. This skeleton of speech production provides the basis for the major class features, that is, the features that subdivide speech sounds into vowels, consonants, obstruents, sonorants, glides, and liquids. Each of the three major class features —sonorant, vocalic, consonantal—focuses on a different aspect of the open-versus-closed phase.

3.1. SONORANT—NONSONORANT (OBSTRUENT)

Sonorants are sounds produced with a vocal tract cavity configuration in which spontaneous voicing is possible; obstruents are produced with a cavity configuration that makes spontaneous voicing impossible.

As we noted above, spontaneous voicing may be suppressed by narrowing the air passage to a point where the rate of flow is reduced below the critical value needed for the Bernoulli effect to take place. Constrictions more radical than those found in the glides [y] and [w] will have this result. Hence sounds formed with more radical·constrictions than the glides, i.e., stops, fricatives, and affricates, are nonsonorant, whereas vowels, glides, nasal consonants, and liquids are sonorant.

In this connection it should be observed that there appear to be differences in the degree of constriction with which [l]- and [r]-sounds are produced. In the better known cases these sounds are produced with a very moderate degree of constriction and are therefore clearly sonorants. There are, however, liquids which are produced with a quite radical constriction and which have to be regarded as obstruents. Such is the case, apparently, in Chipewyan, in certain Caucasian languages, and in those languages with strident liquids, such as the Czech [ř].

3.2. VOCALIC—NONVOCALIC

Vocalic sounds are produced with an *oral* cavity in which the most radical constriction does not exceed that found in the high vowels [i] and [u] and with vocal cords that are positioned so as to allow spontaneous voicing; in producing nonvocalic sounds one or both of these conditions are not satisfied.

Vocalic sounds, therefore, are the voiced vowels and liquids, whereas glides, nasal consonants, and obstruents, as well as voiceless vowels and liquids, are nonvocalic.[7]

3.3. CONSONANTAL—NONCONSONANTAL

Consonantal sounds are produced with a radical obstruction in the midsagittal region of the vocal tract; nonconsonantal sounds are produced without such an obstruction.

It is essential to note that the obstruction must be at least as narrow as that found in the fricative consonants and must, moreover, be located in the midsagittal region of the cavity. This feature, therefore, distinguishes liquids and consonants, both nasal and nonnasal, from glides and vowels. It has been observed by Sievers (1901) that an essential characteristic of vowels is their "dorsal articulation"; that is, vowels commonly are produced with the blade of the tongue some distance from the roof of the mouth. When the blade of the tongue is raised close enough to the roof of the mouth to produce the requisite obstruction, the result is a true consonant or a liquid. Thus an [l]-sound is produced when the tip of the tongue touches the roof of the mouth, thereby blocking the midsagittal region of the vocal tract. In the case of the common lingual [r]-sounds, the raised tongue narrows the passage sufficiently to produce a

---

[7] Recent work indicates that in place of "vocalicness" the phonetic framework should contain a feature of "syllabicity"—see Chapter Eight, pages 353–55.

consonantal obstruction even if it does not make complete contact with the roof of the mouth. The uvular [R] is produced in a quite similar fashion, but in this case the lowered uvula rather than the raised tongue forms the obstruction in the midsagittal region of the vocal tract.

The presence of an obstruction in the midsagittal region is not necessarily accompanied by sufficient closure of the entire passage to suppress spontaneous voicing. The liquids are therefore consonantal sonorants. In producing the consonantal nonsonorants (obstruents), the passage is narrowed to a point where spontaneous vocal cord vibration is impossible; among the latter types of sounds are the plosives, affricates, and fricatives. On the other hand, not every sound produced with a raised tongue tip is consonantal. The so-called retroflex vowels are formed with a raised tongue tip, which, however, is not close enough to the palate to constitute a consonantal obstruction. These vowels are thus nonconsonantal.

The major class features therefore define the categories of speech sounds shown in Table 1.

TABLE 1. *The major class features*

	sonorant	consonantal	vocalic
voiced vowels	+	−	+
voiceless vowels	+	−	−
glides (I): *w, y*	+	−	−
glides (II): *h, ?*	+	−	−
liquids	+	+	+
nasal consonants	+	+	−
nonnasal consonants	−	+	−

4. Cavity features

4.1. PRIMARY STRICTURES

There are several ways in which primary strictures have been treated in the phonetic literature. The most widely known approach, that of the International Phonetic Alphabet, utilizes different features to characterize the strictures in vowels and in consonants. Vowel strictures are described with the help of the features " front-back " and " high-low," whereas consonantal strictures are characterized by means of a single multivalued parameter that refers to the location of the constriction. The disadvantage of this method is that it fails to bring out the obvious parallels between vocalic and consonantal strictures. Thus, the difference between palatal and velar consonants clearly parallels that between front and back vowels, for in both cases there are the same differences in the position of the body of the tongue. There is, however, no mechanism in the IPA framework to capture this and similar facts.

One of the many contributions of R. Jakobson is a phonetic framework in which many of these parallels are properly captured. As is well known, the salient characteristic of the Jakobsonian framework is that the same three features—" gravity," " compactness," and " diffuseness "—are used to describe the primary strictures in both vowels and consonants. This complete identification of vowel and consonant features seems in retrospect to have been too radical a solution, for reasons that we briefly outline below. We have therefore made a number of changes in the framework, in particular, with regard to the primary cavity features. The revised framework is quite likely to appear to depart from the earlier framework much more radically than it in fact does. This deceptive impression is the result of the unfortunate need to change terminology once again and replace the by now reasonably familiar terms "compact," "diffuse," and "grave" in part by totally new terms, in part by terms that are a return to the status quo ante. We discuss the relationship between the two frameworks in Section 4.2.1.

4.1.1. CORONAL—NONCORONAL

Coronal sounds are produced with the blade of the tongue raised from its neutral position; noncoronal sounds are produced with the blade of the tongue in the neutral position.[8]

The phonetic classification effected by this feature is all but self-evident. The so-called dental, alveolar, and palato-alveolar consonants are coronal, as are the liquids articulated with the blade of the tongue. The uvular [R] and the consonants articulated with the lips or with the body of the tongue are noncoronal. The glides [y] and [w] are noncoronal. Finally, the so-called retroflex vowels which are found in some languages of India—e.g., Badaga (H. L. Gleason, personal communication)—as well as in many English dialects in the position before [r] are coronal. Nonretroflex vowels are, of course, noncoronal.

4.1.2. ANTERIOR—NONANTERIOR

Anterior sounds are produced with an obstruction that is located in front of the palato-alveolar region of the mouth; nonanterior sounds are produced without such an obstruction. The palato-alveolar region is that where the ordinary English [š] is produced.

It follows from the proposed characterization that vowels, which are formed without constrictions in the oral cavity, are always nonanterior. Consonants and liquids are anterior when they are formed with an obstruction that is located farther forward than the obstruction for [š]. The consonants that in traditional terminology are described as palato-alveolar, retroflex, palatal, velar, uvular, or pharyngeal are therefore nonanterior, whereas labials, dentals, and alveolars are anterior.

4.2. FEATURES RELATING TO THE BODY OF THE TONGUE: HIGH—NONHIGH, LOW—NONLOW, BACK—NONBACK

The three features "high," "low," "back" characterize the placement of the body of the tongue. Recall that in the neutral position the body of the tongue was assumed to be raised and fronted, approximating the configuration found in the vowel [e] in English *bed*. In characterizing these three features, we shall be concerned with the various displacements of the tongue body from the neutral position.

HIGH–NONHIGH. High sounds are produced by raising the body of the tongue above the level that it occupies in the neutral position; nonhigh sounds are produced without such a raising of the tongue body.

---

[8] The term "coronal" is used here in the sense of the German *Vorderzungenlaut* and the Russian *peredne-jazyčnyj*. Sievers (1901) distinguished two types of linguo-palatal sounds with nonlateral articulation:
  "(1) Coronale Articulation: die Articulation wird durch den vorderen Zungensaum bewirkt, welcher sich als eine mehr oder weniger scharfe Kante dem Gaumen entgegenstellt . . .
  (2) Dorsale Articulation: die nothwendigen Engen bez. Verschluesse werden durch Emporheben eines Theiles des Zungenrueckens . . . zum Gaumen gebildet" (p. 59).
In much the same way the term is defined by Broch (1911): "Wird die charakteristische Enge oder der Verschluss durch den Vorderrand der Zunge gebildet, wobei sich ihre Oberflaeche gewoehnlich auf einer groesseren oder kleineren Strecke als konkav bezeichnen laesst, so wird die Artikulation koronal genannt" (pp. 11 f.)
  We differ somewhat from Sievers and Broch in that we regard as coronal all types of sounds formed with the blade of the tongue; Sievers and Broch did not use this term when speaking of sounds formed with the flat part of the blade (Sweet's "laminal"). (See note 6.) The latter distinction is handled in the present framework with the help of the feature "distributed" (see Section 4.4 of this chapter).

LOW–NONLOW. Low sounds are produced by lowering the body of the tongue below the level that it occupies in the neutral position; nonlow sounds are produced without such a lowering of the body of the tongue.

BACK–NONBACK. Back sounds are produced by retracting the body of the tongue from the neutral position; nonback sounds are produced without such a retraction from the neutral position.

The characterization of the vowels in terms of the three features above is quite straightforward and differs little from that found in most traditional phonetics books. We must observe only that the phonetic characterization of "low" and "high" rules out sounds that are $\begin{bmatrix} +\text{low} \\ +\text{high} \end{bmatrix}$, for it is impossible to raise the body of the tongue above the neutral position and simultaneously lower it below that level.

The characterization of the consonants in terms of these same features is equally straightforward, though perhaps somewhat unfamiliar. Consider first the consonants where the primary constriction is formed with the body of the tongue, in other words, those that are both noncoronal and nonanterior: the palatals, velars, uvulars, and pharyngeals. These four "points of articulation" are readily captured with the help of the three features under discussion, as shown in Table 2.

TABLE 2.

	palatals	velars	uvulars	pharyngeals
high	+	+	−	−
low	−	−	−	+
back	−	+	+	+

The absence of nonhigh nonback consonants is a direct consequence of the fact that the body of the tongue can form a constriction only if it is high or back.

While no language known to us has all four types of consonants in Table 2, there are quite a number of languages in which three of the four classes are attested. Serer, a West African language, has palatal, velar, and uvular voiceless stops.[9] Ubykh, a Caucasian language, distinguishes pharyngeal, uvular, velar, and perhaps also palatal obstruents (Vogt, 1963; Allen, 1964). In Ubykh, as in many other languages, such as Gilyak (see Zinder and Matusevič, 1937; Halle, 1957), the difference between velar and uvular points of articulation is paralleled by the difference between nonstrident and strident. This, however, is by no means universal. For instance, the spectrographic evidence published by Ladefoged (1964, p. 22) shows that in Serer the velar and uvular stops are both nonstrident plosives. Distinctions among palatal, velar, and uvular obstruents are also found in Chinook (Boas, 1911) and are mentioned by Trubetzkoy (1958, p. 122) as attested in certain Nilotic languages (Herero, Nuer, Dinka).

We must now inquire into the role that the features "high," "low," and "back" play in the remaining class of consonants, which in terms of the present framework are anterior and/or coronal. We observe that the three features may be used in a natural manner to characterize subsidiary consonantal articulations such as palatalization, velarization, and pharyngealization. These subsidiary articulations consist in the superimposition of vowel-like

---

[9] The following contrasting forms are cited by Ladefoged (1964, p. 46; see also pp. 21–22): [$k_1$it] "gift," [kid] "eyes," [qos] "leg," where the symbol k_1 represents the voiceless palatal stop equivalent to the IPA *c*.

articulations on the basic consonantal articulation. In palatalization the superimposed subsidiary articulation is [i]-like; in velarization, [ɨ]-like; and in pharyngealization, [a]-like. The most straightforward procedure is, therefore, to express these superimposed vowel-like articulations with the help of the features "high," "low," and "back," which are used to characterize the same articulations when they appear in the vowels. We shall say that palatalized consonants are high and nonback; velarized consonants are high and back; the pharyngealized consonants (e.g., the Arabic "emphatic" consonants) are low and back. On the other hand, consonants neutral with respect to palatalization, velarization, and pharyngealization are $\begin{bmatrix} -\text{high} \\ -\text{back} \end{bmatrix}$, since such configurations lack a constriction formed by the body of the tongue. Incidentally, it is not clear what role the feature "low" plays in such configurations since we do not know of any language with uvularized dentals or labials. If such consonants exist, however, they will be characterized in terms of our framework as nonhigh, nonlow, and back.

The palato-alveolars differ from the labial and dental consonants in that they are redundantly [+high]. In place of the four-way contrast found in the labials and dentals, the palato-alveolars, therefore, exhibit only a two-way contrast of palatalized ([−back]) and velarized ([+back]). The phonetic contrast can be seen very clearly in the X-ray tracings given by Fant (1960) of the two [š] sounds of standard Russian.

Table 3 (p. 307) gives the feature composition of the most important classes of speech sounds.

4.2.1. ON THE RELATIONSHIP BETWEEN THE FEATURES "DIFFUSENESS," "COMPACTNESS," AND "GRAVITY" AND THE FEATURES OF THE PRECEDING SECTIONS

The features discussed in the preceding sections are basically revised versions of "diffuseness," "compactness," and "gravity," which are well known from earlier presentations of the distinctive feature framework where they served to characterize the main articulatory configurations in the vowels as well as the consonants. As more and more languages were described within this framework, it became increasingly clear that there was a need for modification along the lines discussed in the preceding section. In this section we shall examine some of the problems that arose within the earlier framework and outline the way in which these problems are overcome by the revised features presented above. This question has recently been examined also by McCawley (1967a).

The revisions proposed in the last few pages have the following main effects:

(1) Features specifying the position of the body of the tongue are now the same for vowels and consonants.

(2) In the characterization of vowel articulations, the features "high," "low," "back" correspond to the earlier "diffuse," "compact," and "grave," respectively. In consonants, the same three revised features correspond to palatalization, velarization, and pharyngealization in the manner discussed above.

(3) The feature "anterior" mirrors precisely the feature "diffuse" in consonants.

(4) The feature "coronal" corresponds most closely to the feature "grave" in consonants but with opposite value. Except for the palatals ([k₁], etc.), consonants that were classified as nongrave in the earlier framework are coronal in the revised framework, whereas those that were classified as grave are noncoronal. The palatals, which in the earlier framework were nongrave, are noncoronal.

We recall that in the earlier framework the feature "diffuse" was used to characterize

TABLE 3. *Feature composition of the primary classes of speech sounds*

	anterior	coronal	high	low	back
CONSONANTS					
labials	+	−	−	−	−
dentals	+	+	−	−	−
palato-alveolars	−	+	+	−	−
(does not exist)	−	−	−	−	−
palatalized labials	+	−	+	−	−
palatalized dentals	+	+	+	−	−
palatals	−	−	+	−	−
velarized labials	+	−	+	−	+
velarized dentals	+	+	+	−	+
velarized palato-alveolars	−	+	+	−	+
velars	−	−	+	−	+
(?) uvularized labials	+	−	−	−	+
(?) uvularized dentals	+	+	−	−	+
uvulars	−	−	−	−	+
pharyngealized labials	+	−	−	+	+
pharyngealized dentals	+	+	−	+	+
pharyngeals	−	−	−	+	+
VOWELS (nonretroflex)					
high front	−	−	+	−	−
high back	−	−	+	−	+
mid front	−	−	−	−	−
mid back	−	−	−	−	+
low front	−	−	−	+	−
low back	−	−	−	+	+
GLIDES					
y	−	−	+	−	−
w	−	−	+	−	+
h,ʔ	−	−	−	+	−
LIQUIDS					
dental	+	+	−	−	−
palatal	−	−	+	−	−
uvular	−	−	−	−	+
palato-alveolar	−	+	+	−	−

both the distinction between high and nonhigh vowels and that between what we have called anterior and nonanterior consonants. As a result the articulatory and acoustical characterization of the feature became quite complex and rather implausible. (See, for example, the discussion of diffuseness in Halle (1964).)

A further consequence of the same fact was the need to characterize palatalization, velarization, and pharyngealization by means of independent features. This, in turn, failed to explain why these subsidiary articulations are not found with consonants that are formed with the body of the tongue, i.e., consonants that are noncoronal and nonanterior in the present framework. In the former framework this was a mere accident; in the revised framework the gap is structurally motivated, as shown in Section 4.2. It is worthy of note that rounding (labialization), which is also a subsidiary articulation, is not subject to similar restrictions. All classes of consonants, including labials, may be rounded.

A related inadequacy of the former framework is that it provided no explanation for the fact that palatalization, velarization, and pharyngealization are mutually exclusive. In the revised framework the co-occurrence of these articulations is a logical impossibility since a given sound cannot be back and nonback. In the former framework, on the other hand, this is no more than a coincidence.

The former framework, furthermore, did not bring out the fact that palatalization and velarization characteristically occur before front and back vowels, respectively; the connection between palatalization and front vowels and between velarization and back vowels was no more motivated than a connection between glottalization or voicing and front vowels. In the revised framework, on the other hand, palatalization and velarization are obvious cases of regressive assimilation.

The earlier framework failed to account for the appearance of palatal, in place of velar, consonants in precisely the same environments where other classes of consonants undergo palatalization. (Recall that palatalization preserves the point of articulation, whereas the change of velar to palatal constitutes a change in the point of articulation.) In the revised framework these two superficially distinct processes are shown to be a result of the same change, that is, [+back] to [−back]. A parallel argument can be given for the treatment of velarization and pharyngealization in the two frameworks.

The earlier framework made it impossible in principle to distinguish velar from uvular or pharyngeal consonants by means of their points of articulation. Such distinctions instead had to be made by the use of some subsidiary feature such as "stridency." There are, however, languages (Serer, for example—see p. 305 and note 9) in which velar and uvular consonants do not differ in any such subsidiary feature and which therefore could not be accounted for. This shortcoming is easily taken care of in the revised framework, in which the different points of articulation in velar, uvular, and pharyngeal consonants are specified with the help of the features "high," "low," and "back."

4.2.2. DEGREES OF NARROWING IN THE VOCAL TRACT

In our discussion of the features up to this point, we have spoken at length about the location of strictures in the vocal tract but we have said nothing about differences in the degree of narrowing that can readily be observed in the strictures found in different sounds. This omission has been due to the tacit assumption that the degree of narrowing is determinable from other features of a particular sound. This approach is perfectly familiar in phonetics; for example, no phonetics book does more than remark that in rounded vowels the degree of lip narrowing is most radical for high vowels and least radical for low vowels. While degree of narrowing never functions as the sole cue for differentiating two otherwise identical utterances, it is not true that in all languages the degree of narrowing involved in a particular sound is always predictable from universal phonetic principles. This becomes quite clear if we examine velarized consonants, which appear in various languages with radically different degrees of velar constriction.

In Russian a moderate narrowing in the velar region is present in the articulation of the so-called "hard" consonants, where concomitant with velarization we find a certain degree of lip rounding.[10]

Velarization with more radical narrowing has been reported by C. M. Doke (1931) as occurring in Shona:

> Velarization is brought about by an abnormal raising of the back of the tongue towards the soft palate (velum), instead of the usual slight raising effected in

[10] See Broch (1911, pp. 224 ff.) and X-ray pictures in Fant (1960, pp. 140, 163, 170, 186).

pronouncing the velar semivowel *w* . . . The extent to which the tongue is raised differs with the dialects. If the back of the tongue is so far raised as to effect contact with the velum, the velarization will appear as *k, g,* or ŋ . . . Similarly if the raising of the tongue is not so great, corresponding fricative sounds will replace the explosives . . . (p. 109).

Similar phenomena have been noted by Ladefoged (1964) in West African languages. Velarization in which there is complete closure in the velar region was found in Effutu and Nkonya (pp. 51–54). Kom, moreover,

> has the velarized forms *bγ, dγ* which are clearly sequences from the auditory point of view; but equally the articulatory gestures overlap, in that the velar stricture is formed during the stop closure. In this language there are strong grounds for saying that this is a kind of additive component or secondary articulation . . . (p. 31).

The most striking instance of extreme velarization is that of the Bushman and Hottentot clicks, all of which are produced with complete closure at the velum.[11] The clicks, however, differ from other velarized consonants in that in addition to complete closure they involve a special suction mechanism. The clicks will therefore be discussed when we deal with suction mechanisms in Section 5.3.1.

We know of no languages that exhibit parallel variations in degree of narrowing concomitant with palatalization or pharyngealization, but, as will be shown in the next section, parallel variations are found with the feature of "rounding."

4.3. ROUNDED—NONROUNDED

Rounded sounds are produced with a narrowing of the lip orifice; nonrounded sounds are produced without such a narrowing.

All classes of sounds may manifest rounding. In glides and nonlow vowels, rounding is commonly correlated with the feature "back": sounds that are back are also round, those that are nonback are nonround. This association is not obligatory, however, and there are many instances where the features "round" and "back" combine freely. Turkish, for example, has all of the four possible feature combinations contrasting among its high vowels, as shown in Table 4.

TABLE 4. *Turkish high vowels*

	i	ɨ	ü	u
back	−	+	−	+
round	−	−	+	+

French distinguishes three glides phonetically: nonround nonback [y], as in *les yeux,* "the eyes"; round back [w], as in *les oiseaux,* "the birds"; and round nonback [ẅ], as in *tuer,* "to kill."

In consonants, rounding, which is usually designated by the term "labialization," is

---

[11] In our analysis of the clicks as instances of extreme velarization, we follow a suggestion made by Trubetzkoy (1958, p. 129). We differ from Trubetzkoy, however, in postulating a special feature (suction) to account for the peculiar release of these secondary constrictions.

not uncommon, especially in velars. Labialized velars are found, for example, in Southern Paiute (Sapir, 1930), Chippewyan (Li, 1946), and Navaho (Hoijer, 1945). Labialized dentals and palato-alveolars are found in certain West African languages, such as Effutu, Gã, and Krachi (Ladefoged, 1964). Finally, contrasting labialized and nonlabialized labials are attested in Kutep (Ladefoged, 1964) and in certain Caucasian languages such as Ubykh (Vogt, 1963).

Labialization combines quite commonly with velarization, but we do not know of any examples where these two features act independently in a given phonological system. On the other hand, there appear to be a number of languages where labialization and palatalization function independently. Trubetzkoy (1939) notes that in Dungan Chinese rounding may be distinctive for dental continuants and affricates that are $\begin{bmatrix} +\,\text{high} \\ -\,\text{back} \end{bmatrix}$, i.e., palatalized, as well as those that are not. Similar observations have been made in Kashmiri (Jakobson, Fant, and Halle, 1963, p. 35), and in certain West African languages such as Twi and Late (see Ladefoged (1964), plate 9, which reproduces excellent records made of a "labialized and palatalized pre-palatal affricate" (p. 20)).

The degree of rounding is always determinable from other features. In the vowels and glides it is correlated with the maximum degree of constriction in the oral cavity. Glides and high vowels have most rounding; low vowels, least.

There are parallel variations in the degree of rounding in consonants. These vary from a degree that is equivalent to that of the glides to complete closure. Thus, we find rounded consonants with a moderate degree of lip constriction in such languages as Chipewyan (Li, 1946), Hausa (Ladefoged, 1964, p. 64), and Rutulian (Trubetzkoy, 1958, p. 125), whereas in languages such as Ewe and Kpelle we find rounded consonants implemented with complete closure at the lips. The latter are the consonants that are commonly represented orthographically as *kp* and *gb*.[12]

In addition to rounded consonants with moderate constriction and those with total closure, there appear to be consonants of this type which involve an intermediate degree of labial constriction. Thus, Ladefoged (1964) reports that Kom:

> has a labiodental fricative which seems to be superimposable on other articulations. The sounds observed in this language include k^f, g^v, j^v ... A similar secondary articulation also occurs in Kutep; but in this language labiodentalization occurs only after fricatives (including those in affricates) and is in complementary distribution with labialization, which occurs after stops and nasals (p. 31).[13]

A parallel instance of different degrees of rounding being contextually distributed may be cited from Margi, a language spoken in Nigeria. In this language moderate degrees of rounding occur with noncoronal consonants (labials and velars), and extreme degrees of

---

[12] In some African languages—e.g., Effutu, Nkonya (as noted by Ladefoged, 1964, pp. 51–54)—these symbols represent, rather, velarized labials. There are, moreover, different ways in which the secondary closure is released in these sounds, as discussed in Section 5.2.

[13] Quite similar facts are reported by Doke (1931) for Shona: "Labialized alveolar fricatives and affricates occur in all Shona dialects ... In several of the Manyinka dialects and in Tavara, the lip rounding of these sounds is so extreme that the explosive element in the affricates has an acoustic bias towards *p* ... In Northern Tavara the lip contact in the affricates is complete with many speakers, and the resultant forms are actually [pʂ] and [bʐ] ... " (p. 47).

rounding with coronal (dental and palato-alveolar) consonants.[14] This language is interesting also because of the fact that the extreme degree of rounding is superimposed on dentals and palatal consonants, whereas in most other languages extreme rounding (i.e., total lip closure) is a feature of velars. In addition, in Temne (Ladefoged, 1964, p. 47), a voiceless plosive with a moderate degree of rounding, [kʷ], is paired with a voiced plosive with extreme rounding, [gᵇ], the degree of rounding being dependent on voicing.

In sum, in consonants there are at least three phonetically different degrees of rounding. It appears, however, that the particular degree of rounding that obtains in each instance can be determined by the phonological rules of the language so that it is sufficient to indicate in the lexicon whether the given segment is or is not rounded.

An interesting question arises with regard to the labiovelars. We may ask whether these are labials with extreme velarization or velars with extreme rounding, or, in feature terms, whether they should be represented as (1) or as (2):

$$(1) \qquad \begin{bmatrix} +\text{anterior} \\ -\text{coronal} \\ +\text{back} \\ +\text{high} \end{bmatrix}$$

$$(2) \qquad \begin{bmatrix} -\text{anterior} \\ -\text{coronal} \\ +\text{back} \\ +\text{high} \\ +\text{round} \end{bmatrix}$$

We cannot determine this by direct phonetic observation since these two feature configurations seem to result in the same articulatory gesture. Sometimes, however, it is possible to make a decision between such configurations on the basis of the facts of the language. In Nupe (N. V. Smith, personal communication) round (labialized) labials are distinguished from nonround labials; e.g., [pʷ] is distinct from [p]. In addition Nupe has two types of labiovelars, rounded and unrounded. The existence of both types immediately resolves the question as to how they are to be represented. We must regard them as labials with extreme velarization (i.e., as having the feature configuration (1)), which may or may not also be rounded. The reason is that if we chose to represent one of the two labiovelars with the feature configuration (2), we should then be unable to represent its phonetic cognate with the same set of features (except for rounding).

Incidentally, in Nupe there is the further interesting fact that all obstruents palatalize before front vowels. Velars become palatals, and the labials become palatalized, that is, show the characteristic [i]-like transition to the adjacent vowel. The labiovelars show the same type of [i]-like transition as the labials. This fact further supports the decision to regard labiovelars as labials with extreme velarization.

---

[14] See Hoffmann (1963, pp. 27–29). In his list of phonemes Hoffmann also cites a number of dental consonants with superimposed rounding of a moderate degree, which he symbolizes by di- and tri-graphs ending with the letter *w: sw, tw, tlw.* Hoffmann believes that these are in contrast with dentals with labial closure. A good many of the examples quoted, however, seem to be instances of a plain dental being followed by the suffix /wa/ and hence are not really relevant. For example, *swá,* "to shut (without locking)," is given on page 149 as *s(ú)wá* and compared with the stem *sú,* "to contract (disease)"; *tlwá,* "to cut in two (with knife)," is derived on page 148 from *tlá,* "to cut (with knife)."

4.4. DISTRIBUTED—NONDISTRIBUTED

The features "anterior" and "coronal" provide for a four-way classification of consonants corresponding to the four main points of articulation: labial, dental, palato-alveolar, and post-alveolar (palatal, velar, uvular, pharyngeal). We have seen (Section 4.2) that in the fourth class—i.e., in the $\begin{bmatrix} -\text{anterior} \\ -\text{coronal} \end{bmatrix}$ consonants—additional points of articulation are provided for by the features "back," "high," and "low." The same is not true of the other classes of consonants, where these three features instead account for supplementary articulations such as palatalization, velarization, and pharyngealization. Thus we have in effect recognized three points of articulation in the pre-palatal region. The question that must now be considered is how the proposed framework will treat various languages that appear to distinguish more than these three points of articulation.

There are quite a number of languages with the obstruent system in (3):

$$\left(3\right) \qquad\qquad\qquad \text{p} \quad \underset{\smile}{\text{t}} \quad \text{t} \quad \underset{\cdot}{\text{t}} \quad \text{k}_1$$

where $\underset{\smile}{t}$ represents a dental, t an alveolar, $\underset{\cdot}{t}$ a retroflex, and k_1 a palato-alveolar plosive. Such systems have been reported for Aranta (K. Hale, personal communication), Araucanian (Echeverría and Contreras, 1965), Madurese (A. M. Stevens, 1965), Toda (Emeneau, 1957), and many other languages. In at least some of these languages (Araucanian and Aranta, for instance), these distinctions must be directly represented in the lexicon since they function as the sole distinguishing mark among items belonging to identical grammatical categories. We must, therefore, add a feature to the framework, and the next problem to consider is the phonetic nature of this feature. At first sight it may appear that in each of the three "points of articulation" so far established we must recognize a forward and back region. This, however, does not reflect all the facts since in most cases the subsidiary differences in point of articulation are also accompanied by characteristic differences in the length of the zone of contact. The length of a constriction along the direction of the air flow has obvious acoustical consequences, and it would be highly plausible that these should be controlled by a special feature, which we shall call "distributed."

Distributed sounds are produced with a constriction that extends for a considerable distance along the direction of the air flow; nondistributed sounds are produced with a constriction that extends only for a short distance in this direction.

The distinction that we are trying to capture here has by no means gone unrecognized in the past. Phonetics books traditionally distinguish apical from laminal and retroflex from nonretroflex consonants.[15] As a first approximation (to be further refined below), we class the former as [−distributed] and the latter as [+distributed].

In postulating the feature "distributed," we are in effect claiming that subsidiary differences in points of articulation are in all cases describable with the help of low-level phonetic rules, rules which, like the stress rules of English, assign numerical values to the different features. This is by no means an empty claim. It would be controverted if, for example, a given language were shown to have dental and alveolar consonants which both had apical articulations. This question has been investigated by Ladefoged (1964, pp. 19 f. and

---

[15] Zwicky (1965) has argued convincingly that in Sanskrit the retroflex $\underset{\cdot}{s}$ is [−anterior] ([+compact] in the framework used by Zwicky), like the palato-alveolar ς, and not [+anterior] like the dental s. This view was apparently shared by Whitney (1941), who comments: "This very near relationship of $\underset{\cdot}{s}$ and ς is attested by this euphonic treatment which is to a considerable extent the same."

passim), with results that are of great interest. In what we may term the denti-alveolar region, Ladefoged distinguishes three areas: (1) teeth and teeth-ridge; (2) front of teeth-ridge; (3) back of teeth-ridge. In each of these areas Ladefoged finds consonants produced with and without a distributed constriction. In Table 5 we summarize the relevant data given by Ladefoged.

TABLE 5.

	teeth and teeth-ridge	front of teeth-ridge	back of teeth-ridge
Twi		apical	laminal
Ewe	laminal		apical
Temne	apical	laminal (affricated)	
Isoko	laminal (affricated)	apical	

It is immediately clear from the table above that no single language has more than two consonants in the denti-alveolar region, of which one is apical and the other laminal. The simplest situation is that in Twi, where we have the common contrast between alveolar and palato-alveolar consonants (in our terms, anterior and nonanterior consonants). This solution is in accord with Ladefoged's comment that "it was only an arbitrary decision to symbolize the pre-palatal position by a symbol indicating a retracted alveolar rather than an advanced palatal" (p. 19).

The situation is equally simple in Ewe, where dental consonants contrast with retroflex consonants. In our terms the former would be characterized as $\begin{bmatrix} +\text{anterior} \\ +\text{distributed} \end{bmatrix}$; the latter as $\begin{bmatrix} -\text{anterior} \\ -\text{distributed} \end{bmatrix}$. Ladefoged notes that the Ewe retroflex consonant "sounds slightly different from the retroflex stop found in Indian languages such as Hindi" (p. 18). If this difference is systematic, it would clearly have to be reflected in the grammars of these languages. It is, however, quite sufficient to note that the point of contact between the tongue and the roof of the mouth is somewhat more advanced in one language than the other. This fact would presumably be reflected in low-level phonetic rules that assign numerical values to the different features. The existence of a systematic phonetic difference does not, therefore, in itself constitute a necessary and sufficient condition for postulating an additional point of articulation.

In both Temne and Isoko we find a contrast between distributed and nondistributed anterior consonants. In Temne the nondistributed consonant is articulated at the teeth, whereas the distributed consonant is articulated somewhat farther back. In Isoko the situation is the reverse: the distributed consonant is articulated in the front part of the dental region and the nondistributed consonant is articulated farther back. In both cases the facts can be readily accounted for by low-level phonetic rules, provided that the distinction between [+distributed] and [−distributed] is given.

We noted above that the difference characterized by distributed versus nondistributed does not correspond precisely to the distinction between laminal and apical. The relevant distinction is not between articulations made with parts of the tongue other than the apex and those made with the apex, but rather between sounds made with long constrictions and those made with short constrictions. The dividing line between nondistributed and distributed articulations seems to us to be best exemplified by the articulatory distinction between the Polish "hard" and "soft" dentals. Wierzchowska (1965) describes this difference in the following terms:

> The contact made by the tongue with the roof of the mouth in articulating [the "soft" dentals—NC/MH] ć ʒ́ as well as ś ź is considerably wider than the contact made in the hard c ʒ s z. The closure in the forward portion of the region of contact includes in the case of ć ʒ́ the teeth ridge and extends to the forward part of the hard palate . . . The groove in ś ź is longer than in the hard consonants c ʒ s z extending not only across the teeth ridge but also across the forward part of the hard palate . . . [The groove} is formed by a part of the tongue that is farther back than that used in the case of the hard consonants . . .

The excellent illustrations (palatograms, linguograms, and X-ray tracings) contained in the book appear to indicate that the critical difference in the length of the stricture is in the vicinity of 1.5 cm. It is this longer stricture that accounts for the striking hushing quality that is observed in the Polish "soft" dentals.[16]

Finally a word must be said about the distinction between labials and labiodentals. As these fit rather naturally under the proposed distinction, we shall assume that labials are [+distributed], labiodentals are [−distributed]. The fact that there are other feature distinctions between these two classes of sounds makes this distinction in the length of stricture somewhat peripheral, though no less real.

Since phonetic features induce categorizations of segments, one expects these categorizations to be reflected in the phonological rules. This has clearly been the case with all features that have been discussed so far. Since it is, however, less obvious with regard to the feature "distributed," an example is called for here. The feature "distributed" provides a natural characterization of the alternation between the dental and retroflex consonants that are found in Sanskrit. If it is assumed, as is usual, that the Sanskrit dentals are [−distributed], then the alternation can be characterized by the following rule:[17]

$$
(4) \qquad \begin{bmatrix} -\text{distributed} \\ +\text{coronal} \end{bmatrix} \rightarrow [-\text{anterior}] \ / \ \begin{bmatrix} -\text{anterior} \\ -\text{low} \end{bmatrix} \underline{\qquad}
$$

4.5. COVERED—NONCOVERED

In many West African languages there is vowel harmony in terms of a feature that has been variously described as "tenseness" (Ladefoged, 1964), "heightening" (Welmers, 1946), "brightness" (Sapir, 1931). The X-ray tracings published by Ladefoged (1964, p. 38) clearly show that in one set of these vowels the pharynx is more constricted than in the other and that the constriction in the pharynx is accompanied by a noticeable elevation of the larynx. We venture to suggest that this difference corresponds to the difference between the vocal tract positions in open and covered singing. The particular dull quality associated with covered voice production appears not to be present in all cases. Sapir (1931) observed it in Gweabo, and Berry (1957) mentions it for Twi, but other observers, including Ladefoged (1964), have

---

[16] In Russian the "soft" [s,] lacks this hushing quality. It is also formed with a much shorter stricture. (See the X-ray tracing in Fant (1960, p. 172), where the length of the stricture is 1 cm.) The Russian sound is therefore to be regarded as [−distributed].

[17] We assume here that the [r] in Sanskrit, as in English, is [−anterior] and that all vowels are universally [−anterior]. The feature [−low] in the rule excludes the environment after the vowel [a].

failed to notice it. In view of the uncertain status of our data, the proposed description of this feature must be taken as tentative (but see Stewart (1967) for recent strong supporting evidence).

We shall assume that covered sounds are produced with a pharynx in which the walls are narrowed and tensed and the larynx raised; uncovered sounds are produced without a special narrowing and tensing in the pharynx.

As far as we know, this feature is restricted to vowels and is found primarily in the West African languages exhibiting vowel harmony. It is possible, however, that it has a wider utilization. For example, the two rounded front vowels of Swedish represented as [y] and [ʉ] may perhaps differ in that the latter is covered whereas the former is not. The X-ray tracings published by Fant (1959) lend some plausibility to this suggestion.

4.6. GLOTTAL CONSTRICTIONS

Glottal constrictions are formed by narrowing the glottal aperture beyond its neutral position. Such constrictions may accompany many different types of supraglottal articulatory configurations. Included among the sounds with glottal constriction are both the implosives and the ejectives, as well as certain types of clicks. Since phonetically the most interesting factor is the manner in which the glottal closure is released and the motion of the glottis that may precede the release, we shall discuss these different types of glottalized sounds in Section 5.2, which deals with release features.

Glottal constrictions are commonly of an extreme degree, i.e., they involve total closure. There are, however, instances where glottal constrictions of lesser degree occur. Thus, for instance, in the dialect of Korean described by Kim (1965), the tense glottalized stops represented by Kim as p^* t^* k^* have glottal constriction, but not glottal closure, for otherwise it would be impossible to account for the buildup of oral pressure during the stop phase that was observed by Kim. That the vocal cords are, on the other hand, not wide open is shown by the timing of the voicing onset in the adjacent vowel. This begins in these stops as soon as the primary stop closure is released, whereas in the stops without glottal constriction the onset of voicing is delayed. (For further discussion of this point, see Section 6.2.) It follows from the preceding that in sounds produced with glottal constriction voicing can occur only after the glottal constriction has been released.

Several African and Caucasian languages exhibit the so-called laryngealized or "creaky" voice (Knarrstimme), which seems to be an instance of glottal constriction. This phenomenon has been described by Ladefoged (1964):

> In this state of the glottis there is a great deal of tension in the intrinsic laryngeal musculature, and the vocal cords no longer vibrate as a whole. The ligamental and arytenoid parts of the vocal cords vibrate separately . . . Laryngealized voicing often occurs during an implosive consonant . . . [but] need not occur in implosive consonants; and equally it [laryngealized voicing— NC/MH] can occur without the downward movement of the larynx which must by definition be present in an implosive. We can, therefore, separate out two kinds of glottalized consonants: what we are here calling voiced implosives (as in Igbo and Kalabari), in which there is always a downward movement of the glottis—and there may or may not be laryngealized voicing; and what we are here calling laryngealized consonants (as in Hausa), in which there is always a particular mode of vibration of the vocal cords—and there may or may not be a lowering of the larynx (p. 16).

In describing the actual production of one of these sounds, Ladefoged noted:

> The vocal cords were apparently tightly closed for at least 30 msec in between the two syllables . . . then, when they did start vibrating, there were four glottal pulses irregularly spaced in a little under 20 msec; these pulses were followed by a gap of almost 17 msec; the next pulse was the first of a series recurring at regular intervals of about 12 msec. During some of the 17 msec before the regular vibrations began the vocal cords must have been held together; I have no criteria for deciding whether the vocal cords were together for long enough for this part of the sequence to be called a glottal stop. It is often not possible to make an absolute distinction between laryngealization and glottal closure . . . (pp. 16–17).[18]

4.7. SECONDARY APERTURES

4.7.1. NASAL—NONNASAL

Nasal sounds are produced with a lowered velum which allows the air to escape through the nose; nonnasal sounds are produced with a raised velum so that the air from the lungs can escape only through the mouth.

The most common type of nasal sounds are the anterior nasal consonants [m] and [n], where nasalization is superimposed upon a plosive articulation, i.e., on that of [b] and [d], respectively. These are found in the overwhelming majority of languages. Less common are the nonanterior nasals [ɲ] and [ŋ]. Nasal consonants of other types are quite uncommon. Ladefoged (1964, p. 24) reports that Tiv has nasal affricates which contrast with both nasal and nonnasal plosives. We do not know of any certain examples of nasal continuants such as a nasal [z] or [v]. Nasal vowels are, of course, quite common. In the best known cases, such as in the Romance and Slavic languages, however, the nasality of vowels is contextually determined and would not appear in the representation of items in the lexicon.

In Yoruba, Nupe, and other African languages, nasality can be superimposed on glide as well as liquid articulation; i.e., the language exhibits nasal cognates of the nonnasal [y], [w], [r]. These, however, are contextual variants of the nonnasal phonemes. (See Ladefoged, 1964, p. 23). The superimposition of nasality on the lateral [l] is phonetically attested in modern French in such words as *branlant*, "shaking," where [l] appears between two nasal vowels. Nasalized [r] is attested phonetically in Yoruba (Siertsema, 1958).

Nasal sounds are normally voiced because the open nasal passage does not permit sufficient pressure buildup inside the vocal tract to inhibit spontaneous vocal cord vibration. There are rare instances of contrast between voiced and voiceless nasals. (See Westermann and Ward, 1933, p. 65).

PRENASALIZED CONSONANTS. In many rather widely scattered languages of Africa there are prenasalized consonants, which contrast with both voiced plosives and the familiar type of nasal consonant. Ladefoged (1964) reports the existence of prenasalized consonants in Serer, Fula, Mende, Sherbro, Tiv, Kutep, and Margi among the West African languages. They occur also in other parts of Africa; e.g., in Kikuyu[19] and in Xhosa (McLaren, 1955).

---

[18] All but the first of the durations in the above quotation have been reduced by us by a factor of 10 to conform to the facts as shown in Ladefoged's oscillogram on which the passage is an extended comment (Plate 1B).

[19] L. E. Armstrong (1940). In Kikuyu prenasalized consonants do not occur initially in verbal stems (note 2, p. 40). On the other hand, there are hardly any nasals of the familiar type in initial position in noun stems. The noun stems beginning with a prenasalized labial, a large number of which are listed in the glossary of Armstrong (1940), appear in almost every case to consist of a special nasal prefix plus stem.

Phonetically, prenasalized consonants differ from the more familiar type of nasal consonant in that the velum, which is lowered during the period of oral occlusion, is raised prior to the release of the oral occlusion, whereas in the more common type of nasal consonant the velum is raised simultaneously with or after the release of the oral occlusion. It would appear, therefore, that phonetically we have to recognize a feature that governs the timing of different movements within the limits of a single segment. As an alternative to this, it has been suggested to us by R. Carter that the difference between prenasalized and ordinary nasal consonants might be regarded as an instance of instantaneous versus delayed release (see Section 5.2). This suggestion appeals to us but we are at present unable to provide serious arguments in its favor.[20]

4.7.2. LATERAL—NONLATERAL

This feature is restricted to coronal consonantal sounds. Lateral sounds are produced by lowering the mid section of the tongue at both sides or at only one side, thereby allowing the air to flow out of the mouth in the vicinity of the molar teeth; in nonlateral sounds no such side passage is open. Laterality is compatible both with vocalic (liquid) and nonvocalic sounds, the difference being that in the vocalic lateral (liquid) the passage is wider and less obstructed than in the nonvocalic lateral. Among the lateral nonvocalic sounds we have continuants opposed to affricates, whereas there does not seem to be any such subdivision among the vocalic laterals. A good example of the nonvocalic affricates is provided by Chipe-wyan (Li, 1946), where a lateral series exactly parallels the different manners of articulation found in nonlateral series. Thus, nonlateral series such as (5) are paralleled by lateral series such as (6).

$$\left(5\right) \qquad \begin{matrix} t & d & t' \\ \check{c} & j & \check{c}' & \check{s} & \check{z} \end{matrix}$$

$$\left(6\right) \qquad t\mathfrak{l} \quad d\mathfrak{l} \quad t\mathfrak{l}' \quad \mathfrak{l} \quad l^{21}$$

Of the laterals only the vocalic [l] occurs with any frequency among the languages of the world. Nonvocalic laterals, which often are strident, are found in various widely scattered areas of the globe: the Caucasus, Africa, and among the languages native to the American continent.[22]

5. Manner of articulation features

5.1. CONTINUANT—NONCONTINUANT (STOP)

In the production of continuant sounds, the primary constriction in the vowel tract is not narrowed to the point where the air flow past the constriction is blocked; in stops the air flow through the mouth is effectively blocked.

Among the stops are the plosives (nasal as well as oral), the affricates, and the glottal

---

[20] J. D. McCawley (personal communication) has suggested that prenasalized consonants be regarded as obstruent nasals, as opposed to the familiar types of nasals which are sonorant.

[21] *t'* represents a glottalized *t*, and ɫ a voiceless *l*.

[22] For the Caucasian languages, see Trubetzkoy (1922); for African languages, Ladefoged (1964); and for instances of laterality in American Indian languages, Li (1946).

stops, as well as various types of sounds with closure not only at the point of primary constriction but also at supplementary constrictions, including clicks, other doubly articulated plosives (labiovelars), and implosive and ejective stops.

The status of the liquids with regard to this feature requires some comment. The fricative varieties of [r] do not represent any particular difficulty; they are clearly continuant. The trilled [r] is more difficult, for here there is interruption of the air stream during at least part of the duration of the sound. The vibrations of the tongue tip, however, are produced by the drop in pressure which occurs inside the passage between the tip of the tongue and palate when the air flows rapidly through it (Bernoulli effect). The trill is thus a secondary effect of narrowing the cavity without actually blocking the flow of air. Consequently there is good reason to view the trilled [r] as a continuant rather than as a stop. The distinction between the tap [r] and the trilled [r] is produced by a difference in subglottal pressure: the trilled [r] is produced with heightened subglottal pressure; the tap [r], without it. (See also Section 6.1.)

It may be noted parenthetically that the tap [r] may be produced by a different mechanism than the so-called "tongue flap" [D] which greatly resembles the tap [r]. Whereas the latter is the result of the aerodynamic mechanism just described, it is quite possible that the tongue flap [D] is produced by essentially the same muscular activity that is found in the dental stop articulation, except that in the case of the tongue flap the movement is executed with great rapidity and without tension.

The characterization of the liquid [l] in terms of the continuant-noncontinuant scale is even more complicated. If the defining characteristic of the stop is taken (as above) as total blockage of air flow, then [l] must be viewed as a continuant and must be distinguished from [r] by the feature of "laterality." If, on the other hand, the defining characteristic of stops is taken to be blockage of air flow *past the primary stricture*, then [l] must be included among the stops. The phonological behavior of [l] in some languages supports somewhat the latter interpretation. As noted above (Section 4.7.2), in Chipewyan the lateral series parallels the nonlateral series if [l] is regarded as a continuant. Moreover, continuants (including [l]) are subject to voicing alternations which do not affect noncontinuants (Li, 1946). On the other hand, there are other facts in different languages which suggest that [l] is best regarded as a noncontinuant (with the definition of the feature adjusted accordingly). Thus, for instance, in certain dialects of English spoken in Scotland, diphthongs are lax before noncontinuants and tense before continuants (Lloyd, 1908). Thus there is [rʌjd] but [r'ajz]. The liquids [l] and [r] pattern in parallel fashion, the former with the noncontinuants and the latter with the continuants: [t'ʌjl] but [t'ajr].

5.2. RELEASE FEATURES: INSTANTANEOUS RELEASE— DELAYED RELEASE[23]

These features affect only sounds produced with closure in the vocal tract. There are basically two ways in which a closure in the vocal tract may be released, either instantaneously as in the plosives or with a delay as in the affricates. During the delayed release, turbulence is generated in the vocal tract so that the release phase of affricates is acoustically quite similar to the cognate fricative. The instantaneous release is normally accompanied by much less or no turbulence.

Though restricted to sounds produced with a closure, the release is of significance

[23] These terms have been suggested to us by R. Carter.

not only for closures at the primary stricture but also for closures at the secondary stricture. Our phonetic framework must therefore contain two release features.

5.2.1. RELEASE OF PRIMARY CLOSURES

As already noted the release feature of the primary constriction distinguishes the affricates from the plosives: plosives such as English [p b t d k g] are produced with an abrupt release; affricates such as English [č j] are produced with a delayed release. Quite similar to the gesture involved in the production of these fairly common affricates is the gesture that produces the lateral affricates found in the Athabaskan languages of North America (Li, 1946; Hoijer, 1945), and in some Caucasian languages (Trubetzkoy, 1922). The closure in these sounds is commonly produced by contact between the blade of the tongue and the dental or palatal region of the mouth. During the delayed release of this closure, the sides of the tongue, but not its tip, are lowered, thereby allowing the air to flow sideways across the molar teeth. As stated above, the lateral affricate differs from other laterals in that it requires complete closure (which is then followed by a lateral release); in the other laterals, the lateral aperture is open all through the articulation of the sound.

5.2.2. RELEASE OF SECONDARY CLOSURES

The chief examples of the role played by the release of secondary closures are provided by the clicks. Clicks are formed with two or even three simultaneous closures. In the terms of the framework developed here, clicks are noncontinuants with extreme velarization, i.e., $\begin{bmatrix} +\text{high} \\ +\text{back} \end{bmatrix}$. They may or may not be glottalized. In this section our attention will be focused on the release mechanisms, and we shall therefore touch only in passing upon such major aspects of the clicks as the suction produced by the backward movement of the secondary closure or the order in which the different closures are released. These matters are discussed more fully in Section 5.3.

Our discussion is based primarily on the detailed description of clicks given in D. M. Beach (1938). Beach views the articulation of a click as composed of two separate parts, an " influx " and an " efflux." Under the term " influx " he subsumes the features that are relevant for the primary constriction; all other click features are subsumed under the heading " efflux." Beach finds that in Hottentot there are four types of influx: (1) the dental affricative ⱶ, (2) the denti-alveolar implosive ꞙ, (3) the lateral affricative ꞵ, (4) the alveolar implosive type C. As the palatograms in Beach clearly show, the first two are dentals and the latter are " post-alveolar " or " palato-alveolar " (p. 81). In the terms developed here, all clicks are [+coronal]; the former two are [+anterior], the latter two [−anterior]. Each of the pairs has one member which is plosive and one member which is affricative. In our terms we characterize the former as being formed with an instantaneous release, and the latter as being formed with a delayed release. In the nonanterior clicks the delayed release is lateral rather than frontal.[24] We summarize the preceding discussion in Table 6 (p. 320).

---

[24] "The principal difference between ⱶ and ꞙ is not in the *place* but rather in the manner of influx. ⱶ is affricative, whereas ꞙ is plosive, in other words, the lowering of the tip and blade of the tongue is sudden for ꞙ, but more gradual for ⱶ. Doke . . . uses the term *instantaneous* and *drawn out* for *plosive* and *affricative*, respectively" (Beach, 1938, p. 77). "Although there is very little difference in tongue-position between C and ꞵ there are two other very great differences. In the first place, C is "frontal," whereas ꞵ is lateral. For C the tip of the tongue is lowered first, while for ꞵ the release is made at the side (or sides) of the tongue. And in the second place C is implosive ("instantaneous"), whereas ꞵ is affricative" (ibid., p. 80).

Each of these four classes of influx is paired with some efflux to produce a particular click. The number of different effluxes differs somewhat from dialect to dialect. We shall discuss here the Korana dialect which has the largest number of effluxes—six. These are, according to Beach, (1) nasal symbolized by *N*, (2) "weak unvoiced velar plosive" symbolized by *k*, (3) "strong unvoiced velar affricative" symbolized by *kxh*, (4) "glottal plosive"

TABLE 6.

	ⱶ	ꜰ	ꜱ	C
anterior	+	+	−	−
coronal	+	+	+	+
delayed primary release	+	−	+	−
lateral	−	−	+	−

symbolized by ʔ, (5) "glottal fricative" symbolized by *h*, (6) "velar glottalic affricative" symbolized by *kx*. Since each of the four influxes discussed in the preceding paragraph can be combined with each of these six types of efflux, there are twenty-four different clicks in Korana. (Nama, the other Hottentot dialect discussed by Beach, lacks the "velar glottalic affricative efflux" and hence has only twenty distinct clicks.) We must now characterize the features of the different effluxes.

Of the six effluxes, the one termed nasal by Beach presents no serious difficulty.

> In clicks containing this type of efflux the [nasal—NC/MH] efflux commences during the lingual occlusion before either the prevelar or velar release has been made. The prevelar influx then occurs, followed by a silent release of the velar closure. The nasal efflux continues throughout both of these releases, and to a lesser extent throughout the following vowel (p. 87).

This evidently is a click with nasalization, whereas the other five types of click are nonnasal.

Of the remaining five clicks, two are of the velar "affricative" type, whereas the others —and also the nasal type—have a "plosive" or "silent" velar release. The velar affricative release is described by Beach as being somewhat more gradual than the velar plosive release "so that an affricate . . . is heard instead of a pure plosive" (p. 85). It is clear that we are dealing with sounds differing in the manner of release of the secondary closure. The two affricative types have a delayed release of the secondary closure; all other types have instantaneous release. The two types with affricative secondary releases are further subdivided into an aspirated and a glottalized type. The aspirated type of efflux shall be classified as being produced with heightened subglottal pressure (aspiration), but without glottal constriction, whereas the glottalized type of efflux is produced with glottal constriction and presumably without heightened subglottal pressure. This type of efflux is described by Beach as being

> made by making two airtight chambers, an outer or mouth-chamber formed by placing the rim of the tongue . . . in the position for making the required influx, and an inner pharynx-chamber having as its boundaries the velar closure and the closed glottis. Suction is created in the outer or mouth-chamber by lowering the "front" of the tongue (still keeping the rim in contact with the roof of the mouth), and pressure is created in the inner or pharynx-chamber by raising the larynx (p. 232).

The glottalized type of efflux is marked, therefore, not only by glottal closure but also by an upward movement of the larynx which is the main characteristic of glottalized or ejective sounds. (See Section 5.3.2.)

Thus, of the three nonnasal types with plosive efflux, one is aspirated and the other two are nonaspirated. Of the latter, one is made with glottal closure, but apparently without movement of the larynx, and the other is made without glottal closure. We have been unable to determine the role, if any, that is played by tenseness in the production of clicks.

The feature characterization of the six types of efflux given above are summarized in Table 7.

TABLE 7.

	N	*k*	*kxh*	*ʔ*	*h*	*kxʔ*
nasal	+	−	−	−	−	−
delayed release of secondary closure	−	−	+	−	−	+
glottal (tertiary) closure	−	−	−	+	−	+
heightened subglottal pressure	−	−	+	−	+	−
movement of glottal closure	n	n	n	−	n	+

n = not applicable

The click system of Xhosa, perhaps the best known of the click languages, is somewhat different from that of Hottentot. Of the four different types of influx found in Hottentot, Xhosa has only three, lacking the dental plosive types. Each of the three influxes may be produced with or without nasalization. Both nasal and nonnasal clicks may be aspirated or unaspirated. The unaspirated nonnasal clicks are, in turn, subdivided into voiced and voiceless. It appears, thus, that the release of the secondary closure plays no role in Xhosa; all secondary closures have an instantaneous release. The parallelism between voicing in Xhosa and glottal closure in Hottentot is found in many nonclick languages.

5.2.3. COMMENTS ON THE RELEASE FEATURES

COMMENT 1. We have seen that each closure in the vocal tract may be released instantaneously or with a delay. There are, however, important restrictions on the release features. Only sounds produced with closure can have different types of release. Ladefoged (1964) describes a labiodental flap (in Margi) which consists in effect of a labiodental fricative terminating in an instantaneous release. This sound, however, occurs only in "ideophones," e.g., in utterances such as *bə́v^bú*, "describing sudden appearance and flight," *háv^báwù*, "describing escape of an animal," *káv^báhù*, "describing intruding into a place" (Hoffmann, 1963, pp. 25 f.), which occupy a clearly marginal position in the phonological system.

It appears that there are no clicks formed with laryngeal voice. In view of this we propose the following general restriction: in a sound formed with all three of the possible types of closure, only the primary and secondary can have both types of release while the tertiary closure must be released instantaneously.

COMMENT 2. In Jakobson, Fant, and Halle (1963), the difference between plosives and affricates was characterized by means of the feature "stridency." Plosives were characterized as nonstrident stops, affricates as strident stops. Thus no allowance was made for the existence of nonstrident affricates. Such sounds do, however, exist; for example, in the American Indian language Chipewyan, there are contrasting dental strident and nonstrident affricates (Li, 1946). The device for characterizing these differences is already available. Since the manner of release is clearly relevant for the secondary and tertiary closure, there is little reason not to extend it to include the primary closures, as was done above. In this way we can fill the gap just noted: plosives are stops with instantaneous (primary) releases, affricates are stops with delayed releases. The feature "stridency" can then be used to distinguish strident from nonstrident affricates. Stops with instantaneous releases are universally nonstrident.

5.3. *SUPPLEMENTARY MOVEMENTS*

In sounds formed with two simultaneous closures, such as the clicks, the labiovelars, or the glottalized sounds, there may be movements of the velar or glottal closures during the period of closure. If these movements are in a direction toward the lungs, the volume of the space between the two closures is increased and the pressure inside that space decreases. As a result, when the primary closure is released there will be a suction effect produced and air will flow into the mouth. If, on the other hand, the movement of the constriction is in a direction away from the lungs, the volume between the two closures will be reduced and the air pressure inside the cavity will increase.

These two opposite motions underlie the phonetic properties "suction" and "pressure," respectively. In the case of both suction and pressure we find that they can be produced by motions either of the velar or of the glottal closure. In fact, there are sounds (e.g., the imploded labiovelars observed by Ladefoged (1964, p. 9) in Idoma and Bini) where both closures move during the articulation of a single sound.

5.3.1. SUCTION

It must be noted that the velar closure that produces suction need not necessarily be a secondary closure but may also be a primary closure. In the Hottentot or Xhosa clicks, the velar closure is secondary, since, as we have seen, it combines with different primary articulations. In the labiovelar suction stops of such languages as Kpelle, on the other hand, the closure at the velum is primary and the closure at the lips secondary (rounding). The velar nature of the sound in question is clearly indicated by the fact that a preceding nasal, which always assimilates to the primary point of articulation of the following stop, is velar before labiovelars as well as before velars (Welmers, 1962).

CLICKS AND IMPLOSIVES. Since suction is produced by a downward movement of velar or glottal closures, it is necessary from a phonetic point of view to postulate two distinct suction features, one (the "click" feature) is associated with velar closure and the other (the "implosion" feature) with glottal closure. As noted above, the clicks have primary constrictions in the dental and alveolar region, but there are also clicklike sounds which have a labial closure. Moreover, there appear to be labiovelar suction sounds with glottal implosion. In his discussion of the African labiovelars, Ladefoged notes:

> These sounds are formed in at least three different ways . . . The first type occurs in many Guang languages (Late, Anum). It consists of simply the simultaneous articulation of *k* and *p* or *g* and *b*, superimposed on a pulmonic airstream. [In the terms of the preceding discussion, these are sounds without suction and glottal closure—NC/MH.] The second type, which is found in

Yoruba, Ibibio, and many other languages, is more complicated. After the two closures have been made, there is a downward movement of the jaw, and a backward movement of the point of contact of the back of the tongue and the soft palate; these movements cause a lowering of the pressure in the mouth. Thus from the point of view of the release of the closure at the lips, there is an ingressive velaric airstream. But there is still a high pressure behind the velar closure owing to the outgoing air from the lungs . . . This combination of a velaric and pulmonic airstream mechanism has been described very accurately by Siertsema . . . who concluded that Yoruba $\widehat{kp}$ 'is implosive at the lips, "explosive" at the back.' [These sounds, then, are produced with suction at the velar closure, but, like the first type of labiovelar, without glottal closure— NC/MH.] . . . In the third type of $\widehat{kp}$, which is found in Idoma and sometimes in Bini, all three airstream mechanisms are involved. After the two closures have been made there is a backward movement of the tongue . . . and during the latter part of the sound there is also a downward movement of the vibrating glottis . . .[25] [This type of labiovelar is produced with closures at the velum and the glottis, and with suction movements at both closures—NC/MH.]

An interesting side effect of the lowering of the glottis in the implosives is that it is usually accompanied by vocal cord vibration. This vibration is the direct consequence of the drop in supraglottal pressure and the rise in subglottal pressure which result from the increase in the supraglottal volume and the decrease in the subglottal volume that are produced by the lowering of the glottis.

5.3.2. PRESSURE

Like suction motions, pressure motions can be executed by the velar or by the glottal closure. We must therefore postulate two pressure features, a "velar pressure" feature and a "glottal pressure" feature. We shall refer to the latter by its traditional name "ejection," in view of its greater familiarity.

VELAR PRESSURE. The existence of velaric pressure stops, which is occasionally mentioned in the literature (see Heffner, 1950), could not be substantiated.

EJECTION. Ejection is produced by an upward movement of the glottal closure. Ejective consonants have been described in languages all over the globe—in India, in the Caucasus, and in American Indian languages.[26] It has also been observed that ejectives and implosives differ in the effect on the transition of the second formant in the adjacent vowel. Ejectives have a transition with a somewhat higher termination frequency than the corresponding nonejectives, and resemble palatalized consonants in this respect; in the implosives (as in rounded or velarized consonants), the termination frequency is somewhat lower. This is a direct consequence of the fact that in the ejectives the glottis is raised above its normal position and is therefore being lowered during part of the vowel articulation, whereas in the implosives, at the beginning of the vowel articulation the glottis is lower than its normal position and moves upward. As a result, after the ejectives there is a lengthening and after

[25] Ladefoged (1964, p. 9). See also Beach's description of clicks with a "velar glottalic affricative efflux" on page 320. Note the close similarity between this type of click and Ladefoged's third type of labiovelar.

[26] On ejectives in the languages of India, see citations in Trubetzkoy (1958, pp. 146–150), where ejection is designated by the term *Rekursion*. On ejectives in the Caucasian languages, see Trubetzkoy (1931) and, more recently, Kuipers (1960). On ejectives in American Indian languages, see Sapir (1949b). In the West African languages surveyed by Ladefoged (1964), ejectives were found only in Hausa (p. 5).

implosives a shortening of the vocal tract, which is directly translated into a falling or rising, respectively, transition in the second formant of the adjacent vowel.[27]

5.3.3. ORDER OF RELEASES IN SOUNDS WITH MULTIPLE CLOSURES

The order of release of the different closures is governed by a simple rule. In sounds without supplementary motions, the releases are simultaneous. In sounds produced with supplementary motions, closures are released in the order of increasing distance from the lips. The reason for this ordering is that only in this manner will clear auditory effects be produced, for acoustic effects produced inside the vocal tract will be effectively suppressed if the vocal tract is closed.

5.4. *TENSE—NONTENSE (LAX)*

The feature "tenseness" specifies the manner in which the entire articulatory gesture of a given sound is executed by the supraglottal musculature. Tense sounds are produced with a deliberate, accurate, maximally distinct gesture that involves considerable muscular effort; nontense sounds are produced rapidly and somewhat indistinctly. In tense sounds, both vowels and consonants, the period during which the articulatory organs maintain the appropriate configuration is relatively long, while in nontense sounds the entire gesture is executed in a somewhat superficial manner.[28]

Dealing first with vowels, we find examples of tense versus nontense sounds in modern German, for instance, where this feature plays a differentiating role in pairs such as *ihre*, "her," versus *irre*, "err"; *Huhne*, "chicken," versus *Hunne*, "Hun"; *Düne*, "dune," versus *dünne*, "thin"; *wen*, "whom," versus *wenn*, "if"; *wohne*, "reside," versus *Wonne*, "joy"; *Haken*, "hook," versus *hacken*, "hack."

One of the differences between tense and lax vowels is that the former are executed with a greater deviation from the neutral or rest position of the vocal tract than are the latter. It has been observed, for instance, that the tongue constriction in tense [i] is narrower than that in lax [i]. This difference in tongue height is superficially rather similar to that observed between high [i] and nonhigh [e]. The mechanism involved, however, is quite different in the two cases, a fact which was already well known to Sievers (1901), who explicitly warned against confusing the two:

> Man hüte sich auch davor, die Begriffe "gespannt" (oder "eng") und "unge-
> spannt" (oder "weit") mit denen zu verwechseln, welche die althergebrachten
> Ausdrücke "geschlossen" und "offen" bezeichnen sollen. Diese Letzteren
> wollen nur aussagen dass ein Vocal geringere oder grössere Mundweite habe als

---

[27] Sonagrams of implosives which show these transitions clearly can be found in Ladefoged (1964, Plate 4B). Note also the comment of Trubetzkoy (1931): "Was die Verkürzung des Resonanzraumes des Mundes betrifft, so geschieht sie in den ostkaukasischen Sprachen mit aktivheller Eigentonauffassung (*positive transition*) nicht durch die gewöhnliche Palatalisierung, d.h., Vorschiebung der Zungenmasse nach vorne, wie in vielen Sprachen der Welt, sondern durch die Verschiebung des Kehlkopfes nach oben" (pp. 10–11); as well as the observation of Ladefoged (1964) that in Igbo, at least, implosives are "velarized as well as usually involving lowering of the glottis" (p. 6), i.e., they exhibit secondary movements that bring about a negative transition in the adjacent vowel.

[28] This difference was well brought out in one of the earliest phonological studies, Winteler (1876): ". . . diejenigen Artikulationen, welche Lenes [lax—NC/MH] erzeugen, [werden] in demselben Augenblicke wieder aufgegeben . . . in welchem sie ihre Kulmination erreicht haben. . . . Bei der Bildung der Fortes [tense—NC/MH] verharren die Sprachwerkzeuge fühlbar in ihrer Kulminationsstellung . . ." (p. 27).

ein anderer, aber ohne alle Rücksicht auf die Verschiedenheit der Articulations-
weise, welche die Differenzen der Mundweite im einzelnen Fall hervorruft,
speciell also ohne alle Rücksicht darauf ob die specifische Mundweite auf
grössere oder geringere Erhebung oder auf grösserer oder geringerer Spannung
der Zunge beruht ... (p. 100).

The greater articulatory effort in the tense vowels is further manifested by their greater
distinctiveness and the markedly longer duration during which the articulatory configuration
remains stationary. This fact has been documented by the detailed studies of X-ray motion
pictures of speech conducted by Perkell (1965), who comments that:

> the pharynx width remains relatively stable throughout the tense vowels
> whereas there is a change in this width during the lax vowels. ... It is as though
> the tongue shape in the lower pharynx is relatively unconstrained during a lax
> vowel, and is free to be influenced by the adjacent phonetic segment. For a tense
> vowel, on the other hand, the tongue position and shape in this region are rather
> precisely defined.

Turning now to consonants, we note that the differences between tense and lax
consonants also involve a greater versus a lesser articulatory effort and duration. The
greater effort is produced by greater muscular tension in the muscles controlling the shape
of the vocal tract. Evidence supporting this comes primarily from X-ray studies and from
observations on the onset of voicing in vowels following a stop consonant. It is obvious that
voicing can occur only if two conditions are met: the vocal cords must be in a position that
will admit voicing, and there must be a flow of air through the glottis. When a stop is produced
and the oral cavity is blocked while the vocal cords are in the appropriate configuration for
voicing, pressure will build up in the cavity and will very rapidly—within about 20 msecs,
under normal conditions—increase to the point where it is approximately equal to the
subglottal pressure. This will halt the flow of air through the glottis, thereby making further
vocal vibrations impossible. Under these conditions there is only one way in which the
pressure buildup inside the vocal tract can be slowed down and voicing allowed to take place
during the closure phase of a stop, that is, by allowing the vocal tract to expand. If the walls
of the tract are rigid as a result of muscular tension, this expansion of the cavity volume
cannot take place, and, therefore, tense stops will not show any voicing during the closure
phase. If, on the other hand, the walls of the cavity are lax, the vocal tract can expand and
voicing can occur even during the closure phase. In fact, X-ray motion picture studies conducted by Perkell (1965) show precisely this behavior.

In analyzing the behavior of the pharynx in the nonsense words [hət′ɛ] and [həd′ɛ] as
spoken by American subjects, Perkell found that during the period of closure there was a
significant increase in the pharynx width when the nontense [d] was articulated but not when
the tense [t] was articulated. This increase in pharynx volume in the nontense obstruent was
also accompanied by the presence of voicing during the period of oral closure, which, however,
died off toward the end of the stop gap. Perkell commented:

> The tense vocal-tract configuration for /t/ would imply a rigid vocal-wall, which
> would not expand to permit the increase in volume needed for a voiced stop.
> Presumably a similar tense configuration exists for the voiceless unaspirated
> stop consonants occurring in certain languages ... For such stop configurations
> an instruction to the larynx musculature to assume a configuration appropriate

for voicing would not result in vocal-cord vibration until the release of the stop, whereas a lax vocal-tract configuration would permit a limited amount of air to pass through the glottis, with consequent glottal vibration.[29]

6. *Source features*

6.1. *HEIGHTENED SUBGLOTTAL PRESSURE*

In discussions concerning tenseness it is usually observed that tense sounds are produced with greater subglottal pressure and that this fact accounts for the well-known presence of aspiration in the tense voiceless stops of many languages. Since, however, the tenseness of the supraglottal muscles is evidently controlled by a different mechanism than is tenseness in the subglottal cavities, these two properties cannot be combined into a single phonetic feature. Instead we must set up in addition to tenseness a feature of "heightened subglottal pressure."

It must further be noted that heightened subglottal pressure may be used in the production of a speech sound without involving tenseness (in the supraglottal musculature). This is the situation in the aspirated voiced stops of languages such as Hindi, where, according to Lisker and Abramson (1964), voicing commonly occurs during the period of oral closure. As explained in the preceding section, this is possible only when the vocal tract is allowed to expand during the stop closure; but this expansion *cannot* occur if the supraglottal musculature is tense. We shall say, therefore, that the voiced aspirated stops of Hindi are produced without tenseness but with heightened subglottal pressure.[30]

Heightened subglottal pressure is a necessary but not a sufficient condition for aspiration. Aspiration requires, in addition, that there be no constriction at the glottis. If there is a glottal constriction, aspiration will not occur. Stops of this type—produced with (supraglottal) tension, heightened subglottal pressure, and glottal constriction—are found in Korean, for example, where they constitute the third class of stops, in addition to the heavily aspirated tense stops produced without glottal constriction and the slightly aspirated stops produced with no heightened subglottal pressure and no glottal constriction. (For pressure measurements see Kim (1965).)

6.2. *VOICED—NONVOICED (VOICELESS)*

In order for the vocal cords to vibrate, it is necessary that air flow through them. If the air flow is of sufficient magnitude, voicing will set in, provided only that the vocal cords not

---

[29] The fact that the supraglottal vocal tract musculature is under greater tension in sounds such as the English [p t k] in initial position would provide a straightforward explanation for the observation made by Lisker (1963, p. 382) that "the rate of pressure build-up is significantly slower for voiced stops than for voiceless." The lesser rigidity of the walls in the "voiced" stops (which are nontense) would allow the cavity to expand after the buccal closure is made. This increase in volume would result in a slowing down of the pressure buildup inside the cavity. Since the volume would remain more or less fixed in the "voiceless" stops, which are tense, the pressure buildup after buccal closure would be more rapid in these consonants.

[30] The question of how this obvious relationship should be expressed in the phonetic framework is of great importance. It has been suggested that there be set up a hyper-feature of "strength of articulation" under which tenseness, heightened subglottal pressure, and, perhaps, certain phonetic features would be subsumed as special cases. While certain facts such as the treatment of Spanish consonants in different contexts (see J. Harris, 1967) make this suggestion quite attractive, we have not adopted it here as it conflicts with our conception of phonetic features as directly related to particular articulatory mechanisms. Instead we have chosen to reflect the interrelatedness among these different features with the help of marking rules (see Chapter Nine).

be held as widely apart as they are in breathing or in whispering. As has been demonstrated in the various high-speed motion pictures of the vocal cords, glottal closure or a constriction of the glottis is not required for voicing; it is necessary only that the glottis not be wide open. On the other hand, vocal cord vibration will also result when the glottis is constricted, as long as there is an air flow of sufficient magnitude or the vocal cords are not held so tight as to prevent vibrating, as they are in the case of sounds produced with glottal constrictions.

In Section 2.1 it was suggested that when the vocal tract is in its neutral speech position, the vocal cords are placed in a configuration that will cause them to vibrate if air flows through them. The vocal cords may also be spread farther apart than in the neutral position, in which case voicing will not occur. We shall restrict the term " nonvoiced " or " voiceless " to sounds produced with a glottal opening that is so wide that it prevents vocal vibration if air flows through the opening. This widening of the glottis is a sufficient condition to suppress vocal cord vibration, but, as suggested in the discussion above, it is not a necessary condition. It should be noted that the narrowing of the glottis in voiced sounds can be quite moderate and may never attain complete closure.

Our understanding of the mechanism of voicing has recently been advanced by the investigations of Lisker and Abramson (1964) of the onset time of vocal cord vibrations in the following vowel relative to the moment of release of the stop closure. We do not share Lisker and Abramson's view that it is the timing of the onset of vocal cord vibrations that is being controlled in implementing the various feature complexes that in the phonetic literature have often been subsumed under the term " voicing." The data on the onset of vocal vibration that have been gathered by Lisker and Abramson can be readily accounted for in terms of the present framework. It is to such an account that the remainder of this section is devoted.

From their measurements Lisker and Abramson conclude that the onset times of vocal vibrations fall into three distinct categories:
(1) onset of voicing precedes stop release
(2) onset of voicing substantially coincides with stop release
(3) onset of voicing lags after stop release

In an investigation of onset times of voice after Korean stops, Kim (1965) has found, moreover, that at least for Korean there are two distinct types of lag, a short lag and a con-siderable lag. In particular, he found that for the glottalized stop, voice onset occurred 12 msecs after the stop release (substantial coincidence); for the weakly aspirated stops, it was 35 msec (moderate lag); and for the heavily aspirated stops, it was 93 msec (considerable lag). (The cited values are mean values for about 800 sample words.) Re-examination of the Lisker and Abramson data shows such a moderate lag to be present at least after the velar stops of Korean, and also, somewhat less convincingly, after the labials and dentals; in addition, the unaspirated velar stops of Cantonese and English also show a short lag. We now have, therefore, four distinct categories:
(1) onset of voicing precedes stop release
(2) onset of voicing substantially coincides with stop release
(3) onset of voicing lags moderately after stop release
(4) onset of voicing lags considerably after stop release

To account for these facts we have at our disposal four phonetic features: voicing, tense-ness, glottal constriction, and subglottal pressure. The simplest case to deal with is case (1)—the stops with voicing lead. All these must be produced with vocal cords in voicing position and without tenseness. The aspirated stops will, moreover, have high subglottal pressure and no glottal constriction. The unaspirated voiced stops will be produced with normal subglottal pressure; the data do not allow us to draw conclusions about glottal constriction, but we suspect that none is present. Next in complexity is case (4)—the sounds with greatly delayed voicing onset. These are all produced with vocal cords *not* in voicing position and hence without glottal constriction but with tenseness and marked subglottal pressure. The sounds of case (3)—those with slight or no aspiration and moderate delay of voicing onset—are produced with vocal cords not in voicing position, normal or low muscular tension in the vocal tract, and low or moderate subglottal pressure. It is significant that, as noted by Lisker and Abramson, it is precisely this category of stops in Korean that is "voiced through" in intervocalic position, rather than the stops with simultaneous voicing onset, which at first sight might seem more reasonable candidates. Observe, however, that it is the former rather than the latter type of stop that is produced without strong muscular tension in the vocal tract. In order for a stop to be "voiced through," it is necessary that the cavity be allowed to expand during the period of stop closure. Consequently one should expect the Korean lax stops to be "voiced through" rather than the tense stop with glottal constriction. Finally, there is case (2), the category where the onset of voicing substantially coincides with the stop release. These sounds are produced with a glottis that either is in the voicing position or has

TABLE 8.

	Voicing leads	Voicing coincides substantially	Voicing lags moderately	Voicing lags considerably
tense	No	Yes, if glottal constriction	No	Yes
voice	Yes	Yes	No	No
heightened subglottal pressure	Yes, if aspirated No, if unaspirated	Either	No	Yes
glottal constriction	No	Yes, if heightened subglottal pressure; otherwise, optional	No	No
Examples in Lisker and Abramson (1964) and Kim (1965)[a]	Dutch Spanish Tamil English[b] Thai Eastern Armenian Hindi Marathi[c]	Dutch Spanish Hungarian English Cantonese Korean Thai Eastern Armenian Hindi Marathi	Korean	English Cantonese Korean Thai E. Armenian Hindi Marathi

[a] When the name of a language appears in a particular column, this indicates that in the cited studies the language was found to have had stops of this type in contrast with stops of some other type. Thus, Dutch was found by Lisker and Abramson to have stops with voice onsets that precede the release as well as stops where the voice onset coincides with the release.

[b] Almost all instances of stops with voicing onset preceding stop release came from a single speaker, who, however, lacked stops where the voicing onset coincided with the release. All other speakers used the second type of stop almost exclusively. (See Lisker and Abramson, 1964, pp. 395–97.)

[c] Hindi and Marathi have two distinct types of stops in which voicing onset leads the stop release; these two types are distinguished by the presence or absence of aspiration.

a constriction. They may or may not be produced with heightened subglottal pressure. If they are produced with heightened pressure, they will be tense and may or may not have a glottal constriction.

We summarize this discussion in Table 8.

6.3. STRIDENT—NONSTRIDENT

Strident sounds are marked acoustically by greater noisiness than their nonstrident counterparts. When the air stream passes over a surface, a certain amount of turbulence will be generated depending upon the nature of the surface, the rate of flow, and the angle of incidence. A rougher surface, a faster rate of flow, and an angle of incidence closer to ninety degrees will all contribute to greater stridency. Stridency is a feature restricted to obstruent continuants and affricates. Plosives and sonorants are nonstrident.

Examples of nonstrident versus strident sounds are bilabial versus labiodental continuants in Ewe: *éɸá*, "he polished," *éfá*, "he was cold"; *ɛβὲ*, "the Ewe language," *ɛvὲ*, "two" (Ladefoged, 1964, p. 53); interdental versus alveolar continuants in English: [θin], "thin," [sin], "sin"; post-alveolar versus palatal continuants in German: [liçt], "light," [lišt], "extinguishes"; interdental versus dental affricates in Chipewyan: *tθɛ*, "stone," *tsá*, "beaver."

Strident liquids, which are nonvocalic (see Section 3.1) are found, for example, in Czech *řada*, "row," versus *rada*, "council," in which strident and nonstrident [r] contrast; in Bura and Margi we find contrasts of strident and nonstrident [l] (Ladefoged, 1964).

7. Prosodic features

Our investigations of these features have not progressed to a point where a discussion in print would be useful. Some recent work by W. S-Y. Wang seems to us promising. For a report of some early results, see Wang (1967).

Chapter eight

PRINCIPLES OF PHONOLOGY

1. On the evaluation procedure and the form of phonological rules

In this chapter we survey the formal devices that we propose for phonological description. These formal devices are a part of the theory of language underlying the description of English that we have presented. There are several conditions of adequacy that they must meet, and there are functions of various sorts that they must fulfill. They must, for example, make it possible to present the data precisely and clearly. They must, moreover, permit us to formulate general statements about the language which are true and significant, and must provide a basis for distinguishing these from other generalizations which are false, or which are true but not significant. Thus, if our analysis is correct, the rules in Chapter Five represent true and significant generalizations; they characterize the native speaker's competence, his idealized ability to produce and understand an unlimited number of sentences. The theory of English of which this study presents a part is based on a certain set of data, but it goes beyond these data, as any grammar must, both in depth and in scope—in depth insofar as it expresses the facts that underlie the data, and in scope insofar as it deals with other potential data, with linguistic forms that we did not specifically consider, including indefinitely many that have never been produced.

In terms of the formal devices that we permit, there are many rules that can be formulated that are incorrect for English. Obviously, a proper choice of formal devices does not guarantee selection of the correct grammar. It is to be expected that there will be many grammars which are statable in terms of the given formal devices and which are all compatible with whatever data are available from a certain language; thus selection among the alternatives will require a procedure of evaluation of some sort. Certainly this is true of any proposal that can now be envisioned with regard to the formalism for the statement of grammars. Furthermore, with other formal devices than those we allow it is possible to express "generalizations" that are consistent with the data but that are not, we would maintain, linguistically significant. When we select a set of formal devices for the construction of grammars, we are, in fact, taking an important step toward a definition of the notion "linguistically significant generalization." Since this notion has real empirical content, our particular characterization of it may or may not be accurate as a proposed explication. This point is important but often overlooked, and it may be useful to touch on the matter briefly here.

To clarify the empirical status of the formal devices selected for the theory of language, it is helpful to set the problem within the framework of psychological theory. The child is presented with certain "primary linguistic data," data which are, in fact, highly restricted and degraded in quality. On the basis of these data, he constructs a grammar that defines his language and determines the phonetic and semantic interpretation of an infinite number of sentences. This grammar constitutes his knowledge of his language. It will, in particular, specify that the primary linguistic data are, in large measure, ill-formed, inappropriate, and contrary to linguistic rule.

These rather obvious facts pose the problem to which the linguist addresses himself, that is, to account for the child's construction of a grammar and to determine what preconditions on the form of language make it possible. Our approach to this problem is two-pronged. First we develop a system of formal devices for expressing rules and a set of general conditions on how these rules are organized and how they apply. We postulate that only grammars meeting these conditions are "entertained as hypotheses" by the child who must acquire knowledge of a language. Secondly, we determine a procedure of evaluation that selects the highest valued of a set of hypotheses of the appropriate form, each of which meets a condition of compatibility with the primary linguistic data. We will not concern ourselves here with the nontrivial problem of what it means to say that a hypothesis—a proposed grammar—is compatible with the data, but will restrict ourselves to the other two problems, namely, the specification of formal devices and of an evaluation procedure. In other words, we make the simplifying and counter-to-fact assumption that all of the primary linguistic data must be accounted for by the grammar and that all must be accepted as "correct"; we do not here consider the question of deviation from grammaticalness, in its many diverse aspects. Given this simplifying assumption, we face the empirical problem of selecting a set of formal devices and an evaluation procedure which jointly meet the empirical condition that the highest valued grammar of the appropriate form is, in fact, the one selected by the child on the basis of primary linguistic data. Even with this idealization, a proposed theory that specifies formal devices and an evaluation procedure can be proven false (all too easily, in actual fact) by confronting it with empirical evidence relating to the grammar that actually underlies the speaker's performance. There is such a grammar, and it is an empirical problem to discover it and to determine the basis for its acquisition. However difficult it may be to find relevant evidence for or against a proposed theory, there can be no doubt whatsoever about the empirical nature of the problem. We stress this fact because the problem has so often been misconstrued as one of "taste" or "elegance."

A further word of caution is perhaps necessary in connection with this formulation of the general problems that guide our study of language. Apart from the idealization mentioned in the preceding paragraph, there is another, much more crucial, idealization implicit in this account. We have been describing acquisition of language as if it were an instantaneous process. Obviously, this is not true. A more realistic model of language acquisition would consider the order in which primary linguistic data are used by the child and the effects of preliminary "hypotheses" developed in the earlier stages of learning on the interpretation of new, often more complex, data. To us it appears that this more realistic study is much too complex to be undertaken in any meaningful way today and that it will be far more fruitful to investigate in detail, as a first approximation, the idealized model outlined earlier, leaving refinements to a time when this idealization is better understood. The correctness of this guess, of course, will have to be judged by the long-range effectiveness of a research program of this sort, as compared with alternatives that might be imagined. In the meantime, this idealization must be kept in mind when we think about the problem of the "psychological reality" of the postulated mental structures.

To take a concrete example, consider the matter of the synchronic residue of the

English Vowel Shift, discussed in detail in Chapter Six. We have argued that the underlying lexical forms in English contain vowels in pre-Vowel-Shift representation, and that these forms are what would have psychological reality given the other assumptions in our model—in particular, the assumption of instantaneous language acquisition. To the extent that these assumptions are false to fact, the conclusions that follow from them may also be false to fact. In particular, it is no doubt the case that the linguistic forms that justify our postulation of the Vowel Shift Rule in contemporary English are, in general, available to the child only at a fairly late stage in his language acquisition, since in large measure these belong to a more learned stratum of vocabulary. Since the order of presentation of linguistic data is, for the moment, an extrinsic factor that has no place in our theory, we cannot take account of this fact, and we can therefore state our conclusion about psychological reality only in hypothetical form: *if it were the case that language acquisition were instantaneous, then the underlying lexical forms with pre-Vowel-Shift representations would be psychologically real.* This, we propose, is a true statement about language—ultimately, about mental processes and the particular way in which they function. But an empirical conclusion of this sort will, naturally, be more difficult to verify, will require more indirect and subtle means of verification, than a simple categorical assertion. To us it seems that for the foreseeable future, the study of language and mental processes will have to be carried out at such a level of abstraction if it is to make significant progress.

With these background comments in mind, let us turn to the formal devices that we have been using in our exposition of English sound structure.

The rules that we assign to the phonological component have generally been presented in terms that can be symbolized by the formula:

$$\left(1\right) \qquad\qquad A \;\rightarrow\; B \;/\; X\!\!-\!\!\!-\!\!\!-Y$$

where A and B represent single units of the phonological system (or the null element); the arrow stands for "is actualized as"; the diagonal line means "in the context"; and X and Y represent, respectively, the left- and right-hand environments in which A appears. These environments may be null, or may consist of units or strings of units of various sorts, and may also include labeled brackets representing the syntactic category of the string to which the rule is applied.

Consider the hypothetical languages A and B which have identical phonological systems consisting of the vowels /i u æ a/ and the other phonological units shown in Table 1. Assume that language A has the rules of (2), whereas language B has the rules of (3).

TABLE 1.   *The sound systems of languages A and B*[a]

	i	u	æ	a	r	l	p	t	k	s	m	n	y	w
vocalic	+	+	+	+	+	+	−	−	−	−	−	−	−	−
consonantal	−	−	−	−	+	+	+	+	+	+	+	+	−	−
high	+	+	−	−	(−)	(−)	(−)	(−)	(+)	(−)	(−)	(−)	(+)	(+)
back	−	+	−	+	(−)	(−)	(−)	(−)	(+)	(−)	(−)	(−)	−	+
anterior	(−)	(−)	(−)	(−)	−	+	+	+	−	+	+	+	(−)	(−)
coronal	(−)	(−)	(−)	(−)	(+)	(+)	−	+	(−)	+	−	+	(−)	(−)
continuant	(+)	(+)	(+)	(+)	(+)	(+)	(−)	−	(−)	+	(−)	(−)	(+)	(+)
nasal	(−)	(−)	(−)	(−)	(−)	(−)	−	−	(−)	(−)	+	+	(−)	(−)
strident	(−)	(−)	(−)	(−)	(−)	(−)	(−)	(−)	(−)	(+)	(−)	(−)	(−)	(−)

[a] The meaning of the parenthesization will be discussed directly.

$\begin{pmatrix}2\end{pmatrix}$

RULES OF LANGUAGE A

i → y / ——p
i → y / ——r
i → y / ——y
i → y / ——a

$\begin{pmatrix}3\end{pmatrix}$

RULES OF LANGUAGE B

i → y / ——p
r → l / ——r
t → p / ——y
s → n / ——a

The difference between (2) and (3) lies in the fact that the statements in (2) are partially identical, whereas those in (3) are totally different from one another. This difference, which is clearly of linguistic interest, would be expressed if we introduced into our formalism a device akin to conjunction in ordinary English, which would permit us to coalesce two partially identical rules into a single rule without repeating the parts that are identical. We therefore establish the convention (4):

$\begin{pmatrix}4\end{pmatrix}$ Two partially identical rules may be coalesced into a single rule by enclosing corresponding nonidentical parts in braces: { }.

This convention enables us to rewrite (2) as (5):

$\begin{pmatrix}5\end{pmatrix}$

$$i \rightarrow y / \underline{\quad} \begin{Bmatrix} p \\ r \\ y \\ a \end{Bmatrix}$$

However, it does not permit (3) to be similarly abbreviated. Let us call (5) a " schema " which " expands " to the sequence of rules (2). The convention (4) is one of a set of notational conventions that allow certain sequences of rules (or schemata) to be abbreviated by schemata. In informal discussion, when no confusion can arise, we will not consistently maintain the distinction between the terms " rule " and " schema," extending " rule " to schemata as well.

Implicit in the brace notation is the assumption that languages tend to place partially identical rules such as those in (2) next to one another in the ordered sequence of rules that constitutes the phonological component of a grammar: it is only when partially identical rules are adjacent to one another that the brace notation can be exploited. It has been noted by Kiparsky (forthcoming) that phonological change provides evidence in support of this assumption. One of the examples discussed by Kiparsky is the evolution of the rules laxing vowels before consonant clusters (see (20III), Chapter Five) and in the pre-penultimate syllables of a word (see (20IV), Chapter Five). The historical antecedents of these two rules differed from their modern counterparts in that preconsonantal laxing took place before three (instead of two) or more consonants, whereas trisyllabic laxing required that the vowel be followed by two (instead of one) consonant. The historical change, then, was that both of these rules decreased by one the number of consonants that must follow the vowel to be laxed. This parallelism may be regarded as a mere coincidence, as has been the approach in every treatment of English historical phonology known to us. Alternatively, and more satisfactorily, in view of the fact that there is no evidence to show that the changes in the two rules were due to separate processes, the parallelism may be regarded as being the result of a single change: the generalization of the schema (6) to the schema (7) by deletion of one of the consonants that must follow the vowel to be laxed.

$$\left(6\right) \qquad \qquad V \;\rightarrow\; [-\text{tense}] \;\Big/\; \underline{\quad\quad} CC \begin{Bmatrix} C \\ VC_0V \end{Bmatrix}$$

$$\left(7\right) \qquad \qquad V \;\rightarrow\; [-\text{tense}] \;\Big/\; \underline{\quad\quad} C \begin{Bmatrix} C \\ VC_0V \end{Bmatrix}$$

The characterization of the change as a single process, however, presupposes the existence of rule schemata as entities to which phonological changes may apply. Since schemata exist in a grammar only by virtue of conventions such as those discussed in this section, the examples just cited might be regarded as evidence in support of the reality of rule schemata and the conventions governing their use.

We can make use of notational conventions such as (4) to provide an evaluation procedure for grammars if we supplement the conventions with the following definition:

$$\left(8\right)$$ The "value" of a sequence of rules is the reciprocal of the number of symbols in the minimal schema that expands to this sequence.[1]

where the minimal schema is the one with the smallest number of symbols. More generally, let us say that if the schema Σ_1 expands to the sequence of rules $R_1, \ldots, R_m$ and the schema Σ_2 expands to the sequence of rules $S_1, \ldots, S_n$, then the sequence of schemata Σ_1, Σ_2 expands to the sequence of rules $R_1, \ldots, R_m, S_1, \ldots, S_n$; and let us accept the analogous convention for a sequence of schemata $\Sigma_1, \ldots, \Sigma_p$ of arbitrary length. Let us now say that the "minimal representation" of a sequence of rules is the sequence of schemata with the smallest number of symbols that expands to this sequence of rules.[2] We can then restate definition (8) as (9):

$$\left(9\right)$$ The "value" of a sequence of rules is the reciprocal of the number of symbols in its minimal representation.

Let us return now to the rules of (2) and (3). Given the conventions (4) and (9), the sequence of rules (2) is more highly valued than the sequence of rules (3): the minimal representation of (2) is (5) and the minimal representation of (3) is (3) itself, and (5) has fewer symbols than (3). Within the general framework of our theory, as described above, the conventions (4) and (9) imply that a linguistically significant generalization underlies (2) but not (3). Although in this case the fact may seem too trivial to require extensive comment, as we proceed further along the same lines we soon reach conclusions that are quite non-trivial, such as some of those discussed in the preceding chapters.

It should be observed in this connection that although definition (9) has commonly been referred to as the "simplicity" or "economy criterion," it has never been proposed or intended that the condition defines "simplicity" or "economy" in the very general (and

---

[1] We take the value to be $\frac{1}{n}$, where n is the number of symbols, so that the phrase "higher valued" will have its natural intuitive and numerical meaning.

[2] We give a more precise statement of these definitions in the Appendix to this chapter. Notice that the minimal representation may not be unique.

still very poorly understood) sense in which these terms usually appear in writings on the philosophy of science. The only claim that is being made here is the purely empirical one that under certain well-defined notational transformations, the number of symbols in a rule is inversely related to the degree of linguistically significant generalization achieved in the rule. In other words, definition (9), together with a specific choice of an alphabet from which the symbols are selected (see Section 2) and a specific set of notations for formulating rules and schemata, provides a precise explication for the notion "linguistically significant generalization" (Halle, 1962; Chomsky, 1964; Chomsky and Halle, 1965). Like all empirical claims, this can be tested for correctness and accuracy and can readily be controverted by evidence showing that it fails to hold true in certain clear cases.

2. *Segments as feature complexes*

We have as yet said nothing about the symbols that are used to represent the entities in our rules. In the present study speech sounds, or, more technically, segments, as well as all boundaries, are formally treated as complexes of features rather than as further unanalyzable entities. We assume, in other words, that the units or strings of units represented by the letters A, B, X, Y in (1) consist of feature columns or sequences of feature columns such as those shown in Table 1. The symbols referred to in the evaluation criterion (9) will, then, naturally be taken as distinctive feature specifications such as [+vocalic] or [−nasal].

The decision to regard speech sounds as feature complexes rather than as indivisible entities has been adopted explicitly or implicitly in almost all linguistic studies. Specifically, it is almost always taken for granted that phonological segments can be grouped into sets that differ as to their "naturalness." Thus, the sets comprising all vowels or all stops or all continuants are more natural than randomly chosen sets composed of the same number of segment types. No serious discussion of the phonology of a language has ever done without reference to classes such as vowels, stops, or voiceless continuants. On the other hand, any linguist would react with justified skepticism to a grammar that made repeated reference to a class composed of just the four segments [p r y a]. These judgments of "naturalness" are supported empirically by the observation that it is the "natural" classes that are relevant to the formulation of phonological processes in the most varied languages, though there is no logical necessity for this to be the case. In view of this, if a theory of language failed to provide a mechanism for making distinctions between more or less natural classes of segments, this failure would be sufficient reason for rejecting the theory as being incapable of attaining the level of explanatory adequacy.

Translated into feature terms, rule (5) will appear as (10) (p. 336), where the feature complexes representing a given unit (segment) are enclosed in square brackets: [ ].

By viewing segments as complexes of a fixed language-independent set of features, we have established a part of a mechanism which is required to distinguish more natural from less natural sets of segments; we can now say that sets of segments that have features in common are more natural than sets of segments that have no common features. What remains to be decided is the "metric of naturalness," that is, whether sets of segments sharing a large number of features are more "natural" than sets of segments sharing fewer features, or whether the reverse or perhaps some totally different relationship is the appropriate formal expression of this concept. Before making this decision, it is useful to state certain

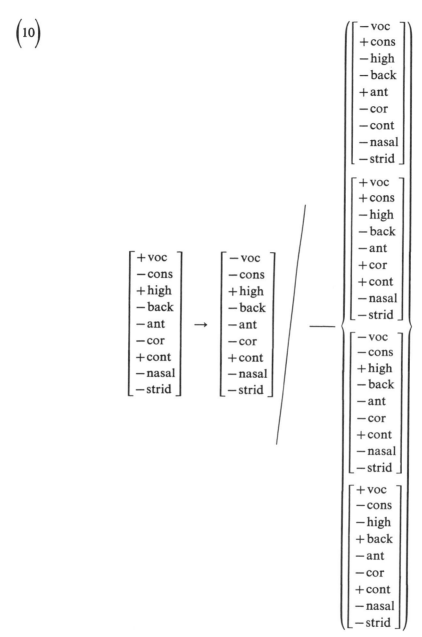

conventions governing the representation of units as feature complexes and their utilization in rules. Among these conventions are the following:

$\begin{pmatrix}11\end{pmatrix}$ Two units U_1 and U_2 are distinct if and only if there is at least one feature F such that U_1 is specified $[\alpha F]$ and U_2 is specified $[\beta F]$ where α is plus and β is minus; or α and β are integers and $\alpha \neq \beta$; or α is an integer and β is minus. Two strings X and Y are distinct if they are of different lengths, that is, if they differ in the number of units that they contain, or if the ith unit of X is distinct from the ith unit of Y for some i. (We assume "distinct" to be symmetrical.)

$\begin{pmatrix}12\end{pmatrix}$ A rule of the form $A \to B \,/\, X \underline{\quad} Y$ applies to any string $Z = \dots X'A'Y' \dots$, where X', A', Y' are not distinct from X, A, Y, respectively; and it converts Z to $Z' = \dots X'B'Y' \dots$, where B' contains all specified features of B in addition to all features of A' not specified in B.

With these conventions we can replace (10) with a higher-valued representing schema, in ways which are empirically significant, as can be seen by the following considerations.

Notice first that we have specified more features in (10) than are necessary to identify the four environments unambiguously. In particular, all the features that are parenthesized in Table 1 may be omitted without in any way affecting the operation of the rule. In accordance with conventions (11) and (12), we can reformulate (10) as (13), which has the same empirical content as (10):

$$
\begin{pmatrix}13\end{pmatrix}
\begin{bmatrix} +\text{voc} \\ -\text{cons} \\ +\text{high} \\ -\text{back} \end{bmatrix}
\rightarrow
\begin{bmatrix} -\text{voc} \\ -\text{cons} \\ -\text{back} \end{bmatrix}
\Big/ \underline{\quad}
\left\{
\begin{bmatrix} -\text{voc} \\ +\text{cons} \\ +\text{ant} \\ -\text{cor} \\ -\text{nasal} \end{bmatrix}
\begin{bmatrix} +\text{voc} \\ +\text{cons} \\ -\text{ant} \end{bmatrix}
\begin{bmatrix} -\text{voc} \\ -\text{cons} \\ -\text{back} \end{bmatrix}
\begin{bmatrix} +\text{voc} \\ -\text{cons} \\ -\text{high} \\ +\text{back} \end{bmatrix}
\right\}
$$

The conventions that permit us to replace (10) by (13) are quite natural; they imply that the value of a rule, as a measure of the linguistically significant degree of generalization it achieves, increases as the number of features required to identify the contexts in which it applies decreases.

The schema (13), however, is still not empirically adequate. Putting aside the question of the context of the rule, the conventions (11) and (12) permit the change that the rule effects to be formulated as (14), without any alteration of meaning:

$$
\begin{pmatrix}14\end{pmatrix}
\begin{bmatrix} +\text{voc} \\ -\text{cons} \\ +\text{high} \\ -\text{back} \end{bmatrix}
\rightarrow
[-\text{voc}]
$$

Thus the change effected by rule (13) is minimal, involving only a single feature. But compare the change $i \to y$ effected by (10) (i.e., (14)) with the changes $i \to w$ and $i \to r$. These, in terms of our conventions, must be stated as (15) and (16), respectively:

$$
\begin{pmatrix}15\end{pmatrix}
\begin{bmatrix} +\text{voc} \\ -\text{cons} \\ +\text{high} \\ -\text{back} \end{bmatrix}
\rightarrow
\begin{bmatrix} -\text{voc} \\ +\text{back} \end{bmatrix}
$$

$$\left(16\right) \qquad \begin{bmatrix} +\text{voc} \\ -\text{cons} \\ +\text{high} \\ -\text{back} \end{bmatrix} \rightarrow \begin{bmatrix} +\text{cons} \\ +\text{cor} \\ -\text{high} \end{bmatrix}$$

The rules (15) and (16) have a lower value than (14), reflecting the fact that the changes $i \rightarrow w$ and $i \rightarrow r$ are more radical, that is, less to be expected in the grammar of a language, than is the change $i \rightarrow y$. Here too, then, the conventions have the natural and desired consequences. We return in Chapter Nine to a further discussion of this sort of distinction.

Two further comments must be made here concerning the formulation of the schema (13). First we note that if we omit the feature [+vocalic] on the left-hand side of the arrow, then the schema will also apply to the glide /y/. Since in the cases under discussion the application of the rule to this glide is vacuous, the minimal representing schema will make no reference to the feature "vocalic" in this position.

Notice that the class containing the glide /y/ and the vowel /i/ is a more natural class in our terms than the class containing the vowel /i/ alone. In fact, this class plays a role in the grammars of numerous languages—for example, all Slavic languages, in which velars undergo precisely the same type of palatalization before the glide /y/ as before the front (nonback) vowels.[3] We have noted a similar phenomenon in English, with velar softening before nonback nonlow vowels and glides.

Returning to schema (13), we may make a second observation: it would be quite reasonable to modify our conventions so that any part of the feature complex on the left-hand side of the arrow can be transferred to the environment by being placed under the dash that indicates the location of the segment subject to the rule. In accordance with this revision, the facts expressed in (13) may be alternatively formulated as (17):

$$\left(17\right) \qquad \begin{bmatrix} -\text{cons} \\ +\text{high} \end{bmatrix} \rightarrow [-\text{voc}] \; \Big/ \; \begin{bmatrix} \underline{\quad\quad} \\ -\text{back} \end{bmatrix} \left\{ \begin{matrix} \begin{bmatrix} -\text{voc} \\ +\text{cons} \\ +\text{ant} \\ -\text{cor} \\ -\text{nasal} \end{bmatrix} \\ \begin{bmatrix} +\text{voc} \\ +\text{cons} \\ -\text{ant} \end{bmatrix} \\ \begin{bmatrix} -\text{voc} \\ -\text{cons} \\ -\text{back} \end{bmatrix} \\ \begin{bmatrix} +\text{voc} \\ -\text{cons} \\ -\text{high} \\ +\text{back} \end{bmatrix} \end{matrix} \right\}$$

The possibility of moving features in this way from the left of the arrow into the environment has significant empirical consequences, for it allows us to express partial identities between rules that could not otherwise be captured (but see also the discussion in Chapter

---

[3] In many of the standard handbooks of Slavic this fact is overlooked, and palatalization before the glide /y/ is treated in a separate chapter from palatalization before front vowels. See, e.g., Leskien (1919), Bräuer (1961); see also comments on page 422.

Nine). For example, assume that the language under discussion, in addition to containing (13) (= (17)), also contains (18):

$\begin{pmatrix}18\end{pmatrix}$ /w/ and /u/ are actualized as [u] before /p r y a/

This rule could be formulated as (19):

$$\begin{pmatrix}19\end{pmatrix} \qquad \begin{bmatrix} -\text{cons} \\ +\text{high} \\ +\text{back} \end{bmatrix} \rightarrow [+\text{voc}] \Big/ \underline{\quad} \begin{Bmatrix} p \\ r \\ y \\ a \end{Bmatrix}$$

Rule (19) shows only a limited resemblance to (13). Suppose, however, that, taking advantage of the possibility of transferring part of the feature complex from the left-hand side of the arrow to the environment, we write the relevant parts of (13) and (19) as (20a) and (20b), respectively:

$$\begin{pmatrix}20\end{pmatrix} \qquad \begin{array}{l} \text{(a)} \; \begin{bmatrix} -\text{cons} \\ +\text{high} \end{bmatrix} \rightarrow [-\text{voc}] \Big/ \begin{bmatrix} \underline{\quad} \\ -\text{back} \end{bmatrix} \\[2em] \text{(b)} \; \begin{bmatrix} -\text{cons} \\ +\text{high} \end{bmatrix} \rightarrow [+\text{voc}] \Big/ \begin{bmatrix} \underline{\quad} \\ +\text{back} \end{bmatrix} \end{array}$$

The formulation (20) brings out the fact, previously obscured, that both (13) and (19) affect the natural class $\begin{bmatrix} -\text{cons} \\ +\text{high} \end{bmatrix}$. This can now be readily captured by a double use of the brace notation:

$$\begin{pmatrix}21\end{pmatrix} \qquad \begin{bmatrix} -\text{cons} \\ +\text{high} \end{bmatrix} \rightarrow \begin{Bmatrix} [-\text{voc}] \; / \begin{bmatrix} \underline{\quad} \\ -\text{back} \end{bmatrix} \\ [+\text{voc}] \; / \begin{bmatrix} \underline{\quad} \\ +\text{back} \end{bmatrix} \end{Bmatrix} \begin{Bmatrix} p \\ r \\ y \\ a \end{Bmatrix}$$

To be precise, we must specify an order of expansion for the two sets of braces (see the Appendix to this chapter) and add the notational convention (22):

$\begin{pmatrix}22\end{pmatrix}$ Where C is a unit,[4] the schema (a) is equivalent to (b):

$$\text{(a)} \quad A \rightarrow B \;/\; X \begin{bmatrix} \underline{\quad} \\ C \end{bmatrix} Y$$

$$\text{(b)} \quad \begin{bmatrix} A \\ C \end{bmatrix} \rightarrow B \;/\; X \underline{\quad} Y$$

Consider, now, a language that differs from the language subject to rule (2) (or, equivalently, (17)) in that it is instead subject to rule (23):

$$\begin{pmatrix}23\end{pmatrix} \qquad i \rightarrow y \Big/ \underline{\quad} \begin{Bmatrix} i \\ u \\ æ \\ a \end{Bmatrix}$$

---

[4] By the term "unit" we now and henceforth refer to any feature matrix with just a single column, and not necessarily a matrix which is specified with respect to each feature. Thus [+vocalic] is a unit, for example.

An important difference between (17) and (23) is that in (23) the environment is a highly natural class of segments, that is, all vowels of the language, whereas the environment in (17) is a very unnatural class. This distinction must, of course, be brought out formally by an adequate linguistic theory. In fact, the theory as developed to this point is adequate in this respect. An examination of Table 1 shows that the four segments in the context of (23) can be uniquely identified in the language in question by specifying the two features $\begin{bmatrix} +\text{vocalic} \\ -\text{consonantal} \end{bmatrix}$; and in view of the evaluation criterion (9), it is this most abbreviated schema that determines the value of the rules summarized by (23). In short, the theory requires that these rules be formally represented by the minimal schema (24):

$$(24) \qquad \begin{bmatrix} -\text{cons} \\ +\text{high} \\ -\text{back} \end{bmatrix} \rightarrow [-\text{voc}] \ / \ \underline{\hspace{1cm}} \begin{bmatrix} +\text{voc} \\ -\text{cons} \end{bmatrix}$$

The required empirical distinction is thereby expressed, as a comparison of (24) and (17) readily shows.

3. *The ordering of the rules*

Consider again a language with a sound system such as that in Table 1. Assume that in this language:

(25)
   (a) The plosives /p t k/ are actualized as their (nonstrident) voiceless continuant congeners [φ θ x] if preceded by but *not* followed by a vowel.
   (b) The plosives /p t k/ are actualized as their (nonstrident) voiced continuant congeners [β ð γ] if preceded by *and* followed by a vowel.
   (c) The continuant /s/ is actualized as its voiced congener [z] if followed by a vowel.[5]

Compare this language to another language having the same sound system as the former (Table 1) in which instead of (25), the very similar allophonic alternations (26) obtain:

(26)
   (a) Same as (25a).
   (b) The plosives /p t k/ are actualized as their (nonstrident) voiced congeners [β ð γ] if preceded by a consonant and followed by a vowel.
   (c) The continuant /s/ is actualized as its voiced congener [z] if preceded by a liquid.

The essential difference between (25) and (26) is that in (25), but not (26), the alternations occur in partially identical environments; that is, in (25) alternation (b) shares one part of its environment with (a) and another part of its environment with (c), whereas in (26) the environments are quite unrelated. This difference between (25) and (26) must somehow be reflected in their respective grammars.

    A more formal statement of (25) and (26) would be given as (27) and (28), respectively:

---

[5] As the attentive reader will no doubt have observed, the alternations presented in (25) are slightly modified forms of Grimm's and Verner's Laws.

$$
(27) \quad
\begin{bmatrix} -\text{voc} \\ +\text{cons} \\ -\text{nasal} \end{bmatrix}
\rightarrow
\begin{cases}
[+\text{cont}] & / \begin{bmatrix} +\text{voc} \\ -\text{cons} \end{bmatrix} \underline{\quad} \begin{Bmatrix} \# \\ [-\text{voc}] \\ [+\text{cons}] \end{Bmatrix} & \text{(a)} \\[2em]
\begin{bmatrix} +\text{cont} \\ +\text{voice} \end{bmatrix} & / \begin{bmatrix} +\text{voc} \\ -\text{cons} \end{bmatrix} \begin{bmatrix} \underline{\quad} \\ -\text{cont} \end{bmatrix} \begin{bmatrix} +\text{voc} \\ -\text{cons} \end{bmatrix} & \text{(b)} \\[2em]
[+\text{voice}] & / \begin{bmatrix} \underline{\quad} \\ +\text{cont} \end{bmatrix} \begin{bmatrix} +\text{voc} \\ -\text{cons} \end{bmatrix} & \text{(c)}
\end{cases}
$$

$$
(28) \quad
\begin{bmatrix} -\text{voc} \\ +\text{cons} \\ -\text{nasal} \end{bmatrix}
\rightarrow
\begin{cases}
[+\text{cont}] & / \begin{bmatrix} +\text{voc} \\ -\text{cons} \end{bmatrix} \underline{\quad} \begin{Bmatrix} \# \\ [-\text{voc}] \\ [+\text{cons}] \end{Bmatrix} & \text{(a)} \\[2em]
\begin{bmatrix} +\text{cont} \\ +\text{voice} \end{bmatrix} & / \begin{bmatrix} -\text{voc} \\ +\text{cons} \end{bmatrix} \begin{bmatrix} \underline{\quad} \\ -\text{cont} \end{bmatrix} \begin{bmatrix} +\text{voc} \\ -\text{cons} \end{bmatrix} & \text{(b)} \\[2em]
[+\text{voice}] & / \begin{bmatrix} +\text{voc} \\ +\text{cons} \end{bmatrix} \begin{bmatrix} \underline{\quad} \\ +\text{cont} \end{bmatrix} & \text{(c)}
\end{cases}
$$

It is obvious that the above-noted differences between the two sets of rules are not formally brought out in (27) and (28). We propose, therefore, the convention (29):

(29) Rules are applied in linear[6] order, each rule operating on the string as modified by all earlier applicable rules.

Now rule (27) can be significantly abbreviated without affecting the results produced by it:

$$
(30) \quad
\begin{bmatrix} -\text{voc} \\ +\text{cons} \\ -\text{nasal} \end{bmatrix}
\rightarrow
\begin{cases}
[+\text{cont}] & / \begin{bmatrix} +\text{voc} \\ -\text{cons} \end{bmatrix} \underline{\quad} & \text{(a)} \\[2em]
[+\text{voice}] & / \begin{bmatrix} \underline{\quad} \\ +\text{cont} \end{bmatrix} \begin{bmatrix} +\text{voc} \\ -\text{cons} \end{bmatrix} & \text{(b)}
\end{cases}
$$

Applying (30) to sequences such as those in the first line of (31), we obtain the required results:

(31)

#ap#	#apa#	#sa#	
#aφ#	#aφa#		RULE 30a
	#aβa#	#za#	RULE 30b

Rule (26) (= (28)), on the other hand, cannot be abbreviated in a corresponding fashion; but this is precisely the result that we wish to obtain, for an adequate theory of grammar should allow for abbreviations where an actual generalization is to be observed and should prevent abbreviations when no true generalizations are to be found. Given the phenomena described in (25) and (26), any linguist would understand (25) but not (26) to express a linguistically significant generalization, and this distinction is accurately reflected by convention (29); the generalizations in the present instance are the result of taking explicit account of partial identities in the rules. A theory of grammar which fails to provide for the expression of such regularities must clearly be judged unsatisfactory.

It should be observed that an abbreviation such as is achieved in (30) is possible only when the subrules in question are adjacent in the order of the rules. If other subrules

[6] This will be modified presently (see (39), p. 344).

intervene, then it is impossible to coalesce the various parts of the rule into one schema by the conventions we have so far established. In this respect too, then, these conventions express an empirical hypothesis concerning the notion "linguistically significant generalization."

Convention (29) is evidently not the only logically possible condition on the ordering of rules. It is possible, for instance, to require that rules apply in an arbitrary order or that they apply simultaneously. Neither alternative, however, provides for the required distinction in the case of (25), (26), which is representative of innumerable well-studied examples.

Consider first the proposal that rules be applicable in an arbitrary order. With respect to (30) this would mean that the same results would have to be obtained if we applied subpart (b) before subpart (a). This clearly is not the case, for subpart (b) must apply to the output of subpart (a) or else /apa/ will yield [aφa] rather than the required [aβa]. In (27) or (28), on the other hand, the order of application is immaterial: the same results would be obtained were the subparts to be applied in any order. However, (27) is not the appropriate formulation of the facts described in (25), since it fails to express the underlying generalization.

Consider next a possible convention that all rules apply simultaneously. This would mean that all rules apply to the input string rather than to the string as modified by earlier rules. In the example under discussion, then, all rules would apply to the sequences as given in (31). Under this convention rule (30) could not produce the sequence [aβa] from /apa/, though, once again, (27), which does not reflect the appropriate generalizations, would yield the correct results. In this case too, then, the relevant distinction between (25) and (26) is expressed only on the assumption that rules are linearly ordered.

The hypothesis that rules are ordered, formulated tentatively as convention (29), seems to us to be one of the best-supported assumptions of linguistic theory. In earlier chapters, we saw many examples of how linearly ordered rules may interact to yield quite unexpected results. As we noted previously (see Chapter Two, note 5), it is easy to invent examples that require unordered rules or rules that are organized in some different fashion; but it is striking that no real examples of this sort have yet been discovered, whereas many cases are known where linear ordering captures significant generalizations.

Further supporting evidence for the hypothesis of rule ordering comes from the study of dialectal variation. Several cases have been discovered of dialects that contain the same rules but with different ordering. An interesting example has been described by Joos (1942). He considers certain Canadian dialects which have the Diphthong Laxing Rule (32a) and the rule (32b) voicing intervocalic [t]:

$$
\binom{32}{} \quad
\begin{array}{l}
\text{(a) } \bar{a}y \;\rightarrow\; {\scriptstyle\Lambda}y \;/\; \underline{\hspace{1.5em}}[-\text{voice}] \\
\text{(b) } t \;\rightarrow\; [+\text{voice}] \;/\; V\underline{\hspace{1.5em}}V
\end{array}
$$

However the dialects differ in the order of rules (32a) and (32b). In dialects where the rule of Diphthong Laxing precedes the rule voicing intervocalic [t], words such as *typewriter* are pronounced with the same diphthong in both positions—[tʌyprʌydɚ]—whereas in dialects where *t*-Voicing precedes Diphthong Laxing, such words have phonetically distinct diphthongs—[tʌyprāydɚ].

The same phenomenon can be demonstrated in artificial, invented examples, such as the well-known children's "secret language," Pig Latin. This "language" is defined by adding to the normal grammar of English a rule which moves the initial consonant sequence in the word, if any, to the end, and which then adds the sequence [ēy] to its right. More concisely, this rule might be stated as (33):

$$(33) \qquad \#\#C_0VX\#\# \quad \rightarrow \quad \#\#VXC_0\bar{e}y\#\#$$

As a result of this rule, the word *Latin*, for example, becomes [æt\overset{1}{\text{ə}}nlēy], and the word *day* is [\overset{1}{\text{ē}}ydēy].

Consider now the Pig Latin form of an English dialect that contains the Diphthong Laxing Rule (32a), which produces the diphthong [ʌy] in words such as *ice, sight, life*, while leaving the diphthong [āy] in words such as *sigh, side, time, strive*. It appears that speakers of the dialect in question divide into two groups: some keep the two words *ice* and *sigh* distinct in Pig Latin, as [\overset{1}{\text{ʌ}}ysēy] (*ice*), [\overset{1}{\text{ā}}ysēy] (*sigh*), while others actualize both words as [\overset{1}{\text{ʌ}}ysēy]. Evidently, the two "subdialects" differ in the ordering that they assign to the Diphthong Laxing Rule (32a) and the Pig Latin Rule (33). In the first "subdialect" the Diphthong Laxing Rule precedes the Pig Latin Rule, whereas the order is reversed in the second subdialect. In this artificial "language," choice of one or the other order would be expected to be fairly random for speakers of English, and our casual observations seem to bear out this expectation.

If we were to accept the hypothesis that rules are unordered, applying simultaneously, we would no longer be able to use the the same rules for the two "subdialects." Rules (32a) and (33) would characterize the first "subdialect"; but for the second, we would have to replace (32a) by the rule (34):

$$(34) \qquad \bar{a}y \rightarrow \text{ʌy} \quad / \quad \left\{ \begin{array}{l} \text{\underline{\hspace{1em}}[-\text{voice}]} \\ \#\#[-\text{voice}]X\text{\underline{\hspace{1em}}}\#\# \end{array} \right\}$$

This description of the phenomena implies that the speakers of the second dialect of Pig Latin not only mastered rule (33) but also modified the Diphthong Laxing Rule (32a), which is a part of their normal English grammar. This hardly seems likely, and thus, along with the mass of attested linguistic evidence, indicates that the assumption that rules are unordered at this level of the grammar is untenable.

Convention (29) provides only a first approximation to the set of conditions that determine ordering constraints on phonological rules. We saw in earlier chapters that under certain well-defined circumstances ordering is "disjunctive," in the sense that the application of certain rules precludes the application of certain others, formally related to them in a way to which we will return directly. Still another departure from the principle of strict linear ordering, as specified by convention (29), seems called for under other circumstances, also well-defined, in which simultaneous applicability of rules is required. A very simple example is provided by the rules (35) and (36), which are to be found in many languages:

$$(35) \qquad C \rightarrow \phi \quad / \text{\underline{\hspace{1em}}}C_0\#$$

$$(36) \qquad C \rightarrow \phi \quad / V\text{\underline{\hspace{1em}}}C_0\#$$

Rule (35) deletes word-final consonant clusters of arbitrary length; rule (36), on the other hand, deletes the first (or only) consonant of a word-final consonant sequence. To achieve this intention, we must specify with care the meaning of the formalism in (35) and (36). We have taken (35) and (36) each to be a schema representing an infinite set of rules, where (35) stands for (37) and (36) for (38):

$$\begin{pmatrix} 37 \end{pmatrix}\qquad \begin{aligned} C &\to \phi \;/\; \text{———} \# \\ C &\to \phi \;/\; \text{———} C\# \\ C &\to \phi \;/\; \text{———} CC\# \\ C &\to \phi \;/\; \text{———} CCC\# \\ &\qquad\qquad\vdots \end{aligned}$$

$$\begin{pmatrix} 38 \end{pmatrix}\qquad \begin{aligned} C &\to \phi \;/\; V\text{———} \# \\ C &\to \phi \;/\; V\text{———} C\# \\ C &\to \phi \;/\; V\text{———} CC\# \\ C &\to \phi \;/\; V\text{———} CCC\# \\ &\qquad\qquad\vdots \end{aligned}$$

Consider now a string of the form $XVCCC\#$. This string satisfies the first three rules of (37) but only the third rule of (38). We must interpret (35) as implying that each applicable rule of (37) abbreviated by (35) takes effect; thus the schema (35) converts $XVCCC\#$ to $XV\#$, as intended. Similarly, each applicable rule of (38) takes effect, so that (36) converts $XVC_aC_bC_c\#$ to $XVC_bC_c\#$, with only the third rule of (38) actually applying. Underlying this interpretation of schemata (35) and (36) are certain conventions of rule application:

$\begin{pmatrix} 39 \end{pmatrix}$ To apply a rule, the entire string is first scanned for segments that satisfy the environmental constraints of the rule. After all such segments have been identified in the string, the changes required by the rule are applied simultaneously.

$\begin{pmatrix} 40 \end{pmatrix}$ In the case of a schema standing for an infinite set of rules, convention (39) is applied to each rule of the set and all changes are made simultaneously rather than in sequence.

Let us now slightly extend our notations to permit a uniform way of presenting infinite schemata, interspersed among the rules. We define the notation $(X)^*$, where X is an arbitrary matrix, as follows:

$\begin{pmatrix} 41 \end{pmatrix}$ Where Z and W contain no braces, parentheses, or angled brackets, $Z(X)^*W$ is an abbreviation for the infinite set $ZW, ZXW, ZXXW, ZXXXW$, etc.

We extend this, in the obvious way, to notations of the form $Z(X_1)^*W_1(X_2)^*W_2$, etc. Clearly, we can define such notations as C_0, C_1, and so on in these terms. We now permit schemata involving $(X)^*$ to appear among the linearly ordered rules of the grammar, governed by convention (40).

Notice that convention (39) permits a rule to apply several times to a given string, the several applications being simultaneous; and (40) generalizes this to an infinite set of rules.

It should be stressed here that the existence of exceptions to linear ordering does not in any way affect the arguments advanced here to establish the need for such an order. The conditions under which linear ordering does not hold have been defined precisely. The examples adduced to show the need for linear ordering do not satisfy these special conditions and remain, therefore, unaffected by the existence of ordering other than linear.

To conclude this consideration of different types of rule ordering, we will discuss a classical phonological example presented by Sapir (1949a) that involves rule ordering of both the sequential and the simultaneous kind, along with several other intricacies.[7] In this

---

[7] Our discussion has benefited from a close study of Harms (1966). We have, however, proposed a quite different solution here which seems to us to be preferable to that of Harms.

paper, Sapir compared what he called the "phonological orthography" of Southern Paiute with its "phonetic orthography," commenting that "the phonetic forms result from the phonologic only by the application of absolutely mechanical phonetic laws of spirantizing, alternating stress, and unvoicing." Rather than discussing these "laws," Sapir illustrates their effects by a table which we reproduce as (42), with the following modifications. We

(42)		PHONETIC ORTHOGRAPHY	PHONOLOGICAL ORTHOGRAPHY
	1.	páWA	papa
	2.	pawáA	papaa
	3.	paáWA	p̣aapa
	4.	paáwaA	paapaa
	5.	páppA	pappa
	6.	pApáA	pappaa
	7.	paáppA	paappa
	8.	paáppaA	paappaa
	9.	mawáWA	mapapa
	10.	mawáwaA	mapapaa
	11.	mawáaWA	mapaapa
	12.	mawáawàA	mapaapaa
	13.	mawáppA	mapappa
	14.	mawáppaA	mapappaa
	15.	mawáappA	mapaappa
	16.	mawáApàA	mapaappaa
	17.	MApáWA	mappapa
	18.	MApáwaA	mappapaa
	19.	MApáaWA	mappaapa
	20.	MApáawàA	mappaapaa
	21.	MApáppA	mappappa
	22.	MApáppaA	mappappaa
	23.	MApáappA	mappaappa
	24.	MApáApàA	mappaappaa

represent Sapir's long vowels and geminate obstruents by sequences of identical segments and indicate the stress on the mora on which it is placed by the Alternating Stress Rule (see (47)). We interpret Sapir's β and φ as, respectively, the voiced and voiceless variants of the back glide [w]. We give voiceless vowels in word-final position everywhere, whereas Sapir represents voiceless vowels in postvocalic position by '. Like Sapir we represent voiceless vowels, nasals, and glides by capital letters. Finally, we give in the phonetic transcription the full effect of the alternating stress rule which Sapir (1930) describes as follows:

> According to this all odd moras are "weak" or relatively unstressed, all even moras are "strong" or relatively stressed. The theoretically strongest stress of the word comes on the second mora. Hence all words beginning with a syllable containing a long vowel or diphthong ... are accented on the first syllable ... On the other hand, all words beginning with a syllable containing an organic short vowel ... are accented on the second syllable, unless the second syllable is final, and therefore unvoiced, in which case the main stress is thrown back on the first syllable (p. 39).

Southern Paiute possesses the following consonant system:

$$\left(43\right)$$

$$
\begin{array}{llll}
m & n & \eta & \eta^w \\
p & t & k & k^w \\
  & c & & \\
  & s & &
\end{array}
$$

"When these consonants, by the processes of derivation and composition, take up a medial position and are immediately preceded by a vowel, voiced or unvoiced, they assume, in part, one of three distinct forms" (Sapir, 1930, p. 62). These three distinct forms, which will be detailed below, are the result of processes which Sapir designated as spirantization, gemination, and nasalization. According to Sapir the factor that decides which of the three processes a consonant is to undergo is "the nature of the preceding stem or suffix, which, as far as a descriptive analysis of Paiute is concerned, must be credited as part of its inner form, with an inherent spirantizing, geminating, or nasalizing power ..." (p. 63).

How, exactly, are we to interpret this analysis of stems as spirantizing, geminating, or nasalizing, by virtue of their "inner form"? One possibility would be to regard these properties as extrinsic to the segmental analysis, an arbitrary three-part categorization of morphemes. Alternatively, we might interpret "inner form" in terms of an abstract segmental representation. The latter interpretation is quite straightforward in this case. Let us assume that morphemes can end not only in vowels, as they generally do in the phonetic output, but also in nasals and obstruents. Thus we postulate a rule that deletes morpheme-final consonants at the end of the word or before vowels. This rule, which generalizes rule (4b) of Harms (1966), can be stated as follows:

$$\left(44\right) \qquad [+\text{cons}] \;\rightarrow\; \phi \;/\; \underline{\quad\quad} \left\{ \begin{array}{c} \# \\ +\text{V} \end{array} \right\}$$

As a consequence of (44), morphemes will appear in the output with final consonants only if the following morpheme begins with a consonant. These consonant sequences are, moreover, subject to the restriction (again generalizing a rule first proposed by Harms—his rule (17)) that the first consonant assimilates from the second consonant the so-called point of articulation features:[8]

$$\left(45\right) \qquad [+\text{cons}] \;\rightarrow\; \begin{bmatrix} \alpha\text{ant} \\ \beta\text{cor} \\ \gamma\text{high} \\ \delta\text{back} \end{bmatrix} \;/\; \underline{\quad\quad} + \begin{bmatrix} +\text{cons} \\ \alpha\text{ant} \\ \beta\text{cor} \\ \gamma\text{high} \\ \delta\text{back} \end{bmatrix}$$

In view of (44) and (45), it is impossible to determine the point of articulation of the morpheme-final consonant. We shall assume, then, that the features "anterior," "coronal," "high," and "back" are unspecified in such consonants. Certain general considerations to which we return in Chapter Nine will lead us to conclude that these consonants are actually dentals, that is, anterior, coronal, nonhigh, and nonback.

---

[8] The treatment of the two strident obstruents /s/ and /c/ is not completely clear to us, and it is conceivable that the assimilation rule is more complicated. Since this does not affect the theoretical points that are of primary interest here, we have chosen to restrict ourselves to sequences of nonstrident consonants, which, incidentally, are the only ones exemplified in (42).

    The use of variables as feature coefficients is discussed in Section 4.

    As discussed in Chapter Nine, the assimilation rule would be of a much simpler form if the marking conventions involving rule linking were observed.

Rules (44) and (45) account for the behavior of Sapir's geminating and nasalizing morphemes, on the assumption that these are morphemes that have obstruent stops and nasals, respectively, as their final consonants. Thus, when the morpheme-final consonant is a nasal, we derive such sequences as [mp], [nt], [ŋk] at morpheme boundaries; and when it is an obstruent stop, we find such sequences as [pp], [tt], [kk] at morpheme boundaries. We can therefore dispense with the morpheme categories "geminating" and "nasalizing" on the assumption that morphemes can terminate, phonologically, with obstruents and nasals as well as vowels. This enables us to dispense as well with the third morphological category, "spirantizing morphemes," since these are now simply the morphemes terminating in a vowel in the underlying phonological representation. By a general rule, which we give as (46), the first consonant following such morphemes will be spirantized. In the case of labial and velar stops, spirantization results in a nonstrident voiced continuant glide; in the case of a dental stop, it results in [r]. Formally, we may state this process as follows:

$$
\left(46\right) \qquad
\begin{bmatrix} -\text{son} \\ -\text{strid} \\ \alpha\text{cor} \end{bmatrix}
\rightarrow
\begin{bmatrix} +\text{cont} \\ +\text{voice} \\ +\text{son} \\ \alpha\text{cons} \\ \alpha\text{voc} \end{bmatrix}
\ / \ \text{V}+\underline{\hphantom{--}}
$$

We see the operation of this rule in examples 2, 4, and 9–16 of (42). The rule does not affect either the geminated obstruent or the strident /s c/, for, as Sapir (1930) noted, "spirantized *-tc-, -ts-* can be most convincingly differentiated from geminated *-t·c-, -t·s-* by the failure of weak moras to lose their voice before it" (p. 64), i.e., by providing a context for a rule which devoices vowels (see rule (53)), rather than by overt phonetic differences.

Southern Paiute is subject to an Alternating Stress Rule, the effects of which are detailed in the passage from Sapir (1930) which we had occasion to quote on page 345. Sapir explains that the stress is placed not on some phonetic syllable, but rather on an abstract entity, the mora, which can be equated with a vowel in a representation where long vowels are represented as sequences of two vowels. As can be seen from such examples as 1, 5, and 7 of (42), Sapir's formulation of the Alternating Stress Rule is not quite correct, since stress is not placed on word-final vowels. Moreover, in bisyllabic words, stress is placed on the first mora. The Alternating Stress Rule must, therefore, be given as in (47):

$$
\left(47\right) \qquad \text{V} \rightarrow [1 \text{ stress}] \ / \ \# \langle \text{C}_0\text{V}(\text{C}_0\text{VC}_0\text{V})^* \rangle \text{C}_0 \underline{\hphantom{---}} \langle [+\text{seg}]_0 \rangle \text{C}_0\text{V} \#
$$

Schema (47) involves angled brackets. As before, we understand these to enclose the parts of a discontinuous environment; thus we take (48a) to be an abbreviation for the sequence (48b):

$$
\left(48\right) \qquad
\begin{array}{ll}
\text{(a)} & X\langle Y \rangle Z \langle W \rangle Q \\
\text{(b)} & XYZWQ \\
& XZQ
\end{array}
$$

Under this convention, (47) is an abbreviation for the sequence of schemata (49):

$$
\left(49\right) \qquad
\begin{array}{lll}
\text{(a)} & \text{V} \rightarrow [1 \text{ stress}] & / \ \#\text{C}_0\text{V}(\text{C}_0\text{VC}_0\text{V})^*\text{C}_0 \underline{\hphantom{--}} [+\text{seg}]_0\text{C}_0\text{V}\# \\
\text{(b)} & \text{V} \rightarrow [1 \text{ stress}] & / \ \#\text{C}_0 \underline{\hphantom{--}} \text{C}_0\text{V}\#
\end{array}
$$

Schema (49a) is, in turn, an abbreviation for an infinite set of rules of the form (50) (where, in fact, there is an infinite set of rules corresponding to each occurrence of C_0 and $[+\text{seg}]_0$):

$$\left(50\right) \quad \begin{aligned} \text{V} &\rightarrow [1\ \text{stress}] \ / \ \#C_0VC_0 \text{——} [+\text{seg}]_0C_0V\# \\ \text{V} &\rightarrow [1\ \text{stress}] \ / \ \#C_0VC_0VC_0VC_0 \text{——} [+\text{seg}]_0C_0V\# \\ \text{V} &\rightarrow [1\ \text{stress}] \ / \ \#C_0VC_0VC_0VC_0VC_0VC_0 \text{——} [+\text{seg}]_0C_0V\# \end{aligned}$$

The schema (47) thus abbreviates the infinite set (50), the rules of which apply simultaneously, followed by the rule (49b) (itself, of course, actually standing for an infinite set of simultaneously applying rules). The effect, then, is that in a string with three or more vowels, [1 stress] is assigned to every even-numbered vowel, with the exception of the final vowel; and in a bisyllabic word, stress is assigned to the first vowel. We must also add a rule weakening all stresses to the right of a main stress to secondary (i.e., a rule which reassigns primary stress to the leftmost stress), since "the theoretically strongest stress comes on the second mora" (Sapir, 1930, p. 39).

To account for the appearance of nongeminate obstruents in intervocalic position, as in examples 6, 16, and 17–24 of (42), we must postulate the Degemination Rule (51):

$$\left(51\right) \quad [-\text{son}] \ \rightarrow \ \phi \ / \ [-\text{son}] \text{——} \begin{bmatrix} +\text{voc} \\ -\text{cons} \\ +\text{stress} \end{bmatrix}$$

Thus the second of two obstruents is deleted *if followed by a stressed vowel*. Observe, now, the intricate interaction of this rule with the stress assignment rule (47). Since stress is not assigned to word-final vowels, the geminate obstruent remains in example 5 of (42), whereas it is simplified in example 6. For precisely the same reason the geminate remains in example 15 but is simplified in example 16. Since stress falls on the vowel following the first (geminate) obstruent in examples 17–24, it is always simplified. If there is a second geminate obstruent in the word, it is simplified again under the same conditions as above; thus, compare the two simplified geminates of example (24) with the other examples.

The examples can be readily accounted for if it is assumed that the Degemination Rule applies after the Alternating Stress Rule (47), as well as after the Spirantization Rule (46). But consider how the Degemination Rule would have to be stated if rules were to be applied simultaneously. We would have to include in the Degemination Rule the environment that we have specified for the Alternating Stress Rule. Instead of (51) we would have to have:

$$\left(52\right) \quad [-\text{son}] \ \rightarrow \ \phi \ / \ \# \langle C_0V(C_0VC_0V)^*\rangle [-\text{son}] \text{——} \langle [+\text{seg}]_0\rangle C_0V\#$$

This complication, however, would not allow us either to dispense with the Stress Rule or to simplify it, since stress assignment is independent of degemination, though not vice versa. The environment for the Stress Rule would have to figure twice in the grammar only because of the decision to utilize rules that apply simultaneously rather than linearly ordered rules. Such a theory, then, implies that the similarity of environments is completely fortuitous, that the rules would be no less general, in the linguistically significant sense of "generality," if some totally different environment were to appear in the latter case.

The complexity of simultaneous rules increases with every increase in the depth of ordering of the linearly ordered rules which the simultaneous rules replace. This is well illustrated by the next rule mentioned by Sapir, the Devoicing Rule, which incorporates two separate rules. The first, (53), devoices vowels in word-final position and in position before a nongeminate obstruent; and the second, (54), devoices nonstrident continuants before voiceless vowels:

$$(53) \qquad V \rightarrow [-voice] \ / \ \underline{\hspace{1cm}} \left\{ \begin{array}{c} \# \\ [-son] \ V \end{array} \right\}$$

$$(54) \qquad \begin{bmatrix} +son \\ -voc \end{bmatrix} \rightarrow [-voice] \ / \ \underline{\hspace{1cm}} \begin{bmatrix} -cons \\ -voice \end{bmatrix}$$

Observe that if rules were to apply simultaneously, these rules would have to be complicated quite considerably. The obstruents referred to in (53) are those which are produced by degemination; consequently the environment for the Degemination Rule (51) would have to be incorporated into (53). We know, however, from the discussion above that if the rules were to apply simultaneously, the Degemination Rule itself would have to include the environment for the Alternating Stress Rule. Moreover, by the same argument, rule (54) would have to include all the environments mentioned, and, in addition, the environment for the Vowel Devoicing Rule (53). The reason for this is that the voiceless nonconsonantal segments before which the devoicing in (54) takes place are produced by the Vowel Devoicing Rule; consequently, the simultaneous analog of rule (54) would have to incorporate the environments of the Vowel Devoicing Rule. In addition, the rule would also have to incorporate the environment for the Spirantization Rule (46).

Examples of this type can be found in almost any language with which we are familiar. They are handled quite naturally if rules are applied in accordance with the ordering conventions we have postulated, but require endless repetition of environments if the rules are made to apply simultaneously. The theory of ordering presented here, along with the evaluation measure (9), provides for generalizations of just this sort, and implies that phonological processes will, in general, take place in similar or identical environments only when the restricted means made available by this theory suffice to collapse the statement of environments in a single schema. Collectively these devices thus express an empirical hypothesis of a complex and abstract but quite specific sort. It seems to us that the evidence now available suggests that this hypothesis is quite close to the correct one, and that no radically different alternative that might be invented has real plausibility.

In Chapter Three we presented examples of rule interactions that are more complicated than the ones just reviewed. The cases discussed there involved order relations of a cyclical kind. Rule A must be applied before rule B in certain examples, whereas rule B must precede rule A in other examples. To account for such relationships we introduced the convention of the transformational cycle:

$$(55)$$ Phonological rules apply in linear sequence to each phrase of the surface structure, beginning with the smallest, and proceeding to successively larger phrases until the maximal domain of phonological processes is reached.

Putting it in slightly different terms, we require that the domain of a rule be the maximal string containing no internal brackets; and, furthermore, after the last rule of the phonological component applies, we erase innermost brackets and return to the first rule of the phonological component, continuing in this manner until the maximal domain of phonological processes is reached.

Examples of cyclical application of rules seem to be restricted to prosodic features and segmental modifications associated closely with prosodic features (e.g., the *i–y* alternations discussed in Chapter Four, Section 6). We have experimented with cyclical rules in accounting for segmental features (see, e.g., Halle, 1963), but we are at present inclined to believe that all cases explored can be handled better with noncyclical rules. It would, however, be premature to rule out the possibility that cyclical rules may play a role in the segmental phonology as well.

4. *Variables as feature coefficients*

We investigate next the manner in which the familiar phonological processes of assimilation and dissimilation are to be characterized formally. In terms of the apparatus developed here, assimilation is a process in which two segments are made to agree in the value assigned to one or more features, whereas dissimilation is a process in which two segments are made to disagree in the value assigned to one or more features. An example of assimilation is provided by the Southern Paiute rule (45), according to which a morpheme-final consonant assimilates the "point of articulation" features of the following consonant. Since Southern Paiute has only labial, dental, and velar consonants, rule (45) expresses the facts stated in (56):

$$
(56) \quad [+\text{cons}] \;\rightarrow\;
\left\{
\begin{array}{l}
\begin{bmatrix} +\text{ant} \\ -\text{cor} \\ -\text{high} \\ -\text{back} \end{bmatrix} \Big/ \underline{\quad} + \begin{bmatrix} +\text{ant} \\ -\text{cor} \\ -\text{high} \\ -\text{back} \end{bmatrix} \\[4ex]
\begin{bmatrix} +\text{ant} \\ +\text{cor} \\ -\text{high} \\ -\text{back} \end{bmatrix} \Big/ \underline{\quad} + \begin{bmatrix} +\text{ant} \\ +\text{cor} \\ -\text{high} \\ -\text{back} \end{bmatrix} \\[4ex]
\begin{bmatrix} -\text{ant} \\ -\text{cor} \\ +\text{high} \\ +\text{back} \end{bmatrix} \Big/ \underline{\quad} + \begin{bmatrix} -\text{ant} \\ -\text{cor} \\ +\text{high} \\ +\text{back} \end{bmatrix}
\end{array}
\right\}
$$

The formulation (56), however, fails to bring out the essential difference between a case of assimilation such as that under discussion and the following totally implausible process:

$$
(57) \quad [+\text{cons}] \;\rightarrow\;
\left\{
\begin{array}{l}
\begin{bmatrix} +\text{ant} \\ -\text{cor} \\ -\text{high} \\ -\text{back} \end{bmatrix} \Big/ \underline{\quad} + \begin{bmatrix} -\text{ant} \\ +\text{cor} \\ -\text{high} \\ +\text{back} \end{bmatrix} \\[4ex]
\begin{bmatrix} +\text{ant} \\ +\text{cor} \\ -\text{high} \\ -\text{back} \end{bmatrix} \Big/ \underline{\quad} + \begin{bmatrix} +\text{ant} \\ -\text{cor} \\ +\text{high} \\ +\text{back} \end{bmatrix} \\[4ex]
\begin{bmatrix} -\text{ant} \\ -\text{cor} \\ +\text{high} \\ +\text{back} \end{bmatrix} \Big/ \underline{\quad} + \begin{bmatrix} -\text{ant} \\ +\text{cor} \\ +\text{high} \\ -\text{back} \end{bmatrix}
\end{array}
\right\}
$$

Clearly, some formal means is required to express the fact that in the Southern Paiute case the agreement of the consonants in terms of the features "anterior," "coronal," "high," and "back" is linguistically significant, whereas in the case exemplified by (57) the relation between the change effected and the determining context is entirely fortuitous. Given the evaluation measure specified in (9), we can meet this requirement by adopting the convention of using variables ranging over the values of the feature coefficients $+$, $-$, 1, 2, ... It is readily seen that (56) can be abbreviated with the help of the variable convention, and the schema (45), where Greek letters are used as variables, is just this abbreviation; the facts expressed in (57), on the other hand, cannot be similarly abbreviated. But this is precisely the result needed, given the measure (9), to distinguish assimilation from a set of arbitrary rules like (57).

In fact, the schema (45) implicitly includes, in addition to the three subparts of (56), several other subparts, namely:

$$
\left(58\right) \quad [+\text{cons}] \rightarrow \left\{
\begin{array}{l}
\begin{bmatrix} -\text{ant} \\ -\text{cor} \\ +\text{high} \\ -\text{back} \end{bmatrix} \Big/ \underline{\quad} + \begin{bmatrix} -\text{ant} \\ -\text{cor} \\ +\text{high} \\ -\text{back} \end{bmatrix} \\[4em]
\begin{bmatrix} +\text{ant} \\ -\text{cor} \\ +\text{high} \\ -\text{back} \end{bmatrix} \Big/ \underline{\quad} + \begin{bmatrix} +\text{ant} \\ -\text{cor} \\ +\text{high} \\ -\text{back} \end{bmatrix} \\[4em]
\begin{bmatrix} +\text{ant} \\ +\text{cor} \\ +\text{high} \\ +\text{back} \end{bmatrix} \Big/ \underline{\quad} + \begin{bmatrix} +\text{ant} \\ +\text{cor} \\ +\text{high} \\ +\text{back} \end{bmatrix} \\[2em]
\vdots
\end{array}
\right\}
$$

Since these feature complexes—i.e., palatals, palatalized labials, velarized dentals, etc.—do not occur in Southern Paiute, this special case of the schema is vacuous. There is no point in complicating the rule in order to prevent (58) from applying since the situation in which it applies can never arise. More precisely, our formalism implies that the sequence of rules (56), (58) is simpler, in the technical sense, than the sequence (56) itself; and since there is no empirical reason to reject the more highly valued sequence (56), (58) (with the minimal representation (45)), we are required to accept it as part of the grammar. We are thus led to predict that if, through some process of linguistic change, palatal stops were introduced into the language (the phenomena of (56) remaining constant), then palatality would also be assimilated by a preceding consonant.

As long as we are dealing with features having one of the two values plus or minus, we can also handle dissimilation by an extension of the above convention. All that is needed is to permit specifications of the form $[-\alpha \text{ Feature X}]$, where α is a variable and where, moreover, the convention holds that $-- = +$, $-+ = -$.

A simple example of dissimilation is found in Gothic, where, after an unstressed vowel, voicing in continuants dissimilates with that in the preceding obstruent. Thus, we find *hatiza*, "hatred" (dat. sg.), *riqiza*, "darkness" (dat. sg.), but *agisa*, "fright"; and, similarly, *fastubni*, "position," *fraistubni*, "temptation," but *waldufni*, "force," and *wundufni,* "wound." Formally, the rule underlying these facts (Thurneysen's Law) would be stated in our terms as (59):

$$\left(59\right) \qquad \begin{bmatrix} -\text{son} \\ +\text{cont} \end{bmatrix} \rightarrow [\alpha\text{voice}] \ / \ \begin{bmatrix} +\text{cons} \\ -\alpha\text{voice} \end{bmatrix} \begin{bmatrix} +\text{voc} \\ -\text{cons} \\ -\text{stress} \end{bmatrix} \underline{\qquad}$$

In the cases of assimilation and dissimilation that have been discussed here, variables were associated with the same feature in different segments. The question arises, therefore, whether the use of variables should be formally restricted in this manner or whether the theory should admit a freer use of variables. An example that has bearing on this question is the dialect of German spoken in the city of Vienna. In this dialect, nonback (front) vowels are nonround before /r/ and round before /l/: e.g., Standard German *vier,* "four," and *für,* "for," are pronounced [fīr]; *Heer,* "army," and *hör,* "listen!" are pronounced [hēr]; whereas *viele,* "many," and *fühle,* "feel," are pronounced [fǖlə], and *hehlen,* "hide," and *Hölen,* "caves," are pronounced [hȫlən] (Trubetzkoy, 1958, p. 209). These observations are naturally formalized as follows:

$$\left(60\right) \qquad \begin{bmatrix} +\text{voc} \\ -\text{cons} \\ -\text{back} \end{bmatrix} \rightarrow [\alpha\text{round}] \ / \ \underline{\qquad} \begin{bmatrix} +\text{voc} \\ +\text{cons} \\ \alpha\text{lateral} \end{bmatrix}$$

Trubetzkoy (1958) treated these facts in a somewhat different fashion. He assumed that assimilation can occur only between identical features and argued that the examples just cited show that "vom Standpunkt der genannten Mundart darf *r* als die hellere, und *l* die dunklere Liquida definiert werden" (p. 209). This inference is based on the following considerations. In Trubetzkoy's system every speech sound is said to have its "proper pitch" (*Eigenton*), and speech sounds may be ordered in terms of their "proper pitches" from high (*hell*) to low (*dunkel*). Among the vowels the "proper pitch" corresponds to the frequency of the second formant; hence [i] has the highest "pitch," [ü] the next highest, and [u] the lowest. Since the relative "pitches" of the liquids [r] and [l] were not known to phoneticians of the 1930s, Trubetzkoy proposes to determine them indirectly. He assumes that assimilation can occur only between identical features and thus concludes that the "pitch" of [r] is higher than that of [l], since [i] occurs before [r] and [ü] before [l]. However, the assumption on which the inference is based is nowhere justified, and no other evidence is presented in favor of the proposition that [r] is "higher pitched" than [l]. Thus neither Trubetzkoy's solution nor the assumption that underlies it is well grounded. Moreover, such a common process as that of length being governed by the voicing or voicelessness of the following consonant shows that assimilation cannot be restricted to the same feature in different segments and that assimilation between cognate or related features at least will have to be allowed. In part, this was recognized by Trubetzkoy and others who made use of the feature of "proper pitch" (*Eigenton*), for this feature subsumes the phonetically quite different features of rounding and backness.

Nevertheless, there is empirical evidence in favor of imposing a limitation on the use of variables with different features in different segments. The great majority of examples involve only a single feature, and in other cases there clearly seems to be some intrinsic connection between the features involved in the process of assimilation. At the present juncture, however, we are in no position to formulate these restrictions.

Variables can be used quite naturally to characterize intrasegmental as well as intersegmental constraints. For example, the vowel system of the Uzbek dialect of the city of Tashkent consists of six vowels, of which three are back and round, and three are nonback and nonround (Trubetzkoy, 1958, p. 90). They are thus subject to the rule (61):

$$
(61) \qquad \begin{bmatrix} +\text{voc} \\ -\text{cons} \\ \alpha\text{back} \end{bmatrix} \rightarrow [\alpha\text{round}]
$$

Actually, we will suggest later (see Chapter Nine) that this common phenomenon has a rather different status.

The use of variables as coefficients of features allows us to capture in a very natural manner a number of other phonological regularities. For example, in contemporary French (under certain conditions which are of no interest here), vowels are truncated before vowels and glides, and consonants are truncated before consonants and liquids; glides and liquids, on the other hand, are not truncated. Thus we have forms such as those in (62) (where the truncated segments are in boldface):

$$
(62)
$$

petit garçon	*petit livre*	*petit enfant*	*petit oiseau*
cher garçon	*cher livre*	*cher enfant*	*cher oiseau*
le garçon	*le livre*	*l(e)'enfant*	*l(e)'oiseau*
pareil gâchis	*pareil livre*	*vieil ami*	*vieil oiseau*

To characterize these facts, we might propose the following two rules (where # represents a word boundary):

$$
(63)
$$

(a) $\begin{bmatrix} +\text{voc} \\ -\text{cons} \end{bmatrix} \rightarrow \phi \ / \ \text{——} \# \ [-\text{cons}]$

(b) $\begin{bmatrix} -\text{voc} \\ +\text{cons} \end{bmatrix} \rightarrow \phi \ / \ \text{——} \# \ [+\text{cons}]$

This formulation, however, would miss the symmetry inherent in (62) and would fail to distinguish it from a totally unsymmetrical pair of rules such as (64):

$$
(64)
$$

(a) $\begin{bmatrix} +\text{voc} \\ -\text{back} \end{bmatrix} \rightarrow \phi \ / \ \text{——} \# \ [-\text{cons}]$

(b) $\begin{bmatrix} +\text{cons} \\ -\text{high} \end{bmatrix} \rightarrow \phi \ / \ \text{——} \# \ [+\text{nasal}]$

As was noted by Schane (1965), the introduction of variables allows us to capture the symmetry of (62) in a quite natural fashion:

$$
(65) \qquad \begin{bmatrix} -\alpha\text{voc} \\ \alpha\text{cons} \end{bmatrix} \rightarrow \phi \ / \ \text{——} \# \ [\alpha\text{cons}]
$$

Excursus. It has been pointed out to us by J. C. Milner and C. J. Bailey that the rule of liaison and elision does not operate in precisely the manner of (65) when the second word belongs to the "foreign" vocabulary. In "foreign" words, glides pattern like consonants and liquids rather than like vowels. Thus, for instance, we have no elision in *le yogi* and no liaison in *les yogis*. This observation requires at the very least that we introduce a diacritic category "foreign" and restrict (65) to occur before words which are [−foreign]. In addition we should have to formulate a special rule for [+foreign] words. This rule would have to have the effects of (66):

$$\left(66\right)$$

(a) $\begin{bmatrix} +\text{voc} \\ -\text{cons} \end{bmatrix} \rightarrow \phi \ / \ \underline{\quad} \# \begin{bmatrix} +\text{voc} \\ -\text{cons} \end{bmatrix}$

(b) $\begin{bmatrix} -\text{voc} \\ +\text{cons} \end{bmatrix} \rightarrow \phi \ / \ \underline{\quad} \# \begin{Bmatrix} [-\text{voc}] \\ [+\text{cons}] \end{Bmatrix}$

We observe, however, that unlike (65), this pair of rules cannot be abbreviated. Given the feature system adopted in this study, there is no way to express the obvious symmetry of two related processes such as those in (66), one of which occurs before vowels and the other before nonvowels. To overcome this serious inadequacy, Milner and Bailey have suggested that the feature system be somewhat modified; i.e., the feature "vocalic" might be replaced by a feature "syllabic" which would characterize all segments constituting a syllabic peak. Obstruents would by definition be excluded from forming syllabic peaks; vowels would normally be syllabic peaks, whereas the remaining sonorants—i.e., liquids, glides, nasal consonants—would normally be nonsyllabic, but could become syllabic under special circumstances, as, for example, between obstruents. When vowels become nonsyllabic, they turn into glides: high vowels turn into the high glides [w] and [y]; nonhigh vowels into the nonhigh glides symbolized by [h]. In sum, we propose the following major class features in place of those of Chapter Seven:

$$\left(67\right)$$

	sonorant	syllabic	consonantal
vowels	+	+	−
syllabic liquids	+	+	+
syllabic nasals	+	+	+
nonsyllabic liquids	+	−	+
nonsyllabic nasals	+	−	+
glides: *w, y, h, ʔ*	+	−	−
obstruents	−	−	+

Before applying (67) to liaison and elision, we should note that the consonants that are deleted in preconsonantal position are all obstruents, for word-final nasals are deleted by other rules that are independently required. We can now restate the facts of elision and liaison before native words as follows:

$$\left(68\right)$$

(a) $\begin{bmatrix} +\text{son} \\ +\text{syll} \\ -\text{cons} \end{bmatrix} \rightarrow \phi \ / \ \underline{\quad} \# \begin{Bmatrix} \begin{bmatrix} +\text{son} \\ +\text{syll} \\ -\text{cons} \end{bmatrix} \\ \begin{bmatrix} +\text{son} \\ -\text{syll} \\ -\text{cons} \end{bmatrix} \end{Bmatrix}$

(b) $\begin{bmatrix} -\text{son} \\ -\text{syll} \\ +\text{cons} \end{bmatrix} \rightarrow \phi \ / \ \underline{\quad} \# \begin{Bmatrix} \begin{bmatrix} -\text{son} \\ -\text{syll} \\ +\text{cons} \end{bmatrix} \\ \begin{bmatrix} +\text{son} \\ -\text{syll} \\ +\text{cons} \end{bmatrix} \end{Bmatrix}$

This pair of rules readily abbreviates to:

$$
(69) \qquad \begin{bmatrix} -\alpha\text{syll} \\ \alpha\text{cons} \end{bmatrix} \rightarrow \phi \ / \ \underline{\qquad} \ \# \begin{bmatrix} \alpha\text{cons} \\ -\text{foreign} \end{bmatrix}
$$

Before foreign words, we find:

$$
(70) \qquad \text{(a)} \begin{bmatrix} +\text{son} \\ +\text{syll} \\ -\text{cons} \end{bmatrix} \rightarrow \phi \ / \ \underline{\qquad} \ \# \begin{bmatrix} +\text{son} \\ +\text{syll} \\ -\text{cons} \end{bmatrix}
$$

$$
\text{(b)} \begin{bmatrix} -\text{son} \\ -\text{syll} \\ +\text{cons} \end{bmatrix} \rightarrow \phi \ / \ \underline{\qquad} \ \# \left\{ \begin{matrix} \begin{bmatrix} -\text{son} \\ -\text{syll} \\ +\text{cons} \end{bmatrix} \\ \begin{bmatrix} +\text{son} \\ -\text{syll} \\ +\text{cons} \end{bmatrix} \\ \begin{bmatrix} +\text{son} \\ -\text{syll} \\ -\text{cons} \end{bmatrix} \end{matrix} \right\}
$$

Rules (70a, b) in turn abbreviate to:

$$
(71) \qquad \begin{bmatrix} -\alpha\text{syll} \\ \alpha\text{cons} \end{bmatrix} \rightarrow \phi \ / \ \underline{\qquad} \ \# \begin{bmatrix} -\alpha\text{syll} \\ +\text{foreign} \end{bmatrix}
$$

The appearance of two such similar rules as (69) and (71) in a given grammar is quite unusual. J. C. Milner (1967) has argued that (69) can be dispensed with and that by appropriate ordering (71), generalized by omitting the feature [+foreign], can account for all cases of liaison and elision.

This example is, thus, of the greatest importance for our feature framework. If, as it now appears to us, (71) is indeed the correct formulation of the phonetic facts just discussed, and if, moreover, this example is shown to be more than an isolated instance, the feature framework will have to be revised along the lines sketched in (67).

The final class of cases to be considered is that in which a variable used for a single feature in a single segment is affected. Evidently, the only significant case will be a rule such as (72):

$$
(72) \qquad [\alpha\text{Feature X}] \ \rightarrow \ [-\alpha\text{Feature X}]
$$

The schema (72) would serve as the abbreviation for the two rules:

$$
(73) \qquad \begin{matrix} \text{(a)} & [+\text{Feature X}] & \rightarrow & [-\text{Feature X}] \\ \text{(b)} & [-\text{Feature X}] & \rightarrow & [+\text{Feature X}] \end{matrix}
$$

Clearly, it would be quite arbitrary to assign an ordering to rules (a) and (b). Let us then assume, tentatively, that they apply simultaneously. (Further justification for this assumption will appear directly, and we shall see below that it is a natural consequence of other, independent assumptions about the form of rules.) Under this assumption, rule (72) describes a process in which two segments exchange position in the phonological pattern, as it were; for example, voiced segments become voiceless while voiceless segments become voiced. Rules of this type certainly are to be found. The Africanist Meinhof (1912) discussed such rules more than fifty years ago, and coined for them the appropriate term "polarity rules."[9]

Although Meinhof's main examples of polarity rules—those of Fula—have apparently been shown to be invalid by Klingenheben (1963), there are clear cases of such rules in a number of languages. One example from Menomini has been discussed by Bever (1963).[10] A second example of the polarity principle is provided by the West Semitic languages, Arabic, Hebrew, and Aramaic. In the conjugation of these languages, the verbal stem vowel, which is the vowel between the second and third consonants of the stem, undergoes Ablaut. In the perfect, which is formed by suffixation alone, we find one vowel, whereas a different vowel is found in the imperfect forms, which involve prefixation and suffixation. Typical of this situation is Biblical Hebrew, as illustrated by (74):[11]

$$(74)$$

	PERFECT	IMPERFECT	
	a	o	*lamad–yilmod* (learn)
	o	a	*qaton–yiqtan* (be small)
	e	a	*zaqen–yizqan* (age)

Examination of (74) shows that if we have the nonlow vowel /o/ or /e/ in the perfect, we find the low vowel /a/ in the imperfect; whereas if in the perfect we have the low vowel /a/, we find the nonlow vowel /o/ in the imperfect. Notice that the conditions under which these alternations occur are precisely the same, so that the context is of no assistance in distinguishing between the two types of interchange. It is, of course, possible to assume an intermediate stage. Thus we might postulate that /a/ becomes high as a first step, that the nonlow nonhigh vowels /e/ and /o/ then become /a/, and that, finally, the high reflex of original /a/ lowers to /o/. However, there appears to be no justification for this account other than that it avoids utilizing a polarity rule. Since polarity rules are implicit in our notation and since there seems no reason to suppose that they are somehow objectionable, there is also no reason to handle the facts of Hebrew in the roundabout way just described or with any similar artifice. Instead we propose the polarity rule (75):[12]

$$(75) \qquad \begin{bmatrix} +\text{voc} \\ -\text{cons} \\ \alpha\text{low} \end{bmatrix} \rightarrow \begin{bmatrix} -\alpha\text{low} \\ \alpha\text{round} \\ +\text{back} \end{bmatrix} \Big/ \underline{\quad\quad} C + \textit{Imperfect}$$

The situation described is not restricted to Hebrew, but arises as well in other West Semitic languages. Consider, for example, the following description from Grande's

---

[9] "Suppose that under certain conditions A becomes B and under the same conditions B becomes A. I call this process polarity, for the following reasons. The magnet has a positive pole (A) and a negative pole (B). If, under the influence of a more powerful magnet, the positive pole becomes negative—i.e., A becomes B—then simultaneously the negative pole becomes positive, namely, B becomes A" (Meinhof, 1912, p. 19—our translation NC/MH).

[10] It was Bever who first drew our attention to the fact that the possibility of "polarity" rules is implicit in our notation.

[11] Other examples can be found in Harper (1910), pages 73 and 76.

[12] Speiser (1938) has argued that the origin of these alternations in Semitic can be explained without recourse to the principle of polarity, in terms of grammatical analogy. Apart from the fact that analogy as a motivating principle for linguistic change is of dubious validity (see discussion in Kiparsky, 1965), Speiser's argument, even if correct, can have no bearing on the issue under discussion, which concerns the synchronic grammar of Biblical Hebrew after it had acquired the alternations in question. As we note in Chapter Six, polarity rules may arise in a language in a great many ways in addition to being added directly to the grammar. Hence, even if, as Speiser suggests, the historical process did not involve any polarity rules, the synchronic facts reviewed above would still require the postulation of the polarity rule (75).

Arabic grammar (1963):

> The class vowel (the vowel after the second stem consonant) can be /a/ /i/ or /u/ in verbs of the first conjugation. If in the perfect the class vowel is /a/, then according to the polarity principle the imperfect will be either /i/ or /u/, whereby /u/ will appear in the majority of verbs: /a/ also occurs relatively frequently but primarily in such verbs in which the second or third stem consonants are guttural or velar consonants; e.g.

to uncover	fataḥa	yaftaḥu
to read	qaraʔa	yaqraʔu
to doze	naʕasa	yanʕasu
to strike	faĵaʕa	yafĵaʕu

> If the class vowel is /i/ then in accordance with the same principle of polarity it will be /a/ in the imperfect and in rare cases /i/; e.g.

to be ill	mariḍa	yamraḍu
to be sad	ḥazina	yaḥzanu

but

to consider	ḥasiba	yaḥsibu

> If the class vowel is /u/ then in the imperfect it is always /u/, for instance, "to be handsome" ḥasuna yaḥsunu (p. 150).

The polarity rule thus applies only to stems with unrounded stem vowels.

A further instance of polarity rules is known to us from Kasem, a West African language, where in the noun classes A, B, and C the singular and plural suffixes are correlated so that if the singular suffix is /i/ or /u/, the plural suffix is /a/, whereas if the singular suffix is /a/, the plural suffix is /i/ (Callow, 1965, p. 32).

Rules with variables are not, strictly speaking, single rules, but rather schemata that stand for sets of rules. Thus (72), for example, stands for the two rules (73a), (73b); and (65) is in fact a schema that abbreviates the two rules in (63). If we survey the rules that have been discussed up to this point, we observe that there are no examples in which ordering is crucial. However, in the case of polarity rules, it is essential that the two rules apply disjunctively, for otherwise the second rule will undo the effects of the first rule. Generalizing upon these observations, we might impose the condition that rules abbreviated in a single schema by the use of variables cannot apply in sequence (in a given stage of cyclic application). This idea can be made precise in various ways. Looking ahead to later developments, we state the convention in the following form:

$$\left(76\right)$$ Suppose $\Sigma(\alpha)$ to be a schema involving the variable α. Then $\Sigma(\alpha)$ represents the sequence $\Sigma(+)$, $\Sigma(-)$ formed by replacement of α by $+$ and $-$, respectively, in $\Sigma(\alpha)$, and the schemata $\Sigma(+)$, $\Sigma(-)$ are "disjunctively ordered," in the sense that application of a rule derived by expanding $\Sigma(+)$ (or of $\Sigma(+)$ itself, if it is a rule) precludes the application of any rule derived by expanding $\Sigma(-)$ (or of $\Sigma(-)$ itself, if it is a rule) in the same stage of the cycle.

This, of course, is the notion of disjunctive ordering studied in detail, in its application to English, in Chapters Two, Three, and Four. We propose, then, that the variable convention also imposes disjunctive ordering, with, in fact, an arbitrary choice in the ordering of the rules derived from the schema with variables. We return to this matter in the Appendix to this chapter.

5. *Metathesis, contraction, and elision*

The phonological rules that have been discussed in the preceding sections of this chapter have been characterized by having a single segment on the left-hand side of the arrow. There are, however, a number of phonological processes that simultaneously affect more than one segment in the string. Of particular interest are the phenomena of metathesis, contraction, and elision.

One of the most interesting examples of metathesis and contraction that have come to our attention is in Kasem. According to Callow (1965), the language has the following consonants:

$$
\left(77\right)
\qquad
\begin{array}{llll}
p & t & č & k \\
b & d & ǰ & g \\
m & n & ɲ & ŋ \qquad\qquad l \quad w \quad y \\
f & s \\
v & z
\end{array}
$$

Its vowel system consists of two parallel sets of five vowels, a set of "upper" vowels and a set of "lower" vowels, which meet a condition of vowel harmony, namely, that the vowels in any word are exclusively drawn from one set or the other. (On the phonetic distinction between the sets, see Chapter Seven, Section 4.5.) Since the vowel harmony rule is a late rule which has no effect on the processes we are interested in here, we shall not indicate the difference between the two sets of vowels in our transcription of the examples cited by Callow. The vowel system appearing in our transcription will therefore consist of two high vowels [i u] and three low vowels [æ a ɔ]. Our discussion is further restricted to nouns of the type belonging to Callow's class C, and it must, of course, be regarded as suggestive only, since our information about the language is limited. We do not discuss the other four noun classes of Kasem because Callow provides very little information about three of the classes and the facts of the fourth class hold little additional interest.

The nouns of Callow's class C add to the stem the suffix /a/ in the singular and the suffix /i/ in the plural. Thus we have:

$$
\left(78\right)
$$

SINGULAR	PLURAL		SINGULAR	PLURAL	
bakada	*bakadi*	(boy)	*kukuda*	*kukudi*	(dog)
sada	*sadi*	(grass mat)	*fana*	*fani*	(knife)
mimina	*mimini*	(thin)	*čana*	*čani*	(moon)
fala	*fali*	(white man)	*bakala*	*bakali*	(shoulder)
tula	*tuli*	(granary)			

When a word ends in two identical vowels, one of these is truncated. Thus, for instance, parallel to (78) we find examples such as (79):

$$
\left(79\right)
$$

kambia	*kambi*	(cooking pot)
pia	*pi*	(yam)

Were there not such a truncation rule, the expected plurals would be [kambii] and [pii].[13]

Stems ending in velars lose the velar consonant before the [i] of the plural. Thus, we

---

[13] The form [daa], "stick," cited by Callow, which contradicts the rule mentioned here, may be an error in the transcription. In the absence of further information we shall assume that this is the case and that the form is actually [da].

get forms such as [buga]–[bwi], "river," and [diga]–[di], "room"—from [digi]→[dii]→ [di]. To account for the appearance of the glide [w] in [bwi], we need, in addition to a rule of Velar Elision, the Glide Rule (80), which turns a high vowel into its cognate glide before another vowel. (Actually the rule is not quite as general as stated here—see p. 363.)

$$\left(80\right) \quad \text{GLIDE RULE}$$

$$\begin{bmatrix} -\text{cons} \\ +\text{high} \end{bmatrix} \rightarrow [-\text{voc}] \quad / \quad \underline{\qquad} \begin{bmatrix} +\text{voc} \\ -\text{cons} \end{bmatrix}$$

Before formulating the elision rules, we will extend our formalism to provide for the deletion of units and the introduction of units into strings. In accordance with widely used conventions, we now permit rules such as (81) and (82):

$$\left(81\right) \qquad A \rightarrow \phi \quad / X \underline{\qquad} Y$$

$$\left(82\right) \qquad \phi \rightarrow B \quad / X \underline{\qquad} Y$$

We stipulate that (81) has the effect of rewriting a string $\ldots X'A'Y'\ldots$ as $\ldots X'Y'\ldots$, and that (82) has the effect of rewriting a string $\ldots X'Y'\ldots$ as $\ldots X'BY'\ldots$, where X', A', Y' are not distinct from X, A, Y, respectively.[14]

The two deletion rules in Kasem mentioned above will therefore be stated as follows:

$$\left(83\right) \quad \text{VELAR ELISION}$$

$$\begin{bmatrix} +\text{cons} \\ -\text{ant} \\ -\text{cor} \end{bmatrix} \rightarrow \phi \quad / \quad \underline{\qquad} \begin{bmatrix} +\text{voc} \\ -\text{cons} \\ +\text{high} \\ -\text{back} \end{bmatrix}$$

$$\left(84\right) \quad \text{TRUNCATION}[15]$$

$$\begin{bmatrix} -\text{cons} \\ \alpha\text{high} \\ \beta\text{back} \end{bmatrix} \rightarrow \phi \quad / \quad \underline{\qquad} \begin{bmatrix} +\text{voc} \\ -\text{cons} \\ \alpha\text{high} \\ \beta\text{back} \end{bmatrix}$$

As we examine the velar stems cited by Callow, we find that Velar Elision is accompanied by phonological processes that are considerably more complex, as is seen in the following forms:

$$\left(85\right) \qquad \begin{array}{lll} la\eta a & læ & \text{(song)} \\ naga & næ & \text{(leg)} \end{array}$$

---

[14] We might, as a notational device, represent the identity element as [−unit] rather than as ϕ, regarding segments and boundaries as elements with the feature [+unit]. This would be natural, given our use of the term "unit" to cover segments and boundaries (and would suggest that ϕ should count in the evaluation just as another feature), but would also be confusing, given the ordinary mathematical meaning of the term "unit."

[15] The reason for omitting the specification [+vocalic] on the left-hand side of the arrow is that in prevocalic position there can be no contrast between vowels and glides (see rule (80)). We can also omit the specification of all vowel features except "high" and "back," for in the lexical representations of Kasem, only three vowels are in contrast, as will be shown directly.

Since the plural marker for the nouns of this class is [i], we must assume that the plurals in (85) have the underlying representations:

$$\left(86\right) \qquad\qquad\qquad laŋi$$
$$nagi$$

We know that the velars will be elided by rule (83), yielding:

$$\left(87\right) \qquad\qquad\qquad lai$$
$$nai$$

These two strings, however, appear in the output as [læ] and [næ], respectively. We have here a phenomenon familiar from many languages—e.g., *guṇa* in Sanskrit—where a sequence of two vowels is contracted into a third vowel which keeps the lowness of the first vowel and the backness of the second vowel. Informally such a contraction rule would be stated:

$$\left(88\right) \qquad\qquad\qquad ai \;\rightarrow\; æ$$

This rule, however, deviates from the rules so far considered in that it must have two segments rather than one on the left-hand side of the arrow. To state contraction rules, therefore, we must admit into the phonology rules that are most naturally formulated as transformational rules.[16] Rule (88) may then be stated as (89):

$$\left(89\right)$$ VOWEL CONTRACTION

$$\text{Structural Description (SD):} \begin{bmatrix} +\text{voc} \\ -\text{cons} \\ -\text{high} \\ +\text{back} \\ -\text{round} \end{bmatrix}, \begin{bmatrix} -\text{cons} \\ +\text{high} \\ -\text{back} \end{bmatrix}$$
$$\qquad\qquad\qquad\qquad\qquad 1 \qquad\qquad\qquad 2$$

$$\text{Structural Change (SC):} \; 1 \; 2 \; \rightarrow \; \begin{bmatrix} 1 \\ -\text{back} \end{bmatrix}, \begin{bmatrix} 2 \\ \phi \end{bmatrix}$$

We shall tentatively adopt the convention that the complexity of such rules is to be measured in the same way as that of all other rules of the phonology; i.e., in the case of (89), the complexity is ten features (counting the identity element as a feature—see note 14).

Returning now to the discussion of Kasem nominals, we note as somewhat puzzling the following pairs of forms, particularly in view of the form [pia]–[pi], " yam," cited in (79):

$$\left(90\right) \qquad\qquad pia \quad pæ \quad \text{(sheep)}$$
$$babia \quad babæ \quad \text{(brave)}$$

Since the grammar already contains the Vowel Truncation Rule (84), [pia] can also be derived from an underlying [piaa]; and [pæ] can be derived not only from an underlying [pai] but also from an underlying [paii]. Our underlying forms, then, show different stems in the singular and plural:

$$\left(91\right) \qquad\qquad\qquad pia+a \quad pai+i$$

These stems are obviously related by metathesis, and we shall assume (and justify later)

---

[16] For a discussion of such rules, see Chomsky (1961) and many other references that examine the kinds of rules that are necessary for syntactic description.

that the underlying form is [pia] and that metathesis takes place in the plural but not in the singular. Like the Vowel Contraction Rule (89), the Metathesis Rule requires two segments on the left-hand side of the arrow, and it will therefore be given in the same format as (89):

$$\left(92\right) \quad \text{METATHESIS}$$

$$\text{SD:} \quad \begin{bmatrix} +\text{voc} \\ -\text{cons} \end{bmatrix} , \quad [-\text{cons}] , \quad \begin{bmatrix} +\text{voc} \\ -\text{cons} \end{bmatrix}$$
$$\qquad\qquad\quad 1 \qquad\qquad 2 \qquad\qquad 3$$

$$\text{SC:} \quad 1\ 2\ 3 \;\rightarrow\; 2\ 1\ 3 \;\; except\ when\ 2 = 3 = [a]$$

By formulating metathesis in this manner, we raise a problem for our evaluation measure, for if we evaluate (92) by counting nothing but the features in it, its " cost " is less than that of a rule with the same structural description (SD) and with a minimal structural change (SC) of one feature, for example, in the vowel. It would be simple to institute a special convention so that metathesis rules would cost more. For instance, we could require that all or some segments mentioned in the metathesis rule be supplied with a special abstract feature [+Metathesis]. The "cost" of such a rule would then be equal to the number of features mentioned in the SD plus the number of segments to which we have assigned the feature [+Metathesis]. If this turned out to be unsatisfactory, we could easily invent any number of different conventions. For the present, however, we do not know of any crucial cases that would allow us to decide among the alternatives. We therefore leave the question open.

By extending the notational system to permit rules such as the Metathesis Rule (92), and by supposing the cost of such a rule to be not too great, we have, in effect, postulated that such mechanisms are readily available to the child as he attempts to construct the grammar of his speech community. We could, of course, have decided otherwise and established conventions that would have made the formulation of metathesis extremely "costly," but this would not properly harmonize with the fact that metathesis is a perfectly common phonological process. Though the device of metathesis, like all linguistic universals, is in principle available to speakers of any language, it does not, of course, follow that every language must actually present examples.

Returning again to our discussion of Kasem nominals, we first give in detail the derivation of the singular and plural forms of the noun [pia] meaning "sheep" (as opposed to the noun meaning "yam," which will have the underlying forms /pi+a/ and /pi+i/):

$$\left(93\right)$$

	pia+a	*pia+i*	
		pai+i	METATHESIS (92)
	pia	*pai*	TRUNCATION (84)
		pæ	VOWEL CONTRACTION (89)

We recall that we have blocked the Metathesis Rule from applying to the string [Vaa], and we must now justify this decision. To this end, consider forms such as:

$$\left(94\right)$$

nanjua	*nanjwæ*	(fly)
yua	*ywæ*	(hair)

At first sight it might appear that these present no difficulty and could be derived in a straightforward fashion from underlying strings such as:

$$\left(95\right)$$

nanjua+a	*nanjua+i*
yua+a	*yua+i*

This solution, however, requires that Metathesis be blocked both in the singular and the plural, whereas in (93) Metathesis is needed in the derivation of the plural form [pæ]. To allow Metathesis to apply to [pia +i] but to block it in [yua +i] would require a rule of very great complexity. We propose, therefore, that the underlying forms are not those given in (95) but rather:

$$\begin{pmatrix} 96 \end{pmatrix} \quad \begin{array}{ll} nan\check{j}au{+}a & nan\check{j}au{+}i \\ yau{+}a & yau{+}i \end{array}$$

These strings are converted by the Metathesis Rule into the strings given in (95), and the phonetic forms are then derived by the rules already discussed.

The above considerations provide some justification for our proposal to allow the Metathesis Rule to apply except if the second and third vowels in the SD are both [a]. The mechanism for handling such exceptional behavior is dealt with in Section 7. Here we shall only provide evidence that makes it rather unlikely that some simpler condition for the application of the Metathesis Rule (92) can be found. Callow gives examples of metathesis taking place under the following conditions:

$$\begin{pmatrix} 97 \end{pmatrix} \quad \begin{array}{lll} Vai & pæ & \text{(SEE (93))} \\ Vui & ywæ & \text{(SEE (96))} \\ Vua & yua & \text{(SEE (96))} \\ Viu & lili\flat & \text{(SEE BELOW)} \end{array}$$

The forms [lili\flat]–[lilæ:du], "saliva," belong to Callow's class D: these nouns form their singular by the addition of /u/ and their plural by the addition of /du/ together with secondary lengthening of the last or only vowel of the stem. Hence the underlying form for the plural must be assumed to be /lilai +du/. From this we must further assume that the singular has the underlying form /lilai +u/, which is converted into the required [lili\flat] by the Metathesis Rule and Vowel Contraction (appropriately revised—see (100)), applying in this order. This is, then, an instance of metathesis taking place in a string of the form *Viu*, as shown in (97). The variety of the sequences presented in (97) makes it highly unlikely that the Metathesis Rule can be constrained in any less complicated manner than the one proposed here.

Further support for the suggested analysis comes from a consideration of the following velar stems:

$$\begin{pmatrix} 98 \end{pmatrix} \quad \begin{array}{lll} k\flat ga & kwæ & \text{(back)} \\ \check{c}\flat\eta a & \check{c}wæ & \text{(path)} \end{array}$$

The rules already given would readily yield the plural forms if we assumed as underlying representations /kaug +i/, /čaun +i/, as shown below:

$$\begin{pmatrix} 99 \end{pmatrix} \quad \begin{array}{lll} kaug{+}i & \check{c}au\eta{+}i & \\ kau{+}i & \check{c}au{+}i & \text{VELAR ELISION (83)} \\ kua{+}i & \check{c}ua{+}i & \text{METATHESIS (92)} \\ kuæ & \check{c}uæ & \text{VOWEL CONTRACTION (89)} \\ kwæ & \check{c}wæ & \text{GLIDE RULE (80)} \end{array}$$

A problem is presented by the singular forms, since we have as yet no way to account for the stem vowel [\flat] (which also appeared in the form [lili\flat]). In view of the plural forms, we should expect the underlying form to contain the diphthong [au] in place of [\flat]. The change from [au] to [\flat], however, is very similar to the change in (88), and, in fact, a very straightforward generalization of the Vowel Contraction Rule (89) will yield the required result:

$$(100) \quad \text{VOWEL CONTRACTION}$$

SD: $\begin{bmatrix} +\text{voc} \\ -\text{cons} \\ -\text{high} \\ +\text{back} \\ -\text{round} \end{bmatrix}$, $\begin{bmatrix} -\text{cons} \\ +\text{high} \\ \alpha\text{back} \end{bmatrix}$

$\qquad\qquad 1 \qquad\qquad 2$

SC: $1 \; 2 \;\rightarrow\; \begin{bmatrix} 1 \\ \alpha\text{back} \\ \alpha\text{round} \end{bmatrix}, \begin{bmatrix} 2 \\ \phi \end{bmatrix}$

The Contraction Rule makes it unnecessary to postulate /ɔ/ and /æ/ in the underlying representations, for these will now be derived from /au/ and /ai/. We have thus reduced the vowel inventory in the lexical representations of Kasem to the three vowels /i u a/.

A few minor facts must still be taken account of. We note that among the velar stems cited by Callow are the following two:

$$(101) \qquad \begin{array}{lll} \text{ĭiŋa} & \text{ĭĩ} & \text{(hand)} \\ \text{zuŋa} & \text{zwĩ} & \text{(calabash)} \end{array}$$

To account for these forms, we follow Callow's suggestion and postulate the Nasalization Rule (102):

$$(102) \quad \text{NASALIZATION}$$

$\begin{bmatrix} +\text{voc} \\ -\text{cons} \\ -\text{back} \end{bmatrix} \rightarrow [+\text{nasal}] \;/\; \begin{bmatrix} +\text{voc} \\ -\text{cons} \\ +\text{high} \end{bmatrix} \begin{bmatrix} +\text{cons} \\ +\text{nasal} \\ -\text{ant} \\ -\text{cor} \end{bmatrix} \underline{\qquad}$

In other words, /i/ is nasalized after a high vowel followed by a nasal velar. The plural forms cited in (101) are then derived as follows:

$$(103) \qquad \begin{array}{lll} \text{ĭiŋ}+\text{i} & \text{zuŋ}+\text{i} & \\ \text{ĭiŋĩ} & \text{zuŋĩ} & \text{NASALIZATION (102)} \\ \text{ĭiĩ} & \text{zuĩ} & \text{VELAR ELISION (83)} \\ \text{ĭĩ} & & \text{TRUNCATION (84)} \\ & \text{zwĩ} & \text{GLIDE RULE (80)} \end{array}$$

Observe that the Nasalization Rule does not affect the operation of either of the deletion rules (83) (Velar Elision) or (84) (Truncation), since nasality is not mentioned in these rules.

Examination of the forms cited by Callow reveals that the Glide Rule does not function everywhere as postulated in (80). In particular, it appears that the rule does not apply before the singular suffix /a/. Thus we find forms such as [pia], "yam," [yua], "hair," [kua], "bone," [nua], "finger," without the expected glide, although in the plural forms [ywæ], [kwi], [nwi] the glide appears, as expected. The absence of the glide in the plural [pi] is, of course, due to the prior application of the Truncation Rule (84).

To complete our discussion of the Kasem nominals belonging to class C, we list below the rules developed, in the order of their application:

$$\begin{pmatrix} 104 \end{pmatrix} \quad \begin{array}{l} \text{Nasalization (102)} \\ \text{Velar Elision (83)} \\ \text{Metathesis (92)} \\ \text{Vowel Contraction (100)} \\ \text{Truncation (84)} \\ \text{Glide Rule (80)} \end{array}$$

6. Boundaries

The terminal string produced by the syntax consists of units of two types, segments and boundaries (or junctures). To distinguish these two classes of units, we shall utilize the feature "segment," marking boundaries [−segment] and segments [+segment]. Like segments, different types of boundaries are designated by the utilization of a special set of features, which are distinct from the segmental features. The boundary features, like the segmental features, are given in the universal theory of language; but unlike the latter, boundary features do not have universal phonetic correlates, except perhaps for the fact that word boundaries may optionally be actualized as pauses.

6.1. *FORMATIVE BOUNDARY*: +

The most elementary boundary is the formative boundary, which we have symbolized in our informal transcription by the plus sign. The formative boundary is characterized by the features $\begin{bmatrix} +\text{formative boundary} \\ -\text{segment} \end{bmatrix}$; it indicates the point at which a given formative begins and ends. It is, therefore, part of the representation of every formative in the lexicon. In this respect the formative boundary differs from all other boundaries, for the latter are introduced by means of special rules, some universal, others language-specific. These rules introduce boundaries that have the feature [−formative boundary] and as many other features as are required. There can be no rule in the grammar that introduces or deletes the feature [+formative boundary] (except as part of a longer string of units).

As already noted in preceding chapters, in view of the unique status of formative boundary, we shall treat it quite differently from all other boundaries. In particular, we shall establish the following convention:

$$\begin{pmatrix} 105 \end{pmatrix} \quad \text{Any rule which applies to a string of the form } XYZ \text{ also applies to strings of the form } X+Y+Z, XY+Z, X+YZ, \text{ where } X, Y, Z \text{ stand for sequences of zero or more units and } + \text{ represents formative boundary.}$$

In other words, a rule in which the presence of formative boundary is not explicitly indicated applies also to strings containing any number of formative boundaries. The converse is not true, however: a rule that applies to the string $X+Z$ does not also apply to the string XZ. This formal asymmetry expresses a certain empirical hypothesis, namely, that processes operating within formatives normally also apply across formative boundary, whereas processes may be restricted to the position where two formatives come together. Under this empirical assumption, the grammar must be complicated in some way to permit a process to apply only when there is no formative boundary present.

Suppose that we have the rule (106):

$$\left(106\right) \qquad A \;\rightarrow\; B \;\mid\; X\text{——}Y$$

According to convention (105), this rule applies to the strings $X+A+Y$, $XA+Y$, $X+AY$, and XAY. But it may be crucial for an order to be determined among these subrules of (106). Within our framework, it is natural to take (106) to be an abbreviation for the schema (107), which stands for the sequence of disjunctively ordered rules (108):

$$\left(107\right) \qquad A \;\rightarrow\; B \;\mid\; X(+)\text{——}(+)Y$$

$$\left(108\right) \qquad
\begin{array}{ll}
\text{(a)} & A \;\rightarrow\; B \;\mid\; X+\text{——}+Y \\
\text{(b)} & A \;\rightarrow\; B \;\mid\; X\text{——}+Y^{17} \\
\text{(c)} & A \;\rightarrow\; B \;\mid\; X+\text{——}Y \\
\text{(d)} & A \;\rightarrow\; B \;\mid\; X\text{——}Y
\end{array}$$

We will, then, assume that convention (105) is satisfied as a consequence of the somewhat more explicit convention (109):

$\left(109\right)$ A schema of the form

$$A \;\rightarrow\; B \;\mid\; X_1 \ldots X_m \text{——} X_{m+1} \ldots X_n$$

where $X_1, \ldots, X_n$ are units, is an abbreviation for the schema

$$A \;\rightarrow\; B \;\mid\; X_1(+)X_2(+)\ldots(+)X_m(+)\text{——}(+)X_{m+1}(+)\ldots(+)X_n$$

In particular, then, (106) stands for (107) (hence for the disjunctively ordered sequence (108)), if X and Y are units; and convention (105) is satisfied.

As an illustration of this convention, consider the rule of Latvian phonology which (omitting certain details) converts high vowels into glides before vowels (see Halle and Zeps, 1966):

$$\left(110\right) \qquad
\begin{bmatrix} -\text{cons} \\ +\text{high} \end{bmatrix} \;\rightarrow\; [-\text{voc}] \;/\; \text{——} \begin{bmatrix} +\text{voc} \\ -\text{cons} \end{bmatrix}$$

The expression (110) is, by convention, a schema that expands to the pair of disjunctively ordered rules (111):

$$\left(111\right) \qquad
\begin{array}{ll}
\text{(a)} & \begin{bmatrix} -\text{cons} \\ +\text{high} \end{bmatrix} \;\rightarrow\; [-\text{voc}] \;/\; \text{——}+\begin{bmatrix} +\text{voc} \\ -\text{cons} \end{bmatrix} \\[2.5em]
\text{(b)} & \begin{bmatrix} -\text{cons} \\ +\text{high} \end{bmatrix} \;\rightarrow\; [-\text{voc}] \;/\; \text{——}\begin{bmatrix} +\text{voc} \\ -\text{cons} \end{bmatrix}
\end{array}$$

Let us now consider how rule (110) yields the correct phonetic outputs from the underlying representations in the forms shown in (112):

$\left(112\right)$

(a) $/\#$iāi$+$a$\#/$	(rides)	[yāy]
(b) $/\#$kuru$+$iai$\#/$	(basket (gen. sg.))	[kurwya]
(c) $/\#$aui$+$a$\#/$	(puts on (footgear))	[auy]

In the derivation of the phonetic representation of (112a), the second [y] is produced by (111a), and the first [y] by (111b). The absence of the final /a/ in the phonetic output is due

---

[17] The ordering of cases (b) and (c) is arbitrary; we have no examples to motivate one or the other ordering. The relation between disjunctive ordering and the notational device of parenthesization is discussed in Section 1.2 of Chapter Three. We return to it in the Appendix to this chapter.

to the operation of a word-final-vowel truncation rule:

$$(113) \qquad\qquad V \rightarrow \phi \ / \text{———} \#$$

This example brings out an indeterminacy in our formalism. Rules (111a) and (111b) are disjunctively ordered; nevertheless, both apply in the derivation of [yāy] from /iāi + a/ in (112a). The point is that rule (111a) applies to the rightmost occurrence of /i/ and rule (111b) to the leftmost occurrence. We must, then, define the notion of disjunctive ordering so as to permit such a case of joint application of disjunctively ordered rules but to exclude the cases discussed earlier. Clearly we must stipulate that if rules R_1 and R_2 are disjunctively ordered—R_1 preceding R_2—and if R_1 applies to the substring Y of a string XYZ but is independent of X and Z, then R_2 may apply to X and Z but not to Y in a stage of the cycle in which R_1 applies. More precisely, if R_1 is the rule $A \rightarrow B \mid P \text{———} Q$, and R_1 applies to a string $XP'A'Q'Y$ (where P', A', Q' are not distinct from P, A, Q, respectively), converting it to $XP'B'Q'Y$ in the usual manner, then R_2 may apply to a string contained in X or in Y but not to a string that is included in (or, in particular, identical with) $P'B'Q'$. No doubt this convention must be extended to permit R_2 to apply not only to X or Y, but also to a string that is derived by other rules from X or Y (but not to a string that is derived, even in part, from $P'B'Q'$). When we try to make this notation precise, we immediately face a variety of cases where a specific decision arises as to how the formalization should proceed. There is no difficulty in principle in resolving these cases, one way or another, but having so little relevant information, it would be pointless to make these decisions. We therefore leave the matter in this semiformalized state, noting simply that further empirical evidence is needed to determine just how the relevant conventions should be formulated. Some steps toward a formalization will be found in Bever (1967).

Example (112b) is derived in a fashion parallel to (112a). First (111a) accounts for the appearance of [w], and then (111b) produces the [y]. Example (112c) is somewhat more complicated. The [y] results from (111a), with the consequence that when (111b) becomes applicable, [u] no longer precedes a vowel, and the rule therefore does not apply. Thus, the presence of + between two high vowels in /#kuru + iai#/ and its absence in /#aui + a#/ account for the different phonetic interpretations that the sequence of two high vowels receives in the two examples.

6.2. *THE BOUNDARY* # *AND THE NOTION* "*WORD*"

In addition to formative boundary, every language has a boundary characterized by the feature complex:

$$(114) \qquad \begin{bmatrix} -\text{segment} \\ -\text{formative boundary} \\ +\text{word boundary} \end{bmatrix}$$

We postulate that this boundary, which we will symbolize as #, appears in the phonological surface structure primarily, but not exclusively, as the result of the general convention (115):

(115) The boundary # is automatically inserted at the beginning and end of every string dominated by a major category, i.e., by one of the lexical categories "noun," "verb," "adjective," or by a category such as "sentence," "noun phrase," "verb phrase," which dominates a lexical category.[18]

---

[18] We can formulate this convention in terms of a more abstract notion of major category that does not presuppose a fixed universal set of lexical and other categories. The matter is not relevant here, and we will continue to suppose that the stronger assumption is justified.

In addition to convention (115), there are language-specific rules governing the presence of #. Conceivably, there may be rules that introduce # in various positions not specified by convention (115), although we know of no clear examples of this; but there are, as we shall see, rules that delete # in various positions.

The boundary # plays a role in defining the notion "word," which, as we have seen, is crucial for phonology since it constitutes the domain of application of the noncyclic rules. It is important to bear in mind, however, that a word, in the phonologically relevant sense, is not simply determined as a string bounded by occurrences of #. The situation is somewhat more complex. Consider, for example, the "neutral affixes" of English, which we discussed in Chapter Three, Section 7. Expressions such as *differing, ringing, metalanguage, establishment* are single words from the point of view of the phonological rules, and the definition of "word" must certainly be designed so as to express this fact. But convention (115) will assign an internal # boundary in these expressions because they contain the elements *differ, ring, language, establish,* each of which belongs to a lexical category. Thus convention (115) gives the forms:

$$\left(116\right)$$
(a) $[_V \# \ [_V \# \textit{differ} \# \ ]_V \ \textit{ing} \# \ ]_V$
(b) $[_V \# \ [_V \# \textit{ring} \# \ ]_V \ \textit{ing} \# \ ]_V$
(c) $[_N \# \textit{meta} \ [_N \# \textit{language} \# \ ]_N \ \# \ ]_N$
(d) $[_N \# \ [_V \# \textit{establish} \# \ ]_V \ \textit{ment} \# \ ]_N$

The occurrence of internal # is quite important, as we have noted several times. It accounts for the syllabicity of [r] in case (a) (compare [difəriŋ], "differing," with [difrənt], "different," in which the # boundary is deleted by a language-specific rule); the deletion of final /g/ in *ring* in case (b); the shift of stress to the first syllable in case (c); and the fact that the affix does not shift stress to the penultimate syllable in case (d). Nevertheless, we want to regard the full forms of (116) as single words.

It seems that an appropriate definition of "word" can be given in the following way. Let us assume, as throughout this book, that surface structures are represented with labeled bracketing indicating categorization (as in Chapter One), and let us suppose further that # is introduced by convention (115) and then perhaps dropped in certain positions by whatever language-specific rules there may be.

Let us next define the "terminus" of a word as being any configuration of boundaries and brackets having the form (117) (where S is the category "sentence" and X contains no segments):

$$\left(117\right)$$
$$_S[\# X [\#$$
$$\#] X \#]_S$$
$$\#] X [\#$$

Suppose that we have a string $\ldots Y \ldots = \ldots Z [\# W \#] V$, where $Z [\#$ and $\#] V$ are termini as defined in (117), and Y contains no other termini. Then $[\# W \#]$ is a word.

For example, the sentence (118) would have the surface structure (119) (where D stands for the category "determiner," P stands for "preposition," PP stands for "prepositional phrase," and the other letters stand for categories already mentioned—see Chapter One) after the application of convention (115) and would consist of the three words listed in (120), where brackets are deleted:

$$\left(118\right)$$ *the book was in an unlikely place*

$\left(119\right)$ $[_S\# \ [_{NP}\# \ [_D the]_D \ [_N \# book\#]_N \ \#]_{NP} \ [_{VP}\# \ was \ [_{PP}\# \ [_P in]_P \ [_{NP}\# \ [_D an]_D$
$[_A \# un \ [_A \# likely\#]_A \ \#]_A \ [_N \# place\#]_N \ \#]_{NP} \ \#]_{PP} \ \#]_{VP} \ \#]_S$

$\left(120\right)$ (a) $\# the \# book \#$
         (b) $\# was \# in \# an \# un \# likely \#$
         (c) $\# place \#$

In other words, the rules of word-level phonology in English will apply in the derivation initiated by (119) at the point in the cycle when we reach one of the three elements *the book*, *was in an unlikely*, and *place*.

As is illustrated by the second element of (120), the word as defined here need not be a constituent of the surface structure. This causes a difficulty for the theory of rule application. We have assumed that word-level (noncyclic) rules apply when the level of words is reached in the cycle; thus, if a certain word is not a constituent, the word-level rules will never apply to it under this formulation. We can remedy this inadequacy by a convention which readjusts surface structure so as to guarantee that words, as just defined, will in fact be constituents. Suppose that we have a string $\dots WX[_\alpha YZ]_\alpha \dots$, where $[_\alpha$ and $]_\alpha$ are paired brackets, $X[_\alpha Y$ is a word, and W contains no units. Then this will be readjusted, by convention, to $\dots [_\alpha WXYZ]_\alpha \dots$. Similarly, a string $\dots [_\alpha XY]_\alpha ZW \dots$, where $Y]_\alpha Z$ is a word and W contains no units, will be readjusted to $\dots [_\alpha XYZW]_\alpha \dots$. Where this convention is relevant several times, we apply it in such a way as to preserve proper parenthesization. Applied to (119), this readjustment convention will give (121):

$\left(121\right)$ (a) $[_S\# \ [_{NP}\# \ [_D the]_D \ [_N \# book\#]_N \ \#]_{NP}$
         (b) $[_{VP} \ [_{PP} \ [_{NP} \ [_A \# was\# \ [_P in]_P \ \#[_D an]_D \ \#un \ [_A \# likely\#]_A \ \#]_A$
         (c) $[_N \# place\#]_N \ \#]_{NP} \ \#]_{PP} \ \#]_{VP} \ \#]_S$

With this modification, the three words are (with internal brackets deleted) as in (120); they belong to the categories NP, A, N, respectively. In effect, we are treating the elements *was, in, an* as proclitics to the adjective *unlikely*.

This definition seems appropriate for English, as well as for other cases with which we are familiar. The orthographic conventions for Hebrew and Arabic, for example, are consistent with the phonetics in not separating prepositions or articles from the following word. Similarly, a common error of semiliterate writers of Russian is to omit the space after a preposition. In fact, certain phonetic effects correlated with the word terminus as defined in (117) are not found before the # boundary that follows a preposition. In particular, final obstruents in prepositions are not subject to the general rule of Russian that devoices word-terminal obstruents before sonorants: in word-terminal position before sonorant we find only voiceless consonants, e.g., [v,os# #atca], "he drove the father"; in preposition-final position before sonorant, on the other hand, we find both voiced and voiceless consonants, e.g., [b,iz#atca], "without the father," and [s#atcom], "with the father." This distinction is readily correlated with the fact that a single occurrence of # boundary separates the preposition from the following noun, whereas a word terminus intervenes between adjacent lexical categories. Many other examples could be cited.

These proposals, if tenable, characterize the analysis of a surface structure into a sequence of elements, each a constituent and each of which is the domain of the noncyclic processes of word phonology—processes of the sort discussed, for English, in Chapter Four. We are supposing this characterization to be universal, except for the language-specific rules that replace certain occurrences of # by +, i.e., that convert $\begin{bmatrix} -\text{FB} \\ +\text{WB} \end{bmatrix}$ (where FB stands for "formative boundary" and WB for "word boundary") to [+FB] in certain contexts (and, perhaps, that introduce #—see p. 367). Apart from these rules, we are suggesting that the elements to which the noncyclic rules of word phonology apply are determined by certain formal properties of surface structures, as indicated above. It seems to us that these proposals capture the main usages of the term "word," and that other, minor usages of the term can be readily accounted for by slight extensions and modifications. Thus, if we wish to regard compound nouns, adjectives, and verbs as words, we may extend the above definition so that the string in question is dominated by a lexical category which is *not* dominated by a lexical category. It has on occasion been proposed (see, e.g., Milewski, 1951) that words exist in a language only if specific phonetic effects are correlated with word boundaries; languages where such phonetic effects are absent are then said to possess no words but only phrases. It is easy enough to modify our definition of "word" to accommodate this usage, but the requirement that phonetic effects of some sort be associated with word boundary appears to us as insufficiently motivated, and we have not incorporated it into our theory of language.

In preceding chapters we have had occasion to note that the surface structure required as input to the phonological component will not in all cases be identical with the surface structure that can by syntactically motivated. Thus in English *Fifth Avenue* has a different stress pattern from *Fifth Street*. The rules of the phonological component will yield this difference if *Fifth Avenue* is not dominated by the node "noun." Syntactically, however, there is no justification for treating *Fifth Avenue* any differently from *Fifth Street*. We must therefore assume that there exist special "readjustment rules" which modify the syntactically justified surface structure of a sentence so that it will be appropriate as an input to the phonological component. As already noted, the primary effect of these readjustment rules is to delete structure from the syntactically motivated surface structure.[19]

The universal convention (115) governing the placement of the # boundary will insert this unit in inflected forms, as we have noted. Thus, for example, the inflected forms of English verbs will contain a single # boundary, by virtue of this convention, and we will have forms such as those of (122) (see also (116a,b)):

$$\left(122\right) \quad \begin{array}{ll} \text{(a)} & [_\text{V} \# \; [_\text{V} \# \text{sing} \# \;]_\text{V} \; \text{ing} \# \;]_\text{V} \\ \text{(b)} & [_\text{V} \# \; [_\text{V} \# \text{wīp} \# \;]_\text{V} \; \text{d} \# \;]_\text{V} \\ \text{(c)} & [_\text{V} \# \; [_\text{V} \# \text{kēp} \# \;]_\text{V} \; \text{d} \# \;]_\text{V} \end{array}$$

The # boundary internal to /sing#ing/ causes deletion of the word-medial /g/ and indicates, moreover, that /ing/ is a neutral suffix as far as stress placement is concerned, which is essential in verbs such as *contemplating* or *signifying*. This boundary also exempts the form *wiped* from the laxing rule which normally operates before nondental consonant clusters. Thus we have [wāypt] rather than [wipt] as the phonetic representation of *wiped*. But in example (c) of (122), *kept*, this laxing rule does operate, indicating that the # boundary must have been eliminated by a language-specific rule, the applicability of which defines the subcategory of irregular verbs that contains *keep*, *lose*, *weep*, etc. Similarly, the comparative and superlative forms of adjectives are not subject to the rule deleting /g/ after nasal in final

---

[19] One might argue, on grounds of a theory of performance, that a "well-designed language" for humans should contain rules for reducing the complexity of surface structure, where this does not interfere with recoverability of the full syntactic and semantic representation of a sentence. In fact, it seems that this is a primary function of grammatical transformations. See Miller and Chomsky (1963, especially part II) and Chomsky (1965, Chapter 1) for some discussion of this matter. See also, in this connection, the discussion by Ross (1967) of general conditions under which nodes are deleted in derived phrase markers.

position; thus we have [lɔŋ]–[lɔŋgər]–[lɔŋgəst], *long–longer–longest*, contrasting with [siŋ]–[siŋər], *sing–singer*, etc., as is well known. Here too, then, we must have a language-specific rule that eliminates #, thereby making the rule deleting /g/ inapplicable.

The elimination of # in these exceptional forms could be carried out in various ways. One possibility, once again, would be to eliminate a certain category from the surface structure—in this case, the innermost constituent—before the application of convention (115), which inserts # boundaries. Thus if $[_V [_V kēp]_V d]_V$ and $[_A [_A long]_A ər]_A$ are replaced by $[_V kēp+d]_V$, $[_A long+ər]_A$ before # boundaries are introduced, then the phonological processes will apply in just the desired way.[20] Since deletion of categories of the surface structure is required for other cases as well, one might inquire into the possibility of dispensing entirely with rules deleting # and relying solely on rules deleting parts of the surface structure to achieve the required results in all cases such as those just discussed.

This proposal does not seem feasible, however, for there are instances where word boundaries must be deleted but constituent structure maintained. Consider, for example, words such as *advocacy, condensation, compensation*, discussed in .Chapter Three. After the application of convention (115), these will be represented as in (123):

$$\left(123\right) \qquad \begin{array}{l} [_N \# \ [_V \# \ advocate \# \ ]_V \ y \# \ ]_N \\ [_N \# \ [_V \# \ condens \# \ ]_V \ at+ion \# \ ]_N \\ [_N \# \ [_V \# \ compensate \# \ ]_V \ ion \# \ ]_N \end{array}$$

In these cases the internal constituent analysis is essential for the correct operation of the phonological rules, as was observed in Chapter Three. However, it is also necessary for the # boundary to be eliminated before application of the stress placement rules in the second cycle, since the affixes are not neutral with respect to stress placement. Therefore, the elimination of internal # in these examples can be taken care of by a lexical rule which will be automatic with these and various other affixes and which will affect the boundary but not the constituent structure.

It is no doubt possible to find rules of some generality governing the deletion of # before affixes, rules which will perhaps reflect (or even sharpen) the traditional distinction of derivational and inflectional processes and which may depend on a distinction between affixes added by transformation and affixes that are assigned by processes internal to the lexicon. But there are many obscure questions here involving the proper dividing line between the lexical and transformational components of a generative grammar, and, since we have arbitrarily excluded problems of syntax from consideration in this study, we must leave this matter in its present unsettled state.[21]

---

[20] Such awkward forms as *cunningest* and *willingest*, with initial stress and deleted /g/, indicate that the rule deleting constituent structure in adjectives must be restricted to monosyllabic adjectives. If structure were deleted in these forms, they would receive penultimate rather than initial stress. We should, therefore, represent these as $_A[\# _A[\#cunn+ing\#]_A \ est\#]_A$, etc.

    The underlying forms for the comparative and superlative apparently must be /Vr/, /Vst/, rather than /r/, /st/ which become syllabic, because of forms such as *happier, happiest*, i.e., [hæpīyər] (not *[hæpīyr]) and [hæpīyəst] (not *[hæpīyst]).

[21] One critical syntactic problem has to do with the processes of nominalization that give forms such as *proof, advice, sincerity, conviction*. Although phrases such as *John's proving the theorem, John's advising Bill about the matter, John's being sincere, John's being convinced that...* are no doubt derived from underlying sentence-like structures by nominalization transformations, there are quite a few reasons to suppose that *John's proof of the theorem, John's advice to Bill, John's sincerity, John's conviction that...* have a very different origin, involving lexical processes and various other transformations (relativization, possessive). (See Chomsky (1965, pp. 219–220) for a brief discussion and Chomsky (forthcoming).) The matter deserves much fuller study.

6.3. *THE BOUNDARY =*

All languages, we are assuming, have the two boundaries $\begin{bmatrix} -\text{seg} \\ +\text{FB} \\ -\text{WB} \end{bmatrix}$ and $\begin{bmatrix} -\text{seg} \\ -\text{FB} \\ +\text{WB} \end{bmatrix}$, designated as $+$ and $\#$, respectively. In several cases with which we are familiar, there is also a need for a third boundary, designated as $=$, to which we have assigned the feature analysis $\begin{bmatrix} -\text{seg} \\ -\text{FB} \\ -\text{WB} \end{bmatrix}$. (Clearly what we are assuming to be the universal system of boundaries is redundant, with respect to feature specification, if the $=$ boundary is lacking.) This boundary, it will be recalled (see Chapter Three, Section 10), is necessary in the phonology of English in order to account for stress placement, *s*-voicing, and several other facts in forms such as *per=mit, contra=dict, re=semble, con=de=scend, com=bat*. It is introduced by special rules which are part of the derivational morphology of English.

6.4. *BOUNDARIES AS UNITS*

In our treatment, boundaries are units in a string, on a par in this sense with segments. Like segments, each boundary is a complex of features. Boundaries function rather differently from the various types of constituent markers (labeled brackets) that play a role in determining the application of the phonological rules of the transformational cycle. The phonological rules apply in a domain that is delimited by a given pair of labeled brackets, inside of which there are no other labeled brackets. All brackets internal to the domain in question will have been erased on a previous pass through the transformational cycle.

Suppose that we place boundaries in the natural hierarchy $\#$, $=$, $+$. It is then possible to formulate many phonological rules in such a way that they apply only within the domain of a given boundary, but not across this boundary or across any other boundary that takes precedence over it in the hierarchy. Thus in certain languages the stress placement rule can be thought of as applying in the environment $\# X \#$, where X contains no word boundaries but may contain the other boundaries, $+$ or $=$, which are lower in the hierarchy. This observation has prompted McCawley (1965) to propose that boundaries be regarded not as units in the string, but rather on a par with the labeled brackets, as elements delimiting the domain in which a given phonological rule applies. This is an attractive idea, but it seems to us that it cannot be maintained in general; there are fairly clear cases for which boundaries must be regarded as units in the string.

A case in point is the Alternating Stress Rule of English (see (75), Chapter Three), which assigns main stress to the antepenult in words such as *advocate, eliminate, anecdote*. This rule is blocked in forms such as *con=de=scend, contra=dict, inter=ject* because of the appearance of a $=$ boundary. This boundary per se does not block the rule, as shown by forms such as *con=gregate, inter=rogate, per=colate*; it is only when $=$ appears before the final syllable that the rule does not apply.

6.5. *READJUSTMENT RULES*

It seems clear that the grammar must contain readjustment rules that reduce surface structure, but it is very difficult to separate the study of these processes from the study of the theory of performance in any principled way. Consider, for example, sentences such as

(124), where the three bracketed expressions are the three noun phrases in the predicate:

$\begin{pmatrix} 124 \end{pmatrix}$ This is [the cat that caught [the rat that stole [the cheese]]]

Clearly, the intonational structure of the utterance does not correspond to the surface structure in this case. Rather, the major breaks are after *cat* and *rat*; that is, the sentence is spoken as the three-part structure *this is the cat—that caught the rat—that stole the cheese*. This effect could be achieved by a readjustment rule which converts (124), with its multiply embedded sentences, into a structure where each embedded sentence is sister-adjoined in turn to the sentence dominating it. The resulting structure appears then as a conjunction of elementary sentences (that is, sentences without embeddings). This allows us to say that intonation breaks precede every occurrence of the category S (sentence) in the surface structure and that otherwise the ordinary rules prevail. But it can certainly be argued plausibly that this "flattening" of the surface structure is simply a performance factor, related to the difficulty of producing right-branching structures such as (124). The various restrictions on the use of right-branching structures certainly seem to be a matter of performance limitations rather than of grammatical structure, just as the well-known conditions on self-embedding (see Chomsky, 1965, Chapter 1, §2) are obviously a matter of performance rather than of grammatical structure. Hence it can certainly be argued that these problems do not belong to grammar—to the theory of competence—at all.

Similar questions arise in connection with the notion of "phonological phrase," which we have mentioned several times. It is clear that the rules of the phonological component do not apply to strings that exceed a certain level of complexity or a certain length, and that therefore certain readjustment rules must apply to the syntactically generated surface structure to demarcate the strings to which the rules are limited, that is, the strings that we have called "phonological phrases." We might, for example, try to incorporate into the grammar certain readjustment rules which assign the feature [+ phonological phrase boundary] to the # boundaries associated with certain constituents and then impose the condition that the transformational cycle cannot apply to a string containing this feature (which, of course, would have to be assigned along with conventions that guarantee that the full utterance will be analyzed into a sequence of phonological phrases, each a constituent of the adjusted surface structure). The rules that introduce this feature will have to take account of syntactic structure, but they will also involve certain parameters that relate to performance, e.g., speed of utterance. An interesting attempt to develop such rules has been made by Bierwisch (1966). We have nothing to add to his proposals, and we therefore omit any further discussion of phonological phrases.

This discussion by no means exhausts the topic of readjustment rules. We could go on to list many examples of constructions that seem to show a discrepancy between the syntactically motivated surface structure and what is apparently required as an input to the phonological component. We do not have any further substantive proposals or analyses, however. In fact, as noted earlier, our discussion of syntactically determined phonological processes has been extremely restricted in scope. We have attempted to give a systematic presentation of a very limited range of intonational phenomena. Although there is a substantial literature on intonational and prosodic features in English, it is largely restricted to citation of examples, and we cannot draw on it for any significant insight into processes of a general nature. Our inability to provide a more explicit theory of readjustment rules is in part a consequence of the limitations of our investigation of syntactic determination of phonetic shape.

7. Diacritic features

Many grammatical rules apply only to certain lexical items. For example, in a language with a rich inflectional system, such as Latin or Russian, it is necessary to divide all noun stems into several declensional classes to account for the phonetic realization of the gender, number, and case features. These classes may play no other role in the grammar; in particular, they generally have no syntactic function. We shall represent this rather peripheral classification with special "diacritic features" in lexical entries. Thus, in the grammar of Russian there will be, for example, a diacritic feature associated with all feminine nouns which will differentiate the "third declension" stem /dal,/, "distance," from the "second declension" stem /dol,/, "portion."

In the phonology proper, we also find quite commonly that rules apply in a selective fashion and thus impose an idiosyncratic classification on the lexicon. Often there is a historical explanation for this idiosyncratic behavior, but this is obviously irrelevant as far as the linguistic competence of the native speaker is concerned. What the speaker knows is, simply, that a given item or set of items is treated differently from others by the phonological component of the grammar.

In English, for example, we have noted that it is necessary to classify many lexical items in terms of a feature that, roughly, distinguishes items of Germanic origin from other items; and for certain rules, such as Velar Softening, we need a further classification of the non-Germanic part of the vocabulary into items of Greek and Romance origin, roughly. This classification is functional in the language and must be presumed to be represented in the internalized grammar. It is justified not by the historical development of the language but by the applicability of phonological and morphological rules.

Parallel instances may be cited from a great variety of languages. For example, in his study of Turkish phonology, Lees (1961) makes use of a classification that corresponds closely to Turkic or Arabic origin. Similarly, Lightner (1965a) has shown that the phonological component of Modern Russian requires at least the following three classes of lexical formatives: [−Slavic], $\begin{bmatrix} +\text{Slavic} \\ +\text{Russian} \end{bmatrix}$, $\begin{bmatrix} +\text{Slavic} \\ -\text{Russian} \end{bmatrix}$ (= Church Slavonic).[22] Thus, for instance, Russian has the "second conjugation" verbs [vərɔčú], "I turn," and [vɔz # vraščú], "I return." These two verbs are derived from an underlying root /uərt/, which figures both in the "Russian" and in the "Church Slavonic" components of the Russian lexicon. All [+ Slavic] forms undergo "liquid metathesis" in the environment ——C_1. The [+ Russian] forms, however, are first subject to vowel doubling (i.e., /ər/ → [əər], whereas the [− Russian] forms are first subject to tensing (i.e., /ər/ → [ɔ̄r]). Since tense vowels are unrounded, and ultimately laxed, we find in the Church Slavonic forms the derivation /ər/ → [ɔ̄r] → [rɔ̄] (and ultimately) → [ra]; whereas in the Russian forms we derive /ər/ → [əər] → [ərə]. In addition, in the Russian forms stem-final /t/ alternates with [č] in the first person singular present tense of this class of verbs, whereas in the Church Slavonic forms the stem-final /t/ alternates with [šč].

In these instances the categories to which lexical items are assigned account not only for their phonological peculiarities but also for their behavior with respect to various

---

[22] The names we give to the categories designate their major historical source, but, of course, are not etymologically justified in detail.

morphological processes such as the choice of derivational affix and freedom of compounding.

Lexical items may also belong to categories that are much less general than those just illustrated. In fact, not infrequently an individual lexical item is exceptional in that it alone fails to undergo a given phonological rule or, alternatively, in that it is subject to some phonological rule. The copula is an example of such a highly deviant item in many languages.

The natural way to reflect such exceptional behavior in the grammar is to associate with such lexical items diacritic features referring to particular rules, that is, features of the form [αrule n], where α is, as before, a variable ranging over the values + and − and n is the number of the rule in question in the linear ordering. We must then establish precise conventions that will have the effect of excluding an item specified as [−rule n] from the domain of rule n. This can be done in various slightly different ways.

A reasonable approach within our framework seems to be the following. Suppose that rule n is (125):

$$\left(125\right) \qquad\qquad A \;\rightarrow\; B \;\;|\;\; X \text{——} Y$$

By convention, one of the features contained in A will be [+rule n], thus requiring that any segment to which the rule applies be specified as [+rule n]. Secondly, we assume that for each rule m of the phonology, the feature specification [+rule m] is automatically assigned to each unit of each lexical matrix.[23] After this obligatory assignment of [+rule m], for each m, to each unit in the lexicon, we apply convention (126):

$$\left(126\right) \quad \text{All nonphonological features of a given lexical item are distributed to every unit of this item.}$$

In particular, if a given lexical item is a human noun in the kth declensional class which is an exception to rule n, then the feature specifications [+noun], [+human], [+k^{th} declensional class], [−rule n], now reinterpreted as on a par with phonological features, are assigned to each unit in this lexical item. The assignment of [−rule m], for any m, modifies the specification [+rule m] determined by the preceding convention.[24] The ordinary conventions of rule application will now prevent the application of rule n to any of the phonological units of an item marked in the lexicon as an exception to rule n.

A few comments are necessary about this particular way of handling exceptions. First, we assume that the readjustment rules that convert a syntactically generated structure to an appropriate input to the phonology may modify or introduce diacritic features. In particular, then, they may affect specifications of the type [αrule m]. One might also raise the question whether the rules of the phonology themselves may modify these features; for example, should we permit rules of the form (127):

$$\left(127\right) \qquad\qquad A \;\rightarrow\; [\text{−rule } n] \;\;|\;\; Z \text{——} W$$

Such rules add greatly to the power of the phonology. Suppose, for example, that rule (125)

---

[23] In terms of the system developed in Chapter Nine, we assume, simply, that [+rule m] is the "unmarked" value for the feature [rule m], for each m.

[24] Convention (126) makes it possible for phonological rules to refer to any syntactic or semantic property and is thus, no doubt, far too strong. Various modifications might be proposed, but we will not go into this matter.

applies as indicated except in the context Z——W. By ordering rule (127) before rule (125), we achieve exactly this effect. Therefore rules of the form (127) permit us to formalize the notion "except"; in other words, they permit us to refer to contexts in which a rule does *not* apply, as well as to those in which it does apply. This is true even if we permit a rule such as (127) only when it is rule $n-1$ in the ordering, so that it can be reformulated as (128):

$$\left(128\right) \qquad\qquad A \;\rightarrow\; [-\text{next rule}] \;\; / \; Z \text{——} W$$

If we permit rules such as (127) to appear more freely, we add still greater power to the phonology. At various stages of our work we have experimented with rules of the form (128) and of the more powerful type (127), but we have not found any convincing example to demonstrate the need for such rules. Therefore we propose, tentatively, that rules such as (127), (128), with the great increase in descriptive power that they provide, not be permitted in the phonology: the feature [$-$rule n] must either be introduced by readjustment rules or appear as a diacritic feature in the lexical representation of an item.

Furthermore, observe that our first convention assigned the feature [$+$rule n] only to the unit A in (125), and not to the units of X and Y. Suppose, then, that we have a string $\ldots X'A'Y'\ldots$ such that A' is nondistinct from A, and X', Y' are nondistinct from X, Y except with respect to the feature [rule n]. Suppose further that X' and Y' contain units which are specified as [$-$rule n] but that A' is specified [$+$rule n]. The convention we have suggested would permit rule n to apply to $\ldots X'A'Y'\ldots$ under these circumstances; but the application of rule n to this string would be prevented if we were to adopt an alternative convention which assigned the feature [$+$rule n] to each unit of A, X, and Y in rule (125), thus requiring not only that any segment to which the rule applies be specified as [$+$rule n] but that the contextual segments be so specified as well. In brief, the issue is whether the context in which a segment appears should be permitted to block the application of a rule to this segment, even if the segment itself is not specified as an exception to this rule. It is easy to invent examples that militate against this assumption, but we have no clear cases in a real language. Considerations of plausibility, admittedly weak, have led us to adopt the convention proposed above which blocks application of a rule only when the segment to which the rule applies is itself identified as an exception to this rule. There is, in fact, one sort of example that suggests that our convention is inexact. Suppose that we have a rule of epenthesis such as (129):

$$\left(129\right) \qquad\qquad \phi \;\rightarrow\; B \;\; / \; X \text{——} Y$$

Suppose further that a lexical item $W = XY$ is an exception to this rule and is lexically marked as such. Our convention does not permit us to express this fact, but the alternative that we have rejected would allow it to be expressed readily. Such examples suggest that we reformulate the convention slightly, so that rule (125) is inapplicable to a string $\ldots X'A'Y'$ $\ldots$ (where X, A, Y are nondistinct from X', A', Y', respectively, except with regard to the feature [rule n]) if A' is specified [$-$rule n], as in the earlier convention, or if the formative containing A' is specified [$-$rule n]. This modification, which we will not take the trouble to make precise here, would account for examples such as the exceptions to epenthesis without permitting the full range of difficulties that appear to be possible consequences of the convention we have rejected, which assigns [$-$rule n] to each unit of A, X, and Y in (125). Obviously, additional empirical material is needed before this matter can be settled.

Finally, notice that our conventions imply that in a given lexical item either all segments that otherwise satisfy the condition for application of some rule will be subject to the rule or no such segments will be subject to the rule; for it is the lexical item rather than an individual segment that constitutes an exception, at least insofar as exceptions are indicated in the lexicon. For example, if a language has a rule voicing intervocalic stops and a given lexical item containing several intervocalic stops[25] is marked as exempt from this rule, then, in general, all intervocalic stops in the lexical item will be exempt from voicing. We shall not exclude the possibility that in the situation just presented an item is doubly exceptional in that one of its intervocalic stops *is* subject to the voicing rule; however, this will be quite costly, for a special readjustment rule will be required to supply the intervocalic stop in question with the feature [+Intervocalic Voicing Rule]. The diacritic features, as noted earlier, will thus have two sources, the lexicon and the readjustment rules. An example illustrating the way in which readjustment rules operate in such cases is discussed at the end of this section.

With the help of diacritic features, we can deal with many phenomena involving prosodic features—for example, the behavior of stress in languages such as Russian or Bulgarian, and pitch in languages such as Japanese or Serbo-Croatian. The salient property that distinguishes stress in Russian or Bulgarian from other phonological features is that once it is determined which vowel in the word receives the main stress, the stress contour of the word is also determined. The fact that stress must be indicated for only one vowel of a word suggests that this vowel be designated by means of a diacritic feature associated with the root of the word. There appears to be a fair amount of evidence—although a definitive demonstration is still lacking—that the location of this vowel in Russian words can be determined by quite simple rules, given the structure of the word and some idiosyncratic information about the stress behavior of the root (in particular, whether or not the root takes stress; if not, whether main stresses must be placed on the suffix following the root or on the case ending; etc.) Once these facts are known, the location of the main-stressed vowel is directly determined. In terms of the framework that has been developed here, this means that the root will have to be provided in the lexicon with a few (perhaps two or three) diacritic features which will then provide enough information for the rules to locate the main stress on some vowel in the word. Subsequent rules then determine the stress contour of the word.

The situation is rather similar in Serbo-Croatian and Japanese. As has been shown by Browne and McCawley (1965) for Serbo-Croatian and by McCawley (1965) for Japanese, the tonal contour of the word can be determined by simple rules, once the location of the vowel with high pitch is determined. As in the case of Russian stress, these facts suggest that we utilize a diacritic feature associated with the lexical formative rather than phonological features associated with a given vowel in a word. Similar mechanisms have been shown by Heeschen (1967) to account for the very intricate prosodic features of Lithuanian words.

The situation in these languages thus differs from that obtaining in true tone languages, such as Chinese or Mixtecan, where, as observed by McCawley (1965), "the number of possible pitch shapes [our 'tone contours'—NC/MH] increases geometrically as the length of the morpheme increases, rather than arithmetically as is the case in Japanese."

---

[25] These segments may not be intervocalic stops in the lexicon but only at the point where the rule in question is reached in derivations; correspondingly, we are not concerned here with intervocalic stops of the lexicon if they do not have this property at the point in derivations where the rule in question applies.

In languages such as Japanese or Russian, one need at most determine the location of a single vowel in the word in order to determine the tonal contour of the word, whereas in languages such as Mixtecan or Chinese, each vowel in the word may have its own distinctive prosodic features. Only in the latter case might it be proper to mark the prosodic features for each vowel in the lexicon rather than associating a few diacritic features with the lexical item as a whole.

Another type of phenomenon that is appropriately handled with diacritic features is vowel harmony, which is found in languages in all parts of the world. A particularly instructive example occurs in Nez Perce, an American Indian language. According to Aoki (1966), on whose study the following remarks are based, Nez Perce has, phonetically, the five vowels [i u o a æ]. The [o] is always round, but in the high back vowel [u] rounding appears to vary a great deal. The words of Nez Perce fall into two classes with regard to their utilization of vowels; in the words of the first class the vowels are selected from the set [i a o]; in the words of the second class the vowels are chosen from the set [i æ u]. Nez Perce words are composed of strings of morphemes. The morphemes themselves constitute two mutually exclusive categories: morphemes of the first category, to which we shall attribute the diacritic feature [+H], appear in words of the first class only, whereas morphemes of the second category, which we shall designate as [−H], appear in words of both classes. Hence [+H] morphemes show no vowel alternations and select their vowels from the set [i a o], whereas [−H] morphemes exhibit the vowel alternations *a–æ* and *o–u*, depending on whether the morpheme appears in a word of the first or the second class. For example, the first person possessive pronoun morpheme [na ʔ]–[næ ʔ] is [−H]; we therefore have [na ʔ+tó·t], "my father," but [næ ʔ+mǽx], "my paternal uncle." On the other hand, the morpheme for *father* appears everywhere with the vowel [o], and must therefore belong to the category [+H]. Since morphemes containing the vowel [i] may be either [+H] or [−H], this property must be indicated with the help of a diacritic feature rather than derived from the phonetic features of the vowels. Moreover, the sets of vowels in the two classes of words—[i a o] and [i æ u]—are not natural classes in any reasonable phonetic framework. This represents further evidence that the categorization should not be based on phonetic features.

In order to account for the facts just sketched, it is necessary to postulate a readjustment rule that distributes the feature [+H] to all segments of a *word* containing a single [+H] segment. (As noted above, a universal convention distributes all diacritic features to all segments of a given *lexical item*.) This readjustment rule might have the following form:

$$(130) \qquad [+\text{seg}] \;\rightarrow\; [+\text{H}] \;\bigg/ \begin{Bmatrix} \#\,X\,[+\text{H}]\,Y\text{---} \\ \text{---}Z\,[+\text{H}]\,W\,\# \end{Bmatrix}$$

As a consequence of (130), words containing a [+H] morpheme will have all their segments marked [+H]; all other words will contain only segments marked [−H]. We now need to postulate in the lexicon only the three vowels /i u a/. The phonological rules (131) will then supply the correct output:

$$(131) \qquad V \;\rightarrow\; \begin{Bmatrix} [-\text{back}] & \Big/ & \begin{bmatrix} +\text{low} \\ -\text{H} \end{bmatrix} \\[12pt] [-\text{high}] & \Big/ & \begin{bmatrix} +\text{back} \\ +\text{H} \end{bmatrix} \end{Bmatrix}$$

A certain amount of support for this analysis may be derived from comparing Nez Perce with Sahaptin, which is closely related to Nez Perce genetically. Sahaptin has the three-vowel system /i u a/, which corresponds to the Nez Perce system as illustrated in (132):

$$\left(132\right)$$

	Nez Perce	i	u	o	a	æ
	Sahaptin	i	u		a	

It is obvious that the relationship between the two vowel systems corresponds to the effects of the vowel harmony rule (131). Since Sahaptin lacks vowel harmony, this correspondence is precisely what one would expect.

A rule similar to (131) would account for the vowel harmony in such African languages as Igbo (Carnochan, 1960), Twi (Fromkin, 1965), and Fanti (Welmers, 1946). There are, however, a number of differences between the vowel harmony in these West African languages and that in Nez Perce. In the first place, in Nez Perce the diacritic feature is distributed to the entire word only if it has the coefficient + ; in the West African languages the diacritic feature is distributed to the word if it has either + or −. This can readily be effected by use of the variable notation. In the West African languages, moreover, the diacritic feature is distributed from stems alone (but see below), whereas in Nez Perce the source of the [+H] feature may be any element in the word; if a word contains a single [+H] morpheme, the entire word is marked [+H]. Finally, in the West African languages the diacritic feature in question is fully correlated with the phonological feature "covered." (See Chapter Seven, Section 4.5, for a discussion of the phonetic correlates of this feature.) As a result, instead of (131), we have the much simpler rule (133) (where H represents the diacritic feature governing harmony):

$$\left(133\right) \qquad \begin{bmatrix} +\text{voc} \\ -\text{cons} \\ \alpha\text{H} \end{bmatrix} \rightarrow [\alpha\text{covered}]$$

Rule (133), incidentally, fails to account for a curious assimilation phenomenon which has been observed in the West African languages mentioned above. According to Carnochan (1960, pp. 161–62), if a noun ending with a high vowel immediately precedes a verb that is [−H], the high vowel is [−covered], even if the noun is [+H] and the vowel should therefore have been [+covered]. This can readily be accounted for by a special readjustment rule which assigns the feature [−H] to high vowels in the position stated above, or by a phonological rule that makes the vowel [−covered].

It would appear that vowel harmony in the Ural-Altaic languages can be characterized by structurally similar rules. In a language such as Turkish there are four classes of harmonizing words, rather than two as in Nez Perce or Igbo. This fact requires that we supply each lexical item with two diacritic features instead of the single feature that was required in Nez Perce and in Igbo. Ural-Altaic vowel harmony appears to be a process that propagates from left to right, from the first vowel of the word to the last, rather than being a nondirectional property inherent in each word by virtue of its containing a particular type of morpheme. This seems to us to be only a superficial phenomenon, however, resulting from the fact that in these languages prefixation is not utilized and words are formed by suffixation alone. The evidence brought forward by Zimmer (1967) with regard to Lightner's analysis (1965b) of vowel harmony in Mongolian, which proceeded along the lines sketched here, shows that there are certain cases where the evaluation measures that have been developed up to this point would fail to decide the issue clearly one way or the other. As Zimmer notes, in order to resolve the matter in favor of the approach advocated here, one would have to enrich the descriptive machinery in some way so as to make readjustment rules such as (130) formally less complex, that is, more economical, than the phonological rules having the equivalent effect. This seems to us the proper solution; since vowel harmony is a process available to languages, this fact should be formally recognized by incorporating into the theory a device especially designed to reflect it. At the present time we are unable to make specific suggestions as to the nature of this device. The problem, however, is not one of principle but rather one of a scarcity of data for choosing among the many alternatives that readily come to mind.

It was observed above that diacritic features may be assigned to particular segments by readjustment rules. This possibility may be illustrated by the following example from the Russian conjugation.

It has been shown by Lightner (1965a) that in the underlying representations of Russian there are two parallel sets of vowels, tense and nontense. The nontense high vowels never appear in the output; they are either deleted by rule (134), or they are lowered by rule (135) and thus appear phonetically as [e] or [o]:

$$
(134) \quad
\begin{bmatrix} +\text{voc} \\ -\text{cons} \\ -\text{tense} \\ +\text{high} \end{bmatrix}
\rightarrow \phi \; / \; \underline{}
\left\{
\begin{matrix}
\# \\
C_1 \begin{bmatrix} +\text{voc} \\ -\text{cons} \\ \left\{ \begin{matrix} -\text{high} \\ +\text{tense} \end{matrix} \right\} \end{bmatrix}
\end{matrix}
\right\}
$$

$$
(135) \quad
\begin{bmatrix} +\text{voc} \\ -\text{cons} \\ -\text{tense} \end{bmatrix}
\rightarrow [-\text{high}]
$$

Thus, high nontense vowels are deleted at the end of a word or if followed in the next syllable by a vowel which is tense or nonhigh; elsewhere, they become nonhigh. These two rules account for alternations such as the following, in the nominative and genitive singular:

$$
(136) \quad
\begin{matrix}
/\text{rut}+\text{u}/ & \rightarrow & [\text{rot}] & & /\text{rut}+\text{a}/ & \rightarrow & [\text{rta}] & & (\text{mouth}) \\
/\text{lid}+\text{u}/ & \rightarrow & [\text{l,ed}] & & /\text{lid}+\text{a}/ & \rightarrow & [\text{l,da}] & & (\text{ice}) \\
& & (\rightarrow & [\text{l,od}]) & & & & &
\end{matrix}
$$

Among the exceptions to rule (134) is the suffix /isk/. The vowel of this suffix is not deleted by the rule if the stem to which the suffix is attached ends with a velar or palatal consonant, that is, a consonant which is [−anterior, −coronal]. In the output, velars in this position are usually actualized as strident palato-alveolars because velars before front vowels undergo the so-called "first palatalization" (see Chapter Nine). Thus we have [s,ib,írskəy], "Siberian," [r,ímskəy], "Roman," [uč,ít,il,skəy], "teacher" (adj.), but [gr,éč,iskəy], "Greek," [manášiskəy], "monkish," [múžiskəy], "masculine" (gram.) In addition there is a further layer of exceptions to the exceptions just cited, namely, forms in which the suffix /isk/ follows a nonanterior consonant but in which the vowel of the suffix is deleted: e.g., [mušskóy], "manly," [vólšskəy], "Volga" (adj.), [čéšskəy], "Czech" (adj.)

To account for the above facts, we may postulate a readjustment rule with the effects of (137):

$$
(137) \quad \begin{bmatrix} +\text{voc} \\ -\text{cons} \\ +\text{high} \\ -\text{back} \\ -\text{tense} \end{bmatrix} \rightarrow [-\text{rule (134)}] \quad / \quad \begin{bmatrix} +\text{cons} \\ -\text{ant} \\ -\text{D} \end{bmatrix} + \underline{\quad} \text{sk} +
$$

This rule exempts the vowel of the suffix /isk/ from deletion by rule (134) if the stem to which the suffix is attached ends with a velar or palatal consonant, unless the stem is marked with the special diacritic feature [+D] which indicates that it is an exception to the readjustment rule (137).

8. Lexical representation

A language contains a stock of items which, under various modifications, constitute the words of the language. Associated with each such item is whatever information is needed to determine its sound, meaning, and syntactic behavior, given the system of grammatical rules. Hence this information ultimately determines the sound and meaning of particular words in specific linguistic contexts. Evidently, this knowledge constitutes part of the knowledge of the speaker of the language. He makes use of it not only in his normal linguistic behavior, but also in explaining the meaning of a word, in distinguishing rhyming from nonrhyming pairs of words, in determining whether verse is properly constructed (given certain canons), in seeking a word with a particular meaning, and so on. To represent this aspect of linguistic competence, the grammar must contain a lexicon listing the items which ultimately make up the words of the language. Clearly, the lexicon may contain different items for different individuals, and a given speaker may revise and expand his lexicon throughout his life.

As noted above, knowledge of lexical structure goes beyond familiarity with a list of lexical items. For example, speakers can distinguish in various ways among items that are not in their lexicon. Certain "nonsense" forms are so close to English that they might be taken by the speaker to be accidental gaps in his knowledge of the language: e.g., *brillig, karulize, thode*. Other forms, such as *gnip, rtut*, or *psik*, will almost certainly be ruled out as "not English." To account for these and other facts, we must assume that there is more structure to the internalized lexicon than merely the list of known items. An examination of the additional structure that must be presupposed is the subject of the present section.

In order for a lexical item to be used in a well-formed sentence, two types of information are required. First, we must have information about the syntactic and morphological characteristics of the item; we must know, for example, that the item *write* is a verb, that it takes an inanimate object, that it is an irregular verb of a specific subtype, and so on. As we have seen, information of this type can be provided by the syntactic and diacritic features that form part of each lexical entry. The second type of information required for proper use of a lexical item relates to its physical, phonetic actualization. Such information is embodied in a classificatory matrix in which the columns stand for the successive segments, the rows represent features, and the entry at the intersection of a particular column and row indicates whether the item in question belongs to the category of items that are positively specified or to the category of items that are negatively specified for the given feature in the particular segment. As indicated above, classificatory matrices are ultimately converted into phonetic matrices, in which the columns represent successive phonetic segments and the rows represent specific phonetic features, that is, aspects of vocal tract behavior that are under the voluntary control of the speaker,[26] and into internally produced elements that play a role in perceptual processing.

Other things being equal, the more direct the relationship between classificatory and phonetic matrices, the less complex—the more highly valued—will be the resulting grammar. Insofar as language-specific rules are proposed that express an indirect relation between classificatory and phonetic matrices, these rules must be justified by showing that they lead to economies in other parts of the grammar that more than compensate for the complexity that they introduce.

Languages differ with respect to the sounds they use and the sound sequences they permit in words. Thus each language places certain conditions on the form of phonetic matrices and hence on the configurations of pluses and minuses (indicating membership in one of a pair of complementary categories) that may appear as entries in the classificatory matrices of the lexicon. These constraints make it possible to predict, in a given language, the specification of features in particular segments. Such predictability applies to segments in isolation (e.g., in Finnish, all obstruents are voiceless) as well as to segments in particular contexts (e.g., in English, /s/ is the only true consonant admissible before a true consonant in word-initial position). Rules describing these constraints can readily be formulated within our framework, and can be interpreted as specifying the coefficients of particular features in particular environments. It is therefore natural to propose that such rules be incorporated in the grammar and that the features that are predictable be left unspecified in lexical entries (Halle, 1959). If we then extend the simplicity criterion to the lexicon, we can distinguish between admissible and inadmissible matrices (possible and impossible words) in what seems a natural way. Thus, when a rule specifying coefficients of features in certain configurations is added to the lexicon, the predicted values can be left unspecified in lexical entries. We might propose that if the number of predicted coefficients is greater than the number of specified features in the rule in question, then the addition of the rule to the grammar represents a true generalization. Once added to the grammar, this rule excludes certain unattested configurations that would be inconsistent with it. On the other hand, when all such rules are added, there will still be many unattested configurations consistent with this "simplest set" of rules; these, then, would be the "accidental gaps," the

---

[26] The interaction among successive segments and specific features may be complex, and the principles that relate a phonetic matrix to a physical event obviously involve processes that go well beyond a segment— that may even involve whole utterances. Hence it should be understood that when we speak of successive phonetic segments we do not refer to simple temporal succession, and when we refer to aspects of vocal tract behavior we do not presuppose independence of these aspects.

admissible, unrealized matrices. Thus we can draw the distinction between admissible and inadmissible configurations in terms of a rather natural extension of the method of evaluation to the lexicon.[27]

The rules that describe lexical constraints in this fashion have been called "morpheme structure rules" or "lexical redundancy rules" and form a part of the readjustment component. In many respects, they seem to be exactly like ordinary phonological rules, in form and function. Thus certain regularities are observed within lexical items as well as across certain boundaries—the rule governing voicing in obstruent sequences in Russian, for example—and to avoid duplication of such rules in the grammar it is necessary to regard them not as redundancy rules but as phonological rules that also happen to apply internally to a lexical item. Nevertheless, there are certain difficulties in formulating redundancy rules within the framework outlined for ordinary phonological rules, difficulties which suggest that the conception just sketched is in need of revision.

It was observed by Lightner (1963) that the appearance of unspecified features in lexical representations allows for specious simplifications. The problem arises in connection with the convention for application of the rule $A \rightarrow B \mid X$——Y to a matrix when features mentioned in A, X, or Y are unspecified in this matrix. For example, consider the rule (138):

$$(138) \qquad\qquad [+A] \quad \rightarrow \quad [+B]$$

A convention must be established to determine whether or not the rule should apply to a one-segment matrix unspecified for the feature A. Two fairly natural conventions suggest themselves. Let R be the rule $A \rightarrow B \mid X$——Y.

(139) The rule R applies to a matrix M only if XAY is a *submatrix* of M.

(140) The rule R applies to a matrix M unless M is distinct from XAY, in the sense of distinctness defined in (11).

Under convention (139), the rule (138) would not apply to a segment unspecified for the feature A; under convention (140), on the other hand, the rule (138) would apply to such a segment. However, Lightner showed that both conventions lead to specious simplifications in that they make it possible to distinguish items that are not represented as distinct in the lexicon. We can see this from the following examples.

Consider two segments which are nondistinct, one totally unspecified except for the feature [segment], and the other specified only for the feature [X]:

$$(141) \qquad\qquad [+\text{seg}] \, , \quad \begin{bmatrix} +\text{seg} \\ +X \end{bmatrix}$$

Suppose that the two segments of (141) are subject to rules in accordance with the convention (139). Given the rules (142), we obtain the derivations (143):

$$(142) \qquad\qquad
\begin{array}{lll}
\text{(a)} & [+\text{seg}] & \rightarrow \quad [-Y] \\
\text{(b)} & [+X] & \rightarrow \quad [+Y] \\
\text{(c)} & [-Y] & \rightarrow \quad [-X]
\end{array}$$

---

[27] For additional discussion, see Halle (1959), Chomsky (1964), Chomsky and Halle (1965).

$$\left(143\right)$$

$$[+\text{seg}] \qquad \begin{bmatrix} +\text{seg} \\ +X \end{bmatrix}$$

$$\begin{bmatrix} +\text{seg} \\ -Y \end{bmatrix} \qquad \begin{bmatrix} +\text{seg} \\ +X \\ -Y \end{bmatrix} \qquad \text{RULE (142a)}$$

$$\begin{bmatrix} +\text{seg} \\ +X \\ +Y \end{bmatrix} \qquad \text{RULE (142b)}$$

$$\begin{bmatrix} +\text{seg} \\ -X \\ -Y \end{bmatrix} \qquad \text{RULE (142c)}$$

Thus the rules (142) have converted nondistinct segments into segments that are distinct with respect to all features.

Assume now that the two segments of (141) are subject to rules under the distinctness interpretation of convention (140). Then these segments can be rendered distinct by the rule (144):

$$\left(144\right) \qquad\qquad [-X] \;\rightarrow\; [-X]$$

If rules of the type (144) are disallowed on general grounds, the same incorrect result as in (143) can be obtained by the set of rules (145):

$$\left(145\right)$$

$$\begin{array}{lll} \text{(a)} & [+\text{seg}] & \rightarrow \;\; [+Y] \\ \text{(b)} & [-X] & \rightarrow \;\; [-Y] \\ \text{(c)} & [-Y] & \rightarrow \;\; [-X] \end{array}$$

With these rules, we have the derivation (146):

$$\left(146\right)$$

$$[+\text{seg}] \qquad \begin{bmatrix} +\text{seg} \\ +X \end{bmatrix}$$

$$\begin{bmatrix} +\text{seg} \\ +Y \end{bmatrix} \qquad \begin{bmatrix} +\text{seg} \\ +X \\ +Y \end{bmatrix} \qquad \text{RULE (145a)}$$

$$\begin{bmatrix} +\text{seg} \\ -Y \end{bmatrix} \qquad \text{RULE (145b)}$$

$$\begin{bmatrix} +\text{seg} \\ -X \\ -Y \end{bmatrix} \qquad \text{RULE (145c)}$$

It is clear that derivations such as (143) and (146) must not be allowed, since they permit us to distinguish three entities with the use of a single binary feature: the rules (142) or (145) allow us to distinguish $[+\text{seg}]$ from $\begin{bmatrix} +\text{seg} \\ +X \end{bmatrix}$; an analogous set of rules will allow us to distinguish $[+\text{seg}]$ from $\begin{bmatrix} +\text{seg} \\ -X \end{bmatrix}$, which is, of course, distinct from $\begin{bmatrix} +\text{seg} \\ +X \end{bmatrix}$ by definition.

If derivations such as (143) and (146) are allowed, the classificatory features are no longer binary, but rather ternary, for an unspecified feature can be distinguished from both a positively and a negatively specified feature. Hence, in a system such as this, the fact that no cost attaches to unspecified features represents a specious simplification, since lack of specification is treated as a value distinct from—and thus on a par with—the values plus and minus.

As a matter of fact, in our descriptive practice no such illicit simplifications were ever made; the grammars were always so devised that at the point at which a rule $A \rightarrow B \mid X \underline{\hspace{1em}} Y$ was applied, all features mentioned in A, X, Y had already been specified by prior rules if they had not already been specified in the lexicon. It might therefore be proposed that this be made a formal requirement on grammars; i.e., that we impose the condition (147):

$\left(147\right)$ A grammar is not well-formed if in any derivation the rule $A \rightarrow B \mid X \underline{\hspace{1em}} Y$ is available for application to a matrix M which is not distinct from XAY and of which XAY is not a submatrix.

The imposition of condition (147) fails to resolve the difficulty properly, however, since it makes it impossible to determine whether a grammar is well-formed by an elementary inspection of the grammar itself; instead it is necessary to examine a large class of derivations permitted by this grammar. This is surely an unacceptable consequence. A grammar represents a particular speaker's competence in some language. Since only well-formed grammars are acquired and since such grammars are acquired in a reasonably short time, the question of well-formedness must be decidable by a procedure that terminates quite rapidly. Under condition (147), this is not the case; therefore, it follows that this condition cannot realistically be imposed on grammars.[28]

As an alternative to (147) it has been proposed that we impose the condition (148):

$\left(148\right)$ Lexical entries must be pairwise distinct.

This requirement would rule out pairs of matrices such as those in (141). It would, however, give rise to problems of a different sort, as pointed out by Stanley (1967).

Consider the following observations about lexical items in English:

$\left(149\right)$ (a) The segment preceding a final string consisting of a liquid followed by one or more consonants is always a vowel.

(b) The segment following an initial liquid is always a vowel.

More formally, these two facts might be embodied in the following two redundancy rules:

$\left(150\right)$ (a) $[+\text{seg}] \rightarrow \begin{bmatrix} +\text{voc} \\ -\text{cons} \end{bmatrix} \Big/ \underline{\hspace{1em}} \begin{bmatrix} +\text{voc} \\ +\text{cons} \end{bmatrix} \begin{bmatrix} -\text{voc} \\ +\text{cons} \end{bmatrix}_1 +$

(b) $[+\text{seg}] \rightarrow \begin{bmatrix} +\text{voc} \\ -\text{cons} \end{bmatrix} \Big/ + \begin{bmatrix} +\text{voc} \\ +\text{cons} \end{bmatrix} \underline{\hspace{1em}}$

It is clear that given these two rules it should be unnecessary to specify in a lexical entry that the initial segment in an item such as *ilk* or the second segment of an item such as *rip*

---

[28] The discussion of rule (20) in Chapter Nine presents further difficulties associated with this convention.

is $\begin{bmatrix} +\text{vocalic} \\ -\text{consonantal} \end{bmatrix}$. We should therefore represent the features "vocalic" and "consonantal" in the two lexical items as in (151):

$\left(151\right)$

(a) *rip*

vocalic	+		−
consonantal	+		+

(b) *ilk*

vocalic		+	−
consonantal		+	+

We note immediately that the two matrices in (151) are not distinct and therefore violate condition (148). In order to make the matrices distinct, we have to specify the feature "consonantal" in one of them. This specification, however, is redundant in the sense that it is predicted by (150); furthermore, the choice of the lexical entry to be specified in this way is quite arbitrary. These facts suggest that condition (148) is not altogether appropriate.

Observe that the choice of the item in which the redundant feature is to be specified in (151) depends on the order that we establish among the rules in (150), if we accept some analog of (147) as an appropriate requirement for grammars. If we let (150a) precede (150b), then the redundant feature must be specified in the representation of *rip*; if the order is reversed, the redundant feature must be specified in the representation of *ilk*. In neither case, however, can one provide a motivation for the order chosen. This would seem to indicate that there is something wrong with a requirement that redundancy rules apply in a fixed order.

It has also been pointed out by Stanley (1967) that ordering of redundancy rules can be used to effect specious simplifications of yet another sort. Consider a language which admits only lexical items with the structure CVCVCVCV.... For such a language we should postulate the redundancy rules (152a,b) (see page 344 for discussion of the ( )* notation):

$\left(152\right)$

(a) $[+\text{seg}] \rightarrow \begin{bmatrix} -\text{voc} \\ +\text{cons} \end{bmatrix} \Big/ + ([+\text{seg}][+\text{seg}])^* ——$

(b) $[+\text{seg}] \rightarrow \begin{bmatrix} +\text{voc} \\ -\text{cons} \end{bmatrix} \Big/ —— ([+\text{seg}][+\text{seg}])^* +$

That is to say, counting segments from the beginning of the item, every odd-numbered segment is a consonant; and counting segments from the end, every odd-numbered segment is a vowel. As a result of these rules, the features "vocalic" and "consonantal" need not be specified in any lexical entry of this language. Assume now that we decide to "simplify" the lexicon even further by omitting a particular consonant X from the initial position in all lexical entries of the form X.... At first sight, it would appear that such an illegitimate "simplification" would be ruled out on the grounds that it destroys the very far-reaching generalization about the structure of lexical items embodied in rule (152). Thus it would seem that if the consonant X is omitted in initial position, this rule can no longer be a redundancy rule, and therefore it will be necessary to specify in lexical representations features which otherwise could have been left unspecified. This, however, is not true. As noted by Stanley, nothing prevents us from reintroducing the (incorrectly) omitted consonants by a rule that applies before (152). Hence, by the time (152) applies, the *status quo ante* is restored.

It is, of course, possible to rule out specious simplifications of the type just discussed by the simple expedient of prohibiting redundancy rules that insert segments. Alternatively, it is possible to achieve the same result by requiring that redundancy rules apply simultaneously rather than in sequence. The latter decision would make the redundancy rules formally quite different from the true phonological rules.

The requirement that redundancy rules apply simultaneously is attractive in several respects. For one thing, no good examples have been discovered of empirically significant generalizations that result from ordering these rules. Hence any ordering that has been presented has actually been rather unmotivated. In contrast, the ordering of phonological rules has generally been discovered to be well motivated, and very narrowly constrained. Furthermore, there are difficulties beyond those just mentioned that can be avoided if the redundancy rules are regarded as unordered. As a case in point, Stanley (1967) cites the restrictions on obstruents in Indo-European obstruent-vowel-obstruent roots. Since Indo-European possessed the three series of obstruents in (153), we expect to find nine distinct types of roots of the form obstruent-vowel-obstruent, as in (154): ·

$$
(153) \qquad
\begin{bmatrix} -\text{voice} \\ -\text{aspirated} \end{bmatrix}
\begin{bmatrix} +\text{voice} \\ -\text{aspirated} \end{bmatrix}
\begin{bmatrix} +\text{voice} \\ +\text{aspirated} \end{bmatrix}
$$

$$
(154) \qquad
\begin{array}{ccc}
\text{tek} & \text{teg} & \text{*teg}^{\text{h}} \\
\text{dek} & \text{*deg} & \text{deg}^{\text{h}} \\
\text{*d}^{\text{h}}\text{ek} & \text{d}^{\text{h}}\text{eg} & \text{d}^{\text{h}}\text{eg}^{\text{h}}
\end{array}
$$

As is well known, forms of the types starred in (154) are not found. With ordered redundancy rules, we might express these facts as in (155):

$$
(155) \qquad
[-\text{son}] \ \rightarrow \
\begin{cases}
[-\text{asp}] & / \ + \begin{bmatrix} -\text{son} \\ -\text{voice} \end{bmatrix} \begin{bmatrix} +\text{voc} \\ -\text{cons} \end{bmatrix} \underline{\quad} + \\[2ex]
[\alpha\text{voice}] & / \ + \begin{bmatrix} -\text{son} \\ +\text{voice} \\ -\text{asp} \end{bmatrix} \begin{bmatrix} +\text{voc} \\ -\text{cons} \end{bmatrix} \begin{bmatrix} \underline{\quad} \\ \alpha\text{asp} \end{bmatrix} + \\[2ex]
[+\text{voice}] & / \ + \begin{bmatrix} -\text{son} \\ +\text{asp} \end{bmatrix} \begin{bmatrix} +\text{voc} \\ -\text{cons} \end{bmatrix} \underline{\quad} +
\end{cases}
$$

There is, however, no reason to assume that the restriction has directionality, i.e., should be formalized to operate from left to right. Equivalently we could propose restrictions where the last obstruent determines the first:

$$
(156) \qquad
[-\text{son}] \ \rightarrow \
\begin{cases}
[-\text{asp}] & / \ + \underline{\quad} \begin{bmatrix} +\text{voc} \\ -\text{cons} \end{bmatrix} \begin{bmatrix} -\text{son} \\ -\text{voice} \end{bmatrix} + \\[2ex]
[\alpha\text{voice}] & / \ + \begin{bmatrix} \underline{\quad} \\ \alpha\text{asp} \end{bmatrix} \begin{bmatrix} +\text{voc} \\ -\text{cons} \end{bmatrix} \begin{bmatrix} -\text{son} \\ +\text{voice} \\ -\text{asp} \end{bmatrix} + \\[2ex]
[+\text{voice}] & / \ + \underline{\quad} \begin{bmatrix} +\text{voc} \\ -\text{cons} \end{bmatrix} \begin{bmatrix} -\text{son} \\ +\text{asp} \end{bmatrix} +
\end{cases}
$$

As Stanley correctly remarks, the facts sketched in (154) can be expressed more naturally by stating that items of the form (157) are excluded:

$$
(157) \qquad
\begin{bmatrix} -\text{son} \\ \alpha\text{voice} \\ \beta\text{asp} \end{bmatrix}
\begin{bmatrix} +\text{voc} \\ -\text{cons} \end{bmatrix}
\begin{bmatrix} -\text{son} \\ -\beta\text{voice} \\ -\alpha\text{asp} \end{bmatrix}
$$

Equivalently, this constraint can be stated as a positive condition requiring that every item of the type in question be of the form:

$$
(158) \quad
\begin{bmatrix} -\text{son} \\ \alpha\text{voice} \\ \beta\text{asp} \end{bmatrix}
\begin{bmatrix} +\text{voc} \\ -\text{cons} \end{bmatrix}
\begin{bmatrix} -\text{son} \\ \gamma\text{voice} \\ \delta\text{asp} \end{bmatrix}
$$

where $\alpha = \delta$ or $\beta = \gamma$

We have no notion of "simplicity" available that has any bearing on the choice between these alternative and equivalent formulations. We therefore adopt the positively stated condition (158), in conformity with our general practice.

The redundancy rules of the type considered heretofore (e.g., (150)) express certain "if-then" constraints: they state that if some segment (or configuration) of a matrix is specified in accordance with condition C_1, then some segment (or configuration) must be specified in accordance with condition C_2. Thinking of a redundancy rule in this way, we may say that (158) expresses an "if-and-only-if" constraint: it states that the first segment meets a certain condition if and only if the last segment meets a corresponding condition, there being four possibilities, all told. Hence such examples indicate that "biconditional constraints" exist alongside of the "conditional constraints" expressed by redundancy rules of the form discussed earlier.

An interesting example of a biconditional constraint combined with a conditional constraint on the structure of lexical items is found in the Central African language Ngbaka. This language is reported to have the seven-vowel system in (159):

$$
(159) \quad
\begin{array}{ccc}
\text{i} & & \text{u} \\
\text{e} & & \text{o} \\
\varepsilon & \text{a} & \mathrm{\mathopen{}\mathopen{}ɔ} \\
\end{array}
$$

Since there are seven vowels in the language, one might expect 49 different vowel-vowel patterns in bisyllabic formatives. In fact, only 35 patterns are admitted, for "if a disyllabic word contains /i/, it does not also contain /u/; if /e/, it does not also contain /ɔ/, /ɛ/, or /o/; if /u/, it does not also contain /i/; if /o/, it does not also contain /e/, /ɛ/, or /ɔ/; and if /ɔ/, it does not also contain /ɛ/, /e/, or /o/" (Wescott, 1965). These constraints do not affect /a/ but only vowels in which the coefficients for roundness and backness agree. The restriction on lexical items of Ngbaka, therefore, reads as follows:

$$
(160) \quad C_0
\begin{bmatrix} +\text{voc} \\ -\text{cons} \\ \alpha\text{back} \\ \beta\text{round} \\ \gamma\text{high} \\ \delta\text{low} \end{bmatrix}
C_0
\begin{bmatrix} +\text{voc} \\ -\text{cons} \\ \varepsilon\text{back} \\ \zeta\text{round} \\ \eta\text{high} \\ \theta\text{low} \end{bmatrix}
$$

Condition: if $\alpha = \beta$ and $\varepsilon = \zeta$, then either $\gamma = -\eta$
or ($\alpha = \varepsilon$, $\beta = \zeta$, and $\delta = \theta$).

That is, in bisyllabic formatives containing no /a/, the vowels either differ with regard to the feature "high" or they are identical.

Conditions such as (158) and (160) are directly formulable in terms of the notions discussed in the Appendix. We note there that certain truth-functional conditions are required for the phonological rules; the conditions now being discussed make rather extensive use of these possibilities. The essential innovation required by the last set of examples is that the redundancy rules be interpreted as conditions on the lexicon, rather than as rules to be applied in sequence in the manner of phonological rules. They can be thought of as filters that accept or reject certain proposed matrices but that do not modify the feature composition of a matrix as a phonological rule does.

Continuing to follow Stanley's exposition, we next turn to the question of how redundancy conditions are integrated into the lexical component of the grammar. Suppose that the language to be described has a lexicon in which the longest item contains *l* segments. We can thus form a finite set U containing all matrices of logically possible fully specified segments which are less than or equal to *l* segments in length. From the set U we now form a smaller set M(U) containing all the matrices that satisfy the redundancy conditions for the language being described. These redundancy conditions thus function as a set of filters, passing only acceptable matrices; and the set of these acceptable matrices constitutes M(U).

The set M(U), however, is not identical with the set of items found in the lexicon. We must now relate lexical entries to the matrices in M(U). Since the lexical entries will be incompletely specified matrices whereas the matrices in M(U) are fully specified, it will be the case that every lexical entry will be a submatrix of at least one matrix in M(U).[29] We now impose the condition (161):

$$\left(161\right) \quad \text{Every lexical entry Q must be so specified as to be distinct from all but one fully specified matrix in M(U).}$$

We call the one matrix in M(U) that is not distinct from Q the "systematic phonemic matrix" of Q. Condition (161) is weaker than the requirement (148) that any two lexical matrices must be distinct. To see this, consider the redundancy condition (150). This condition admits into M(U) the two matrices of (162) but excludes matrices that have nonvowels in the relevant positions:

$$\left(162\right)$$

(a)
vocalic	+	+	−
consonantal	+	−	+

(b)
vocalic	+	+	−
consonantal	−	+	+

Observe now that the lexical representations (151) are not distinct; however, (151a) is distinct from (162b) and (151b) is distinct from (162a).

We now adopt the convention that a lexical matrix which is incompletely specified is automatically supplied with all features specified in the matrix of M(U) which is the systematic phonemic representation of the lexical entry in question. In other words, (151a) will be supplied with all the features of (162a), and (151b) will be supplied with all the features of (162b).

---

[29] We must expect to find that certain lexical entries are distinct from all items in M(U). These are the true exceptions, examples of which in English are such words as *pueblo* and *sthenic*, as well as numerous proper nouns and foreign borrowings that have found their way into normal use. Notice that if the lexicon is subdivided into several major categories (native and foreign, Romance and Germanic, etc.) by diacritic features such as those discussed in Section 7, then differences in the redundancy conditions for these sets can be characterized directly within the framework just outlined by truth-functional conditions on feature specifications.

We might handle exceptions in the following way. Given a set M(U) of fully specified matrices which satisfy the redundancy conditions, we can also consider a set M'(U) which is larger than M(U) and satisfies all but one, or several, of the conditions. If an entry is an exception to a particular condition C, it can be so marked in the lexicon, and this will mean that this entry will have to select its "systematic phonemic representation" (see the discussion of (161)) not from the set M(U), but rather from the larger set M'(U).

It is obvious that each new redundancy condition will make the set M(U) smaller; if it did not have this consequence, there would be no point in adding it to the grammar. Moreover, the smaller the set M(U), the smaller, in general, the number of features that will have to be specified in a lexical entry in order to satisfy the condition that it be distinct from all but one matrix in M(U). Thus, we are able to extend the evaluation measure to the lexicon in a natural way, for we can require that each redundancy condition result in a saving of features in the lexical representations that is larger than the number of features required to state the condition itself.

This concludes our discussion of the organization of the lexicon and of the devices required for the statement of regularities in the structure of lexical items. We shall not state the redundancy conditions for English, since we believe that the above is but an interim solution to the difficulties that have been sketched. A more adequate solution will require a more radical revision of the conception of phonology than has been presented in this book, and it is to a brief discussion of this new conception that we devote the final chapter.

Appendix: Formalism

In this Appendix we shall restate succinctly the formalism used for presenting phonological rules and the schemata that represent them, the interpretation of this formalism, and the system of evaluation that we have proposed. Our general assumption is that the phonology consists of a linearly ordered sequence of rules that apply to a surface structure in accordance with the principle of the transformational cycle, within the phonological phrase. Certain of these rules, the rules of word phonology, apply only when the level of a word (as defined in Section 6.2) is reached in the cycle. Under formal conditions of a highly abstract sort, the relation of disjunctive ordering is assigned to certain pairs of rules. The sequence of rules is represented by a minimal schema that assigns a value to this sequence and also determines the relationship of disjunctive ordering. As we have noted, it is a significant fact that the same formal notions are involved in the very different functions of determining an evaluation measure and assigning disjunctive ordering.

Throughout this book we have been thinking of rules as certain formal expressions to which certain notational operations can be applied, forming schemata. Continuing along these lines, we can regard rules as expressions built up out of the following primitive elements:

$$\begin{pmatrix}1\end{pmatrix}$$ PRIMITIVES

   (a) *features*: $F_1, \ldots, F_q$ (F_1 is the feature "segment")
   (b) *specifications*: $+, -, 1, 2, \ldots, N$
   (c) *categories*: $C_1, \ldots, C_t$
   (d) ϕ ("zero")
   (e) $\rightarrow$ ("rewrite as")

The features of (a) are, we propose, those listed in Chapter Seven, Section 2, along with a certain stock of diacritic features.[1] The number N in (b) indicates the maximal degree of differentiation permitted for any linguistic feature. The categories $C_1, \ldots, C_t$ are provided by the theory of universal grammar; these are the categories "sentence," "noun phrase," "noun," "verb," etc., which we assumed to be characterized in a uniform, language-independent fashion and to be available for any syntactic description.[2] The zero symbol of (d) is not to be confused with the identity element of the system of concatenation, which we designate by the conventional symbol e.

We can form strings from the primitive symbols of (1) by concatenation. We say that X is a substring of Y if $X = X_1 \ldots X_n$ and $Y = Y_1 X_1 \ldots Y_n X_n Y_{n+1}$ (where any of the Y_i's may be null). For example, among the strings that can be formed are (2) and (3), (3) being a substring of (2):

$$\begin{pmatrix}2\end{pmatrix} \quad \rightarrow + -F_1 + F_5 + \rightarrow F_1 + F_6 F_3 C_3 - \rightarrow + F_1 - F_2 + F_1 - \rightarrow F_4 + + F_3 C_3 +$$

---

[1] Technically speaking, the number of diacritic features should be at least as large as the number of rules in the phonology. Hence, unless there is a bound on the length of a phonology, the set (a) should be unlimited. There is no point of principle involved here, and to simplify exposition slightly we shall assume the set to be limited by an a priori condition. A similar comment applies to (1b).

[2] See Chomsky (1965, pp. 115 f.) for some discussion of this matter.

$$\left(3\right) \quad +F_1+F_5+F_1+F_3C_3 \rightarrow +F_1-F_2+F_1+F_3C_3$$

Of these, an interpretation will be assigned only to (3), (2) being totally meaningless. The string (3) will be interpreted as (4), which would be written as (5) in the notation that we have been using so far:

$\left(4\right)$ A segment specified as $[+F_5]$ is further specified as $[-F_2]$ when it is followed by a segment specified $[+F_3]$ at the right-hand end of a phrase of the type C_3.

$$\left(5\right) \qquad \begin{bmatrix} +F_1 \\ +F_5 \end{bmatrix} \rightarrow [-F_2] \ / \ \underline{\hspace{2em}} \begin{bmatrix} +F_1 \\ +F_3 \end{bmatrix}]c_3$$

Of the various strings that can be constructed, we are concerned only with those of the following types:

$\left(6\right)$
(a) *specified feature*: αX, where α is a specification and X is a feature.
(b) *unit*: $\alpha F_1 \beta_1 F_{i_1} \ldots \beta_m F_{i_m}$, where $\alpha = +$ or $-$, β_i is a specification, and $F_1 F_{i_1} \ldots F_{i_m}$ is a substring of $F_1 \ldots F_q$.
(c) *matrix*: $X_1 \ldots X_m$, where X_i is a unit.
(d) *rule*: $ZXAYW \rightarrow ZXBYW$, where A and B may be ϕ or any unit; $A \neq B$; X and Y may be matrices; Z or W may be C_i, for some i; Z, X, Y, W may be null; and where these are the only possibilities.[3]

We say that the unit defined in (6b) is "composed of" the specified features αF_1, $\beta_1 F_{i_1}, \ldots, \beta_m F_{i_m}$.

What we have so far defined is simply a linearized version of rules of the form we have been discussing all along, the only difference being that we now insist that the feature [segment] be specified in every column (i.e., every unit) of a matrix, and that the features in a unit be given in a fixed order, as determined by (1a) (a condition that we will modify—see p. 397). Thus (3) is a rule of the form (6d), with Z and X null, $A = +F_1+F_5$, $B = +F_1-F_2$, $Y = +F_1+F_3$, and $W = C_3$.

We say that X is "contained in" Y under the following condition:

$\left(7\right)$ $X = X_1 \ldots X_m$ and $Y = Y_1 \ldots Y_m$, where X_i and Y_i are units and the specified features of which X_i is composed constitute a subset of the specified features of which Y_i is composed.

Furthermore, we extend the notion "contained" so that ϕ is contained in e and e is contained in e.

We must now explain how a rule applies to a matrix bounded by category symbols, that is, to a domain of the sort we have been considering throughout.

Let R be the rule $ZXAYW \rightarrow ZXBYW$, where Z, X, A, B, Y, W are as in (6d). We say that R "is applicable to" a string D, which is its domain, if $D = C_i \varphi_1 \psi_1 \psi_2 \psi_3 \varphi_2 C_i$, where the following conditions are met:

$\left(8\right)$
(a) X, A, and Y are contained in ψ_1, ψ_2, ψ_3, respectively.
(b) If $Z = C_k$, then $k = i$ and $\varphi_1 = e$; if $W = C_k$, then $k = i$ and $\varphi_2 = e$.
(c) $\varphi_1 \psi_1 \psi_2 \psi_3 \varphi_2$ is a matrix.

Under these conditions, we say, more explicitly, that R "is applicable to D with the analysis" C_i, φ_1, ψ_1, ψ_2, ψ_3, φ_2, C_i.

[3] Note that if $Z = C_i$ and $W = C_j$, then $i = j$.

Under the same conditions on R and D, we say that the "result of applying R to D" is the string $D' = C_i\varphi_1\psi_1\omega\psi_3\varphi_2C_i$, where ω is determined by ψ_2 and B in the following way:

$\begin{pmatrix}9\end{pmatrix}$ (a) If $B = \phi$, then $\omega = e$.
  (b) If B is a unit, then ω is a unit containing each specified feature that appears in B and each specified feature αF_j of ψ_2 such that F_j does not appear in B.

If R is not applicable to D, we say that the "result of applying R to D" is D itself.

Observe that the result of applying R to D may not be uniquely defined if Z or W is null. For example, consider the rule $A \rightarrow B$ and the domain C_iAAC_i. As we have defined "result of applying," the result of applying this rule to this domain is C_iBAC_i and it is also C_iABC_i; but what we want, clearly, is rather the unique result C_iBBC_i. The problem is that there are two ways of analyzing C_iAAC_i in such a way that the rule $A \rightarrow B$ will apply. Similarly, suppose that we have the rule $A \rightarrow B \mathbin{/} A \text{———} A$ (in primitive notation, the rule $AAA \rightarrow ABA$) and the domain C_iAAAAC_i. Again, "result of applying" is not uniquely defined since both the second and the third occurrences of A in this domain are in the context $A \text{———} A$. Presumably, here, too, we want the result of applying the rule to affect both of the occurrences of A that are in the appropriate context, even though each forms part of the appropriate context for the other; that is, we want the result of applying the rule to be: C_iABBAC_i.

To achieve these results, we extend the definition of "result of applying" in the following way. Let R be as above—that is, $ZXAYW \rightarrow ZXBYW$—and let D be the domain $C_i\varphi_1A_1 \ldots \varphi_mA_m\varphi_{m+1}C_i$, where for each $j \leq m$, R is applicable to D with the analysis $C_i, \sigma_1, \sigma_2, A_j, \sigma_3, \sigma_4, C_i (\sigma_1\sigma_2 = \varphi_1A_1 \ldots \varphi_{j-1}A_{j-1}\varphi_j$ and $\sigma_3\sigma_4 = \varphi_{j+1}A_{j+1} \ldots A_m\varphi_{m+1})$, and m is the largest number such that this is true. Thus $A_1, \ldots, A_m$ are the units containing A that are in the context $X \text{———} Y$ in D, in the obvious sense of this notion. In this case, we say that the "result of applying R to D" is the string D' formed from D by replacing each A_j by ω_j, where ω_j is determined by A_j and B exactly as ω is determined by ψ_2 and B by (9).

The phonological component of a grammar is a sequence of rules of the form just described that apply successively to a certain domain in the manner just indicated, each rule applying to the string resulting from the application of the rules that precede. Before precisely defining "application of a sequence of rules to a surface structure," we must develop the crucial notion of "disjunctive ordering." We will delay this step for a moment, however, and turn to the matter of evaluation.

As we have observed several times, the problem of evaluation is basically that of explicating the notion "linguistically significant generalization." We must, in other words, state in a precise way the formal relations among rules that indicate the extent to which rules express such a generalization. We must then go on to assign a numerical value to a system of rules which directly reflects the degree to which they achieve linguistically significant generalizations. The general method we have been pursuing is this: we define certain "notational transformations" that permit rules to be collapsed when they are similar in certain ways and appropriately ordered; we then assign to the system of rules, as its value, the number of features that appear when all notational transformations have applied.

This approach can be made fully explicit in several different ways. The most straightforward seems to be as follows. We will consider a certain class of expressions, called "schemata," which are constructed from the symbols that appear in rules and certain auxiliary expressions such as parentheses, braces, variables over integers, and conditions on integers. We will not define the class of well-formed schemata directly; rather, we will give certain rules of expansion that eliminate auxiliary symbols, and we will then define the "well-formed schemata" to be the ones that can be expanded, in the manner provided, into a sequence of rules. For each sequence of rules, there will be some schema that expands into this sequence and that is optimal, in the sense that it contains a minimal number of feature occurrences. The number of feature occurrences in the optimal schema will be the value of the original sequence of rules. In this way, each sequence of rules is assigned an integral value, and grammars can be compared with respect to the degree to which they achieve linguistically significant generalization, this fundamental concept being defined, implicitly, by the notational system used in constructing schemata.

We will now consider strings which contain, in addition to the symbols that appear as primitives in the formulation of rules, the following auxiliary expressions:

$\begin{pmatrix} 10 \end{pmatrix}$ AUXILIARY EXPRESSIONS
(a) a variable ranging over categories: K
(b) braces: { }; comma: ,
(c) parentheses with indices drawn from the set of symbols $a_1, a_2, \ldots$:), $(_{a_1}, (_{a_2}, \ldots$
(d) expressions of truth-functional conditions $C(a_{k+1}, \ldots, a_{k+n})$, $k \geq 0$, with the predicate $=$, the constants 0, 1, and the variables $a_{k+1}, \ldots, a_{k+n}$; we separate C from the preceding string by a colon.
(e) slash and dash: /, ——

Schemata will be certain strings consisting of primitive symbols and auxiliary expressions. All unexpanded schemata are, first of all, of one of the forms of (11):

$\begin{pmatrix} 11 \end{pmatrix}$
(a) $X \rightarrow Y:C$
(b) $X \rightarrow Y/Z_1:C$
(c) $X \rightarrow Y/Z_1/Z_2:C$
.
.
.

where C is a condition (perhaps vacuous), and $X, Y, Z_1, Z_2, \ldots$ contain no occurrences of $\rightarrow$, /, or truth-functional conditions, and X and Y contain no occurrences of ——. Furthermore, each Z_i is of the form W_i——W_i', where W_i, W_i' contain no occurrences of ——.

We define the class of well-formed schemata by giving certain "expansion conventions": a string that is converted into a sequence of rules by recursive application of the expansion conventions is a well-formed schema. Before giving these conventions, we define the following notions:

$\begin{pmatrix} 12 \end{pmatrix}$
(a) Let $(p_1, \ldots, p_m)$ and $(q_1, \ldots, q_m)$ be m-tuples of the binary digits 0, 1. We say that $(p_1, \ldots, p_m)$ precedes $(q_1, \ldots, q_m)$ if either (i) or (ii) holds:

(i) $\sum_{i=1}^{m} p_i > \sum_{i=1}^{m} q_i$

(ii) $\sum_{i=1}^{m} p_i = \sum_{i=1}^{m} q_i$; there is a j such that $p_i = q_i$ for $i \leq j$, $p_{j+1} = 1$, and $q_{j+1} = 0$

(b) We say that $(p_1, \ldots, p_m)$ "satisfies" the truth-functional condition $C(a_{k+1}, \ldots, a_{k+n})$, $m \leq n$, if C is either true or of the form φ and ψ, where φ is true and ψ still contains variables,[4] when p_i is substituted for a_{k+i} in C.

(c) If $S = X\{Z\}W : C$ is a schema, then $\{Z\}$ is "maximal" in S unless it is contained within paired braces or paired parentheses, in the obvious sense, or unless $W = W_1/W_2$, where W_2 contains auxiliary expressions.

We now give conventions for expanding schemata:

$\left(13\right)$ EXPANSION CONVENTIONS

(a) Where S(K) is a schema containing the category variable K, S(K) expands into the sequence of schemata $S(C_1), \ldots, S(C_t)$ ($C_1, \ldots, C_t$ being the category symbols of (1c)), where $S(C_i)$ is formed by replacing K by C_i in S(K).

(b) Where X_1 and X_2 are strings (possibly null) containing no occurrences of K and where $\{Y_1, \ldots, Y_m\}$ is maximal in the schema (i), the schema (i) expands into the sequence of schemata (ii):
 (i) $X_1 \{Y_1, \ldots, Y_m\} X_2$
 (ii) $X_1 Y_1 X_2, \ldots, X_1 Y_m X_2$

(c) Let S be the schema
$WX_1(_{a_{k+1}}Y_1)X_2 \ldots X_m(_{a_{k+m}}Y_m)X_{m+1} : C(a_{k+1}, \ldots, a_{k+n})$
where $X_1, \ldots, X_{m+1}$ contain no auxiliary expressions, $C(a_{k+1}, \ldots, a_{k+n})$ is an expression of (10d), $m \leq n$, and W is either null or $W = Z/$, where Z contains no occurrences of $a_{k+1}, \ldots, a_{k+n}$. Let $N_1, \ldots, N_r$ be the m-tuples satisfying C in the sense of (12) and ordered in terms of the relation "precedes" defined in (12). Where $N_i = (p_1, \ldots, p_m)$, form Z_i by carrying out the following formal operations on S: for each $j \leq m$:
 (i) if Y_j is not a feature, then replace $(_{a_{k+j}}Y_j)$ by null if $p_j = 0$ and by Y_j if $p_j = 1$.
 (ii) if Y_j is a feature, then replace $(_{a_{k+j}}Y_j)$ by $+ Y_j$ if $p_j = 1$ and by $- Y_j$ if $p_j = 0$.
 (iii) substitute p_j for a_{k+j} in $C(a_{k+1}, \ldots, a_{k+n})$.
 (iv) if the result of (i)–(iii) is the schema $\varphi : C$, where φ is a rule, then delete $: C$.[5] Then S expands into the sequence of schemata $Z_1, \ldots, Z_r$.

(d) If X_3 and X_4 contain no occurrences of / or ———, and X_5 is either null or is $/X_6$, then the schema (i) expands to (ii):
 (i) $X_1 \rightarrow X_2 / X_3 \text{———} X_4 X_5$
 (ii) $X_3 X_1 X_4 \rightarrow X_3 X_2 X_4 X_5$

---

[4] Perhaps to be replaced by integers at a later stage of expansion, if the schema contains parentheses embedded within other parentheses; see (13c) and example (17).

[5] In this case, C will be either a true statement or of the form ψ and $C(a_{k+m+1}, \ldots, a_{k+n})$ (ψ a true statement).

Notice that there is a left-right asymmetry in our notion of schema which can be eliminated by considering S in the case of Expansion Convention (c) to be the schema:

$$X_1(_{b_1}Y_1)X_2 \ldots X_m(_{b_m}Y_m)X_{m+1} : C(a_{k+1}, \ldots, a_{k+n})$$

where $(b_1, \ldots, b_m)$ is a permutation of $(a_{k+1}, \ldots, a_{k+m})$ and everything else remains the same. With this extension, the class of interpretable schemata broadens in a natural way. Other extensions are also possible. For example, we might allow $(b_1, \ldots, b_m)$ to be a permutation of a subsequence $(a_{c_1}, \ldots, a_{c_m})$ of $(a_{k+1}, \ldots, a_{k+n})$, and we might then modify the notion "satisfy" and correspondingly step (iii) of Expansion Convention (c) so that p_j substitutes for a_{c_j} in $C(a_{k+1}, \ldots, a_{k+n})$. As noted earlier, we have no empirical evidence to settle these questions.

Expansion Convention (c) generalizes considerably the angled bracket notation used earlier (i.e., $\langle\,\rangle$—see Chapter Three, p. 77); where the truth-functional condition C is vacuous in S and case (ii) of (13c) is excluded, we have the ordinary parenthesis notation of our earlier usage. No doubt, the class of conditions C of (10d) can be narrowed considerably, but we will not attempt a further refinement here. Note, incidentally, that the ordering imposed by (12aii) is quite arbitrary, since we have, at the moment, no relevant examples. In this and several other cases, then, the formalization is premature. Case (ii) of Expansion Convention (c) incorporates a generalized version of our use of variables for feature specifications. For example, the rule (14) of our informal usage would be given as the schema (15):

$$\left(14\right) \qquad \begin{bmatrix} \alpha F_1 \\ \beta F_2 \end{bmatrix} \rightarrow \begin{bmatrix} -\beta F_1 \\ \alpha F_4 \end{bmatrix}$$

$$\left(15\right) \quad (a_1 F_1)(a_2 F_2) \rightarrow (a_3 F_1)(a_4 F_4) : a_1 = a_4 \text{ and } a_2 \neq a_3$$

The quadruples that satisfy (15) in this case are $(1,1,0,1)$, $(1,0,1,1)$, $(0,1,0,0)$, $(0,0,1,0)$, in this order of precedence. Expansion Convention (c), case (ii), thus expands (15) into the sequence of four rules (16):

$$\left(16\right) \quad \begin{aligned} +F_1 + F_2 &\rightarrow -F_1 + F_4 \\ +F_1 - F_2 &\rightarrow +F_1 + F_4 \\ -F_1 + F_2 &\rightarrow -F_1 - F_4 \\ -F_1 - F_2 &\rightarrow +F_1 - F_4 \end{aligned}$$

Furthermore, Expansion Convention (c) permits conditions on features to be intermingled with conditions on occurrence and nonoccurrence of strings (i.e., it permits our former angled bracket notation to be used to form conditions that also involve variables on features) in a very flexible way—no doubt, in too flexible a way.

To illustrate Expansion Convention (c) further, consider the schema (17), with parentheses embedded within parentheses:

$$\left(17\right) \quad (a_1 X (a_3 Y) Z (a_4 W) V) P (a_2 Q) : a_1 = a_2 \text{ and } a_3 = a_4$$

One application of Expansion Convention (c) to (17) will give the sequence of schemata (18):

$$\left(18\right) \quad \begin{aligned} &\text{(a)} \;\; X(a_3 Y) Z (a_4 W) V P Q : 1 = 1 \text{ and } a_3 = a_4 \\ &\text{(b)} \;\; P : 0 = 0 \text{ and } a_3 = a_4 \end{aligned}$$

Schema (18a) is subject to another application of Expansion Convention (c), which gives the sequence of schemata (19):

$$\left(19\right) \quad \begin{aligned} &\text{(a)} \;\; XYZWVPQ : 1 = 1 \text{ and } 1 = 1 \\ &\text{(b)} \;\; XZVPQ : 1 = 1 \text{ and } 0 = 0 \end{aligned}$$

If $XYZWVPQ$, $XZVPQ$, and P are rules, then we now apply case (iv) of Expansion Convention (c), giving (20) as the full expansion of (17):

$$\left(20\right) \quad \begin{aligned} &\text{(a)} \;\; XYZWVPQ \\ &\text{(b)} \;\; XZVPQ \\ &\text{(c)} \;\; P \end{aligned}$$

If the conventions expand the schema X_i to the sequence of schemata $Z_1, \ldots, Z_m$, we will say that these conventions expand the sequence of schemata $X_1, \ldots, X_i, \ldots, X_n$ to the sequence $X_1, \ldots, X_{i-1}, Z_1, \ldots, Z_m, X_{i+1}, \ldots, X_n$. If the expansion conventions expand the sequence $X_1, \ldots, X_m$ to $Z_1, \ldots, Z_n$, and they expand $Z_1, \ldots, Z_n$ to $W_1, \ldots, W_p$, we will say that they expand $X_1, \ldots, X_m$ to $W_1, \ldots, W_p$.

We will say that the schema X is "well-formed" if it expands to the sequence of rules $Y_1, \ldots, Y_m$; in this case we will say that X "represents" $Y_1, \ldots, Y_m$. If X does not expand to a sequence of rules, it is not well-formed.

If $Y_1, \ldots, Y_m$ is a sequence of rules represented by X and X contains n occurrences of features (i.e., of the symbols $F_1, \ldots, F_q$), then X assigns the index n to the sequence $Y_1, \ldots, Y_m$. The "optimal index" of $Y_1, \ldots, Y_m$ is the minimal index assigned to it by some representing schema.[6]

Finally, we state the empirical hypothesis on rule applications that we proposed earlier in terms of the parenthesis and angle notations:

$\left(21\right)$ ORDERING HYPOTHESIS

If the schema X is expanded to the sequence of schemata $Y_1, \ldots, Y_n$ by application of Expansion Convention (c), then for each i, j ($i \neq j$), the rules into which Y_i expands (or Y_i itself, if Y_i is a rule) are disjunctively ordered with respect to the rules into which Y_j expands (or Y_j itself, if Y_j is a rule).

Notice that rules expanded from schemata involving variables for feature specifications are disjunctively ordered, as are rules expanded by the use of the parenthesis and angled bracket notations (generalized as above). These conventions are what we have been assuming all along.

We now have the conceptual apparatus needed to state precisely the way in which a sequence of rules applies to a surface structure. Given a surface structure Σ and a sequence of rules $X_1, \ldots, X_n$, we derive a phonetic representation in the following way. First, find the optimal schema representing $X_1, \ldots, X_n$.[7] Define disjunctive ordering among the rules $X_1, \ldots, X_n$ in accordance with the Ordering Hypothesis (21). Now find some string in Σ of the form $C_i W C_i$, where W is a matrix.[8] Call this the string D. Let D_1 be the result of applying X_1 to D (recall that the result of applying a rule to a string is always well-defined). After having applied (or skipped) the rule X_i to form D_i, turn to the rule X_{i+1} and apply it to D_i to form D_{i+1} (as the result of its application to D_i), if X_{i+1} is not disjunctively ordered with respect to one of the rules that has already applied in this cycle. If X_{i+1} is disjunctively ordered with respect to a rule that has already applied in this cycle, then skip X_{i+1} and form $D_{i+1} = D_i$. Continue in this way until rule X_n has either been applied or skipped. At this point, erase the occurrences of C_i in D_n, forming D_{n+1}. This terminates the cycle. We now begin a new cycle, applying $X_1, \ldots, X_n$ to Σ', in just the same way, where Σ' is formed from Σ by replacing D in Σ by D_{n+1}. Rules designated as rules of word phonology will be applied when the domain is a word, as defined in Section 6.2. Continue in this way until the phonological phrase is reached. Boundaries are now automatically deleted. At this terminal point, we have a phonetic representation—the phonetic representation associated with Σ by the sequence of rules $X_1, \ldots, X_n$.

There are, in fact, several other notational devices that we have used in presenting schemata. These require additional expansion rules of essentially the sort just given.

---

[6] Recall that a system is more highly valued as its index, in this sense, is smaller.

[7] We here assume this to be unique; if it is not, the mapping defined by the phonological component might, correspondingly, be one-many.

[8] In the notation we used earlier, a minimal string of the form $[_{C_i} \ldots]_{C_i}$.

Consider first the schema (22), which, by Expansion Convention (13d), expands to (23):

$$\left(22\right) \qquad X \;\rightarrow\; Y \;/\; Z\text{---}W$$

$$\left(23\right) \qquad ZXW \;\rightarrow\; ZYW$$

In our earlier, informal usage, we employed this device to abbreviate a rule such as (24) with the schema (25):

$$\left(24\right) \qquad X\begin{bmatrix}+F_1\\+F_2\\+F_3\end{bmatrix}Y \;\rightarrow\; X\begin{bmatrix}+F_1\\-F_2\\+F_3\end{bmatrix}Y$$

$$\left(25\right) \qquad \begin{bmatrix}+F_1\\+F_2\end{bmatrix} \;\rightarrow\; \begin{bmatrix}+F_1\\-F_2\end{bmatrix} \;/\; X\begin{bmatrix}\text{---}\\+F_3\end{bmatrix}Y$$

In our present system, rule (24) would appear as (26), and would, accordingly, be represented by the schema (27), corresponding to (25):

$$\left(26\right) \quad X+F_1+F_2+F_3\,Y\rightarrow X+F_1-F_2+F_3\,Y$$

$$\left(27\right) \quad +F_1+F_2\rightarrow+F_1-F_2/X\text{---}+F_3\,Y$$

Suppose, however, that the rule in question modifies the value of F_4 as well as F_2. Thus instead of (25) we have (28):

$$\left(28\right) \qquad \begin{bmatrix}+F_1\\+F_2\\+F_4\end{bmatrix} \;\rightarrow\; \begin{bmatrix}+F_1\\-F_2\\-F_4\end{bmatrix} \;/\; X\begin{bmatrix}\text{---}\\+F_3\end{bmatrix}Y$$

In our present formalism, the rule in question is (29):

$$\left(29\right) \quad X+F_1+F_2+F_3+F_4\,Y\rightarrow X+F_1-F_2+F_3-F_4\,Y$$

We have no way to abbreviate this as a schema involving $/$, ———. Thus, if we were to construct (30) (corresponding to (27)), we would find that it expands not to (29) but to (31):

$$\left(30\right) \quad +F_1+F_2+F_4\rightarrow+F_1-F_2-F_4/X\text{---}+F_3\,Y$$

$$\left(31\right) \quad X+F_1+F_2+F_4+F_3\,Y\rightarrow X+F_1-F_2-F_4+F_3\,Y$$

But (31) is not well-formed, because of our earlier assumption (see p. 391) that the order of features in a unit be fixed by (1a). What we need is a trivial modification of our earlier definitions, replacing "is a substring of $F_1, \ldots, F_q$" by "is a substring of some permutation of $F_1, \ldots, F_q$" in the definition (6b) of "unit," other definitions being adjusted accordingly.

We must also formalize the convention regarding formative boundary, utilizing for this purpose the parenthesis convention, along the lines outlined in Section 6.1. Furthermore, we must provide the device $[X]_m^n$, m and n numerals, $m \leq n$. The appropriate expansion convention will replace a schema (32) by the sequence of schemata (33), where X^i is the schema $X \ldots X$ containing i occurrences of X, and X^0 is null.

$$\left(32\right) \qquad\qquad Z\,[X]_m^n\,W$$

$$\left(33\right) \qquad\qquad ZX^nW, \ldots, ZX^mW$$

The convention that expands (32) must be ordered in its application with respect to the other conventions. Apparently, it must be last in the ordering. That is to say, we must impose the condition that Z and W contain no auxiliary expressions in (32). Thus the string (34) will be an abbreviation for the sequence (35):

$$\left(34\right) \qquad\qquad \ldots C_0^1(\varphi) \ldots$$

$$\left(35\right) \qquad\qquad \ldots C\varphi \ldots, \ldots \varphi \ldots, \ldots C \ldots, \ldots\ldots$$

We have, in fact, made use of this convention in presenting rules (see, for example, pp. 70–71, Chapter Three).

Still another notation that must be incorporated is the notation (36), which we have used as an abbreviation for an infinite set of simultaneously applicable schemata (37):

$$\left(36\right) \qquad\qquad X(Y)^*Z$$

$$\left(37\right) \qquad\qquad XZ,\ XYZ,\ XYYZ,\ XYYYZ, \ldots$$

The conditions under which this kind of formulation is appropriate are strictly limited. (See p. 344 for some discussion.) Furthermore, since an infinite set is involved, and since there is no ordering among the represented schemata, it would seem appropriate to introduce this device as a primitive notation rather than as an auxiliary expression, and to restate the principle of rule applicability accordingly. Since we have so few examples to illustrate this device, we leave the matter with no further clarification.

There are a few other conventions in common use—for example, a convention of indexed braces that makes use of (38) as a representation for (39), where n is a numeral:

$$\left(38\right) \qquad\qquad Z\{_nX_1, \ldots, X_m\}V\{_nY_1, \ldots, Y_m\}W$$

$$\left(39\right) \qquad\qquad ZX_1VY_1W, \ldots, ZX_mVY_mW$$

Formalization is straightforward. It is also necessary to add a provision for rules such as those discussed in Section 5, which are rather similar to transformations in their formal properties. Again, this is a straightforward matter.

The devices just outlined should no doubt be restricted in various ways to reduce their expressive power. For example, we might require that a schema be of the form

(40), where *A* and *B* are units (or φ), or involve at most parentheses around specified features (i.e., variables over feature specifications):

$$\left(40\right) \qquad\qquad A \;\rightarrow\; B \;\;/\;\; X$$

Other conditions might be suggested. Such refinements are pointless and arbitrary in the absence of any real linguistic material that would provide crucial, or at least relevant, evidence concerning their correctness. We emphasize, once again, that the choice of notations is an empirical matter with factual consequences, within the framework just outlined.

Chapter nine

EPILOGUE AND PROLOGUE:
THE INTRINSIC CONTENT
OF FEATURES

1. *Some unresolved problems*

The entire discussion of phonology in this book suffers from a fundamental theoretical inadequacy. Although we do not know how to remedy it fully, we feel that the outlines of a solution can be sketched, at least in part. The problem is that our approach to features, to rules, and to evaluation has been overly formal. Suppose, for example, that we were systematically to interchange features or to replace $[\alpha F]$ by $[-\alpha F]$ (where $\alpha = +$, and F is a feature) throughout our description of English structure. There is nothing in our account of linguistic theory to indicate that the result would be the description of a system that violates certain principles governing human languages. To the extent that this is true, we have failed to formulate the principles of linguistic theory, of universal grammar, in a satisfactory manner. In particular, we have not made any use of the fact that the features have intrinsic content. By taking this intrinsic content into account, we can, so it appears, achieve a deeper and more satisfying solution to some of the problems of lexical redundancy as well as to many other problems that we have skirted in the exposition.

For example, we have suggested that the "naturalness" of a class (in the empirically significant sense as discussed in Chapter Eight, Section 1) can be measured in terms of the number of features needed to define it. Thus the class C of nonvowels (consonants, liquids, and glides) is more natural than the class (C,L) containing the low vowels as well as nonvowels. Correspondingly, the class C is defined with two features, as the class of segments which are [+consonantal] or [−vocalic]; whereas (C,L) has a three-feature definition as the class of segments which are [+consonantal], [−vocalic], or [+low].

Up to a point this measure gives the desired results, but in many cases it fails completely. For example, the class of voiced obstruents is, intuitively, more natural than the class of voiced segments (consonant or vowel), but the latter has the simpler definition. The class of vowels which are the same in backness and rounding (i.e., the class [αback, αround]) is more natural than the class of vowels which have the same coefficient for the features "low" and "round" (i.e., the class [αlow, αround], which contains [i e ɨ ʌ æ ɔ]); in spite of this the same number of features enters into each characterization. The class of segments which are [αvocalic, αhigh] has a simpler definition in terms of number of features than either of the last two classes mentioned, but it is far less natural. Counterexamples of this sort are quite easy to find. It would be a mistake to try to eliminate them by a sharper definition of "naturalness" that makes use only of formal properties of features and feature specifications, for it is actually the content of the features and not the form of the definition that decides these questions of naturalness.

Similar problems can be noted with regard to rules of the grammar. Compare, for example, the pairs of rules in (1):

$$\begin{pmatrix}1\end{pmatrix}$$

(a) (i) i → u
    (ii) i → ɨ

(b) (i) t → s
    (ii) t → θ

(c) (i) $[+\text{nasal}] \rightarrow \begin{bmatrix}\alpha\text{ant}\\ \beta\text{cor}\end{bmatrix} / \underline{\quad} \begin{bmatrix}\alpha\text{ant}\\ \beta\text{cor}\\ C\end{bmatrix}$

    (ii) $[+\text{nasal}] \rightarrow \begin{bmatrix}+\text{ant}\\ \alpha\text{cor}\end{bmatrix} / \underline{\quad} [\alpha\text{cor}]$

(d) (i) ɸ → ə / C——[+son] #
    (ii) ɸ → k / C——[+son] #

(e) (i) [k, g] → [č, ǰ] / ——[i, e]
    (ii) [p, b] → [t, d] / ——[i, e]

(f) (i) k → č / $\underline{\quad} \begin{bmatrix}-\text{cons}\\ -\text{back}\end{bmatrix}$

    (ii) č → k / $\underline{\quad} \begin{bmatrix}-\text{cons}\\ +\text{back}\end{bmatrix}$

In each of the examples (a)–(f), case (i) involves more features than or at least as many features as case (ii); but in each pair case (i) is more to be expected in a grammar than case (ii) and should therefore be "simpler" in terms of an empirically significant evaluation measure. In fact, although rules (ai)–(fi) are observed in many languages, examples (cii)–(fii) (though not (aii) and (bii)) are quite extraordinary despite their "simplicity." Once again, additional examples are easy to construct, and they strongly suggest that the intrinsic content of features and feature specifications must be taken into account in determining the value of a grammar.

A different type of example is provided by phonological processes which reflect the effects of a coherent system of rules. Thus, in Tswana (Cole, 1955; see also Fudge, 1967), in position after nasals voiced stops becomes ejectives, nonobstruent continuants become voiceless aspirated plosives, and obstruent continuants become voiceless aspirated affricates. Cole rightly subsumes these changes under the single heading of "strengthening." In the present framework, however, there is no device available that would allow us to bring out formally the fact that these three processes are somehow related.[1]

The study of lexical redundancy provides a fourth class of examples of the same general sort. Thus, although a vowel system such as (2) would be more natural, in some

---

[1] For further remarks that have a bearing on this problem see J. W. Harris (1967), McCawley (1967a), and Postal (1968).

significant sense, than one such as (3) or (4), our measures of evaluation make no distinction among them.

$\begin{pmatrix}2\end{pmatrix}$

	i		u
	e		o
		a	

$\begin{pmatrix}3\end{pmatrix}$

	i		u
	e		o
	æ		

$\begin{pmatrix}4\end{pmatrix}$

	ü		ɨ
			ʌ
	œ		a

To take another example, our evaluation measure makes no distinction between a language in which all vowels are voiced and one in which all vowels are voiceless, or between a language in which obstruent clusters are redundantly voiced and a language in which they are redundantly voiceless. But surely one case is much more natural than the other.

All of these examples, and many others like them, point to the need for an extension of the theory to accommodate the effects of the intrinsic content of features, to distinguish "expected" or "natural" cases of rules and symbol configurations from others which are unexpected and unnatural. In the linguistically significant sense of the notion "complexity," a rule that voices vowels should not add to the complexity of a grammar but a rule that unvoices vowels should, whereas in the case of obstruents the opposite decision is called for. Similarly, if a language has a five-vowel system, the rules that determine the configuration (2) should not add to the complexity of the grammar; rather, the complexity should increase if these rules, or at least some of them, do *not* appear in the grammar. The same is true of the rules and configurations discussed earlier; and it may even be the case that there are optimal orderings of rules that can be determined in terms of their form and content.[2] Obviously these matters are significant not only for synchronic description but also for historical linguistics. They do not, however, fall into the theoretical framework that we have so far outlined.

2. *A theory of "markedness"*

Certain aspects of this general problem can be dealt with if we incorporate the Praguian notion of "marked" and "unmarked" values of features into our account in some systematic way,[3] and if we then revise the evaluation measure so that unmarked values do not contribute to complexity. As a first step, suppose that we take the specifications in a matrix that constitutes a lexical entry to be not $+$, $-$, 0 as in the earlier exposition, but u (for

---

[2] See Kiparsky (1966) for an interesting discussion of this question.

[3] A great many of the problems discussed in this chapter were first investigated by the phonologists of the Prague Circle, notably Trubetzkoy and Jakobson. After a promising start, the exploration of these problems was not continued, largely because it seemed impossible to surmount the conceptual difficulties that stemmed from the taxonomic view of linguistics, which was all but universally accepted at that time. The attempts to break out of the confines of this view, which can be seen in studies such as Trubetzkoy (1936a, 1936b), elicited little positive response and almost no interest among contemporary workers, and the notion of markedness is hardly mentioned in the phonological literature of the 1940s and 1950s.

"unmarked") and m (for "marked"), along with $+$ and $-$ (see pp. 404, 409). We then add universal rules of interpretation which systematically replace the symbols u and m by the symbols $+$ and $-$. Being universal, these rules are not part of a grammar but rather conventions for the interpretation of a grammar; they do not affect the complexity of a grammar, as determined by the evaluation measure, any more than the rules for interpreting $\rightarrow$ or $\{\ \}$.

Assuming that the unmarked value of the feature "segment" is [−segment], a lexical entry that contains only u's (that is, the simplest lexical entry) will be phonologically vacuous; it will contain no segments. If a lexical entry is nonvacuous—i.e., contains segments—the universal interpretive conventions will assign to it a particular phonological structure in terms of $+$ and $-$ entries. The complexity of the lexical item will depend on the number of features that are not left unmarked in its matrix representation; each such marked entry will distinguish the item from the "neutral," simplest lexical item. Adding an item to the lexicon, in this sense, is a matter of distinguishing the item from the neutral case, and from the other items already incorporated in the lexicon, by a minimal number of marked features.

For instance, let us imagine a language in which lexical items are all one segment long. If such a language has a lexicon of two items, these can be distinguished from each other by marking—specifying m for—some one feature in one item; in the other item there will be no marked feature, except, of course, for the feature "segment." If the language has a lexicon of three items, another feature will have to be marked. The lexicon will then consist of the entries in (5):

$$\begin{pmatrix}5\end{pmatrix} \qquad \begin{bmatrix} u\mathrm{F}_1 \\ u\mathrm{F}_2 \\ u\mathrm{F}_3 \\ \cdot \\ \cdot \\ \cdot \\ u\mathrm{F}_n \end{bmatrix} \quad \begin{bmatrix} m\mathrm{F}_1 \\ u\mathrm{F}_2 \\ \cdot \\ \cdot \\ \cdot \\ u\mathrm{F}_n \end{bmatrix} \quad \begin{bmatrix} u\mathrm{F}_1 \\ m\mathrm{F}_2 \\ \cdot \\ \cdot \\ \cdot \\ u\mathrm{F}_n \end{bmatrix}$$

If a fourth item is added to the lexicon, there will have to be another marked feature in its lexical representation, and so on. Since unmarked features do not add to the complexity of a grammar, there is no point in allowing unspecified features in the lexicon. In this way, the conception of markedness resolves the difficulties with regard to unspecified features that were discussed in Chapter Eight, Section 8.

2.1. THE MARKING CONVENTIONS

We now turn to the interpretive conventions, which we shall also refer to as "marking conventions." Consider the set given as (6) on pages 404–407. As a first approximation, which will later be somewhat refined, we may think of each rule of (6) as analogous to a phonological rule, except that each schema $[u\mathrm{F}] \rightarrow [\alpha\mathrm{F}]\ /\ X \underline{\hspace{1cm}} Y$ (where $\alpha = +$ or $-$, and X and Y may be null) is interpreted as a pair of rules, the first of which replaces $[u\mathrm{F}]$ by $[\alpha\mathrm{F}]$ in the context $X \underline{\hspace{1cm}} Y$ and the second of which replaces $[m\mathrm{F}]$ by $[-\alpha\mathrm{F}]$ (where $--=+$ and $-+=-$) in the context $X \underline{\hspace{1cm}} Y$. Let us also assume that the leftmost and rightmost unit of each lexical entry is $+$ (the formative boundary). The interpretive conventions can therefore be viewed as a fixed way of interpreting a given lexical matrix. Whenever the normal (unmarked) interpretation is not to apply, i.e., when instead of the expected $[\alpha\mathrm{F}]$, $[-\alpha\mathrm{F}]$ is required, a special symbol must appear in the matrix, and it is natural that the symbol that blocks the expected interpretation should increase the complexity of the description. Observe, moreover, that the interpretive conventions have been defined so as to supply + or − not only for [uF], but also for [mF].[4] It turns out, however, that in certain contexts (see (6X) and accompanying discussion) it is not possible to specify the value of the unmarked feature (and hence also of the marked feature) by a universal convention. In these cases the value will be specified directly in the lexical representation. Such a directly specified feature will be viewed as increasing the complexity of the description to the same extent as a feature that has the coefficient m; thus only unmarked features add nothing to the complexity. Finally, there are cases where the coefficient of a feature is determined by the universal constraints on feature combinations; for instance, it is impossible, by definition,

to have segments which are $\begin{bmatrix} +\text{low} \\ +\text{high} \end{bmatrix}$. To reflect this fact in our framework, we utilize con-

ventions such as (6VII) and (6IX), which specify the coefficient of a given feature regardless of whether or not it has been marked for that feature. This is but another way of expressing the fact that the feature in question is not subject to marking and will therefore always remain unmarked.

(6) A TENTATIVE STATEMENT OF SOME MARKING CONVENTIONS

(I)   [u seg]   →   [−seg]

(II)

$$[u\text{ cons}] \rightarrow \begin{cases} [+\text{cons}] & / \left\{ \begin{cases} \left\{ \begin{array}{c} + \\ \begin{bmatrix} +\text{voc} \\ -\text{cons} \end{bmatrix} \end{array} \right\} \underline{\quad} \\ \begin{bmatrix} \underline{\quad} \\ -\text{voc} \end{bmatrix} \end{cases} \right\} \\ [-\text{cons}] & / \begin{bmatrix} \underline{\quad} \\ +\text{voc} \end{bmatrix} \end{cases}$$

(a)
(b)
(c)
(d)

(III)

$$[u\text{ voc}] \rightarrow \begin{cases} [+\text{voc}] & / \text{ C}\underline{\quad\quad} \\ [-\text{voc}] & / \left\{ \begin{array}{c} \begin{bmatrix} \underline{\quad} \\ +\text{cons} \end{bmatrix} \\ \left\{ \begin{array}{c} + \\ V \end{array} \right\} \underline{\quad} \end{array} \right\} \end{cases}$$

(a)
(b)
(c)
(d)

(IV)   [+voc]   →   [+son]

---

[4] A major difference between the Praguian conception of markedness and our own is that in the former the marked coefficient of a feature was assumed always to be + and the unmarked coefficient always −. This severe restriction limited the usefulness of the markedness notion and was one of the reasons for the failure of the earlier attempt to apply it. It should be noted that this restriction loses force unless it is coupled with the assumption of a fixed set of phonological features so that it is impossible to replace in the description of a particular language a given feature by its complement—for example, the feature "tense" by "lax," "voice" by "voicelessness," or "rounding" by "unroundedness." Without this further assumption, the proposal concerning the relationship between marked and positively specified features is weakened, but it is still stronger than the position taken here since it does not permit the marked value of a particular feature to depend on a particular context.

SOME CONVENTIONS FOR VOWELS:

(V)
$$\begin{bmatrix} +\text{voc} \\ -\text{cons} \end{bmatrix} \rightarrow \begin{bmatrix} -\text{ant} \\ -\text{strid} \\ +\text{cont} \\ +\text{voice} \\ -\text{lateral} \\ \textit{etc.} \end{bmatrix}$$

(VI)
$$[u\ \text{low}] \rightarrow \left\{ \begin{array}{ll} [+\text{low}] & / \begin{bmatrix} \overline{} \\ u\ \text{back} \\ u\ \text{round} \end{bmatrix} \quad \text{(a)} \\ [-\text{low}] & \text{(b)} \end{array} \right.$$

(VII) $\quad [+\text{low}] \rightarrow [-\text{high}]$

(VIII) $\quad [u\ \text{high}] \rightarrow [+\text{high}]$

(IX) $\quad [+\text{high}] \rightarrow [-\text{low}]$

(X) $\quad [u\ \text{back}] \rightarrow [+\text{back}] \, / \begin{bmatrix} \overline{} \\ +\text{low} \end{bmatrix}$

(XI)
$$[u\ \text{round}] \rightarrow \left\{ \begin{array}{ll} [\alpha\text{round}] & / \begin{bmatrix} \overline{} \\ \alpha\text{back} \\ -\text{low} \end{bmatrix} \quad \text{(a)} \\[3ex] [-\text{round}] & / \begin{bmatrix} \overline{} \\ +\text{low} \end{bmatrix} \quad \text{(b)} \end{array} \right.$$

(XII) $\quad [u\ \text{tense}] \rightarrow [+\text{tense}]$

SOME CONVENTIONS FOR CONSONANTS:

(XIII) $\quad [u\ \text{nasal}] \rightarrow [-\text{nasal}]$

(XIV) $\quad [-\text{nasal}] \rightarrow [-\text{son}]$

(XV)
$$[+\text{nasal}] \rightarrow \begin{bmatrix} +\text{son} \\ -\text{cont} \\ -\text{strid} \end{bmatrix}$$

(XVI) $\quad [u\ \text{low}] \rightarrow [-\text{low}]$

(XVII) $\quad [+\text{low}] \rightarrow [-\text{high}]$

(XVIII)
$$[u\ \text{high}] \rightarrow \left\{ \begin{array}{ll} [-\text{high}] & / \begin{bmatrix} \overline{} \\ u\ \text{ant} \\ u\ \text{back} \end{bmatrix} \quad \text{(a)} \\[4ex] [+\text{high}] & / \left\{ \begin{array}{ll} \begin{bmatrix} \overline{} \\ m\ \text{ant} \end{bmatrix} & \text{(b)} \\[3ex] \begin{bmatrix} \overline{} \\ u\ \text{ant} \\ m\ \text{back} \end{bmatrix} & \text{(c)} \end{array} \right. \end{array} \right.$$

(XIX) $\qquad$ $[+\text{high}] \rightarrow [-\text{low}]$

(XX)

$$[u\ \text{back}] \rightarrow \begin{cases} [-\text{back}] & / \begin{bmatrix} \rule{1.5em}{0.4pt} \\ u\ \text{ant} \\ -\text{low} \end{bmatrix} & \text{(a)} \\[3em] [+\text{back}] & / \begin{cases} \begin{bmatrix} \rule{1.5em}{0.4pt} \\ m\ \text{ant} \end{bmatrix} & \text{(b)} \\ \begin{bmatrix} \rule{1.5em}{0.4pt} \\ +\text{low} \end{bmatrix} & \text{(c)} \end{cases} \end{cases}$$

(XXI) $\qquad$ $[u\ \text{voice}] \rightarrow [-\text{voice}] / \begin{bmatrix} \rule{1.5em}{0.4pt} \\ -\text{son} \end{bmatrix}$

(XXII)

$$[u\ \text{ant}] \rightarrow \begin{cases} [-\text{ant}] & / \begin{bmatrix} \rule{1.5em}{0.4pt} \\ +\text{high} \\ +\text{cor} \\ \alpha\text{cont} \end{bmatrix} & \text{(a)} \\[3em] [+\text{ant}] & & \text{(b)} \end{cases}$$

(XXIII)

$$[u\ \text{cor}] \rightarrow \begin{cases} [-\text{cor}] & / \begin{bmatrix} \rule{1.5em}{0.4pt} \\ -\text{ant} \\ +\text{nasal} \end{bmatrix} & \text{(a)} \\[2.5em] [\alpha\text{cor}] & / \begin{bmatrix} \rule{1.5em}{0.4pt} \\ -\alpha\text{back} \\ -\text{ant} \end{bmatrix} & \text{(b)} \\[2.5em] [+\text{cor}] & / \begin{bmatrix} \rule{1.5em}{0.4pt} \\ +\text{ant} \\ \begin{cases} [+\text{nasal}] \\ [m\ \text{cont}] \end{cases} \end{bmatrix} & \text{(c)} \end{cases}$$

(XXIV) $\qquad$ $[u\ \text{cont}] \rightarrow \begin{cases} [+\text{cont}] & / +\rule{1.5em}{0.4pt}[+\text{cons}] & \text{(a)} \\ [-\text{cont}] & & \text{(b)} \end{cases}$

(XXV) $\qquad$ $[+\text{cont}] \rightarrow [+\text{delayed release}]$

(XXVI)

$$[u\ \text{delayed release}] \rightarrow \begin{cases} [+\text{del rel}] & / \begin{bmatrix} \rule{1.5em}{0.4pt} \\ -\text{ant} \\ +\text{cor} \end{bmatrix} & \text{(a)} \\[2.5em] [-\text{del rel}] & & \text{(b)} \end{cases}$$

(XXVII)

$$[u \text{ strid}] \rightarrow \begin{cases} [-\text{strid}] & / \begin{cases} \begin{bmatrix} \underline{} \\ +\text{son} \end{bmatrix} \\ \begin{bmatrix} \underline{} \\ -\text{ant} \\ -\text{cor} \end{bmatrix} \end{cases} & \begin{matrix} \text{(a)} \\ \\ \text{(b)} \end{matrix} \\ \\ [\alpha\text{strid}] & / \begin{bmatrix} \underline{} \\ \alpha\text{del rel} \\ \left\{ \begin{matrix} [+\text{ant}] \\ [+\text{cor}] \end{matrix} \right\} \end{bmatrix} & \text{(c)} \end{cases}$$

SOME CONVENTIONS FOR LIQUIDS:

(XXVIII)

$$\begin{bmatrix} +\text{voc} \\ +\text{cons} \end{bmatrix} \rightarrow \begin{bmatrix} -\text{nasal} \\ +\text{son} \end{bmatrix}$$

(XXIX)

$$[u \text{ ant}] \rightarrow [+\text{ant}]$$

(XXX)

$$[+\text{ant}] \rightarrow [+\text{cor}]$$

(XXXI)

$$[u \text{ cor}] \rightarrow [+\text{cor}]$$

(XXXII)

$$[-\text{cor}] \rightarrow [-\text{lateral}]$$

(XXXIII)

$$[u \text{ lateral}] \rightarrow [+\text{lateral}]$$

(XXXIV)

$$[u \text{ cont}] \rightarrow [+\text{cont}]$$

SOME CONVENTIONS FOR GLIDES:

(XXXV)

$$\begin{bmatrix} -\text{voc} \\ -\text{cons} \end{bmatrix} \rightarrow \begin{bmatrix} +\text{son} \\ -\text{ant} \\ -\text{cor} \\ -\text{nasal} \end{bmatrix}$$

(XXXVI)

$$[u \text{ low}] \rightarrow [-\text{low}]$$

(XXXVII)

$$[u \text{ high}] \rightarrow [+\text{high}]$$

(XXXVIII)

$$[u \text{ back}] \rightarrow [+\text{back}] \; / \begin{bmatrix} \underline{} \\ +\text{low} \end{bmatrix}$$

(XXXIX)

$$[u \text{ round}] \rightarrow \begin{cases} [-\text{round}] & / \begin{bmatrix} \underline{} \\ -\text{high} \end{bmatrix} \\ \\ [\alpha\text{round}] & / \begin{bmatrix} \underline{} \\ \alpha\text{back} \\ +\text{high} \end{bmatrix} \end{cases}$$

Let us assume that these conventions are applied to a given lexical item L in the following way. We proceed through the conventions (I)–(IV) in order, applying those that are applicable. We then return to convention (I) and proceed through conventions (II), (III), and (IV) again, in the given order. We continue in this way until none of the four conventions is applicable. We then proceed to conventions (V)–(XXXIX) and apply these in order, each convention being applied only once. Conventions (I)–(IV), which express the universal constraints on syllable structure, thus differ from the other marking conventions not only in their content but also in the principles governing their application. Given a complete set of conventions, the matrix representing L will contain only + and − entries once the entire set of conventions has been systematically applied.

2.2. CONVENTIONS FOR THE MAJOR CATEGORIES

The conventions of (6) embody certain empirical assumptions about the value of grammars. Convention (I) asserts that short lexical items are simpler than long ones. We could sharpen this convention to provide for the fact that lexical entries consisting of a single formative are simpler than those containing more than one formative (for example, *worship* is simpler than *permit* /pVr=mit/), but we omit this qualification here.

Conventions (II) and (III) deal with the major categories "true consonant," "vowel," "glide," "liquid." They will interpret initial segments as follows: the configuration [*u* consonantal, *u* vocalic] will be a true consonant; [*m* consonantal, *m* vocalic], a vowel; [*m* consonantal, *u* vocalic], a glide; and [*u* consonantal, *m* vocalic], a liquid. Thus in initial position the conventions select true consonants as the unmarked segments, vowels as the fully marked segments, and glides and liquids as intermediate in complexity. After a consonant, vowels are fully unmarked and glides fully marked. After a vowel, true consonants are fully unmarked and vowels fully marked. We might easily extend these rules to distinguish additional cases.

Convention (IV) specifies that [+vocalic] segments are sonorants. This convention differs from the preceding three in that it does not involve marking at all. It is to be interpreted as applying regardless of marking: all vocalic segments are sonorants. Since we always select the least complex lexicon, the feature "sonorant" will therefore never be marked for vocalic segments.

2.3. CONVENTIONS FOR VOWELS AND THE REPRESENTATION OF VOWELS IN THE LEXICON

Conventions (V)–(XII) apply to vowels only, and the following comments concerning these conventions are similarly restricted.

Convention (V) contains an incomplete listing of all features that are not available for marking in vowels.

Convention (VI) specifies that the vowel unmarked for the feature "low" is [+low] if the vowel is also unmarked for the features "back" and "round"; otherwise it is [−low].

Conventions (VII) and (IX) reflect the fact that there can be no segments that are $\begin{bmatrix} +\text{high} \\ +\text{low} \end{bmatrix}$. Given the discussion up to this point, it may appear that one of these two conventions is redundant. However, we shall see that this is not the case when we examine the function of the marking conventions in the interpretation of phonological rules (Section 4).

Convention (VIII) characterizes the feature "high" in nonlow vowels. The restriction need not be stated explicitly in the marking convention since at the point at which (VIII) applies, no low vowels will be unmarked for the feature "high" (see (VII)). As we shall see, this fact has other important consequences.

Convention (X) specifies the feature "back" for low vowels. It should be noted that there is no parallel specification of "back" for the nonlow vowels. It follows from this that in nonlow vowels the feature "back" will have to be specified as + or − in lexical representations, or, in other words, will not remain unmarked. We shall see that as a result of these conventions the feature "back" in the nonlow vowels will not be subject to various further conditions imposed on features that appear as marked or unmarked in lexical representations.[5]

Convention (XI) specifies "round" for low and nonlow vowels. In nonlow vowels the features "back" and "round" have the same coefficient if the vowel is [*u* round]; the low vowel unmarked for rounding is [−round].

Convention (XII) is the first of a set of conventions that specify the values for the remaining features. Since we have not investigated these conventions in any detail, we shall say nothing here about their content.

Observe now the effects of these conventions on the representation of vowel systems. We give in (7) the lexical representation that will result in the assignment by conventions (V)–(XII) of the correct feature specifications for the vowels indicated:

$\begin{pmatrix}7\end{pmatrix}$

	a	i	u	æ	ɔ	e	o	ü	ɨ	œ	ö	ʌ
low	*u*	*u*	*u*	*m*	*m*	*u*	*u*	*u*	*u*	*m*	*u*	*u*
high	*u*	*u*	*u*	*u*	*u*	*m*	*m*	*u*	*u*	*u*	*m*	*m*
back	*u*	−	+	*m*	*u*	−	+	−	+	*m*	−	+
round	*u*	*u*	*u*	*u*	*m*	*u*	*u*	*m*	*m*	*m*	*m*	*m*
complexity	0	1	1	2	2	2	2	2	2	3	3	3

As noted previously, a vowel system such as (2) (p. 402) is simpler in some significant sense than either (3) or (4). Suppose that the complexity of a system is defined as in (8):

$\begin{pmatrix}8\end{pmatrix}$ The complexity of a system is equal to the sum of the marked features of its members.

The system /a i u e o/ of (2) will then have a complexity of six; the system /i u e o æ/ of (3), a complexity of eight; and the system /ü ɨ ʌ œ a/ of (4), a complexity of ten. We can therefore say that (2) is less complex than either (3) or (4). On the same basis we can say that the three-vowel system /a i u/ is the simplest possible, a conclusion that seems to be supported by its predominance over other three-vowel systems in the languages of the world.

Definition (8), however, is hardly adequate in itself as a principle for selecting the optimal system. There are no doubt overriding considerations of symmetry and feature hierarchy that must be brought to bear in establishing what consititutes an optimal phonological system. This becomes quite apparent when one examines five-vowel systems. The simplest such system will certainly contain /a i u/; but given (8) as the only basis of selection, the choice of any two of the vowels /æ ɔ e o ü ɨ/ will lead to an equally complex system. This surely is incorrect; the conventions should select /a i u e o/ as the optimal five-vowel system.

---

[5] The difference between the two situations is somewhat similar to the one that Trubetzkoy (1958, p. 67) sought to capture by distinguishing between privative and equipollent oppositions and by restricting neutralization to privative oppositions.

To achieve the desired result, we propose the following two general conditions on the choice of representations of vowels in the lexicon:

$\begin{pmatrix} 9 \end{pmatrix}$ No vowel segment can be marked for the feature "round" unless some vowel segment in the system is marked for the feature "high."

$\begin{pmatrix} 10 \end{pmatrix}$ Other things being equal, a system in which more features have only the specification u is preferable to a system in which fewer features have only the specification u.

Condition (9) establishes a hierarchy in the availability of features for marking vowels in the lexicon. There are doubtless other conditions of this sort. Thus one would expect a hierarchy in which the feature "segment" is above "consonantal" and "vocalic," and the latter two are above the features listed in (7). Incidentally, it appears to us that the proper extension of (9) would make the availability for marking of the features "high" and "low" depend on the prior marking of the feature "back," resulting in the hierarchical structure shown in (11):

$\begin{pmatrix} 11 \end{pmatrix}$

$$\text{high} \swarrow \overset{\text{back}}{} \searrow \text{low}$$
$$\downarrow$$
$$\text{round}$$

If this proposed extension is incorporated into the theory, it will make the same choices in the cases reviewed as the complexity measure (8). This, however, does not render the latter superfluous: as we shall see in the discussion of consonant systems, all other things being equal, there is a clear preference for systems utilizing less complex segments over those utilizing more complex segments.

Condition (10) builds into our framework a "symmetry" condition of the sort that has often been mentioned in the literature. The condition asserts that one should minimize the number of features available for distinguishing lexical items. Given conditions (9) and (10), the system /a i u e o/ is the optimal five-vowel system, as desired.

Further modifications are required, however. In this regard, consider four-vowel systems. Again, the optimal system must contain /a i u/. The fourth vowel must be selected from among those of complexity 2 if the total complexity is to be minimized. By convention (9) the fourth vowel cannot be marked for the feature "round" unless it is also marked for "high" since none of /a i u/ is marked for the latter. This consideration rules out the choices /ɔ ü i/, leaving /æ e o/ as possibilities. Neither condition (10) (which in this case allows the fourth vowel to be any vowel marked for "back" and one other feature) nor the proposed extension (11) of condition (9) supplies any reason for making a choice among these three possibilities. However, it does not seem implausible that there is an optimal four-vowel system—namely, /a i u æ/; there should, then, be a principled way of selecting it. There are various means by which this result could be achieved. For instance, parallel to (10) we might impose a "symmetry" condition on systems which would be expressed in terms of specified features rather than in terms of markedness. This would be our analog to the traditional conception of "filling holes in the phonological pattern." We shall not attempt to state this alternative formally, however, since we do not feel that we have a sufficient understanding of the empirical issues involved; in particular, we are not certain that the system /a i u æ/ occupies the privileged position that we have suggested it does.

Let us now clarify the empirical content of the various assumptions sketched above.

Our general theory of evaluation leads to certain conclusions, on syntactic and phonological grounds, about the optimal set of inputs to the phonological component. Suppose that these considerations have led to the conclusion that for a given language this optimal set involves an *n*-vowel system. We want to know just how complex this *n*-vowel system is. Let us assume that the lexical entries must be represented in terms of the *optimal n*-vowel system (or one such, if there are several) as defined by conventions of the sort we have just been considering. Then the language must contain certain redundancy rules converting the optimally represented matrices into those required for the phonological rules. The complexity of these rules, measured in accordance with the system of evaluation outlined in the Appendix to Chapter Eight, is the measure of the complexity of this language with respect to its vocalic system. Similar considerations will determine the complexity of the lexical system in general. The simplest language with a five-vowel system will have the set /a i u e o/ as the input to the phonological component; thus it will have no phonological redundancy rules of the sort just mentioned.

We would expect, naturally, that systems which are simpler, in this sense, will be more generally found among the languages of the world, will be more likely to develop through historical change, etc. In fact, the hierarchy that we have so far established seems roughly in harmony with the results of studies of a great variety of vowel systems. (See, for example, the review of vowel systems given in Trubetzkoy (1958, Chapter IV, sec. 3).) Further refinements will no doubt be necessary, but they seem to us premature at this point in our investigation.

It must be emphasized that what we are discussing here is only one aspect of the evaluation of a lexicon, and, in principle, this aspect cannot be developed in isolation. For example, it might be possible to select either an *n*-vowel or an *n*+1-vowel system for a lexicon, consistent with certain assumptions about the phonological rules, in such a way that the *n*-vowel set is less optimal in the category of *n*-vowel systems than the *n*+1-vowel set is in the category of *n*+1-vowel systems. A method must be developed for weighing the extra complexity inherent in a larger inventory of segments against the advantages of having a more nearly optimal lexical system. There are many other questions of this sort, but we are not yet in a position to propose answers for them here.

2.4. *CONVENTIONS FOR TRUE CONSONANTS AND THE REPRESENTATION OF CONSONANTS IN THE LEXICON*

Returning now to our discussion of the marking conventions (6), we consider briefly cases (XIII)–(XXVII), which apply to true consonants only. Most of these are either self-explanatory or can best be discussed when we examine the manner in which consonants are represented in the lexicon. There are a few matters, however, that can be clarified at this point. We note, first of all, that conventions (XVII) and (XIX) are identical with conventions (VII) and (IX), respectively. These conventions are repeated in (6) for expository reasons only. Furthermore, it is important to draw attention to the fact that the order in which the different features are specified in consonants agrees with that obtaining in the vowel system as far as comparable features are concerned. This is surely no accident, but unfortunately its full significance cannot be brought out, given the present rudimentary state of our understanding of the marking conventions.

As in the case of vowels, the environments in which the marking conventions apply may be expressed in terms of marked and unmarked features, as well as in terms of features specified as + or −. The ordering of the conventions plays a crucial role, as already noted.

It is for this reason that the environments must be specified in the two ways just mentioned. Note that convention (XXIIa) will never find application in interpreting a matrix given in terms of marked and unmarked features. The reason is to be found in the specification [αcontinuant] in the context of the convention. Recall that α is a variable ranging over + and − and not over *m* and *u*. Note further that the feature "continuant" is not specified for + or − until convention (XXIV). Hence, at the point at which (XXIIa) becomes applicable as a marking convention, there will be no segment which is [αcontinuant], i.e., [±continuant]. We shall see later (in the discussion of (42), p. 429) that convention (XXIIa) plays a very special role in the functioning of the marking conventions.

The feature "continuant" is contextually determined (see (XXIV)). In initial position before a consonant, the consonant that is [*u* continuant] is interpreted as [+continuant]; in other positions it is interpreted as [−continuant]. In other words, the unmarked consonant in preconsonantal position is a continuant, whereas elsewhere it is a stop. It will be recalled that conventions (II) and (III) are also dependent on the phonological characteristics of adjacent segments. Convention (XXIVa), however, will not be assumed to be subject to the special principles of application that were imposed in the case of conventions (I)–(IV) (see p. 408).

Conventions (XXVI) and (XXVII) interpret the unmarked palato-alveolar consonant as an affricate but the unmarked consonants in all other points of articulation as plosives. Additional conventions not given here specify the values for tenseness, glottal constriction, etc.

In (12) the major types of consonantal segments are given with the markings imposed by conventions (6XIII–XXVII). The blank boxes represent unmarked features, i.e., features which are to be taken as having the specification *u*.

$\left(12\right)$

	m	n	ɲ	ŋ	p	f	t	t,	t°	θ	s	c	č	š	t_1	k_1	k	x	q
nasal	*m*	*m*	*m*	*m*															
low																			*m*
high								*m*											
back			*m*						*m*			*m*	*m*	*m*	*m*				
anterior			*m*	*m*								*m*	*m*	*m*	*m*	*m*	*m*	*m*	
coronal	*m*				−	*m*	+	+	+			+			*m*				
continuant						*m*				*m*	*m*			*m*				*m*	
delayed release													*m*		*m*				
strident										*m*									

The symbol /t,/ represents a palatalized [t], /t°/ a velarized [t], /t_1/ a palato-alveolar plosive (see Jones, 1956b, fig. 28, p. 46), /k_1/ a palatal plosive (IPA *c*), and /q/ a pharyngeal plosive.

Application of the marking conventions (6XIII–XXVII) to (12) yields the fully specified distinctive feature complexes shown in (13).

(13)

	m	n	ɲ	ŋ	p	f	t	t,	t°	θ	s	c	č	š	t_1	k_1	k	x	q
nasal	+	+	+	+	−	−	−	−	−	−	−	−	−	−	−	−	−	−	−
low	−	−	−	−	−	−	−	−	−	−	−	−	−	−	−	−	−	−	+
high	−	−	+	+	−	−	−	+	+	−	−	−	+	+	+	+	+	+	−
back	−	−	−	+	−	−	−	−	+	−	−	−	−	−	−	−	+	+	+
anterior	+	+	−	−	+	+	+	+	+	+	+	+	−	−	−	−	−	−	−
coronal	−	+	−	−	−	−	+	+	+	+	+	+	+	+	+	−	−	−	−
continuant	−	−	−	−	−	+	−	−	−	+	+	+	+	+	−	−	−	+	−
delayed release	−	−	−	−	−	+	−	+	−	−	−	+	+	+	+	−	−	−	−
strident	−	−	−	−	−	+	−	−	−	−	+	+	+	+	−	−	−	−	−

A difference between (12) and the analogous representation for vowels (7) is that while there is an "unmarked" vowel, there is no "unmarked" consonant. A few words should be said about the reasons for this disparity. In view of the fact that the unmarked nasal must be /n/ and the unmarked continuant /s/, the unmarked plosive—if there were to be one—would have to be /t/. This conclusion, however, seems unacceptable to us; in particular, the choice of the dental over the labial plosive appears incorrect. Furthermore, if the dental plosive is taken as "unmarked," then dental plosives with "supplementary" articulation—voicing, palatalization, velarization, rounding, etc.—will have a single marked feature each. As a result, the "supplementary" articulations of these consonants will have a different status, formally, from those of all other consonants. Finally, as will be seen in Section 4, some of the marking conventions also play a role in the interpretation of phonological rules. The formulation of convention (XXIIIc), which is forced upon us if "unmarked" consonants are not to be admitted, prevents this convention from affecting the phonological rules and restricts it to serving only in the interpretation of lexical items. As far as we can tell at the present stage of our knowledge, this restriction has the correct effects on the form and nature of the phonological rules.

As can be seen in (12), there are, therefore, five consonants, /p t k s n/, that are marked for just one feature. It is significant that these five consonants are rarely absent in the phonological system of a language. Trubetzkoy (1958, p. 135) notes that languages without apicals (dentals) are unknown to him, and that languages without velars and labials are extremely rare. He cites certain Slovene dialects as lacking velars; but this is, at most, a low-level phonetic fact, since the lexical representations of Slovene dialects, as of all Slavic languages, will clearly require velars. Tlingit is cited as the only language without labials. However, Jakobson (1940, pp. 357–58) notes that the absence of labials in the speech of women in a few Central African languages is caused by the ritualistic mutilation of the lips, and such mutilation also occurs among the Tlingit, where both men and women wear labrets. The dental continuant /s/ is equally common. Trubetzkoy lists only Eastern Nuer of the Egyptian Sudan as lacking this sound. Jakobson (1940, p. 360) cites P. Schmidt as his source for the absence of this sound in a series of "Australian, Tasmanian, Melanesian, Polynesian, African, and South American languages," and notes that in Karakalpak and Tamil fricatives appear only as combinatory variants of the stops. But such cases are obviously unusual. Finally, the absence of nasals is as uncommon among the languages of the world as is the absence of the other types of sounds just reviewed. Hockett (1955, p. 119) cites Quileute, Duwamish, Snoqualmie, and "probably also . . . a few other southern Coast Salishan dialects, as lacking nasal consonants altogether." He reports, moreover, that "languages with but a single nasal have an /n/, and usually have no labial consonant at all."

It was observed previously that the least marked segment, given the conventions outlined here, is the vowel /a/, which in many contexts requires only the lexical marking [*m* segment]. All other segments will require additional markings. In accordance with (7) and (12), there are two vowels, /i u/, and five consonants, /p t k s n/, that require only a single marking in addition to [*m* segment]. These eight sounds constitute, as it were, the minimal phonetic inventory available to a language. While many details must remain open for the present, it seems to us that the conception of a basic phonetic inventory and the proposed membership are, in the main, correct.

Given the theory of markedness as developed up to this point, the complexity of a specific phonological pattern—an inventory of segments—is related to the sum of the complexities of the individual segments. However, we have already noted with regard to vowel systems (see pp. 409–410) that certain systematic properties such as symmetry (in some sense that has yet to be made precise) must also play a role in determining complexity. This is true in the case of consonant systems as well. Thus, if the complexity of a system were merely the sum of the markedness values of its elements, a phonological system containing the five basic consonants /p t k s n/ and the voiced obstruents /b d g z/ would be as complex as a system which contained the five basic consonants and /b c x f/, each of which requires only one additional marking beyond that of the basic set. But this is surely incorrect. Such conventions as those proposed for vowel systems (see (9) and (10)) might provide the correct results in this case, but our understanding of the situation is too rudimentary for a detailed proposal to be of much value.

2.5. CONVENTIONS FOR LIQUIDS

Conventions (XXVIII)–(XXXIV) apply to liquids. It should be noted that in view of conventions (II) and (III) vowels and consonants may be unmarked for both the features "vocalic" and "consonantal" in certain positions. However, this is not true for the liquids and the glides; these will always have to be marked for at least one of the two features.

Convention (XXVIII) supplies the features that are phonetically fixed for liquids: liquids are sonorant, nonnasal, etc. Conventions (XXIX) and (XXXI) specify that the unmarked liquid is a dental. Convention (XXX) rules out labial liquids and convention (XXXII) excludes lateral uvulars. Conventions (XXXIII) and (XXXIV) specify that the unmarked coronal liquid is lateral (i.e., /l/ rather than /r/) and continuant.

2.6. CONVENTIONS FOR GLIDES

Conventions (XXXV)–(XXXIX) are a few of the conventions that apply to the glides. Convention (XXXV) specifies that glides are sonorant, nonanterior, noncoronal, and nonnasal.

These conventions are quite similar to the vowel conventions except that noncontinuant glides are permitted. It may also be noted that the conventions as given here admit both high and nonhigh glides. They therefore provide a slot for the glide /ɛ/, for which we found some evidence in English (see Chapters Three and Four). Note finally that, as in the vowel system, backness is specified by the marking conventions only for the low glides, /h ʔ/. Among the nonlow glides the feature "back" is always marked.

3. *Markedness and lexical representation*

Let us now consider the consequences for lexical representation of a system of interpretive conventions such as (6). The least complex lexical entry will be the single-segment entry /a/, which in this case will have but one marked feature, [*m* segment]; when it is not a separate lexical entry it may be marked as a vowel as well. Lexical entries consisting of more than one segment will, by conventions (II) and (III), have the form CVCVCV ..., where C is a true consonant, unless further marked. Each of the consonants may be one of the five belonging to the basic set [p t k s n] in the simplest possible lexical entry. Thus, we have such items as /pata/, /tata/, /kata/, /sasa/, /nana/.

To consider a real example, the English word *stun* would be represented in the lexicon by the matrix (14):

$\begin{pmatrix}14\end{pmatrix}$

segment	*m*	*m*	*m*	*m*
consonantal				
vocalic		*m*		
nasal				*m*
low				
high				
back			+	
round				
anterior				
coronal			+	
continuant				
delayed release				
strident				

The conventions of (6) (plus a few other straightforward conventions) will then apply to this matrix, yielding (15):

$\begin{pmatrix}15\end{pmatrix}$

segment	+	+	+	+
consonantal	+	+	−	+
vocalic	−	−	+	−
nasal	−	−	−	+
low	−	−	−	−
high	−	−	+	−
back	−	−	+	−
round	−	−	+	−
anterior	+	+	−	+
coronal	+	+	−	+
continuant	+	−	+	−
delayed release	+	−	+	−
strident	+	−	−	−

As already observed, the problems connected with the appearance of unspecified features in lexical matrices alongside of features specified + and − (see Section 8 of Chapter Eight) will no longer arise, since all matrices are now fully specified at all times. Notice, moreover, that many redundancy rules that were necessary in the earlier version of the theory are now replaced by universal conventions and can therefore be dispensed with in grammars of individual languages. For example, convention (V) specifies that all vowels are nonanterior, nonstrident, etc.; this is now no longer presented as a fact specific to English but rather as a universal convention for interpreting grammars. The same is true of the conventions that, unlike (V), are not absolute but that assign segments and phonological systems to a hierarchy of complexity. The interpretive conventions are the major devices for expressing the various interdependencies among features. They express in a natural way both the fact that certain feature complexes are impossible ((V), for example) and the fact that certain feature combinations are less complex than others ((X), for example, which indicates that among the low vowels, the back vowels are less complex than their nonback counterparts, except under the conditions discussed on page 410).

The interpretive conventions state not only constraints on feature combinations within segments, but also constraints on segment sequences. Thus convention (XXIV) eliminates the necessity for a redundancy rule in English stating that in initial preconsonantal position the only admitted consonant is /s/. A consonant in this position may now be totally unmarked, as in (14), and the proper feature values will be supplied by the universal conventions.

Some language-specific redundancy rules remain, of course—for example, those that introduce truly idiosyncratic properties such as [−rule *n*] in certain contexts. Furthermore, if our analysis of English is correct, there will be several redundancy rules that are specific to English. The rules that determine the distribution of /o/ and /ɔ/ in lexical entries (see Chapter Four) provide one example. For the most part, however, those redundancy rules that have any wide applicability in the grammar are simply eliminated in favor of universal interpretive conventions.

Although the replacement of particular rules by general conventions is, if tenable, an obvious step forward, there is one difficulty that arises from this new conception of redundancy. In the earlier version, we were able to make a distinction between phonologically admissible and phonologically inadmissible matrices in terms of the redundancy rules. Thus we had a three-way distinction among such items as /brik/ (in the lexicon), /blik/ (accidental gap), and /bnik/ (inadmissible). The "accidental gaps" were the items that did not appear in the lexicon but were not ruled out by the redundancy rules. Now that we have eliminated most redundancy rules, the category of "accidental gaps" is no longer defined in any reasonable way.

Before we turn to this new problem, we should note that the discussion of accidental gaps, both in our comments in Section 8 of Chapter Eight and in all of the recent literature on the subject, has been oversimplified in one important respect. It is not true that potential lexical items are simply divided into the three categories just mentioned: occurring, accidental gaps, and inadmissible. Items that do not appear in the lexicon differ strikingly in their "degree of admissibility."[6] Thus the matrices /bnik/ and /bnzk/ are both inadmissible in English, but the difference between them is at least as linguistically significant as the difference between these two matrices and /brik/, /blik/. Hence a real solution to the problem of "admissibility" will not simply define a tripartite categorization of occurring, accidental gap, and inadmissible, but will define the "degree of admissibility" of each potential

---

[6] Furthermore, in any real grammar, the lexicon will actually contain certain items that are "inadmissible." In English, for example, there are items such as *Tlingit*, *tsetse*, *kook*. There are also words such as *sphere*, *sphincter*, which violate restrictions on initial clusters, and *adze*, *smaragd*, which violate restrictions on final clusters, etc. We return to this matter directly. (See note 7.)

lexical matrix in such a way as to distinguish /blik/ from /bnik/, and /bnik/ from /bnzk/, and to make numerous other distinctions of this sort.

Given a lexicon L, which determines a set of interpreted lexical matrices of the form (15), we can define the "distance" from L of a lexical matrix μ in the following way. Let us say that rule (16) *distinguishes* μ from L if (16) does not change any member of L (i.e., given ν ε L, either (16) is inapplicable to ν or it leaves ν unaltered) but (16) does change μ; and furthermore, (16) is minimal in that any other rule meeting these conditions contains at least as many features F specified [+F] or [−F] as does (16):

$$\left(16\right) \qquad\qquad X \; \rightarrow \; Y \; / \; Z \text{---} W$$

Let us define the distance of μ from L as $1/n$, where n is the number of features specified as [+F] or [−F] in a rule that distinguishes μ from L in this sense. Where the distance is undefined in this way (there being no such rule), let us say that it is zero.

For example, let L be the lexicon of English and consider the distance of /brik/, /blik/, /bnik/, /bnzk/ from L. The distance of /brik/ from L is zero since there is no rule distinguishing it from L. The distance of /blik/ from L is 1/17 since the minimal rule distinguishing /blik/ from L is (17), which has 17 specified features. The distance of /bnik/ from L is 1/5, since the distinguishing rule is (18). The distance of /bnzk/ from L is 1/4 since the distinguishing rule is (19).

$$\left(17\right) \qquad [+\text{cons}] \; \rightarrow \; [-\text{lateral}] \; / \; [-\text{seg}] \begin{bmatrix} +\text{cons} \\ -\text{voc} \\ +\text{ant} \\ -\text{cor} \\ +\text{voice} \end{bmatrix} \text{---} \begin{bmatrix} +\text{high} \\ -\text{back} \\ -\text{tense} \end{bmatrix} \begin{bmatrix} +\text{cons} \\ -\text{voc} \\ -\text{ant} \\ -\text{cor} \\ -\text{cont} \\ -\text{voice} \end{bmatrix}$$

$$\left(18\right) \qquad [+\text{cons}] \; \rightarrow \; [-\text{nasal}] \; / \; [-\text{seg}] \begin{bmatrix} +\text{cons} \\ -\text{cont} \end{bmatrix} \text{---}$$

$$\left(19\right) \qquad [+\text{seg}] \; \rightarrow \; [+\text{voc}] \; / \; [+\text{cons}][+\text{nasal}] \text{---}$$

In short, to determine the distance of a matrix μ from L, we find the simplest rule which is "true of L," in the obvious sense, but not true of μ, and we take the distance of μ from L to be inversely related to the complexity of this rule. This measure of distance can be refined in various ways. For example, certain distinguishing rules may be universal and may be taken as defining an absolute "maximal" distance; we can take into account the natural hierarchy of features discussed on page 410 and consider the position of X in (16) in this hierarchy in determining distance, etc. Furthermore, we can assign special status to rules that make use of "natural" environments, such as "initial cluster," "vocalic nucleus," etc. Without going into these and other refinements, however, it is clear even from the very simple examples given that an interesting and linguistically significant characterization of "degree of phonological admissibility" can be given in quite general terms, even if grammars contain no redundancy rules. We feel, therefore, that the proposed measure of distance is an improvement over the tripartite categorization that was discussed in earlier treatments of this problem, although it still falls short of providing a fully adequate explication of phonological admissibility.[7]

Notice that this approach to phonological admissibility leads to certain asymmetries that should be studied further. For example, we need no redundancy rule to account for the unvoicing of clusters in English. Consonant clusters in lexical entries will simply not be marked for voicing, and a marking convention will specify that all obstruents unmarked for voicing are unvoiced. In other words, the lexicon of English will be the simplest possible, in this respect.[8] Items with voiced clusters will be at a certain "distance" from the lexicon, as indicated in the preceding discussion. But consider a language in which all clusters are voiced in the lexicon. If we are correct in our general assumption that [−voice] is the unmarked value of voicing for obstruents, then in this language it will be necessary to add a rule that voices obstruents in clusters. Whereas in English an item with a voiced cluster violates no rules but is only semi-admissible on very general grounds, in this hypothetical language an unvoiced cluster will violate a rule of the phonology and will therefore be an exception of a very different sort. In fact, it will have to be characterized by a feature of the type [−rule n]. We would therefore expect that in such a case cluster-unvoicing would, in general, be a property of formatives rather than of individual clusters. We have no examples at hand to suggest whether this interpretation of these phenomena is correct or incorrect, but the problem is quite clear, and it should be possible to find crucial examples.

Let us turn now to some of the other consequences of the approach to redundancy that we have outlined.

In Chapter Four, Section 2.2, we discussed the fact that in English a vowel becomes lax before a consonant cluster within the same formative unless the cluster in question consists of dental consonants.[9] Thus we cannot have formatives such as *[dūwkt] or *[tāypt], but we can have *hoist*, *find*, etc. We accounted for this fact by a readjustment rule, which we repeat here as (20), that excludes certain vowels from the application of the laxing rule n.

---

[7] The analogy between degree of phonological admissibility and degree of grammaticalness is obvious. Just as certain sentences that are semi-grammatical can find a more natural use than others that are fully grammatical (e.g., many common metaphors), so, analogously, we expect to find certain items in a lexicon that depart from the regularities of that lexicon and, correspondingly, depart from phonological admissibility. In defining the degree of deviation of a sentence from a corpus or an item from a lexicon, we must therefore provide for "semi-grammaticalness" of occurring items; we might, for example, define the distance of an item from a normalized set (lexicon or corpus) from which certain items are systematically excluded. List frequency of exceptions, in the lexicon, would therefore be a relevant factor in determining degree of admissibility. The problems are nontrivial, but various approaches can be suggested.

[8] As noted in Chapter Three, Section 16, there are a few exceptions to this generalization. The words listed there will, as a group, be phonologically deviant. As pointed out in the preceding note, the question of how list frequency of certain configurations in the lexicon should be introduced into considerations of admissibility is not trivial, but there is little doubt that such considerations are necessary.

If a measure is precisely defined, it will, of course, make sharp distinctions, many of which will not be independently motivated. Such distinctions, then, will be motivated only indirectly, in terms of the plausibility of the general metric and, ultimately, the empirical considerations on which it is based. Clearly, the lack of independent motivation for the sharp distinctions themselves provides no evidence one way or another for the proposed measure of evaluation. We mention this because there has been much confusion and idle controversy over the matter. For example, it has been maintained that the theory of admissibility discussed on pages 381 f., which defined a tripartite division into occurring, admissible, and inadmissible, was ill-conceived because the addition of one item to the lexicon might well imply a redistribution of matrices among these three categories. As noted, we now feel that this theory must be abandoned, for other reasons; but surely the objection just mentioned has no force whatsoever. It is simply an objection to precision in the development of a procedure of evaluation for grammars.

[9] We actually extended the exception slightly—see page 241, note 2—but this is not relevant here.

$$\left(20\right) \qquad\qquad V \rightarrow [-\text{rule } n] \Big/ \underline{\hspace{1cm}} \begin{bmatrix} +\text{cons} \\ +\text{ant} \\ +\text{cor} \end{bmatrix} \begin{bmatrix} +\text{cons} \\ +\text{cor} \end{bmatrix}$$

Although we did not discuss the matter in Chapter Four, there is a certain difficulty in the application of this rule. In order for it to apply correctly in forms such as *find, faint,* etc., it is necessary for /n/ to be specified as dental (i.e., as [+anterior, +coronal]) at the point of application of (20), that is, in the lexicon. Notice, however, that the well-known rule of assimilation with respect to point of articulation applies to nasals before stops. Thus we have [n] in *lint, wind*; [m] in *lamp, ramble*; [ŋ] in *sink, mingle*. Consequently nasals in this position should appear in the lexicon as unspecified with respect to the features "anterior" and "coronal." Furthermore, the rule that assimilates point of articulation must be a relatively late rule of the phonology, occurring after the stress rules, since it involves position of stress. (Compare *Concord* [káŋkərd]–*concordance* [kankɔ́rdəns]; *congress* [káŋgrəs]–*congressional* [kəngréšənəl]; etc.)

This problem could not really be solved within the framework that was presupposed previously. It would have been necessary to specify /n/ fully in the context ——"dental," while leaving /n/ in other pre-stop contexts unspecified with respect to point of articulation. The general assimilation rule would then apply to all nasals before stops, but application would be vacuous in the pre-dental position. Now, however, within the framework of conventions (6), this difficulty is resolved in a straightforward way. Nasals will be unmarked before stops, as required, and will be specified as /n/ by the marking conventions (XXIIb) and (XXIIIc), which realize unmarked nasal consonants as [+anterior] and [+coronal]. The late phonological rule that determines the point of articulation of nasals before stops remains as before, but the fact that nasals must be specified as dental in order for rule (20) to apply properly no longer involves an unmotivated cost in complexity.

Supporting evidence for this approach comes from another property of point-of-articulation assimilation of nasals before stops. Consider words such as *congress–congressional* in which [ŋ] alternates with [n]. As was just noted, the application of the assimilation rule depends on stress. Thus, in *cóngress* there is assimilation of the features "anterior" and "coronal" from the velar stop to the preceding nasal, but not in *congréssional*. In the latter form the nasal is $\begin{bmatrix} +\text{anterior} \\ +\text{coronal} \end{bmatrix}$. Obviously, then, the "neutral" position for nasals is dental, as is, in fact, indicated by conventional orthography.[10]

4. Markedness and phonological rules: linking

In introducing the discussion in this chapter, we noted that certain rules are more plausible than others, although the distinction cannot be made in purely formal terms. Thus, in either synchronic or diachronic description one might expect such rules as those of (1i), but the corresponding rules of (1ii) are somewhat less natural (and, in some cases, quite impossible). We now have machinery for making some of these distinctions.

---

[10] Thus, from the point of view of our earlier discussion, the spelling *sink, sing* is no more natural than would be the spelling *simk, simg* for these words. It might be possible, incidentally, to develop an independent test of the linguistically motivated decisions as to marking by examining the relative ease with which alternative spelling conventions, in such cases as these, can be learned by children.

Suppose that the phonology contains the rule (21) and that one of the universal marking conventions is (22), where α, β = + or −, *Y, Z, Q, W* may be null, and the feature G is distinct from F.

$$\left(21\right) \qquad\qquad X \;\rightarrow\; [\alpha F] \;\Big/\; Y\left[\overline{}_{\,Q}\right] Z$$

$$\left(22\right) \qquad\qquad [uG] \;\rightarrow\; [\beta G] \;\Big/\; \left[\begin{array}{c}\overline{} \\ \alpha F \\ W \end{array}\right]$$

Suppose that we were now to say that when a rule and a convention are formally related as are (21) and (22), they are "linked." We will interpret such linkage in the following manner. When rule (21) applies to a segment containing *X* in the context $Y\left[\overline{}_{\,Q}\right]Z$, it assigns to this segment the feature specification [αF] in the usual way. If, furthermore, the segment to which (21) has applied meets the condition *W* of (22), then the feature specification [βG] is automatically assigned to that segment. In order to prevent the assignment of [βG], rule (21) will have to be made more complex in some way. The natural proposal is to stipulate that linkage of (21), (22) is blocked if (21) is revised with [αF, γG] replacing [αF]. Thus, given the convention (22), a process that rewrites *X* as [αF, βG] is more plausible, more highly valued in the grammar, than an otherwise identical process that rewrites *X* as [αF]; the latter rule will be more complex in that it will have to mention G to the right of the arrow. We are thus making the very strong empirical claim that the marking conventions, which were established for an entirely different purpose, contribute significantly to determining the concept "rule plausibility."

It is readily seen that marking conventions such as (6XXa, b), where the context *W* includes features that are specified in terms of the values *u* or *m*, can never serve as linking rules, since the conditions on the linking of rules and conventions will never be satisfied. Moreover, conventions such as (6XVI), which specify the unmarked value of the feature independently of context, will not function as linking rules. On the other hand, conventions such as (XXIIa) will function only as linking rules. We have expressed this fact by including [αcontinuant] in the environment of this convention. As noted above, since α is a variable ranging over + and − only, (XXIIa) cannot apply as a marking convention because no segment will be specified [±continuant] at the point where (XXIIa) becomes applicable as a marking rule. We will extend and refine the account of linking as we proceed.

To illustrate with a concrete and well-known example, let us consider in detail the so-called palatalizations of Slavic.[11] Although usually presented as fossilized historical processes, the palatalizations are, in fact, productive in most modern Slavic languages. (For a demonstration of this fact in modern Russian, see Lightner (1965a).) We may therefore be dealing with a quite recent stage of the language. However, since the dating of the palatalization processes is irrelevant for the purposes of the following discussion, we shall not concern ourselves with this question any further; we shall simply assume that we are examining the stage in the development of the Slavic languages at which the palatalizations were productive.

---

[11] The factual material on which this discussion is based is readily available in the standard handbooks such as Meillet (1924), Vaillant (1950), and Bräuer (1961). The interpretations offered here, which in part deviate from traditional accounts, are discussed in Halle and Lightner (forthcoming).

We wish to account for the facts shown in (23):[12]

$\begin{pmatrix}23\end{pmatrix}$

	FIRST VELAR PALATALIZATION			SECOND VELAR PALATALIZATION			DENTAL PALATALIZATION			
underlying segment	k	g	x	k	g	x	t	d	s	z
South Slavic	č	ǰ	š	c	3	s	t₁	d₁	š	ž
East Slavic	č	ǰ	š	c	3	s	č	ǰ	š	ž
West Slavic	č	ǰ	š	c	3	š	c	3	š	ž

Of interest in the following discussion will be the interpretive conventions (XIX)–(XXVII), which for the reader's convenience we reproduce here as (24) (omitting (XXI), which is irrelevant here):

$\begin{pmatrix}24\end{pmatrix}$

(XIX) $\qquad\qquad [+\text{high}] \rightarrow [-\text{low}]$

(XX)

$$[u \text{ back}] \rightarrow \begin{cases} [-\text{back}] & / \begin{bmatrix} \rule{1em}{0.4pt} \\ u \text{ ant} \\ -\text{low} \end{bmatrix} & \text{(a)} \\[2em] [+\text{back}] & / \begin{cases} \begin{bmatrix} \rule{1em}{0.4pt} \\ m \text{ ant} \end{bmatrix} & \text{(b)} \\[1em] \begin{bmatrix} \rule{1em}{0.4pt} \\ +\text{low} \end{bmatrix} & \text{(c)} \end{cases} \end{cases}$$

(XXII)

$$[u \text{ ant}] \rightarrow \begin{cases} [-\text{ant}] & / \begin{bmatrix} \rule{1em}{0.4pt} \\ +\text{high} \\ +\text{cor} \\ \alpha\text{cont} \end{bmatrix} & \text{(a)} \\[2em] [+\text{ant}] & & \text{(b)} \end{cases}$$

(XXIII)

$$[u \text{ cor}] \rightarrow \begin{cases} [-\text{cor}] & / \begin{bmatrix} \rule{1em}{0.4pt} \\ -\text{ant} \\ +\text{nasal} \end{bmatrix} & \text{(a)} \\[2em] [\alpha\text{cor}] & / \begin{bmatrix} \rule{1em}{0.4pt} \\ -\alpha\text{back} \\ -\text{ant} \end{bmatrix} & \text{(b)} \\[2em] [+\text{cor}] & / \begin{bmatrix} \rule{1em}{0.4pt} \\ +\text{ant} \\ \{[+\text{nasal}]\} \\ \{[m \text{ cont}]\} \end{bmatrix} & \text{(c)} \end{cases}$$

[12] In order not to complicate the discussion unduly, we shall exclude from consideration here the fact that the voiced stop /g/ alternates with strident continuants rather than with strident noncontinuants. We shall assume that this adjustment is taken care of by a phonological rule that does not concern us here. We shall also assume that the products of all palatalizations are palatalized, i.e., $\begin{bmatrix} -\text{back} \\ +\text{high} \end{bmatrix}$. Thus /c/, for example, will be [+high] in this case.

The term "Second Velar Palatalization" is used ambiguously in the literature. We use it here to refer to the palatalization of velars before front vowels derived from underlying diphthongs beginning with a back vowel. We do not discuss the velar palatalization discovered by Baudouin de Courtenay (1894), which is a separate phenomenon. (See Halle and Lightner, forthcoming.)

(XXIV) $[u \text{ cont}] \rightarrow \begin{cases} [+\text{cont}] & / & + \underline{\quad} [+\text{cons}] \\ [-\text{cont}] \end{cases}$ (a)
(b)

(XXV) $[+\text{cont}] \rightarrow [+\text{delayed release}]$

(XXVI)

$[u \text{ delayed release}] \rightarrow \begin{cases} [+\text{del rel}] & / & \begin{bmatrix} \underline{\quad} \\ -\text{ant} \\ +\text{cor} \end{bmatrix} \\ \\ [-\text{del rel}] \end{cases}$ (a)

(b)

(XXVII)

$[u \text{ strid}] \rightarrow \begin{cases} [-\text{strid}] & / & \begin{cases} \begin{bmatrix} \underline{\quad} \\ +\text{son} \end{bmatrix} \\ \begin{bmatrix} \underline{\quad} \\ -\text{ant} \\ -\text{cor} \end{bmatrix} \end{cases} \\ \\ [\alpha\text{strid}] & / & \begin{bmatrix} \overline{\alpha\text{del rel}} \\ \begin{cases} [+\text{ant}] \\ [+\text{cor}] \end{cases} \end{bmatrix} \end{cases}$

(a)

(b)

(c)

As shown in (23), the First Velar Palatalization produces the same results in all three major dialect areas. The environment in which this process takes place is usually given as "before front vowels and before /y/." Some students—e.g., Meillet (1924)—treat this as a single phenomenon; others—e.g., Leskien (1919), Bräuer (1961)—treat palatalization before front vowels as distinct from palatalization before /y/, and combine the latter with other alternations that take place before /y/, such as the palatalization of dentals and labials. Since, however, the dental and labial palatalizations yield different results from the palatalization of velars before /y/, it is clearly incorrect to combine these phenomena, especially in view of the fact that palatalization of velars before /y/ produces precisely the same results as palatalization of velars before front vowels. Moreover, as noted in Section 2 of Chapter 8, the distinctive feature framework provides us with a ready-made device to characterize the environment in question.

At the point in derivations at which the First Velar Palatalization takes place, velars will be the only type of nonanterior consonants that appear in the representations. We would therefore expect to formulate the First Palatalization as (25):[13]

$\left(25\right)$ $[-\text{ant}] \rightarrow \begin{bmatrix} -\text{back} \\ +\text{cor} \\ +\text{del rel} \\ +\text{strid} \end{bmatrix} / \underline{\quad} \begin{bmatrix} -\text{cons} \\ -\text{back} \end{bmatrix}$

It is easy to understand why a velar would be fronted—i.e., replaced by $/k_1/$—before a front glide or vowel; it is not so easy to see why the other features should also change. Recall that in (12) the palato-alveolar /č/ is less marked than either the palato-alveolar plosive $/t_1/$ or the

---

[13] We omit, here and below, specification of the features [−vocalic, +consonantal] for the segments undergoing the rules.

The reader may find it helpful to refer to table (13) (p. 413).

palatal plosive $/k_1/$. The less-marked status of $/\check{c}/$, as well as the marking conventions (24), reflects the fact that in consonant systems with four points of articulation, the fourth point (in addition to labial, dental, and velar) is commonly occupied by the palato-alveolar affricate $/\check{c}/$ rather than by $/t_1/$ or $/k_1/$. As noted on page 420, the marking conventions affect not only lexical representation but also the interpretation of phonological rules to which they are linked. An examination of conventions (24) immediately reveals that several are linked to the phonological rule (25), namely, one case of (24XXIIIb), (XXVIa), and one case of (XXVIIc). These conventions govern the features "coronal," "delayed release," and "strident," which are just the ones whose status is at issue in rule (25). The marking conventions, then, functioning successively in linkage, provide the desired values for these three features. They tell us that when velar obstruents are fronted, it is simpler for them also to become strident palato-alveolars with delayed release.

Notice that to achieve this result, we must extend the notion of "linking" given earlier and permit the *successive* application of marking conventions functioning as linking rules. Thus the conclusion regarding rule plausibility that we have just formulated (namely, that fronting of velar obstruents will normally convert them to strident palato-alveolars with delayed release) requires, in our framework, that the process (25) be stated as rule (26):

$\left(26\right)$ FIRST VELAR PALATALIZATION

$$[-\mathrm{ant}] \quad \rightarrow \quad [-\mathrm{back}] \ / \ \underline{\quad\quad} \begin{bmatrix} -\mathrm{cons} \\ -\mathrm{back} \end{bmatrix}$$

Convention (24XXIIIb) links directly to this rule, so that rule (26) is interpreted as also assigning the feature specification $[+\mathrm{coronal}]$. But we must now extend the notion of "linkage," in an obvious way, so that convention (24XXVIa), introducing the feature $[+\mathrm{delayed\ release}]$, links to convention (24XXIIIb) and hence applies at this point. And, by the same extension of the notion "linkage," convention (24XXVIIc), introducing $[+\mathrm{strident}]$, links to (24XXVIa) and also applies, completing the process (25).

According to our earlier definition, (28) links to (27), where (28) is a marking convention and (27) a phonological rule:

$\left(27\right)$
$$X \ \rightarrow \ [\alpha F] \ / \ Y \begin{bmatrix} \underline{\quad\quad} \\ Q \end{bmatrix} Z$$

$\left(28\right)$
$$[uG] \ \rightarrow \ [\beta G] \ / \ \begin{bmatrix} \underline{\quad\quad} \\ \alpha F \\ W \end{bmatrix}$$

Let us now say that the same is true not only when (27) is a rule but also when it is a marking convention, in which case $X = [uF]$.

Suppose now that (27) is again a phonological rule, and that $C_1, \ldots, C_n$ is a sequence of marking conventions such that for each $i \geq 1$, C_i is the convention (29), where $G_0 = F$ and $\alpha_0 = \alpha$ of (27):

$\left(29\right)$
$$[uG_i] \ \rightarrow \ [\alpha_i G_i] \ / \ \begin{bmatrix} \underline{\quad\quad} \\ \alpha_{i-1} G_{i-1} \\ W_i \end{bmatrix}$$

Thus C_1 is linked to (27), and for each $i > 1$, C_i is linked to C_{i-1}. Suppose further that for each $i, j \geq 0$, $G_i \neq G_j$. Suppose now that the rule (27) applies to some segment S and that for each $i < n$, S, when modified to contain the feature complex $[\alpha_0 G_0, \ldots, \alpha_i G_i]$, satisfies the condition W_{i+1}. Suppose, finally, that $C_1, \ldots, C_n$ is the longest sequence meeting these conditions. Then we interpret rule (27) as assigning to the segment S the feature complex $[\alpha_0 G_0, \ldots, \alpha_n G_n]$. In the special case $n = 1$, we have the situation of linkage that was defined earlier.

In the case of the First Velar Palatalization, (27) is (26), and C_1, C_2, C_3 are (30), (31), (32), respectively:

$$\left(30\right) \qquad [u \text{ cor}] \quad \rightarrow \quad [+\text{cor}] \quad / \quad \begin{bmatrix} \rule{1.5em}{0.4pt} \\ -\text{back} \\ -\text{ant} \end{bmatrix} \qquad \text{ONE CASE OF (24XXIIIb)}$$

$$\left(31\right) \qquad [u \text{ del rel}] \quad \rightarrow \quad [+\text{del rel}] \quad / \quad \begin{bmatrix} \rule{1.5em}{0.4pt} \\ -\text{ant} \\ +\text{cor} \end{bmatrix} \qquad \text{(24XXVIa)}$$

$$\left(32\right) \qquad [u \text{ strid}] \quad \rightarrow \quad [+\text{strid}] \quad / \quad \begin{bmatrix} \rule{1.5em}{0.4pt} \\ +\text{del rel} \\ +\text{cor} \end{bmatrix} \qquad \text{ONE CASE OF (24XXVIIc)}$$

With this quite natural concept of "linkage," the process (25) is stated simply as (26), a simple assimilation rule, and hence is highly "plausible" in the required sense.

Consider next the so-called "Second Velar Palatalization" as it manifests itself in South and East Slavic. This alternation is produced by the replacement of velars by strident dentals (i.e., $/k/ \rightarrow [c]$, $/g/ \rightarrow [\mathrecstrict{3}]$, $/x/ \rightarrow [s]$) before certain front vowels that derive from the diphthongs $/oy/$ and $/ay/$. We shall assume that following the First Velar Palatalization (26), the grammars of South and East Slavic contain the Diphthong Rule (33):

$$\left(33\right) \qquad \begin{Bmatrix} \text{oy} \\ \text{ay} \end{Bmatrix} \quad \rightarrow \quad \text{nonback vowels}$$

Since rule (33) applies after the First Velar Palatalization Rule (26), velars before front vowels deriving from diphthongs are not subject to First Palatalization. If the Second Velar Palatalization is made to apply after the Diphthong Rule, it can then be stated quite simply as applying before front vowels. Note, however, that the strident palato-alveolars resulting from the First Palatalization, which are nonanterior, are not subject to the Second Palatalization. Thus, the Second Palatalization, unlike the First Palatalization, cannot apply to all nonanterior consonants; instead it is restricted to nonanterior consonants that must be specified either as $[+\text{back}]$ or $[-\text{strident}]$. We shall assume that the additional specification should be $[-\text{strident}]$ rather than $[+\text{back}]$, and shall provide some motivation for this assumption in the discussion that follows. Since we have thus excluded the palato-alveolars produced by the First Palatalization, we may somewhat generalize the environment in which the Second Palatalization applies. It is no longer necessary to exclude specifically the environment before the glide $/y/$, and we may therefore allow the Second Palatalization to apply before $[-\text{consonantal}, -\text{back}]$, that is, in the same environment as the First Palatalization.

Having characterized the context in which the process applies, we must turn to the question of the modification that it effects. The difference between the results of the First and Second Palatalizations is that the former produces nonanterior strident coronals, whereas the latter results in strident coronals which are $[+\text{anterior}]$. This naturally suggests a rule of the form (34).

$\left(34\right)$ SECOND VELAR PALATALIZATION (SOUTH AND EAST SLAVIC)

$$\begin{bmatrix} -\text{ant} \\ -\text{strid} \end{bmatrix} \rightarrow \begin{bmatrix} -\text{back} \\ +\text{ant} \end{bmatrix} / \underline{\quad\quad} \begin{bmatrix} -\text{cons} \\ -\text{back} \end{bmatrix}$$

We would like to be able to interpret rule (34) so that it links to the conventions that introduce the features [+coronal], [+delayed release], and [+strident], analogous to the case of the First Palatalization. Certainly it seems natural to assume that these features are determined in the same manner in both processes of palatalization, that a linguistically significant generalization underlies the appearance of these three specified features in the two cases. However, the theory of linkage that we have just developed does not, in general, provide for cases such as (34) in which two features appear on the right-hand side of the arrow. Since this seems to us the appropriate form of the rule, we shall attempt to extend the theory of rule application so as to permit the required linkage.

The first suggestion that comes to mind is that we analyze (34) into two rules, the first of which shifts the feature "back," and the second the feature "anterior." The marking conventions will now link properly, as before, to the first of these two rules. Thus we replace (34) by the sequence of rules (35), (36):

$\left(35\right)$
$$\begin{bmatrix} -\text{ant} \\ -\text{strid} \end{bmatrix} \rightarrow [-\text{back}] / \underline{\quad\quad} \begin{bmatrix} -\text{cons} \\ -\text{back} \end{bmatrix}$$

$\left(36\right)$
$$\begin{bmatrix} -\text{ant} \\ +\text{cor} \\ +\text{del rel} \\ +\text{strid} \end{bmatrix} \rightarrow [+\text{ant}] / \underline{\quad\quad} \begin{bmatrix} -\text{cons} \\ -\text{back} \end{bmatrix}$$

Rule (35) converts /k/ to [k_1], which automatically becomes [č], as discussed above in connection with the First Palatalization. Rule (36) will then convert this [č] to [c] (which in this case is also [+high]—see note 12).

This proposal is unworkable, however. Since the environment in which (36) applies is the same as that of the First Palatalization (25), rule (36) would also affect the [č] produced by the First Palatalization, converting it, incorrectly, to [c].

It seems to us that the correct solution to this problem lies in an extension of the theory of rule application along the following lines. Let us make the very general assumption that two successive lines of a derivation can differ only by a single feature specification. A rule such as (34) must then be interpreted in two steps, that is, in one of the two ways which we can represent as (37) and (38):

$\left(37\right)$
$$\begin{bmatrix} -\text{ant} \\ -\text{strid} \end{bmatrix} \rightarrow [-\text{back}] \rightarrow [+\text{ant}] / \ldots$$

$\left(38\right)$
$$\begin{bmatrix} -\text{ant} \\ -\text{strid} \end{bmatrix} \rightarrow [+\text{ant}] \rightarrow [-\text{back}] / \ldots$$

We will select the interpretation (37), returning to the justification for this choice directly. Rule (34), interpreted as (37), is to be understood as follows: first, the appropriate instances of /k/ are converted to [k_1]; second, the linking rules apply in the manner discussed above; third, those segments which have been formed in steps one and two are converted to their anterior counterparts; fourth, the linking rules apply as before. What is new in rule (37) is its "non-Markovian" character. That is, rule (37) differs from the sequence of rules (35), (36) in that its second step applies only to segments which are formed by its first step; whereas in the case of the sequence of rules (35), (36), the second rule (i.e., (36)) has no "memory" and cannot distinguish those occurrences of [č] formed from (35) and the marking conventions from other occurrences of [č] that may be present in the relevant environment at this point in a derivation—from occurrences of [č] resulting from the First Palatalization, for example.

Under this new interpretation, rule (34) has precisely the effects required by the facts of the Second Velar Palatalization in South and East Slavic, as we can see from (23) (p. 421). Note especially that conventions (24XXa) and (24XXIIIc) are not linking rules and that none of the linking rules are sensitive to shifts from [−anterior] to [+anterior].

The facts of the Second Velar Palatalization in West Slavic are readily accounted for by restricting the second step in the derivation to noncontinuants:

$$\left(39\right) \quad \text{SECOND VELAR PALATALIZATION (WEST SLAVIC)}$$

$$\begin{bmatrix} -\text{ant} \\ -\text{strid} \\ \langle -\text{cont} \rangle \end{bmatrix} \rightarrow \begin{bmatrix} -\text{back} \\ \langle +\text{ant} \rangle \end{bmatrix} / \underline{\qquad} \begin{bmatrix} -\text{cons} \\ -\text{back} \end{bmatrix}$$

The schema (39) abbreviates two rules, the first of which applies to nonanterior nonstrident noncontinuants in two steps, as illustrated by (37), and the second of which simply fronts nonanterior nonstrident segments in the manner of (26). It is quite natural for (34) and (39) to be so similar since they characterize similar phenomena in closely related languages. Therefore, the fact that the rules for West Slavic differ in such a minor way from those for South and East Slavic may be regarded as providing a certain amount of support for the analysis proposed here and for the theory underlying this analysis.[14]

Before continuing with the topic under discussion, we note that the process of Velar Softening in English (see (6) and (114), Chapter Four, where [−back] was omitted since it was not crucial to the discussion there) is very similar to (39). Under the theory of rule application that we have now developed, Velar Softening would be characterized by the schema (40):

$$\left(40\right) \quad \text{VELAR SOFTENING (ENGLISH)}$$

$$\begin{bmatrix} -\text{ant} \\ -\text{cont} \\ +\text{deriv} \\ \langle -\text{voice} \rangle \end{bmatrix} \rightarrow \begin{bmatrix} -\text{back} \\ \langle +\text{ant} \rangle \end{bmatrix} / \underline{\qquad} \begin{bmatrix} -\text{back} \\ -\text{low} \\ -\text{cons} \end{bmatrix}$$

Under the proposed interpretation, the two velars in the derivable word *regicide* will be converted to [g₁] and [k₁], respectively, by the first step of (40), and then to [ǰ] and [č] by marking conventions which link to this rule. The second step of the first rule abbreviated by (40) will then convert unvoiced [č] formed by the first step to [c]. Note that other instances of [č], not formed by the first step of rule (40), will not be affected by the second

---

[14] We noted above that if the Second Palatalization were not restricted to nonstrident consonants, it would affect the segments produced by the First Palatalization Rule, turning these, as well as the remaining velars, into strident dentals. If this were actually the desired result, there would then be no need for the First Palatalization Rule, since the output of the grammar would be the same whether or not it included this rule. These considerations are of more than abstract interest since the well-known *mazurzenie* phenomenon of Polish is precisely of this type and would be formally characterized in the manner just outlined.

step. Thus, in the word *cherub*, for example (which is [+derivable]—cf. *cherubic*—and has [č] before a nonback nonlow vowel), the initial segment will not be converted to [c] by the second part of the Velar Softening Rule.

In the cases just reviewed, then, the proposed modification of the theory of rule application has just the right consequences. It seems, moreover, to be a very natural modification. The one step in this account that is still not motivated by any general consideration is the choice of (37) rather than (38) as an interpretation of (34) and the corresponding choice in the case of Velar Softening in English.

Here, too, however, there is a rather natural enrichment of the theory that will lead to the desired conclusion. At the outset of this discussion we noted that certain rules are more plausible than others which may be just as complex or even less complex, when complexity is measured in terms of number of features. In particular, we noted that rule (1ei) (see p. 401), which converts velars to palato-alveolars before nonlow nonback vowels, is much "simpler," in some linguistically important sense, than rule (1eii), which converts labials to dentals in this context. Similarly, it seems correct, in general, that a rule converting palatal stops to dentals should be simpler than a parallel rule converting velar stops to labials. Quite apart from the problem we are now discussing, these distinctions must somehow be built into the grammar. However, if these distinctions are incorporated into general linguistic theory, then we can also suggest a very natural principle for interpreting a rule such as (34) which introduces two feature modifications: namely, interpret the rule in the way that is simplest, given the general theory of simplicity of rules. On these grounds, (37) is a simpler interpretation of (34) than is (38), since (37) involves a change of velars to palato-alveolars (before high front vowels) and of palato-alveolars to dentals, whereas (38) involves a change of velars to labials and labials to palatalized labials. These considerations suggest the direction in which an overall solution to this problem might be sought. Unfortunately, they do not solve the problem in general, or even in this case, since we have simply established the correct ordering of rule plausibility by fiat. To give a general solution to the problem in these terms, we would have to extend the theory of rule plausibility so that it would automatically provide a "simplest interpretation" for each possible case.

A possible direction in which one might look for such an extension of the theory is suggested by certain other facts that are not handled with complete adequacy in the present theory. Consider first the manner in which the process of metathesis was treated in Chapter Eight, Section 5. As will be recalled, we were forced there to take advantage of powerful transformational machinery of the sort that is used in the syntax. This increase in the power of the formal devices of phonology did not seem fully justified since it was made only to handle a marginal type of phenomenon. An alternative way to achieve the same results is to introduce a special device which would be interpreted by the conventions on rule application as having the effect of permuting the sequential order of a pair of segments. It goes without saying that if this were done, the conventions on rule application would have to be considerably extended, both in scope and in character, beyond the type of marking conventions and linking rules discussed in this chapter. If it should prove possible to define a reasonably short list of such "plausible" phonological processes and show that all—or the majority of—the phonological processes encountered in different languages belong to this set, this would constitute a very strong empirical hypothesis about the nature of language.

We are clearly quite far from achieving this goal, but certain facts suggest that this may be a fruitful direction in which to pursue further inquiry. Consider, for example, the phenomenon of assimilation, of which the Slavic palatalizations are a special case. In assimilation the coefficients of a given feature or feature set in one segment are made to agree with the coefficient of the same feature or feature set in a nearby segment. The fact that it is the same feature or feature set in both segments is crucial. In the framework of this book, however, we are unable to reflect this fact with complete adequacy, for formally a rule such as (26) is not sufficiently different from (41):

$$\left(41\right) \qquad\qquad [-\text{ant}] \;\rightarrow\; [-\text{back}] \;\Big/\; \underline{\qquad} \begin{bmatrix} -\text{cons} \\ -\text{voice} \end{bmatrix}$$

Rule (41), however, in which backness is made to agree with voicing, expresses a type of assimilation that is unknown and implausible. If assimilation were a special process which was available for use whenever necessary, it could be restricted so as to affect only the same features in different segments, or it could be further constrained to affect particular features or sets of features in particular environments. Thus, nasals seem to be quite prone to assimilate the point of articulation of a succeeding consonant, while continuants are apparently all but immune to such assimilation. It would seem plausible to establish a hierarchy of assimilation processes ranging from complete assimilation of all features to assimilation of only a single feature. Processes such as palatalization and velarization would be characterized as assimilations which affect the features "high" and "back."

As already noted in Section 1, there are also processes which involve coherent sets of rules. In addition to the processes of "strengthening" mentioned previously, there are various types of "weakening" processes. We may also include here such processes as "compensatory lengthening," "raising" (and "lowering") of vowels, and perhaps also phonological shifts such as the Great Vowel Shift of English.

It does not seem likely that an elaboration of the theory along the lines just reviewed will allow us to dispense with phonological processes that change features fairly freely. The second stage of the Velar Softening Rule of English (40) and of the Second Velar Palatalization (34) of Slavic strongly suggests that the phonological component requires wide latitude in the freedom to change features, along the lines of the rules discussed in the body of this book.

It should be pointed out that the proposal that we have made concerning "plausible" phonological processes is much more substantial than our proposal concerning "plausible" phonological systems. We have seen that the conventions required to define "plausible" segments could also be utilized to define "plausible" phonological rules. Thus, the marking rules had two sources of empirical support. On the one hand, they were supported by the fact that the most "plausible" phonological segments seemed to reappear constantly in the phonological systems of different languages. On the other hand, the marking conventions in their function as linking rules were justified by the facts of the grammars of individual languages. Confirmation that arises from considerations internal to a grammar is much more significant than any observations on what is commonly to be found. While internal confirmation is available for the proposed "plausible" phonological processes, such independent confirmation is lacking in the case of "plausible" phonological systems. This is a serious shortcoming which reflects our limited understanding of the problem.

Returning now to the Dental Palatalizations in Slavic (see (23), p. 421), we observe that Dental Palatalization takes place before /y/, i.e., before a glide that is nonback and high. In East Slavic, in this environment, the dentals turn into strident palato-alveolars (/t/ → [č], /s/ → [š], etc.) At first sight it would appear that there was a change here in the point of articulation, from anterior to nonanterior. This observation, however, is quite superficial: it states the facts but provides no insight into them. Consider, therefore, the possibility of treating this palatalization as an instance of regressive assimilation, just as we did the other two palatalizations. Let us assume that what is being assimilated here is the high position of the tongue body that is characteristic of the following glide. More formally:

$$(42) \quad \text{DENTAL PALATALIZATION (EAST SLAVIC)}$$

$$[+\text{cor}] \quad \rightarrow \quad [+\text{high}] \Big/ \underline{\quad\quad} \begin{bmatrix} -\text{voc} \\ -\text{cons} \\ -\text{back} \\ +\text{high} \end{bmatrix}$$

Since the dentals are coronals, the immediate consequence of this rule will be to invoke the linking rule (24XXIIa), which has the effect of converting the segments to [−anterior]. This, in turn, makes the segments subject to conventions (24XXIIIb) (vacuously), (24XXVIa), and (24XXVIIc), yielding the required strident palato-alveolars as the final output.

The linking rule (XXIIa) reflects the assumption that when dental consonants " palatalize " they most commonly turn into strident palato-alveolars. The hypothesis embodied in the conventions is that under these conditions it is more complicated for dental obstruents to retain their original point of articulation and, if applicable, their original nonstridency than for them to undergo the shift in point of articulation and stridency.[15]

Consider next Dental Palatalization in South Slavic. The results differ from those in East Slavic in that the plosive does not become an affricate. This fact is treated quite readily by the same device that was employed in (39) above:

$$(43) \quad \text{DENTAL PALATALIZATION (SOUTH SLAVIC)}$$

$$\begin{bmatrix} +\text{cor} \\ \langle -\text{cont} \rangle \end{bmatrix} \quad \rightarrow \quad \begin{bmatrix} +\text{high} \\ \langle -\text{del rel} \rangle \end{bmatrix} \Big/ \underline{\quad\quad} \begin{bmatrix} -\text{voc} \\ -\text{cons} \\ -\text{back} \\ +\text{high} \end{bmatrix}$$

The change to [−delayed release] in the second step of the first rule abbreviated by (43) blocks (24XXVIa), in accordance with the suggestion made at the beginning of this section. Convention (24XXVIIc) now applies vacuously, yielding the nonstrident plosive [t₁], as required. Rule (43) is in need of modification, however, as can be seen from the following considerations. The environment in which Dental Palatalization takes place is a special case of the environment of the two Velar Palatalizations. The nonstrident palato-alveolars [t₁, d₁] which are produced by Dental Palatalization would therefore be subject to the First Velar Palatalization if Dental Palatalization preceded the latter, and they would be subject to the

---

[15] It should be noted that crucial to the discussion of the preceding paragraphs is the assumption that the neutral dentals are $\begin{bmatrix} -\text{high} \\ -\text{back} \end{bmatrix}$. If, instead, we had assumed that the neutral dentals were $\begin{bmatrix} -\text{high} \\ +\text{back} \end{bmatrix}$, rule (42) would have linked these to convention (24XXIIIb) nonvacuously and to convention (24XXVIIb), thereby producing nonstrident velars instead of strident palato-alveolars. It has been observed by J. D. McCawley (1967a) that this phenomenon takes place in the Ripuarian dialects of German, which include the dialect of the city of Cologne. In these dialects dentals are replaced by velars after high vowels; for example, [huŋk] (standard [hunt]), "dog"; [kiŋk] (standard [kint]), "child"; [lük] (standard [lɔytə]), "people"; [cik] (standard [cayt]), "time." To describe this phenomenon, it would be necessary to assume that in these dialects a prior rule made dentals [+back].

Second Velar Palatalization if Dental Palatalization were placed after the First and before the Second Velar Palatalization. To avoid this consequence, it is necessary to order Dental Palatalization in South Slavic after the two Velar Palatalizations.[16] Once this is done, however, a further problem arises. Rule (43) will apply to [čy] and [jy] (from underlying /ky/ and /gy/) and convert these to [t₁y] and [d₁y]. This consequence can readily be blocked by restricting the Dental Palatalization in South Slavic to [+anterior] segments:

$\left(44\right)$ DENTAL PALATALIZATION (SOUTH SLAVIC)

$$
\begin{bmatrix} +\text{cor} \\ +\text{ant} \\ \langle -\text{cont}\rangle \end{bmatrix} \rightarrow \begin{bmatrix} +\text{high} \\ \langle -\text{del rel}\rangle \end{bmatrix} \Big/ \underline{\quad} \begin{bmatrix} -\text{voc} \\ -\text{cons} \\ -\text{back} \\ +\text{high} \end{bmatrix}
$$

Consider now what would happen if Dental Palatalization were formulated so that all of its products were nonstrident, rather than just the noncontinuants as in South Slavic. If Dental Palatalization were ordered before the Second Velar Palatalization, all of its products would merge with those of the Second Palatalization. But this is precisely the result that we have in West Slavic (see (23)). Dental Palatalization in West Slavic must therefore be of the form (45) and be ordered before the Second Palatalization (39):

$\left(45\right)$ DENTAL PALATALIZATION (WEST SLAVIC)

$$
\begin{bmatrix} +\text{cor} \\ +\text{ant} \end{bmatrix} \rightarrow \begin{bmatrix} +\text{high} \\ -\text{strid} \end{bmatrix} \Big/ \underline{\quad} \begin{bmatrix} -\text{voc} \\ -\text{cons} \\ -\text{back} \end{bmatrix}
$$

To sum up the discussion of the Slavic Palatalizations, we observe that the processes differ only in relatively minor respects in the three major dialect areas. There are two slightly different variants of Second Velar Palatalization (i.e., (34) and (39)), and there are three obviously related variants of Dental Palatalization ((42), (44), and (45)). Finally, the dialects differ with regard to the order in which the rules have to apply:

$\left(46\right)$

South Slavic	*East Slavic*[17]	*West Slavic*
First Velar (26)	First Velar (26)	First Velar (26)
Second Velar (34)	Second Velar (34)	Dental (45)
Dental (44)	Dental (42)	Second Velar (39)

Turning now to a different topic, we note that the marking convention (24XXVIIc) will be involved when stops alternate with continuants. Thus, in modern Russian, for instance, /t, d/ → [s, z] before a dental stop, as in the infinitive /met+ti/ → [m,ist,i], "to sweep." Formally such a rule would be expressed as (47):

$\left(47\right)$

$$
\begin{bmatrix} +\text{ant} \\ +\text{cor} \\ -\text{nasal} \end{bmatrix} \rightarrow [+\text{cont}] \Big/ \underline{\quad} \begin{bmatrix} +\text{ant} \\ +\text{cor} \\ -\text{nasal} \\ -\text{cont} \end{bmatrix}
$$

[16] In East Slavic analogous problems of ordering do not arise. Since the First Velar Palatalization and the Dental Palatalization have identical results, it is irrelevant whether the output of one rule is subject to the other rule. Moreover, the Dental Palatalization in East Slavic results in strident obstruents which are, therefore, exempt from the Second Velar Palatalization. Hence there is no reason within East Slavic for ordering Dental Palatalization with respect to the two Velar Palatalizations.

[17] The relative ordering of Dental Palatalization in East Slavic is not justified here. See note 16.

Rule (47) converts /t, d/ to [θ, ð]. The conventions (XXV) and (XXVIIc) supply stridency to the segments [θ, ð] formed by rule (47), and we derive [s, z]. Precisely the same is true of English Spirantization, as we have seen (Chapter Four, (120), p. 229).

There are, however, well-known cases in various languages in which stops become continuants or continuants become stops without the concomitant shift in stridency implied by marking convention (24XXVIIc). A good example of this is spirantization in Semitic, where in postvocalic position and certain other environments nonemphatic (nonpharyngealized) obstruents become continuants. Thus we have a rule such as (48):

$$
\left(48\right) \qquad [-\text{son}] \;\rightarrow\; [+\text{cont}] \;/\; \begin{bmatrix} +\text{voc} \\ -\text{cons} \end{bmatrix} \begin{bmatrix} \underline{} \\ -\text{low} \end{bmatrix}
$$

However, a segment undergoing this spirantization rule is not further modified by the marking convention (XXVIIc) as might be expected. Thus, whereas rule (47) produces the change /t/ → [s], rule (48) results in the change /t/ → [θ], with nonstridency preserved.[18] *All* segments subject to (47) are also subject to the marking convention (XXVIIc). We make this observation the basis for the formal principle (49):

$$
\left(49\right) \qquad \text{A linking rule applies either to all or to none of the segments formed by a given rule.}
$$

In view of principle (49), we are required to apply the linking rule (24XXVIIc) in the case of (47), since all segments are subject to the convention; but principle (49) blocks application of (24XXVIIc) in the case of rule (48) since certain segments formed by the rule— e.g., the velars, which are [−anterior, −coronal]—are not subject to this convention.

Thus principle (49) states that if a spirantization rule applies only to dentals, it will (in the simplest case) make them strident; whereas if it applies to velars as well, it will (in the simplest case) leave all of the segments produced unchanged in stridency (but see note 18). This observation seems factually correct and supports our assumption that (49) is a proper principle governing the interpretation of rules. Notice, furthermore, that (49) is an entirely natural condition. Its effect is to build a consideration of symmetry into the interpretation of phonological rules. It guarantees that the segments formed by a rule will differ among themselves exactly in those respects in which the corresponding segments to which the rule applied differed among themselves. If, for example, we have the situation shown in (50), with segments A and B differing from segments C and D in the feature F_1, and segments A and C differing from segments B and D in the feature F_2, and if, furthermore, the rule (51) applies to the segments A, B, C, D, changing their value with respect to the feature F_3, then the segments A', B', C', D' of (52), formed by the application of (51) to (50), will differ from one another as indicated in (52):

$$\left(50\right)$$

	A	B	C	D
F_1	+	+	−	−
F_2	+	−	+	−
F_3	+	+	+	+

[18] We shall assume that the same is true of the labials, and that the appearance of [f] and [v] instead of the expected [φ] and [β] is due to a low-level phonetic rule, which no doubt itself involves a universal marking convention. Note, incidentally, that Grimm's Law consists in part of a process analogous to (48), stridency not being supplied by the marking conventions since the law applies to all obstruents, not only to anterior ones.

$$(51) \qquad\qquad [A, B, C, D] \;\rightarrow\; [-F_3]$$

$$(52)$$

	A'	B'	C'	D'
F_1	$+$	$+$	$-$	$-$
F_2	$+$	$-$	$+$	$-$
F_3	$-$	$-$	$-$	$-$

Thus the structure of (50) is carried over under rule (51), except for the change that it itself introduces. Were we not to adopt principle (49), this consequence would not necessarily result. Thus, if the language in question contained a marking convention that converted A', B' to $[-F_1]$, or that converted A' alone to $[-F_1]$, etc., the result of the application of (51) would be a formal structure which differed from the system to which it applied, even apart from the change introduced by the rule. The effect of this principle, then, is to preserve whatever symmetries of structure exist in more abstract representations. In other words, this principle implies that, *ceteris paribus*, processes that destroy underlying symmetry will be more costly than processes that preserve them. Since there are also various conventions that lead us to favor abstract systems with certain underlying symmetries (see the discussion on page 410), it follows that even phonetic outputs can be expected to preserve a certain measure of phonological structure of the type associated with phonological representations.

An interesting parallel to the example of spirantization is provided by the application of marking convention (6XIa) to the segments subject to the back-front shift in English, and the nonapplication of this convention in the case of the Umlaut of Modern Standard German. To facilitate the following discussion, we reproduce here as (53) a number of the marking conventions for vowels:

$$(53)$$

(VI)
$$u \text{ low} \;\rightarrow\; \begin{cases} [+\text{low}] \;/\; \begin{bmatrix} \rule{1.2cm}{0.4pt} \\ u \text{ back} \\ u \text{ round} \end{bmatrix} & \text{(a)} \\[2em] [-\text{low}] & \text{(b)} \end{cases}$$

(VII)
$$[+\text{low}] \;\rightarrow\; [-\text{high}]$$

(VIII)
$$[u \text{ high}] \;\rightarrow\; [+\text{high}]$$

(IX)
$$[+\text{high}] \;\rightarrow\; [-\text{low}]$$

(X)
$$[u \text{ back}] \;\rightarrow\; [+\text{back}] \;/\; \begin{bmatrix} \rule{1.2cm}{0.4pt} \\ +\text{low} \end{bmatrix}$$

(XI)
$$[u \text{ round}] \;\rightarrow\; \begin{cases} [\alpha\text{round}] \;/\; \begin{bmatrix} \rule{1.2cm}{0.4pt} \\ \alpha\text{back} \\ -\text{low} \end{bmatrix} & \text{(a)} \\[2em] [-\text{round}] \;/\; \begin{bmatrix} \rule{1.2cm}{0.4pt} \\ +\text{low} \end{bmatrix} & \text{(b)} \end{cases}$$

(XII)
$$[u \text{ tense}] \;\rightarrow\; [+\text{tense}]$$

The phonology of English contains an early Backness Adjustment Rule that applies to such exceptional items as *sing, run, mouse, wind* (verb), with the underlying representations /sing/,

/run/, /mūs/, /wind/, and converts them to [suŋ], [rin], [mis], [wūnd], respectively. By application of Vowel Shift and other rules in the paired forms, we derive ultimately the phonetic forms [siŋ]–[sæŋ], [rʌn]–[ræn], [māws]–[māys], [wāynd]–[wāwnd], in the manner described in Chapter Four, Section 4.3.7. We can formulate the Backness Adjustment Rule as (54):

$$
\left(54\right) \qquad [+\text{high}] \quad \rightarrow \quad [\alpha\text{back}] \quad / \quad \left[\begin{array}{c} \underline{\hspace{1.5cm}} \\ -\alpha\text{back} \end{array}\right] \text{ in certain contexts}
$$

Convention (53XIa) applies to all segments formed by (54). Applying rule (54) to /run/ and /mūs/, we derive [rün] and [mǖs], which automatically become [rin] and [mis] by convention (XIa). Applying rule (54) to /sing/ and /wind/, we first obtain [siŋ] and [wind], which automatically become [suŋ] and [wūnd] by the same convention.

Consider, by way of contrast, the Umlaut of modern German, where in certain morphologically defined environments *all* vowels are fronted, so that $u \rightarrow \ddot{u}$, $o \rightarrow \ddot{o}$, $a \rightarrow \ae$ ($\rightarrow e$).[19] The rule characterizing the German Umlaut can be stated as (55):

$$
\left(55\right) \qquad \left[\begin{array}{c} +\text{voc} \\ -\text{cons} \end{array}\right] \quad \rightarrow \quad [-\text{back}] \quad / \text{ in certain contexts}
$$

Rule (55) forms certain segments (i.e., the [+low] vowels) that are not subject to (53XIa). Hence, by principle (49), the linking rule (53XIa) will not apply to *any* segments formed by rule (55), and the rounding of the original nonlow back vowels will remain in the output. Observe that if we wished to characterize a situation in which $u \rightarrow \ddot{u}$ without concomitant fronting of low vowels, we would have to give a rule that is more complex than (55); for example, the rule (56):

$$
\left(56\right) \qquad [+\text{high}] \quad \rightarrow \quad \left[\begin{array}{c} -\text{back} \\ +\text{round} \end{array}\right] \quad / \text{ in certain contexts}
$$

where [+round] on the right-hand side of the arrow represents the extra cost in complexity that must be paid to undo the effects of the linking rule (XIa).[20]

Summarizing, we are assuming that all phonological rules are presented in the form (57):[21]

$$
\left(57\right) \qquad \left[\begin{array}{c} \alpha_1 F_1 \\ \cdot \\ \cdot \\ \cdot \\ \alpha_m F_m \end{array}\right] \quad \rightarrow \quad \left[\begin{array}{c} \beta_1 G_1 \\ \cdot \\ \cdot \\ \cdot \\ \beta_n G_n \end{array}\right] \quad / \quad Y \left[\begin{array}{c} \underline{\hspace{1cm}} \\ W \end{array}\right] Z
$$

Certain general conditions of rule plausibility force us, we have suggested, to interpret such a rule as a non-Markovian block, with a uniquely determined ordering of $G_1, \ldots, G_n$, let us say, as given in (57). We interpret (57) in the following way. Given a segment specified as $[\alpha_1 F_1, \ldots, \alpha_m F_m, W]$ in the context $Y \underline{\hspace{1cm}} Z$, we assign it the feature specification $[\beta_1 G_1]$, exactly as before. We next apply the longest sequence of linked marking conventions, in the

---

[19] We disregard here the raising of /a/ that is normally a concomitant phenomenon of the German Umlaut. For a discussion of Umlaut in modern German from the viewpoint of generative phonology, see Zwicky (1964).

[20] The phenomenon of vowel harmony in the Ural-Altaic languages provides a further example of the nonapplication of convention (XIa) in a situation that precisely parallels that of the German instance.

[21] In fact, as suggested on page 427, the choice of W may be automatically determined by conditions of rule plausibility, so that the distinction between $[F_1, \ldots, F_m]$ and the other features of the unit $[\alpha_1, \ldots, \alpha_m F_m, W]$ may not have to be expressed directly in the rule.

manner described on pages 423–44.[22] We then proceed to assign to every segment subject to (57) the feature specification $[\beta_2 G_2]$ and again apply the marking conventions. We repeat the process for every $[\beta_i G_i]$ given on the right-hand side of the arrow in (57). We have seen that quite a few intricate phonological processes can be described in very simple terms if these assumptions about rule application are adopted.

To complete this preliminary and tentative discussion of the role of marking in phonology, we now examine processes associated with the Vowel Shift, which play such a prominent role in the word-level phonology of English. The Vowel Shift Rule and the associated Adjustment Rules illustrate rather graphically the changes in the formulation of our rules that are necessitated by the introduction of the marking conventions and the attendant principles of rule interpretation.

As we shall see, there is no need to modify the Vowel Shift Rule itself at all. Rather, the introduction of linking rules and markedness considerations will make unnecessary certain parts of the Rounding Adjustment and the Backness Adjustment Rules which were introduced in Chapter Four in order to bring about the change from /ɔ̄/ and /æ/ to [ā]. The considerations introduced in this section allow us, therefore, to achieve significant simplifications in our description of English. This fact provides further empirical support for the proposals that have been sketched in the preceding pages. Moreover, the fact that the rules proposed here link naturally to the marking conventions has bearing also on the history of the Great Vowel Shift. In the light of the marking conventions, the historical process that we have postulated makes use of rules that are quite natural, whereas the alternative rules that we rejected in Chapter Six would be highly complex and implausible. If correct, the marking conventions, therefore, are important evidence in favor of the account that we have advanced.

We give here the Vowel Shift Rule in a slightly different form from that of (33) in Chapter Five:

$$
\left(58\right) \quad
\left\{
\begin{array}{ccc}
\begin{bmatrix} \alpha\text{high} \\ -\text{low} \end{bmatrix} & \rightarrow & [-\alpha\text{high}] \\[1.5em]
\begin{bmatrix} \beta\text{low} \\ -\text{high} \end{bmatrix} & \rightarrow & [-\beta\text{low}]
\end{array}
\right\}
\;\Big/\;
\left\{
\begin{array}{c}
\begin{bmatrix} +\text{tense} \\ +\text{stress} \end{bmatrix} \\[1em]
\begin{bmatrix} \underline{} \\ +\text{F} \end{bmatrix} \\[1em]
\begin{bmatrix} \underline{} \\ -\text{tense} \\ +\text{back} \\ +\text{high} \end{bmatrix}
\end{array}
\right\}
\;\Big/\;
\begin{bmatrix} \underline{} \\ +\text{voc} \\ -\text{cons} \\ \gamma\text{back} \\ \gamma\text{round} \end{bmatrix}
$$

We now ask whether the rule needs any modification in view of the considerations of this section. It should be noted, first, that both parts of the Vowel Shift Rule are schemata which abbreviate two rules each; i.e., the relevant parts of (58) must be rewritten as (59):

$$\left(59\right)$$

(a) (i) $[+\text{high}] \rightarrow [-\text{high}]$
    (ii) $[-\text{high}] \rightarrow [+\text{high}]$
(b) (i) $[+\text{low}] \rightarrow [-\text{low}]$
    (ii) $[-\text{low}] \rightarrow [+\text{low}]$

---

[22] Notice that such conventions as (6IIa, b), (6IIIa, c), which involve sequential constraints, never play a role in interpreting the application of phonological rules. Thus, if a glide becomes vocalic in initial position by a phonological rule, it is not subject to the marking conventions that govern initial position, etc. This conclusion is essential if absurdities are not to result.

This is important for the correct application of principle (49) since that principle refers to rules and not to schemata and hence to the form (59) rather than (58). It is readily seen that none of the conventions in (53) are applicable to vowels that become [−high]. Conventions (IX) and (XIa) are applicable to vowels that become [+high]; their effects in the cases under consideration are vacuous. Thus there is no need to change part (a) of the Vowel Shift Rule.

The situation is somewhat different with respect to part (b) of the Vowel Shift Rule. Here most of the conventions (VII)–(XII) function as linking rules. The segments affected by (59bi) are the tense vowels /ǣ/, /ɔ̄/, which as a consequence of the rule become nonlow. It is immediately clear that except for (53XIa) none of the marking conventions apply. Convention (XIa) could conceivably function in the case under discussion; its effects would be vacuous, however. As R. Stanley has pointed out to us, in view of principle (49) the decision as to whether or not (XIa) applies here depends on whether schemata are treated as single conventions or as abbreviations of several individual conventions. If the former decision is made, then convention (XIa) will apply in the case under discussion. If, on the other hand, the latter decision is made, principle (49) will block the application of (XIa). Since the same consequences follow from either decision in the present instance, it is impossible to know which choice is correct. The issues involved, however, are clear.

The segments affected by (59bii) are the tense vowels /ē/ and /ō/, which are converted by the rule into low vowels:

$$\left(60\right) \qquad \begin{array}{ccc} \bar{e} & \to & \bar{æ} \\ \bar{o} & \to & \bar{ɔ} \end{array}$$

Marking convention (53VII) then applies vacuously. Next, convention (53X) applies, with the effects shown in (61):

$$\left(61\right) \qquad \begin{array}{ccc} \bar{æ} & \to & \bar{a} \\ \bar{ɔ} & \to & \bar{ɔ} \end{array}$$

Finally, convention (53XIb) applies, yielding the required results:

$$\left(62\right) \qquad \begin{array}{ccc} \bar{ɔ} & \to & \bar{a} \\ \bar{a} & \to & \bar{a} \end{array}$$

BIBLIOGRAPHY

Allen, W. S., 1964, Review of Vogt (1963), in *Language, 40,* no. 3, 500–502.

Aoki, H., 1966, "Nez Perce Vowel Harmony and Proto-Sahaptian Vowels," *Language, 42,* no. 4, 759–767.

Armstrong, L. E., 1940, *The Phonetic and Tonal Structure of Kikuyu,* Oxford University Press, Humphrey Milford, London.

Avanesov, R. I., 1956, *Fonetika sovremennogo russkogo literaturnogo jazyka,* Izdatel'stvo Moskovskogo Universiteta, Moscow.

Batchelor, T., 1809, *An Orthoepical Analysis of the English Language,* Didier and Tebbett, London.

Baudouin de Courtenay, J., 1894, "Einiges über Palatalisierung (Palatalisation) und Entpalatalisierung (Dispalatalisation)," *Indogermanische Forschungen, 4,* 45–52.

Beach, D. M., 1938, *The Phonetics of the Hottentot Language,* Heffer, Cambridge.

Berry, J., 1957, "Vowel Harmony in Twi," *Bulletin of the School of Oriental and African Studies,* University of London, *19,* 124–130.

Bever, T. G., 1963, "Theoretical Implications of Bloomfield's 'Menomini Morphophonemics,'" *Quarterly Progress Report of the Research Laboratory of Electronics,* Massachusetts Institute of Technology, no. 68, 197–203.

Bever, T. G., 1967, *Leonard Bloomfield and the Phonology of the Menomini Language,* unpublished Doctoral dissertation, Massachusetts Institute of Technology.

Bierwisch, M., 1966, "Regeln für die Intonation deutscher Sätze," *Studia Grammatica, 7,* 99–201.

Bloch, B., and G. L. Trager, 1942, *Outline of Linguistic Analysis* (Linguistic Society of America: Special Publications), Waverly Press, Baltimore.

Bloomfield, L., 1933, *Language,* Holt, New York.

Bloomfield, L., 1939, "Menomini Morphophonemics," *Travaux du Cercle Linguistique de Prague, 8,* 105–115.

Boas, F., 1911, "Chinook," *Handbook of American Indian Languages,* Bulletin 40, Smithsonian Institution, Bureau of American Ethnology, Washington, D.C., Part 1, 559–676.

Bolling, G., 1934, Reply to Kent's review of Bloomfield (1933), in *Language, 10,* no. 1, 48–52.

Bräuer, H., 1961, *Slavische Sprachwissenschaft I* (Sammlung Göschen Band 1191/1191A), Walter de Gruyter, Berlin.

Broch, O., 1911, *Slavische Phonetik,* Carl Winter, Heidelberg.

Browne, E. W., and J. D. McCawley, 1965, "Srpskohrvatski akcenat," *Zbornik matice srpske za filologiju i lingvistiku* (Novi Sad, Yugoslavia), *8,* 147–151.

Brunner, K., 1960, *Die englische Sprache,* Max Niemeyer, Tübingen.

Callow, J. C., 1965, "Kasem Nominals—A Study in Analyses," *The Journal of West African Languages, 2,* no. 1, 29–36.

Carnochan, J., 1960, "Vowel Harmony in Igbo," *African Language Studies, 1,* 155–163.

Chomsky, N., 1951, *Morphophonemics of Modern Hebrew,* unpublished Master's thesis, University of Pennsylvania.

Chomsky, N., 1955a, *Semantic Considerations in Grammar,* Monograph No. 8, Georgetown University Institute of Languages and Linguistics, Washington, D.C.

Chomsky, N., 1955b, *The Logical Structure of Linguistic Theory,* on microfilm at the reference department, Massachusetts Institute of Technology library.

Chomsky, N., 1957a, *Syntactic Structures,* Mouton, The Hague.

Chomsky, N., 1957b, Review of Jakobson and Halle (1956), in *International Journal of American Linguistics, 23,* no. 3, 234–242.

Chomsky, N., 1961, "On the Notion 'Rule of Grammar,'" in Fodor and Katz (1964), 119–136.

Chomsky, N., 1964, *Current Issues in Linguistic Theory,* Mouton, The Hague.

Chomsky, N., 1965, *Aspects of the Theory of Syntax,* Massachusetts Institute of Technology Press, Cambridge, Mass.

Chomsky, N., 1966a, *Cartesian Linguistics,* Harper & Row, New York.

Chomsky, N., 1966b, "Topics in the Theory of Generative Grammar," in T. Sebeok, ed., *Current Trends in Linguistics, 3: Linguistic Theory,* Indiana University Press, Bloomington. Also appears separately in the *Janua Linguarum* series, no. 56, Mouton, The Hague.

Chomsky, N., 1967, "Some General Properties of Phonological Rules," *Language, 43,* no. 1.

Chomsky, N. (forthcoming), "Remarks on Nominalization," in R. Jacobs and P. Rosenbaum, eds., *Readings in Transformational Grammar.*

Chomsky, N., and M. Halle, 1965, "Some Controversial Questions in Phonological Theory," *Journal of Linguistics, 1,* no. 2, 97–138.

Chomsky, N., M. Halle, and F. Lukoff, 1956, "On Accent and Juncture in English," *For Roman Jakobson,* Mouton, The Hague, 65–80.

Cole, D. T., 1955, *Introduction to Tswana Grammar,* Longman's, London.

Cooper, C., 1687. See Sundby, 1954.

Danielsson, B., 1955, 1963, *John Hart's Works on English Orthography and Pronunciation* (Stockholm Studies in English), Almqvist and Wiksell, Stockholm (1955, Part I; 1963, Part II).

Dobson, E. J., 1957, *English Pronunciation 1500–1700,* Oxford University Press, London.

Doke, C. M., 1931, *A Comparative Study in Shona Phonetics,* Witwatersrand University Press, Johannesburg.

Echeverría, M. S., and H. Contreras, 1965, "Araucanian Phonemics," *International Journal of American Linguistics, 31,* no. 2, 132–135.

Elphinston, J., 1765, *The Principles of the English Language Digested; or, English Grammar Reduced to Analogy,* James Bettenham, London.

Emeneau, M. B., 1944, *Kota Texts I* (Publications in Linguistics, *2,* no. 1), University of California Press, Berkeley and Los Angeles.

Emeneau, M. B., 1957, "Toda, a Dravidian Language," *Transactions of the Philological Society,* 15–66.

Fant, G., 1959, "The Acoustics of Speech," in L. Cremer, ed., *Proceedings of the Third International Congress on Acoustics, Stuttgart, 1959,* Elsevier, Amsterdam, 188–201.

Fant, G., 1960, *Acoustic Theory of Speech Production,* Mouton, The Hague.

Fodor, J. A., and J. J. Katz, 1963, "The Availability of What We Say," *Philosophical Review, 72,* 57–71.

Fodor, J. A., and J. J. Katz, 1964, *The Structure of Language: Readings in the Philosophy of Language,* Prentice-Hall, Englewood Cliffs, N.J.

Fromkin, V., 1965, "On System-Structure Phonology," *Language, 41,* no. 4, 601–609.

Fudge, E. C., 1967, "The Nature of Phonological Primes," *Journal of Linguistics, 3,* 1–36.

Garde, P., 1965, Review of *American Contributions to the Fifth International Congress of Slavists, Vol. I: Linguistic Contributions,* in *Word, 21,* no. 1, 141–147.

Gil, A., 1621, *Logonomia Anglica,* London. Re-edited by O. L. Jiriczek, Strassburg, 1903.

Gleason, H. A., Jr., 1961, *An Introduction to Descriptive Linguistics,* Holt, Rinehart and Winston, New York.

Grande, B., 1963, *Kurs arabskoj grammatiki v sravnitel'no-istoričeskom osveščenii,* Akademija Nauk SSSR, Institut Narodov Azii, Moscow.

Halle, M., 1957, "In Defense of the Number Two," *Studies Presented to Joshua Whatmough on his 60th Birthday,* Mouton, The Hague, 65–72.

Halle, M., 1959, *The Sound Pattern of Russian,* Mouton, The Hague.

Halle, M., 1962, "Phonology in a Generative Grammar," *Word, 18,* 54–72. Reprinted in Fodor and Katz (1964), 334–352.

Halle, M., 1963, "On Cyclically Ordered Rules in Russian," *American Contributions to the Fifth International Congress of Slavists,* Mouton, The Hague, 113–132.

Halle, M., 1964, "On the Bases of Phonology," in Fodor and Katz (1964), 324–333.

Halle, M., and S. J. Keyser, 1966, "Chaucer and the Study of Prosody," *College English, 28,* no. 3, 187–219.

Halle, M., and S. J. Keyser (forthcoming), *The Evolution of Stress in English.*

Halle, M., and T. M. Lightner (forthcoming), "The Slavic Palatalizations."

Halle, M., and K. N. Stevens, 1967, "On the Mechanism of Glottal Vibration for Vowels and Consonants," *Quarterly Progress Report of the Research Laboratory of Electronics,* Massachusetts Institute of Technology, no. 85, 267–270.

Halle, M., and V. J. Zeps, 1966, "A Survey of Latvian Morphophonemics," *Quarterly Progress Report of the Research Laboratory of Electronics,* Massachusetts Institute of Technology, no. 83, 105–113.

Halpern, A. M., 1946, "Yuma," *Linguistic Structures of Native America* (Viking Fund Publications in Anthropology, 6), New York, 249–288.

Harms, R., 1966, "Stress, Voice, and Length in Southern Paiute," *International Journal of American Linguistics, 2,* no. 3, 228–235.

Harper, W. R., 1910, *Elements of Hebrew by an Inductive Method,* Scribner, New York.

Harris, J. W., 1967, *Spanish Phonology,* unpublished Doctoral dissertation, Massachusetts Institute of Technology.

Harris, Z. S., 1951, *Methods in Structural Linguistics,* University of Chicago Press, Chicago.

Heeschen, C., 1967, "Lithuanian Morphophonemics," *Quarterly Progress Report of the Research Laboratory of Electronics,* Massachusetts Institute of Technology, no. 85, 284–296.

Heffner, R.-M. S., 1950, *General Phonetics,* University of Wisconsin Press, Madison.

Hill, A. A., 1958, *Introduction to Linguistic Structures,* Harcourt, Brace & World, New York.

Hill, A. A., ed., 1962, *The Second (1957) Texas Conference on Problems of Linguistic Analysis in English,* University of Texas Press, Austin.

Hockett, C. F., 1955, *A Manual of Phonology* (*International Journal of American Linguistics,* Memoir 11), Waverly Press, Baltimore.

Hockett, C. F., 1965, "Sound Change," *Language, 41,* no. 2, 185–204.

Hoenigswald, H. M., 1964, "Graduality, Sporadicity, and the Minor Sound Change Processes," *Phonetica, 11,* 202–215.

Hoffmann, C., 1963, *A Grammar of the Margi Language,* Oxford University Press, London.

Hoijer, H., 1945, *Navaho Phonology* (Publications in Anthropology, no. 1), University of New Mexico Press, Albuquerque.

Horn, W., 1912, "Probleme der neuenglischen Lautgeschichte," *Anglia, 35,* 357–392.

Horn, W., and M. Lehnert, 1954, *Laut und Leben,* Deutscher Verlag der Wissenschaften, Berlin.

Jakobson, R., 1939, "Observations sur le classement phonologique des consonnes," *Proceedings of the Third International Congress of Phonetic Sciences,* Ghent. Reprinted in Jakobson (1962), 273–279.

Jakobson, R., 1940, "Kindersprache, Aphasie und allgemeine Lautgesetze," in Jakobson (1962), 328–401.

Jakobson, R., 1957, "Mufaxxama, the 'Emphatic' Phonemes of Arabic," *Studies Presented to Joshua Whatmough on his 60th Birthday,* Mouton, The Hague, 105–115. Reprinted in Jakobson (1962), 510–522.

Jakobson, R., 1962, *Selected Writings I,* Mouton, The Hague.

Jakobson, R., and M. Halle, 1956, *Fundamentals of Language,* Mouton, The Hague.

Jakobson, R., and M. Halle, 1964, "Tenseness and Laxness," in D. Abercrombie *et al.,* eds., *In Honour of Daniel Jones,* Longmans, London, 96–101. Reprinted in Jakobson (1962), 550–555.

Jakobson, R., G. Fant, and M. Halle, 1963, *Preliminaries to Speech Analysis,* Massachusetts Institute of Technology Press, Cambridge, Mass.

Jespersen, O., 1909, *A Modern English Grammar on Historical Principles, Part 1: Sounds and Spellings,* Carl Winter, Heidelberg.

Jones, D., 1950, *The Phoneme: Its Nature and Use,* Heffer, Cambridge.

Jones, D., 1956a, *Outline of English Phonetics,* Dutton, New York.

Jones, D., 1956b, *The Pronunciation of English,* Cambridge University Press, Cambridge.

Jones, J. D., 1912, *Cooper's Grammatica Linguae Anglicanae (1685),* Max Niemeyer, Halle.

Joos, M., 1942, "A Phonological Dilemma in Canadian English," *Language, 18,* no. 2, 141–144.

Joos, M., 1962, "The Definition of Juncture and Terminals," *The Second (1957) Texas Conference on Problems of Linguistic Analysis in English,* University of Texas Press, Austin, 4–38.

Jordan, R., 1934, *Handbuch der mittelenglischen Grammatik I,* Carl Winter, Heidelberg.

Katz, J. J., 1966, *The Philosophy of Language,* Harper & Row, New York.

Katz, J. J., and P. M. Postal, 1964, *An Integrated Theory of Linguistic Descriptions,* Massachusetts Institute of Technology Press, Cambridge, Mass.

Kauter, H., 1930a, "Englische Lautlehre nach Richard Hodges' 'The English Primrose' (1644)" (Beiträge zur Erforschung der Sprache und Kultur Englands und Nordamerikas, 6), Breslau, 1–60.

Kauter, H., ed., 1930b, *Richard Hodges' "The English Primrose" (1644),* Carl Winter, Heidelberg.

Kent, R. G., 1934, Review of Bloomfield (1933), in *Language, 10,* no. 1, 40–48.

Kenyon, J. S., 1958, *American Pronunciation,* Wahr, Ann Arbor.

Kenyon, J. S., and T. A. Knott, 1944, *A Pronouncing Dictionary of American English,* Merriam, Springfield, Mass.

Keyser, S. J., 1963, Review of Kurath and McDavid (1961), in *Language, 39,* no. 2, 303–316.

Kim, C.-W., 1965, "On the Autonomy of the Tensity Feature in Stop Classification," unpublished paper presented at the summer meeting of the Linguistic Society of America, Ann Arbor.

Kingdon, R., 1958, *The Groundwork of English Stress,* Longmans, Green, London.

Kiparsky, P., 1965, *Phonological Change,* unpublished Doctoral dissertation, Massachusetts Institute of Technology.

Kiparsky, P., 1966, "Über den deutschen Akzent," *Studia Grammatika, 7,* 69–98.

Kiparsky, P. (forthcoming), "Universal Grammar and Linguistic Change," in E. Bach and R. Harms, eds., *Proceedings of the Texas Conference on Language Universals.*

Klingenheben, A., 1963, *Die Sprache der Ful,* J. J. Augustin, Hamburg.

Kuipers, A. H., 1960, *Phoneme and Morpheme in Kabardian,* Mouton, The Hague.

Kurath, H., 1964, *A Phonology and Prosody of Modern English,* University of Michigan Press, Ann Arbor.

Kurath, H., and R. I. McDavid, Jr., 1961, *The Pronunciation of English in the Atlantic States,* University of Michigan Press, Ann Arbor.

Kuroda, S.-Y., 1967, *Yawelmani Phonology,* Massachusetts Institute of Technology Press, Cambridge, Mass.

Ladefoged, P., 1964, *A Phonetic Study of West African Languages* (West African Language Monographs, 1), Cambridge University Press, Cambridge.

Lamb, S. M., 1964, "On Alternation, Transformation, Realization, and Stratification" (Monograph Series on Languages and Linguistics, *17*), Georgetown University Press, Washington, D.C., 105–122.

Lees, R. B., 1960, *The Grammar of English Nominalizations* (Indiana University Research Center in Anthropology, Folklore, and Linguistics, no. 12), Indiana University Press, Bloomington.

Lees, R. B., 1961, *The Phonology of Modern Standard Turkish* (Indiana University Publication: Uralic and Altaic Series, *6*), Indiana University Press, Bloomington.

Lehiste, I., 1964, "Juncture," *Proceedings of the Fifth International Congress of Phonetic Sciences, Münster, 1964,* S. Karger, Basel.

Lehnert, M., 1936, *Die Grammatik des englischen Sprachmeisters John Wallis (1616–1703)* (Sprache und Kultur der germanischen und romanischen Völker, A: Anglistische Reihe, *21*), Breslau.

Leskien, A., 1919, *Grammatik der altbulgarischen Sprache,* Carl Winter, Heidelberg.

Leslau, W., 1941, *Documents Tigrigna,* Klincksieck, Paris.

Li, F. K., 1946, "Chipewyan," *Linguistic Structures of Native America* (Viking Fund Publications in Anthropology, *6*), New York, 398–423.

Lieberman, P., 1965, "On the Acoustic Basis of the Perception of Intonation by Linguists," *Word, 21,* no. 1, 40–54.

Lieberman, P., 1966, *Intonation, Perception, and Language,* Massachusetts Institute of Technology Press, Cambridge, Mass.

Lightner, T. M., 1963, "A Note on the Formulation of Phonological Rules," *Quarterly Progress Report of the Research Laboratory of Electronics,* Massachusetts Institute of Technology, no. 68, 187–189.

Lightner, T. M., 1965a, *Segmental Phonology of Modern Standard Russian,* unpublished Doctoral dissertation, Massachusetts Institute of Technology.

Lightner, T. M., 1965b, "On the Description of Vowel and Consonant Harmony," *Word, 21,* no. 2, 244–250.

Lisker, L., 1963, "On Hultzen's 'Voiceless Lenis Stops in Prevocalic Clusters,'" *Word, 19,* 376–387.

Lisker, L., and A. S. Abramson, 1964, "A Cross-Language Study of Voicing in Initial Stops: Acoustical Measurement," *Word, 20,* 384–422.

Lloyd, R. J., 1908, *Northern English,* Stechert, New York.

Luick, K., 1898, "Beiträge zur englischen Grammatik, III: Die Quantitätsveränderungen im Laufe der englischen Sprachentwicklung," *Anglia, 20,* 335–362.

Luick, K., 1907, "Beiträge zur englischen Grammatik, V: Zur Quantierung der romanischen Lehnwörten und den Quantitätsgesetzen überhaupt," *Anglia, 30,* 1–55.

McCawley, J. D., 1965, *The Accentual System of Modern Standard Japanese,* unpublished Doctoral dissertation, Massachusetts Institute of Technology.

McCawley, J. D., 1967a, "The Role of a Phonological Feature System in a Theory of Language," *Langages,* no. 6.

McCawley, J. D., 1967b, "Sapir's Phonological Representation," *International Journal of American Linguistics, 33,* 106–111.

McIntosh, M. M. C., 1956, *The Phonetic and Linguistic Theory of the Royal Society School from Wallis to Cooper,* unpublished Bachelor's thesis, Oxford University.

McLaren, J., 1955, *A Xhosa Grammar,* Longmans, Green, Capetown.

Malmberg, B., 1956, "Distinctive Features of Swedish Vowels: Some Instrumental and Structural Data," *For Roman Jakobson,* Mouton, The Hague, 316–321.

Marchand, H., 1960, *The Categories and Types of Present-Day English Word-Formation: a Synchronic-Diachronic Approach,* Harrassowitz, Wiesbaden.

Marouzeau, J., 1943, *Lexique de la terminologie linguistique,* Librairie Orientaliste Paul Geuthner, Paris.

Martin, S. E., 1951, "Korean Phonemics," *Language, 27,* no. 4, 519–533. Reprinted in M. Joos, ed., 1957, *Readings in Linguistics,* American Council of Learned Societies, Washington, D.C., 364–371.

Martinet, A., 1936, "Neutralisation et archiphonème," *Travaux du Cercle Linguistique de Prague, 6,* 46–57.

Matthews, G. H., 1965, *Hidatsa Syntax* (Papers on Formal Linguistics, no. 3), Mouton, The Hague.

Meillet, A., 1924, *Le Slave commun,* Librairie Honoré Champion, Paris.

Meinhof, C., 1912, *Die Sprachen der Hamiten,* Friederichsen, Hamburg.

Milewski, T., 1951, "The Concept of Word in the Native Languages of America," *Lingua Posnaniensis, 3,* 248–267.

Miller, G. A., 1956, "The Magical Number Seven, Plus or Minus Two: Some Limits on our Capacity for Processing Information," *Psychological Review, 63,* no. 2, 81–97.

Miller, G. A., and N. Chomsky, 1963, "Finitary Models of Language Users," in R. D. Luce, R. R. Bush, and E. Galanter, eds., *Handbook of Mathematical Psychology,* Vol. 2, Wiley, 419–492.

Milner, J. C., 1967, "French Truncation Rule," *Quarterly Progress Report of the Research Laboratory of Electronics,* Massachusetts Institute of Technology, no. 86, 273–283.

Newman, S. S., 1946, "On the Stress System of English," *Word, 2,* 171–187.

Perkell, J. S., 1965, "Cineradiographic Studies of Speech: Implications of a Detailed Analysis of Certain Articulatory Movements," *Reports to the Fifth International Congress of Acoustics, 1,* A32, Université de Liège.

Pollack, I., and L. Ficks, 1954, "Information of Elementary Multidimensional Auditory Displays," *Journal of the Acoustical Society of America, 26,* no. 2, 155–158.

Postal, P. M., 1962, *Some Syntactic Rules in Mohawk,* unpublished Doctoral dissertation, Yale University.

Postal, P. M., 1964a, "Mohawk Prefix Generation," in H. Lunt, ed., *Proceedings of the Ninth International Congress of Linguists,* Mouton, The Hague, 346–357.

Postal, P. M., 1964b, "Boas and the Development of Phonology: Comments Based on Iroquoian," *International Journal of American Linguistics, 30,* no. 3, 269–280.

Postal, P. M., 1968, *Aspects of Phonological Theory,* Harper & Row, New York.

Postal, P. M. (forthcoming), *Mohawk Grammar.*

Ross, J. R., 1967, *Constraints on Variables in Syntax,* unpublished Doctoral dissertation, Massachusetts Institute of Technology.

Sapir, E., 1930, *Southern Paiute, a Shoshonean Language* (Proceedings of the American Academy of Arts and Sciences, *65,* nos. 1–3).

Sapir, E., 1931, "Notes on the Gweabo Language of Liberia," *Language, 7,* no. 1, 30–41.

Sapir, E., 1949a, "The Psychological Reality of Phonemes," in D. G. Mandelbaum, ed., *Selected Writings of Edward Sapir in Language, Culture, and Personality,* University of California Press, Berkeley and Los Angeles, 46–60.

Sapir, E., 1949b, "Glottalized Continuants in Navaho, Nootka, and Kwakiutl," in D. G. Mandelbaum, ed., *Selected Writings of Edward Sapir in Language, Culture, and Personality,* University of California Press, Berkeley and Los Angeles, 225–250.

Schane, S. A., 1965, *The Phonological and Morphological Structure of French,* unpublished Doctoral dissertation, Massachusetts Institute of Technology.

Siertsema, B., 1958, "Problems of Phonemic Interpretation, I: Nasalized Sounds in Yoruba," *Lingua, 7,* 356–366.

Sievers, E., 1901, *Grundzüge der Phonetik,* Breitkopf and Härtel, Leipzig.

Sledd, J. H., 1966, "Breaking, Umlaut, and the Southern Drawl," *Language, 42,* no. 1, 18–41.

Smith, N. V., 1968, "Tone in Ewe," *Quarterly Progress Report of the Research Laboratory of Electronics,* Massachusetts Institute of Technology, no. 90.

Speiser, E. A., 1938, "The Pitfalls of Polarity," *Language, 14,* no. 3, 187–202.

Stanley, R., 1967, "Redundancy Rules in Phonology," *Language, 43,* no. 1.

Stanley, R. (forthcoming), *The Phonology of the Navaho Verb,* unpublished Doctoral dissertation, Massachusetts Institute of Technology.

Stevens, A. M., 1965, "Language Levels in Madurese," *Language, 41,* no. 2, 294–302.

Stewart, J. M., 1967, "Tongue Root Position in Akan Vowel Harmony," *Phonetica, 16,* 185–204.

Stockwell, R. P., 1960, "The Place of Intonation in a Generative Grammar of English," *Language, 36,* no. 3, 360–367.

Stockwell, R. P., 1964, "Realism in Historical English Phonology," unpublished paper presented at the winter meeting of the Linguistic Society of America at the University of California at Los Angeles.

Stockwell, R. P., 1966, "Problems in the Interpretation of the Great English Vowel Shift," unpublished paper presented at Austin, Texas.

Stockwell, R. P., J. D. Bowen, and I. Silva-Fuenzalida, 1956, "Spanish Juncture and Intonation," *Language, 32,* no. 4, 641–665.

Sundby, B., 1954, *Christopher Cooper's English Teacher (1687),* Munksgaard, Copenhagen.

Sweet, H., 1891, *A Handbook of Phonetics,* Henry Frowde, Oxford.

Teeter, K. V., 1964, *The Wiyot Language* (University of California Publications in Linguistics, no. 37), University of California Press, Berkeley and Los Angeles.

Trager, G. L., and H. L. Smith, 1951, *An Outline of English Structure* (Studies in Linguistics: Occasional Papers, 3), Battenburg Press, Norman, Okl.

Trubetzkoy, N. S., 1922, "Les consonnes latérales des langues caucasiques-septentrionales," *Bulletin de la Société de Linguistique de Paris, 23,* 184–204.

Trubetzkoy, N. S., 1926, "Studien auf dem Gebiete der vergleichenden Lautlehre der nord-kaukasischen Sprachen," *Caucasica, 3,* 7–37.

Trubetzkoy, N. S., 1931, "Die Konsonantensysteme der ostkaukasischen Sprachen," *Caucasica, 8,* 1–52.

Trubetzkoy, N. S., 1933, "La phonologie actuelle," *Journal de psychologie, 30,* 227–246.

Trubetzkoy, N. S., 1936a, "Essai d'une théorie des oppositions phonologiques," *Journal de psychologie, 33,* 5–18.

Trubetzkoy, N. S., 1936b, "Die Aufhebung der phonologischen Gegensätze," *Travaux du Cercle Linguistique de Prague, 6,* 29–45.

Trubetzkoy, N. S., 1939, "Aus meiner phonologischen Kartothek, I: Das phonologische System der dunganischen Sprache," *Travaux du Cercle Linguistique de Prague, 8,* 22–26.

Trubetzkoy, N. S., 1958, *Grundzüge der Phonologie,* Vandenhoeck and Ruprecht, Göttingen.

Tucker, A. N., 1940, *The Eastern Sudanic Languages, I,* Oxford University Press, London.

Vaillant, A., 1950, *Grammaire comparée des langues slaves, I,* IAC, Lyon.

Vogt, H., 1963, *Dictionnaire de la langue Oubykh,* Universitetsforlaget, Oslo.

W. S.-Y. Wang, 1967, "Phonological Features of Tone," *International Journal of American Linguistics, 33,* 93–105.

Welmers, W. E., 1946, *A Descriptive Grammar of Fanti,* Supplement to *Language, 22,* no. 3.

Welmers, W. E., 1962, "The Phonology of Kpelle," *Journal of African Languages, 1,* no. 1, 69–93.

Wescott, R. W., 1965, Review of J. M. C. Thomas, *Le parler Ngbaka de Bokanga: Phonologie, morphologie, syntaxe,* in *Language, 41,* no. 2, 346–347.

Westermann, D., and I. C. Ward, 1933, *Practical Phonetics for Students of African Languages,* Oxford University Press, London.

Wetmore, T. H., 1959, *The Low-Central and Low-Back Vowels in the English of the Eastern United States* (Publication of the American Dialect Society, no. 32), 6 and 100 ff.

Whitney, W. D., 1941, *Sanskrit Grammar*, Harvard University Press, Cambridge, Mass.

Wierzchowska, B., 1965, *Wymowa polska*, Panstwowe zaklady wydawnictw szkolnych, Warsaw.

Williamson, K., 1967, "Pitch and Accent in Ịjọ," unpublished paper.

Winteler, J. C., 1876, *Die kerenzer Mundart des Kantons Glarus in ihren Grundzügen dargestellt*, Carl Winter, Heidelberg.

Wright, J., 1905, *The English Dialect Grammar*, Oxford University Press, Henry Frowde, New York.

Wyld, H. C., 1927, *A Short History of English*, Verry, Lawrence, London.

Zachrisson, R. E., 1913, *Pronunciation of English Vowels 1400–1700*, W. Zachrisson, Göteborg.

Zimmer, K., 1967, "A Note on Vowel Harmony," *International Journal of American Linguistics, 33*, no. 2, 166–171.

Zinder, L. R., and M. I. Matusevič, 1937, "Eksperimental'noe issledovanie fonem nivxskogo jazyka," in E. S. Krejnovič, *Fonetika nivxskogo (giljackogo) jazyka* (Naučno-issledovatel'skaja associacija instituta narodov severa, Trudy po lingvistike, 5), Moscow.

Zwicky, A. M., 1964, "Noun Plurals and Umlaut in German," unpublished paper presented at the winter meeting of the Linguistic Society of America, New York.

Zwicky, A. M., 1965, *Selected Topics in Sanskrit Phonology*, unpublished Doctoral dissertation, Massachusetts Institute of Technology.

INDEXES

LANGUAGE INDEX

WORD INDEX

AFFIX INDEX

SUBJECT INDEX

Abramson, A. S., 326, 327–28
Admissibility, phonological, 150n, 380, 381–82, 416–18
   degree of, 416–18
Affix Rule of Main Stress Rule, 31, 32–34, 36, 39, 40–41, 42–43, 81–83, 84–85, 88–89, 98, 103, 126–29, 130–35, 142n, 144, 158
   formulation, 31, 32–33, 35, 42, 82, 84, 99, 103, 110, 126, 132–33
Affixes, 370
   neutral, 84–87, 129, 134n, 142n, 154, 159–60, 367, 369–70
   and stress, 23n, 31, 32–34, 37n, 38–43, 59n, 63, 80–83, 86–89, 112, 115–25, 126–45, 158–62
   tense, 107–108, 152–58
   See also AFFIX INDEX
Affricates, 302, 303, 317, 318, 319–20, 321–22, 329, 412, 422–23
Alternating Stress Rule, 77–79, 86–87, 95–96, 153, 156, 157–58, 227, 371
   formulation, 78, 84, 96, 240
   similarity to Stressed Syllable Rule, 237–38
Alveolar consonants, 304, 312, 313
Anderson, S., 234
Aoki, H., 377
Apical consonants, 312–14, 413
Archi-segment, 64, 85, 86n, 94, 116n, 148n, 166
Archi-unit, 64
Articulation base, 295
Aspiration, 26, 320–21, 326, 327–28
Assimilation, 178, 208–209, 346, 350–51, 352, 428
   in English, diphthongization as, 208–209
   nasal, 116n, 209, 222, 234, 419

   with prefixes, 149, 222, 238
   voicing, 178, 229
   palatalization and velarization as, 307, 423–24
   and use of variables, 178, 350–51, 352

Backness Adjustment, 189, 215, 244, 288, 434–35
   in irregular forms, 209, 238, 432–33
Bailey, C. J., 353, 354
Baudouin de Courtenay, J., 421
Beach, D. M., 319–20
Bernoulli effect, 301, 302, 318
Bever, T. G., 18n, 356n
Bierwisch, M., 372
Biuniqueness, 169
Bloomfield, L., 18n, 137n, 251
Boundaries, 66–68, 160n, 364–72
  + (formative), 5n, 8, 9, 29, 33, 66, 364, 403
    and applicability of English rules, 13, 85, 95, 104–105, 108n, 134n, 137n, 138n, 139n, 142n, 154, 155, 159–60, 161–62, 171, 172, 180–81, 210, 226–27, 226n, 231, 369–70
    and rule application, 67, 85, 364–66, 397
  #, 14, 21, 29, 66–67, 85–87, 366–70
    and applicability of English rules, 27, 75, 85–87, 89, 94, 95, 105–106, 115, 129, 134n, 137n, 142n, 154, 158n, 159–60, 171n, 172, 182n, 196n, 210, 367, 368–70
    and the word, 13–14, 27, 60, 89, 159, 160, 163, 366–70
  =, 37, 67, 94–95, 371
    and applicability of English rules, 94–95, 98, 99, 106, 115, 118, 121, 128–